Communication Research

ASKING QUESTIONS, FINDING ANSWERS

FOURTH EDITION

Joann Keyton

North Carolina State University

COMMUNICATION RESEARCH: Asking Questions, Finding Answers, FOURTH EDITION

Published by McGraw-Hill Education, 2 Penn Plaza, New York, NY 10121. Copyright © 2015 by McGraw-Hill Education. All rights reserved. Printed in the United States of America. Previous editions © 2011, 2006, and 2001. No part of this publication may be reproduced or distributed in any form or by any means, or stored in a database or retrieval system, without the prior written consent of McGraw-Hill Education, including, but not limited to, in any network or other electronic storage or transmission, or broadcast for distance learning.

Some ancillaries, including electronic and print components, may not be available to customers outside the United States.

This book is printed on acid-free paper.

2 3 4 5 6 7 8 9 0 DOC/DOC 1 0 9 8 7 6 5

ISBN 978-0-07-803691-0
MHID 0-07-803691-7

Senior Vice President, Products & Markets: *Kurt L. Strand*
Managing Director: *David Patterson*
Vice President, Content Production & Technology Services: *Kimberly Meriwether David*
Executive Director of Development: *Lisa Pinto*
Managing Editor: *Penina Braffman*
Marketing Specialist: *Alexandra Schultz*
Content Production Manager: *Terri Schiesl*
Brand Coordinator: *Adina Lonn*
Content Project Manager: *Judi David*
Buyer: *Jennifer Pickel*
Cover Credit: *Lisa Zador/Getty Images*
Cover Designer: *Studio Montage, St. Louis, MO*
Compositor: *MPS Limited*
Typeface: *10/12 Times*
Printer: *R. R. Donnelley*

All credits appearing on page or at the end of the book are considered to be an extension of the copyright page.

Library of Congress Cataloging-in-Publication Data

Keyton, Joann.
   Communication research : asking questions, finding answers / Joann Keyton,
North Carolina State University.—Fourth Edition.
      pages cm.—(Communication Research)
   Includes bibliographical references and indexes.
   ISBN-13: 978-0-07-803691-0 (acid-free paper)
   ISBN-10: 0-07-803691-7 (acid-free paper)
   1. Communication–Research. I. Title.
   P91.3.K49 2014
   302.2072–dc23

                                                            2013043703

The Internet addresses listed in the text were accurate at the time of publication. The inclusion of a website does not indicate an endorsement by the authors or McGraw-Hill Education, and McGraw-Hill Education does not guarantee the accuracy of the information presented at these sites.

www.mhhe.com

CONTENTS

Preface   xx

SECTION 1: RESEARCH BASICS

CHAPTER 1   Introduction to Communication Research   1
CHAPTER CHECKLIST   1

WHAT IS RESEARCH?   2
Your Relationship with Research   3

SCHOLARLY RESEARCH   4
Goals of Research   5
Research and Theory   7

COMMUNICATION AS A SOCIAL SCIENCE   7
The Scientific Approach   9
Characteristics of Science   11
Methodological Extremes   13

WHAT KINDS OF QUESTIONS DO COMMUNICATION SCHOLARS ASK?   13
The Nature of the Questions   14

SUMMARY   16

KEY TERMS   17

BOXED FEATURES
AN ETHICAL ISSUE: Is Communication Public or Private?   4
TRY THIS! Evaluating Communication Questions   15

CHAPTER 2   The Research Process: Getting Started   18
CHAPTER CHECKLIST   18

CONSIDERING THEORY IN RESEARCH   19
Developing Theory   19
Utility of Theory–Research Link   21

THE RESEARCH PROCESS MODEL   22
Deductive Research Model   23
Inductive Research Model   23
Research as a Process   23

IDENTIFYING THE RESEARCH PROBLEM   24
Formulating Research Ideas   24
Turning Communication Problems into Preliminary Questions   25
Evaluating Your Questions   26

USING LIBRARY AND DATABASE RESOURCES   27
Scholarly Journals   27
Books   28
Online Resources   29
Analyzing Your Resources   29
Adjusting the Question   30

USING AND ORGANIZING YOUR RESOURCES   31
Tracking Others' References   32
Organizing What You Have Found   32
Summarizing What You Have Found   32

WRITING THE LITERATURE REVIEW   33
Introduction to the Literature Review   33
Body of the Literature Review   34
Organizing the Literature Review   35
Concluding the Literature Review   36

SUMMARY   36

KEY TERMS   37

BOXED FEATURES
TRY THIS! Finding Theory in Journal Articles   21
TRY THIS! Developing Initial Questions to Guide the Research Process   26
TRY THIS! Searching for Sources   30
AN ETHICAL ISSUE: Using the Ideas of Others   31
DESIGN CHECK: Evaluating the Literature You Found   32
TRY THIS! Analyzing What You Have Found   36

CHAPTER 3   Research Ethics   38
CHAPTER CHECKLIST   38

ETHICAL QUESTIONS IN PLANNING RESEARCH   40
Institutional Review Board   44
Informed Consent   45
Informed Consent and Quantitative Research   49
Informed Consent and Qualitative Research   50

ETHICAL ISSUES IN CONDUCTING RESEARCH   50
Intentional Deception   51
Using Confederates   52
Physical and Psychological Harm   53
Upholding Anonymity and Confidentiality   54
Using Online Technology   56
Videotaping and Audiotaping Participants   57
Debriefing Participants   57

ETHICAL ISSUES IN REPORTING RESEARCH   58
Ensuring Accuracy   58
Avoiding Plagiarism   58
Protecting the Identities of Participants   59

SUMMARY   60

KEY TERMS   61

BOXED FEATURES
AN ETHICAL ISSUE: *Professional Association Guidelines for Conducting Research   42*
AN ETHICAL ISSUE: *Do Research Participants Have Any Ethical Responsibilities?   46*
DESIGN CHECK: *Do You Need Informed Consent for Your Research Project?   47*
AN ETHICAL ISSUE: *Would You Participate?   49*
DESIGN CHECK: *Private or Public?   51*
TRY THIS! *What Would You Include?   56*
AN ETHICAL ISSUE: *Ethics in Proprietary Research   60*

SECTION 2: QUANTITATIVE COMMUNICATION RESEARCH

CHAPTER 4   Introduction to Quantitative Research   62

CHAPTER CHECKLIST   62

WHAT IS QUANTITATIVE RESEARCH?   63
Examples of Quantitative Research   63
Deductive Reasoning   65
A Model for Conceptualizing Quantitative Research   65

CREATING THE FOUNDATION FOR QUANTITATIVE RESEARCH   67

RESEARCH HYPOTHESES FOR QUANTITATIVE RESEARCH   68
Directional Hypotheses   70
Nondirectional Hypotheses   70
Assessing Hypotheses   70
Null Hypotheses   71
Research Traditions in the Use of Hypotheses   71

RESEARCH QUESTIONS IN QUANTITATIVE RESEARCH   71

TYPES OF VARIABLES   72
Independent Variables   73
Dependent Variables   74
The Relationship Between Independent and Dependent Variables   75

OPERATIONALIZING VARIABLES   76

MAKING THE CASE FOR QUANTITATIVE RESEARCH   78
Advantages of Quantitative Research   78
Limitations of Quantitative Research   79

ISSUES OF RELIABILITY AND VALIDITY   79
Threats to Reliability and Validity   80

SUMMARY   82

KEY TERMS   82

BOXED FEATURES
AN ETHICAL ISSUE: Giving Your Children Permission to Participate in a Research Study   64
DESIGN CHECK: What Is Sex? What Is Gender?   73
TRY THIS! Identifying Independent and Dependent Variables   77
TRY THIS! Operationalizing Variables   79

CHAPTER 5   Measurement   83

CHAPTER CHECKLIST   83

MEASUREMENT PRINCIPLES   84

LEVELS OF MEASUREMENT IN COMMUNICATION RESEARCH   86
Discrete Data   86
Continuous Level Data   88
Ordinal Data   89
Interval Data   90
Likert-Type Scales   90
Semantic Differential Scales   90
Ratio Data   92

ISSUES OF VALIDITY AND RELIABILITY   93
Validity   93
Face Validity   94
Content Validity   94
Criterion-Related Validity   94
Construct Validity   95
Reliability   96
Internal Reliability   97
Test–Retest Reliability   98
Improving Reliability   99

The Relationship Between Validity and Reliability 99
Threats to Validity and Reliability 100
   Issues of Data Collection 100
   Issues of Sample Representativeness 101
   Summary of Threats 102

ISSUES OF DATA INTERPRETATION 103

SUMMARY 104

KEY TERMS 105

BOXED FEATURES
AN ETHICAL ISSUE: *What Am I Willing to Reveal About Myself?* 88
TRY THIS! *Changing Levels of Measurement* 91
DESIGN CHECK: *Questioning Measurement Techniques* 92
DESIGN CHECK: *Will These Results Apply to Me?* 101

CHAPTER 6   Populations, Samples, and Sample Size   106

CHAPTER CHECKLIST 106

POPULATION AND SAMPLE 107
Identify the Population 108
Addressing Generalizability 109
Probability Sampling 110
   Simple Random Sampling 112
   Systematic Sampling 112
   Stratified Random Sampling 113
   Cluster Sampling 113
Nonprobability Sampling 114
   Convenience Sampling 115
   Volunteer Sampling 115
   Inclusion and Exclusion Criteria 116
   Snowball Sampling 116
   Purposive Sampling 117
   Quota Sampling 117
Sample Size 118
A Final Word on Sampling 118

SUMMARY 120

KEY TERMS 121

BOXED FEATURES
AN ETHICAL ISSUE: *Participant Selection Can Make a Difference* 114
DESIGN CHECK: *Justifying Nonprobability Sampling* 116
TRY THIS! *Identifying Populations, Generating Samples* 119
AN ETHICAL ISSUE: *Selected, But Not Required to Participate* 120

CHAPTER 7   Quantitative Research Designs   122

CHAPTER CHECKLIST   122

THE EXPERIMENTAL FRAMEWORK   124

The Classical Experiment   125
Random Assignment of Participants   126
Creating Treatment and Control Groups   127
Manipulation Checks   128
Types of Experimental Design   129
Posttest Only   129
Pretest–Posttest   130
Factorial Design   132
Longitudinal Designs   133
Strengths of Experimentation   134
Limitations of Experimentation   134

QUASI-EXPERIMENTS   135

Field Experiments   138
Strengths and Limitations of Quasi-Experimental Research Designs   139

DESCRIPTIVE DESIGNS   139

Strengths and Limitations of Descriptive Research Designs   141

ONLINE EXPERIMENTS   141

RESEARCHER EFFECTS AND PROCEDURAL BIAS   142

COMPARING RESEARCH DESIGNS   143

SUMMARY   144

KEY TERMS   144

BOXED FEATURES
AN ETHICAL ISSUE: *Would You Ask Participants To . . . ?   128*
TRY THIS! *Designing an Experiment   135*
DESIGN CHECK: *Is One Study Ever Enough?   138*

CHAPTER 8   Surveys and Questionnaires   146

CHAPTER CHECKLIST   146

WHAT IS A SURVEY?   147

Types of Surveys   147
Self-Reports   147
Face-to-Face Interviews   148
Phone Surveys   148
Online Surveys   148
Comparing Survey Types   150

DESIGNING A SURVEY   151

Evaluating Existing Questionnaires or Surveys   152
Writing Your Own Questionnaire   153

Designing Survey Items   153
  Closed Questions   154
  Response Sets for Closed Questions   155
  Likert-Type Scales   156
  Semantic Differential Scales   158
Open Questions   159
Choosing Between Open and Closed Questions   160

DESIGNING THE FLOW OF THE SURVEY   161
  How the Survey Looks   161

PRETESTING THE SURVEY OR QUESTIONNAIRE   162

SAMPLING ISSUES FOR SURVEYS   167
  Response Rate   167

SURVEY RELIABILITY AND VALIDITY   167

ANALYZING AND REPORTING SURVEY DATA   168

SUMMARY   169

KEY TERMS   170

BOXED FEATURES
DESIGN CHECK: *Are All Polls the Same?   150*
TRY THIS! *Survey Design   152*
DESIGN CHECK: *Racial and Ethnic Group Identification   156*
TRY THIS! *How Different* Are Usually, Sometimes, *and* Seldom?   161
TRY THIS! *Does This Questionnaire Need Modification?   164*
AN ETHICAL ISSUE: *Would You Participate?   166*

CHAPTER 9 Descriptive Statistics, Significance Levels, and Hypothesis Testing   171

CHAPTER CHECKLIST   171

NUMBERS INTO STATISTICS   172

NORMAL CURVE   173
  Skewed Distributions   173
  Distributions of Data   174

DESCRIPTIVE STATISTICS   176
  Number of Cases   176
  Measures of Central Tendency   177
    Mean   177
    Median   177
    Mode   177
  Measures of Dispersion   178
    Range   179
    Standard Deviation   179

APPLICATION OF DESCRIPTIVE STATISTICS   180
  Frequencies   181
  Percentages   182

CRUNCHING THE NUMBERS   182

SIGNIFICANCE LEVELS   183

HYPOTHESIS TESTING   185

A FINAL WORD   187

SUMMARY   188

KEY TERMS   188

BOXED FEATURES
TRY THIS! Are the Data Normal or Skewed?   177
AN ETHICAL ISSUE: Mistakes in Calculations   181
DESIGN CHECK: Describing Variables   182

CHAPTER 10   Testing for Differences   189

CHAPTER CHECKLIST   189

INFERENTIAL STATISTICS   190
  Alternative and Null Hypotheses   191
  Degrees of Freedom   191
  Four Analytical Steps   192

CHI-SQUARE   193
  One-Dimensional Chi-Square   193
  Contingency Analysis   194
  Limitations of Chi-Square   196

THE *t*-TEST   196
  Common Forms of t-Test   197
  Two-Tailed t-Test   198
  One-Tailed t-Test   199
  Limitations of the t-Test   199

ANALYSIS OF VARIANCE   199
  ANOVA Basics   200
  One-Way ANOVA   202
  Two-Way ANOVA   203
  Factorial ANOVA   205
  Limitations of ANOVA   206

ASKING FOR STATISTICAL HELP   206

SUMMARY   207

KEY TERMS   207

BOXED FEATURES
DESIGN CHECK: *Interpreting Chi-Squares*   *196*
DESIGN CHECK: *Interpreting t-Tests*   *198*
AN ETHICAL ISSUE: *Are Two Categories Fully Representative?*   *200*
TRY THIS! *Should Differences Be Significant or Practical?*   *204*
DESIGN CHECK: *Interpreting F*   *205*

CHAPTER 11   Testing for Relationships   208

CHAPTER CHECKLIST   208

BASIC ASSUMPTIONS   210
Alternative and Null Hypotheses   *210*
Degrees of Freedom   *211*
Four Analytical Steps   *211*

CORRELATION   211
Interpreting the Coefficient   *212*
   Amount of Shared Variance   213
   Plotting the Data   214
Examples of Correlation   *214*
Limitations of Correlation   *216*

REGRESSION   216
Linear Regression   *218*
Multiple Regression   *218*
   Interpreting Multiple Regressions   219
Regression Examples   *219*
   Other Forms of Multiple Regression   222
Limitations of Regression   *225*

STRUCTURAL EQUATION MODELING   225
SEM Example   *225*
Other Forms of SEM   *226*

CAUTIONS IN USING STATISTICS   226

SUMMARY   228

KEY TERMS   228

BOXED FEATURES
DESIGN CHECK: *Paying Attention to Details*   *210*
DESIGN CHECK: *Interpreting Correlations*   *217*
DESIGN CHECK: *Interpreting Multiple Regression*   *222*
TRY THIS! *Identifying Independent Variables for Multiple Regression*   *223*

CHAPTER 12 Quantitative Analysis of Text   229

CHAPTER CHECKLIST   229

CONTENT ANALYSIS   230
What Content Can Be Analyzed?   232
The Content Analysis Process   233
Selecting What to Code   233
Developing Content Categories   235
Units of Analysis   235
Training Coders   237
Coding Reliability   237
Validity   240
Interpreting the Coding Results   241
Computers and Content Analysis   241
Strengths of Content Analysis Research   242
Limitations of Content Analysis Research   243

INTERACTION ANALYSIS   243
Gathering and Preparing the Interaction for Coding   243
Coding the Interaction   245
Analyzing and Interpreting the Coding   245
Strengths of Interaction Analysis   245
Limitations of Interaction Analysis   245

DESIGN CONSIDERATIONS   246

SUMMARY   246

KEY TERMS   247

BOXED FEATURES
DESIGN CHECK: Content Analyzing Big Data   231
DESIGN CHECK: What Content Can Be Analyzed?   232
TRY THIS! Identifying Themes of Freshman Socialization   239
DESIGN CHECK: How Did the Researcher Perform the Content Analysis?   240
AN ETHICAL ISSUE: Taking Content Out of Context   242

CHAPTER 13 Reading and Writing the Quantitative Research Report   248

CHAPTER CHECKLIST   248

REVIEWING THE LITERATURE REVIEW   249
Reviewing the Research Questions and Hypotheses   249

THE METHOD SECTION   250
Describing Participants   250
Describing the Research Procedure   251
Describing the Variables   251

THE RESULTS SECTION   252
Using Tables and Graphs   252

THE DISCUSSION SECTION 253
  Developing Interpretations from Results 253
  Manner of Presentation 255
  Presenting the Limitations 255
  Recommending Future Research 256

FINISHING THE QUANTITATIVE RESEARCH REPORT 256
  Title 256
  Title Page 256
  Abstract 256
  References 257

USING APA STYLE 257
  Citing Others' Work 257
  Creating the Reference List 257

ISSUES IN WRITING 259
  The Revision Process 259

SUMMARY 260

KEY TERMS 260

BOXED FEATURES
DESIGN CHECK: *Do You Have the Basic Information?* 251
AN ETHICAL ISSUE: *Dealing with Unexpected Results* 254
TRY THIS! *How to Read a Research Report* 255
TRY THIS! *Submit Your Research Paper to a Communication Convention* 258

SECTION 3: QUALITATIVE COMMUNICATION RESEARCH

CHAPTER 14 Introduction to Qualitative Research 261

CHAPTER CHECKLIST 261

WHAT IS QUALITATIVE RESEARCH? 262
  Examples of Qualitative Research 263
  Inductive Analysis 266
  A Model for Qualitative Research 266
  Issues of Credibility in Qualitative Research 269

CONCEPTUALIZING RESEARCH QUESTIONS FOR QUALITATIVE RESEARCH 270
  Assessing Research Questions 271

WHAT COUNTS AS DATA IN QUALITATIVE RESEARCH? 272
  Interpreting Meaning 272
  Level of Evidence 273

MAKING THE CASE FOR QUALITATIVE RESEARCH   273
> *Advantages of Qualitative Research   273*
> *Limitations of Qualitative Research   274*
> *Threats to Credibility in Qualitative Research   274*

ONE LAST THOUGHT   275

SUMMARY   275

KEY TERMS   276

BOXED FEATURES
TRY THIS! *Identifying Contexts for Qualitative Research   265*
DESIGN CHECK: *What If Research Questions Are Not Presented?   271*
AN ETHICAL ISSUE: *Is Anything Off-Limits?   275*

CHAPTER 15   Designing Qualitative Research   277

CHAPTER CHECKLIST   277

RESEARCHER SKILLS FOR QUALITATIVE METHODOLOGIES   278

THE RESEARCHER'S ROLE IN QUALITATIVE METHODOLOGIES   278
> *Forms of Participant Observation   279*
>> Complete Participant   279
>> Participant as Observer   280
>> Observer as Participant   280
>> Complete Observer   281
>> Committed Membership   282
>> Researcher as Interviewer   282
>> Moving Between Researcher Roles   282

IDENTIFYING THE RESEARCH FOCUS   283
> *Consulting the Literature   284*
> *Concept Map   284*
> *Research Questions and Objectives   286*

SAMPLING IN QUALITATIVE DESIGNS   286
> *Sample Size   287*
> *Special Considerations for Sampling in Qualitative Research   288*

GAINING ACCESS   289
> *Becoming Familiar with People and Places   290*
> *Developing Trust   291*
>> Developing Rapport   291
>> Locating Key Informants   292
> *Stumbling Onto Something Interesting   292*

DESIGNING A QUALITATIVE RESEARCH PROJECT   293
> *What Constitutes Data in Qualitative Research?   294*
> *Your Impact as a Researcher   294*

FINALIZING THE RESEARCH DESIGN   296

SUMMARY   296

KEY TERMS   297

BOXED FEATURES
AN ETHICAL ISSUE: One Role? Or Two?   281
TRY THIS! Assuming Researcher Roles   282
DESIGN CHECK: Why Was the Researcher There?   289
DESIGN CHECK: Are the Data Credible?   295

CHAPTER 16   Qualitative Methods of Data Collection   298

CHAPTER CHECKLIST   298

COLLECTING QUALITATIVE DATA   299
Observation Strategies   299
The Seamless Container   299
Ask Questions to Aid Observation   300
Taking Notes   301
Describing versus Analyzing in Fieldnotes   302
Digital Note Taking   302
Transcribing Fieldnotes   304
What If You Cannot Take Notes?   304

FIELD INTERVIEWING   304
Online Interviewing   306
The Interview Process   307
Conceptualizing the Interview Study   307
Designing the Interview   307
Conducting the Interview   308
Asking Questions   309
Interviewing Technique   311
Concluding the Interview   312
Transcribing the Interview   312
Strengths and Limitations of Interview Research   313

FOCUS GROUPS   313
Planning Focus Group Research   316
The Focus Group Schedule   316
Selecting Participants   317
Conducting Focus Group Research   317
Guiding and Maintaining the Conversation   318
Data from Focus Group Discussions   319
Focus Group Strengths and Limitations   319

COLLECTING NARRATIVES   321
Sources for Stories   322
Strengths and Limitations of Narrative Research   323

ETHNOGRAPHY   324
    Entering the Scene   325
    Strengths and Limitations of Ethnographic Research   326

SUMMARY   326

KEY TERMS   327

BOXED FEATURES
TRY THIS! *Your Classroom as a Seamless Container   300*
DESIGN CHECK: *Where Did the Interviews Occur?   307*
AN ETHICAL ISSUE: *Research or Selling?   314*
TRY THIS! *Motivating Attendance at Focus Groups   320*
DESIGN CHECK: *The Difference Between the Research Question and Asking Questions   323*
DESIGN CHECK: *Reading Ethnography   326*

CHAPTER 17   Analyzing Qualitative Data   328

CHAPTER CHECKLIST   328

AN OVERVIEW   329
    Choosing An Analytic Method   330

THE PROCESS OF ANALYSIS AND INTERPRETATION   330
    Analytical Memos   331
    Diagramming the Data   333
    Coding and Categorizing Data   333

GROUNDED THEORY   335

THEMATIC ANALYSIS   338

CODING AND ANALYZING WITH SOFTWARE   338

THE PROCESS OF INTERPRETATION   339
    Evaluating Interpretation   339
        Participant Quotes   339
        Credibility   340
        Triangulation   341

A FINAL WORD   341

SUMMARY   342

KEY TERMS   342

BOXED FEATURES
AN ETHICAL ISSUE: *Considering Relational Ethics with Participants During Data Analysis   336*
DESIGN CHECK: *How Are Participant Quotes Used?   340*

CHAPTER 18 Reading and Writing the Qualitative Research Report 343

CHAPTER CHECKLIST 343

REPRESENTING QUALITATIVE RESEARCH 344
Beginning the Research Report 345
The Literature Review 345

WRITING ABOUT THE METHOD 346
Revealing the Identity of Participants 347

PRESENTING THE DATA 347
Authorial Voice 348

FINDINGS AND INTERPRETATION 349
Balancing Description and Analysis 349
Strategies for Writing the Findings and Analyses 350
Using Participants' Quoted Material 352

DRAWING AND SUPPORTING CONCLUSIONS 353
Revisiting Your Analysis 353

FINISHING THE QUALITATIVE RESEARCH REPORT 354
Title 354
Abstract 355
Using the APA Style Manual 356

SUMMARY 356

KEY TERMS 356

BOXED FEATURES
AN ETHICAL ISSUE: Creating Something from Nothing 348
DESIGN CHECK: Who Did What? How? When? 349
TRY THIS! Describe, Then Analyze 350
DESIGN CHECK: Letting Participants Speak 352
TRY THIS! Submit Your Paper to a Communication Journal 354

Glossary G-1

References R-1

Name Index I-1

Subject Index I-7

PREFACE

Thank you for picking up this book and reading the preface. I am a communication researcher who conducts and publishes quantitative and qualitative research. I am always learning something new about research methods, and, perhaps, most central to this preface—I really enjoy teaching research methods courses. I designed this research methods book to help students overcome their fear of research methods and to provide instructors with foundational material for their classroom use. Over the previous editions, including this one, I have received a substantial amount of feedback of how the book could be more effective for both instructors and students. Most directly, I receive feedback from my students when I teach undergraduate and graduate research methods courses. More formal feedback has come from the publisher who seeks professional reviews of textbooks before an author begins work on a new edition. Other times, feedback has come informally from conversations at conferences, or in e-mails from instructors or students using the book. I'm grateful for everyone who has taken the time to comment, to point out what's good or bad, and to suggest what they would like to see in a new edition—and what they hope I will remove.

So, simply, the goal of this book is to be helpful to instructors in teaching research methods, and to be supportive to students who are learning research methods.

My other goal is to focus on communication research. I emphasize *communication*, as all of the examples used in book are drawn from the published research of communication scholars in communication or communication-related journals. I hope you will (and you will encourage your students to) go back to these cited sources.

I've written this book to be most useful to students (undergraduate or beginning graduate level) who have little or no familiarity with communication research. I have used previous editions at both the undergraduate and graduate levels, and know others have done the same. I hope that the book hits a middle ground that is engaging for undergraduates but can also provide a foundation for beginning graduate students (with the help of additional reading material and more sophisticated in-class exercises). Across the chapters, I've selected techniques and methods that are foundational to more advanced methods and ones that students can learn to use in research settings.

What I've learned from the publisher's examination of the research methods book market and from my conversations with colleagues who teach research methods is that no two instructors teach the research methods course in the same way. Some faculty focus on quantitative; some faculty focus on qualitative; and some do a mix of the two. Some of us insist that students *do the math*; others of us want statistics presented conceptually. Some of us want more of the philosophical traditions that are the underpinning of quantitative and qualitative methods; some don't. Thus, I've had to make choices. But my choices were guided by a principle I've long believed in: Researchers must have a broad understanding and appreciation of all methodologies—quantitative and qualitative—to conduct their research effectively.

To that end, the fourth edition of this book continues to emphasize three important points:

1. All research starts with an initial research question or problem.
2. Research is a process in which the researcher makes important decisions at crucial points about what to do and how to do it. This is in contrast to viewing research simply as a series of steps to be completed.

3. To answer the varied nature of questions about communication, one must be familiar with both quantitative and qualitative methodologies.

Communication Research: Asking Questions, Finding Answers covers basic research issues and processes for both quantitative and qualitative approaches appropriate for communication students with little or no previous research methods' experience. The text's guiding principle is that methodological choices are made from one's research questions or hypotheses. This avoids the pitfall in which students learn one methodology or one methodological skill and then force that method to answer all types of questions.

WHAT'S NEW TO THE FOURTH EDITION AND ORGANIZATION OF THE TEXT

The book presents a balance of quantitative and qualitative research because the communication scholarship embraces both approaches. In addition to updating the published research examples and research references sources (161 new references are included), the biggest change to the fourth edition is its organization and the continuation of the increased focus on qualitative research. More examples are given; more direction is provided in how to design and conduct a qualitative study and collect (Chapters 14, 15, and 16) and analyze qualitative data (Chapter 17), as well as writing a qualitative research report (Chapter 18). Information in each of these chapters has been strengthened with greater depth and more examples, and this information has been reorganized for improved flow that better mirrors the qualitative research process.

Based on feedback from reviewers, the book is now divided into three sections. In the first section, Research Basics, students are introduced to the research process, its basic principles, and research ethics. Chapters in this first section are introductory to research in general and are neutral with respect to methodology. The issues raised in these initial chapters are issues that both quantitative and qualitative researchers must address. Section 2 focuses on quantitative communication research methods whereas Section 3 focuses on qualitative communication research methods.

Across all chapters, emphasis was placed on updating examples and reference sources to align the book with current research practices in the communication discipline. All of the new references are from the 2011 through 2013 published literature. Across all of the chapters, I also worked to be more inclusive of examples drawn from research conducted in other parts of the world, and by researchers outside the USA. Likewise I updated technology examples to reflect the current mediated environment.

The book remains in APA 6th, as that is the style requirement of most social science communication journals.

Material from the appendixes has been moved to the book's website, www.mhhe.com/keyton4, where instructors and students will also find PowerPoint presentations for each chapter and short online quizzes for which results can be e-mailed to instructors. As with the last edition, a note about online resources available to students concludes each chapter (www.joannkeyton .com/CommunicationResearchMethods.htm). I update these resources each academic year. Whether you assign students to work with these resources inside or outside of class, or expect students to use these materials on their own, the online resources provide students with ways to enhance and test their knowledge of research methods.

FEATURES

The primary purpose of this textbook is to introduce students to communication research methods by meeting two objectives. The first objective is to help students become better consumers of the communication research literature by emphasizing effective methods for finding, consuming, and analyzing communication research. This objective is important because students are consumers of the communication literature through their participation in communication courses. The second objective is to provide a path for students who wish to develop and conduct research projects. To those ends, this book provides coverage of the entire research process: how one conceptualizes a research idea, turns it into an interesting and researchable question, selects a methodology, conducts the study, and writes up the study's findings. I believe that students who can effectively navigate, select, and use the communication research literature can become effective researchers, and, reciprocally, that students engaged in communication research will be able to more effectively use the existing research literature. Regardless of the role in which students use their research knowledge, they must be able to read and understand the communication research literature.

This book provides several features to help students succeed in both roles.

1. The research process is situated in communication research about symbols, messages, and meanings.

2. 161 new research and reference source citations were added; these new citations were pulled from the 2011 through 2013 published communication and communication-related journals found on Communication and Mass Media Complete.

3. Examples cover the breadth of the discipline (for example, persuasion, interpersonal, group, health, organizational, and mass communication and public relations).

4. A boxed feature labeled *Design Check* alerts students to the practical and logistical issues that student researchers should consider when designing a study. These are the same issues that students should ask of the research studies they read, as how these issues are addressed by researchers influences study outcomes and data interpretations.

5. A boxed feature labeled *An Ethical Issue* alerts students to issues of research ethics and integrity. Not only must researchers balance practical and logistical issues, they must do so while addressing ethical issues that occur when *people* and their communication artifacts are used as the basis of research. *Chapter Checklists* begin each chapter to highlight for students the essential learning objectives for each chapter. End-of-chapter summaries provide point-by-point summaries of information presented in the chapter. Stated simply,

these factual statements can help direct students' study of the material. Key terms are boldfaced within the text and listed at the end of chapter. Key term definitions can be found in the glossary at the end of the book.

6. Continuing the active pedagogy approach of the book, *Try this!* boxes are placed throughout the chapters to engage students in short research activities that can be used in the classroom with individuals or groups, or as short homework assignments. Finally, the book focuses on students. It is written for them—to their level of knowledge and understanding about human communication, the communication research literature, and the relative research processes.

My goal in writing the chapters was to explain the research steps and identify the steps researchers take in developing and conducting communication research. With study and instruction, students should be able to use this material and integrate it with what they know and are familiar with from their other communication courses to accomplish two objectives: (1) to be more analytical and make more sophisticated interpretations of the communication research they read, and (2) to design and conduct basic quantitative and qualitative research studies.

TEACHING AND LEARNING SUPPLEMENTS

Detailed instructor's materials are available at the Instructor Center website that accompanies the book (www.mhhe.com/keyton4). The password-protected instructor's center includes an Instructor's Manual with sample syllabi, teaching tips, chapter and course assignments, exercises, and worksheets for each chapter. Typically one or two pages in length, worksheets can be used as a homework or in-class assignment for students to review their knowledge and understand about the material presented. Also included on the website are PowerPoint outlines for each chapter and a test bank. Question types include objective (for example, fill in the blank), comprehension (for example, explain how academic research differs from proprietary research), and behavioral (for example, given a set of variables the student is asked to write research questions and hypotheses). For those chapters that cover statistics or the analysis and interpretation of qualitative data, additional worksheets are available, which provide students with the opportunity to work several examples from raw data through to interpretation.

The Student Center can also be found at the same website (www.mhhe.com/keyton4). This site is not password-protected and includes PowerPoint outlines for each chapter, as well as online, self-grading chapter quizzes, outlines, checklists, and summaries.

ABOUT THE AUTHOR

Joann Keyton (B.A., Western Michigan University; M.A., Ph.D., The Ohio State University) is Professor of Communication at North Carolina State University. She specializes in group communication and organizational communication. Her current research examines the collaborative processes and relational aspects of interdisciplinary teams, participants' use of language in team meetings, the multiplicity of cultures in organizations, and how messages are manipulated in sexual harassment. Her research is field focused and she was honored with the 2011 Gerald Phillips Award for Distinguished Applied Communication Scholarship by the National Communication Association.

Her research has been published in *Business Communication Quarterly, Communication Studies, Communication Theory, Communication Yearbook, Journal of Applied Communication Research, Journal of Business Communication, Management Communication Quarterly, Small Group Research, Southern Communication Journal,* and numerous edited collections including the *Handbook of Group Communication Theory and Research* and the *Handbook of Organizational Communication.*

In addition to publications in scholarly journals and edited collections, she has published three textbooks for courses in group communication, research methods, and organizational culture in addition to co-editing an organizational communication case book. Keyton was editor of the *Journal of Applied Communication Research,* Volumes 31–33, and founding editor of *Communication Currents,* Volumes 1–5. Currently, she is editor of *Small Group Research.* She is a founder and vice-chair of the Interdisciplinary Network for Group Research.

For more information, contact Joann at *jkeyton @ncsu.edu* or www.joannkeyton.com

ACKNOWLEDGMENTS

In writing this book, I have benefited from the generosity of researchers, scientists, and scholars from many disciplines around the world. Unlike many other bodies of knowledge, the Web has become a cornucopia of information about research methods and statistics. When contacted by e-mail, these colleagues were both prompt and generous.

I have also benefited from the many undergraduate and graduate students in my research methods course who continued to say that they did not understand after I had explained a concept or technique. Their questioning and my inability to always provide them an appropriate and acceptable answer provided the motivation for this text.

This fourth edition has benefited from the many instructors and students who have e-mailed me with questions or issues they would like me to address or explain further. I appreciate this feedback-in-progress and much of it has been incorporated here.

I also thank the scholars who reviewed this text during its development for the encouragement and wisdom they extended. Reviewers for the fourth edition were: Christina Anderson, Coastal Carolina University; Gary Beck, Old Dominion University; Merry Buchanan, University of Central Oklahoma; Lovette Chinwah, Central State University; Janet Colvin, Utah Valley University; Leda Cooks, University of Massachusetts; Douglas Ferguson, College of Charleston; Eileen S. Gilchrist, University of Wyoming; Chia-Fang Hsu, University of Wyoming; Angela La Valley, Bloomsburg University; Danielle Leek, Grand Valley State University; Rick Olsen, University of North Carolina Wilmington; James O. Olufowote, The University of Oklahoma; Sachiyo Shearman,

East Carolina University; Laurel Traynowicz, Boise State University; Nicholas A. Valentino, University of Michigan; Margaret Wills, Fairfield University.

Thanks to the McGraw-Hill team, including Penina Braffman, managing editor; Judi David, project manager; and Alexandra Schultz, marketing manager, as well as to the developmental editing team at **ansr**source. They helped me produce the finished product.

In the first edition, I thanked my colleagues— Tommy Darwin, Steve Rhodes, and Pradeep Sopory. In the second edition, I added Ron Warren, Debbie Ford, and Tracy Russo. Each of these six people have enriched and challenged my role as researcher. For the third edition, I added Paul Schrodt, Ryan Bisel, Stephenson Beck, and Renee Meyers for always returning the e-mails in which I proposed a methods question or conundrum. The book has benefited from those online discussions. (We miss you, Renee!)

For the fourth edition, I'd like to thank Amber Messersmith for always being kind, friendly, and cheerful. I also thank Joe Bonito whose humor about research methods, communication research, and, particularly, group research, lifts my spirits. Thanks goes to Andrew Ledbetter for his willingness to engage me in Facebook discussions about research methods, especially why the doi is important in a reference citation. I would also like to thank my growing network of research colleagues from other disciplines. Being asked over and over why communication matters and how we study communication are conversations I never mind having.

I would also like to thank the many undergraduate and graduate students who have worked with me at North Carolina State University, University of Kansas, and University of Memphis on research projects and who have worked through research issues (and challenged me) in methodology classes. For me, methodology is the best teaching assignment I can have.

Between the third and fourth editions, my Dalmatian family changed. Cher died shortly after the third edition came out. Sonny was sad and it took a while . . . but we recently found Zoe. Sonny and Zoe are making sure that I live up to my promise that I will not forget what my *real* job is: to let the dogs in, let the dogs out, let the dogs in, let the dogs out. . . .

Jeff—this book is for you. As a student, you would not allow me to let you down. As a friend, you have not let me down. Your invaluable lessons, both professional and personal, helped me write this text in the beginning and through its revisions. Thanks for your continual support and encouragement.

Joann Keyton

CHAPTER ONE

Introduction to Communication Research

Chapter Checklist

After reading this chapter, you should be able to:

1. Identify instances in which you could use or conduct communication research as a student, use or conduct communication research as a professional, and use the results of communication research in your personal life.

2. Explain the goals of research.

3. Explain the relationship of research and theory.

4. Explain communication research as a social science.

5. Describe how communication research from a social science perspective is different from other forms of communication research and other forms of social science research.

6. Differentiate among the characteristics of science.

7. Distinguish between research question and hypothesis.

8. Describe the differences among questions of fact, variable relations, value, and policy.

9. Identify questions about communication that you believe are worth pursuing.

As a student in a research methods course, you have two roles. In one role, you are a consumer of communication research. You read summaries of research in your textbooks. In some courses, you may be required to read and analyze research articles published in the discipline's journals.

In the other role, you are a researcher collecting and interpreting data to answer research questions and hypotheses. These activities may be part of the course for which you are reading this book, an independent study, an upper-division course, or a capstone project. The information in this book can help you succeed in both roles. But before you identify yourself with either or both roles, turn your attention to answering the question "What is research?"

WHAT IS RESEARCH?

In its most basic form, *research* is the process of asking questions and finding answers. You have likely conducted research of your own, even if it wasn't in the formal sense. For example, as you chose which college or university to attend, you asked questions of students, faculty, and staff at the various institutions you were considering. You might also have looked on web sites for answers to your questions or used the survey results from *U.S. News & World Report* that rank America's colleges and universities. As you made choices about your major, you read the college bulletin, talked to students and an advisor, and perhaps even talked to professionals in the field you believed you wanted to pursue. In these activities, you sought answers to your questions. Which school is best for me? Which school has the type of student experience I am looking for? Which schools are affordable? What is the annual income of alumni with my major? What kinds of career opportunities can I expect? By asking these questions, you were taking on the role of a researcher as you tracked down the information needed to make a decision.

Not only were you asking questions and seeking answers, but more than likely you were also relying on the results of research performed by others. It would be impossible for you to answer your set of questions without such input. For example, for the question "What is the annual income of alumni with my major?" it would not be realistic for you to survey graduates in your major field to discover their annual income. More likely you relied on a survey conducted by a professional association, an alumni association, or a news organization. You used the reported findings of their research to answer your question. Although someone else did the research, you still needed to evaluate the efficacy of their research to gauge the usefulness of their findings in answering the question.

You are also familiar with other types of research. News reports profile the results of research each day. You have heard the results of medical research reported in the news. During political campaigns, the results of preference polls are reported in the news and archived on news organization websites. And, no doubt, you have heard the results of research on drug use and underage drinking. If you work, your company may have conducted research on the preferences of its customers or the quality of its products.

The point here is that research is all around us, often presented in ways that we would not recognize as research. Thus, **research,** as we will study it, is the discovery of answers to questions through the application of scientific and systematic procedures. Given this basic definition of research, you can see that you probably come into contact with several forms of research on a daily basis. You probably also use the results of research in making both personal and professional decisions.

The specific focus of this text is communication research—that is, quantitative or qualitative research conducted by communication scholars about communication phenomena. The focus is also on research conducted from a social science perspective, which is distinct from rhetorical research and also distinct from critical research. Yet, distinctions among these three perspectives—social science, rhetorical, and critical—are not always clear (Craig, 1993), and scholars working from the other perspectives do use some methods more commonly associated with social science research. **Social science research** is conducted through the use of scientific and systematic methods, and it is based on the assumption that research can uncover patterns in the lives of people. When patterns of communication behavior are confirmed or discovered, scholars develop useful theories of communication that speak to the regularity of communication (Bostrom, 2003).

The research techniques and methods presented in this book are used to study the communication behavior of humans and the communication artifacts that people create. Although some people think of social science research as objective research, communication scholars use both quantitative (more objective) and qualitative (more subjective) methods—sometimes separately and sometimes in combination with one another. Both types of methods are **empirical,** meaning that both methods are based on observations or experiences of communication. Both types are needed because it is unlikely that quantitative or qualitative methods alone can provide complete answers to the many questions we have about communication behavior.

Your Relationship with Research

As discussed earlier, your relationship to this material can be conceptualized in two ways—as that of a researcher or as that of a consumer of research. You may take on the researcher role as a student, as an employee, or as a consultant. It is likely that the class for which you are reading this book will develop and conduct a research project as part of a class assignment. You may also decide that the process of research is interesting enough that you plan to take additional courses in research methodology. You might even decide to become a professor and spend much of your professional time as a researcher, finding answers to questions that interest you and matter to others.

After you graduate, you might find yourself in a professional position where research is part of your regularly assigned job responsibilities. Positions in marketing and advertising, as well as jobs in political, organizational, and health communication, are just a few in which research

plays a central role in decision making. Even though their organizational title may not be "researcher," many employees at managerial levels are responsible for collecting and analyzing data to help organizations and employees make more effective and efficient decisions. But are these examples of communication research? They could be. Some organizations conduct surveys or focus groups to discover the degree of effectiveness of their internal communication practices. Media organizations regularly use surveys or focus groups to discover if informational, advertising, or promotional messages are being received as intended.

You could become a consultant and conduct **proprietary research,** research that is commissioned by an individual or organization for its own use. Organizations use consultants to evaluate their internal communication systems and operational effectiveness. Political figures also commission proprietary research to discover how they are doing in the polls and which of their messages have the most influence on potential voters. Marketing and advertising research is also proprietary. Even though the results of proprietary research are private and intended only for the use of whoever pays for the research, the researcher uses the same procedures and practices used in conducting scholarly or academic research.

Your relationship with research can also be conceptualized as that of a consumer. You consume the research of others when you read scholarly books and journals. You also consume research when you see or hear personally or professionally interesting information presented in the media, and use information about goods and services marketed to you. You might trust some sources more than others—or be more cautious—if you knew how the data were collected and analyzed.

Right now, your role as a consumer of research is more immediate than your current or potential role as a researcher. Your status as student forces you into the consumer role as you collect information in the library or online to complete class assignments. Your ability to evaluate the information you collect has a direct impact on your ability to learn and prepare assignments.

AN ETHICAL ISSUE

Is Communication Public or Private?

In general, what ethical issues do you believe are raised when researchers study the communication behavior of others? About what communication situations would you feel comfortable answering questions? In what situations would you feel comfortable having a researcher observe you? Should some communication contexts remain the private domain of participants, closed to researchers' inquiries? What about intimate communication between significant others in the privacy of their bedroom? What about the communication between parent and child when discipline is required? What about communication that occurs among co-workers as they joke about ways to ridicule their boss? How would you respond if a communication researcher asked you questions about your communication behavior during these events? What arguments could you develop both for and against communication scholars conducting research about such events? Should some communication behaviors or contexts be off limits to communication researchers?

As a researcher, you seek answers to questions by collecting data, and then interpreting results and findings to draw conclusions and make recommendations. As a consumer, you sort through results and findings others have provided. In this role you still need to distinguish good information from bad, test assumptions and conclusions drawn by others, and analyze the extent to which the research process others used fits your needs and situation. In this case, you need the skills to determine if the information you are using is misleading or misinterpreted from its original source.

It is easy to feel overwhelmed or intimidated by the particular vocabulary and traditions of research. But if you approach learning about research as another way to find information, you are likely to discover that formal research is an extension of the types of informal asking and answering of questions that you have done all your life. After reading this chapter, you should be able to identify how research acts as an influence on your life and in your decision making. Throughout the rest of this chapter and throughout the book as well, specific examples of communication research will be highlighted as we explore how research is conducted—that is, how research is planned and carried out and how data are collected, analyzed, and reported. The goals

of the book are to provide you with the basic skills of a researcher and to enhance your ability to be a better critic of the research reported by others.

SCHOLARLY RESEARCH

With this introduction to research in general, we will turn our attention to the formal and systematic method of scholarly research. Researchers, or scientists, who have been trained in research methods and procedures conduct research. These scholars formalize their questions into research questions or hypotheses, which provide the scope and direction of the research project as well as guide the researcher in selecting quantitative or qualitative methods to answer the questions. The questions or hypotheses direct what data the researcher collects. After the data are collected, the researcher or research team analyzes the data to draw conclusions about the hypotheses or answer the research questions. Essentially, conducting research is a matter of making claims based upon data (O'Keefe, 2004). Different types of claims require different types of evidence, or data, which may be quantitative data, qualitative data, or both.

But the process is not complete. Scholarly, or academic, research is also public and available to others. However, the process of making it public is certainly different than it is for research conducted by a polling organization, for instance. Scholarly researchers describe what they have done in a paper that is submitted to a conference for presentation or to a journal or book for publication. Other experts in the field review the paper. This review serves as a test. Have the authors used an appropriate methodology to answer their questions or hypotheses? Have the authors explained the results thoroughly and logically? Are there critical flaws in the research process that jeopardize the results? The papers that make it through the review process are then presented at a conference or published in an academic journal or book. This is where the results become consumable.

Pick up a text that is assigned reading for one of your other communication courses. You will find many references to research within the chapters. As an example, the following passage is from my text *Communication and Organizational Culture: A Key to Understanding Work Experiences* (Keyton, 2011):

> For organizations such as AT&T, Cisco, and Red Hat, the culture is technologically grounded. That is, "the organization is not simply a culture that uses a technology; instead, it is a culture whose image, identity, and relationship to its environment are strongly associated with—indeed, dependent upon—the functionality of the technology it produces, services or sells" (Leonardi & Jackson, 2009, p. 397).

The reference to the authors Leonardi and Jackson is called an in-text citation. If you turned to the references listed at the back of the text, you would find the publication information so you could look up the 2009 journal article written by these authors. As the author of the text, I relied on the research of Leonardi and Jackson. As the reader of this passage, you are also a consumer and could verify my interpretation of their work by going to the original source.

Goals of Research

Accumulating knowledge through research is a continuous process. One research study cannot answer all the questions about any one issue or topic. This facet of learning—building on the research of others—is central to any academic discipline. Thus, the primary goal of communication research is to describe communication phenomena as well as discover and explain the relationships among them. Continuing with the example just given, discovery occurred when Leonardi and Jackson conducted qualitative research using three types of data to explore the concept of technological grounding.

These scholars first built a case for their study by drawing on the published research of other scholars. Next, they collected data to be able to analyze each organization's culture before the merger, and the organizational culture of the merged organization. Finally, they provided an explanation of how one company's organizational culture prevailed after the two companies merged. Thus, to put it more formally, research is the process of discovery and explanation.

The research process, if approached systematically, can have one of four results: It allows the researcher to describe behavior, determine causes of behavior, predict behavior, or explain behavior. *Describing behavior* entails describing outcomes, processes, or ways in which variables (another name for the concepts we study) are related to one another. The following example illustrates a research project that enabled a researcher to describe behavior.

Guthrie and Kunkel (2013) analyzed participants' diary entries to answer the research question, "What are the motives for using deception in long-term romantic relationships?" (p. 145). Across 68 participants who kept diaries about the use of deception with their romantic partners, 332 motives for using deception were identified. Across these, the researchers identified six overarching categories for using deception. These were: engaging in relational maintenance (e.g., engaging in deception to avoid a fight), managing face needs (e.g., protecting the partner's feelings), negotiating dialectical tensions (e.g., balancing the need for independence vs. togetherness), establishing relational control (e.g., ensuring that the partner behaves as desired), continuing previous deception (e.g., continuing a lie from the past), and motive unknown (e.g., a participant could not identify their motive for using deception). Guthrie and Kunkel asked a descriptive question; that is, what motives do people give for deceiving their partner? Their coding and analysis of that coding produced five different types of motives for lying. Thus, their results describe why people use untruthful messages in long-term relationships.

Determining the cause or causes of behavior is of interest to communication scholars because knowing the cause of something allows scholars to later plan interventions or develop training to increase the effectiveness of communication. For example, Nan and Zhao (2012) wanted to determine if self-affirmation messages, or positive messages about one's self, influence participants' response to anti-smoking messages. What the researchers found has interesting implications as the results were not straightforward. For example, participants who smoke who were asked to think and write about their personal values believed the anti-smoking messages to be overstated and felt that the anti-smoking message was annoying; on the other hand, the same manipulation had little influence for nonsmokers. The authors explain the findings this way: Because the anti-smoking messages are not relevant for nonsmokers, these participants did not process the antismoking messages carefully. Applying this finding more generally, the authors conclude that some variables influence smokers in a way that does not occur for nonsmokers. They argue that paying attention to these types of variables is necessary to produce effective health communication messages.

If researchers can describe communication events and identify their causes, then they can turn to *predicting behavior*. If behaviors are predictable, then we can anticipate what will happen in the future. In turn, this knowledge can help us make better decisions. Working from the principles of cultivation theory, Aubrey and colleagues (2013) wanted to test the prediction that watching interpersonal conflict on television would influence how people use control in their romantic relationships. Participants rated how frequently they watched 100 popular television shows. Participants also responded to questionnaires to capture how often

they used relational control in their romantic relationships, how many hours of television they watched per week, and their perceptions of television realism (e.g., television programming presents things as they are in life). Next, raters evaluated each show for how much interpersonal conflict was depicted. Some of the shows with the most interpersonal conflict included *The Real World*, *Nip/Tuck*, and *Sex and the City*. Some of the shows with fewer depictions of interpersonal conflict included *The Simpsons*, *American Idol*, and *7th Heaven*. The researchers used statistics to test the prediction that those participants who perceive television programming to be realistic would use more control in the relationships. Their prediction was verified: participants who watched more television that depicted interpersonal conflict used more control in their romantic relationships.

Going beyond describing, determining causes, and predicting, *explaining behavior* means understanding why a behavior occurs. For example, if researchers were able to determine how and why health campaigns work, more effective campaigns would ultimately result in a healthier society that spends less money on health care. But finding such an explanation is difficult and often requires a series of sophisticated research projects. Working from a well-developed and validated theoretical basis is an effective way to develop explanations for communication behavior. For example, A. J. Roberto, Meyer, Boster, and H. L. Roberto (2003) surveyed 488 junior high students about four aggressive behaviors: watching a fight, telling friends about a fight that is going to happen, insulting others, and fighting. For each of the aggressive behaviors except fighting, the explanatory model provided by the theory of reasoned action (i.e., the best determinant of actual behavior is behavioral intention) explained students' participation in aggressive behaviors. That is: students' attitudes about a behavior created behavioral intention, which, in turn, caused their participation in that behavior.

These four outcomes—description, determination of causes, prediction, and explanation—are closely related. New knowledge in one area will affect how questions are asked and answered in another.

Research and Theory

When researchers discover that one explanation about the relationship between phenomena occurs regularly, a theory can be constructed. Although many definitions exist for the term *theory*, in general, a **theory** is a related set of ideas that explains how or why something happens. In other words, a theory provides a way for thinking about and seeing the world (Deetz, 1992). More formally, a theory is a set of interrelated concepts, definitions, and propositions that presents a systematic view of phenomena. A theory specifies the relationships among the concepts with the objective of explaining and predicting the phenomena being studied (Kerlinger, 1986). As a result, theory helps us understand or make sense of the world around us. Of course, communication theories can help us understand our own communication behaviors as well as the communication behaviors of others (Miller & Nicholson, 1976).

With respect to communication, a theory is one or more propositions about people's communication behavior that enables a communicator to figure out how to communicate with particular individuals or in a given situation. The term *theory*, however, does not have one precise meaning. Rather, different definitions of the term are used because they promote different approaches to research (Craig, 1999; Miller & Nicholson, 1976). The best research is driven by theory, validates a theory, further explains a theory, challenges an existing theory, or aids in the creation of theory. Theoretically driven research is built on the results of previous researchers, and it provides a foundation for subsequent researchers. Theory cannot be formulated, tested, and verified in one research study. Rather, theory is developed and tested over time. What we come to know as *the theory* to explain some phenomenon is the result of many research studies and the efforts of many researchers.

Cushman (1998, p. 9) points out that "human communication is one of the most creative, flexible, and thus anti-theoretic processes in which human beings engage." Why? The complexity of communicating in multiple cultures with multiple, and sometimes conflicting, social goals provides the opportunity for multiple individual interpretations. Moreover, communication occurs in multiple languages with different sets of rules and practices. According to Cushman, this variability is one important reason communication scholars must look for the mechanisms or constructs that are constant regardless of the language used to communicate. Thus, communication researchers use systematic procedures and scientific principles to conduct research about how and why humans communicate as they do.

COMMUNICATION AS A SOCIAL SCIENCE

There are many methods of discovery and explanation, or many ways to view communication problems. Scholars conduct their research from paradigms that provide different explanations and functions for the role of symbols, messages, and meanings in the process of communication. These paradigms also create differences in what researchers count as data. You have probably explored these different paradigms in courses on communication and rhetorical theory.

Broadly, this book explores the social scientific study of communication for which a wide variety of methods is available. This text will introduce you to both **quantitative methods** (generally speaking, research that relies on numerical measurement) and **qualitative methods** (generally speaking, research in which the researcher observes participants first hand in naturally occurring contexts). Both methods are part of the social science research tradition as practiced in the communication discipline and reported in communication and related-discipline journals and scholarly books. Both quantitative and qualitative methods of research are empirical; that is, both methodologies are based on or are derived from experiences with observable phenomena. This is the critical element of research. Both quantitative and qualitative methodologies can observe and describe human communication. And both can help researchers in explaining or interpreting what was observed.

The study of communication from a social science perspective uses quantitative or qualitative methods to look for patterns of messages or communication behaviors. These patterns can be based on observations or measurements across the experiences of many individuals or on the in-depth observations from one case over time. Either way, the data must be empirical; that is, the data must be able to be verified through observations or experiences.

How does the study of communication as a social science differ from humanistic and critical studies of communication? The study of communication from a rhetorical perspective often focuses on how language is used to persuade in a particular case (for example, a specific speech by a specific person or other one-time event from which a text can be drawn or developed; a website that represents the views of a specific group of people). In addition to the rhetorical event itself, an analysis would include the historical, cultural, and social contexts surrounding it. Probably the most useful distinction is that rhetoric is planned for a specific goal for a specific audience, whereas the social science study of communication focuses on the interactive moment between and among conversational participants. A rhetorical study is more focused on one case, whereas the social science study of communication looks for patterns across people or situations.

From a critical perspective, the research emphasis is on the hidden assumptions of broad social structures that serve the interests of some people (those in power) more than others. Critical communication scholarship focuses on understanding the domination, inequality, and oppression that can occur through communication practices and structures. (For example, what ideological structures in our society control or dominate the dissemination of new media technology?) Some critical scholars use qualitative methods in their research, and some of these examples are included in this book. Critical communication research can also be rhetorical.

The definitional boundaries for what constitutes these three perspectives for studying communication (social science, rhetorical, critical) are blurry, and not mutually exclusive. But, broadly speaking, this text focuses on the social scientific methods for conducting communication research.

How does the study of communication differ from the study of other social sciences? Generally, the social sciences are defined as those areas of scientific exploration that focus on the study of human behavior. Psychology, sociology, and political science are other fields in the social sciences. As a social scientist, the communication scholar focuses on symbols used to construct messages, messages, the effects of messages, and their meanings. So, as you read communication research in journal articles and books, and as you design research projects, you should ask yourself, "What characterizes scholarship as communication research?" More specifically, what communicative component (e.g., symbols, messages, or meanings) is being studied? Does the research address social problems as communication problems? Is the research based upon communication theory or contributes to the development of communication theory? How does the research position communication in relationship to our social and cultural lives? (Buzzanell & Carbaugh, 2010).

The social sciences are different from the natural sciences in that the social scientists focus on the study of human behavior. Problems that are significant for study in the social sciences involve several important variables, and untangling the effects of one variable from another is difficult. Moreover, the social sciences recognize that the researcher is a human instrument with biases and subjective interpretations that can affect the individuals or processes under investigation. Finally, seldom can an entire system of human behavior (for example, an entire organizational communication system) be observed. Even if it could be, human systems are always subject to new influences; thus, what is being observed is dynamic. As a result of these differences, the study of human behavior is difficult to isolate and control even if the examination is done in the laboratory setting.

One last point is that social science research is contextually and culturally bound. Research is contextualized first by the number and type of people participating and by the type of communication being investigated. Second, research is contextualized by where the investigation occurs—in the lab or in the field. Third, research is contextualized by the culture in which it occurs. Researchers and participants bring cultural norms and values to what they do and how they communicate. All these contextual and cultural factors influence the research investigation, the data produced, and the interpretation of results.

The Scientific Approach

So how do communication researchers incorporate scientific characteristics into the process of conducting research? Generally, research follows procedural traditions that have been tested, validated, confirmed, and accepted by social scientists of many disciplines over time. The research process has five general steps (Kerlinger, 1986). Figure 1.1 illustrates this process.

First, researchers start with a question that interests them. A question may arise from reading the scholarly literature or a communication issue they've seen or heard in the media. Or, a question may arise from their personal experiences or from experiences reported to them by others. In other words, some question, or curiosity, has not been explained or had been explained inadequately.

A question may also be stated as a problem. In either form, the researcher cannot continue the research process without identifying and specifying the question or problem. For example, my own curiosity about why sexual harassment continues to occur in organizations despite clear societal and organizational signals that a perpetrator faces employment, legal, and even financial consequences for sexually harassing another employee caused me to pursue this area in several research projects.

Second, the researcher uses the question or problem to formulate a **hypothesis,** or a tentative, educated guess or proposition about the relationship between two or more variables. Oftentimes, hypotheses take the form of statements such as, "If x occurs, then y will follow" or "As x increases, so will y." With respect to our sexual harassment research, we used previous scholarship to help direct our inquiry. One of our hypotheses proposed that participants who identified themselves as targets of sexual harassment would identify more verbal and nonverbal cues as harassment (Keyton & Rhodes, 1999).

If the researcher cannot formulate a tentative proposition after reviewing the existing literature, then a research question is developed. A **research question** asks what the tentative relationship among variables might be or asks about the state or nature of some communication phenomenon. For example, we used the research question "Will there be a relationship between ethical ideology and the ability to accurately distinguish between verbal and nonverbal behaviors that have been shown to be associated with flirting and sexual harassment?" (Keyton & Rhodes, 1997, p. 135). Although numerous studies had been published on both ethical ideology and sexual harassment, no study had explored the relationship between these two issues. Thus, we posed a question to help us determine if a relationship occurred. We could not propose what type of relationship would exist.

In the third step, which is often underemphasized, the researcher uses reason and experience to think through the hypotheses or research questions that are developed. A researcher might ask, "Do the research questions and hypotheses I've generated capture the essence of the problem?" or "Are there other variables that affect the relationship between the two variables I've identified?"

This step of reasoning, or thinking through, may, in fact, change the research agenda. It may broaden the nature and scope of research, or it may more narrowly focus the researcher's inquiry. By taking this step in refining and formulating the research question or hypothesis, researchers discover the most significant issue that can be addressed given their initial questions or problems. By using the experience we gained in developing sexual harassment training for organizations and by searching the literature, we discovered that one of our proposed hypotheses ("participants who identified themselves as targets of sexual harassment would identify more verbal and nonverbal cues as harassment") would not adequately explain why some employees view behaviors as sexual harassment and others do not. In other words, an employee's perceptions of sexual harassment would not

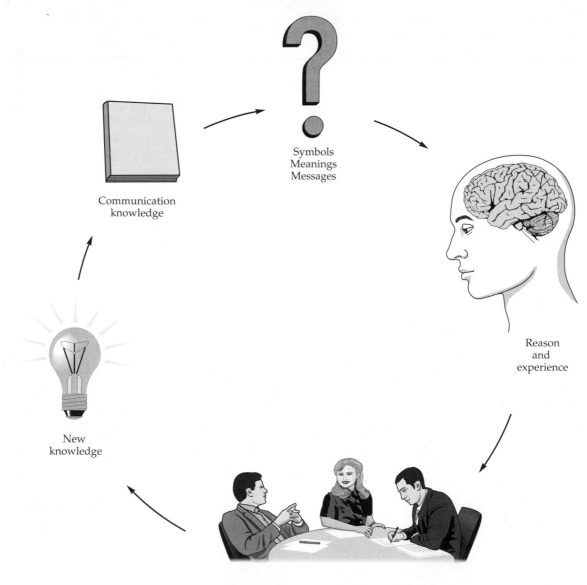

FIGURE 1.1 General Steps of the Scientific Approach.

simply turn on whether she or he had been sexually harassed. As a result, we tested three other explanations.

Fourth, the researcher designs and conducts the observation, measurement, or experiment. Although each variable or element identified in the research question or hypothesis must be observed or measured, it is actually the relationship between them that is assessed. Fifth, the data are analyzed and interpreted in reference to the question or hypothesis posed in step 2 and refined in step 3.

Thus, the social scientific approach to communication research starts with a problem, a question, or an idea as the researcher identifies a barrier or gap in knowledge. Then, the research question or hypothesis is formulated. Once developed, the research question or hypothesis is revisited and refined. Only then can the methodology be designed and carried out. The results are interpreted and fed back into our knowledge of the original problem. As a result, the problem is resolved, completely or partially, or new questions arise. Recognize that the five steps described are not necessarily discrete. One step blends into another. Work in one step may require the researcher to go back and revise what was previously completed.

Characteristics of Science

In pursuing these five steps of the research process, researchers can select from a variety of quantitative and qualitative methods. Although individual methods vary in the extent to which they encompass the following 12 characteristics, over time these characteristics have distinguished scholarly research from everyday, or informal, ways of knowing (Andersen, 1989; Bostrom, 2003; Katzer, Cook, & Crouch, 1978; Kerlinger, 1986). These characteristics are not unique to the study of communication. Rather, scientists of all disciplines have accepted them. Thus, the tradition of science rests with these 12 characteristics:

1. *Scientific research must be based on evidence.* Even experts can disagree. That is why evidence, or data, is paramount to the research process. Further, scientific research is based on the principle of empiricism. This means that careful and systematic observation must occur. What is observed and measured—the data—serves as the evidence researchers use in making their claims.

2. *Scientific research is testable.* This means that the proposition, research question, or hypothesis must be able to be probed or investigated with some qualitative or quantitative methodology. If the proposition cannot be tested or challenged in a research study, only speculations about the validity of the claim can be made.

3. *Researchers must explore all possible explanations in an effort to demonstrate that their proposition cannot be disproved.* If a proposition can be shown to be false, then, logically, it cannot be true, or valid. If the proposition and its explanation hold up over time, scientists come to accept the finding as true or real, until shown otherwise.

4. *The results of a research study are replicable, or repeatable.* Ideally, different researchers in different settings and with different participants should conduct replication studies—studies that repeat the same procedures. The results of any one study could be wrong for many reasons. Repeating the same or a very similar study many times and obtaining the same or very similar results ensures that the finding is real and can be counted on.

5. *For replication to occur, research must be part of the public record.* This is why communication scholars publish their work in academic journals and scholarly books. Scholars typically are not paid for these publications, but their work is supported through their universities and sometimes by government agencies and other funding organizations. As part of the public record, university and college libraries provide access to these journals and books so you can scrutinize what researchers did and how they did it. Scientific study is available to other researchers and the general public. It is not private, or proprietary, research conducted for the exclusive use of those who paid for the research to be done. Because scientific research is part of the public record, scholars build onto as well as challenge each other's work. All published research includes a section describing the methods by which the data were collected and interpreted. This allows others to evaluate the methods used for potential weaknesses and to replicate the study for further validation.

6. *Because scientific research is part of the public record, it is also self-correcting.* This characteristic means that the scholars who conducted the original study as well as the scholars who replicate or challenge studies are continually improving the methods by which they observe or measure the phenomenon of interest. Improving on the methods is one way to develop a greater understanding and more detailed explanations.

7. *Scientific research relies on measurement and observation.* Researchers can measure your communication apprehension, for example, by asking you to fill out a questionnaire. Or they can observe your apprehension by counting the number of times you lose your place when you are speaking and have to refer to your notes. When something is not directly observable, researchers develop and rely upon other methods (such as questionnaires) to capture participants' attitudes, perceptions, and beliefs.

8. *Scientific research recognizes the possibility of error and attempts to control it.* When things are measured or observed, we expect that some error will occur. For example, errors occur when a researcher does not see the participant lose her place while speaking because his attention is distracted by loud voices in another room or when a mistake is made in transferring data from the coding sheet to a spreadsheet. Errors can occur in many places in the research process. Quantitative research limits and accounts for error through the use of systematic procedures and statistics. Qualitative research accounts for error by providing detailed description to allow the reader to draw his or her own conclusions and interpretations. Most procedures have been standardized over time and across disciplines. Such formality in procedure acts as a form of control to help the researcher eliminate error, bias, and other explanations for the result found. Despite these control mechanisms, it is impossible to eliminate all bias and error in conducting research. Recognizing that bias and error can occur, researchers must take every precaution in helping to minimize it.

9. *Scientific objectivity requires the researcher to minimize personal bias and distortion.* Despite the passion for their topic and the time devoted to the project, researchers cannot be so committed to their own point of view and expectations that they fail to see other explanations when they appear. In essence, the objectivity of science distinguishes it from conclusions based solely on opinion. Too frequently, objectivity is associated only with quantitative research, and subjectivity is associated only with qualitative research. In reality, all researchers, regardless of method, must demonstrate objectivity in conducting research.

Even though qualitative research is more subjective due to the greater intimacy of the researcher–participant relationship, scholars doing this type of research must be able to describe their role in the research process, and this act requires a certain amount of objectivity. Alternatively, statistics must be selected and statistical findings must be interpreted—both subjective decisions. The point here is not to quibble over the alignment of objectivity/subjectivity to quantitative/qualitative method. Rather, it is to introduce the concept of scientific objectivity as practiced by all researchers regardless of which methodology they choose.

10. *Science by its nature rests on an attitude of skepticism.* By their nature, researchers are suspicious; they do not rely on what appears to be obvious or on common sense. Within the social science research tradition, researchers rely on data compiled from quantitative and qualitative methodologies to answer their questions and support their claims. This element of skepticism is what allows, even encourages, researchers to put their assumptions through a process of testing or verification.

11. *Scientific research has an interest in the generalizability of findings, or the extension of the findings to similar situations or to similar people.* In quantitative research, findings have greater external validity if they apply to a range of cases, people, places, or times. In other words, are the results of studies that use traditional college-age students as research participants applicable to nontraditional college-age students? What about teenagers? Or retired adults? All studies have limitations, but by using discipline-accepted procedures, researchers can help strengthen the generalizability of their results. In qualitative research, findings are typically less generalizable because they are more case-specific. However, the generalizability of qualitative results can also be strengthened as a researcher spends greater lengths of time observing research participants.

12. *The final characteristic of science is its* **heuristic** *nature.* This means that research findings lead to more questions. At the conclusion of most journal articles, scholars identify new questions that surface from their findings. The ability of a

finding to suggest additional questions or new methods of conducting the research is its heuristic ability. The ultimate objective of science should be to lead scientists to future discoveries and investigations.

Methodological Extremes

This introductory chapter is a good place to also introduce you to a methodological extreme that you should be aware of as you learn about research methodology (Bouma & Atkinson, 1995). A child given a hammer for the first time is likely to run around the house and hammer anything and everything. The child hammers because it is new and novel.

Unfortunately, this same phenomenon can exist when anyone is learning about research methods (see Cappella, 1977; Janesick, 1994). With each new technique, there is the tendency to believe that this particular method can answer any question. However, think of the method as a tool and recognize that there are appropriate tools for different purposes. To expand the tool metaphor, hammers are good for pounding in nails, but screwdrivers are better for twisting in screws. The point here is that the substantive content of the research question or hypothesis drives the selection of the methodological tool (Hackman, 1992; Janesick, 2000).

Methods are useful or effective only to the degree that they help the researcher answer a specific question or explore a specific hypothesis. In fact, the answers produced through any method of investigation are influenced by the specific methodological technique used in the investigation (Clark, 1990). So, if you let the method drive the research questions you ask or the hypotheses you test, then your results are more likely to be tied to the method you selected than to represent a valid response to the question or test of the hypothesis. No one research method can answer all questions. Although you will find that you are drawn to some methods more naturally than others, you will develop stronger analytical skills, both as a researcher and as a consumer of research, if you develop skills collecting and interpreting data from a variety of methodological techniques.

WHAT KINDS OF QUESTIONS DO COMMUNICATION SCHOLARS ASK?

Among the variety of questions that can be asked about communication are both important questions and trivial ones (Miller & Nicholson, 1976). How do researchers determine the significance of a question? There are three criteria: theoretical significance, social importance, and personal interest. The first criterion is theoretical significance. Questions that initiate the development of or contribute to the further development of communication theories are significant (Miller & Nicholson, 1976) because they deepen our understanding and explanation of communication behavior. When these questions are posed and answered by research, we gain new knowledge.

Because communication is a social activity, significant questions are those that have a general social importance (Miller & Nicholson, 1976). For example, questions that satisfy this second criterion might be, "What media campaigns would decrease the likelihood that children try drugs and alcohol?" or "What negotiation strategies work best in resolving intercultural differences in international negotiations?" Finding the answers to questions like these could have a powerful impact on many lives. Questions that drive research do not have to relate to all members of society. But we should ask who would be affected by the answer. If enough people are affected by or could use the answer to the question, then the question has social importance.

The third criterion focuses on which interests or perplexes the researcher (Miller & Nicholson, 1976). Questions that interest me include: (1) How do children learn to communicate in groups? (2) Why do some employees persist in sexually harassing other employees given the individual, relational, professional, financial, and legal consequences that are likely to result? (3) To what extent does the relational development among group members affect the task effectiveness of a group? Some of the studies my colleagues and I have conducted in these areas are used as examples in this book.

What questions interest you? They may be questions you have considered in another course, or questions that arise from your experiences with others. Your interests may be idiosyncratic, not coinciding with the interests of others. This demonstrates why the first and second criteria of theoretical significance and social importance are valuable and necessary. Keeping these three criteria in mind can help us respond to the "So what?" question. Many times, people read research reports and have difficulty finding any significance or utility for the findings. If your research project has societal significance, and is driven by personal interest—and if these issues are described in the research report—then the "So what?" has been answered.

The Nature of the Questions

As you read the communication research literature, you will notice several types of questions (Stacks & Salwen, 2009). The first type, **questions of definition,** provides definitions for phenomena in which we are interested. Whereas you may believe that all definitional issues have been addressed, remember that new communication situations and environments and changing societal values create new areas to explore and define. As a question of definition, Keyton and colleagues (2013) asked adults which communication skills they observe or hear in their workplace. In a subsequent study, working adults evaluated how effective they were at using the skills identified in study 1. Interestingly, what the first group of participants identified as the most frequently used communication skills were ones that participants in the second study admitted were not their most effective. These studies addressed definitional questions in that they were designed to, first, identify from an employee's perspective what communication skills are more frequently used; and second, to evaluate how effective employees believed they were in using these skills. Questions of definition, or *what* questions, move the phenomena from the abstract realm into the specific. Rather than guessing which communication skills employees use frequently and how effective they are in using these skills, the research team used online survey methods to answer the question, "What verbal workplace communication behaviors are routinely performed at work?" (p. 156).

After the *what* has been adequately defined, researchers generally turn to questions of relationships or questions of cause and effect. **Questions of relationships** examine if, how, and the degree to which phenomena are related. For example, adult online daters who had dating profiles on popular dating sites participated in a lab-based study so that the researchers could ask participants to assess the accuracy of their online profile; researchers also objectively assessed the online profile against characteristics they could observe about the person or verify through another source (e.g., their driver's license). As the researchers predicted, the more online daters lied in their profiles, the more they distanced themselves psychologically from these deceptions by using fewer self references, such as "I," "my," "me," or "mine," and more negations, such as "no," "not," or "never" in their online profiles. Thus, the researchers looked at the relationship between online daters' use of deception and how they presented themselves in their online profiles.

By understanding how variables are related, we have a greater understanding of our world and the role of communication behavior in it. Most important, questions of variable relations help the community of communication scholars build and develop theory.

Questions of cause and effect ask and answer if one or more variables is the cause of one or more outcome variables. These types of questions explore *why* one aspect of communication is connected to another. As an example, one research team (Paek, Oh, & Hove, 2012) predicted that exposure to a nationwide multimedia campaign directed toward children ages 9 to 13 would influence their attitudes toward physical activity. Children who saw the campaign

> were more prone to perceive that they can control their behavior of doing physical activity, that their family and parents think they should engage in physical activity, that their peers consider physical activity to be important and fun, and that physical activity is prevalent among their peers. Also, teens who reported greater exposure to the VERB campaign were more likely to form a favorable attitude toward physical activity. (p. 877)

TRY THIS! ### Evaluating Communication Questions

For each of the questions listed, evaluate your personal interest in the question and the question's social importance. Use the table to capture your evaluations. Rate your personal interest on a scale of 1 to 5, with 1 being "little or no personal interest" and 5 being "high personal interest." Rate social importance on a scale of 1 to 5, with 1 being "little or no social importance" and 5 being "high social importance."

Preliminary Research Question	*Personal Interest*	*Social Importance*
What is the relationship between social support and perceived stress of college students who use Facebook? (From Wright, 2012)		
Are personalized tweets from politicians more effective for message recognition and message recall than non-personalized tweets? (From Lee & Oh, 2012)		
How effective are campus organ donation campaigns in persuading college students to sign organ donation consent forms? (From Weber & Martin, 2012)		
How does task difficulty, leadership and peer communication influence the uncertainty volunteers can feel during their volunteering activities? (From Kramer, Meisenbach, & Hansen, 2013)		
What tactics do employees report using when expressing disagreement or contradictory opinions to their supervisors and managers? (From Kassing, 2009b)		
What coping strategies do people use when dealing with unfulfilled standards, or preexisting beliefs, about what makes a good dating relationship? (From Alexander, 2008)		

Compare your evaluations with those of other students. How are your evaluations similar or different? What other questions about communication do you believe merit researchers attention?

Thus, the researchers predicted, or demonstrated, that messages in the campaign had positive effects on children's beliefs about physical activity. **Questions of value** ask for individuals' subjective evaluations of issues and phenomena.

Questions of value examine the aesthetic or normative features of communication, asking, for example, how good, right, or appropriate a communication phenomenon or practice is. Questions of value are inherent in a study that explores how everyday discourse stigmatizes teenagers who are homeless. Harter, Berquist, Titsworth, Novak, and Brokaw (2005) interviewed homeless teens, educators, and social service providers. These teens, often called the hidden homeless, try to disguise the fact that they are homeless when talking with others to avoid being stigmatized or labeled. Other interviews revealed that community members are generally unaware of this homeless population and the difficulties the teens encounter trying to continue their education. This study raises the question of how this type of public discourse inhibits conversations that could bring awareness to the problem and help the teens and their families.

Finally, there are **questions of policy**. Communication researchers seldom test policy issues directly, but the results of research studies are often used to recommend a course of action. Roberto, Carlyle, Zimmerman, Abner, Cupp, and Hansen (2008) tested a 7-week intervention program designed to prevent pregnancy, STDs, and HIV in adolescents. The intervention included six computer-based activities. Over 300 10th graders at two high schools participated in the study. Students at one high school completed the intervention activities; students at the other high school served as the control group and did not participate in the intervention activities. Students who participated in the intervention program outperformed students in the control group on disease knowledge, condom effectiveness, how to negotiate condom use, and attitudes toward waiting to have sex. The study demonstrated that modest computer-based interventions could be effective. Because this type of intervention can be used to reach a large number of teens, the findings have policy implications for agencies considering how to allocate funds for these types of health-related programs.

As you can see, communication research varies widely in its subject matter. Some research has implications for the development of communication theory, some has more practical application, and some contributes to both theory and practice. But all research starts with a basic question about communication that needs an answer, and all research uses some form of scientific and systematic research methodology in providing those answers.

SUMMARY

1. Research is asking questions and finding answers.
2. Scholarly research is the discovery of answers to questions through the application of scientific and systematic procedures.
3. Academic research follows accepted norms and procedures that have been adopted by scholars from many disciplines.
4. In the process of scientific discovery and explanation, four outcomes are sought: describing behavior, determining causes of behavior, predicting behavior, and explaining behavior.
5. The best research is that which is driven by theory, validates a theory, further explains a theory, challenges an existing theory, or aids in the creation of theory.
6. As a social science, communication researchers use both quantitative and qualitative methods.
7. The study of communication from a social science perspective looks for patterns across cases and focuses on symbols used to construct messages, messages, the effects of messages, and their meanings.
8. Communication scholars start with an interesting question and then formulate a formal research question or hypothesis.
9. A hypothesis is a tentative, educated guess or proposition about the relationship between two or more variables.
10. A formal research question asks what the tentative relationship among variables might be, or asks about the state or nature of some communication phenomenon.
11. Research is judged to be scientific by 12 characteristics: its empirical nature, its ability to be tested, the extent to which it can be falsified or disproved, the ability to replicate or repeat findings, the public nature of findings, its self-correcting nature, the ability to measure or observe the phenomenon of interest, the ability to minimize error through the control of procedures, its level of objectivity, the skepticism it raises, the generalizability of findings, and its heuristic nature.
12. Questions suitable for communication research are those with theoretical significance, of social importance, and in which the researcher has personal interest.
13. Questions suitable for communication research may be questions of fact, questions of variable relations, questions of value, or questions of policy.

KEY TERMS

empirical

heuristic

hypothesis

proprietary research

qualitative methods

quantitative methods

questions of cause and effect

questions of definition

questions of policy

questions of value

questions of relationships

research

research question

social science research

theory

See the website www.mhhe.com/keyton4 that accompanies this text. For each chapter, the site contains a:

- chapter outline
- chapter checklist
- chapter summary
- short multiple-choice quiz
- PowerPoint presentation created by Dr. Keyton

For a list of internet resources, visit http://www.joannkeyton.com/CommunicationResearch-Methods.htm.

CHAPTER TWO

The Research Process: Getting Started

Chapter Checklist

After reading this chapter, you should be able to:

1. Describe what a theory is and its role in communication research.

2. Explain why the research process starts with identifying a research problem.

3. Develop a preliminary question from a topic or issue.

4. Explain why a preliminary question is superior to a topic in conducting library research.

5. Evaluate preliminary questions for their completeness and clarity.

6. Conduct a search for print and online scholarly resources.

7. Glean the basic ideas from reading the abstract, literature review, and discussion sections of a research article.

8. Track a citation back to its original source.

9. Effectively summarize and report what you have found in the library.

CONSIDERING THEORY IN RESEARCH

Research revolves around theory. Thus, the journal articles and book chapters you find in the library use research as a basis for developing or challenging theory. *Theory* is a set of interrelated propositions that present a systematic view of phenomena. The purpose of those propositions is to describe, predict, or explain the phenomena. For communication research, theory creates propositions about symbols, messages, and meanings.

Research is necessary to validate theory. Generally, quantitative research starts with a theory. Then researchers conduct a research study to demonstrate if a theory holds true for a set of data. If it does not, the theory is altered or discarded. In this theory–research link, theory is the map by which the researchers conduct their studies. This type of research relies on *deductive* thinking or reasoning in that theory presumes what will result and the research verifies those claims. Theory directs the researcher in developing hypotheses and questions and in selecting the method for testing them.

Research is also necessary to develop theory. In this case, research is inductive. Researchers start with a research question and examine their collected data for both patterns and anomalies to first answer the question and then contribute to theory development. In this theory–research link, the theory, or map, is drawn from the patterns uncovered by the research. This type of research relies on *inductive* thinking or reasoning in that theory, or generalization, is derived from the cases explored.

As you can see, research and theory are necessary complements to one another. Theorizing is important to research in two additional ways (Brooks, 1970). First, researchers cannot observe the entire universe. Rather, researchers must select a subset of phenomena to be observed. Theory directs researchers' attention to particular communication patterns, functions, themes, processes, and so on. For example, it would be impossible for a communication researcher to study every aspect of how communication is used in political campaigns. Thus, theory helps us define and isolate a communication phenomenon for study. Second, theory helps "integrate data which otherwise would remain mere collections of facts" (Brooks, p. 4). In a theory, research findings are integrated into a system of description, prediction, and perhaps explanation that help us answer questions of "What?" "Why?" "How?" and sometimes "What if?"

Developing Theory

We engage in informal theorizing when we try to make sense of the past, operate effectively in the present, or anticipate events in the future (Lustig, 1986). Although theorizing is a common and fundamental human activity practiced every day, formal theorizing as a scientific process is quite different. Formal theory building (Lustig) involves six basic steps:

In step 1, the researcher describes an event or observation that needs understanding. The event must be observable, interesting, important, and remarkable to come to the attention of the researcher or someone else who desires an understanding of it. This first step begins to identify the "what."

In step 2, the researcher creates an explanation for the event. Although anyone can create an explanation, it is the scientist's job to formalize and test explanations. In this step the answer to "Why?" begins to be formulated.

In step 3, the researcher moves from the specific event or observation to a more generalized form. In other words, if the event of interest is family decision making around the dinner table, the researcher could move to the more generalized communication event of decision making or the more generalized communication event of family interaction. The researcher must decide which type of communication event is more interesting and intriguing to investigate. By moving to a more abstract level, the researcher can now look for similar events to see if the answer to "Why?" developed in step 2 is also suitable for explaining these other, different but similar events. Instead of focusing on one specific interaction event, the researcher must develop answers suitable for a class of similar events. This characteristic of theory moves it from an informal

TABLE 2.1 Theory Development—Steps 1 Through 4

	Task	*Example*
Step 1	Describe event or observation	Family members (2 adults, 2 children) eat dinner and discuss their daily activities. Father introduces family activity for weekend, which generates considerable discussion from children. Although the discussion initially has both positive and negative points introduced, eventually the children agree that they do not want to pursue the weekend activity suggested.
Step 2	Create explanation for event	Explanation 1: Children are likely to reject ideas presented by parents during dinnertime discussions. Explanation 2: Parents introduce ideas for family dinnertime discussion to obtain family members' preferences.
Step 3	Move from specific to more generalized form	General form 1: Children's rejection or acceptance of parental input. General form 2: Parents desire input from other family members.
Step 4	Derive predictions from explanations	Focus 1: Children are likely to reject ideas presented by parents. Focus 2: Parents will seek input about family matters from other family members.

to a formal level. Although you are comfortable with the way informal theorizing describes and explains events that happen in your daily life, you would not be comfortable applying others' informal theories to the events that you experience. Thus, the researcher's job is to discover the commonalities among events that allow them to be classified and then to develop and test theories that describe and explain all events belonging to a class. Thus, a theory of decision making should apply to many people's experiences of decision making, not just one's own.

In step 4, the researcher begins to derive predictions from the explanation developed in step 3. To do this, the researcher asks, "What else would be true, or observable, if the explanation was correct?" Continuing with our family decision-making example, the researcher could make several propositions that are testable. Examine Table 2.1 to see the progression from step 1 through step 4.

Now, in step 5, the researcher must select a focus and test the proposed theory. Most communication observations are complex enough to support multiple attempts at theory building. The researcher must develop a plan for and collect data that can test the predictions or propositions.

Step 6 of the theory-building process uses the obtained data to confirm, revise, expand, generalize, or abandon the proposition tested (Lustig, 1986). Notice that collecting the data in step 5 is distinct from interpreting the data in step 6. If the results are consistent with the proposition, the theoretical framework is confirmed for the time being. If the results are not consistent with the proposition, the discrepancy must be explained by critically examining the methodological process or by reworking the theoretical framework. If the theoretical framework is revised or if two alternative and competing explanations are present, the theory-building process starts again. If methodological problems are identified, the researcher repeats steps 5 and 6 using different and improved methodological procedures.

Even after these six steps, the theory-building process is not complete or final. Theory is developed over time, and this theory-building process is repeated many times as different scholars test theoretical propositions in their research. Both quantitative and qualitative research contribute to theory development.

Theories are developed and tested incrementally. After a basic theoretical notion is presented

TRY THIS!   Finding Theory in Journal Articles

Find two or three communication journal articles for a communication problem that interests you. Carefully read the literature review of each article. Does the author identify by name the theory or theories that are providing the foundation for the research study? Does the author point to a description, cause, prediction, or explanation as the reason for conducting the research? If so, this is likely the theoretical basis of the study. Next, read the discussion and implication sections of the articles. In this part of the journal article, authors discuss the implications of the study as a challenge to the theory or as further development or expansion of the theory.

as a proposition in the scholarly literature, scholars develop studies to test the propositions. This is possible because the results of scholarly research are presented in a public forum. Theory is confirmed only after many studies, usually conducted by different scholars with different methodologies, achieve similar results. Even at that point, theories are still considered tentative. A theory that was at one time believed to be valid can be questioned in the future. For example, new technologies can create new opportunities and circumstances for communication. Thus, theories of how and why interpersonal relationships develop over time may need to be reexamined in light of the extent to which these technologies are used in developing relationships.

Utility of Theory–Research Link

To the extent that a community of scholars accepts research findings and can agree on the theoretical propositions, theory has been achieved. But all theory should be judged by some aspect of utility (Lustig, 1986). The knowledge gained from the process of theory-building should be used "to suggest new questions that are worth answering, develop more accurate theories about human communication, communicate more effectively, teach others to communicate more effectively, create better human relationships, and improve the cultures and the environments within which we all live" (Lustig, p. 457). When the utility criterion is added as a test of the theory-building process, you can see not only

that the theory–research relationship is reciprocal, but also that it is grounded in the practical issues of human communication (Keyton, Bisel, & Ozley, 2009).

In fact, theory is used four ways in the research process (Hoover & Donovan, 1995). First, theory provides patterns for interpreting data. Without working from or toward theory, research could produce results without an organizing framework. Second, theory links one study to another, helping to provide a continual conversation about our understanding of communication phenomena. Third, theory provides a framework for understanding how concepts and issues are important or significant in our interactions. For example, theorizing about communication apprehension and then conducting studies to validate those expectations helped researchers uncover the role apprehension plays in nearly every communication event in which we participate. Fourth, theory helps us interpret the larger meaning of research findings. For example, reading about how observers react to an apprehensive individual may cause you to monitor and manage your own apprehensiveness when speaking in public.

Scientific and systematic inquiry is a process of developing and testing theory. Direct relationships exist among questions asked, data observed, and theory development (Miller & Nicholson, 1976). Examine the deductive and inductive research models (see Figure 2.1 and 2.2). See how theory drives quantitative research? Alternatively, in qualitative methodology, observations

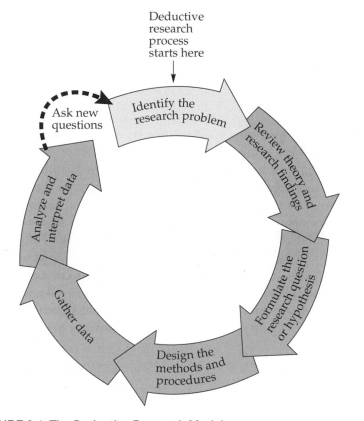

FIGURE 2.1 The Deductive Research Model

tend to drive theory development. However, the selection of any particular quantitative or qualitative methodology does not guarantee that a study will result in theoretical development. Rather, a study must be designed to illuminate and examine underlying principles and propositions (Shapiro, 2002). Only then can its findings contribute to theoretical development.

Also recognize that the process of inquiry is not always linear. Nor can theory be developed or challenged in one study. Recall that science can be characterized by its replicable and self-correcting nature. Multiple studies are needed to replicate findings, just as multiple studies are needed to challenge and alter existing theory.

Theory, or less formalized versions of theory called *models*, *frameworks*, or *taxonomies*, is the basis of the research process and the literature

review you conduct before designing a study and collecting data. As you conduct your library search be aware that not all theories have the word *theory* in their title.

THE RESEARCH PROCESS MODEL

Doing research means joining the conversation. Whether you are conducting a literature review for a class assignment or developing a literature review to support a research project you design and conduct, you will need to know what exists in the research literature. Much of what you will find in the library will be related to the theories researchers use to describe, predict, and explain communication behavior and processes.

Researchers seek answers to questions. There are two possibilities regarding the information they need. First, an answer may already exist, but that information is not known to the researcher. In this case, library research usually provides the answer. Second, an answer is neither known nor available. In this case, the researcher must develop and conduct research to uncover an answer. In either case, finding an answer depends on the researcher's skills to search and track down information that fits his or her needs.

Working from what you already know and understand, your objective as a researcher is to find information that answers your question. Yet, obstacles and pitfalls along the way may keep you from accomplishing your goal. You must be vigilant and pay attention throughout because your ability to integrate new information that you find is really the key issue and determines whether you are successful in answering your question. To help you, the library search you do for your research study can be guided by two scholarly traditions. Each is described next.

Deductive Research Model

Take a look at the first research model, presented in Figure 2.1, to see how the deductive research process is structured. Notice how the model is circular and cyclical. Each of the steps must occur for the research process to be complete. In this case, after identifying the research problem, the researcher begins with a theory and then gathers evidence, or data, to assess whether the theory is correct. This type of research process is **deductive** because the researcher is moving from a position that has already been worked out by others. From theory, the researcher develops hypotheses or research questions, which are then tested by collecting data. Ultimately, the collected data are interpreted against the theoretical position.

After entering the research process at "identify the research problem," the researcher uses theory to guide the investigation. Next, based upon theory and the research findings accumulated, the literature review is developed and presented as a foundation for the research project. The literature review is also the basis for formulating the research question or hypothesis. The researcher

then selects the research methods that will help in answering the questions or hypotheses. Then data are gathered and interpreted. Although the researcher will be able to answer the initial questions at this point, the research process is not necessarily complete.

Recall that research is prized for its heuristic characteristic. If research has heuristic significance and values building on the work of others, answering one question should lead to other questions for which answers are needed. Thus, as answers are developed from the interpretation of data, the research process starts over again with a new question.

Inductive Research Model

Alternatively, a researcher suspends judgment in beginning his or her research study and develops a plan for seeking literature and gathering data that is framed around the foundation of a research question (Figure 2.2). After the data are gathered and examined, theories are developed in response to what the data reveal. This type of research process is **inductive** because the researcher is moving from the specifics of the data to the more general explanation of theory. Again, the research process is complete, but only temporarily. Reports of these findings are likely to encourage researchers to uncover new problems and start the process again.

Research as a Process

Regardless of where one enters the research process, all of the steps are linked together. The steps are interdependent. At times, researchers believe they have completed a step and proceed to the next—only to find that they do not have the most effective foundation from which to proceed. And so they must go back and work through the preceding step again. As you will discover in the class for which you are reading this book, research is not evaluated solely on its outcomes. Rather, the process that leads to the outcome, or research result, is equally important.

Whether a researcher uses the deductive or inductive process, the first research activity is to identify the research problem, often stated as a broad question. Formulating the problem or

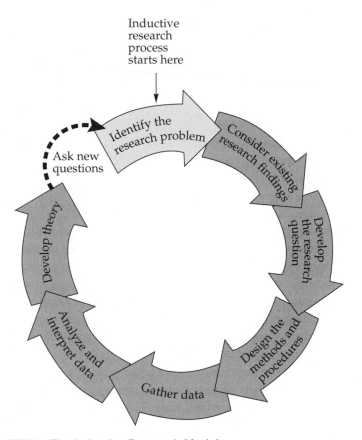

FIGURE 2.2 The Inductive Research Model

question into a research question or hypothesis formalizes the research as social science. Research conducted according to the deductive model, which typically relies on quantitative methods, is described in greater detail in Chapter 4. Research conducted according to the inductive model, which typically relies on qualitative methods, is described in greater detail in Chapter 14. Throughout the research process, researchers must be concerned with issues of ethics and integrity. Communication research is conducted on, with, or through others. Thus, the communication researcher must seriously consider and evaluate the integrity of the research proposed. Moreover, the research must balance the scientific needs of the researchers (as well as society's need for knowledge) with the physical, psychological, and emotional needs of those who participate in the research. These issues are addressed in Chapter 3. But, for now, let's turn to the ways in which researchers identify the communication problem or question of interest.

IDENTIFYING THE RESEARCH PROBLEM

Remember that research is the process of asking questions and finding answers. Identifying the research problem or broad research question is always the first activity in the research process.

Formulating Research Ideas

If you cannot think of a communication problem or broad question, think back to the theories you have discussed in other courses. In reading and learning about theory that describes, explains, and predicts communication behavior, did one strike you as being particularly relevant to your personal or professional life? Did one cause you to ask questions differently than you had in the past? Did a theory intrigue you because it provided a description, explanation, or prediction that seem incomprehensible? Or did a theory help you understand your desired profession in a different way?

Another way to begin to develop a communication problem or broad question to study is to think of what happened today to you, or in front of you, that illuminated a communication dilemma, problem, or question? What are your family, friends, and colleagues talking about? How are their issues related to communication? Answering questions like these can help you think of a communication problem. Often we tend to think that the daily problems of living we experience are unique to us. In reality, individual experiences may differ in some ways, but generally they are connected to and mirror the experiences of others. Thus, consider whatever problems you are facing as a good source for research ideas.

Still unsure about a communication problem to pursue? A good way to survey contemporary problems and issues is to check what topics are being featured by news sources. Many of the major news outlets—*The New York Times, USA Today,* ABC News, CBS News, NBC News, CNN, Fox News, and others—update their websites throughout the day.

Turning Communication Problems into Preliminary Questions

With the communication problem identified, you can begin to frame preliminary questions, which will help you search through library holdings and electronic databases. The preliminary question is not the final research question you will see in both the deductive and inductive models. The research question is more formal, and the foundation for the research project. The preliminary question is still important, however, because it can certainly lead you to the formal research question or research hypothesis. Before you seek library resources, use the following steps to evaluate your preliminary question. Taking this step will help make your library search more effective.

Let's say you are interested in the impact of divorce on children's abilities to communicate their feelings. Closer examination shows that there are two issues here: The first is impact of divorce; the second is children's abilities to express their feelings. You could do library research on each topic separately, but doing so might not lead you to the answer. By formulating your interest in this topic into a preliminary question, "How does divorce affect children's abilities to communicate feelings?" you are more likely to uncover resources that can answer your question or that will help you determine that the question has not been adequately answered.

But take another look at that question. What does the question assume? The question asks "how" divorce impacts children's abilities. A better first step would be to find out *if* divorce affects children's abilities to communicate. Thus, "Does divorce affect children's abilities to communicate feelings?" will be a better place to start, for it keeps you from falsely assuming that divorce does influence children in this way.

As another example, you might recognize that the team leader of your shift at work has difficulty in organizing and conducting meetings. You wonder if there is anything you can do as a team member to help. In this case, questions could be, "Are leaders the only team members responsible for how meetings are conducted?" or "In what ways can a team member maintain the role of team member and help the leader conduct more effective meetings?" or "What risks do team members take when they help facilitate meetings?" Now look at these questions for the assumptions embedded within them. In the first, you are asking about the basic assumption of who is responsible for conducting team meetings. But notice in the second and third questions that the answer to the first question is assumed.

Rephrasing the communication problem as a preliminary question is the first step in seeking answers. Phrasing your question helps define your research area and narrow your search. Most important, questions help you uncover the links between concepts and help you identify assumptions you have made. And, as they frequently do,

TRY THIS!

Developing Initial Questions to Guide the Research Process

Read the example given in the table for the topic of instant messaging (IM). Notice how the general topic is developed as a communication problem and then stated as a preliminary question. Then the question is analyzed for any underlying assumptions. With these assumptions uncovered, the preliminary question should be restated so that it is more specific. Use the topics and communication problems listed in the following table to develop the preliminary questions to start the research process.

Topic	State as Preliminary Question(s)	Examine Question(s) for Assumptions	Restate Preliminary Question(s)
Texting	What are teenagers texting when they drive?	All teenagers have access to texting. All teenagers who drive, text.	What do teenagers explain as their motivation for texting while driving?
Parents talking with their children about guns and violence			
Careers for communication graduates			
Encouraging someone who is going through a difficult personal situation.			

questions lead to more questions. If you end up with several questions, try to order them into a list of which questions must be addressed first, second, and so on. Or if questions in one area suggest questions in another area, try to draw a diagram of the relationship of the questions to one another. Regardless of how you identified your problem, remember to formulate it into a question that focuses on communication. For example, a news report on the prevalence of bullying in schools might end up as "In what ways do playground and recess activities promote or inhibit the occurrence of verbal bullying among children?"

Take a look at the examples of communication problems in the Try This! box "Developing Initial Questions to Guide the Research Process." When you have finished revising a few of the examples listed, do the same with communication issues that interest you.

Evaluating Your Questions

After you have developed your preliminary question, it's time for evaluation. Use these questions to make a final assessment before you spend time searching the research literature:

1. Is the question clearly stated?
2. Do others agree about the clarity of the question?

3. Have you asked only one question? Not two, three, or four?

4. What is the communication orientation of the question? In other words, what communication practice, policy, rule, procedure, or consequence is being investigated? Is your focus on symbols, messages, or meanings?

5. Is the question phrased in such a way that it is not biased toward a particular answer or solution?

6. Is there some way to observe or measure the communication phenomenon of interest?

7. Can you research this question given the limitations of time and resources?

8. Who would be interested in the answer to the question?

9. How could those who are interested use the information?

If you are satisfied that you are asking the preliminary question in the most effective way and that the question is appropriate for communication research, you should identify the keywords or phrases to use in your search of library resources.

USING LIBRARY AND DATABASE RESOURCES

With preliminary questions developed, you are now ready to conduct your search for resources. It is tempting to conduct all your research online, but working in the library has advantages as well. The most important advantage: You can ask a librarian for help.

If your library has the *International Encyclopedia of Communication* or the *Encyclopedia of Communication Theory* in print or online, these are good first steps in looking for resources for your preliminary question. The encyclopedic entries cover all aspects of communication. Each entry provides definitions, major themes of research, and several key citations. Regardless of where you gather resources, ask questions about the credibility, authority, and relevance. Also consider how current the source is. Look for more recent sources if necessary. How something is presented (in print or online) does not necessarily make a source good or bad. If you select a source for your literature review or research project, you should feel confident that it is the best source for your project. It is also important to gather several resources so you can compare definitions and research findings. The next section describes several ways to find resources for a literature review or for a research project.

Scholarly Journals

Generally, your initial search should be for scholarly articles published in academic journals. Articles in journals give you the opportunity to see what research questions and hypotheses have been studied by communication scholars. You can read their arguments for the research study they designed, and read how they collected and analyzed their data. Most important, you can read about what they learned in conducting the study.

Journals are edited and published by scholarly professional associations, universities, or publishing houses dedicated to scholarly work. Scholars submit their manuscripts to a journal. The journal editor sends the manuscript out for review to at least two reviewers who do not know the identity of the author. This process allows reviewers to give their honest and critical feedback about the manuscript. After this peer review, the editor makes a decision about revision and publication. Often, journal articles are published only after an extensive review and revision process. In addition, most journals have a very high rejection rate, generally 80 to 90 percent. As a result, journal articles are regarded as quality research written by knowledgeable experts. Some of the journals specific to the discipline of communication that publish social science research include

American Communication Journal	*Communication Quarterly*
Communication Education	*Communication Reports*
Communication Monographs	*Communication Research*
Communication Research	*Communication Research Reports*

The Communication Review

Communication Studies

Communication Theory

Electronic Journal of Communication

Health Communication

Howard Journal of Communications

Human Communication Research

International Journal of Listening

Journal of Applied Communication Research

Journal of Broadcasting & Electronic Media

Journal of Communication

Journal of Computer-Mediated Communication

Journal of Family Communication

Journal of Public Relations Research

Journal of Social and Personal Relationships

Journalism & Communication Monographs

Journalism & Mass Communication Quarterly

Mass Communication & Society

Political Communication

Public Relations Review

Qualitative Research Reports in Communication

Research on Language and Social Interaction

Southern Communication Journal

Western Journal of Communication

Women's Studies in Communication

Of course, there are other journals in the communication discipline as well as journals that are multidisciplinary (such as *Business Communication Quarterly, Cultural Studies ↔ Critical Methodologies, Journal of Business Communication, Journal of Contemporary Ethnography, Journal of Health Communication, Management Communication Quarterly, Qualitative Inquiry, Small Group Research*). Finally, journals in other disciplines (for example, management, psychology, and sociology) do publish research of interest to communication scholars. In some cases, the research of communication scholars can be found there as well.

Journals can be accessed in a number of ways. First, your library subscribes to article databases that index communication research. *Communication & Mass Media Complete* (often shortened to CMMC) contains abstracts or full text for articles published in more than 600 journals in

communication, mass media, and related fields. Many times, the full text of journal articles is available through that database. If an article you want is not in full text through this or another database, look directly for the journal. Your library may subscribe to print and online issues of hundreds, maybe thousands, of journals.

Should you look for journal articles on your library website? Or through a Google search? Accessing journals through your library's website is recommended. You are likely asking, "Why not use Google?" You can. But if your assignment is to be based only on academic sources, the university library online resources are the best place to get the most comprehensive return on your time spent searching. Why? Your library has purchased journal subscriptions. Thus, there is no cost to you for reading the online or print version. Check with your instructor or librarian to identify the journals that will satisfy your needs during your literature search.

Books

Your library also has a collection of books and edited books. Communication scholars often write or edit books about their research expertise. If you have identified an author who writes in the area you are conducting research, use his or her name in a search of the library catalog. Or use one of your keywords as part of a title or subject area search in the library catalog.

You should also check to see if your library carries *Communication Yearbook*. This annual series is an edited collection of literature reviews and topical critiques. For example, in Volume 36 (2013), *Communication Yearbook* published literature reviews on the influence of advertising and media on the alcohol consumption of children and teens, use of social media in organizations, and many other communication issues. You will have to check the table of contents of each *Yearbook*. If you find a chapter that helps you, be sure to review the resources in the reference section.

Finally, check to see if your library has a handbook related to your area of research. Handbooks are focused on one context of communication and provide extensive reviews and critiques of literature, theories, and methods in a particular area (examples are *Handbook of Family Communication, Handbook of Communication and Aging Research, Handbook of Political Communication Research, Handbook of Interpersonal Communication,* and *Handbook of New Media*). To find which handbooks your library carries, use the keywords *handbook* and *communication* to search your university's catalog database. If you find a chapter that helps you, be sure to review the resources in the reference section.

Online Resources

Because anyone can post a website and because so many websites are posted, finding information on the Web is not a problem. But finding credible, authoritative information can be. Remember that all search engines are not the same; each search engine has a different mechanism for finding websites even when you use the same keywords for searches.

There is nothing wrong with doing resource searches on the Web. Online materials are not necessarily unreliable. To find credible and authoritative sources online, use this list of questions.

1. What type of domain does the site come from? Generally, .edu and .gov sites are considered more trustworthy than .org and .com sites.

2. Who publishes or owns the site? How can you tell? Look for this information between http:// and the next /.

3. Is this a personal website? One way to tell is to look for a tilde (~). Tildes often signify a personal website. If a tilde is used with an organizational name, often what follows is the website of a specific person of that organization.

4. Can you tell who (a person or institution) created the site? Is there a name, e-mail address, or an *about us* or *contact us* link? Where do those links take you?

5. Are the author's credentials or affiliations displayed on the website?

6. What is the purpose of the website? To inform? Persuade? Sell? Is advertising clearly labeled as such?

7. How current is the website? Look for dates to indicate when the site was created and updated.

8. If a source is quoted or paraphrased on the web page, is information about that source provided so you can independently verify the accuracy of the information?

Anyone can produce a website. This means that you must carefully assess what is presented. A website can present research that appears to be scholarly. But unless the site includes citations and identifies the author and his or her qualifications, it may be very difficult to gauge the authenticity or validity of the material.

Analyzing Your Resources

After you have found several articles, books, book chapters, or websites, you need to evaluate these sources. For journal articles and chapters, read through the abstracts, and then read the discussion section. Read the foreword or introduction and first chapter of each book. Check the list of references at the end of the articles or chapters. Could any of the sources listed there be helpful to you? Are you able to answer your question? Should your question be revised based upon what you have found? At this point, you have reached another decision point. If you can answer your question to your satisfaction, your search is over. If you cannot satisfactorily answer your question, or if you found conflicting answers in your search, you can write your question in its final form. You are ready to develop your research project.

Answering the following questions can help determine if you have enough information or if you need to continue on with a detailed search. Your library search has been adequate if you are satisfied with your answers to the following questions:

1. How much has been written on your issue?

2. How recent or relevant is the material?

3. Has some critical event occurred or societal value changed that could challenge the interpretation of the answers to the questions asked?

TRY THIS!   ## Searching for Sources

1. Using the keywords *media* and *ethics,* perform a database search (e.g., *Communication and Mass Media Complete*) available through your university library. Do the same keyword search on Google. How would you describe and explain the differences?

2. Your question is "What nonverbal behaviors demonstrate confidence in public speaking?" What keywords would you use in your basic search? What synonyms could be used? Conduct this search and report on your findings.

3. In your basic search for references on communication in stepfamilies, you have found that communication scholar Paul Schrodt is the author of several studies. How do you interpret this information? How would you use this information in your detailed search?

---

4. Who has done the most work on your issue?
5. Where has research on the topic been published?
6. What aspects of the issue received the most attention?
7. What questions about the issue have been answered?
8. What aspects of the issue have been ignored?
9. Are there reasons to replicate, or repeat, studies that have been conclusive?
10. What other issues have you found related to your primary one?

If you have searched thoroughly and diligently, you are likely to have uncovered the materials you need to answer your question or to develop your research project. Remember, however, that it is nearly impossible to find all the available literature. Finding everything is not a prerequisite for most student research projects. But you should have information available from a variety of authors, from a variety of publication outlets, and from sources published over time. Analyze your resources for their breadth and depth of coverage.

As you review the literature you have found, take good notes and save or print all the relevant pages. Check out the table of contents as well as subject and author indexes of books. Identify books that are helpful by noting the authors' names, complete book title, year of publication, place of publication, publisher, and call number. Identify journal articles that are helpful by noting the authors' names, complete article title, year of publication, complete journal title, volume number, and page numbers of the journal article. You will need all this information to develop a reference list if you cite the material in your research project.

Adjusting the Question

As you work through the search strategies, don't hesitate to adjust your preliminary question. As you discover new information, you will develop a more sophisticated appreciation and understanding of the problem. Incorporate the information you read into your preliminary question. In particular, did your search uncover theories that can help you make sense of your question? Could several theories provide the basis for competing claims or solutions to your preliminary question? As you find new sources of information, it is likely that your preliminary question will become more narrowly focused. Keep a list of all resources that you are using. You will use these again as you develop your research project and as you write up your research report.

It is time to stop adjusting the preliminary research question when two conditions are satisfied.

First, you should be comfortable that your question is specific enough to be interesting. Second, you should be comfortable with the quality and quantity of resources you can use to help you answer your question. At this point, it is time to move on to analyzing the resources you have collected.

USING AND ORGANIZING YOUR RESOURCES

Getting started on a stack of resources is not easy. The first step is to read the title and abstract or summary of each resource. Next, read the problem statement, which is usually part of the literature review or precedes the literature review in a journal article or book chapter. It identifies the research objectives. Although the exact research questions or hypotheses may not be presented here, the problem statement generally suggests them. The problem statement answers the question "Why did the researchers conduct this study?" Generally, reading this section will help you decide if the article or research report will be helpful to you.

In the literature review, the authors present the literature that supports their formal research questions and hypotheses. Read the research questions and hypotheses carefully because the results or conclusions from the study are tied directly to them. For now, skim the methods and results section, and then move on to the discussion section. What did the scholars find? What

---

AN ETHICAL ISSUE

Using the Ideas of Others

Anytime you use the work of others, you must provide a citation indicating in the text of your paper what idea you are using and whose idea it was. This is called an in-text citation. There are two types. The first is the citation for a direct quotation. In this case, you indicate with quotation marks the exact words you copied from the original work and provide the page number in addition to the author's last name and the year of the publication. This way, anyone who reads your paper can locate the exact source.

d'Haenens and Ogan (2013) performed analyses of data from EU Kids Online to determine if ethnic minority children living in Turkey used the Internet differently than native Turkish children and their peers in the European Union. On page 42 of their article, they use the following direct quote in-text citation as they describe online usage in Asia and Latin America as "becoming the dominant nations online, having the greatest number of users" (Dutta, Dutton, & Law, 2011, p. 3).

The second type of in-text citation is for situations in which you have summarized or paraphrased the ideas or conclusions of others. This in-text citation is documented with the author's last name and year of publication. An example of an indirect in-text citation from the same article on the same page is

> Lack of internet access is still an issue in EU countries, despite the fact that in six of its member countries, regular internet use was reported by 80% of the population. Seven other countries, however, reported use levels below 60% (Seybert, 2011).

A complete list of your references must be provided at the end of your paper. This enables the reader to locate the source of any in-text citation you used. Most social science researchers use the citation and reference style of the American Psychological Association (6th ed.), which is the style used in this book. Check with your instructor to see which style you should use.

DESIGN CHECK

Evaluating the Literature You Found

As you can see, the research process starts with your identification of a research topic, and then examines the topic further as a communication problem through your search of the research literature. You will use the articles and chapters that you find in the literature review for your study. Communication research is indexed on several databases, so if you cannot find what you need, be sure to ask your reference librarian for help. As you search the literature, be sure that you are collecting studies that are published in communication journals or are authored by communication scholars. Scholars in many disciplines study communication, but the most complete and thoughtful focus on communication is published by communication scholars.

were the answers to the research questions? Did they confirm or not confirm the hypotheses they proposed? Remember that the conclusion to the investigation is found in the discussion section. When a research question or hypothesis is presented in the literature review, it is still tentative.

Tracking Others' References

As you read the articles, books, and chapters, you will find in-text citations. This documentation device provides information within parentheses for the research work cited by the author. Each in-text citation includes the authors' last names, year of publication, and the page number if material is quoted word for word. To track down this citation, turn to the reference list at the end of the article, book, or chapter. This is labeled with the heading "References," "Bibliography," or "Works Cited." For each citation you will find a complete bibliographic entry—all the information necessary for you to find the article, book, or chapter. Look at the "References" section at the end of this book for an example.

Why would you want to track down the articles, books, and chapters that other authors have used? There are several reasons. First, these published works are part of an ongoing scholarly conversation. Something briefly mentioned in one article might lead you to another article that could provide valuable background information for you. Second, you may have missed this source in your library search. Tracking down the references used by others gives you the

opportunity to fill in the gaps of your literature search. Third, authors draw conclusions about the work of others and then base their arguments on those conclusions. If you are not familiar with the literature, you have to take the authors' conclusions for granted. Rather than relying on their evaluative biases, you could track down the reference, read it, and draw your own conclusions.

Organizing What You Have Found

Now, how will you organize the resources you have found so you can write a research report or a research proposal? First, look at the body of literature you have collected. Are there one or two authors whose names appear several times? If so, start your reading there. Researchers tend to work on lines, or streams, of research. This means that scholars become known for conducting research on certain issues. If the names of one or two scholars don't stand out, organize your literature by publication date. To get a historical overview, read from the older literature through to the newer literature. Another way to begin is with an article or chapter that reviews or summarizes a particular line of research. If you find conflicting ideas, theories, or findings, organize resources into similar categories.

Summarizing What You Have Found

One method is to arrange the material using major and minor points as primary and secondary headings, much like a traditional outline. A second method is to arrange the findings in chronological order, usually working from the oldest to the most recent. This is particularly helpful if you want to demonstrate how a question was answered or how an issue developed over time. A third method is to ask a series of questions and respond with what you found for each question. In this case, working from the broadest question to the narrowest question is recommended. A final method for organizing your material is to work from general to specific (a deductive approach), or build from the specific to the general (an inductive approach).

Whatever approach you take to summarizing what you found in your literature search, the primary question should be—"Have I answered my question?" If you have, you will need to think creatively about how to replicate, extend, or challenge those conclusions as the basis for a research project. Generally, there is little value in repeating the work of others if you agree with their conclusions and find no major faults in how they conducted the research. However, there is value in replication when the original study is dated, when societal values and practices surrounding the issue have changed or are changing, or when you find a flaw in the study that makes you question the results. For example, societal values about many adult relationships (such as same-sex marriage, living together, divorce, single parenting, adoption) have changed significantly. Research in these areas may be necessary to see if the conclusions drawn in the past about communication in these relationships are relevant now.

As you read and sort the literature you found, you might find that scholars disagree. Or you might find that research conclusions have been drawn about most, but not all, of the issues surrounding your issue. If scholars disagree, you could develop a research study to examine the disagreement. If some, but not all, issues are answered, you could develop and conduct the study that fills in this gap. Remember that one of the characteristics of science is that it is heuristic. This means that conclusions, or answers to questions, help identify new questions to be answered. You are now ready to write the literature review, which is described next.

WRITING THE LITERATURE REVIEW

The **literature review** is the framework of the research investigation (Katzer et al., 1978). More specifically, it interprets, integrates, and critically analyzes the published literature relevant to your study (Northey, Tepperman, & Albanese, 2012). It includes a summary of the scholarly literature the researcher studied to design and develop his or her research study. Thus, it provides the structure and orientation for the research project and the rest of the written research report.

Although there are many ways to organize a literature review, all have an introduction, a body, and a conclusion (Northey, Tepperman, & Albanese, 2012). The introduction of the literature review describes the communication problem to be examined and notes very briefly the significant research results or theory that exists. The body of the literature review provides detail about existing studies—those that both support and contradict the position you are advocating. Most important, the literature should be developed as an argument—one that leads the reader to the research questions or hypotheses you are examining or testing, which is the conclusion of your literature review.

Introduction to the Literature Review

The problem statement is usually positioned at or near the beginning of the literature review. It describes the communication problem you are investigating and broadly describes the research objectives. For example, the first paragraph of the literature review should be a road map for the rest of the review. Specify what you are going to cover and what you hope to accomplish. Although the exact research question or hypotheses are not stated directly here, they are suggested. The problem statement answers the questions, "What precisely is the problem?" and "Why is this problem worthy of study?" In other words, the problem statement explains why the researchers conducted the study and why you and others should be interested.

Look at how van Swol (2009) presents the problem statement for a study on group decision making:

> Decision making in groups involves discussing and receiving information about the decision alternatives, but researchers have found that groups often focus on information that all members know and share in common before the group discussion. Because groups are often used to make decisions precisely because groups potentially could have a more diverse pool of information than an individual, the fact that groups focus on shared information has concerned researchers and practitioners. Therefore, researchers have examined ways to increase the focus on unshared information in groups. This paper examines if structuring the group as a Judge-Advisor System can increase the focus upon unshared information. (p. 99)

From this paragraph, a reader would know what the problem is and how severe the problem is perceived to be. This type of problem statement presents a compelling argument for the study that follows.

Body of the Literature Review

The literature review is a historical account of the variables and concepts used in the study. In some cases, this history can be substantial. While it can always be succinctly summarized; it should never be excluded. A good literature review also includes the latest research, generally including publications within the last year. But a good literature review goes beyond a simple description of previously published work to include analysis, synthesis, and a critique of this work (Ryan, 1998). It should provide an assessment of previous efforts and suggest why these issues should be explored again or in new ways. The literature review is also the place to point out gaps in previous research, or to develop new arguments by integrating or considering the research literature in new ways.

In addition to acknowledging themes and gaps in the literature, a good literature review seeks to identify and establish relationships among previously published work and the study presented.

The writer should address the major assumptions that have guided earlier work and address how the current study accepts or rejects those assumptions. Finally, the literature review should state clearly how the current study contributes to the understanding of theory or theoretical assertions (Ryan, 1998). The literature review will become the first section of your research report. So it should focus on theory, theories, or findings from research studies that provide a foundation for the study.

One way to introduce theory into your literature review follows this pattern (Creswell, 2009). First, identify the theory by name. Next, describe the central hypothesis or argument of the theory. This doesn't need to be detailed; rather provide a general description of what the theory describes, explains, or predicts. Third, describe who has used the theory and and their findings and conclusions. Finally, explain how the theory will be adapted to your study and research context.

As you select articles for your literature review, you are likely to see certain authors, or even one article, cited over and over. This is an indication that the author is central to the discussion of this research issue or that this one article is considered a landmark or classic study (Galvan, 1999). Another way to identify noted authors or classic studies is to turn to a textbook in the area of your research study. These authors and studies are often highlighted there. Locate the published article so you can read it in its original form and in its entirety. Otherwise, you will have to rely on others' summaries and evaluations.

Finally, as you include the work of other researchers, be careful to distinguish between assertions made in the literature review and conclusions supported with evidence in the discussion section (Galvan, 1999). It is easy to confuse the two. In the literature review, researchers often make predictions or claims as they set up their research questions and hypotheses. But these claims can be different from conclusions found in the discussion section. Claims made in the discussion section are based on data from the research study. So, even though a researcher may hypothesize something in the literature review, support for that claim is not known until the study is completed and the data analyzed and interpreted.

TABLE 2.2 Ways of Organizing a Literature Review

Organizing Framework	Description and Uses
Chronological order	In temporal order based on publication dates. Especially good for tracing the development of an issue, concept, or theory.
General to specific	Information about the broadest issue is presented first, followed by research that deals with more narrow aspects of the issue.
Contrast-comparison	Research that is similar is separated into sections to highlight differences among the types or topics of studies.
Trend identification	Research is separated into identifiable trends. Trends are placed in order of importance to the study.
Methodological focus	Studies using the same methodology are grouped together and compared to other methodologies.
Problem-cause-solution	Description of the problem is followed by description of its cause and suggestion of a solution.
Topical order	All information about a topic is presented in separate sections. Topics are introduced sequentially in order of importance or in order of appearance in research questions or hypotheses.

Thinking of a literature review as describing the relationships among previous studies helps authors avoid long strings of references or quotations, which could lead readers to miss the trends or themes that the researcher found in the literature. In essence, the literature review is effective to the degree that the researcher helps the reader see and understand key terms and phrases, and relationships among issues that the researcher saw in his or her development of the research project.

Organizing the Literature Review

There are different forms for organizing a literature review. Table 2.2 reviews several of the most common approaches.

Writing a literature review is no small task. Actually, it is much like writing a paper or essay for a class that does not require you to collect data to support your claims. Many of the writing techniques useful for that type of paper are also helpful in research reports.

Use headings and subheadings to structure the review and to distinguish among its major and minor sections. Use internal summaries to signal the end of one section, and use transitions to signal that another section of the literature review is beginning. Within sections, major points can be enumerated with "first," "second," "third," and so on. Finally, remember that a literature review is not a long string of quoted material. Your evaluations and summaries of the literature are important elements of the literature review because your opinions and arguments shape the research project.

Literature reviews are written in the third person. Some communication scholars use the first person, although the third person still appears to be preferred. Because research reports are considered formal writing, some other advice includes

- Spell out acronyms the first time they are used.
- Avoid contractions; instead write out both words completely.
- Avoid slang expressions (for example, "you know").
- Eliminate bias in your writing with respect to sex, gender, sexual orientation, racial or ethnic group, disability, or age.

TRY THIS!   ## Analyzing What You Have Found

As you read through the resources you have found, these questions can help you identify the most important aspects for your research project. In each journal article or book:

1. Look for the definitions of important concepts and ideas.
2. Identify the arguments the author is making. What evidence (i.e., data, theory) does the author present for those arguments?
3. What examples does the author give?
4. What insights can you draw from the article or chapter? What is new, useful, or has implications for your research project?
5. It is not likely that any study will be exactly like the one you want to design and conduct. How can you adapt ideas from this article or chapter to your study?

(Adapted from Berger, 2011).

Concluding the Literature Review

The literature review concludes with a presentation of the research questions or hypotheses. Typically, the research questions and hypotheses served as a summary of your analysis of the existing literature. Each hypothesis or research question should be separately stated as a simple sentence or simple question. And each hypothesis or research question should be identified as such, usually with the notations H1, H2, or RQ1, RQ2, and so on. Besides helping to identify specific questions and hypotheses, this notation form creates a shortcut later in the results section because the researcher can simply refer to H1, or the first hypothesis, without restating it again.

SUMMARY

1. Researchers seek answers to questions.
2. Theory is developed and tested through research.
3. Research can be a deductive or an inductive process.
4. The steps of the deductive process are identifying the research problem, reviewing existing theory, formulating a research question or hypothesis, designing the

methods and procedures, gathering data, and analyzing and interpreting data.

5. The steps of the inductive research process are identifying the research problem, considering existing research findings, developing the research question, designing the methods and procedures, gathering data, analyzing and interpreting data, and developing a theoretical explanation.

6. Both the deductive and inductive research processes are circular and cyclical as the final step, asking new questions, starts the research process again.

7. The first step in both the deductive and inductive research processes—identifying the research problem—consists of identifying a communication issue, turning this into a preliminary question or set of questions, conducting a library search, and adjusting the question, if necessary.

8. Library research can reveal if the answer to your question is available, but not known to you.

9. If the answer is neither known nor available, research must be conducted to uncover the answer.

10. Evaluate your preliminary questions for their underlying assumptions,

completeness, and clarity prior to conducting the library search.

11. Find scholarly articles published in academic journals or scholarly books.

12. When you find an article or book that may be helpful, take notes and document all the citation information.

13. Your preliminary question may require adjustment as you discover new information.

14. Using what you found in the library search, organize your material by major and minor points, in chronological order, by answering a series of questions, or from the general to the specific or from specific to general.

15. A literature review is your integrated analysis of the scholarly literature and concludes with the statement of the research questions or hypotheses.

KEY TERMS

deductive   literature review

inductive

See the website www.mhhe.com/keyton4 that accompanies this text. For each chapter, the site contains a:

- chapter outline
- chapter checklist
- chapter summary
- short multiple-choice quiz
- PowerPoint presentation created by Dr. Keyton

For a list of internet resources, visit http://www.joannkeyton.com/CommunicationResearchMethods.htm.

CHAPTER THREE

Research Ethics

Chapter Checklist

After reading this chapter, you should be able to:

1. Address potential ethical issues during the design phase of the research project.
2. Explain how your research project minimizes risk and enhances benefits to participants.
3. Find alternative research procedures to avoid physical or psychological harm to participants.
4. Design a research project that demonstrates beneficence, respect for persons, and justice.
5. Follow procedures and guidelines required by your university's institutional review board.
6. Write an informed consent form that is understandable for participants.
7. Use deception and confederates only if other alternatives are unavailable, and only if these practices do not cause undue harm for participants.
8. Devise data collection procedures that maintain participants' confidentiality and anonymity.
9. Identify ethical concerns when a research study uses online technology.
10. Understand any risks associated with videotaping and audiotaping participants' interactions.
11. Provide an adequate debriefing for research participants.
12. Ensure the accuracy of data and findings.
13. Write a research report that does not plagiarize the work of others.
14. Write a description of research participants in such a way as to conceal their identities.

This chapter explores issues of ethics and integrity associated with the research process. Researchers, including student researchers, have a responsibility to conduct their investigations without harming research participants and report their findings without misrepresenting the results. As a consumer of research, you should be aware of the ethical principles that guide researchers in the development, execution, and reporting of research studies. Knowing this information will help you identify where ethical breaches could occur and influence a study's findings.

Various standards and guidelines have been developed in specific scientific fields, particularly to guide researchers who use participants in their studies. In some instances the phrase *human subjects* is used, but many researchers consider this term pejorative and prefer the term *research participants*. Communication researchers generally follow or adapt the more specific ethical guidelines of research adhered to by psychologists or sociologists. Additionally, most universities require their researchers—faculty and students—to adhere to guidelines of ethical research promoted by the National Institutes of Health whether or not the research project is funded by that agency.

It is the researcher's responsibility not only to adhere to the guidelines but also to be familiar with the most recent developments. Ethical standards change in response to changes in research practices. For example, changes were required because the increased use of technology to collect data focused attention on privacy and identity concerns. Ethical standards have also changed due to research misconduct. Whereas many people are familiar with ethical problems that have occurred in medical research, a survey has documented ethical problems in the social sciences (Swazey, Anderson, & Lewis, 1993) and with researchers whose work is funded by the National Institutes of Health (Martinson, Anderson, & de Vries, 2005). If ethical standards exist for research, why does this happen?

Research designs are developed and research is conducted through a series of decisions—decisions made by the researcher or research team. These decisions require researchers to evaluate what to do or how to proceed based on the setting or context of their research. Also, researchers, just like others, view ethical standards differently. Major ethical violations, such as plagiarism or falsifying data, occur infrequently. But more minor ethical violations, such as not fully describing a research design or keeping inadequate records for the research process, are more common (Martinson, Anderson, & de Vries, 2005).

As a result of these problems, communication researchers in the United States are required to use the general research guidelines from the Office for Human Research Protections (OHRP), a unit of the U.S. Department of Health and Human Services. These guidelines have been adopted by universities and funding agencies. Communication researchers who study communication about health issues or in health contexts are also required to follow the Health Insurance Portability and Accountability Act (HIPAA) guidelines established by the U.S. Department of Health and Human Services. These guidelines provide comprehensive federal protection for the privacy of personal health information. The website URLs for these guidelines and others of interest to communication researchers are listed on the author's website at http://joannkeyton.com/CommunicationResearchMethods.htm. Other countries have developed similar ethical guidelines (see Israel & Hay, 2006).

It may be helpful to think of protection for research participants in this way. "Given that social researchers intrude in the social lives of human beings, they must ensure that rights, privacy, and welfare of the people and communities involved in the study are protected" (Ntseane, 2009, p. 296). In addition, most studies conducted by researchers promises some degree of social benefit for participants, directly, or for similar people, more broadly. If participants give the researcher information, then researchers should provide protections for them (Mabry, 2009). But who would ensure that those protections are provided? Typically, governments step in to develop and administer regulations about research like that conducted by communication scholars. But it would be inefficient, for example, for the Federal government to do this for all scholarly research conducted in the United States. Thus, the responsibility for ensuring that protections for research participants are upheld has been delegated to the institutional home of the researcher conducting the study. Researchers also are responsible for securing the well-being of participants and this means being sensitive to how burdens and benefits are distributed among researcher and participants in data collection. What are you asking of participants? What are you giving back? Leeman (2011) describes the sensitivity with which he conducted ethnographic interviews in a homeless shelter; he also describes the way in which the interview process offered a voice to the participants he interviewed. The balance between seeking and collecting data, and providing protections to participants is delicate and must be carefully thought through.

Researchers generally agree that protections should be provided to participants (Ntseane, 2009). However, there are some difficulties with how human subject protections are administered. Two issues are prominent. First of these is that each college or university implements their own interpretation and applications of the federal regulations (Mabry, 2009). This means that a research design allowed at one university may be disallowed at another. The second issue is that the federal guidelines were developed for medical research, not necessarily social science research. Thus, it can be difficult to apply these standards to the types of quantitative and especially qualitative research that communication scholars and students conduct. You will be reminded throughout this chapter to consult with your college or university's Institutional Review Board before designing and conducting any research project to learn about their required forms and approvals.

It's worth mentioning that the ethical regulations and guidelines presented below are general so that they can apply to a variety of types of studies. Thus, the regulations and guidelines cannot address the details of each research study. Rather, they point out important ethical features that should be examined and considered (Carusi & De Grandis, 2012). Before you collect any data, quantitative or qualitative, be sure to check with your professor to determine which guidelines you must follow.

ETHICAL QUESTIONS IN PLANNING RESEARCH

Without question, all the ethical issues of conducting and reporting research are the responsibility of the researcher. Researchers must have integrity and be honest and fair in interacting and working with research participants. Additionally, researchers must be concerned with how their research topic and procedures could create physical or psychological harm to participants. While there is a tendency to think of ethical responsibility in terms of regulatory standards, researchers should also contemplate what ethical standards are upheld by their communities and larger societal groups. The study of ethics has long been a part of studying communication. Thus, ethics is not something that is added to our research projects because we are required to add it (Cheney, 2008). Rather, ethical issues guide all our decisions, including those about whether to conduct research and how, who will be asked to participate and why, and what the benefits are that they and others will accrue. Essentially, it is the social responsibility of researchers to ethically plan and conduct their research (Resnik, 2007).

The researcher has two broad ethical responsibilities (Kvale, 1996). The first responsibility is scientific. This means that researchers are responsible to their profession and discipline. Guidelines developed and prescribed by the researcher's sponsor (for example, department, university, professional association, or funding agency) must be followed. Further, researchers have a responsibility for developing and conducting research projects that will yield knowledge worth knowing. As part of this ethical responsibility, researchers should write their research reports in a transparent manner. This means that the researcher should write so readers can understand the logic and activities that led to the development of the topic, problem, hypothesis, or research question; understand the definitions of what is being studied; be able to follow the collection, and analysis of data or empirical evidence; and clearly identify the results of the study ("Standards for Reporting," 2006). Adhering to this responsibility ensures that participants' time and energy are not wasted or abused.

Second, researchers must consider the ethical issues that arise from their relationships with research participants. Regardless of how close or distant those relationships are, researchers must assess the extent to which the nature of the researcher–participant relationship is affecting the collection, interpretation, and reporting of data.

At the beginning of any research project, the researcher must consider the basic ethical issues just described. Although general ethical principles guide the researcher, ethical issues must be considered specific to the design of the study (how data will be collected) and by the nature of the study (for example, what is being studied and with which participants). All researchers should ask and answer the following questions about their research designs (Kvale, 1996; Sieber, 1992):

1. What are the benefits of this study? How can the study contribute to understanding communication? Will the contributions of the study be primarily for participants? For others similar to the participants? Or for people in general?

2. How will the consent of participants to participate in the study be gained? Should consent be given orally or in writing? Who should give the consent? Is the participant capable of doing so? If not, who is? How much information about the study needs to be given in advance? What information can be given afterward?

3. How can the confidentiality and anonymity of research participants be handled? Is there a way to disguise participants' identity? Who will have access to the data?

4. Are the participants appropriate to the purpose of the study? Are they representative of the population that is to benefit from the research?

5. What potential harm—physical or psychological—could come to the participants as a result of the study?

6. What are the consequences of the study for participants? Will potential harm be outweighed by expected benefits? Will reporting or publishing the outcomes of the study create risk or harm for participants?

7. How will the researcher's role affect the study?

8. Is the research design valid or credible? Does it take into account relevant theory, methods, and prior findings?

9. Is the researcher capable of carrying out the procedures in a valid and credible manner?

The answers to these questions will affect how the researcher assesses the developing design and conducts the research study.

Because research participants are people, special attention is paid to how they are treated. In 1991, seventeen federal departments and agencies adopted a set of regulations, known as the *Belmont Report* (National Commission for the Protection of Human Subjects of Biomedical and Behavioral Research, 1979). Three ethical principles—beneficence, respect for persons, and justice—were identified in this report to guide researchers in designing the aspects of the research process that directly affect or involve research participants. These principles not only guide this aspect of research design but must also be simultaneously upheld, as they are the foundation on which Institutional Review Boards evaluate research proposals.

Beneficence means that the well-being of participants is protected. The researcher must protect the participant from harm as well as meet the obligation to maximize possible benefits while minimizing possible harms. How does this work? Ideally, the outcomes of your research would provide immediate benefits for those who participated and longer-term benefits for individuals like those who participated, while minimizing risk for participants. You can justify a research project that does not provide immediate benefits for those who agree to participate in your study if the longer-term benefits improve knowledge or aid in the development of more effective procedures or treatments. In other words, the long-term benefits outweigh the minimal risk participants might encounter.

The balance between risks and benefits must favor the benefits gained. Before research is

AN ETHICAL ISSUE

Professional Association Guidelines for Conducting Research

Communication research takes many forms, and ethical principles have been established for both quantitative and qualitative research methodologies. Quantitative research has traditionally been evaluated with the research guidelines *Ethical Principles of Psychologists and Code of Conduct of the American Psychological Association* (APA). For those using qualitative methodologies, the research ethics guidelines and statement on ethnography of the American Anthropological Association (AAA) and the American Sociological Association (ASA) will be pertinent. For those who conduct research on or through the Internet, the ethical guidelines of the Association of Internet Researchers (AOIR) will be useful. The URLs for these research guidelines and others can be found on the website at http://joannkeyton.com/CommunicationResearchMethods.htm.

Regardless of method, however, the National Communication Association's (NCA) *Code of Professional Ethics for the Communication Scholar/Teacher* presents three guidelines that should inform all communication research activities.

1. In terms of integrity, ethical communication researchers should employ recognized standards of research practice, conducting research that they have been properly trained to do, and avoiding procedures for which they have not been adequately prepared. If in doubt about any ethical matter, they seek advice before proceeding. Their primary goal is to avoid harm to others–whether direct emotional or physical harm or harm to the reputations of those being researched.

2. The value of confidentiality demands that the identity of those being researched be kept confidential except in cases where the research is carried out on public figures or publicly available material. Criticism of another's language, ideas, or logic is a legitimate part of scholarly research, but ethical researchers avoid *ad hominem* attacks. Avoiding personal attack does not mean that critics or reviewers refrain from commenting directly and honestly on the work of others, however.

3. Professional responsibility requires that ethical communication researchers know and comply with the legal and institutional guidelines covering their work. They do not use the work of others as their own, plagiarizing others' ideas or language or appropriating the work of others for which one serves as a reviewer.

conducted, researchers should identify risks—emotional, physical, professional, or psychological—and benefits to participants. It is easy for researchers caught up in designing their research study to assume that their method of data collection will not present any risks for participants. One way to avoid this assumption is to talk with people who are similar to the potential pool of participants about their comfort level with the data collection method planned. You may not mind answering a set of questions, but others can provide insight into how a set of questions or observations may be too

uncomfortable, personal, or revealing—too much of an imposition.

In every case, benefits to participants must outweigh the risks. Saying that knowledge will be gained is not an adequate benefit. Rather, researchers should explain specifically how the knowledge gained from the research study poses benefits to the participants or to similar individuals.

Respect for persons involves two separate principles: (1) treating individuals as capable of making decisions, and (2) protecting those

Responsibility to others entails honesty and openness. Thus, the ethical communication researcher:

- Obtains informed consent to conduct the research, where appropriate to do so.
- Avoids deception as part of the research process, unless the use of deception has been approved in advance by an appropriate review body.
- Provides adequate citations in research reports to support theoretical claims and to justify research procedures.
- Discloses results of the research, regardless of whether those results support the researcher's expectations or hypotheses.
- Does not falsify data or publish misleading results.
- Reports all financial support for the research and any financial relationship that the researcher has with the persons or entities being researched, so that readers may judge the potential influence of financial support on the research results.

Likewise, the value of personal responsibility mandates that:

- Communication researchers will not accept research funding for projects that are likely to create a conflict of interest or where the funder controls any of the research design or procedures. If funding is accepted, communication researchers honor their commitments to finish the work on schedule.
- Communication researchers who work with research participants honor their commitments to their subjects. Those who work with communities honor their commitments to the communities they research.
- Communication researchers share credit appropriately and recognize the contributions of others to the finished work. They decide before research is conducted how authorship will be determined and the order of authorship. They also decide through mutual consultation whether authors should be added or deleted from the finished product.

who are not capable of making their own decisions (National Commission, 1979). Researchers should treat participants as if they are capable of deliberating about personal goals and capable of determining their own actions. In other words, the researcher should refrain from making choices for participants. The research process should be described and explained, and then the participant should make a choice about volunteering to participate. Unfortunately, the heavy-handed demeanor of some researchers leaves the impression that participants have no choice but to participate. When a researcher communicates with research participants this way, the researcher is being disrespectful.

Another issue of respect arises when individuals are not capable of self-determination. Usually, these individuals are those who are sick or disabled or those whose circumstances restrict their opportunity to deliberate freely. Thus, respect for the immature and the incapacitated is evident when the researcher refrains from placing these individuals in the position where they would be asked to make choices about research participation.

Justice is really an issue of fairness (National Commission, 1979). Ideally, all participants would be treated equally. In the past, however, research in disciplines other than communication has violated this criterion by creating risks for participants and, later, using the research results to generate benefits for those not involved in the research study. Thus, justice was not upheld because the benefits were withheld from research participants who took the risk of participating. Sometimes it is difficult to treat all participants equally, especially if the goal of research is to explore differences between and among groups of people (for example, differences between supervisors and subordinates or differences between males and females). But justice and equal treatment should always be the researcher's goal.

This type of inequality can also surface in communication research when training is offered to one group of participants and not another before the outcome measures are collected. At the conclusion of the study, the researcher should offer the same training to those who were initially denied it. Hopf, Ayres, Ayres, and Baker (1995) provided this type of justice in their study of public speaking apprehension. In this study, participants who were apprehensive about public speaking, as identified by their self-report scores, were contacted and asked to participate in a study. In two of the conditions, participants were assigned to workshops to receive some type of intervention for public speaking apprehension, a method for reducing anxiety about communicating. Participants assigned to the third condition were the control group and did not participate in any workshop activities. However, after all data were collected, participants in the control condition were given the opportunity to enroll in a workshop for apprehension reduction.

But the issue of justice raises a larger issue. In selecting individuals to participate in a study, a researcher must carefully examine why he or she made those population and sample choices. The researcher should ask, "Am I systematically selecting one group of people because they are (1) easily available, (2) in a position making it difficult for them to deny participating in the research, or (3) in a position in which they can be manipulated into participating?" Ideally, research participants are selected because they have characteristics relevant to the theoretical or practical issue being examined.

Although the three principles—beneficence, respect for persons, and justice—guide the development of the research design with respect to the use of research participants, they do not prescribe a specific set of ethical rules for researchers to follow. Each research situation is unique, causing unique applications of the three principles. At times, these principles may even be in conflict with one another (Vanderpool, 1996). The researcher's goal, however, is to design a research study that upholds these principles to the fullest degree possible.

As you can see, how the researcher treats or interacts with research participants is a significant element of research ethics. As a result, researcher integrity and the rights of participants in research studies are closely intertwined. These issues are so central to academic research that formalized procedures have been established to ensure both. Universities and funding agencies sponsor most academic research, and they require that research conducted under their sponsorship follow guidelines for informing participants of their rights and the potential risks of participating in research studies. These formal procedures require the researcher to gain permission to conduct research before any aspect of the research is conducted. In most universities and colleges, the institutional review board reviews the research proposal and grants the researcher approval to conduct the research.

Institutional Review Board

Federal agencies that sponsor research (for example, the National Institutes of Health, the National Science Foundation) require that universities have a formal process in place for considering the soundness and reasonableness of research proposals. These formal considerations are usually conducted by groups typically identified as **institutional review boards (IRBs)** or **human subjects review committees**; universities require their faculty and students to develop and submit a research proposal for the board's or committee's approval before any data are collected. Policies and procedures differ among universities, but if you intend to use the data collected to prepare a paper for distribution to any audience other than your professor, or if there is any possibility you will do so in the future, approval is probably needed.

The primary role of such university groups is to determine if the rights and welfare of research participants are adequately protected (Sieber, 1992). By examining a research protocol or proposal before the researcher starts a project, an institutional review board can ensure that the research project adheres to both sound ethical and scientific or systematic principles. After its review, the board or committee can take one of several actions: (1) the research proposal can be approved and the researcher conducts the research as proposed; (2) the committee or board can request the researcher to change some aspect of the research proposal and resubmit the proposal for approval; (3) the research proposal can be denied or not approved.

Each university or college has its own procedures for submitting a research protocol for review. Generally, however, the following items are required in submitting a research protocol proposal:

- The research questions or research hypotheses
- Relevant literature to provide a foundation for the research project
- A description of how participants will be recruited and selected and a copy of the intended informed consent form
- A description of research methods and procedures (for example, copies of questionnaires, measuring instruments, instructions or stimuli given to participants, interview schedules)
- A statement of how benefit is maximized and risk is minimized
- A statement of how subjects' anonymity and confidentiality will be protected
- A description of the investigator's background and education

After your research protocol is approved, it carries legal implications. The protocol must reflect what you will actually do. You must follow the procedures detailed in your proposal.

Even minor changes to your procedures will require a separate approval (Sieber, 1998).

Must all researchers adhere to these responsibilities? Yes, if the researcher will require interaction with other people to collect his or her data. Universities require that researchers, including student researchers, seek approval for their study before any data are collected. If you are conducting a study with the intention of presenting your conclusions in a paper at a professional meeting or convention, or submitting your conclusions in a manuscript for consideration for publication, you must seek approval of your institution's review board.

Fitch (2005) offers advice for preparing your IRB application and for interacting with those who administer your university's IRB or human subject review if they have questions about your proposal. First, carefully consider the risks and complexity of the research you are proposing. Have you designed your study to do good, but do no harm? Second, take the training that your university recommends or requires. Third, read the directions of the IRB application and fill in the information requested. Leaving a section blank will inevitably result in the return of your proposal. In completing the application, pay particular attention to the rationale you present for your study. Fourth, consider asking questions before submitting your proposal and be willing to answer questions from those who administer your university's IRB or human subject review. As you can see, Fitch recommends treating the research proposal process as a communicative process in which both sides (the researcher and IRB) need information from one another.

Informed Consent

Following a form agreed upon by federal agencies, researchers must give research participants **informed consent**. This means that a potential participant agrees to participate in the research project after he or she has been given some basic information about the research study. Of course, a person's consent to participate in a research study must be given voluntarily. No one should be coerced into participating in research against his or her will or better judgment. In other words,

AN ETHICAL ISSUE

Do Research Participants Have Any Ethical Responsibilities?

In terms of designing a research study, the burden of ethical treatment of participants is the responsibility of the researcher—after all, the researcher is in control of the data collection process. But you may be wondering, do participants bear any ethical responsibilities? We would hope that research participants would be truthful in providing data and that they would answer our questions completely and honestly. Some people fear or detest research studies and, as a result, provide answers or behave in a way that essentially undermines the research process. One of the reasons ethical principles for research have been established is to strengthen the relationships between researchers and participants. Researchers hope that if participants feel that they have been treated respectfully, they will reciprocate with truthful and complete answers and will try to behave characteristically (rather than modifying their normal behavior because they are being observed). Do you agree that providing truthful and complete answers and behaving characteristically are the ethical responsibilities of participants? Are there other ethical responsibilities for which participants should be responsible?

participants cannot be threatened or forced into participating.

Informed consent is generally thought of when researchers need to create research relationships with individuals. However, there can be instances in which a community or organization needs to assent, or agree, that you, the researcher, can collect data in that setting (Kaiser, 2012). If you are collecting data in a formal community, such as an organization or town council, or an informal community, such as a support group or a tightly knit neighborhood, asking for and gaining permission for the group to conduct the research is appropriate and can be beneficial. "Although community support does not supercede individual rights to informed consent, community involvement prior to and throughout the project facilitates study recruitment and the identification of potential risks" (Kaiser, 2012, p. 460).

Informed consent creates obligations and responsibilities for the researcher. To gain a potential participant's informed consent, the researcher must provide certain information in writing to participants. This information includes:

- Identification of the principal researcher and sponsoring organization
- Description of the overall purpose of the investigation

- Main features of the research process including a description of what data will be collected
- The expected duration of participation

Not only must these details about the research process be provided, but the consent form should also be written in a manner that participants can easily understand. Thus, the consent form should be written in everyday language rather than scientific language. Finally, a copy of the consent statement should be given to each participant. An example of an informed consent form is shown in Figure 3.1. Whatever form your university or college follows, informed consent should be clear, friendly, and respectful of participants. It should also be an accurate representation of what participants will experience.

The concept of informed consent implies that the researcher knows what the possible effects of conducting the research are before the research is conducted (Eisner, 1991). This is more easily accommodated in quantitative research than in qualitative research. For example, a researcher using unstructured interviews to explore a relatively new research topic would find it quite difficult to develop a complete and comprehensive interviewing guide. The exploratory nature of the study precludes complete planning.

DESIGN CHECK

Do You Need Informed Consent for Your Research Project?

The Office of Human Research Protections of the U.S. Department of Health and Human Services provides an Internet site http://www.hhs.gov/ohrp/policy/checklists/decisioncharts.html that can help guide you in deciding if you need to provide your research participants with informed consent. Most universities follow these standards, but you should also check your university's rules and procedures. Your university's institutional review board will post information about informed consent and research compliance on your school's website. Check to see if you can find it using the key terms *institutional review board, human subjects,* or *research compliance.*

- Any possible risks to and benefits for research participants
- An explanation of how confidentiality and anonymity will be ensured or the limits to such assurances
- Any physical or psychological harms that might occur for participants and any compensation or treatment that is available
- Any incentives for participating
- A statement of whether deception is to be used; if so, the participant should be told that not all details of the research can be revealed until later, but that a full explanation will be given then
- The name and contact information for the principal investigator to whom questions about the research can be directed
- Indication that participation is voluntary
- Indication that a participant can decline to participate or discontinue participation at any time during the research process
- Indication that refusal to participate or to continue to participate will not result in a penalty
- Indication that the participant should keep a copy of the consent form

Additionally, in such situations, the researcher is unable to predict how participants will answer. Thus, there is no way he or she can identify all of the probing and clarification questions that will be needed to conduct the study before the interviews begin. Still, the researcher must design as much of the research project as possible, develop a proposal, and request a review by the IRB.

How does the researcher know that a participant consents? In most cases of communication research, participants can simply refuse to participate. In other words, they can hang up the phone on a telephone survey. Or if data are

being collected in person, a potential participant can turn and walk away from the research room or refuse to answer an interviewer's questions. Thus, a participant's behavior—for example, answering interview questions or filling out a survey—indicates consent.

For most communication research projects, informed consent is adequate. The research protocol is reviewed with participants, they are given a copy, and their participation implies their consent. In cases where the institutional review board requires participant-signed informed consent, participants read and sign one copy of the written consent form, return

North Carolina State University
INFORMED CONSENT FORM for RESEARCH

Title of Study   Communication Tasks at Work

Principal Investigator   Dr. Joann Keyton

What are some general things you should know about research studies?

You are being asked to take part in a research study. Your participation in this study is voluntary. You have the right to be a part of this study, to choose not to participate or to stop participating at any time without penalty. The purpose of research studies is to gain a better understanding of a certain topic or issue. You are not guaranteed any personal benefits from being in a study. Research studies also may pose risks to those that participate. In this consent form you will find specific details about the research in which you are being asked to participate. If you do not understand something in this form it is your right to ask the researcher for clarification or more information. A copy of this consent form will be provided to you. If at any time you have questions about your participation, do not hesitate to contact the researcher(s) named above.

What is the purpose of this study?

The purpose of this study is to identify the communication tasks or activities that individuals engage in throughout their day (shift) at work.

What will happen if you take part in the study?

If you agree to participate in this study, you will be asked to identify on a checklist the communication tasks or activities that you hear or observe others engage in on three different work days (shifts). You will be asked to complete one checklist for each of three days (shifts). Time to complete each checklist should be between 5 and 10 minutes. Across three work days (shifts), your total participation should be no more than 30 minutes. You may choose to complete your checklists at work at the end of your work day(shift) or after you leave the workplace.

Risks

There are no foreseeable risks or discomforts associated with your participation in this study. You will not be asked for your name or the name of your organization. You will receive the checklists in an electronic document. You will be provided a website for its return. All identifying information from your email account will be stripped before the checklists are given to the researchers.

Benefits

There are no direct benefits for your participation in this study. However, you may become more aware of your communication behavior at work and the communication behavior of others by reflecting on and checking off the communication tasks and activities at the end of each work day (shift). Information gained through this study will be used to better understand the communication skills needed for the workplace.

Confidentiality

The information in the records of the study will be kept confidential. Data will be stored securely in electronic files on the researcher's computer at North Carolina State University. The computer is password protected and within a locked office. No reference will be made in oral or written reports which could link you to the study. You will NOT be asked to write your name on any study materials so that no one can match your identity to the answers that you provide.

Compensation

You will not receive anything for participating.

What if you have questions about this study?

If you have questions at any time about the study or the procedures, you may contact the researcher, Dr. Joann Keyton at Dept. of Communication, PO Box 8104, North Carolina State University, Raleigh, NC 27695-8104; 919-513-7402; jkeyton@ncsu.edu

What if you have questions about your rights as a research participant?

If you feel you have not been treated according to the descriptions in this form, or your rights as a participant in research have been violated during the course of this project, you may contact Deb Paxton, Regulatory Compliance Administrator, Box 7514, NCSU Campus (919/515-4514).

Consent To Participate

I have read and understand the above information. I have the opportunity to print and keep a copy of this form. I agree to participate in this study with the understanding that I may choose not to participate or to stop participating at any time without penalty or loss of benefits to which I am otherwise entitled. By completing the checklists, I give my consent to participate in this study.

FIGURE 3.1 Example of Informed Consent Form

AN ETHICAL ISSUE

Would You Participate?

Imagine that one way you can receive extra credit for a communication course is to volunteer to participate in one of three research projects. The first is a study examining how strangers interact. When you sign up for the project, you are told to meet at a certain time and date at the information desk of your university's library. The second research project is described as a study of how relational partners talk about difficult topics. When you sign up for the project, you are asked to bring your relational partner (significant other, wife, husband) with you to the research session. The third project is a study of how people react in embarrassing situations. When you sign up, you are told that you will not be embarrassed, but that you will participate in interaction where embarrassment occurs. For each of these three studies, what information would need to be included in the informed consent for you to agree to participate? Would you be willing to withdraw from a study after it had already started? If yes, what would activate such a response in you?

it to the researcher, and keep a copy for themselves. In extremely risky research, the institutional research board may even require that a witness sign the consent form as well. Signed consent forms create a paper trail of the identities of those who participated in your study. Recognize the difference between the two. For informed consent, participants receive all the information they need to make a decision about participating, based on the written information you provide them. For participant-signed informed consent, participants receive the same information, but they must all sign a copy of the informed consent and return it to you, the researcher. When this is the case, you should keep the consent forms separate from any data collected. In either case, however, you may even want to read the consent form out loud as potential participants follow along.

Recall that one of the ethical principles for conducting research is respect for persons and that some types of research participants may not be able to speak for themselves. This is the case with minor children. In no case can the researcher rely upon the consent of a child to participate in a research project. Rather, the parents or guardian of each child must agree that the child can participate in the research project. If you want to collect data from children in a school environment, you

should get approval for your project from your university's institutional review board, as well as obtain permission for conducting the research from the superintendent of schools, the principal of the particular school, the teacher or teachers of the children you want to use, and the children's parents or guardians.

The committee that reviews research proposals for your university or college will prescribe the type of consent required for your research project. Be careful, however. Even if written, or signed, consent is not needed, a participant's informed consent is still required. A researcher cannot forgo this step in the research process.

Informed Consent and Quantitative Research Traditionally, quantitative communication research conducted in the lab or in field experiments has been associated with informed consent. Quantitative research requires considerable planning. As a result, the consent form is able to describe the exact procedures the participant will encounter. For example, in Dixon and Linz's (1997) study of rap music, participants were told that they might be asked to listen to sexually explicit lyrics, although not all participants were assigned to listen to that type of music. Participants were also told that they could withdraw from the experiment at any time, and one participant did.

Informed Consent and Qualitative Research
How do these standards and traditions apply to qualitative research? Unfortunately, there are no easy answers (Punch, 1994). In some qualitative research settings—for example, watching how teenagers interact as fans of the X Games—asking fans to agree to informed consent would disrupt the naturalness of the interaction. Thus, in these types of public and naturally occurring settings, asking for participants' informed consent would not only disrupt the interaction but would also divulge the identity of the researcher and expose the research purpose—all of which has the potential for stopping the interaction the researcher is interested in observing.

Thus, two questions provide guidelines in considering the necessity for asking participants for informed consent. The first one asks "Is the interaction occurring naturally in a public setting?" Let's look more closely at this question. Hammersley and Traianou (2012) suggest that privacy has several overlapping criteria. First, are observations to occur in a home (or home area) for some group or type of people? Is the place of observation privately or publicly owned? Are there restrictions on who can or cannot enter this place? Does engaging in a private activity in a public place create a temporary sense of privacy? Now, let's look at the second question, "Will my interaction with participants in that setting create negative consequences for any of the participants being observed?" If the answer is "yes" to the first question and "no" or "minimal consequences" to the second, then it is likely that the researcher will not need to adhere to the protocol of informed consent. If the answer to the first question is "in some ways" or "no," and acknowledgeable effects can be discerned, then the researcher must follow the principles of informed consent.

For example, interviewing is one type of qualitative research. The researcher may seek and conduct interviews at the public library, so the interaction is public, but it is not naturally occurring. The researcher is significantly influential in and purposely directing the interaction. Thus, informed consent is needed. Alternatively, a qualitative researcher wants to observe how patients approach the nurses' station in an emergency medical center to ask for help. This interaction is public—everyone in the waiting room has the opportunity to see and hear the interaction—and it is naturally occurring. The researcher is not involved in staging the interaction in any way. But this is an interesting case. Even though the interaction is public, interaction in an emergency medical center may be sensitive, and personal health information may be unintentionally revealed to the researcher. Researchers should be sensitive to private interaction even when it occurs in public spaces. For example, a couple saying goodbye to each other at an airport should be regarded as acting in a private setting, even though the interaction occurs in public (Sieber, 1992). So what is a researcher to do?

Despite the public nature of the interaction you want to observe or your opinion about whether or not informed consent is necessary, it is always wise to take the most prudent course of action. For each research project—quantitative or qualitative—develop a research proposal to be reviewed by your university's IRB. This committee will guide you as to when informed consent is needed and, when it is, as to what type of informed consent is required.

Indeed, Lindlof and Taylor (2002) see applying for IRB approval as an expected and necessary aspect of qualitative research design. Completing the IRB proposal and approval process will strengthen your thinking about and planning for interacting with or observing people in the field. Admittedly, special challenges exist in qualitative research, such as balancing the protection of participant identity against the need to describe unique features and people in the setting. The process can be to your benefit if you view it as a "critical reading of a study's ethical character" (p. 119).

ETHICAL ISSUES IN CONDUCTING RESEARCH

Ethical issues must first be considered in the design and development phase of research. But ethical decisions made in the design phase must be carried out. Six areas of ethical concern—use of deception, use of confederates, the possibility

**DESIGN
CHECK**

Private or Public?

All research participants should have the right to decide what information and how much information researchers may know about them. This aspect of research integrity can be especially tricky when conducting research on the Internet, because it is more difficult to untangle private from public and because issues about informed consent were established before prevalence of online communication (Elm, 2009). As a result, current ethical guidelines, including informed consent, need to be reconsidered for Internet-based data (chat rooms, e-mail, bulletin boards, listservs, and posted videos). Researchers using Internet-based data must address the continuum between private and public domains. In fact, researchers must acknowledge that many of these data are produced in private situations within a larger, public context (Elgesem, 1996). Markham (2004) reminds us that some people who communicate in the public space of the Internet can be angered by intruding researchers or prefer not to be studied. Because technology and societal acceptance of technology changes fairly quickly, a researcher who wants to collect Internet-based data should seek the advice of his or her university's institutional review board early in the design phase of the project. Not only have digital technologies provided new ways to conduct research, but also these technologies allow researchers to invite people to participate in research when previously this would have been impossible (Miller, 2012). Reviewing the recommendations on ethical decision making and Internet research from the Association of Internet Researchers (http://www.aoir.org) will help you make decisions about your research design and help you in describing your research project in your IRB proposal.

of physical or psychological harm, confidentiality and anonymity, video- and audiotaping, and debriefing participants—affect the interaction between research participants and researcher. Each of these can contribute to or detract from developing positive relationships with research participants.

Intentional Deception

When experimentation is the primary method of data collection, deceptive scenarios or practices are often used. Actually, the broad use of intentional deception, particularly in social psychology, caused federal granting agencies to establish guidelines and ask universities to establish human subjects committees to monitor research in which people participate.

With **deception**, researchers purposely mislead participants. Deception should be used only if no other way exists to collect the data and the deception does not harm participants. Deception is used when it is necessary for participants to be uninformed of the purpose of a study so that they can respond spontaneously (Littlejohn, 1991). Communication scholars regularly practice this type of deception. Deception might also be used to obtain data about interactions that occur with very low frequencies.

Researchers who use deception must be sure that it is justified and that the results are expected to have significant scientific, educational, or applied value. Additionally, researchers must give sufficient explanation about the deception as soon as is feasible (Fisher & Fryberg, 1994). Even in these conditions, however, it is never advisable to deceive participants if there would be significant physical risk and discomfort or if the deception would cause participants to undergo unpleasant or negative psychological experiences.

Recall that a major question of informed consent is how much information should be given to research participants and when. If full information is given about the research design and the purpose of the research, procedures that require deception cannot be used. Generally, however, institutional review boards will allow researchers to conceal some aspects of their studies if participants are debriefed and given all the information at the end of their involvement.

Researchers can underestimate as well as overestimate the effects of their techniques. Thus, a good source of information about the potential use of deception in research can come from potential research participants (Fisher & Fryberg, 1994). If you plan to use deceptive techniques, consider discussing them with persons who are similar to those who will be participants in your research project. Specifically, prospective participants can help you determine (1) if some significant aspect of the research procedure is harmful or negative, (2) if knowing some significant aspect of the research would deter their willingness to participate, and (3) the degree of explanation needed after the use of deception.

If you are thinking about using deception in a quantitative study, use it with caution. Answering the following questions will help you determine if your decision to use deceptive practices is justified. Will the deceptive practice cause the data collected to be invalid? Are there other equally effective ways to collect data? Of course, if deceptive practices are used, participants should be informed of this in their debriefing.

Researchers should consider alternatives to the use of deception. In some cases, the same information could be collected through role-playing, observing interaction in its natural settings, or using participant self-reports. However, deceptive practices can also create ethical problems when researchers use qualitative data collection methods.

For example, the extent to which participants in a qualitative study know that the researcher is, in fact, a researcher and that he or she is conducting research on them is an issue of deception. Chapter 15 describes four types of researcher participation in qualitative research. The role of the strict participant—in which the researcher

fully functions as a member of the scene but does not reveal this role to others—is deceptive. Is it ethical? This question can be answered only by examining the entirety of the research design. If the interaction is public and individuals in the interaction scene are accustomed to outsiders visiting, it is doubtful that a question of ethics and integrity would arise. However, if a researcher joins a group for the express purpose of investigating the communication within that environment and has no other reason or motivation for being there, then an ethical question is raised. This type of research design would need a strong justification, and the expected benefits would need to be substantial for an IRB to approve it.

Using Confederates

One type of deceptive practice is for the researcher to use a **confederate,** or someone who pretends to also be participating in the research project but is really helping the researcher. The use of confederates is a type of deceptive practice because research participants do not know that someone is playing the confederate role. In most cases, confederates are used when the researcher needs to create a certain type of interaction context or to provide a certain type of interaction to which an unknowing research participant responds.

To better understand the adequacy of truth and lies, Ali and Levine (2008) used a female undergraduate as a confederate. Participants believed she was also a research participant with whom they would play a trivia game. Partway through the game, the team was interrupted by an emergency in which the researcher had to leave the room. At this point the female confederate attempted to instigate cheating on the game by pointing out the folder on the desk (where she believed the answers were), her desire to win the monetary reward, and that they could improve their scores by cheating. After about 5 minutes, the researcher returned and the game was resumed. When the game concluded, participants (including the confederate) were told that they would be interviewed separately. After answering questions about strategy for playing the game, the researcher asked participants if they had cheated and why they should be believed. The use of a confederate was necessary to create the stimuli conditions for the experiment.

Confederates can also be recruited from participants who agree to participate in a research study. Wanting to examine how people explain their failures, researchers recruited students for a study with the condition that they had to bring along a friend or sign up to be paired with a stranger (Manusov, Trees, Reddick, Rowe, & Easley, 1998). When the dyad came to the research site, the person standing on the left was assigned the confederate role by the researcher, although the researcher did not provide the dyad that information at this point. The individuals were separated and taken to different rooms. While the participant in the confederate role was given instructions to get the partner to discuss a failure event, the unknowing partner completed a questionnaire.

After the confederate was clear about his or her interaction goal, both individuals were brought to a room where they were asked to talk for 10 minutes while being videotaped. Remember that in the role of confederate, one member of the dyad was responsible for bringing up the topic of a failure event and getting the partner to discuss it. After the interaction task was completed, the partners were separated again to fill out questionnaires. After that phase of the data collection, the unknowing partner was debriefed and told that the researchers were interested in the way people offered accounts or explanations for their failures and that the interaction partner had been asked to play the role of the confederate. Participants were further told that the confederates were supposed to get their unknowing partner to talk about a failure, unless the partner offered it without encouragement.

Without using one of the research partners in the role of confederate to encourage the other partner to talk about a failure, this topic may have never occurred in the limited time the interaction was being videotaped. After debriefing, participants in the study did not seem overly concerned with this deceptive practice, because they perceived that talking about failures was commonplace (V. Manusov, personal communication, January 26, 2000). In this case, deception was necessary to create the interaction condition the researchers were interested in studying. Recognize that the deceptive practice did not create any unusual harm for the unknowing partner, who still had control over which failure was discussed and how much detail was given.

Physical and Psychological Harm

Some research has the potential to harm participants. Whether the harm is physical or psychological, harm should always be minimized to the greatest extent possible. In communication research, it is unlikely that research participants would face many instances of physical harm. Researchers in the communication discipline do not engage in the type of invasive procedures more commonly found in medical research. Infrequently, however, communication researchers do take physiological measurements from participants to test how individuals respond to different stimuli. Generally, these are restricted to routine measurements of participants' heart rate, skin temperature, pulse rate, and common blood tests (for example, see Floyd, et al., 2009). Of course, these procedures must be explained to participants as part of the informed consent procedure.

Communication research can create psychological harm when researchers venture into sensitive topics like abortion, the use of animals in laboratory research, or the sexual explicitness of music videos. The sensitive content of such studies seems obvious. Psychological harm can also occur for participants when they are asked to role-play interactions that are uncomfortable or are not normal for them or when they are asked to relive distressing or painful experiences through interviews or focus groups or even in self-report surveys. Such research experiences can create negative reactions with long-term effects (Sapsford & Abbott, 1996).

Researchers also need to realize that even seemingly innocuous topics (for example, talking about a relationship) or generally accepted research procedures (for example, responding to a questionnaire) could cause psychological harm for some participants.

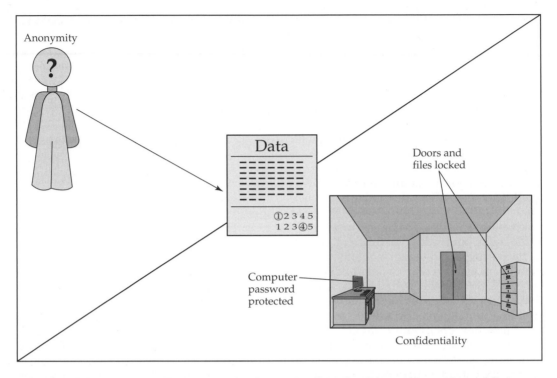

FIGURE 3.2 Researcher Is Responsible for Protecting Both Participant Anonymity and Data Confidentiality

It is doubtful that you would design your research project to include a topic or procedure you find distasteful. But we make attribution errors when we assume that research participants would not find the topic or procedure distasteful either. To help overcome our biases, it is a useful practice to ask at least 10 individuals who are like the people you expect to participate if they would agree to participate in and complete the research experience. Use their feedback to guide you in redesigning the research project to minimize any harm and to guide you in the type of explanations participants are likely to require as part of the informed consent. Some risks are inherent anytime humans participate in research, and we should never assume that our research topics or procedures are immune to this element.

Upholding Anonymity and Confidentiality

In scholarly research, anonymity and confidentiality are two types of protection given to participants (see Figure 3.2). **Anonymity** means that names and other pieces of information that can identify participants are never attached to the data. That is, the source of the message is absent, largely unknown, or unspecified (Scott, 2005). In fact, in many quantitative studies, the researcher has no idea who the participants are. Researchers do not ask participants to reveal information that would aid the researcher in identifying and finding them in the future. For example, in collecting data, a researcher should never ask for the participant's Social Security number as a way to keep track of data.

If your quantitative study requires data collection at multiple times, you can create some type of temporary personal identification number to link data together. Rather than randomly assigning numbers to participants, it is better to create some other unique number that is easily remembered by participants. For example, have participants take the middle two-digit sequence of their Social Security number and use it as a prefix for their birth date. For a participant with the Social Security number 492-58-0429 and the birth date of April 24, the unique identification number would be 580424.

However, even with a unique identification number, some participants will be hesitant to respond to demographic questions for fear that supplying this information will make it easy to trace their responses back to them. Employees, in particular, are sensitive to providing too much information. For example, you ask employees to identify their race or ethnicity and sex, as well as identify whether they are an hourly employee or salaried manager. If there is only one Black female manager, she may be particularly hesitant to provide the researcher with three pieces of data that could potentially identify her and her responses. Even if the information is not used to identify her, the participant may have the perception that the data could be used to do so, causing her to be less than truthful as she responds to the questionnaire. Whereas some demographic information generally is useful to collect, be careful of asking for more demographic information than you really need.

Protecting anonymity in qualitative studies that use interviewing, focus groups, and some participant-observation methods is difficult. In many of these cases, you would need to know the identity of participants to set up the interviews, focus groups, or observation periods. In some instances, knowing who the participants are is important for interpreting and understanding the data they provide. However, even though you may know the full identity of a participant, you can protect her identity in your notes and in your research report by referring to her as Female #1 or in some other way that does not reveal her true identity.

TABLE 3.1 One Method for Ensuring Participant Anonymity

Speaker Sequence	Real Name	Name in Written Research Report
First speaker, male	Ted	Roger
Second speaker, female	Amy	Saundra
Third speaker, female	Shamieka	Tamithra
Fourth speaker, male	Melvin	Upton
Fifth speaker, female	Jamila	Vanessa

If you are taking notes on a focus group, it will probably be more convenient to do so using participants' names. But when you write up the results of the focus group, you will probably want to change the names to pseudonyms. One way to do this is to pick any letter of the alphabet—for example, *R*. Assign the first person that speaks a same-sex name beginning with *R*, such as Roger. Assign the next person who speaks a same-sex name beginning with the next letter of the alphabet—for example, Saundra—and so on. If the ethnicity of participants is important to your study, assign names from the same ethnic group as well. If you use this method, readers of your research report will be able to clearly distinguish among the different participants' comments, and you have provided participants with anonymity. Table 3.1 demonstrates this type of name-change procedure.

Confidentiality is related to privacy. In the research process, **confidentiality** means that any information or data the participant provides is controlled in such a way that it is not revealed to others; nor do others have access to it (Scott, 2005). For example, the data from students participating in a research project are never given to other students or their professors. The data from employees are never given to other employees or their supervisors. In each of these cases, results from all participants may be summarized and distributed as a research report, but in no case should the data provided by any one person be released to anyone except the participant. Providing confidentiality for participants is respectful and protects their dignity. The researcher who provides confidentiality is attempting to ensure that no harm or embarrassment will come to participants.

Recognize that data may be a participant's responses to a questionnaire, an audiotape or videotape of a participant interacting with another person, their comments on a chat log, or your notes from an interview. Confidentiality needs to be expressly addressed in each research situation. Any materials or data you collect from participants should be carefully stored out of sight of others and away from the data collection site. In no instance should you deliver a participant's data to a parent, teacher, colleague, or relative.

Using Online Technology

Some consider technology as a tool, but in the conduct of research online technologies can change how researchers interact with research participants. How both parties create and maintain their identities is one issue. Another issue is how both researcher and participant establish and maintain their relationship. Consider this example from Beaulieu and Estalella (2012).

Estalella's aim was to study bloggers. So he became a blogger to better understand the technology and experience he was researching. Having his own blog also allowed him to present his research and himself. At the same time, his blog was one way to identify participants for his ethnographic research project. Two tensions developed. First, how could he both inform his research participants about his presence and role as an ethnographer, and provide them anonymity in this online environment? Second, being *in the field* in this case meant *being online*. Being in both places at once, Estallela found that boundaries were becoming blurred, as tension was created between his fieldwork and his analysis, and between discussions with informants and discussions with his research colleagues. Given his online presence and activity was in the form of blog postings and responses from others, how could Estalella maintain the anonymity of research participants? Beaulieu and Estalella (2012) argue that in some types of online research, especially qualitative research about online research practices, seeking to maintain participant anonymity may be difficult, if not impossible, to achieve. These researchers suggest that as communication research moves further into the use of online technologies anonymity may not be the most appropriate standard. Questions like these have not been settled. If your research takes you online, be sure to check with your instructor and your Institutional Review Board for guidance.

Videotaping and Audiotaping Participants

Much communication research focuses on the interaction between or among people. Videotaping and audiotaping are good tools for providing researchers with accurate accounts of these processes. But videotaping and audiotaping raise special ethical concerns. First, research participants should be taped only if the researcher has told them what is to be recorded and how. Second, participants' consent to be taped must be specifically obtained through informed or written consent. Third, videotape and audiotape records must be treated like any other data. A videotape or audiotape record is not anonymous. Thus, maintaining the confidentiality of such data is paramount.

One study of patient communication skills illustrates these principles (McGee & Cegala, 1998). Patients with appointments who met the selection criteria for the study were contacted by phone prior to their appointments. The research procedures, including information about videotaping and audiotaping, were described to them. After patients agreed to participate, their physicians were contacted to obtain their permission to record the doctor–patient meetings. When patients arrived at the doctor's office, they were again briefed about the study procedures and asked to sign a consent form. Patients were also told that they could choose not to participate.

For those who agreed to participate in the study, data collection occurred in one of two examination rooms equipped with videotaping and audio-recording equipment. The equipment was unobtrusively placed but visible to both patient and doctor. Especially important in this interaction setting, the video camera and examination table were intentionally placed so the video camera could not capture the patient on the examining table. Thus, the patient's visual privacy was maintained even though verbal interaction with the doctor could still be audiotaped. At the conclusion of the project, the research team maintained the video- and audiotapes, honoring its original agreement with patients about privacy (Cegala, personal communication, January 31, 2000).

Debriefing Participants

Debriefing is the opportunity for the researcher to interact with participants immediately following the research activity. Generally, the researcher explains the purpose of the study and what he or she hopes to find. Any information that was withheld from participants before the research activity began can be shared at this time.

Debriefing can accomplish several other objectives as well (Sieber, 1992). First, this informal interaction is a good opportunity for researchers to obtain participants' observations on taking part in the research project. Information obtained here may help the researcher better interpret the results. Second, debriefing gives participants an opportunity to ask questions and express their reactions to participating in the research.

If your research deals with sensitive matters, each participant should be debriefed separately. Likewise, if several types of people participated in the research—for example, parents, teachers, and children—separate debriefings may need to be held, a different one for each type of research participant. In general, your debriefing should include the purpose of the study, a description of the condition individuals participated in, what is known about the problem and the hypotheses tested or questions asked, and why the study is important. In some cases, you may even want to provide participants with a brief written description, including resources for their follow-up. Regardless of the information provided or the form of debriefing, this step should be a positive one for participants. If negative or difficult information must be conveyed, the researcher should consider providing participants with remedies such as counseling assistance or referrals, reading materials, or personal follow-up.

In some cases as a part of the debriefing, the researcher can promise that the findings of the research project will be made available to participants. Some researchers write a one-page summary of the results and distribute this to participants. Organizational communication researchers often promise to deliver a report of the research results as an incentive for executives to permit entry into the organization. If this is the case, be sure to specify how and when the findings will be delivered and give assurances that all findings will mask the identities of participants.

If delivering research results to participants is difficult or impossible, the researcher could provide a brief summary of the relevant literature and the rationale for the research questions or hypotheses. Prepared in advance, this type of summary sheet could be handed to participants at the conclusion of the study as part of the debriefing to satisfy their curiosity and needs (Sieber, 1994).

ETHICAL ISSUES IN REPORTING RESEARCH

Whether the report of a research study is presented to an instructor as a class paper or submitted to a communication conference or for publication, two long-standing ethical principles are adhered to by scholars in all disciplines. The first principle is ensuring accuracy of the information presented. The second principle is protecting intellectual property rights. A third principle, a carryover from ethical issues that surface in conducting the research, is protecting the identities of individuals.

Ensuring Accuracy

The principle of accuracy is fairly broad. Not only must you present the data accurately, but also data cannot be modified or adjusted in any way to better support a hypothesis or research question. Likewise, you cannot omit any data or results that are difficult to interpret or whose interpretation calls other results into question.

To be accurate in reporting your data, you must have been accurate throughout the research process. One way to increase the accuracy of your reporting is to document every step in the research process—from designing and developing your study, to collecting the data, to the methods used to interpret the data. Complex research projects can take months or even years to complete. Thus, relying on memory for details of the research process may not be adequate.

After your research report is written, you are responsible for checking the manuscript for errors caused in typing or editing. When these aspects of accuracy are achieved, your results should be verifiable by others using the same data or be repeatable with data and procedures similar to those you used.

Avoiding Plagiarism

Researchers protect intellectual property rights and avoid plagiarism in three ways. First, researchers must indicate with quotation marks when they use the exact words of others. Moreover, researchers must give complete citation and reference information for each of these occurrences. Second, citation and reference information must also be given when summarizing or paraphrasing the work of others. Even though the exact words of other researchers may not be used, those researchers deserve to be recognized when their ideas are used. Third, complete citation and reference information must be given when mentioning or making reference to the ideas or significant contributions of others. In any of these cases, it is not permissible to present the work of authors as one's own. Take a look at an example of each of these cases.

Dixon and Linz (1997) studied how listeners make judgments about the offensiveness of sexually explicit lyrics in rap music. Here are three excerpts from their journal article, each one providing an example of the cases described above.

The first example demonstrates how Dixon and Linz directly quote the work of other scholars. A reader is alerted to the fact that these three sentences were written by Dyson, rather than

Dixon and Linz, because quotation marks identify the quoted passage:

> "At their best, rappers shape the tortuous twists of urban fate into lyrical elegies. They represent lives swallowed by too little love or opportunity. They represent themselves and their peers with aggrandizing anthems that boast of their ingenuity and luck in surviving" (Dyson, 1996, p. 177).

The second example demonstrates how Dixon and Linz summarize or paraphrase the work of other scholars. A reader knows that these are not the exact words of Hooks because quotation marks are not used.

> According to Hooks (1992) rap music is a form of male expression that provides a public voice for discarded young Black men, although it has led to the expression of unacceptable levels of sexism.

Finally, in the third example, Dixon and Linz are calling readers' attention to the research on rap music that precedes their study:

> There has been little research on listeners' perceptions of rap music and how these perceptions are related to the components of obscenity law. Only a handful of studies have examined listeners' responses to sexually explicit music in general, and rap music in particular (Hansen, 1995; Johnson, Jackson, & Gatto, 1995; Zillmann, Aust, Hoffman, Love, Ordman, Pope, & Siegler, 1995).

In using these techniques, Dixon and Linz have avoided representing the work of others as their own. Because the citation information is provided in the text for these cases, the reader can turn to the reference section of the manuscript or article and find the complete reference for any work—and then go to the library and find the original information. See Chapters 13 and 18 for more information about citation and reference styles.

Protecting the Identities of Participants

Earlier in this chapter, we discussed ways to protect and conceal participants' identities. Generally, participant identity is not an issue in quantitative research reports because a single participant is not the focus or interest of the research study. Rather, the report is about the findings of a group of people described by their demographic characteristics. For example, most researchers report the number of participants, their age, sex, and any other demographic characteristics important to the study. Seldom would a reader be able to identify exactly who participated. If the researcher reports on participants' organizational affiliation, the name of the participating organization is generally changed or referred to only generically.

Protecting the identities of participants in qualitative research can be more difficult. When identities must be concealed, the advice given earlier about changing names can be applied to the writing of the research report. In other cases, only partial concealment is necessary or preferred.

For example, in Lange's (1990) case study research on Earth First!—a radical environmental group—he changed informants' names, but not those of national leaders who were already publicly visible and associated with the movement. Garner (1999) partially concealed the identities of women who willingly participated in her qualitative Web-based study and revealed information about their childhood and their reading habits as young girls and teenagers. In the journal article, Garner describes the group's demographic characteristics in general terms by giving their age, race, nationality, occupation, and relational status. When Garner specifically quotes women, she uses a real name if the woman requested that she do so. But she does not differentiate these women from those who preferred that their names be changed. Thus, with the use of identifiers like "Sue, 42, writer" or "Cathy, 47, professor," and the vastness of the Web, it is unlikely that anyone reading the journal article could associate a designation with any specific person.

AN ETHICAL ISSUE

Ethics in Proprietary Research

Many of you will graduate and take jobs in business, industry, nonprofit, or government rather than pursue academic careers. How would the ethical issues discussed in this chapter be relevant for research conducted in your organization for your organization? This type of research, called proprietary research, is quite common. In these instances, results are shared only with members of the organization that conducted or outsourced the survey; results are not disseminated to a wider audience. For example, many organizations ask employees to fill out surveys as a way of assessing organizational culture and climate or tracking employee satisfaction. Organizations also have confederates interact with their customer service representatives to determine the level and quality of assistance they provide. Finally, many organizations conduct research with customers or clients to assess corporate image or to determine clients' satisfaction with their services. Which ethical principles do you believe should be upheld in these situations? Why?

SUMMARY

1. Issues of ethics and integrity are an integral part of the research process and must be explored as the research project is designed and developed.

2. Researchers have three broad responsibilities: a scientific responsibility, a responsibility for developing and conducting research that will yield knowledge worth knowing, and a responsibility for verifying or validating the data they collect.

3. Three principles—beneficence, respect for persons, and justice—must be simultaneously upheld.

4. Universities and colleges have institutional review boards, or human subjects committees, that review the research proposals of professors and students to determine if the rights and welfare of research participants are being adequately protected.

5. Obtaining informed consent, or a research participants' agreement to participate in the research project, is almost always required.

6. Informed consent contains information about the research procedures, including any possible risks and benefits.

7. Informed consent should be written in language participants can easily understand, and each participant should receive a copy.

8. Researchers use deception to purposely mislead participants when it is necessary for participants to be naive about the purpose of a study, or when telling participants all the information beforehand would trigger unnatural responses.

9. Identify ethical concerns when a research study uses online technology.

10. Upholding confidentiality and anonymity of research participants during the collection of data is another ethical principle to which researchers must subscribe.

11. Videotaping and audiotaping participants as part of research procedures can be done only with their express knowledge and consent.

12. Debriefing gives researchers the opportunity to provide participants with additional knowledge about the research topic or procedure, especially when deception is used.

13. The ethical issues of ensuring accuracy, protecting intellectual property rights, and protecting the identities of individuals in research reports are researcher responsibilities.

KEY TERMS

anonymity

beneficence

confederate

confidentiality

debriefing

deception

human subjects
   review committee

informed consent

institutional review
   board (IRB)

justice

respect for persons

See the website www.mhhe.com/keyton4 that accompanies this text. For each chapter, the site contains a:

- chapter outline
- chapter checklist
- chapter summary
- short multiple-choice quiz
- PowerPoint presentation created by Dr. Keyton

For a list of internet resources, visit http://www.joannkeyton.com/CommunicationResearch-Methods.htm.

CHAPTER FOUR

Introduction to Quantitative Research

Chapter Checklist

After reading this chapter, you should be able to:

1. Describe quantitative research and its assumptions.

2. Identify examples of quantitative research.

3. Explain analytic deduction.

4. Explain the five-component model for quantitative research.

5. Explain the role of hypotheses in quantitative research.

6. Assess the effectiveness of hypotheses in quantitative research.

7. Explain why research questions are used in quantitative research.

8. Distinguish among concepts, conceptual schemes, constructs, variables, and operationalizations.

9. Identify independent and dependent variables.

10. Explain the relationship between independent and dependent variables.

11. Explain the advantages and disadvantages of quantitative research.

12. Describe issues of reliability and validity that must be addressed in quantitative research.

When you think of research, you may think of a survey or a laboratory experiment, both of which are used in communication research. Both of these methods rely on quantitative research methods, as does content analysis.

This chapter provides a basic introduction to quantitative communication research. You will discover how quantitative methods rely on the identification of variables and the development of testable hypotheses and questions. Moreover, you will discover that the way in which the research question or hypothesis is written actually helps the researcher in selecting the research method.

WHAT IS QUANTITATIVE RESEARCH?

As the label implies, the unit of analysis in quantitative research is quantity (Anderson, 1996). Researchers use measurement and observation to represent communication phenomena as amounts, frequencies, degrees, values, or intensity. After phenomena are quantified, researchers compare or relate them using descriptive or inferential statistics. By using traditional quantitative approaches and statistical techniques, researchers bring greater measuring precision and, as a result, some would argue, greater objectivity to the study of communication phenomena. A few examples will demonstrate the variety of quantitative research methods available to communication researchers.

Examples of Quantitative Research

In part, film ratings (i.e., G, PG, PG-13, R, NC-17) in the United States are based on characters' use of language, especially profanity. Many parents rely on these ratings to make appropriate media choices for their children. Yet, parents, media researchers, and policy makers still have concerns about the use of profanity in films, whereas others question whether the regulations are still needed. Cressman, Callister, Robinson, and Near (2009) designed a quantitative research study to identify what types of profanity were used and their frequency. The research team selected 30 of the top grossing teen films from the 1980s, 1990s, and 2000s that had received G, PG, and PG-13 ratings. G-rated films should not contain offensive language; PG-rated films suggest parent guidance because these films can contain some profanity; and PG-13-rated films caution parents because some of the language in the film may be inappropriate for children under 13.

How were quantitative methods used in this study? To answer their research questions and hypotheses, the research team counted frequencies of occurrence for language in the films that could be described in one of five categories: the seven dirty words that the FCC deems unspeakable for broadcast, sexual words, excretory words, strongly offensive words, or mildly offensive words. Across the 90 films coded, 2,311 instances of profanity were identified. Teen characters spoke about two-thirds (69.1%) of these words; teen males used more profanity than teen females or adults of either sex. While mild profanity was identified more frequently (57.1%), the seven dirty words were the second highest category (22.1%). By first identifying and then interpreting the frequency of occurrence of language in the different categories of profanity, the research team was able to demonstrate that there was a slight decrease in the use of profanity across the three decades. However, the use of profanity was still prevalent in the most recent set of films. Thus, the findings question the influence of the film rating system on films that teens will see.

Other quantitative studies are conducted with questionnaires or surveys. Outbreaks of flu are a serious public health issue, especially at universities where students live and learn in close proximity to one another. To investigate the utility of the Integrative Model of Behavioral Prediction, Kim and Niederdeppe (2013) sent an online survey to students whose emails were randomly selected from the list provided by the university registrar. The survey occurred during a time at which more than 500 students reported having the flu. The survey contained a number of items intended to reveal how frequently students engaged in handwashing and to gauge their beliefs about handwashing as a way to prevent the flu. This allowed the

---

AN ETHICAL
ISSUE

Giving Your Children Permission to Participate in a Research Study

To collect data from participants, researchers must ask for and gain their consent. In addition to getting participants' consent, researchers need the consent of a parent or guardian before individuals under the age of 18 can participate in an academically sponsored research project. If you were the parents of a 13-year-old, would you give your daughter or son permission to participate in a research project on dating? Drinking? Drug use? Sexting? Why would some parents object to their teenager's participation? Is there any way the researcher could overcome these objections? What are the potential benefits of having teenagers participate in research projects like these?

---

researchers to examine if behavioral intentions, normative beliefs, or self-efficacy predicted students' handwashing behavior. Further, their results can help those who create health communication campaigns to more effectively develop messages to encourage students to engage in behaviors that minimize the likelihood that they will get the flu.

Using surveys or questionnaires is a very popular quantitative method. Chapter 8 explores this topic in detail.

Communication researchers also use experimentation to capture quantitative information about communication issues. Most of us use digital technologies and many of us receive our news from one of these technologies. Utz, Schultz, and Glocka (2013) designed an experiment to test the networked crisis communication model. Using the Fukushima Daiichi nuclear disaster as the basis of a simulated crisis, the researchers tested the hypothesis that "crisis communication via Twitter and Facebook leads to a higher [organizational] reputation than crisis communication via newspaper" (p. 41). The researchers manipulated what technology participants used (Twitter, Facebook message, or a newspaper) and the type of crisis condition they read about (if the organization was responsible or if the organization was not responsible). Their findings supported the hypothesis, as organizational reputation was evaluated as higher when participants read the news of the crisis as a posting on Facebook or a tweet on Twitter; those who read the crisis news

in the newspaper format evaluated the organization's reputation significantly lower.

In another experimental design, Ivory and Kalyanaraman (2009) asked participants to think of and then write down the most violent video game with which they were familiar; another set of participants were not asked to identify a video game. Next, participants were asked to rate the degree to which they believed the specific video game, or video games in general, would cause others to be aggressive or violent. The research team wanted to test the hypothesis that "participants' perceptions of violent video games' effects on aggression will be greater when considering a specific game compared to violent video games in general" (p. 4). The research findings did not support the hypothesis. Rather, just the opposite was found. Participants who named a specific video game believed that the game would cause others to be less aggressive or violent than those participants who were not asked to identify a video game.

The point of this experiment was to understand what factors influence people's perceptions about the effects of violent video games. It was an interesting experiment because the research team did not have participants view or play any video games. Rather, the manipulation was invoked by simply asking some participants to think of and write down the title of a violent video game. Thus, the results demonstrate that violent video games in general caused participants to believe that video games were more likely to cause aggression and violence. Alternatively, when participants wrote down the title of a violent video game, their perceptions about potential aggression and violence were lower.

These are just a few examples of ways in which communication researchers use quantitative methods. One element underlying these examples that may not be apparent to you, but that needs discussion, is the pattern of reasoning used by these researchers. We examine that next.

Deductive Reasoning

Quantitative research relies primarily on deductive reasoning (Hawes, 1975). This means that the researchers select a theory, or theories, as the basis of the propositions that are tested in the study. In this case, the logic flows from the generalized (the theory) to the specific (the research conclusion). In general, the researcher hopes that the research process supports, or verifies, what the theory proposes to be true.

If the data and results do not support hypotheses derived from the theory, then the researcher looks for an alternative explanation. Perhaps the theory, as it was developed, is deficient or incomplete. Therefore, the results must be faulty because they are a direct result of testing the theory. Or the methods or procedures followed could be faulty. In this case, the researcher develops a new research design for testing the theoretical propositions and collects new data.

A Model for Conceptualizing Quantitative Research

The deductive research model presented in Chapter 2 is a general overview of the research process: It gives the basic steps and can be applied to most quantitative research projects. But more specialized models are needed to guide us through selecting and developing the research plan for a specific study. The model for conceptualizing quantitative research shown in Figure 4.1 is the model that will guide us now.

Starting at the top left of the model, the first component is the research purpose. Because the researcher is familiar with the research literature

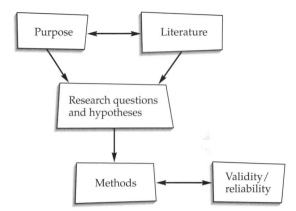

FIGURE 4.1 A Conceptual Model for Quantitative Research

and has developed some questions about communication issues, she or he begins with an overall purpose or objective. For example, I am interested in how a dysfunctional group member can take over a group's interaction to the point that the ineffective member replaces the task as the focus of the group. So my research purpose is to study that communication phenomenon.

Notice that the purpose component alone does not drive the model. The traditions of social science require that researchers use literature as a basis for their research, so my desire to study dysfunctional group members is framed within the context of the research literature and the contexts of real groups that I have observed experiencing this phenomenon. I take information (and motivation) from my original purpose, the research literature, and my experiences with groups. Balancing what I know as an academic and what I know as a group facilitator leads me to the research questions or research hypotheses that will guide my study and selection of quantitative methods.

Research questions and research hypotheses are central to the quantitative research process. No quantitative study can be done without one or a combination of these. This third component dominates the quantitative research methods process. Later in this chapter we will explore these in greater detail. But for now, recognize that without one or several research questions or research hypotheses, there is nothing to direct or define the research process.

The fourth component of the quantitative research model is the selection of the research methods for the project. Generally, quantitative researchers ask questions about differences and relationships. In other words, how are communication phenomena different? Or how are communication phenomena related? Either of these two forms is acceptable, but they require different types of statistical approaches. If I want to study the difference between dysfunctional members and functional, or effective, members, then I choose a quantitative method that will help me examine and illuminate those differences. If I want to study how the dysfunctional member influences the group's decision making and conflict management, I would choose a method that illuminates the relationships among the degrees of dysfunctional decision making and conflict management behaviors.

Looking at some specific examples will help you distinguish between instances in which differences are the focus of the research and instances in which relationships between variables are the focus. Think about your interaction with your romantic partner and your interaction with your supervisor. First, think about how the two relationships are different. Look at Table 4.1 to see what I mean.

In comparing the interaction with a romantic partner to the interaction with a supervisor, it is easy to identify several variables on which

there will be differences (for example, status, motivation, and level of intimacy). Notice how a difference can be extreme, as in the status and motivation examples. Also notice how the differences may be more moderate, as in the level of intimacy of the conversation. In each of these cases, the researcher would quantitatively measure status, motivation, and level of intimacy for each participant twice—once for each relationship type. Then the researcher would compare the scores for interaction with the romantic partner to the scores for interaction with the supervisor to see if a difference existed.

Alternatively, the research project could be designed to explore how the two types of interactions are related to one another. Examine Table 4.2 to find these examples. In looking for how interaction in the two relational types is related or similar, the researcher would again obtain a quantitative measurement of number of conflicts, degree of satisfaction, and frequency of interaction for each relational type. Then the researcher would examine the pairs of scores to see how they relate to one another. Notice how the scores may be very similar, or highly related, as with the number of conflicts. Or the scores can be related, but in opposite directions, as with satisfaction with interaction and frequency of interaction.

Thus, we can look for the differences between these two relational types, or we can look for ways in which interaction in the two relational types is related. The point here is that almost any

TABLE 4.1 Looking for Differences Between Two Types of Interaction

Variables of Potential Differences Between the Two Relational Types	Interaction with Romantic Partner	Interaction with Supervisor
Relative status of other person in the relationship	I consider this person to be *my equal* in terms of power and status.	Due to the organizational hierarchy, this person has *more power* and status in the organization than I do.
Motivation for relationship	I *voluntarily* developed this relationship.	I was assigned to my supervisor's work unit. This relationship *is not voluntary*.
Level of intimacy in conversations	We *share personal information* with one another.	I do *share some personal information* with my supervisor, especially when we eat lunch together.

TABLE 4.2 Looking for Relationships Between Two Types of Interaction

Potential Relationships Between the Two Relational Types	Interaction with Romantic Partner	Interaction with Supervisor
Number of conflicts	I *frequently* have conflicts with my significant other.	I *frequently* have conflicts with my supervisor.
Degree of satisfaction with interaction	I am *very satisfied* with my interaction with my significant other.	I am *not satisfied* with my interaction with my supervisor.
Frequency of interaction	My significant other and I *talk very frequently*.	I *talk* to my supervisor *only when necessary*.

communication phenomenon can be examined for its differences to a similar communication phenomenon, or a communication phenomenon can be examined for how it relates to a similar communication phenomenon. Can you think of other elements that may differ or be related with respect to relationships with romantic partners and supervisors?

Returning to my example of dysfunctional group members, if I focus on differences, I might look for ways in which functional and dysfunctional group members deal with conflict, facilitate the group's decision making, or challenge the group's leadership. If I focus on ways in which these two types of group members are related, I might want to focus on the degree to which each type of group member possesses communication competence, or how similar the types of group members are in their communication style. To highlight differences, one set of statistical techniques is used. To highlight relationships, another set is chosen. These statistical techniques are covered in Chapters 10 and 11.

Notice that the final component of the quantitative research model is connected only to the methods component and that the connection is reciprocal (see Figure 4.1). This last component is an examination of the validity and reliability of the data collected through the method selected. Usually the researcher will make methodological choices and then assess those choices for their impact on *validity*—how truthful the data will be—and *reliability*—how consistent the data will be. These issues must be addressed before the research is undertaken and any data collected, for there is little opportunity to adjust the research

method after the project is started. One of the assumptions of quantitative methods is that all participants are treated similarly; procedures or process should not change as you discover errors or lapses in your planning.

After the researcher has addressed each of these five components, he or she moves through the quantitative research process in a linear fashion. Once the methods are designed, the researcher selects participants, collects and analyzes data, and then writes the research report. As demonstrated in Figure 2.1, findings from the current study are used to extend or challenge the current state of theory. New questions are formulated and the research process begins again. For now, though, we need to return to and examine in detail each step in conceptualizing the research project because these steps provide the foundation for quantitative research projects.

CREATING THE FOUNDATION FOR QUANTITATIVE RESEARCH

After identifying the research problem and turning that topic into a preliminary question or questions, as described in Chapter 2, researchers must further specify the concepts identified in their question. These conceptual definitions are based on theoretical information or past research studies. Generally, researchers build on the work of others and use existing concepts and definitions unless they are inadequate or inappropriate (Katzer et al., 1978).

A **concept,** or the thing you want to study, represents a number of individual, but related, things. It is an abstract way of thinking that helps us group together those things that are similar to one another and, at the same time, distinguish them from dissimilar other things. A concept can be an object, an event, a relationship, or a process. Examples of concepts include a faulty argument, an effective public speaker, a conflict between spouses, leadership, underrepresentation of minorities on prime-time television shows, and so on. Even though they are intended to represent a class of things that have common characteristics, a concept does not have a fixed or precise meaning or definition (de Vaus, 2001). With respect to the research literature, concepts are generally introduced early in the literature review with a general description.

In some cases, a set of concepts can be connected to form a **conceptual scheme.** For example, a researcher could identify ways in which consequence is demonstrated in prime-time television dramas (for example, characters admit guilt and take responsibility, deny responsibility, assign responsibility to others, and so on). Individually, each concept describes a unique process. But as a group, the concepts still retain common characteristics. Together, they form a conceptual scheme that specifies and clarifies the relationships among them (Kibler, 1970).

The theoretical definition of a concept is a **construct.** Concepts can become constructs only when they are linked to other concepts. The linking between and among concepts is part of the theoretical definition. To be used in a research study, however, a construct must also be assigned an observable property, or a way for a researcher to observe or measure it. Obviously, a construct could be observed or measured in many ways. Thus, researchers use the term **variable** to identify the theoretical construct as it is presented in research questions and hypotheses, and the term **operationalization** to denote how the variable is observed and measured. See Figure 4.2 for a visualization of how concepts, constructs, variables, and operationalizations are related to one another in the research process. Sections on identifying and operationalizing variables are presented later in this chapter.

It is important to note that both concepts and constructs are arbitrary creations of researchers

(Kibler, 1970). As a result, in reading many research reports about the same topic, you are likely to find considerable variation in how scholars describe concepts and constructs. Generally, researchers describe the theoretical foundation of a study in the literature review. This is where concepts and constructs are introduced. Then, in the hypotheses and research questions, constructs are further defined as variables. Operationalizations of each variable are presented in the methods section of written research reports.

Variables are the elements of interest to researchers. Finding new descriptions, explanations, or predictions for variables is the primary motivator for conducting scholarly research. To better understand how variables are used in the research process, we need to consider hypotheses and research questions.

RESEARCH HYPOTHESES FOR QUANTITATIVE RESEARCH

Scholars rely on hypotheses to direct their quantitative inquiry. A hypothesis is an educated guess, or a presumption, that is based on a scholar's review of the research literature. It describes a logical explanation of the difference or relationship between two or more variables. To be tested through research, the consequences of the hypothesis must be observable. In fact, the researcher designs the research study to test the difference or relationship described in the hypothesis.

In a study examining college students' stress and their relationships with their grandparents, Mansson (2013. p. 159) hypothesized that:

> Grandchildren's received affection from their grandparents will be related negatively to the grandchildren's stress (Hypothesis 1), depression (Hypothesis 2), and loneliness (Hypothesis 3).

The hypothesis proposes what the relationship will be. When college students receive affection from their grandparents, their stress, depression, and loneliness will decrease. A hypothesis states the nature of the relationship between variables. This is different from phrasing the relationship

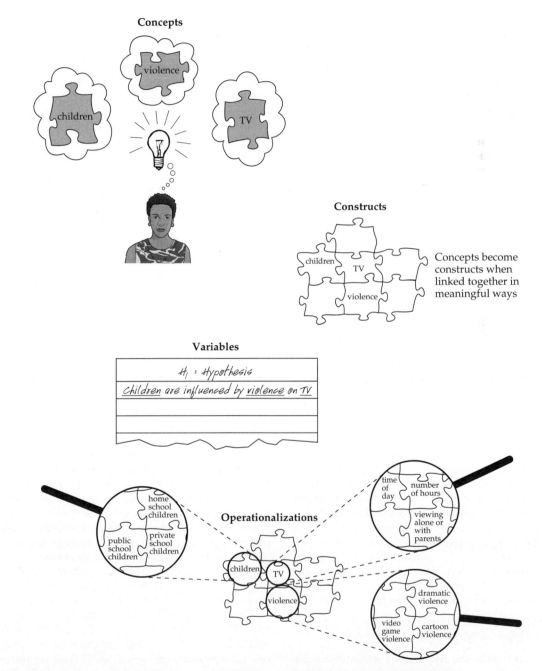

Concepts

violence

children

TV

Constructs

children

TV

violence

Concepts become
constructs when
linked together in
meaningful ways

Variables

H_1 = Hypothesis

Children are influenced by violence on TV

Operationalizations

home
school
children

public
school
children

private
school
children

children

TV

violence

time
of
day

number
of hours

viewing
alone or
with
parents

dramatic
violence

video
game
violence

cartoon
violence

FIGURE 4.2 Moving from Concepts to Constructs to Variables to Operationalizations

as a research question, which would ask what the relationship would be.

As another example, a research team proposed differences in how IM would be used in organizations. Pazos, Chung, and Micari (2013, p. 73) hypothesized that:

> Hypothesis: Individuals are more likely to use IM for collaboration than for conflict tasks.

Collaboration tasks were described as those tasks that employees work toward a solution that benefits all parties, whereas a conflict task was described as one in which employees have a difference in opinion in how to complete a task. Based on the literature on the social presence characteristics of media and how individuals make choices in which media they use, the research team wrote a hypothesis that predicted which type of task employees would choose to use instant messaging more frequently.

Directional Hypotheses

Return to the hypothesis about the use of IM at work. In this case the researchers expect to demonstrate that employees will report using IM more for collaborative tasks than they will for conflict tasks. Because the hypothesis explicitly states which type of task is completed with the use of IM, the hypothesis is directional. That is, IM is used more for one type of work task than another. Thus, a **directional hypothesis** is a precise statement indicating the nature and direction of the relationship or difference between the variables.

Nondirectional Hypotheses

A nondirectional hypothesis is less explicit. Continuing with the use of IM at work example, a nondirectional hypothesis could be:

> Hypothesis: Individuals will report differences in the use of IM based on the type of task.

The **nondirectional hypothesis** states that a difference will occur in employees' use of IM, but does not state in which type of task instant messaging will be used more.

Collaborative and conflict are two categories of the *media type* variable examined in the

study. This nondirectional hypothesis indicates that there will be a difference in the use of IM in the two types of tasks, but does not predict in which task type employees will use IM more. Some researchers judge directional hypotheses to be more sophisticated than nondirectional hypotheses because they more explicitly state what differences will be found. Both types of hypotheses are found in the communication research literature.

Assessing Hypotheses

The following criteria can help you assess the clarity and utility of hypotheses (Hoover & Donovan, 1995; Pyrczak & Bruce, 2007; Salkind, 2008). The first criterion asks evaluative questions about wording, such as, Is the hypothesis simply stated? Is the hypothesis stated as a single declarative sentence? Are at least two variables identified?

The second criterion focuses on the variables in the hypothesis. Are the variables clearly specified? Can the variables be measured by techniques you know how to use? If not, you will need to learn the appropriate measurement or observation method or ask someone to help you with this aspect of the study.

A third criterion for assessing hypotheses is to examine how the differences or relationships between variables are stated. Are they stated precisely? A good way to test this is to explain a hypothesis to someone who is unfamiliar with research methods. If you can describe it to someone else, the difference or relationship in the hypothesis is likely to be precise enough to use in a research study. The fourth criterion asks if the hypothesis reflects a theory or a body of literature. In other words, is the hypothesis logically supported by or based on previous research?

The fifth criterion asks if the hypothesis is testable. In other words, can the difference or relationship between the variables be observed or demonstrated in some way? This criterion is crucial to conducting the research study. The method, or the way in which the study is conducted, must match the hypothesis. Evaluating hypotheses is important because they guide how the research project is developed and structured.

Null Hypotheses

Although a scholar spends time developing research hypotheses from the published literature, these are not directly tested. Rather, a statistical test is performed on the **null hypothesis**, or the implicit complementary statement to the research hypothesis. In using a statistical test, the researcher hopes to reject the null hypothesis and, in effect, validate the alternative, or the research hypothesis. A null hypothesis states that no difference or no relationship, except one due to chance, exists between the variables. As you can see, the null hypothesis is in direct opposition to the research hypothesis. According to the traditions of science, the null hypothesis must be assumed to be true until support for the research hypothesis can be demonstrated.

Although it is unlikely that you would see a null hypothesis presented in scholarly work, it is helpful to think through what the null hypothesis would be. A research team (Maki, Booth-Butterfield, & McMullen, 2012) explored how people use humor (e.g., verbal and nonverbal messages that elicit laughter from others) and how the use of humor influenced their relationships with romantic and platonic partners. One of the research hypotheses was presented as:

H: The higher the HO [humor orientation] discrepancy score of a dyad, the lower the levels of cohesion and satisfaction.

The null hypothesis could be written as

H_0: There will be no difference in levels of cohesion and satisfaction based on dyad's humorous orientation discrepancy score.

It could also be written in one of the following ways:

H_0: Dyads' humorous discrepancy scores will not influence their levels of cohesion and satisfaction.

H_0: Degree of cohesion and satisfaction will not vary based on dyad's humor discrepancy scores.

Notice that the symbol H indicates the research hypothesis and the symbol H_0 indicates the null hypothesis. In some journals, you may also see the symbols H_1 or H_{alt} to indicate the research hypothesis.

Research Traditions in the Use of Hypotheses

You should be aware of several traditions regarding the use of hypotheses (Kibler, 1970). The first is that hypotheses are always tentative. Even when support for a hypothesis is found, support is never considered absolute. Knowledge is developed over time, and the continual efforts of researchers contribute to the development of theory as they seek to confirm or disconfirm hypotheses. Thus, one study cannot absolutely confirm or disconfirm any relationship or difference between or among variables.

Researchers honor the second tradition when they present the research hypothesis. Although not explicitly stated in a journal article, the null hypothesis is assumed to be in direct opposition to the research hypothesis. The research hypothesis, the one the researcher wants to confirm, states the way in which the variables are different or the way in which the variables are related to one another. Alternatively, the null hypothesis, even when not given, implies that no difference exists between the variables or that the variables are not related in any way. In nearly every case, the research, or alternative, hypothesis is the focus of a research project.

RESEARCH QUESTIONS IN QUANTITATIVE RESEARCH

Why would a researcher ask a research question instead of stating an educated guess with a hypothesis? There are several occasions when asking a research question has more utility. The first is when little is known about a communication phenomenon. For example, some communication phenomena—particularly those linked to the use of media or technology—enter the mainstream faster than researchers can study their effects. As a result, early in the adoption of cell phones, Campbell (2008) had few research studies on which to base research hypotheses when he explored how cellphone use in public settings was influenced by cultural and individual differences. Although studies had looked at cellphone use and the perceptions of users, there were few studies upon which to develop hypotheses regarding how individuals interpret rules or norms for mobile phone use in public settings. Thus, the following research question was asked:

RQ: To what extent are individualism and collectivism related to assessments of mobile phone use in public settings that support different levels of focus?

Another opportunity for researchers to use research questions arises when researchers extend existing lines of research to new applications. For example, Jeffres, Neuendorf, and Atkin (2012) argued that the practice of democracy rests on "a reasonably broad distribution of knowledge" (p. 59). As they searched the literature, they discovered that studies generally focused on what people knew, or did not know, about politics, especially presidential campaigns. To broaden the existing research, this research team identified three knowledge domains beyond the public affairs domain, which is most often tested. They identified these knowledge domains as knowledge about the local community, knowledge about international public affairs, and knowledge about the Internet. They asked this research question:

RQ1: Do differences in knowledge by income and education groups persist across three different types of knowledge—international public affairs, Internet, and community knowledge? (p. 64)

A research question makes more sense in this instance because previous research could not help the researchers make an educated and informed guess about knowledge gaps in these three domains. In both of these cases, the research question is an opportunity for the researcher to describe communication phenomena. Research questions are primarily tools of descriptive research.

TYPES OF VARIABLES

In hypotheses and research questions for quantitative studies, researchers make the object of their study more explicit by further specifying a construct as a variable. A *variable* is an element that is specifically identified in the research hypotheses or questions. The literature review may describe several related concepts and constructs, whereas the hypotheses and research questions identify a more limited set of variables to be explored.

The study of communication from a social science perspective borrows heavily from the traditional science disciplines. As a result, quantitative research relies on the study of variables. In social science, variables are the properties or characteristics of people or things that vary in quality or magnitude from person to person or object to object (Miller & Nicholson, 1976).

Simply, to be a variable, the element must vary. In other words, the variable must have two or more levels. For example, sex is a variable as it varies between male and female. Leadership can be a variable, as leaders can be described as autocratic or democratic. Communication apprehension, like other constructs measured by questionnaires, is a variable: Individuals' scores can have many levels, ranging between a potential minimum and a potential maximum score.

Communication phenomena or communication-related phenomena do not always take on the role of variables in communication research. For example, even though sex varies, it cannot be a variable if the researcher studies only the leadership abilities of women. Leadership ability would be a variable; sex would not. In another example, leadership style cannot be a variable if the researcher examines only ways in which democratic leaders encourage group members to participate. In this case, encouragement of group member participation would be a variable; democratic leadership style would not. Something can be identified as a variable only if it fluctuates in the research study (Kibler, 1970). This can be confusing because not every concept that can vary and act as a variable does so in every research study.

Some variables are easy to identify. They are tangible and observable. For example, it is easy to recognize and count what type and how many hand gestures a person makes while arguing. Alternatively, it may not be possible to directly view some variables. In these cases, researchers develop constructs to represent properties that control other events. For example, communication competence is a construct that was developed by communication scholars to represent perceptions of effectiveness and appropriateness of interaction. There is indirect evidence that this construct exists (after all, most people have ideas about what constitutes communication competence), but the construct itself is invisible. Communication researchers willingly accept constructs because they are able to demonstrate differing effects produced by variables. For example, competent communicators produce different effects on their receivers than incompetent communicators do. Similarly, it is impossible to see an attitude about violence on television. But a researcher can see the behavioral effects of your attitude when you report liking shows with violent content or when you change the channel to avoid watching such programming.

Whether they are tangible or constructed, when they are included in research questions or hypotheses, variables must also be identified as independent or dependent. Simply, the independent variable is presumed to have an effect on or cause a change in the dependent variable. The sections that follow describe how the two types of variable are used in research and explain the nature of the relationships between and among variables. In quantitative research, the researcher should specify which variables are independent and which are dependent.

Independent Variables

Variables manipulated by the researcher are called **independent variables.** Presumably, the manipulation, or variation, of this variable is the cause of change in other variables. Technically, the term *independent variable* is reserved for experimental studies (see Chapter 7) in which the researcher has control over its manipulation. In some research reports, independent variables are referred to as **antecedent variables, experimental variables, treatment variables,** and **causal variables.**

The independent variable is manipulated because the researcher wants to assess if different types or values of the variable result in some relationship with another observed phenomenon, or the dependent variable. If the effect or relationship occurs, the researcher presumes that the independent variable caused the change in the dependent variable.

For example, Ploeger, Kelley, and Bisel (2011) wanted to examine how direct employees would be when asked to do something unethical at work. Participants in the study read a hypothetical scenario in which they (in the role of a bookkeeper) were asked how directly they would respond if someone in their organization asked them to write a check from company funds to reimburse a personal lunch (i.e., an organizational practice commonly believed to be unethical). Three scenarios were developed so that some participants

---

DESIGN CHECK

What Is Sex? What Is Gender?

Many quantitative communication studies use sex and gender interchangeably as an independent variable. Unfortunately, many authors do not give their operationalization of this variable. When sex or gender is not operationalized, it is probably safe to assume that the researcher had participants self-report their biological sex—male or female. Of course, biological sex is not the same as one's gender or psychological orientation to sex—for example, feminine, masculine, or androgynous. There is a difference in being female and being feminine. And, one's sex or gender cannot be used to imply sexual orientation. If sex or gender is not operationalized, read the methods section carefully to determine if participants self-reported this information, if researchers assumed this information about participants, or if participants responded to a measuring instrument. If in doubt, use the terms as they are used by the authors of the published research reports.

read the request from one of their employees while others read scenarios in which the request came from their coworker or their boss. Participants were randomly assigned to conditions and engaged the scenarios as supervisor, coworker, or subordinate. The three scenarios manipulated the independent variable *organizational role* so the researchers could test the hypothesis: "Supervisors respond to unethical requests from subordinates more directly than coworkers to coworkers who are more direct than subordinates to supervisors" (p. 469).

Traditionally, the independent variable is manipulated in the context of an experiment to produce a change in the dependent variable. However, communication researchers use experimental, quasi-experimental, and descriptive research designs (each of these is explained in detail in Chapter 7). Whereas experimental research designs use researcher manipulation of the independent variable, other quantitative research designs cannot. In these cases, the researcher relies on natural variation in the independent variable to produce different effects on the dependent variable. In those instances, the term **predictor variable** is preferred and should be used in descriptive research designs (for example, survey research). Researchers are still interested in the predictor variable's effect on other variables, but distinguishing between the two terms helps remind us of this key difference. A few examples will make this distinction clearer.

In a study of how immigrants are socialized into American culture, Erbert, Perez, and Gareis (2003) used country of origin and sex as independent variables in their statistical tests. Obviously, the research team could not alter or change these aspects of the study's participants. Thus, these two variables varied naturally, and the research team used information participants provided to code them as being from one of four world regions (i.e., Americas, Asia, Europe, or Middle East) and as female or male. Thus, both country of origin and sex had two or more levels and could be used as predictor variables.

In a study of how people maintain romantic relationships (Dainton, 2003), relational equity was used as an independent variable. During the data collection procedures, the participants

responded to questionnaire items that allowed the researcher to determine if participants perceived they were in equitable romantic relationships, or in romantic relationships in which they were benefiting more or less than their partner. Thus, the researcher used the natural variation in participants' reports of their relational equity to create this predictor variable for the study.

As you can see, it is better to describe the independent variable as the variable that alters or changes the dependent variable. The researcher does not always manipulate it. In many cases, variation in the independent variable occurs naturally as a characteristic of the population under study. Any change or difference in the independent variable is the presumed cause of a change in the dependent variable if an experimental method is used. Causality is weakened if the researcher does not directly manipulate the independent variable, but it would be impractical to conduct all communication research from the experimental framework. Generally speaking, however, the independent variable is the variable a researcher predicts from, whereas the dependent variable is the one the researcher predicts to (Kibler, 1970).

Dependent Variables

Even though the independent, or predictor, variable causes the change, the dependent variable is of primary interest to the researcher, who is trying to describe, explain, predict, or control changes in it. The **dependent variable** is influenced or changed by the independent variable. Sometimes in descriptive research designs, the terms **criterion variable** and **outcome variable** identify the dependent variable. Regardless of what it is called, logically a researcher cannot have a dependent variable without an independent variable, and vice versa.

Changes in the dependent variable are a consequence of changes in the values or levels of the independent variable. For example, in a study of undergraduate students' compulsive use of the Internet (Mazer & Ledbetter, 2012, p. 407), one hypothesis stated:

H: Online communication apprehension is predictive of CIU [compulsive Internet use].

In this case, the independent variable, online communication attitude, was measured with 31 items examining self-disclosure, social connection, apprehension, miscommunication, and convenience. Researchers measured the dependent variable, compulsive Internet use, with 7 scale items, including "I have been unsuccessful in my attempts to control my Internet use." As described by the hypothesis, the research team wanted to see if attitudes toward communicating online predicted a person's compulsive use of the Internet. This hypothesis was supported, as self-disclosure did predict participants' self-reported compulsive use of the Internet. Thus, the dependent variable is the variable the researcher is trying to explain in a research project (Kibler, 1970).

The Relationship Between Independent and Dependent Variables

In quantitative research, the dependent variable is selected first because it is the primary topic of the research study (Thompson, 2006). Reread the hypothesis just presented. A person's inability to control, reduce, or stop their online behavior, or compulsive use of the Internet is the primary research topic and is the dependent variable. Then, logically, the researchers start to investigate what independent variables would influence or cause change in the dependent variable. When a researcher is looking to describe, predict, or explain differences or relationships, a hypothesis must have at least one independent and one dependent variable. Variables are identified as independent and dependent to establish the presumed relationship between them.

How many independent and dependent variables can a researcher specify? That depends on the nature or complexity of what the researcher wants to explain. Most important, however, the number of independent and dependent variables dictates which statistical test will be used. We will review these distinctions in Chapters 10 and 11 as the most common statistical tests are described and explained. But for now, analyzing a hypothesis from a research report will help you understand the nature of the relationship between independent and dependent variables.

Downs, Boyson, Alley, and Bloom (2011) explored how instructors' use of different media would influence the learning of college students. Their hypothesis was

> H2: Participants who process information disseminated through audio/video modes will achieve higher scores on a cued-recall, research methods cognitive assessment test when compared to those processing information in an audio/text, or audio-only condition. (p. 189)

Because some hypotheses are more complex than others, it can be difficult to clearly identify which variables are independent and which variables are dependent. One way to make this distinction is to look for what changes or varies in the hypothesis statement. Examine Table 4.3. By comparing each mention of each element, we can determine the variables and then assign them as independent or dependent.

The authors made no distinction about who is in the study. The first mention is "participants" and "those" refers back to this label in the hypothesis, so "participants" is not a variable. Likewise, there is no distinction in the use of "processing information." Thus, this is not a variable.

Reread the hypothesis. The authors state that participants who process information disseminated through audio/video modes will achieve higher scores. Also notice their use of the phrase "when compared." This word usage and sentence construction implies that the participants of the audio/video mode are being compared to participants in the audio/text and audio-only modes. So, according to the hypothesis participants' learning (as measured by the recall on the cognitive assessment test) is being compared based on the mode (or condition) they were assigned to. Because the learning can only occur after participating in one of the conditions of the experiment, the mode (or type of media) must be the independent variable and scores must be the dependent variable.

It is always a good idea to read the methodology section of the research report to confirm your identification of variables and assignment of variables as independent and dependent, and to see exactly how the researchers measured or observed their variables.

TABLE 4.3 Determining Variables from the Elements of a Hypothesis

Hypothesis: Participants who process information disseminated through audio/video modes will achieve higher scores on a cued-recall, research methods cognitive assessment test when compared to those processing information in an audio/text, or audio-only condition.

First Mention	Second Mention	Third Mention	Type of Comparison	Type of Variable
Participants	Those (participants)		No distinction	Doesn't vary, not a variable
Process Information	Processing Information		No distinction	Doesn't vary, not a variable
Audio/video Modes	Audio/text	Audio only	Explicit comparison	Independent variable
Scores on a cued-recall, research methods cognitive assessment test	No alternative given		Implied comparison	Dependent variable

OPERATIONALIZING VARIABLES

Whether variables are used as independent or dependent variables in hypotheses or questions, researchers must take one additional step to actually use the variables in a quantitative study. Each variable must be operationalized, or observed or measured in a specified way. Most variables can be operationalized in multiple ways. For example, if you want to measure listening (Bodie, 2013), are you measuring listening as a cognitive process (that is, can you make sense of what you hear), as an affective process (that is, do you have a willingness to listen), or as a behavioral process (that is, do you respond verbally and nonverbally)? Nearly all variables, independent and dependent, can be measured in many ways.

Researchers rely on operationalization to specify the concrete steps or processes for creating and measuring a variable. By specifying what data will represent the variable, the researcher is also specifying what does not represent the variable (Loseke, 2013). Thus, the goal of operationalization is to be specific enough that others reading the description of the operationalization in the research report can follow it (Miller & Nicholson, 1976).

Researchers use three criteria for selecting among available operationalizations. First, which operationalization is practical and useful in their study? Second, can a justifiable argument be developed for this operationalization? Third, does the operationalization selected coincide with the conceptual definition?

A good example of the specificity needed for operationalizations is demonstrated in a study that examined the influence of message design strategies on changes in attitude and use of marijuana (Harrington et al., 2003). The first hypothesis of the study stated:

H$_1$: Compared to low sensation value antimarijuana messages, high sensation value antimarijuana messages will lead to greater attitude, behavioral intention, and behavior change. (p. 22)

Although the research team identifies the variables in the hypothesis, there is not enough information to replicate the research study. What are low sensation value and high sensation value messages? How do you measure attitude, behavioral intention, and behavior change?

In the methods section of their study, the research team specifically defined, or operationalized, these variables. To create the high sensation

TRY THIS!   ## Identifying Independent and Dependent Variables

Following the process shown in Table 4.3, identify the independent and dependent variables for each hypothesis in the following table.

Hypothesis	Independent Variable	Dependent Variable
Family conversation orientation is positively related to adult children's emotional intelligence (From Keaten & Kelly, 2008)	Family conversation orientation	Adult children's emotional intelligence
Higher levels of arousal in corporate blog messages will affect the publics' evaluations of corporate reputation positively. (Kim & Kiousis, 2012)		
Attending orientation will significantly increase a new employee's organizational identification. (Stephens & Dailey, 2012)		
The larger the number of people who use media regularly, the higher their political knowledge and interest levels. (Nir, 2012)		

and low sensation value messages, the research team reviewed public service announcements (PSAs) currently being shown on television. Identifying those that were high and low sensation, the research team then used focus groups to verify their characterizations. With this information, the team created high sensation value PSAs that featured high intensity, loud and driving music, quick and multiple edits, unusual camera angles, and extreme close-ups. Alternatively, low sensation value PSAs featured slower paced music, fewer edits, more typical camera angles, and no extreme close-ups. Thus, the authors clearly described what constitutes a high sensation and a low sensation value message and explained specifically how those messages were created.

The researchers also explained how they operationalized each of the other three variables—attitude change, behavioral intention change, and behavior change. Attitudes toward marijuana use were measured with questionnaire items from a study done as an evaluation of a national drug abuse campaign. Behavioral intention toward using marijuana was measured with this and similar items: "How likely is it that you will use in the next 30 days?" Marijuana use behavior was measured with items that asked if participants had used marijuana in the past 30 days, the past year, or at any time during their lifetime. For each variable the research team provided examples of the items and indicated the direction of the desired change (i.e., should watching a PSA result in a higher or lower score).

Thus, different terms are used as the researcher moves through conceptual, theoretical, and empirical stages. Occasionally, you will notice that the terms are used interchangeably.

But, technically, as the terms move from concept through construct through variable to operationalization, a greater level of specificity should be given.

When you read scholarly journal articles using quantitative methods, you will read about concepts and constructs in the literature review. In this section, the researchers may even present conflicting definitions of the concept of interest. When researchers present their research questions and hypotheses, they will become more specific and treat the concepts and constructs as variables. In the methods section of the journal article, researchers will be precise and provide the operationalization—how the variable will be observed and measured—of each variable.

Both researchers and consumers of research benefit when there is specificity about what is being studied (Miller & Nicholson, 1976). If terms are defined explicitly in operationalizations, it is more difficult for the researcher to draw conclusions beyond the boundaries established. Another advantage is that findings of studies that use the same or similar operationalizations can be compared. When an operationalization is accepted as a standardized way of measuring or observing, there are two consequences. First, preciseness is achieved, which allows our understanding of the communication phenomenon to be enhanced, and this enhancement supports theory development. Second, operationalizations allow other researchers to replicate the research to verify or challenge findings.

MAKING THE CASE FOR QUANTITATIVE RESEARCH

For many of the other social sciences and for a long period of time in communication, researchers conducting their research from the social science perspective relied primarily on quantitative research methods. Traditionally, experimental forms were preferred to other methods in which variables are quantified (for example, surveys). Today, however, communication researchers choose from a variety of quantitative methods. Which method should be chosen is one of the

decisions the researcher must make. By answering the question "What do I want to know in this study?" clearly and completely, the researcher can determine if a quantitative research design is appropriate and then select the best approach. Reviewing the advantages and limitations of quantitative research will help you determine what types of hypotheses and questions are best addressed by quantitative methods.

Advantages of Quantitative Research

The advantages of using quantitative research methods are obvious. First, quantitative methods used in communication research follow the tradition and history of quantitative methods in other disciplines. Thus, the use of quantitative methods implies a certain amount of rigor in the research process. By quantifying and measuring communication phenomena, communication researchers are using the same research language as researchers with whom they share interests. Sharing a research tradition could, for example, strengthen the relationship between communication researchers who study organizational communication and researchers from the management discipline. Likewise, many communication researchers who study interpersonal issues would share a research tradition with psychologists who focus on individuals and their relationships.

A second advantage of quantitative research comes from the use of numbers and statistics. By quantifying communication concepts and using statistical procedures for evaluating differences and relationships, researchers are able to be very precise and exact in their comparisons. This is especially important in the study of microelements of communication. Quantifying abstract concepts provides researchers a way to isolate variables and gain knowledge about concepts that would otherwise remain hidden.

Third, because we can quantify communication phenomena, we can make comparisons, and those comparisons can be made among a large group of participants. As a result, researchers can generalize their findings to other individuals who have the same characteristics as those in the research project.

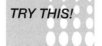

TRY THIS!

Operationalizing Variables

Communication researchers are often interested in studying concepts that are abstract in nature. For example, to study how couples in love communicate and then compare that to how couples not in love communicate, we would first have to describe what love is and then operationalize it. Review the examples that follow; which operationalization do you like best? What is problematic with the two operationalizations? What operationalizations can you develop? Are there other descriptions of love more central to communication?

Description of Love	Operationalization of Love
When two people hold hands in front of others	The number of times a couple holds hands for longer than one minute in public
When two people tell their friends and relatives that they are in love	The degree of vocal intensity in telling friends and relatives that they love the other person The number of reasons given when telling friends and family that they love the other person.
When two people independently feel attracted to each other and decide not to date others	
When two people in a committed relationship do unexpected tasks for each other	

Limitations of Quantitative Research

Of course, with advantages come limitations. And, as is often true, limitations stem from the same sources as the advantages. Because quantitative research can focus on microelements; of communication phenomena, this type of research generally does not lend itself to capturing the complexity or depth of communication over time. The restriction of focusing on just a few variables at a time makes it more difficult for researchers to examine the entirety of the communication process.

Likewise, quantitative research cannot capture communication phenomena that cannot be replicated or simulated in a controlled research environment. Although researchers can use quantitative

methods in the field, all participants must be subjected to the same stimuli and systematic procedures. As a result, questions about a communication phenomenon that occurs spontaneously or sporadically are not as well suited to quantitative methods.

ISSUES OF RELIABILITY AND VALIDITY

All quantitative research hopes to be both reliable and valid. **Reliability** is achieved when researchers are consistent in their use of data collection procedures and when participants react similarly to them. Reliability also means that other researchers using the same measure in another project with comparable participants would get similar results (Hoover & Donovan, 1995).

But reliability is only part of evaluating a quantitative research method. **Validity** is achieved when the measurement does what it is intended to do (Hoover & Donovan, 1995). Validity is related to truth. Thus, within scientific reasoning, the better the technique is at uncovering the reality of the concept, the more valid it is. If a questionnaire presumably assessing your degree of communication competence asks you to respond to an item about your ability to handle conflict, the item would be valid if you and other people in general believe that handling conflict effectively is, in fact, evidence of communication competence.

Reliability and validity are related. Both are evaluations of the utility of a measuring device. When reliability and validity are achieved, the data are free from systematic errors (Selltiz, Jahoda, Deutsch, & Cook, 1959). This is why quantitative researchers must carefully consider reliability and validity in the planning stages of their research project. But doing so is not enough. At the end of data collection, one of the first analytical steps quantitative researchers perform is to assess the reliability and validity of their data. Without reliable and valid measurement, the results of the study, which rely on how the data are collected, are suspect. More detailed information on how to assess reliability and validity can be found in Chapter 5.

Threats to Reliability and Validity

Any measuring device can be faulty—whether the device is a questionnaire or a researcher categorizing and counting the number of times you use "Ms. Wright" while speaking with your boss. Communication research is especially vulnerable to threats to reliability and validity because it measures complex communication phenomena. Let's examine different types of threats to reliability and validity (Selltiz et al., 1959).

First, reliability and validity are threatened if the measuring device cannot make fine distinctions. To what degree can the measuring device capture specificity or exactness? In measuring a person's orientation, or relationship, to organizations, can the measure of organizational orientation (McCroskey, Richmond, Johnson, & Smith, 2004) really distinguish among individuals who have a strong affinity for organizations, those who do not care much about organizations, and those who cannot adapt to organizations well? Second, reliability and validity are threatened if the measuring device cannot capture how people differ. Not only must the organizational orientation measure make distinctions among the three different orientations a person can have to organizations, but it must also provide information about how individuals with those orientations communicate in organizations.

A third threat is present when researchers attempt to measure something that is irrelevant or unknown to the respondent. Anyone can respond to a questionnaire; but if the respondent does not understand the questions or if the respondent is asked to give responses for something for which he or she has no reference, then the measurement is faulty. This is especially true of opinions and attitudes, which are often part of quantitative communication research. Simply, it would not make sense to ask an unmarried and never-married respondent to answer questions about communication satisfaction with a marital partner.

Finally, the complexity of human communication behavior can threaten reliability and validity. Can any measuring instrument really capture the phenomenon? For example, if two researchers are measuring the length of a building and they disagree, together they can remeasure the building. Their individual measures can be verified by each other or a third party. But how can someone verify your organizational orientation? Asking you to respond again to the questionnaire may produce different results, depending on the number and types of interactions you have had in organizations since you last answered the questionnaire or depending on a change in your motivation or employment status. Someone else cannot independently verify your organizational orientation—only you can provide that information. Moreover, what if your organizational orientation is not represented by the three orientations captured by this questionnaire?

As you can see, quantifying communication phenomena provides some difficulties and creates consequences for the validity and reliability of the research. Although researchers want to capture variation across the participants in the research project, the variation should be representative of the true differences among individuals and not result from measurement errors (Selltiz et al., 1959).

Besides the variation that researchers want to capture, there are many other possible sources of variation (Selltiz et al., 1959). Unless these variations are intended to be examined as part of the research design, when they are present, the following must be considered as threats to reliability and validity:

1. Variation due to factors not measured in the research study. For example, you want to measure effects of personality on conflict management strategy choice. A researcher would have to check the research literature to determine if personality is the best choice of independent variable. Rather than personality, could it be that our experiences with conflict help mold our preferences?

2. Variation or differences due to personal factors, such as mood, fatigue, health, time of day, and so on. How would these factors affect your choice of conflict management strategy?

3. Variation or differences due to situational factors. Would your choice of conflict management strategy be different for conflicts at school, at work, at home?

4. Variation due to differences in how the research project is administered. Different researchers may use different communication styles in working with research participants. Would you respond differently to a researcher who appears to be bored than you would respond to a researcher who appears enthusiastic?

5. Variation due to the number of items included in the measuring device. Asking only one question about each of the conflict management styles would not be the same as asking several questions about each style. Multiple items are required to capture the breadth and complexity of most communication phenomena.

6. Variation due to unclear measuring device. As an assistant to a researcher, you are asked to observe students giving speeches and count the number of times students use incomplete sentences. In one speech, the speaker gives an incomplete sentence but before moving on to the next sentence catches the error and restates the incomplete sentence as a full one. Do you count this or not?

7. Variation affected by mechanical or procedural issues. In a research experiment, you are asked to recall your last conflict with your relational partner and write out what you said to him or her. As you recall the conflict incident, you recognize that the conflict was a lengthy one lasting for about 20 minutes. But the researcher left only 3 inches of space on the questionnaire for you to describe what you said. Not knowing what to do, you select the most important things you said and leave out the rest.

8. Variation due to the statistical processing of the data. For example, the researcher accidentally selects the wrong statistical test from the pulldown menu. Or the person who enters the data in the computer pushes "4" every time you have responded with a "5."

Obviously, you want to capture and test variation in your research project. But this type of variation is planned for and identified in your hypotheses and research questions. Other variation is problematic. Look again at the model for quantitative research in Figure 4.1. Notice that selection of methods must be balanced with issues of reliability and validity. That is why researchers using quantitative methods must carefully consider and evaluate their research design, or their procedures and methods, before data are collected. Capturing variation beyond the variation the researchers want to capture is measurement error, which produces threats to reliability and validity.

SUMMARY

1. Quantitative research relies on the use of numbers as a way of observing and measuring communication phenomena.

2. Researchers bring objectivity to the study of communication through the use of traditional quantitative approaches and statistical techniques.

3. Quantitative research relies on deductive reasoning.

4. The primary objective of quantitative research is to test propositions developed from theory.

5. The quantitative research model includes five components: research purpose, literature foundation, research questions and research hypotheses, research methods, and validity and reliability.

6. Quantitative research requires that every phenomenon studied be conceptualized and then explicitly defined. Researchers work from concepts to constructs to variables to operationalizations in providing the degree of objective specificity needed to examine communication phenomena.

7. Operationalizations are the specific way in which researchers observe and measure variables in quantitative research.

8. Quantitative research typically relies on the use of hypotheses to drive the research process.

9. Hypotheses should be simply stated, have variables and their relationships clearly specified, and be testable.

10. Although researchers develop research hypotheses, the null hypothesis is actually the focus of the statistical test.

11. A hypothesis includes both independent and dependent variables.

12. Researchers can also use research questions as a foundation for their quantitative research. Research questions are appropriate to use when there is little known about a communication phenomenon or when previous results are inconclusive.

13. Advantages of quantitative research include a certain degree of rigor, objectivity achieved through the use of numbers and statistics, and ability to make comparisons among a large group of participants.

14. Limitations of quantitative research include difficulty in capturing the complexity or depth of communication over time, and the inability to capture communication phenomenon that cannot be replicated or simulated in a controlled environment.

15. Quantitative research must address threats to reliability and validity, including using imprecise measures of variables, attempting to measure something that is unknown or irrelevant to participants, and difficulty in capturing the complexity of human interaction.

KEY TERMS

antecedent variable	nondirectional hypothesis
causal variable	null hypothesis
concept	operationalization
conceptual scheme	outcome variable
construct	predictor variable
criterion variable	reliability
dependent variable	treatment variable
directional hypothesis	validity
experimental variable	variable
independent variable	

See the website www.mhhe.com/keyton4 that accompanies this text. For each chapter, the site contains a:

• chapter outline

• chapter checklist

• chapter summary

• short multiple-choice quiz

• PowerPoint presentation created by Dr. Keyton

For a list of internet resources, visit http://www.joannkeyton.com/CommunicationResearch-Methods.htm.

CHAPTER FIVE

Measurement

Chapter Checklist

After reading this chapter, you should be able to:

1. Understand that measurement is a process.

2. Explain the principle that numbers have no inherent meaning until the researcher assigns or imposes meaning.

3. Develop categories for nominal data that are mutually exclusive, exhaustive, and equivalent.

4. Distinguish among the three types of continuous level data—ordinal, interval, and ratio—and use them appropriately.

5. Develop effective and appropriate Likert-type scales.

6. Understand the basic principles of validity and reliability and how they affect research results.

7. Understand the relationship between validity and reliability.

8. Consider research design issues that may threaten validity and reliability.

9. Collect, report, and interpret data accurately, ethically, and responsibly.

10. Question the measurement procedures and data interpretations reported by researchers.

Quantitative research relies on measurement, or assigning numbers to data as a way to mark characteristics of data (Vogt & Johnson, 2011). Whether or not you plan to conduct quantitative research, you should have a basic understanding of the concepts presented in this chapter because much of what is known about communication phenomena has been discovered through measurement, and the design and statistical principles that follow from it.

Measurement is a useful process because it aids researchers in identifying and presenting information about communication behavior. It is the link between the conceptual and the empirical. Using measurement principles, researchers can take widely varying phenomena and reduce them to compact descriptions we identify as variables (Judd & McClelland, 1998).

MEASUREMENT PRINCIPLES

You are familiar with using numbers to measure something in order to describe its value, degree, intensity, depth, length, width, distance, and so on. In research, a measurement is simply a descriptive device. Measurement also allows us to evaluate what is described. Even though measurement provides these two functions, the numbers used to measure something have no value until we give meaning to them. For example, the number 99 could be your score on a recent test, in which case you would be proud of your accomplishment if 100 points were possible. But how would you feel about a score of 99 if 200 points were possible? You see, the value we assign numbers is not inherent in the numbers. Rather, the value comes from the meaning we assign or impose, and much of this is done arbitrarily. The goal of this chapter is to help you become comfortable with the way in which numbers are used in research to account for or substitute for the observation of communication concepts and phenomena.

Although numbers are central to measurement, it may be more useful to think of **measurement** as a process that includes everything the researcher does to arrive at the numerical estimates. Thus, measurement includes the measuring device or instrument, how the device or instrument is used, the skill of the person using the device or instrument, and the attribute or characteristic being measured (Katzer, Cook, & Crouch, 1978). Each of these can affect the number obtained by the researcher. Measurement can also be the process of assigning a person, event, or thing to a particular category (Sirkin, 1995). In this way a researcher measures something by describing or identifying it.

Regardless of the type, measurement needs to be accurate because it is the foundation of statistical analyses and the subsequent interpretations made by the researcher. If measurement of a communication phenomenon is flawed, everything that flows from it is flawed as well (Emmert, 1989).

Why measure communication phenomena? When we measure something, we are describing it in some standardized form. Recall from Chapter 4 the discussion about operationalizing variables. Choosing a way to measure something standardizes how the variable is perceived, treated, and handled and, in essence, provides the *operationalization* of the variable. When variables are operationalized, or standardized, they can be used in three types of comparisons (Figure 5.1).

The first type entails comparing many measurements of the same variable. The second type of comparison is especially important to researchers because science is a process of extension and replication. When researchers use the same or similar methods of measurement, the results of one study can be compared to the results of another study. The third type of comparison allows researchers to make more distinct discriminations among elements that might appear to be similar. In making these three types of comparisons, measurement allows researchers to use mathematical techniques to verify the existence of some phenomenon as well as give evidence to the existence of relationships among communication phenomena (Kaplan, 1964).

Figure 5.1 shows a practical example of how researchers use measurement to make three different comparisons. At some point, almost everyone has experienced communication apprehension, or anxiety in interacting with others. The first type of comparison—comparing many measurements of the same variable—can occur

		Apprehension category	PRCA score
1st	**Comparisons among individuals**		
	Kale	high	78
	Dennis	low	56
	Halley	high	79
	Che Su	low	50
2nd	**Comparisons among studies using the same measure**	In previous research, PRCA has demonstrated high internal consistency, with alpha reliability estimates ranging from .93 to .97 (McCroskey, 2009; McCroskey et al., 1985). In this study, the obtained Cronbach's alpha for the overall scale (traitlike CA) was .97. Source: Russ (2012).	
3rd	**Comparisons among similar measures**	The second hypothesis examined the approach-avoidance dimension of unwillingness to communicate. A multiple regression analysis revealed that biological sex, self-esteem, and communication apprehension explained a significant amount of variance in the approach-avoidance dimension of unwillingness to communicate. Source: Pearson, Child., DeGreeff, Semlak, & Burnett (2011).	

FIGURE 5.1 *Measurement Allows Three Types of Comparisons*

in two ways. On the most basic level, we could simply identify people as having or not having communication apprehension. In making these identifications, we have assigned individuals to one of two categories—those who are communicatively apprehensive and those who are not. This type of categorization is the most basic level of measurement. With that information, we would have two groups of people but not know very much about any differences between the two groups or differences among those within each group.

At this first level, we could also make comparisons among many individuals on this variable by using the Personal Report of Communication Apprehension, or the PRCA (McCroskey, Beatty, Kearney, & Plax, 1985). Individuals could answer its 24 questions, and we could calculate their scores of communication apprehension. We could compare the scores of these individuals because this instrument is one way to standardize the measurement of communication apprehension. We could even identify a score that becomes the point for distinguishing between the two groups—those who are communicatively apprehensive and those who are not. Or we could use participants' scores to find subtle variations within groups.

In moving to the second type of comparison, we can compare our results to the results of other researchers who have used the PRCA. We could identify the journal articles that address communication apprehension and report PRCA scores. Then, we could compare findings of our study to the results of studies previously published. In Figure 5.1 see how Russ (2012) compares the internal reliability scores from his study to earlier ones. We could compare our participants' average score to the average scores from similar or different populations.

Communication apprehension is one of the most widely researched communication variables. But it is still only one way to measure participants' predisposition to communication avoidance. So, another type of comparison is to compare participants' PRCA scores to a similar type of measure. As an example, Pearson and her research team (2011) used PRCA scores to predict the approach-avoidance dimension of unwillingness to communicate (Burgoon, 1976). Statistical analyses revealed that PRCA was a significant predictor of unwillingness to communicate.

LEVELS OF MEASUREMENT IN COMMUNICATION RESEARCH

Communication research relies on researchers using measurement and observation to collect and organize data. Researchers use two types of measurement—discrete and continuous. Each produces a different kind of data. How data are collected determines their use in statistical analyses, which are discussed in later chapters.

Perhaps the best way to think of data is that they can represent the name or the value of something. If data only name, or identify, what is being measured, then data are discrete. This level of data is referred to as categorical, or nominal, data. If data represent the value of elements, they are referred to as continuous level data. Ordinal, interval, and ratio are three levels of continuous level data. Both discrete and continuous level data are regularly collected and reported in communication research.

Discrete Data

Some observations and measurements are discrete. In this case, data represent the presence or absence of some characteristic. All the elements with the same characteristic belong to one category; elements with another characteristic belong to another category. This allows the researcher to group similar elements together and, at the same time, to identify these elements as distinct from others. Known as **nominal data,** or **categorical data,** discrete data describe the presence or absence of some characteristic or attribute. In other words, the data give a name to the characteristic without any regard to the value of the characteristic. Sex, political affiliation, class level, and employment status are just a few examples of variables that are measured on the categorical level. The characteristic is present or absent because there is no practical way to express partial presence of the characteristic.

For example, you are male or female. In the United States, your political affiliation can be described as Democrat, Independent, or Republican. Your class level is freshman, sophomore, junior, or senior. You are a part-time or full-time employee, or do not work. An example of discrete measurement appears in Keyton et al.'s (2013) study in which working adults were the respondents to a survey. While it may appear that how long someone has been in their current position is a continuous level variable, few us of talk about it that way. When asked, we are more likely to say, "oh, about 7 years" rather than "6 years, 3 months, and 2 days." So to capture how long participants had been in their current position, the researchers asked participants to identify this by checking one of the following boxes: 1 year or less, 1 to 2 years, 3 to 5 years, or 6 years or more.

Notice here that a discrete variable (e.g., length of time in current position) is represented by several categories. For the variable political affiliation, there could be three categories of Democrat, Independent, and Republican; or there could be more depending on how specifically this variable needed to be measured (for example, five political parties had candidates in the 2012 U.S. presidential election). For the class level variable, its discrete categories are freshman, sophomore, junior, and senior. It is important to remember that within each variable, the different categories reflect different *types* of political affiliation or class rank, not differing *amounts* of political affiliation or class rank. Categorizing people relies on the assumption that participants identified by a particular category are similar and have the same attributes.

Another aspect of categorical data is that the category levels within a particular variable possess no inherent value. Any value imposed on the categories is arbitrary. To avoid biasing responses or to avoid the appearance of a preferred response, researchers frequently arrange categories alphabetically. For example, eye color would be arranged as "black, blue, brown, green, hazel." Some categorical data, such as class level, follow a logical ordering. In this case, it would make sense to list the categories of class level as "freshman, sophomore, junior, senior" rather than in the alphabetical order of "freshman, junior, senior, sophomore." It is generally accepted that you must be a freshman before achieving sophomore standing, and you must be a junior before achieving senior standing. But recognize that in a particular case, being a freshman may be valued more than being a senior. Any value ascribed is arbitrary. Thus, in some cases, societal standards and practices provide guidance in how categorical data are presented to research participants. If no such standard is present or appropriate, then alphabetical listing of categories is preferred. Remember, however, that the ordering of the categories imposes no particular value on any category.

Depending on your familiarity with some nominal variables, you may believe it is easy to identify a nominal variable and its representative categories. Be careful. In data collection, each participant should be identified by only one category of each variable. Thus, where we collect data and from whom can have a major impact on the selection of nominal variables and their representative categories. For instance, Longo et al. (2009) investigated how women from different cultures who survived breast cancer sought and used health-related information. To describe these women, the authors used six nominal variables: stage of cancer at diagnosis, phase of treatment, ethnic/racial background, language, marital status, and education. The categories for each variable are shown in Table 5.1. The research team specifically wanted to compare Latina and

TABLE 5.1 Nominal Variables and Their Categories in Breast Cancer Survivor Study

Stage of Cancer at Diagnosis	Phase of Treatment	Ethnic/Racial Background	Language	Marital Status	Education
Stage 0	Phase 2 (evaluation)	African-American/Black	Spanish only	Married/living as married	8th grade or less
Stage 1	Phase 3 (undergoing treatment)	Asian/Pacific Islander	English or bilingual	Divorced	Some high school
Stage 2	Phase 4 (remission or reoccurrence)	Caucasian/White		Separated	High school diploma or GED
Stage 3	Phase 5 (long term)	Latina		Widowed	Vocational school or some college
Stage 4		Multi-ethnic		Single, never married	College degree
					Professional/graduate school experience

SOURCE: Longo, Ge, Radina, Greiner, Williams, Longo et al. (2009).

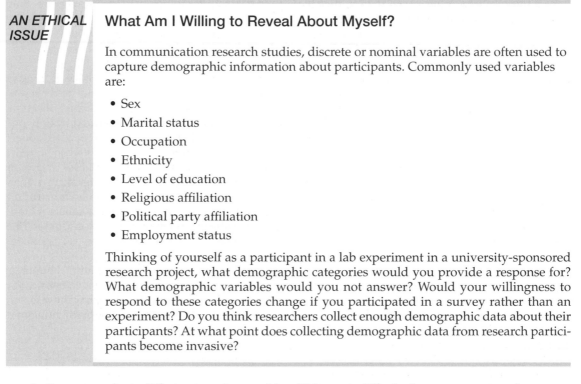

AN ETHICAL ISSUE

What Am I Willing to Reveal About Myself?

In communication research studies, discrete or nominal variables are often used to capture demographic information about participants. Commonly used variables are:

- Sex
- Marital status
- Occupation
- Ethnicity
- Level of education
- Religious affiliation
- Political party affiliation
- Employment status

Thinking of yourself as a participant in a lab experiment in a university-sponsored research project, what demographic categories would you provide a response for? What demographic variables would you not answer? Would your willingness to respond to these categories change if you participated in a survey rather than an experiment? Do you think researchers collect enough demographic data about their participants? At what point does collecting demographic data from research participants become invasive?

non-Latina respondents. What categories would need to be changed or expanded if greater cultural diversity was the goal? Or if another type of disease was examined?

To be both a valid (truthful) and reliable (consistent) measurement, the categories of a nominal variable need to be representative of the people involved. Therefore, categories must be **mutually exclusive;** people should not be able to identify themselves in more than one category. Categories also need to be **exhaustive,** representing the variety of characteristics of the people involved. At the same time, categories must also be **equivalent,** or equal to one another. Finally, a nominal variable must have at least two categories. Otherwise, differentiation is not possible. When these conditions are met, nominal data help researchers classify participants into membership categories.

Continuous Level Data

In contrast to discrete data, other variables take on or assume a quantity, intensity, or magnitude.

Values can differ in degree, amount, or frequency, and these differences can be ordered on a continuum. These are known as **continuous level data,** or **quantitative data.** A person's score on a questionnaire is continuous level data because a score can range from some minimum to a maximum quantity. We can demonstrate this concept with the Computer Mediated Communication Competence Scale (Spitzberg, 2006). Here is one item and the response scale.

I am very knowledgeable about how to communicate through computers.

not at all true of me	mostly not true of me	neither true nor untrue of me; undecided	mostly true of me	very true of me
1	2	3	4	5

A research participant would use the same response scale to answer each of the scale's 77 items. His or her score could range from the minimum possible score to the maximum possible score, with any intermediate position possible. Thus, the data are continuous.

Sometimes, researchers create continuous data by simply counting some element to establish its level or degree of presence or absence. For example, Dennis, Kunkel, and Keyton (2008) studied the types of messages women use to support one another in a breast cancer support group. The research team examined 256 pages of transcripts representing 515 minutes of conversation and categorized them by message type. By counting the number of instances, they found that across the eight support group meetings, these survivors of cancer were almost twice as likely to make negative assessments ($N = 471$; e.g., "I don't know") rather than positive assessments ($N = 277$; e.g., "Without a doubt") of the probability of the success of outcomes or treatments. The data are continuous because the number of probability messages could have been 0 if no probability messages occurred, or be any number between 1 and the total number of messages said in the support group's conversation. There are three types of continuous level data—ordinal, interval, and ratio. They differ in terms of their properties and their abilities to be used in mathematical operations and statistical tests. Each one is more sophisticated than its predecessor because it contains more information about the phenomenon of interest. Each will be discussed in detail in the sections that follow.

Ordinal Data   *Ordinal* means sequence or in order. **Ordinal data** are data measured by ranking elements in logical order from high to low or low to high. Oftentimes, ordinal data are presented as 1st, 2nd, 3rd, and so on. Ordering indicates positioning or sequencing of elements relative to one another. Yet, this type of sequencing often occurs without precise measurement and without knowing to what degree elements are lower or higher than others.

There are three important things to remember about ordinal data. First, ranking positions are relative only to the other ranking positions in that group. As a result, even a participant who has low preferences for all the choices presented will rank one of the low-preference choices as having the highest ranking. Second, the distance between ranked elements is uneven and often unknown. Third, because ordinal data consist of relative rankings, zero cannot exist.

Many times, ordinal measurement is used to make comparison judgments among a set of related topics, things, or issues. Ordinal data, or ranking information, can also be used to demonstrate the relative status or importance of each item in a group of related items. For example, in a study investigating the type of restrictions people prefer for mass-mediated content, Paek, Lambe, and McLeod (2008) asked participants to rank five possible government reactions (e.g., stopping the communication before it happens; imposing fines or other penalties after the communication has taken place; creating time, place, and manner restrictions; not taking action one way or the other; actively ensuring the expression will take place). The higher the rank, the stronger the endorsement for that type of restriction.

In another example, after Hurricane Katrina, a research team (Rold, Honeycutt, Grey, & Fox, 2011) asked participants who suffered the effects of the storm and its aftermath to rank order the people with whom they most talked about the catastrophe. The list included family members, but also friends, teachers, ministers, and God. Participants ranked their fathers as the most likely person they talked with, with mothers, spouse, children, and grandparents ranked as second through fifth. As the researchers explained:

> [The] rank orderings revealed that talking with God in the aftermath of the hurricane was rated number 8 on the list. However, just because God is ranked lower on this list does not mean that a private conversation one has with God is any less impactful than a conversation with a parent or spouse. Certainly one trying to manage strong emotions following a catastrophic event like Hurricane Katrina may experience a great sense of catharsis from praying once a day; whereas, that same person may experience that same sense of catharsis by talking to a parent several times per day. In other words, frequency of conversation does not necessarily equate to impact of conversation. (p. 137)

Ordinal data are not frequently used and this study points out why. Participants can have difficulty in differentiating among what elements, or who, ranks first, second, and so on. Although there are no hard and fast rules, ordinal data can be treated as continuous data and used in some statistical tests if many rank positions are available. If not, ordinal data are best treated as categorical data.

Interval Data   **Interval data** are data measured based on specific numerical scores or values. When using interval data, we can identify which participants scored highest and lowest, and we can determine the exact difference between and among scores. The distance between any two adjacent, or contiguous, data points is called an **interval,** and intervals are assumed to be equal. For example, for the set of scores 50, 60, 70, and 90, the distance between 50 and 60 is 10 units, the same as the distance between 60 and 70. That 10-unit difference is half the 20-unit distance between 70 and 90, or between 50 and 70.

Potential scores	50	60	70	80	90
Actual scores	50	60	70		90

A second important element of interval data is the acknowledgment of zero. Although this zero is arbitrary, these two properties allow researchers to use interval data in mathematical operations. In fact, in some interval data, particularly data from questionnaires, it would be impossible to obtain a zero score. For example, a 24-item questionnaire is used to evaluate the degree of communication flexibility individuals need in their day-to-day communication. Respondents are instructed to use one of five numerical responses as an answer for each question or item. If a respondent strongly agrees with an item, the "5" response is circled; if a respondent strongly disagrees with an item, the "1" response is circled. Thus, an individual's score could range from a minimum of 24 to a maximum of 120. Recognize that it is not possible to produce a score of zero. The lowest score available is 24 (24 items x 1, the lowest possible response), which in this case would be interpreted to mean that the individual has very little communication flexibility. Technically, it would be inappropriate to interpret such a score as representing no communication

flexibility. The highest score available is 120 (24 items x 5, the highest possible response).

As is typical of questionnaire and survey data, an individual's responses across the items on a questionnaire are totaled for a score. Then that score and all other scores are averaged to provide a mean score to represent the sample as a whole.

Likert-Type Scales   One type of interval scale measurement that is widely used in communication research is the Likert, or **Likert-type scale.** Research participants are given a statement and then asked to respond by indicating the degree to which they agree or disagree with the statement. Typically, the response set is like the following:

strongly disagree	disagree	undecided	agree	strongly agree
1	2	3	4	5

The wording can vary considerably, but the responses must be balanced at the ends of the continuum. In this example, "strongly disagree" offsets "strongly agree." It would be inappropriate to balance "strongly disagree" with "agree," or to balance "strongly disagree" with "strongly approve." Most Likert-type scales are 5-point scales, although 7-point scales can be used. This type of measurement is widely used to capture responses about attitudes, beliefs, and perceptions. In some cases, one Likert-type item will represent a variable. More typically, though, a series of Likert-type items will represent a variable. You will find a more complete description of Likert-type scales and their uses in survey research and questionnaires in Chapter 8.

Semantic Differential Scales   Another interval measurement is the **semantic differential scale** (Osgood, Suci, & Tannenbaum, 1957). Using a stimulus statement, participants are asked to locate the meaning they ascribe to a stimulus. The response scale is anchored by two opposites, usually bipolar adjectives. As an example, Kennedy-Lightsey, Martin, Thompson, Himes, and Clingerman (2012) developed a five item 7-point semantic differential scale to capture the

TRY THIS!

Changing Levels of Measurement

Some variables can be observed or measured in several ways. Using the following table, review the example given for classroom communication competence and then develop four levels of measurement for some aspect of intercultural communication competence.

Level	Classroom Communication Competence	Intercultural Communication Competence
Nominal	Identify a behavior that causes others to remark that you communicate competently (for example, you express disagreement tactfully). If another person agrees that you exhibit this behavior, you are competent; if you do not exhibit this behavior, you are not competent. Use this yes–no decision to categorize yourself as competent.	
Ordinal	In your classroom group, select the five members who are best at expressing disagreement tactfully. Rank these five people; the person most competent at this communication task receives the number 1 ranking.	
Interval	Create a statement for which a Likert-type response scale can be used. For example, I can express disagreement tactfully. Response set = strongly agree (5), agree (4), undecided (3), disagree (2), strongly disagree (1).	
Ratio	During a classroom group meeting, count the number of times each member expresses disagreement in a tactful way.	

degree of risk in a recent disclosure to a friend. The items were presented this way:

"The information I shared with my friend is . . ."

high risk	– – – – – – –	low risk
severe	– – – – – – –	not very severe
intense	– – – – – – –	not very intense
dangerous	– – – – – – –	not dangerous
jeopardizing	– – – – – – –	not jeopardizing

As a participant in the study, you would be instructed to place an X in the spot on the line that best represents your evaluation of the risk. In this case, if you believe the information you disclosed to your friend is low risk, you would place an X on one of the lines between the middle and that anchor, or end, of the scale. Likewise, if you believe the information you disclosed was intense, you would place an X between the middle and that anchor on the other end of the scale. The middle space is considered neutral. Notice how the scales do not include descriptors for the

DESIGN CHECK

Questioning Measurement Techniques

Measuring communication phenomena gives the appearance that the identity or value provided by the measurement is fixed, or static; when the identity or value provided is conceptualized this way, it is easy to think of it as being accurate. However, the identity or value is only as good as the measuring device. For example, a questionnaire requests that you check a category describing your ethnicity or race. Being of mixed racial heritage, what do you do? Check one racial category over another? Check both? Check none? In the same questionnaire, you are asked to respond to 20 statements about your most significant interpersonal relationship. By providing a Likert-type response set for each question, the researcher presumes that you think of your interpersonal relationship in a standardized way (for example, "strongly agree," "agree," "undecided," "disagree," "strongly disagree"). But as you read the stimulus statements, you find that you strongly agree to the first item and agree even more strongly to the second. What do you do? Circle "strongly agree" in response to both? Change your response to the first item to "agree" so you can "strongly agree" to the second? How differently do you perceive the space between "strongly agree" and "agree"? Most research participants are unaware of researchers' assumptions about measurement techniques. Is it possible that participants who lack this knowledge will respond differently from participants who understand these assumptions?

intermediate positions. Only the poles of the continuum are anchored, and the anchors must be complete and logical opposites.

As with the Likert-type scales, semantic differential measurement scales can be used singly, or a series of semantic differential scales can represent a variable. To calculate the score, the researcher assigns a numerical value to each position on the semantic differential scale. The spaces would be assigned the values 1 through 7. For this scale, the pole of the continuum labeled "High Risk" would be marked as "7" because risky information is the variable of interest.

Sometimes, semantic differential scales include the numerical values of the response set. Using the first two items of the earlier example, the scale would look like this:

high risk 7 6 5 4 3 2 1 *low risk*
severe 7 6 5 4 3 2 1 *not very severe*

When the response set is configured this way, participants are instructed to indicate their response by circling one of the numbers.

Ratio Data Finally, **ratio data** are similar to interval data except that zero is absolute. This means not only that intervals between data points are equal, but also that if the score is zero, there is a complete lack of this variable. Ratio measurement is not common in communication research. When used, it provides a measurement of the degree to which something actually exists. For example, in a study of media consumption and eating disorders, Moriarty and Harrison (2008) needed to measure children's exposure to television. Participants were asked to report how many hours of television they watched at different points in the preceding week. Response options ranged from 0 to 5 hours. Some children reported watching no television, which would be a true zero on the variable "hours of TV watched." Results from the study demonstrated that, on average, children watched 40.03 hours of TV per week; some watched 0 hours, but others watched as many as 85 hours.

Another way in which communication researchers use ratio measurement would be to capture the length of interaction by audio- or video-recording the conversation. Noting the length of the conversation in minutes and seconds would be a ratio measurement because time has equal intervals and a true zero.

ISSUES OF VALIDITY AND RELIABILITY

Regardless of the type of observation or measurement you use, a measurement is not worthwhile unless it measures a dimension worth measuring (Simon, 1969). With respect to conducting communication research, this means that you are measuring the constructs required by your research questions and hypotheses. Researchers do not measure anything and everything just because they can.

The scientific process also requires that researchers provide valid and reliable measurements. In general, validity speaks to the truthfulness or accuracy of the measurement, and reliability speaks to the consistency or stability of the measurement. Measurements that are not valid or reliable are incapable of helping researchers answer research questions or confirm hypotheses. Thus, measurement validity and reliability are central to the research process. Each of these assessments must be considered in planning the research. After data are collected, one of the first analytic steps researchers perform is to assess the reliability and validity of their data. Without reliable and valid measurement, the results of the study, which rely on how the data are collected, are suspect. Each of these is explored in detail and then in relation to the other.

Validity

Data obtained through measurements that are not valid are worthless data. Measurement has **validity** to the extent that it measures what you want it to measure and not something else (Hoover & Donovan, 1995; Katzer et al., 1978). Many of the variables studied by communication researchers cannot be directly observed. Instead they are inferred from behaviors that are observable (Carmines & Zeller, 1979). Because we often cannot be absolutely certain that measuring devices capture what was intended and only what was intended, validity is a matter of degree. These types of issues are known as **internal validity** because the accuracy of conclusions drawn from the data depends upon how the research is designed and the data collected. Thus, internal validity addresses the relationship between the concept being measured and the process for measuring it (Carmines & Zeller).

Another way to think of validity is as a test of true differences. A measurement is valid to the extent that differences in scores reflect true differences among individuals on the construct measured. If a measurement is ambiguous or unclear, any differences produced by it are due to error, not to the true differences it seeks to measure (Selltiz et al., 1959).

Let's look at an example. Many students participate in public speaking contests. What is a valid measure of public speaking ability? Is it how long students can speak without referring to their notes? Is it how long they can speak without vocal interrupters (*ahh, umm, aaah*)? Or could it be how many people in the audience are persuaded by their arguments? Each of these measures could be valid for selecting the most competent public speaker. Notice, however, that each measures only one aspect of public speaking competence. Which one of these do you believe will make the greatest distinction between a public speaker who is competent and one that is not? Would combining the various measurements be more valid? If we combine the three measurements, should they be equally represented in a composite, or should the measures be weighted in some way? As you can see, anytime something is measured, questions of validity should be raised. There are several types of validity (see Figure 5.2): face, content, criterion-related, concurrent, predictive, and construct. Each is described in the sections that follow.

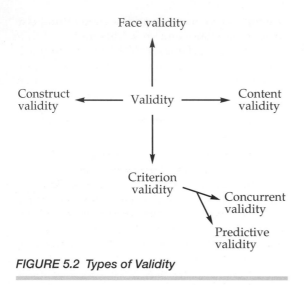

FIGURE 5.2 *Types of Validity*

Face Validity A measure is said to have **face validity** if the items reference the construct we want to measure. We can use the Personal Report of Communication Apprehension, or the PRCA-24 (McCroskey et al., 1985), as an example. The PRCA-24 is a 24-item questionnaire that measures communication apprehension, or the predisposition to avoid communication or suffer anxious feelings, across four contexts (public speaking, small group, meeting, and interpersonal encounters). Thus, in the PRCA, phrases such as "nervous and tense" or, alternatively, "calm and relaxed" are used to describe interaction. On the face of it—by just reading the items of the PRCA-24—it is clear to most individuals who respond to the items and researchers who have experience and expertise in that area that the instrument is measuring some aspect of apprehension as it would be associated with communicating.

In essence, face validity exists if the measurement looks and feels as if it will capture the construct we want to measure. Although face validity is the easiest to establish, most researchers would agree that it is the weakest type of validity. Frequently, researchers constructing questionnaires assert that they believe the measuring instrument has face validity. In other

words, they believe that the questionnaire effectively captures what they want to measure. Face validity can be strengthened when researchers use experts in the content area of the measuring instrument to assess its viability in capturing the construct of interest.

Content Validity The degree to which the items in the measuring device represent the full range of characteristics or attitudes associated with the construct of interest is a measurement's **content validity.** In other words, the measuring items are representative of the universe of items potentially available. Using the PRCA, content validity is achieved if its 24 items represent the complete range of verbal and nonverbal behaviors associated with communication apprehension. Although the PRCA was designed to capture perceptions of communication apprehension in four contexts—groups, meetings, dyads, and public speaking—for a moment, focus on this list of items for public speaking situations (McCroskey et al., 1985):

- I have no fear of giving a speech.
- Certain parts of my body feel very tense and rigid while I am giving a speech.
- I feel relaxed while giving a speech.
- My thoughts become confused and jumbled when I am giving a speech.
- I face the prospect of giving a speech with confidence.
- While giving a speech I get so nervous, I forget facts I really know.

Notice how the six items represent a range of public speaking behaviors. Some items address a person's apprehension or anxiety before the speaking event; others address apprehension during the speech. Some items address a person's attitudes; others address physical behaviors. Content validity is achieved when the measurement covers the universe of possibilities. Can you think of other elements of communication apprehension in the public speaking context?

Criterion-Related Validity **Criterion-related validity,** is achieved when one measurement can be linked to some other external measurement.

Criterion-related validity can be achieved through two procedures—predictive validity and concurrent validity.

For the moment, assume that your research team wanted to develop a new measurement for communication apprehension, one that measured the apprehension workshop leaders and trainers might feel in those situations. You would want scores from your new apprehension measure to be consistent with participant scores on the PRCA. Why? Because the PRCA is an established and accepted measurement of communication apprehension. Collecting data from workshop leaders and trainers on both measuring instruments at the same time (just before a workshop or training session), or concurrently, is one way to demonstrate criterion-related validity. If participants' scores from the two measurements are highly related, or correlated, **concurrent validity** has been achieved. More information about correlation is provided in Chapter 11. Demonstrating that the new measuring instrument and the established measuring instrument—both measuring the same or similar things—are related is one way to establish the validity of your new measurement.

Another way to achieve criterion-related validity is through **predictive validity**. This type of validity is often the most central concern because communication researchers want to be certain that participants' responses to a questionnaire will, in fact, predict their communication behavior. For example, Hall, Carter, Cody, and Albright (2010) wanted to develop and validate a scale that measured how people flirt with one another. Using the literature as a foundation, the research team identified five styles of flirting: traditional, physical, sincere, playful, and polite. To examine the scale's predictive validity, the research team developed another set of behavioral items that measured the number of persons for whom participants felt a romantic interest, the number of those with whom participants flirted, the misreading of sexual interest from others, the frequency of interest expressed from others, and the degree to which flirting and pickup lines are flattering and inviting. The correlation of (or relationship to) participants' scores on the flirting styles inventory with the behavioral items were

used to assess the inventory's predictive validity. For example, "women who score high in the traditional style flirt less with potential romantic interests, are less likely to be flattered by flirting, and are more likely to have difficulty getting men to notice them" (p. 381). The inventory is said to achieve predictive validity as women who use a traditional flirting style would also likely be characterized by these types of behaviors in seeking and attracting romantic interest.

There are other ways to demonstrate predictive validity. In a different setting, Fairhurst (1993) wanted to establish the predictive validity of how conversation patterns distinguished among female leaders' use of personal and positional resources to influence subordinates' performance. To do this, Fairhurst collected two types of data—leaders' self-reports on a Leader-Member Exchange questionnaire and taped routine conversations between leaders and one of their subordinates. Fairhurst's primary interest was to establish how female leaders accomplished and displayed influence in social interaction.

According to Leader-Member Exchange theory, differences should be evident among leaders who maintain and sustain high, medium, or low levels of influence with their subordinates. Thus, the first step in assessing predictive validity was to examine the transcripts for patterns of leader influence. Twelve patterns were identified to distinguish how the leaders used aligning, accommodating, and polarizing behavior to influence their subordinates. Differing uses of these behaviors identified the type of leader–member exchange present in the leader–subordinate relationship. Of the 14 leader–subordinate conversations examined, 11 were consistent with the leaders' self-report scores on the questionnaire. Thus, Fairhurst could claim that her method of measurement did in fact predict leaders' use of influence according to Leader-Member Exchange theory. Thus, the measurement captured the performance, and predictive validity was achieved.

Construct Validity   Researchers rely on **construct validity** to assure themselves that they are measuring the core concept that was intended to be measured and not something else. Often, researchers use a different measure of the same or similar phenomena to establish construct validity. Construct validity rests on the arguments and supporting evidence, provided they are consistent with theoretical expectations (de Vaus, 2001).

Agarwal (2013) describes one way for examining construct validity. The main focus of the research was organizational trust. She identified three different measures of organizational trust. However, the measures differed by their approach. The first scale of trust was grounded in public relations theory. The second scale was grounded in trust of top organizational management. The third scale was grounded in interpersonal trust of top management. The first scale is the target of Agarwal's validity investigation. If the first scale is correlated (or related) to the other two scales, construct validity is achieved. Results of the study indicated that the first scale was strongly and positively related with the second and the third indicating that the first scale had conceptual similarity with the other trust measures.

Now look at a different approach for establishing construct validity. Rogan and Hammer (1994) assessed construct validity in their study of facework, or the presentation of self-image, in crisis negotiations (for example, police officers negotiating with a suicidal individual, an armed man holding his children hostage). Using transcripts of three crisis negotiations as their dataset, the authors identified speaking turns as the unit of analysis; there were 1,814 units across three incidents. Using the research literature as a foundation, the authors created a model of nine facework behaviors and trained research assistants to code the transcripts.

After this coding was complete, the authors turned to a study by Lim and Bowers (1991) that provided a coding scheme for face-supporting and non-face-supporting messages similar to the valence (threat, honor) dimension of the Rogan and Hammer coding scheme. Rogan and Hammer trained assistants to code the same 1,814 units according to the Lim and Bowers scheme. The coders achieved high levels of agreement between the two coding schemes, indicating support for the construct validity of the valence dimension of their coding scheme. Thus, construct validity is theoretically based, because one

measurement is related in a theoretically meaningful way (Emmert, 1989) to another meaningful measurement.

Validity captures the essence of something. Moving closer to capturing the reality or true nature of the phenomenon being studied improves validity. Thus, validity is developed over time. When a measurement is valid, it is truthful or accurate. As you can see, it would be difficult to accept a measurement without a sense of its validity.

Reliability

The **reliability** of a measurement is its degree of stability, trustworthiness, and dependability. If a measuring device varies randomly, there will be greater error, and reliability will be lower. *Consistency* is another word often used to describe reliability. A reliable measure is one that is consistent, that gives very similar results each time it is used. For measuring scales, this means that participants react similarly to the items in the scale. Should reliable measuring devices always produce the same results? That outcome is highly unlikely because some degree of bias or error is always present.

As a result, reliability is expressed as a matter of degree. Rather than use phrases like "completely reliable" and "not reliable at all," researchers use the **reliability coefficient,** a number between zero and one, to express how reliable their measures are. The closer the reliability coefficient is to 1.00, the greater the degree of reliability. The closer the reliability coefficient is to 0, the less the degree of reliability. What is reliable enough?

Generally, communication researchers agree that a reliability coefficient of .70 or above is acceptable. Notice that this is the commonly accepted standard. It is not an absolute. If the construct is easy to measure, as communication apprehension is, then a reliability coefficient of .80 or greater is expected. On the other hand, if a construct is difficult to capture, and thus measure, then a lower reliability coefficient could be acceptable. Generally, this is the case with concepts that are more abstract. There are three primary types of reliability associated with

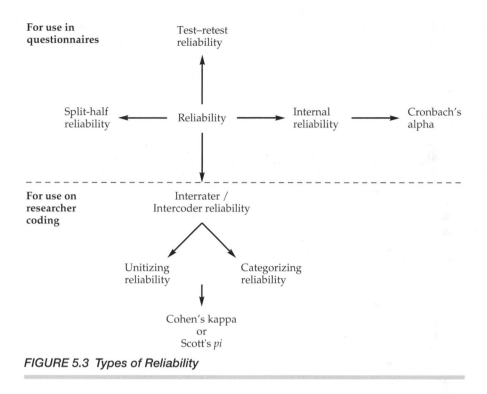

**For use in
questionnaires**

Test–retest
reliability

Split-half
reliability   ←   Reliability   →   Internal
reliability   →   Cronbach's
alpha

**For use on
researcher
coding**

Interrater /
Intercoder reliability

Unitizing
reliability   Categorizing
reliability

Cohen's kappa
or
Scott's *pi*

FIGURE 5.3 *Types of Reliability*

questionnaires or scales—internal reliability, test–retest reliability, and split-half reliability. See Figure 5.3.

Internal Reliability   Many measuring instruments have multiple interval level items to test one construct or variable. Let's go back to the flirting styles inventory. The inventory has 43 items, but each item is connected to only one of the five flirting styles (physical, traditional, polite, sincere, and playful), which are subscales of the inventory. Each item in a subscale was written to measure one aspect of a person's flirting style. The degree to which the items in a subscale, for example, the traditional flirting style, invoke the same response from the person responding to the questionnaire is its degree of **internal reliability.** The traditional flirting style subscale has internal reliability if you respond similarly to each of the items that ask about the man being responsible for initiating flirting or romantic interest.

It is highly unlikely that using any questionnaire will result in perfect reliability. Bias and error can occur in many ways and affect participants' abilities to respond in the same way to similar questions. First, the question or item itself may be ambiguously worded or may contain a word with which participants are unfamiliar. Second, the participant's experience or frame of mind may cause him or her to interpret the question differently from what you intended. Third, where and how the participant fills out the questionnaire can affect the responses given. Perhaps the participant feels rushed because of wanting to quickly finish the online survey to meet his or her friends for coffee. Environmental effects like these can alter a participant's responses. Regardless of its source, imprecision weakens the reliability of a measurement.

Fourth, a participant's mood can be a big factor in the responses given. The participant may have had a particularly bad day or may have just failed at a flirting attempt. Extreme emotions, positive or negative, are likely to alter a participant's responses. Fifth, the participant's interaction with the researcher, or the participant's impression of an online survey, can affect how honestly the participant will respond to a questionnaire. In instances where several members of a research team interact with participants, variation in their manner and style of communication can result in variation in participants' responses. Finally, the participant's familiarity with the questionnaire can affect the consistency of responses. If participants have responded to the same or similar measures when participating in other studies, they may believe they are familiar with the items and not read them or the directions carefully.

How many of these factors will influence participants' responses to your questionnaire varies with each person and each situation. But you should be able to see why it is unlikely that any measuring instrument would achieve perfect reliability. Simply put, there are a variety of sources of bias and error. As the researcher, you should try to control as many of these sources as possible. Pretesting the measuring instrument is under your control. You can also control some aspects of the research environment, including how you interact with participants when they enter the research setting. But it is unlikely that you will reduce all error and bias.

Researchers should calculate the internal reliability of any measuring instrument that includes multiple items. How can you calculate internal reliability? Statistical software programs (such as SAS or SPSS) can compute the internal reliability coefficient for a series of items across all respondents. This test is often referred to as **Cronbach's alpha** (Cronbach, 1951), internal reliability, or internal consistency. The statistic it produces is the coefficient alpha, which is represented as α in research reports. The alpha for each variable is reported in the method or results section of a research report. Recall that researchers generally agree that a coefficient alpha of .70 or greater is sufficient for establishing the internal reliability of a measuring instrument. If the internal reliability of a measuring instrument is not sufficient, the variable may have to be dropped from further analyses.

Ideally, coefficient alpha should be calculated and reported for each variable operationalized with a multiple-item instrument or scale. For example, Horan and Chory (2013) examined the relational implications of same-sex workplace romances and compared those findings to the relational implications of heterosexual workplace romances. To test their research questions and hypotheses, working adults responded to several questionnaires with Likert-type or semantic differential response scales. These internal reliabilities using Cronbach's coefficient alpha were reported as:

- Trust: $\alpha = .94$
- Deception: $\alpha = .79$
- Homophobia: $\alpha = .90$
- Competence: $\alpha = .89$
- Caring: $\alpha = .83$
- Character: $\alpha = .86$

The internal reliability for each of the variables meets or exceeds the generally accepted standard of .70, indicating that the internal reliability of each measuring instrument is sufficient to include in other analyses.

Test–Retest Reliability Communication is an interaction process, and over time the interaction or our perceptions of it can change. Thus, many researchers design their studies to capture measurements at different points in time—sometimes to demonstrate the stability of a measuring instrument. **Test–retest reliability** calculates the relationship, or correlation (see Chapter 11), between scores at two administrations of the same test, or measurement, to the same participants. As with other reliability scores, 1.0 would indicate that the same participants evaluated the stimulus the second time exactly as they did the first time. Alternatively, a score of 0.0 would indicate that the two measurements were no better than chance.

Oliver and Raney (2011) developed a scale to measure why people select the entertainment they do. They theorized that entertainment selection was based on pleasure seeking, or hedonic concerns, as well as a means of truth-seeking, or eudaimonic concerns. That is, entertainment can be pursued for enjoyment, but it can also be pursued to learn about or contemplate life's purpose. The research team believed these constructs (hedonic and eudaimonic concerns) were stable dispositions. That is, although variation within individuals could exist from time to time, the constructs could be predicted to be stable. Each scale was six items. To test this assumption, the research team administered the scales eight weeks apart in a test-retest design. They found that the test-retest scores for both scales were related across time over time (eudaimonia: $r = .89$; hedonism: $r = .72$).

Improving Reliability Generally, reliability can be improved. Here are a few ways that can be accomplished:

- Poorly worded or confusing items on a questionnaire can be rewritten.
- Better instructions can be given to respondents.
- Researchers can take steps to make sure that all measurements occur under similar environmental conditions.

Recognize, however, that reliability is subjective. You must decide what is acceptable to you as a consumer of research and as a researcher. When measurements are not reliable, the findings or conclusions based on them are not warranted or defendable.

The Relationship Between Validity and Reliability

Measuring something sounds easy, but developing a measure that is both valid and reliable is difficult. For a measurement to be useful, it must meet two conditions (Hoover & Donovan, 1995). First, the result of the measurement must fit the meaning of what was intended to be measured. If you want to measure the existence of cultural communication norms (for example, greeting and leave-taking behaviors) to capture cultural differences, then differences among cultural norms should be evident when measurements are complete. This is measurement validity. Second, the measurement of variation must be replicable. Thus, the measurements of cultural norms provided by one

participant on one day should be very similar to his or her measurements provided the next day. This is measurement reliability.

Although reliability and validity are two separate concepts, they are connected in a fundamental way. This connection is diagrammed in Figure 5.4. Measurements and questionnaires should be both reliable and valid. Reliable

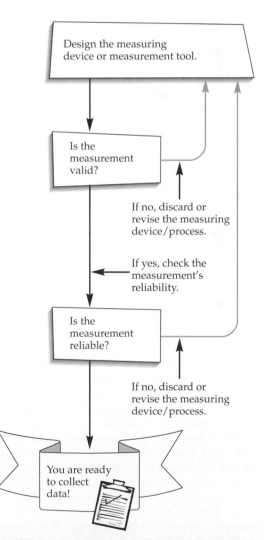

FIGURE 5.4 *Validity and Reliability Are Interconnected in a Fundamental Way—Both Must Be Satisfied to Produce Truthful and Consistent Data*

measurement can be obtained even if the measurement is not valid. For example, a questionnaire could reliably be measuring the wrong thing! Alternatively, valid measures are useful only if they are also reliable. When validity is achieved, reliability is presumed. Thus, validity is primary of the two. If you are not measuring what you want to measure, the consistency of the measurement is pointless. But in developing measurement, validity is more difficult to achieve than reliability. Think of the bathroom scale you use to measure your weight as a metaphor that can help explain this relationship. The scale may weigh you consistently over time at 150 pounds. In other words, it is reliable. But is this reliable measure valid, or accurate? Try your bathroom scale and that of a friend or that at your doctor's office. In no time at all, you will understand the reliability–validity connection!

As you read research reports, you should take careful note of the way in which reliability and validity information is presented. Each researcher makes judgments about the reliability and validity of his or her data. Each consumer must also make judgments: Are the data reliable and valid enough for you to accept the conclusions the researchers offered?

Threats to Validity and Reliability

Should you be concerned about issues of validity and reliability? Yes, if you use research results to make decisions or choices about your communication behavior or to evaluate the communication choices of others. And, yes, if you are conducting research based on the findings of others. Researchers speak of validity and reliability problems as *threats* to validity or reliability. A threat is any data-related problem that could lead you to draw a false conclusion from the data. Both participants and researchers can contribute to these problems. For what kinds of problems should you be on the lookout?

Issues of Data Collection The use of self-report questionnaires or surveys is very popular in communication research. Unfortunately, they are not always the best instruments for collecting data about how people communicate. Suppose a

measuring instrument asks you to think of how you behaved in the past or in a particular communication event. There could be a good deal of difference between how you actually communicated and what you remember about how you communicated (Sypher, 1980). Another type of validity error can occur when researchers use measuring instruments that are dated (Poole & McPhee, 1985), especially instruments that measure communication in relationships that reflect changing social values, like marital relationships or social stigma. In each of these cases, the threat to internal validity, or the degree to which valid conclusions can be drawn from the data, is caused by the researcher's selection of measuring instruments.

Researchers can cause other threats to internal validity by simply being themselves. Here, the researchers unknowingly influence how participants behave or respond to stimuli because of their sex or communication style. On the surface, using only female research assistants in a lab study about interpersonal relationships might not seem problematic. But male participants might be more willing to reveal personal information about their relationships to someone of the same sex and age.

Researchers can unknowingly bias respondents in another way. Continuing with the example of the study about interpersonal relationships, a respondent is describing her interaction in a way that confirms the researcher's expectations. Hearing what she wants to hear from the respondent, the researcher smiles, nods, or gives other confirming behaviors, hoping that the respondent will continue with this type of description. Alternatively, when a respondent is providing descriptions contrary to her expectations, the researcher maintains a straight face and provides few other nonverbal cues. To overcome these types of problems, many researchers make sure that the assistants who are collecting data do not know the hypothesis or purpose of the research project.

Participants can also threaten the internal validity of a research study. For example, in a study that follows a team over a long period of time, two things are likely to happen. First, membership of the group may change. This is known as

DESIGN
CHECK

Will These Results Apply to Me?

Students enrolled in communication classes at a medium-sized Southwestern university were the participants ($N = 210$) in a study that examined if verbal aggressiveness would be higher when participants had arguments with friends, romantic partners, or parents that were about personal or relationship issues than when they had arguments about topics outside the relationship (Johnson, Becker, Wigley, Haigh, & Craig, 2007). These topics were provided to participants as examples of personal arguments: conflicts over romantic partners, leisure time, other friends, household chores, roommate problems, hurt feelings, money/bills, trust and jealousy, showing consideration, alcohol use, apartment space, broken plans, using other's possessions, giving advice, and doing favors. These topics were provided to participants as examples of public arguments: abortion, death penalty, environment, drug legalization, underage alcohol drinking, racial prejudice, sex discrimination, sexual orientation discrimination, religion, gun control, drug testing, military spending, animal experimentation, surrogate mothering, foreign product restriction, sports, movies, etiquette/manners, race discrimination, and politics. The researchers found evidence to support the hypothesis. Verbal aggressiveness was higher in the personal argument condition ($M = 53.51$) than in the public argument condition ($M = 48.75$). What arguments could you make for the validity of using this sample and population? What arguments could you make that would threaten the validity of using such a sample and population? Would the scales used in this 2007 study be relevant today?

participant **mortality,** or **attrition.** Attrition can also occur because participants lose interest or lack the motivation to remain with the study. In some cases, participants move away or die. When participants leave a quantitative research project, either through mortality or attrition, researchers must deal with this loss of data.

Second, participants are likely to change, or mature, over the course of the observations. It would be unusual if some level of participation **maturation** did not occur. Participants can become overly familiar with the same questionnaire when it is presented at different points in time. Or maturation can occur because participants' attitudes and beliefs change due to some element outside the control of the researcher.

Issues of Sample Representativeness Some validity concerns are raised by the way in which researchers find and select their samples. This

is referred to as a threat to **external validity** because the threat weakens the generalizability of the findings. For example, many researchers use sampling techniques, particularly convenience samples, that are not based on the principles of probability (see Chapter 9). This type of sampling limits the generalizability of the results (Rubin & Perse, 1994). Collecting data only from people who are conveniently available to the researcher and who are willing to participate in the research study creates a problem of external validity. What population would the convenience sample represent? In other words, whose truth would these participants reflect?

Another common threat to external validity can occur when researchers use university students as research participants. Although students are a convenient sample for researchers at universities, they do not reflect any population except that of university students. The use of students in lab studies can also threaten external validity. Who is invited to participate in research, where the study is conducted, or how it is controlled can raise serious questions. These are threats to validity because the results for other samples and populations are not known and may be different. This is often referred to as a threat to **ecological validity,** another form of external validity.

Both the degree to which participants are not like those the researcher is really interested in and the degree to which the research setting is artificial and contrived limit the generalizability of the research findings. For example, Kuhn and Poole (2000) wanted to examine if and how organizational teams develop norms about the ways in which conflict spills over into the team's decision making. To increase the external validity of the findings, the researchers used established organizational teams composed of members who regularly worked together on organizational tasks. Studying teams in this naturalistic setting allowed the researchers to follow the teams over a period of time and was more appropriate for the research question than using contrived groups in a laboratory setting.

Summary of Threats   Reliability and validity are threatened if the measuring device cannot make fine distinctions. To what degree can the measuring device capture specificity or exactness? For example, in measuring a person's orientation, or relationship, to organizations, can the measure of organizational orientation (McCroskey, Richmond, Johnson, & Smith, 2004) really distinguish among individuals who have a strong affinity for organizations, those who do not care much about organizations, and those who cannot adapt to organizations well? Second, reliability and validity are threatened if the measuring device cannot capture how people differ. Not only must the organizational orientation measure make distinctions among the three different orientations a person can have toward organizations, but it must also provide information about how individuals with those orientations communicate in organizations.

A third threat is present when researchers attempt to measure something that is irrelevant or

unknown to the respondent. Anyone can respond to a questionnaire; but if the respondent does not understand the questions or if the respondent is asked to give responses for something for which he or she has no reference, then the measurement is faulty. This is especially true of opinions and attitudes, which are often part of quantitative communication research. Simply, it would not make sense to ask an unmarried and never-married respondent to answer questions about communication satisfaction with a marital partner.

Finally, the complexity of human communication behavior can threaten reliability and validity. Can any measuring instrument really capture the phenomenon? For example, if two researchers are measuring the length of a building and they disagree, together they can remeasure the building. Their individual measures can be verified by each other or a third party. But how can someone verify your organizational orientation? Asking you to respond again to the questionnaire may produce different results, depending on the number and types of interactions you have had in organizations since you last answered the questionnaire or depending on a change in your motivation or employment status. Someone else cannot independently verify your organizational orientation—only you can provide that information. Moreover, what if your organizational orientation is not represented by the three orientations captured by this questionnaire?

As you can see, quantifying communication phenomena provides some difficulties and creates consequences for the validity and reliability of the research. Although researchers want to capture variation across the participants in the research project, the variation should be representative of the true differences among individuals and not result from measurement errors (Selltiz et al., 1959). As you read research studies or design one of your own, use this checklist to assess if the measurements chosen, and the procedures by which data are collected, will unexpectedly contribute to a threat to validity and reliability.

1. Variation due to factors not measured in the research study. For example, you want to measure effects of personality on conflict management strategy choice. A researcher would have to check the research literature to

determine if personality is the best choice of independent variable. Rather than personality, could it be that our experiences with conflict help mold our preferences?

2. Variation or differences due to personal factors, such as mood, fatigue, health, time of day, and so on. How would these factors affect your reporting of which conflict management strategy you would use?

3. Variation or differences due to situational factors. Would your choice of conflict management strategy be different at school, at work, at home?

4. Variation due to differences in how the research project is administered. Different researchers may use different communication styles in working with research participants. Would you respond differently to a researcher who appears to be bored than you would respond to a researcher who appears enthusiastic? Would you respond differently to a researcher who looks like you? Or is physically very different?

5. Variation due to the number of items included in the measuring device. Asking only one question about each of the conflict management styles would not be the same as asking several questions about each style. Multiple items are required to capture the breadth and complexity of most communication phenomena.

6. Variation due to unclear measuring device. As an assistant to a researcher, you are asked to observe students giving speeches and count the number of times they use incomplete sentences. In one speech, the speaker gives an incomplete sentence but before moving on to the next sentence catches the error and restates the incomplete sentence as a full one. Do you count this or not?

7. Variation affected by mechanical or procedural issues. In a research experiment, you are asked to recall your last conflict with your relational partner and write out what you said to him or her. As you recall the conflict incident, you recognize that the conflict was a lengthy one lasting for about 20 minutes. But the researcher left only 3 inches of space on the questionnaire for you to describe what you said. Not knowing what to do, will you select the most important things you said and leave out the rest?

8. Variation due to the statistical processing of the data. For example, the researcher accidentally selects the wrong independent variable from the pulldown menu in the statistical software. Or the researcher unexpectedly uses the wrong spreadsheet and not all participant responses are included. What other mistakes could be made in analyzing the quantitative data?

ISSUES OF DATA INTERPRETATION

Recall from earlier in this chapter the idea that numbers hold no meaning until we assign meaning to them. Researchers who use numbers in their data collection are responsible for collecting data accurately and ethically. They also must interpret and report data responsibly. Why? Because most people who read their research reports will take these actions for granted. In fact, most consumers of research will not question what data collection method was used or why, nor will they question how researchers interpreted the data. This is in spite of the fact that scientific traditions require that researchers report their results and interpretations of the data in separate sections of the research report. For many consumers, these are details that are overlooked. These issues are discussed here for two reasons. First, data interpretation is intimately linked to the data collected. The quality of the interpretation cannot be better than the quality of the data. Second, data are also intimately linked to the theory or premise of the study. As a result, measurement is central to the quality of outcomes produced.

When communication phenomena are measured, they are broken down into their constituent parts. This aspect is data collection. Next, the researcher must interpret the data, or give it meaning, to answer research questions and test hypotheses (Kerlinger, 1986). Thus, two areas of concern exist. First, you might take issue with how the data were collected. The following questions can help you assess the researcher's collection of the data:

- Do you agree on how the variables were operationalized? Were the data collection instruments valid and reliable?
- Did the researcher collect data in such a way that what he or she expected to find became overemphasized and obvious to participants?
- Were the researcher's expectations communicated unknowingly to the participants in any way?
- Were the data collection procedures consistently applied?

In other words, do these data make sense given the research questions or hypotheses presented? These really are issues of technical and procedural adequacy.

The second area of concern is the interpretation of the data (Kerlinger, 1986). Even assuming technical and procedural competence, researchers and consumers can still disagree about what data mean. Interpretations of data are subjective to some degree because researchers' interpretations depend somewhat on their backgrounds (culture, education, language, and experiences) and the context in which the interpretation occurs (Katzer et al., 1978). Some typical problems are:

- Drawing sweeping conclusions from nonrepresentative data
- Accepting data results as firm conclusions without examining alternative interpretations
- Not adequately explaining contradictory or unanticipated findings
- Oversimplifying negative or inconclusive results without looking for weakness in the research process (inappropriate theory or hypotheses, inappropriate methodology, poor measurement, faulty analysis)

Too often, consumers of research take authors' conclusions for granted. As you learn more about the research process, however, you can make your own evaluation of the research methods and process. You can make these judgments by reading the method section of the research report. Whether qualitative or quantitative, the researcher should provide you with adequate information about what data were collected, how, and when. Then the analyses of the data should be presented in the results section of the research report. Here is where researchers start to reveal their interpretations of the findings. But the conclusions and implications of the data are not fully revealed until the discussion section of the research report.

As a consumer of research, your role is an active one. It is your job to think through the presentation of how the data were collected and analyzed and to test what you believe it means against what the researcher says it means. A series of questions can help:

- What questions did the researchers ask?
- How much confidence do I have in the data collection methods and statistical analyses?
- What did the researchers find?
- What meaning did the researchers infer from the results?
- How does their interpretation fit with the questions asked?
- Do I agree with their conclusions?
- Do their conclusions fit with other known information about the issue or subject?
- Is there anything missing that might be important?
- To whom do the conclusions apply?

By asking and answering these questions, you can independently come to your own conclusions about the reliability and validity of the data and the conclusions that come from it.

SUMMARY

1. Research relies on measurement.

2. Measurement allows researchers to make comparisons.

3. Discrete data are known as categorical or nominal data and describe the presence or absence of some characteristic or attribute.

4. For categorical data, each variable is comprised of two or more classes or categories that should be mutually exclusive, exhaustive, and equivalent.

5. Continuous level data can be one of three types: ordinal, interval, or ratio.

6. Ordinal data rank the elements in some logical order, but without knowing the relative difference between ranks.

7. Interval data are more sophisticated in that they represent a specific numerical score, and the distance between points is assumed to be equal.

8. Ratio data are the most sophisticated data type; they have the characteristics of interval data and a true zero.

9. Issues of validity and reliability are associated with all types of measurement.

10. Data are valid to the extent that they measure what you want them to measure.

11. Face validity exists when the measurement reflects what we want it to.

12. Content validity exists when the measurement reflects all possible aspects of the construct of interest.

13. Criterion-related validity exists when one measurement can be linked to some other external measurement.

14. Construct validity exists when measurement reflects its theoretical foundations.

15. Reliability is the degree to which measurement is dependable or consistent; it is expressed as a matter of degree.

16. Internal reliability is achieved when multiple items purportedly measuring the same variable are highly related.

17. Test–retest reliability is achieved when measurements at two different times remain stable.

18. Measurement of data must be both valid and reliable.

19. Validity and reliability are threatened by the choices researchers make about how they collect data, and whom or what they choose as their sample, as well as alternative explanations that are plausible.

20. Regardless of how data are collected, they must be collected and reported accurately, ethically, and responsibly.

KEY TERMS

attrition	Likert-type scale
categorical data	maturation
concurrent validity	measurement
construct validity	mortality
content validity	mutually exclusive
continuous level data	nominal data
criterion-related validity	ordinal data
Cronbach's alpha	predictive validity
ecological validity	quantitative data
equivalent	ratio data
exhaustive	reliability
external validity	reliability coefficient
face validity	semantic differential scale
internal reliability	
internal validity	test–retest reliability
interval	unitizing reliability
interval data	validity

See the website www.mhhe.com/keyton4 that accompanies this text. For each chapter, the site contains a:

- chapter outline
- chapter checklist
- chapter summary
- short multiple-choice quiz
- PowerPoint presentation created by Dr. Keyton

For a list of internet resources, visit http://www.joannkeyton.com/CommunicationResearch-Methods.htm.

CHAPTER SIX

Populations, Samples, and Sample Size

Chapter Checklist

After reading this chapter, you should be able to:

1. Describe the distinctions among population, sampling frame, and sample.

2. Identify the population and sampling frame to select an appropriate sample.

3. Argue for how results from a sample are generalizable to its population.

4. Use probability sampling procedures to produce a random sample.

5. Use nonprobability procedures to produce an appropriate sample.

6. Choose an adequate sample size.

Just as researchers make choices about *what* to study, they must make careful choices about *who* to collect data from or *what* to collect data on. In every case, the researcher, then, must make choices and be able to defend his or her choices. Alternatively, a consumer of communication research reports who has a basic understanding of populations, samples, and sample size can more effectively evaluate the significance and potential application of the results. In this chapter, we will explore the relationship of a sample to its population and describe sampling techniques commonly used by communication scholars. Thus, this chapter will help you answer three questions: (1) What is the population to be studied, (2) How should the sample be obtained, and (3) How large does the sample need to be?

POPULATION AND SAMPLE

A **population** consists of all units, or the universe—people or things—possessing the attributes or characteristics in which the researcher is interested. A **sample** is a subset, or portion, of a population. Generally, researchers study the sample to make generalizations back to the population. So, why not study the entire population?

In most cases, it is impossible, impractical, or both to ask everyone to participate in a research project or even to locate everyone or everything in the population. When that is possible, the term **census** is used to refer to the complete count of the population. More realistically, limitations exist to your time and other resources. Normally, a **sampling frame,** or the set of people that have a chance to be selected, must be created. Practically, this is the list of the available population in which you are interested and from which participants are selected. Note the slight but important distinction between the population and the sampling frame: The population is all units possessing the attributes or characteristics in which the researcher is interested, whereas the sampling frame is the list of *available* units possessing the attributes or characteristics of interest. It is highly unusual for the sampling frame and the population to be exactly the same (see Figure 6.1).

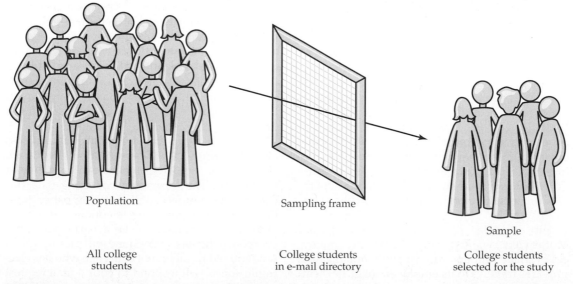

Population	Sampling frame	Sample
All college students	College students in e-mail directory	College students selected for the study

FIGURE 6.1 Creating a Sample from a Population

There are several ways to select a *sample*, which is a portion, or subset, of the larger group, or population. Regardless of how a sample is selected, researchers collect data from the sample to draw conclusions that are used as representative information about the entire population.

Identify the Population

It is easy to be lulled into believing that a researcher simply selects some participants or some set of elements (e.g., tweets) to be examined. Such a process, however, would generate results that are unlikely to be relevant to, or representative of, any other group of people or to apply to another set of elements. Even the most ambitious research project cannot be designed to generalize across all possible dimensions. A researcher must choose which dimension or dimensions are most meaningful or relevant (Katzer et al., 1978) for answering the research questions or hypotheses.

Before a sample can be selected, the population must be identified. Researchers begin by identifying the characteristics they want participants or elements to have or contain based on the research question or hypothesis. There must be at least one common characteristic among all members of a population (Jaeger, 1990). For example, the common characteristic for a population could be adults who work and use e-mail for workplace communication, teenagers who coach summer sports programs, or television shows that include family conversation. Then care must be taken to make sure that every member or element of the sample reflects the population in which the researcher is interested. In other words, the sample must contain the same common characteristic that made the researcher interested in the population. Thus, the population of interest is inherently linked to the hypotheses or research questions the researcher wants to answer.

For example, Faylor, Beebe, Houser, and Mottet (2008) wanted to investigate how employees evaluate trainers. Almost every organization provides training to its employees (e.g., new employee orientation, job or general work skills). Generally, the training literature, however, has used students as training participants rather than employees; obviously, employees who will need to use the training are likely to have different motivations or evaluations of the training and the trainers. In this study, then, the population of interest was employees who had received training at their workplace. The common characteristic among individuals in this group was that they were employees in the same organization and had received training for which they could evaluate the trainer. Thus, these participants could provide the data the research team was looking for.

Generally, it is not possible to use all members of a broadly defined population in a research study. For example, it would be nearly impossible to identify and list all students attending universities. As a result, researchers more narrowly define their populations. In the case of university students, it may be more reasonable to identify a population of sophomores at three private colleges or to identify a population of women in one sorority across universities. A researcher would have to decide which dimension is more important. Are the dimensions of class level and type of college—being a sophomore at a private college—more important? Or are the dimensions of sex and being a member of a sorority more important? The researcher must make this decision based upon the research questions or hypothesis for the study. Does the researcher want to generalize the research findings to sophomores at private colleges or to women in sororities? Identifying the population should be the researcher's primary concern even though the research is actually done on the participants or elements that constitute the sample.

As you can imagine, availability and access also play a role in which individuals are available to be considered as members of a particular population. The format for collecting data (for example, face-to-face, online survey, paper questionnaire, lab experiment, telephone survey) affects who is available to be a participant—not everyone who has a telephone will pick up for an unidentified number; not everyone who has electronic access will respond to your e-mail request to participate in a survey; not everyone will take the time to make a trip to the lab.

The point here is that defining the population for a research project is a necessary first step and must be done before trying to identify and select the sample. Despite the problems caused by limited access or availability, the researcher must define the population on the dimensions most important to the research project and find a way to ensure representative sampling.

Addressing Generalizability

After your population is identified, it is necessary to select a sample, or subset, of the population. There are a variety of ways for doing so, each with its own advantages and disadvantages. But first the issue of generalizability needs to be addressed.

Most communication research is primarily interested in people—how they communicate, why they communicate, how they perceive communication, and so on. As you search the research literature, you are likely to find one or more studies that address the variables or concepts in which you are interested. For example, Cho and Choi (2011) wanted to study if and how males and females were influenced by television messages in reality shows, dramas or soap operas, comedies or sitcoms, and talk shows. Specifically, these researchers were investigating if messages about using tanning salons would influence participants' attitudes about tanning at salons or their intention to tan this way. Cho and Choi invited students at a large Midwestern university to participate, of which 490 completed the survey. Next, the researchers explained that they used the data for only White participants for three reasons: (a) the research literature demonstrates that significant differences exist in the media usage patterns between Whites and other races, (b) Whites and Blacks interpret media images differently, and (c) that it was likely that Whites and those of other races held different perceptions about tanning. The final sample consisted of 365 college students whose average age was 20. Participants provided responses to several scales, including a scale that captured the frequency with which they watch television genres in which tanned images appear, and another scale which captured the frequency to which they believed their peers

(or friends) watch televisions genres in which tanned men and women appear. These measures were used to test the hypothesis: "Self-reported exposure to tanned images on television will be positively associated with perceptions of male and female peers' exposure to the tanned images on television" (p. 510).

The findings suggest that the social perceptual processes underlying young women's tanning tendencies may be more complex than those underlying young men's.

How would the results apply to you? Do you differ from these students with respect to age? With respect to geographical location? Race? Would these differences matter? Of course, other differences may exist with respect to incidence of skin cancer in one's immediate family, socioeconomic status, and so on.

How a sample is selected affects the degree to which the results are generalizable to, or representative of, others. Thus, **generalizability** is the extent to which conclusions developed from data collected from a sample can be extended to the population. A well-defined population and a representative sample diminish generalizability concerns. Theoretically, representative sampling of participants eliminates selection bias. Alternatively, having a poorly defined population and nonrepresentative sample raises concerns about generalizability. In this case, a researcher could not be certain that any differences found were truly results from the research study. The differences might have occurred based on how the sample was identified or the population defined.

Choosing people to study—the sample—who are like the larger group or the population in all essential ways helps establish the generalizability of results. Thus, representativeness is the goal in selecting a sample from a population. To the degree that a sample is representative, all elements in the sample had the same chance for being selected and included as part of the research project. Hence, characteristics of the population should appear to the same degree in the sample as in the entire population. To the degree that a sample is not representative, it is said to be **biased,** to favor one attribute or characteristic of the population more than another. In other words, some elements were more likely to be chosen than others. Representativeness can be ensured only in random sampling. Several methods of random sampling are described in the following sections.

Generalizing results from one set of people to another is strengthened when researchers use **replication**—basing their study on other studies that have investigated the same topic. Three types of replication are available (Lyken, 1968). First, a research study can repeat the exact procedures of a previous study. This is known as *literal replication*. This type of replication is unusual. Second, researchers can use *operational replication*, in which they attempt to reconstruct the procedures used previously. This type of replication is more common. Finally, researchers can use *constructive replication*, in which subsequent studies focus on the same constructs or variables but use different sampling techniques, different populations from which to pull samples, and different research procedures and measures. This type of replication is common in communication research, and it provides strong evidence of generalizability if similar results are found under dissimilar conditions. If several researchers working in different environments, using different populations, employing similar but different methods arrive at the same results, you can be more confident that these results are generalizable to your population. Replication can be powerful. When scholars replicate the findings of previous studies, alternative plausible explanations of outcomes are eliminated—which, in turn, strengthens the generalizability of the findings (Boster, 2002).

Thus, researchers should point out in the written research report how and why their results are similar to or different from earlier but similar studies conducted on different populations. To use this argument for generalizability, however, what you are studying must have a well-developed and published research history.

Whether or not replication is used as a basis for designing a research study, generalizability can be improved by using a principled, or theoretical, basis for the research questions or hypotheses (Shapiro, 2002). "Theoretical knowledge gives us much greater power to predict effects with other people, in other settings, at other times, and with other messages" (p. 495).

Selecting an appropriate population and sample to study is important. Complementing that selection with a theoretically driven design that cleanly explores underlying communication phenomena increases a study's ability to produce valid findings that can be generalized to others.

Probability Sampling

The best sampling procedures produce a representative sample, or model, of the population. These procedures are known as probability or random sampling. Each technique uses some form of random selection. Although no sampling technique is perfect, researchers agree that the techniques described in the following paragraphs ensure that the selected sample is sufficiently representative of the population for the purposes of research.

Probability sampling is a statistical basis, and the most rigorous way, for identifying whom or what to include as part of a sample. What is characteristic of and common to probability sampling techniques is that the probability, or chance, of any element being included in the sample is known for everyone or every element in the sample. So, regardless of who you are, your score on any measurement, or where you are in the sampling frame, you have the same chance of being selected as any other person included in the sampling frame. When the probability for selection is equal, selection is said to be **random.** Random selection procedures decrease bias because other potential systematic selection biases brought to the procedure of selecting participants by the researcher are eliminated. That is, the researcher has no control over who is selected to be in the sample.

With every member of a population assigned a known and nonzero chance of being selected to participate (Henry, 1990), the sampling error can be calculated. Sometimes referred to as the margin of error, **sampling error** is the degree to which a sample differs from population characteristics on some measurement. Sampling error will always occur because the researcher collects data from the sample, not from all the elements in the population. However, as sample size increases and becomes a larger proportion of the population, sampling error is reduced.

TABLE 6.1 Sample Size for Different Populations at 95% Confidence Level

	95% Confidence Level 5% Sampling Error		
Population Size	Sample Size	Population Size	Sample Size
50	44	260	155
75	63	280	162
100	80	300	169
120	92	400	196
130	97	500	217
140	103	1,000	278
150	108	1,500	306
160	113	2,000	322
170	118	3,000	341
180	123	4,000	351
190	127	5,000	357
200	132	10,000	370
220	140	50,000	381
240	148	100,000 & over	384

SOURCE: "Determining Sample Size for Research Activities," by R. V. Krejcie and D. W. Morgan, 1970, *Educational and Psychological Measurement, 30,* pp. 607–610. Reprinted by permission of Sage Publications.

Sample size, population size, and sampling error are intimately connected. These relationships have been worked out by others and are shown in Table 6.1. The sample sizes are based on the use of random sampling, a population's known size, a 95% **confidence level** (the degree of accuracy in predicting the result for the population from the result of the sample), and a 5% sampling error (Krejcie & Morgan, 1970; Meyer, 1973). Notice how sample size increases less rapidly than population size.

The following example explains how sampling error can affect the generalizability of research results. Asked if they will vote in the upcoming presidential election, 70% of participants indicate that they will vote. With a population of 10,000 and a confidence level of 95%, the convention most researchers use, sampling error, would be about 5% in the sample of 370 people. Thus, when inferring the result of the sample—70% indicating that they will vote—to the population, the researcher could state as a generalization that 65% to 75% of the population would vote in the upcoming presidential election. The result of the sample, 70%, is adjusted up and down by the amount of the sampling error, 5% in each direction. That range, in this case 65% to 75%, is known as the **confidence interval.**

Sampling error is dependent upon sample size. Even though you can calculate specific sample size using an equation, the table can help determine sample size for most research projects. If your population size falls in between one of the suggested levels, use the next larger population size and its corresponding sample size. If there is a question or doubt about sample size, it is always best to use a larger rather than smaller sample size.

Although probability sampling is used to ensure the representativeness of the sample selected, there is no guarantee that any one sample selected is representative of its population (Kerlinger, 1986). Each sample selected from a population is unique, and many samples have an equal chance of being selected from the same population. Scientists rely on the principle that a randomly drawn sample is representative of the population. Using one of four common probability sampling techniques—simple random sampling, systematic sampling, stratified random sampling, and cluster sampling—described in the following paragraphs, researchers can increase the likelihood that their sample is representative of the population of interest.

Simple Random Sampling   In **simple random sampling,** every person has an equal chance of being selected to participate in the study. Individuals are selected one at a time and independently. The easiest way to select a random sample is to order the sampling frame and then assign a number to each element, beginning with 1. Then, after deciding on the required sample size, use a random numbers table to generate a set of numbers equal to the number of people you want in the sample. A random numbers table is available at www.mhhe.com/keyton4 in the Student Learning Center. With the random numbers selected or generated, simply select the individuals on the numbered list who correspond to the generated random numbers.

Real (2008) used a variation of this technique to identify potential participants for his study conducted in a manufacturing plant employing 7,000 production workers. The sampling frame consisted of 236 teams—in part because the site utilized a team approach and in part to ensure the anonymity of individual respondents. Real used a random number table to generate a number between one and nine to select randomly

every *n*th team; this number was 6. As a result, every sixth team was chosen out of the sampling frame. This resulted in a random sample of 80 teams with 1,767 members.

Although simple random sampling is the simplest and quickest technique for selecting a sample, it cannot be used in all situations (Barker & Barker, 1989). Simple random sampling should not be used if there are important subgroups to be represented in a population, because the technique lacks the ability to capture distinctions in the population that may be important to the research project. And it cannot be used if it is impossible to generate a complete and accurate sampling frame. This is often a problem if a sample needs to be drawn from a large population for which there is no complete listing (for example, all Internet users, all members of Alcoholics Anonymous).

Systematic Sampling   A second type of random sampling is **systematic sampling.** To select a systematic sample, you need to determine the number of entries of the population, or the sampling frame, and assign a unique number to each element in the sampling frame. Now decide on the number of entries to be selected for the sample. Divide the population size by the sample size to get the sampling interval (for example, a population of 3,600 and a sample of 351 equals 10.26, or every 10th person). Every 10th person on the list needs to be included in the sample. If the sampling frame is randomly organized, systematic sampling results in a truly random sample. However, not all sampling frames are randomized. Many sampling frames, such as e-mail lists or employment rosters, are ordered in some repetitive cycle (for example, residents are listed in alphabetical order by street address; supervisors of each department are listed before hourly workers); in such a case, you will need to carefully analyze how frequently the cycle occurs. Check to see if the random numbers generated to identify the systematic sample can overcome this cycle. If the sampling frame list makes this impractical then use a random numbers table or use a random numbers–generating program to select the first item to be included in the sample.

The obvious advantage to this technique is that it is simple and unbiased and requires little or no technology. It is a particularly effective sampling technique if the elements of the population are randomly listed (Barker & Barker, 1989).

Sometimes a systematic random sampling procedure is used to identify the individuals who will participate in the sample. In other cases, a systematic random sampling procedure is used to select the stimuli participants in the study will evaluate. For example, Austin et al. (2002) used this procedure to select magazine advertisements from 72 popular consumer magazines targeted to the young adult market. First, all advertisements for alcohol were flagged. Then magazines were alphabetized by their titles. Next, the research team selected every third alcohol advertisement. Thus, the research team ended up with 40 alcohol advertisements systematically and randomly selected from popular consumer magazines targeted to the population of interest from the same publication month.

Stratified Random Sampling A third type of random sampling is **stratified random sampling.** In this technique, the population is divided according to subgroups of interest, or homogeneous groups. Then elements are randomly selected from each homogeneous subgroup of the population with respect to its proportion to the whole. This technique is possible because lists of people or elements are available with the stratification information the researcher needs. This sampling technique ensures representativeness for each of the subgroups of interest. The goal of this sampling technique is to first create homogeneous subgroups and then randomly sample from each of them proportionately.

In their study investigating students' beliefs about hygiene practices during an outbreak of influenza, Kim and Niederdeppe (2013) used a stratified random sampling procedure to select participants to invite them to participate in their study. From a list of all student e-mail addresses that were provided by the university registrar, "Students were randomly chosen in proportion to the share of each academic standing (freshman, sophomore, and so on) to ensure that the sample had representation from students in each grade cohort" (p. 210). Recognize, however, that this selection technique was used for choosing

which students to invite to participate in the study. Not every student invited participated.

This technique is recommended when individuals or cases within strata are believed to be similar to one another, yet different from individuals in another strata. Researchers use this sampling technique because sampling frames are available according to strata, or subgroups, that are believed to be related to the expected outcomes (Fink, 1995b). In other words, the strata must be justified with respect to the research.

In some cases, researchers use systematic and stratified sampling techniques together. For example, in a study investigating how the characteristics of cable systems (i.e., ownership, number of basic service, subscribers, and density) influence cable system diversification, Liu (2007) used both stratified and systematic sampling procedures. Starting with the number of cable systems operating in the United States ($N = 6,552$), the cable systems were then stratified by the size of their owners (i.e., number of systems owned) from most cable systems (990) to least (1). Then cable systems were stratified again by the number of their basic service subscribers, again from most to least. Thus, the list of cable systems was organized by the size of their owners and the number of their subscribers. To move from the 6,552 cable systems to the potential list of systems to be studied in the project, Liu then employed a systematic sample to identify the 327 cable systems, which were used as the sample for the research project.

Cluster Sampling Note that the probability sampling techniques described so far require you to obtain a complete listing of the population you want to study. Sometimes, particularly when a population is dispersed over a wide geographical area, that could be difficult or impossible. In that case, cluster sampling can resolve the dilemma. **Cluster sampling** is a two-stage or multistage process. The first stage is accomplished when you can identify the population by groups, or clusters. In the second stage, you use simple random sampling in each cluster to select your sample. There is an inherent strength and weakness to this sampling technique. It captures the diversity of the population, but it also increases

AN ETHICAL ISSUE

Participant Selection Can Make a Difference

Ethical questions arise when researchers make decisions about the research process, especially in the selection of research participants. Many times, communication research is conducted on undergraduate students. Sometimes this is warranted as the research question or hypothesis is directly tied to this population. However, not all college student populations are the same. According to the National Center for Education Statistics, of the 21.6 million students enrolled at colleges and universities, 7.4 million will attend two-year institutions. These students are more likely to attend school part-time and work full- or part-time while attending school. A second issue is the age of college students. The traditional college age is generally represented as 18 to 25. But more than 3 million students are over the age of 25. As consumers of research, you should ask yourself, "Did the population from which participants were chosen, or the way participants were chosen, make a difference in the results or in the interpretation of the results?"

sampling error. Usually, cluster sampling is used because it is cheaper and easier than waiting to develop or purchase a full listing of the population (which, of course, is sometimes impossible). A researcher can always compensate for the increased error by increasing the sample size.

Cluster sampling is ideal when it would be impossible to obtain a complete listing of a population because such records do not exist. A very clear example of cluster sampling is provided by Sriramesh, Moghan, and Wei (2007), whose study required that they survey citizens of Singapore who shopped at local retail stores. Of course, such a list does not exist. So, the research team used a multistage cluster sample. First, the research team compiled an exhaustive list of all 23 shopping malls in Singapore that were next to mass transit stations. Next, shopping malls were categorized into five distinct zones (north, south, east, west, and central); each mall was assigned a number. Using a random numbers table, two malls from each zone were selected. Finally, data were collected from Singaporean shoppers (but not foreigners) who were shopping at these malls and willing to participate in the survey.

The sampling strategies just described are commonly used in communication research. Which one you choose is based on practicality, feasibility,

and costs. The use of probability sampling is preferred when feasible because it provides greater confidence that the sample is representative of the population.

Nonprobability Sampling

Ideally, all samples would be randomly selected from the populations they represent. The alternative is **nonprobability sampling,** or sampling that does not rely on any form of random selection. Although the use of nonprobability samples weakens the sample in regard to population representativeness, these samples are commonly used in communication research when no other sampling technique will result in an adequate and appropriate sample. Nonprobability sampling is also used when researchers study communication variables that are believed to be generally distributed through a population. As you will see, there are also the obvious benefits of ease and efficiency—advantages that may induce researchers to use them.

More commonly, though, researchers use nonprobability sampling because they desire research participants with some special experience or communication ability. Using random selection techniques would not guarantee finding these participants. Finally, sometimes no other alternative to nonprobability sampling exists, because there is no practical way to identify all members of a population or to draw a sample if the population can be determined. Methods of nonprobability sampling are explored in the sections that follow.

Convenience Sampling The easiest way to obtain a sample is to choose those individuals who are convenient to use. In **convenience sampling,** the researcher selects those people who are convenient to locate and identify as potential respondents. While locating research participants in this way, researchers must be careful to not seek individuals who possess traits or characteristics similar to theirs. For example, if you want to conduct a survey about alumni support, you may unconsciously select individuals, like you, who have supported their alma mater in the past. The problem, of course, is that a sample selected this way would be biased and not necessarily include individuals who do not provide alumni support. A convenience sample cannot guarantee that all eligible units have an equal chance of being included in the sample. Moreover, this type of sample makes it more difficult to make inferences because it is impossible to tell to what degree the sample is representative of the population.

Most researchers have immediate access to a body of students who can be encouraged to participate in research studies through requiring research participation as a course responsibility or giving extra credit. Undergraduate students can be easily and efficiently accessed. Second, students are accustomed to the notion that professors conduct research. Although the sample is convenient to the researcher, the sample is also accidental in that participants are available to the researcher by virtue of their selection and schedule of classes. One investigation has demonstrated that students in different disciplines and across stages in their college career responded differently to measures of cultivation (Meltzer, Naab, & Daschmann, 2012). The communication discipline is not unique with respect to this problem. The field of psychology has received the same criticism for using convenience samples of college undergraduates. Some scholars have investigated the extent to which using college students in research differs from using nonstudent participants (Sears, 1986; Wintre, North, & Sugar, 2001).

Unfortunately, the results are not clear. Thus, two perspectives on the use of convenience samples exist. The first suggests that researchers should use convenience samples only when resources are not available for probability sampling. The second suggests that nonprobability sampling can be used if researchers are not trying to apply findings of a sample directly to a population. Some communication research is descriptive rather than predictive. Therefore, some research designs are not intended to infer results from a sample to a population. When this is the case, convenience samples are less problematic (Stanovich, 1986). Of course, using a theoretically driven research design helps counter some of these criticisms (Shapiro, 2002).

Volunteer Sampling Using volunteers is another form of nonrandom sampling. In **volunteer sampling,** the researcher relies on individuals who express interest in the topic or who are willing to participate in research. Initially, you may believe that it is best for people to volunteer to be part of your study. Logistically, their volunteering may expedite the research process. However, evidence suggests that people who volunteer to participate in research studies are "better educated, have higher occupational status, [are] higher in the need for approval, score higher on intelligence tests, [are] less authoritarian, and [are] better adjusted than nonvolunteers" (Katzer et al., 1978, p. 52). So if a research study is examining one of these characteristics or a related characteristic, volunteer participants can certainly bias (although unknowingly) the results.

However, a volunteer sampling procedure may be very helpful in finding participants with specific characteristics that are essential to the research project. For example, Jian, Pettey, Rudd, and Lawson (2007) contacted international students through e-mail lists of two large universities. The e-mail directed recipients to an online survey. This procedure produced 240 surveys representing 55 different cultures, which was essential to studying the influence of gender-based cultural differences on compliance gaining.

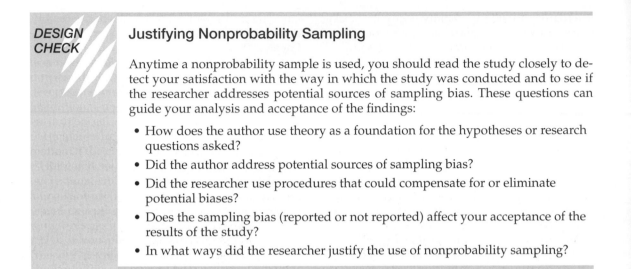

Justifying Nonprobability Sampling

Anytime a nonprobability sample is used, you should read the study closely to detect your satisfaction with the way in which the study was conducted and to see if the researcher addresses potential sources of sampling bias. These questions can guide your analysis and acceptance of the findings:

- How does the author use theory as a foundation for the hypotheses or research questions asked?
- Did the author address potential sources of sampling bias?
- Did the researcher use procedures that could compensate for or eliminate potential biases?
- Does the sampling bias (reported or not reported) affect your acceptance of the results of the study?
- In what ways did the researcher justify the use of nonprobability sampling?

Participants ranged in age from 19 to 47, with an average age of 27; slightly more males than females participated.

Inclusion and Exclusion Criteria   A third way of obtaining a nonprobability sample is to establish an inclusion or exclusion criterion. An **inclusion criterion** identifies the people or elements that meet some specific characteristic. For example, to examine how bloggers with a variety of health conditions derived social support from the supportive communication associated with responses to their blog posts, Rains and Keating (2011) sought individuals who author a personal blog that focused on their health. To satisfy this inclusion criterion, the researchers used search engines to search popular blog-hosting websites. The blogs also had to be written in English and recently updated. Thus, three inclusion criteria had to be met to be included in the sample. These were: (a) a blog authored by an individual who was coping with a health condition that (b) focused on the blogger's personal experience with the condition, and (c) that had been updated in the preceding six weeks.

Alternatively, an **exclusion criterion** rules out people or elements from participating in your survey or study based on some specific characteristic. In some studies, both inclusion and exclusion criteria are used to narrow the sample to represent a very specific population. Inclusion and exclusion criteria set boundaries or limits for a sample. This is still a nonprobability sample because you are including or excluding individuals or elements on a case-by-base basis and not ensuring that all potential members of the population have been identified.

Snowball Sampling   In some cases, snowball sampling or **network sampling** is the only type of sampling to use, particularly when the research topic is controversial or a specific population of participants is difficult to find. **Snowball sampling,** a nonprobability sampling technique, occurs when participants help researchers obtain their sample by identifying other similar participants.

Ancu (2012) used snowball sampling to find Facebook users who were 50 and older. It made sense that people in this age category would be Facebook friends with similar others who matched the participant selection criteria Ancu was seeking. When Ancu found Facebook users in this age category, she invited them to not only take the survey, but to also distribute it among their friends. By using the snowball technique, she was able to increase the sample size of respondents by 82. Thus, the sample grows, or snowballs, as participants help the researcher identify more participants, or forward the survey to others with the same demographic characteristics.

Snowball sampling also occurs when the researcher draws upon his or her network or asks others to help find research participants. For example, Johnson, Kaye, Bichard, and Wong (2008) sent a statement about the research purpose, their biographies, and a link to a Web-based survey to media-focused and politically focused websites, e-mail lists, bulletin boards, and blogs that were likely to attract politically interested users across a range of political ideologies. In addition, the research team asked those who participated to forward the survey to their politically interested friends. This sampling method resulted in 1,399 completed surveys, and a sample that was educated (97.3% with some college), more male (62.6%) than female, and mostly white (91.2%) with average annual incomes over $64,000. The research team described the participants in their survey as very similar to other research studies about blog users and people who seek information from blogs.

Purposive Sampling When researchers want to select cases that are typical of the population of interest, they use **purposive sampling,** which depends on the judgment of the researcher, who hand-picks the cases to be included in the sample. Purposive sampling is completely dependent on the researcher's ability to know what is typical (Selltiz et al., 1959). To help control the bias in such a process, researchers should spend considerable time developing what is typical about the population. From there, the researcher can develop some objective basis for making judgments to include or not include an element in the sample.

Purposive sampling is often used when sensitive topics are of research interest or very specialized populations are sought. For example, Petronio, Reeder, Hecht, and Ros-Mendoza (1996) used purposive sampling techniques to find sexually abused children and adolescents to participate in their research project. With approval from their university's human subjects committee, the research team used a gatekeeper to find appropriate participants. A social service worker who treated sexual abuse survivors identified those children and adolescents under her

care who had already voluntarily disclosed their abuse to peers, family, or friends.

Potential participants for the study had to meet two conditions. First, they had to be victims of sexual abuse, and second, they must have already disclosed this information to others. These children became the population for the study. To select the sample, the social worker then contacted the parents of the children; members of the research team followed up with the parents to discuss the nature of the study. Parental permission for each child was obtained. Obviously, the difficulty and restrictions in obtaining this type of sample required that the research team use purposive sampling as well as the assistance of a gatekeeper. Purposive sampling was required because of the desire to find research participants with unique experiences who were willing to talk about those experiences with researchers.

Quota Sampling In **quota sampling,** the researcher uses the target, or *quota,* as a goal for seeking people or elements that fit the characteristics of the subgroup. After the researcher meets the quota for each subgroup, data collection is complete. Researchers use the following steps to select a quota sample. As in stratified sampling, the population is divided into subgroups that do not overlap. The subgroups must be mutually exclusive. That is, a person or element should not be a member of more than one subgroup. The number of elements in the subgroup is calculated as a proportion of the total population. After sample size is decided, a proportional number of cases or elements from each subgroup becomes a target number of cases to fill.

For example, Webster and Lin (2002) needed to find a way to limit the sample of websites and their users. First, they limited the population to the top 200 websites as reported by Nielsen/NetRatings. Identifying the unit of analysis as pairs of websites, the researchers then had to compare sites based on their content (similar or different; for example, a news site is different from an entertainment site) and structure (similar or different; for example, a website from the same domain of websites). A 2×2 matrix was developed that represented four types of website pairs: similar content and similar structure; different content and different structure; similar content and different structure; or different content and similar structure. Using the statistics of Web use, the research team could select pairs of websites that met these conditions and their quota of 20 for each condition.

Sample Size

Regardless of which technique is used, the size of the sample must also be determined prior to selecting the sample. **Sample size** is the number of people from whom you need to observe or collect data to obtain precise and reliable findings (Fink, 1995b). Notice that this number would be less than the number of people you ask to participate, or the number of people who sign up to participate. It is common for researchers to oversample to ensure that the sample size needed is met. Both practical and theoretical issues must be addressed in considering sample size. Practically, larger samples can take more time and may cost more to administer. This is especially true if the unit of analysis, for example, is a husband and wife as a couple, or a team. It will take longer to find couples willing to participate than it will to find individuals who are married. Likewise, it will take longer to find groups, like boards of directors, for example, for which all members agree to participate than it will to find individuals who are members of organizational boards. If you are sampling television commercials or magazine ads, looking for and coding more information also takes longer.

Identifying the sample size needed for a study is important as it is unusual if you can collect data from everyone or about everything addressed by your research question or hypothesis. But not having an adequate sample size can result in nonsignificant statistical findings. On the other hand, there is a point of diminishing returns. That is, collecting more data may provide little benefit. Theoretically, the larger the sample relative to its population, the less error or bias introduced into the study. Hence, a sample representing a larger proportion of the population results in more accurate data (Kerlinger, 1986). This is particularly true with respect to probability sampling. Simply put, larger samples provide greater opportunity for randomization to work.

The following principles can help you in selecting a sample size for a research project (Barker & Barker, 1989; Fowler, 1993). First, estimate the size of the population. Next, look at the subgroups within the total population. Taking the smallest of the subgroups, estimate how large a sample will be required to provide an adequate sample of this subgroup. What you are doing is looking for the minimum sample size that can be tolerated for the smallest subgroup within the population of interest. Recognize, however, that the greater the number of subgroups you are interested in, the larger the sample must be to ensure representativeness of each subgroup.

There is seldom a definitive answer to how large a sample should be, but Table 6.1 (on p. 111) provides guidelines that most researchers find acceptable for selecting sample size. As you determine your sample size, reflect on its ability to be representative of the population. This is the primary criterion for choosing sample size, whether you are using a probability or a nonprobability sampling technique.

Regardless of how a researcher selects the sample or determines its size, he or she is responsible for justifying both selection and size issues in the written research report. All sampling decisions are subjective and strategic, and most sampling decisions create some type of bias. Thus, sampling decisions should be described and explained in the method section of a research article (Ryan, 1998).

A Final Word on Sampling

As a researcher conducting a study or as a consumer of research reports, you should include or be aware of five pieces of information about sampling issues that should be available in research reports. If you can answer "yes" to the following questions, then **population validity,** or the degree to which the sample represents and can be generalized to the population, exists (Lowry, 1979):

- Is the population, or the aggregation of persons or objects, under investigation defined?
- Is the sampling frame identified?

TRY THIS!   ## Identifying Populations, Generating Samples

For each of the types of participants or elements listed below, specify the population and the sampling frame. Then describe how you would select the sample. Be sure to assess any source of potential bias.

Specify the Population	Specify Sampling Frame	Describe the Selection Procedures	Potential Biases from How Population Was Defined or How Sample Was Selected
Example: Teenagers who play more than 20 hours of massively multi-player online role-playing games (MMORPG) per week	Teenagers between the ages of 13 and 19 who participate in massively multi-player role-playing game competitions in their city or region	Use the roster of competitors signed up to play in the competition to generate a systematic random sample based on player sex and attendance at middle and high schools.	Since teens had to travel to the competition, the sample may not include MMORPG players from all socio-economic groups; sample may not include MMORPG players from rural areas.
Young couples in their 20s who plan to be married in the next 12 months			
Retired men and women who volunteer in their communities			
Manager and employee dyads who have worked together for less than 1 year			
Amateur sports teams that have remained intact despite past losing seasons			
Segments of radio talk-show hosts' interaction with on-air, in-studio guests			

Did you choose probability or nonprobability samples? What arguments could you provide for the choices you made? What are the strengths and weaknesses of your sampling procedures? What procedural or logistical problems would you expect to encounter trying to identify, communicate with, or attract these candidates to participate in a research project?

AN ETHICAL ISSUE

Selected, But Not Required to Participate

In identifying the research population and in selecting the sample, recall that no one can or should be forced to participate in a research project. This ethical principle remains regardless of the difficulty, time, or expense a researcher experiences in locating a sampling frame or in selecting a sample. For many communication research projects, finding enough participants with the characteristics you desire is not a problem. But for research projects requiring a more specialized type of person or experience, it can be frustrating to find a potential participant who meets your criteria, is asked to participate, and refuses. When interacting with potential participants, courtesy and respect is an utmost consideration. Although someone may refuse your request to participate in a research project, perhaps your respectful acceptance of their refusal will encourage them to consider such a request in the future.

- Are the sampling procedures described in detail? Is the type of sampling procedure (probability, nonprobability) described?
- Is the completion, participation, or return rate specified?
- Is the geographic area of the population and sample described?

SUMMARY

1. A population is all units—people or things—possessing the attributes or characteristics that interest the researcher.

2. A sample, or subset, is selected from the population through probability or nonprobability sampling.

3. Generalizability is the extent to which conclusions drawn from a sample can be extended to a population.

4. Sampling error is the degree to which a sample differs from population characteristics.

5. Probability sampling ensures that the selected sample is sufficiently representative of the population because every person or element has an equal chance of being selected.

6. In a simple random sample, every person or element has an equal chance of being selected for a study.

7. In systematic sampling, every nth, for example every 14th, element is selected for the sample.

8. A stratified random sample first groups members according to categories of interest before random techniques are used.

9. Cluster sampling is used when all members of elements of a population cannot be identified and occurs in two stages: (1) the population is identified by its groups, and (2) then random sampling occurs within groups.

10. Nonprobability sampling weakens the representativeness of a sample to the population because it does not rely on random sampling; however, it is used when no other sampling technique will result in an adequate and appropriate sample.

11. Types of nonprobability sampling include convenience, volunteer, inclusion and exclusion, snowball, networking, purposive, and quota samples.

12. Sample size is estimated from the size of the population and the level of error a researcher is willing to tolerate.

KEY TERMS

biased	purposive sampling
census	quota sampling
cluster sampling	random
confidence interval	replication
confidence level	sample
convenience sampling	sample size
exclusion criterion	sampling error
generalizability	sampling frame
inclusion criterion	simple random
network sampling	sampling
nonprobability	snowball sampling
sampling	stratified random
population	sampling
population validity	systematic sampling
probability sampling	volunteer sampling

See the website www.mhhe.com/keyton4 that accompanies this text. For each chapter, the site contains a:

- chapter outline
- chapter checklist
- chapter summary
- short multiple-choice quiz
- PowerPoint presentation created by Dr. Keyton

For a list of internet resources, visit http://www.joannkeyton.com/CommunicationResearchMethods.htm.

CHAPTER SEVEN

Quantitative Research Designs

Chapter Checklist

After reading this chapter, you should be able to:

1. Select and develop the appropriate research design for your hypotheses or research questions.

2. Understand the strengths and limitations of each design form as it relates to research findings, and argue for your design choices.

3. Explain the benefits of experimental forms over quasi-experimental and descriptive forms.

4. Facilitate appropriate random assignment of participants to treatment and control groups.

5. Manipulate independent variables according to their theoretical foundation.

6. Conduct manipulation checks of independent variables.

7. Interpret findings from experimental and quasi-experimental designs with respect to cause–effect relationships.

8. Appropriately interpret findings from descriptive research designs.

9. Consider the appropriateness of using online survey software.

10. Develop a research protocol to limit researcher effects and procedural bias when conducting research studies.

There are three types of quantitative research design: experimental forms, quasi-experimental forms, and descriptive forms. These forms differ in fundamental ways on two characteristics: manipulation of independent variables and random assignment of participants to treatments or conditions (Pedhazur & Schmelkin, 1991). The first characteristic on which quantitative research designs differ—**manipulation** of independent variables—occurs when the researcher intentionally varies or changes how the independent variable is presented to participants. This fundamental characteristic must be satisfied to locate a research study in the classic experimental framework. Manipulation of independent variables also occurs in quasi-experimental research designs but is absent from descriptive forms.

The second characteristic on which quantitative research designs differ—**random assignment** of participants to treatments or conditions—is unique to experimental forms. After being selected to participate in the experiment, the researcher randomly assigns individuals to one of at least two groups. One group is the control group; this group serves as a baseline against which the treatment groups are evaluated. The control group can be used in two ways. First, the control group can receive no treatment. For example, in a study evaluating the effectiveness of public speaking instruction, the control group would not receive any type of instruction. Second, the control group can receive the standard treatment. Using the same example, the control group would receive a routine face-to-face classroom lecture on public speaking. In either case, the control group is the baseline of comparison for the experimental, or treatment groups. Continuing with the public speaking example, one treatment group would receive the same information in an interactive face-to-face lecture on public speaking; a second treatment group would receive the same information in an online self-guided study of public speaking.

Other groups are labeled as experimental groups, or treatment groups, with each group receiving a different treatment or level of the independent variable. This characteristic is absent from both quasi-experimental and descriptive forms. Figure 7.1 demonstrates how these two characteristics differ for the three quantitative research designs.

Initially developed for study in the physical sciences, experimental forms can be found in all disciplines related to communication—education, management, psychology, and sociology. Due to their widespread acceptance, the essential characteristics of the experimental framework have become the standard by which quasi-experimental and descriptive forms of research are evaluated. All three types of quantitative research design are explored, and relevant communication examples are presented in this chapter.

	Experimental forms	Quasi-experimental forms	Descriptive forms
Manipulation of independent variables	Present: researcher controlled	Present: natural variation	Absent
Random assignment of participants to conditions	Present	Absent	Absent

FIGURE 7.1 Three Forms of Quantitative Research Designs

THE EXPERIMENTAL FRAMEWORK

When researchers are curious about causes, they often turn to **experimental research,** which has a long tradition in the social sciences, including communication. This type of research is most often conducted in the laboratory or in other simulated environments that are controlled by researchers. Alternatively, researchers can conduct experiments in the field, or naturally occurring environments. This type of experiment is very popular with communication scholars who study applied communication problems.

The traditional definition of an *experiment,* one often associated with the physical sciences, would characterize it as the manipulation of the independent variable in a controlled laboratory setting conducted on a randomly selected sample of participants who are randomly assigned to control or treatment groups. A broader definition of **experiment,** and one that fits the study of communication phenomena more appropriately, is the recording of measurements and observations made by defined procedures and in defined conditions. The data collected or produced by these procedures are then examined by appropriate statistical tests to determine the existence of significant differences between and relationships among variables.

Experimental research is chosen when a researcher wants to determine causation. In other words, a researcher has developed a hypothesis that asserts that one variable, the independent, causes change in a second variable, the dependent. Experimentation allows a researcher to evaluate hypotheses that have been developed from theories in the literature. In this case, results from previous research studies generate new questions, and the researcher wants to answer the questions "Why?" and "How?" Experimentation is also chosen when researchers want to test a new method or technique. This is especially true of instructional techniques that are believed to have potential application in the classroom. Conducting an experiment allows the researcher to test one technique against another to see if differences between techniques exist. In other cases, experiments are conducted to explore the specific conditions under which a

phenomenon occurs. By varying the conditions of the experiment, researchers can identify which environmental conditions, for example, are most likely to make speakers nervous.

When research is identified as experimental, the goal of the researcher is to establish or explain what caused a person's behavior, feelings, or attitudes to change. Because this is the goal, certain characteristics must be satisfied. First, the research design must have a temporal component, with one element occurring before another. For something to cause something else, the causal agent must precede the change in behavior, feelings, or attitudes. In this way, an experiment provides control of one variable, or the independent variable, to test its effect on another variable, the dependent variable. Second, there are comparisons between at least two groups. Finally, the entire experiment is conducted within a limited time frame, seldom more than 1 hour, with all of the interaction under the control and observation of the researcher.

When the word *experiment* is used, most people think of laboratory experiments. The primary defining characteristic of laboratory experiments is that the researcher structures the environment in which the investigation takes place and in which the data are collected (Miller, 1970). Conducting research in the lab environment serves several purposes. First, it physically isolates the research process from the day-to-day and routine interaction of participants. This isolation gives a researcher greater control over what participants are and are not exposed to. By limiting and controlling exposure in this way, a researcher is attempting to eliminate extraneous variables and influences that are not central to the investigation (Kerlinger, 1986). Second, exploring communication in the lab allows researchers to confine and examine theoretical relationships that would be more difficult to do in the field.

Burgoon, Blair, and Strom's (2008) study of how people rely on mental shortcuts to discriminate truths from lies demonstrates how the lab environment controls for extraneous influences. To set the study up, participants in another study were randomly assigned to the role of thieves or innocent bystanders. Participants assigned the thief role were asked to take a wallet from a classroom on a pre-assigned day and then to make deceptive statements about that act during an interview about the theft. Participants assigned to the innocent bystander role were simply told that a theft would take place in their classroom; they were asked to respond truthfully during the interview. These interviews became the stimuli for the main study. Next, participants for the main study came to a computer lab and were seated in front of a computer. They were told they would see, hear, or read about an interviewee being questioned about the theft of a wallet. They were also told that the interviewee would plead his or her innocence. The participants were told that they should make a determination about whether the interviewee was telling the truth about being innocent or being deceptive.

Without lab experiments, how could researchers carefully make the distinctions between those who tell the truth and those who do not? How could they carefully study the effects of those truths or lies?

To meet these research goals, the research team created two laboratory experiments—the first to create real instances of truth and deception; the second to test the influences of those truth-telling and deceptive messages. By working in the lab environment and using the interviews from the first study, the research team could control what the truth-telling and deceptive messages were about. Being in the lab controlled the interaction environment. Thus, the results of the study can be assumed to result from the conditions of the study rather than from any number of other influences (such as familiarity with the person telling the truth or lies, different motivations for stealing the wallet, theft of a variety of objects).

Many universities and communication departments have rooms equipped as communication laboratories. Some are set up with one-way mirrors so that researchers can view what is going on, although participants cannot see the researchers. Some are equipped with sophisticated audio and video recording equipment, and Internet and other communication technologies. Although some labs are relatively sterile in appearance, others are designed to simulate comfortable interaction environments like a living room, waiting area, or computer lab. Researchers without these types of laboratory environments often use traditional classroom space and temporarily transform it into a lab for research purposes.

Using manipulation and random assignment, researchers design and conduct a study, evaluate the evidence, and then develop a causal explanation for what has occurred. Experimental designs are deliberate, standardized, and used as the research protocol in many disciplines. Their strength lies in the control they provide to researchers, which in turn helps them eliminate rival explanations for the changes they observe and record. Several of the experimental designs more commonly used in communication research are described in the following sections.

The Classical Experiment

Researchers devised the classical, or true, experimental form as a technique to help them in assigning causation. Many researchers believe that the experiment is the most powerful research form for testing cause–effect relationships. The clear logic of its design helps researchers eliminate many of the other explanations that can be given for the results found. In its simplest form, an experiment would be designed to test the influence of one independent variable on one dependent variable. But the social and practical significance of the communication issues studied can seldom be represented so simply.

In a **classical experiment,** the researcher controls the treatment or the manipulation of the independent variable by randomly assigning participants to treatment or control groups. A **treatment,** or manipulation, is one of the ways in which the researcher varies the type of stimuli or the amount or level of stimuli presented to research participants. This fundamental characteristic must be satisfied to locate a research study in the classical experimental framework.

Experiments allow researchers to test two types of hypotheses—those that predict differences and those that predict relationships. Recall from Chapter 4 that hypotheses test differences and relationships between and among variables, not the variables themselves (Kerlinger,

1986). For the first type of hypothesis—the difference hypothesis—the experiment is designed so that the independent variable precedes the dependent variable in temporal order. Thus, the corresponding hypothesis predicts that the independent variable causes changes, or effects, in the dependent variable. For the second type of hypothesis—the relational hypothesis—the experiment is designed so that two variables, the independent and dependent, occur close together. The hypothesis predicts that the two variables exist together in some type of relationship where the value of the independent variable is causing a change in the value of the dependent variable. See Chapters 10 and 11, respectively, for the statistical tests that accompany these hypotheses.

The researcher also controls the order of variables in an experiment. One element, the independent variable, cannot be considered the cause of another element, the dependent variable, if the independent variable occurs after the dependent variable (Selltiz et al., 1959). Simply put, the independent variable can be considered the cause of changes in the dependent only if the independent precedes the dependent or if the two occur close together.

With this level of control, experiments are designed to demonstrate a cause–effect relationship. Still, an experiment may not be able to provide a complete explanation of why an effect occurs. Remember that researchers rely upon a theoretical base to provide a foundation for the variables in the study and from which to develop hypotheses. Thus, for the experiment to reflect a causal relationship, the cause, or independent variable, must come before the effect, or dependent variable. The gap between the two variables can vary greatly—from just a few minutes to years—but the variables must have a time order. The dependent variable must also be capable of change. Some variables cannot be changed in experiments. Your sex, for example, will not be changed by a researcher's intervention. But your attitude toward a public relations campaign can be. Finally, the causal relationship between and among the variables must have theoretical plausibility. In other words, the presumed reason for the causal effect must make sense (de Vaus, 2001).

Random Assignment of Participants In any experiment in which the researcher wants to compare two or more groups, the underlying principle is that individuals in the groups are equivalent before the treatment. To achieve equivalency, participants are *randomly assigned* to treatment or control groups that represent the independet variable. This means that each participant has an equal chance of being assigned to either group. Selecting a random sample from an appropriate population is not the same as randomly assigning individuals to treatment and control groups. The two procedures together help eliminate any true differences between individuals in the groups before the treatment is applied. Thus, the researcher can argue that differences that result after the treatment is applied are caused by the independent variable.

For example, to test the effects of role playing in a video game about the Palestinian-Israeli conflict, student participants were recruited from an American university (Alhabash & Wise, 2012). They were randomly assigned to one of two roles—that of Palestinian president or Israeli prime minister; thus, *nationality assignment* had two conditions and was an independent variable. Participants played the game for about 20 minutes. For this study, it is important to know that playing either role does not change anything about the structure or the content of the game. Because the students were from an American university, the researchers hypothesized that the nationality of the role played would have dissimilar effects on students' attitudes of Israelis as compared to Palestinians.

The hypothesis the researchers tested was: "Participants who play the role of Palestinian president will exhibit unfavorable attitude change toward Israelis, compared to those playing the role of Israeli prime minister, who will not exhibit any considerable attitude change toward Israelis" (Alhabash & Wise, 2012, p. 364). *National attitude* was the dependent variable; students evaluated both Israelis and Palestinians on the same seven characteristics (e.g., sympathy; belief about the national group's intention for peace).

In this experiment, participants were both randomly selected and randomly assigned to different conditions. These procedures maximize the chances that individuals in the treatment and control groups are relatively similar. Thus, any differences between the groups on the dependent variable are said to be caused by the manipulation of the independent variable and not by differences in individual participants. These aspects of the classical experiment give the researcher greater assurance that other alternative explanations for the results are eliminated (Sapsford & Jupp, 1996).

Creating Treatment and Control Groups The **treatment group** is the group of participants who receive a stimulus—anything that the researcher is interested in studying. Alternatively, if a participant is assigned to a **control group,** no treatment or a baseline treatment is offered. In the experimental framework, creation of the treatment and control groups provides the opportunity for the manipulation of the independent variable. It is important to note here that identification of what constitutes a treatment, or condition, is driven by theory (Boruch, 1998); not just any treatment will do.

Returning to Burgoon, Blair, and Strom's (2008) study of detecting deception, the research team formulated its hypothesis on the basis of an extensive literature review and analysis of previous research on the truth bias. From this they hypothesized "observers err in the direction of judging more messages as true than the base rate of truthful and deceptive stimuli being judged" (p. 576). That is, people observing others telling truths and lies are more likely to believe that others are telling the truth. Type of message (truth or lie) was the independent variable manipulated by the research team. Those who took the wallet were told to lie and say that they did not. Those who did not take the wallet were told to tell the truth. In this case, the control group would be those who did not take the wallet and the treatment group would be those who did take the wallet and then lied about doing so. By comparing participants' evaluations of the interviewees' truthfulness, the research team provided support for the hypothesis—that is, when people make deceptive statements about an action, others are more likely to believe they are telling the truth. As you can see, the conditions of the independent variable chosen by the research team were inextricably linked to the theory of interest.

In some communication experiments, multiple treatment groups are used without a control group. Sometimes one group is considered a control group even though participants in it receive some form of the stimulus or treatment. Usually, the more standard, common, or traditional form of the stimulus serves as the control group. In other instances, the treatment groups serve as a control for one another, and the researcher forgoes the use of a pure control group.

Jackob, Roessing, and Petersen (2011) demonstrate this use of treatment groups in their exploration of how different vocal presentations and use of gestures influence the persuasiveness of a presentation. In their experiment, the researchers created three treatment groups by having a presenter make three videos in which vocal emphasis and gesture use was manipulated while making a presentation on globalization. In the first treatment group, participants viewed the professional presenter deliver the speech without vocal emphasis and without gestures. The second treatment group saw the same presenter make the same presentation with vocal emphasis but no gestures. The third treatment group saw the same presenter make the same presentation with both vocal emphasis and gestures. Thus, vocal emphasis was one independent variable, and use of gestures was another independent variable.

Why did the researchers select these treatment groups? Two dual processing theories, like elaboration likelihood model and heuristic systematic model, suggest that two different kinds of persuasion processes exist. One persuasion process is based on the receiver's ability to carefully consider the arguments made and the receiver's ability to focus on the quality of the content in the presentation. Thus, nonverbals of the speaker are less important in evaluating the presentation. Alternatively, other receivers process information and make speaker evaluations based upon the presenter's attractiveness or the presenter's use of nonverbals. By manipulating vocal emphasis and gestures, the research team was able to control the presentation performance.

After watching the video of their condition, participants responded to interval rating scales

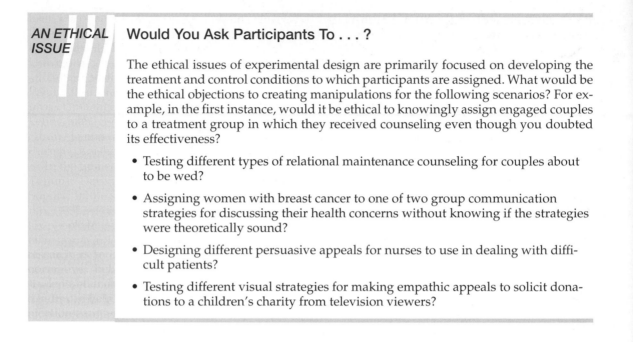

AN ETHICAL
ISSUE

Would You Ask Participants To . . . ?

The ethical issues of experimental design are primarily focused on developing the treatment and control conditions to which participants are assigned. What would be the ethical objections to creating manipulations for the following scenarios? For example, in the first instance, would it be ethical to knowingly assign engaged couples to a treatment group in which they received counseling even though you doubted its effectiveness?

- Testing different types of relational maintenance counseling for couples about to be wed?

- Assigning women with breast cancer to one of two group communication strategies for discussing their health concerns without knowing if the strategies were theoretically sound?

- Designing different persuasive appeals for nurses to use in dealing with difficult patients?

- Testing different visual strategies for making empathic appeals to solicit donations to a children's charity from television viewers?

to assess the dependent variables: the perceived performance of the speaker (e.g., vividness, liveliness), the perceived characteristics of the argumentation (e.g., factual accuracy, thoroughness), and the perceived characteristics of the speaker (e.g., credibility, competence).

Thus, treatment groups are chosen by the researcher based on theory. Researchers must have meaningful reasons for selecting the treatment groups—just trying different things does not uphold the scientific tradition on which experimentation is based. Withholding treatment or the stimulus creates the control group. In cases in which it would not make sense to have a traditional control group, multiple treatment groups can act as controls for one another, or the researcher may designate one treatment group as the standard against which the other treatments will be evaluated.

Manipulation Checks   When an independent variable is manipulated, a researcher should conduct a **manipulation check.** This test, or check, verifies that participants did, in fact, regard the independent variable in the various ways that

the researcher intended. This check is conducted prior to statistical analyses of the hypotheses. Why is this necessary? First, researchers need to confirm that participants were sensitive to the different treatments. Second, researchers need to confirm that differences in treatments as perceived by participants were in line with the differences the researcher intended. Without this confirmation, a researcher might assume that differences in the dependent variable were due to differences in the independent variable when they were, in fact, not.

In their study of students and working adults, Westerman and Westerman (2013) randomly assigned participants to one of four message conditions to examine how participants responded to feedback about a work project. Two independent variables, positive or negative valence, and private or public delivery, were combined to create four conditions: positive/private, positive/public, negative/private, and negative/public. The manipulation check revealed that participants viewed the positive messages as more positive while the negative messages were perceived as more negative. Likewise, evaluations by participants revealed that the e-mail was perceived as more private while a company website was perceived as more public.

Another type of manipulation check should be used when research designs include a confederate. To examine how participants in a group discussion allow nonverbal cues from other members to influence them, Van Swol (2003) used two confederates posing as participants with one naïve participant. Together, the three individuals, role-playing as managers in a pharmaceutical company, were to decide which cholesterol-lowering drug they would market. During the discussion, only one confederate mirrored the nonverbal behavior (posture, hand gestures, facial expressions, adaptors, and head movements) of the naïve participant. To assess the confederates' behaviors, two coders unaware of what the confederates were instructed to do and unaware of the study's hypotheses viewed videotapes of the group discussions and evaluated the coders' smiling behavior, friendliness, persuasiveness, talkativeness, and the degree to which the confederates appeared to like the participant. Statistical tests indicated that the confederates' behaviors were not significantly different on these dimensions, suggesting that the confederates were not acting differently except with respect to the mirroring behavior of one. Manipulation checks should be conducted prior to the statistical testing of any hypothesis in which the manipulated variable is used.

Types of Experimental Design

Several types of experimental design meet the fundamental criteria of random assignment of participants and researcher control of the manipulations of the independent variable. Three of the basic designs commonly used in communication research are described here—posttest only, pretest–posttest, and factorial design. More complex experimental designs exist (for example, see Campbell & Stanley, 1963; de Vaus, 2001). Starting with these basic designs, however, will increase your ability to comprehend complex designs, because they are embedded variations of the basic designs presented here.

Posttest Only   After randomly assigning the sample to treatment and control groups, researchers need to measure the dependent variable either during or after the participants' exposure to the independent variables. This type of research design—the **posttest only,** or simple comparison—allows a researcher to conclude that any significant differences found are due to the fact that the treatment group received some different stimuli or that the treatment group received a stimulus that participants in the control group did not. Thus, this type of design answers the questions, "Do treatment groups differ based on different manipulations of the stimulus?" or "Do the two groups differ after the stimulus is presented to only one group?"

This research design is fairly common in communication research. As an example of a pretest-posttest design, shown in Figure 7.2, Lee and Chen (2013) recruited teenagers between 14 and 20 years old to participate in a lab experiment. Of these participants, 18 self-categorized as moderate drinkers and 45 self-categorized as binge drinkers; 22 indicated they did not drink alcohol. As the first step, participants completed a survey about risky behaviors. Next, participants were randomly assigned to one of three groups: (a) viewing humorous anti-alcohol abuse television ads characterized by proactive-nonrestrictive messages (for example, "Drink responsibly"), (b) viewing humorous anti-alcohol abuse television ads characterized by negative-restrictive slogans (for example, "Don't be a loser. Don't drink"), or (c) the control group in which participants did not view either type of ad. Thus, this posttest only experiment had two treatment groups that manipulated the way in which the television ad used humor to gain attention and deter excessive drinking, and one control group. Finally, all participants filled out surveys about their perceptions of risk of excessive drinking and their intention to change their drinking behavior. Participants in the two conditions that viewed the television ads also responded to items about their interest in the ads, how humorous they found the ads, and their perceptions about the effectiveness of the ads in highlighting the risks of excessive drinking.

Thus, two independent variables were manipulated. First, the researchers manipulated the

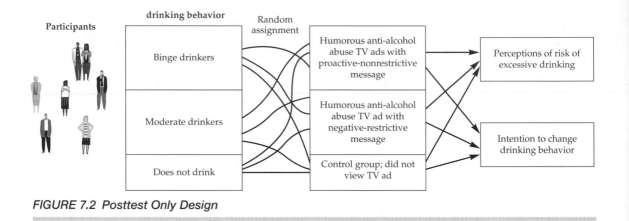

FIGURE 7.2 Posttest Only Design

type of ad, as they randomly assigned participants to one of the two treatment groups. Second, particpants self-categorized their drinking status as binge, moderate, or do not drink. The dependent variables were: interest in the ads (example item: "These ads truly held my interest"), perceived humor of the ads (example item: "I enjoyed the humor used in these ads"), risk perception of excessive drinking (example item: "I consider myself to be at risk of becoming an alcoholic"), and intention to change drinking behavior (example item: "I would very much like to change the fact that I drink excessively"). In designing this type of experiment, the research team was interested in discovering how ads influenced teenagers' perceptions of their risk of drinking excessively and their intention to change their drinking behavior. The objective of this type of experimental research is to demonstrate a cause–effect relationship by looking for differences among scores of participants in the two treatment groups and participants in the control group on the dependent variables.

Pretest–Posttest By adding one step to the posttest-only design, a researcher achieves the **pretest–posttest** experimental form. Here a researcher measures the dependent variable before the treatment group is exposed to the stimulus. After the stimulus is given, the dependent variable is measured again in exactly the same way with the same participants. In some written research reports, the

researcher refers to these measurements as Time 1 and Time 2. Time 1 is the measurement before any stimulus is given to the treatment group, and Time 2 is the measurement after the stimulus.

Adding the pretest, or Time 1, measurement allows the researcher to determine the degree of change in the dependent variable from one measurement to the next and to make more definitive assessments about the influence of the treatment. Although many researchers agree that this experimental form is more powerful, there is one caveat. Because measurements at Time 1 and Time 2 are conducted in the very same way, there is some danger that participants become overly sensitized to the measurement, especially when data are collected through questionnaires. Two different effects can occur. In the first, participants may try to respond at Time 2 as they responded at Time 1, or, in other words, try to be consistent even though a change has occurred. In the second, participants assume that the researcher is looking for differences and may try to make sure they answer differently at Time 2 than at Time 1. In either case, the participants' motivations or expectations can confound the research design.

As an example of a pretest-posttest design, Eyal and Kunkel (2008) recruited undergraduate freshmen to participate in an experiment. As the first step, participants completed a questionnaire, which included a measure of attitudes toward premarital sexual intercourse. At least

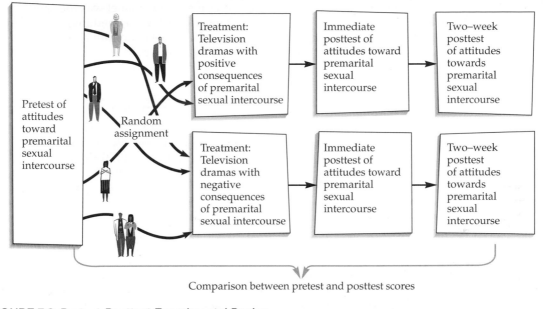

FIGURE 7.3 Pretest-Posttest Experimental Design

one day later, participants were randomly assigned to one of two types of viewing sessions. Each session included two episodes of 1-hour television dramas that were popular with young adults (*Beverly Hills 90210, Dawson's Creek, Party of Five*). All shows included portrayals of young adults engaging in sexual intercourse; shows also depicted the emotional consequences experienced by the characters. In the positive condition, one show ended with a character coming to new conclusions about relationships and about feeling better about himself; the other show dramatized the point that a sexual encounter helped to rekindle passion between the characters, thereby enhancing their relationship. In the negative condition, one show depicts a character who realizes that she became intimate with another character too soon and now feels remorse for her behavior; the characters terminate their relationship. In the second show of the negative condition, one character, who admitted that he did not have sex with his girlfriend, finds himself in an unexpected romantic moment with his female roommate. After their sexual encounter, he expresses guilt and is upset by his behavior

and its implications. Immediately after viewing the shows, participants filled out the measure of attitudes toward premarital sexual intercourse. Two weeks later, participants again filled out the same measure.

Using this research design, the researchers could compare the change in participants' attitudes toward premarital sexual intercourse by comparing first the pretest and immediate posttest scores and then comparing the pretest with the two-week follow-up scores. This pretest–posttest experimental design is presented in Figure 7.3. The objective of this type of experimental design is to demonstrate a cause–effect relationship of attitude change from pretest to immediate posttest and from pretest to two-week following by looking for differences in attitudes between the two types of viewing groups. The researchers found that participants held more negative attitudes of premarital sexual intercourse after viewing the shows in the negative consequence condition both immediately after the viewing and two weeks later. No effect was found for those participants who viewed the shows in the positive consequence condition, as their attitudes toward premarital sexual intercourse did not change.

Factorial Design   In a **factorial design** experiment, treatment groups are based on two or more independent variables. Researchers use this type of research design to investigate complex cause–effect relationships that cannot be adequately tested with only one independent variable. A factorial design allows the researcher to test for the effects of each independent variable. In addition, he or she can test for the **interaction effect,** or how the independent variables can combine to influence the dependent variable.

Because more than one independent variable is of interest, random assignment is necessary on only one. Natural variation on the personal attributes of participants may create assignment for the other independent variable. This is fairly common in communication research in which participants' sex is one of the independent variables of interest. Obviously, a researcher cannot randomly assign sex to participants. Thus, he or she must rely on the participants' natural variation on this independent variable. But then participants must be randomly assigned by the researcher to one of the treatment groups or to the control group on the other independent variable.

Factorial designs allow researchers to test for the treatment effects of each independent variable separately, as well as for the joint effect of the two independent variables together. In research reports, the simple influence of one independent variable by itself is referred to as a **main effect.** In other words, the influence of one independent variable is examined without considering the influence of the other independent variable. A researcher can also examine the interaction effect, or how the dependent variable is jointly affected by the two or more independent variables.

Spack, Board, Crighton, Kostka, and Ivory (2012) used a factorial design to examine the effects of two independent variables—type of argument and presence of an image—on participants' perceptions of the environmental claims on product packaging of a fictional laundry detergent. After being randomly assigned to one of six conditions, participants were brought in small groups to a lab and given one minute and 40 seconds to view a detergent bottle. While the

design of the product label was the same across the six conditions, each condition had different versions of label text and different images of the product seal. This procedure controlled which two independent variables: type of argument presented in the text of the label, and whether an image with the words "Green Seal Certified" was present or absent. With these two variables, or factors, participants were in one of six treatment conditions, as demonstrated in Figure 7.4.

In this case, the factorial design allowed researchers to test for the main effects of each independent variable. In other words, how did participants' perceptions of the arguments on the label influence their perceptions of the *greenness* of the product and their intent to purchase? Figure 7.4 illustrates that significant differences based on the argument (strong, weak, or no argument) would show up as differences among rows. Scores for participants in boxes 1 and 4 would be similar to one another, yet different from scores for participants in boxes 2 and 5, while scores for participants in boxes 3 and 6 would be similar and different from participants in boxes 1 and 4, and boxes 2 and 5.

This design also allowed researchers to test for the main effects of the presence of the label. Here the question would be, "How did participants' perceptions of the seal image influence their perceptions of the *greenness* of the product and their intent to purchase?" Figure 7.4 illustrates that significant differences would show up as differences between the columns. Scores for participants in boxes 1, 2, and 3 would be similar to one another, yet different from scores for participants in boxes 4, 5, and 6.

Testing for the interaction effect could answer the question, "Did viewing the laundry product with a strong argument and no label produce different perceptions of the product's greenness and their intent to buy than when participants viewed the laundry product with a weak argument and the green seal image?" If an interaction effect existed, differences would be between cells in the table, not between rows or columns. Findings from this study did show an interaction effect. Participants' scores for the greenness of the product rose across the no argument, weak argument, and strong argument conditions except when no image of the seal was present. This is

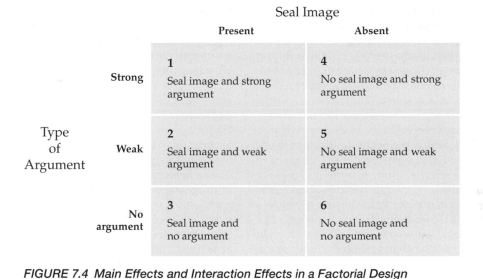

FIGURE 7.4 *Main Effects and Interaction Effects in a Factorial Design*

called an interaction because the differences are not solely dependent on the strength of the argument or solely dependent on the presence of the seal image. However, with regard to participants' intent to purchase the product, only a main effect for presence of the seal image was significant. Strength of arguments on the product label did not influence participants' intent to purchase.

In a factorial design, the minimum configuration requires two independent variables with at least two levels each. But the design can be extended to consist of several factors with as many levels as necessary and feasible for each one. Generally, no more than four independent variables are built into one factorial design. Likewise, seldom are more than four levels of an independent variable considered. When a factorial design is extended to more than two variables, the number of interactions increases as well.

Longitudinal Designs

When experiments of the types just described are designed so that there are multiple measurements of the dependent variable, the design is also labeled as **longitudinal.** Researchers often call for longitudinal experimental designs as they discuss the limitations of their research in the discussion section of the written journal report.

How much time must there be between measurements for a design to be considered longitudinal? That depends on the nature of the communication phenomenon under study. In other words, it is relative to the topic. Days, weeks, sometimes even years could occur between measurement points. Communication scholars frequently use longitudinal experimental designs to test the influence of message design strategies to identify which strategies are more effective in changing participants' attitudes and behaviors. For example, Harrington et al. (2003) designed a pretest–posttest laboratory experiment over 4 weeks to investigate the cumulative effectiveness of different types of antidrug public service announcements. Students who participated were randomly sampled from a university registrar's list of students. To simulate the type of repeated exposure a participant would have to similar messages on television, participants came to the lab to view the conditions twice a week for 4 weeks. Based upon the condition to which they were randomly assigned, participants saw antidrug messages that had high or low sensation value coupled with many arguments against drug use or few arguments against drug use. By designing the study this way, the research team was able to simulate how participants would typically be exposed to public service announcements and how different message strategies influenced participants' attitudes and behaviors toward drug use.

Longitudinal designs are also particularly helpful in determining the degree to which training or instruction has been effective. In one study (Byrne, 2009), 156 fourth- and fifth-grade students participated in a research study over a 10-week period. The study was designed to evaluate two media literacy interventions, both of which were designed to combat the negative effects of media violence. Students were randomly assigned to one of three groups. Both treatment groups received a media literacy lesson that included information on violence in the media and violence in the real world, media effects, how to avoid negative effects, and ways in which to critically evaluate characters that use violence. These lessons were developed around PG-rated violent film clips. In addition, one of the treatment groups also completed a writing activity about what they learned; then they were videotaped reading aloud what they wrote. The control group did not receive instruction; instead they received a lesson on jobs in the film industry and completed a short media production exercise in which they wrote a scene, acted it out, and videotaped it. Measures of the dependent variable, willingness to use aggression, were taken at weeks 1, 2, 4, and 10. By designing the study in this way, the research team conducted a rigorous examination of participants' reactions to two different instructional models. This longitudinal design allowed the research team to examine both the short- and long-term effects of two different interventions. Results of this study demonstrated that children in the treatment group that included the writing and reading aloud activity reduced their willingness to use aggression. Despite this finding, the aggression level of the two treatment groups was not significantly lower than the aggression level of the control group. This type of finding calls into question the use of violent film clips in media literacy instruction.

Strengths of Experimentation

The primary advantage of experimentation is that researchers can manipulate the independent variable to observe changes in the dependent variable. Because the researcher controls the manipulation, and because participants are randomly assigned to treatment and control groups, any significant difference found is assumed to be the cause of variations in the independent variable (de Vaus, 2001). Other primary advantages of experimentation are that the design and researcher control over variable manipulation allows testing of extremes and multiple replications. Operationalizations and measuring techniques are decided on in advance, and a researcher repeats the procedures and methods in exactly the same way for each participant or each group of participants. This leads to precision (Kerlinger, 1986). A less-obvious benefit is that when the lab environment remains static, experimentation can be cost effective and more convenient for the researcher. After a lab environment is secured and outfitted for a particular experiment, the researcher uses it over and over. Seldom can all participants of an experiment be tested at the same time.

Limitations of Experimentation

Despite its strengths, experimentation has several limitations. Not all communication scholarship can be conducted using one of the experimental forms. In some cases it would be immoral or unethical to conduct the research because subjecting participants in one group to some stimuli could be negative or hurtful (de Vaus, 2001). Legal standards might also make experimentation impossible. Thus, moral, ethical, and legal issues prevent a researcher from assigning participants to some categories or from otherwise manipulating an independent variable. In other cases, it is impossible to manipulate the independent variable because these qualities are fixed in the participants. For instance, variables such as sex, socioeconomic class, and age cannot be manipulated. These characteristics and attributes are fixed within participants; the researcher has no control over them. Thus, the first limitation is that experimentation by the nature of its design characteristics will be inappropriate or impossible to use in all situations.

The second major limitation is that even with its stringent design, experimental forms cannot

---

TRY THIS!   ## Designing an Experiment

What social media do you use? Do you know people who do not use it? Or use different social media? Using social media as an independent variable, how would you design a pretest experimental design about social media use? A pretest-posttest design? A longitudinal design? What will you have participants do in the lab? How will that vary depending on the type of experiment you are designing?

- What will you, the researcher, manipulate as the independent variable?
- What are the various treatments or conditions?
- On what dependent variable do you expect the manipulation to have an effect? Why?
- What arguments can you give for the research design choices you have made? What are the limitations of your designs?

---

guarantee that some factor other than the treatment factor produced the significant effect (Sapsford & Jupp, 1996). Researchers can control or minimize the influence of variables they know about. But researchers can never know if they succeeded completely, and they certainly cannot control the influence of a variable that is unknown to them.

Third, laboratory experiments rely on a researcher's manipulation of the independent variable. In some cases, such pure manipulation may not exist in reality. Thus, participants may react to the artificiality of the lab environment as well as to the potentially artificial manipulation of the independent variable.

Another limitation to experimentation is derived from one of its strengths. Experimentation is hailed because it allows researchers to test several variables or combinations of variables at once. Although the variables can be manipulated and measured in the lab, this activity does not always equate with how those variables exist and interact in natural communication settings.

The most frequent complaint about experimentation is the lack of reality in experimental designs. Conducting research in sterile laboratories, available classrooms, or other environments unusual to participants could influence how participants will respond or react, and that may be different from how they would behave in more natural surroundings or environments.

In general, then, experimental research, especially that conducted in laboratories, may be investigating communication behaviors that are less complex than they are in the communication environments in which they are found day to day (Miller, 1970). Other scholars, however, suggest that lab experiments should not attempt to re-create natural interaction. Rather, artificiality is necessary to reduce or eliminate all the confounding variables that exist in the real world (Pedhazur & Schmelkin, 1991).

QUASI-EXPERIMENTS

Because of the limitations mentioned earlier, sometimes researchers rely upon natural variations in the independent variable. Called **quasi-experiments,** or natural experiments, this alternative form of research design is possible because some variation in the independent variable exists naturally. In other words, participants are not assigned randomly to treatment and control groups. Lacking this assignment opportunity, variation in the independent variable is not under the control or direction of the researcher. The three basic designs of posttest only, pretest–posttest, and factorial, can still be used as long as natural variation of the independent variable can be substituted for manipulation of the independent variable.

Longitudinal designs can also be incorporated with quasi-experimentation. Recall that the distinguishing characteristic of this research design is multiple measurements of the dependent variable. Brandtzaeg's (2012) longitudinal study of the use of social networking sites (or SNS) is an example of a longitudinal quasi-experiment. Overall, the goal of the project was to demonstrate the social implications derived from using SNS, as well as the differences between people who use SNS and those that do not. In this example, let's focus on the users of SNS who were recruited and invited to participate in a study over three years. In the first year, 2,000 people participated; in the second year 1,372 participated; and in the third and final year, 708 people participated. This study clearly shows that longitudinal designs are likely (and expected) to lose a significant number of participants across a long term of involvement.

Brandtzaeg (2012) predicted that SNS use would facilitate face-to-face contact with users' close friends and increase over time—so time (or year in this case) is an independent variable. Time varies, but the researcher does not control it; it varies naturally. Another hypothesis in the study predicted that the number of offline acquaintances of SNS users would increase over time. Yet another hypothesis predicted that loneliness among SNS users would decrease from year one to year two. In each year, or wave, of the study participants responded to surveys. What did the researcher find? SNS users did not report an increase in face-to-face interaction over time, but they did show an increase in the number of acquaintances they had; they also reported an increase in loneliness. Thus, this longitudinal study demonstrated that social implications of SNS time were varied. Users of SNS reported both positive (more acquaintances) and negative implications (fewer friends, more loneliness). However, when compared to participants who did not use social networking sites, SNS users reported more face-to-face interactions and a greater number of acquaintances. In these cases, SNS use (yes, no) was also an independent variable that varied naturally.

This study characterizes features of quasi-experimental design because both independent variables (SNS use and time) were based on natural variation rather than researcher assignment of participants to treatments or conditions. This longitudinal quasi-experimental design is presented in Figure 7.5.

Scholars who study the efficacy of research methods differ in the degree to which they support quasi-experimentation. The primary limitation, of course, stems from the lack of control the researcher has over manipulating the independent variable. Although natural variation can be said to be a substitute for this manipulation, there are some concerns about the quality, or the purity, of the manipulation. For example, in communication research, sex is frequently used as an independent variable, which obviously is not under the control of the researcher. Thus, communication researchers rely on individuals to self-identify as females or males. These self-identifications are used to classify participants with respect to sex. It seems simple, but there are inherent problems. Whereas we could agree that there are obvious differences between women and men, there are also differences among women and among men. These differences within categories can confuse any results researchers find. Think of the problem in this way: Just because women and men differ with respect to physical sex does not mean that women and men will differ as distinctly on the communication aspects of gender, such as communicating with feminine, masculine, or androgynous styles.

Thus, the goal for researchers using quasi-experimental forms is to create and communicate clarity about the differences desired in the independent variable (Pedhazur & Schmelkin, 1991). In many quasi-experimental studies, participants are assigned to treatment groups by how they respond to that variable on the questionnaire. For example, participants respond to the questionnaire item that asks them to identify their sex. Males are assigned to the male level of that variable if they check that box on the questionnaire. Likewise, females are assigned to the female level of the variable if they check that box on the questionnaire.

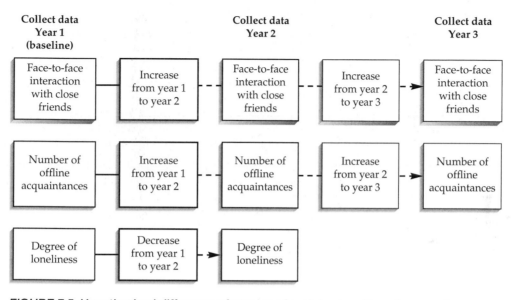

FIGURE 7.5 *Hypothesized differences for users of social networking site users in Longitudinal Quasi-Experimental Design*

In essence, participants self-select into the category of the independent variable to which they belong by labeling themselves. Other variables on which this type of self-selection is common include marital status, political affiliation, race or ethnicity, and university class level. Although researchers can never completely overcome problems associated with self-selection, they can reduce the potential error by providing full and complete descriptions of any categories used and by making sure categories are exhaustive, mutually exclusive, and equivalent.

When treatment groups are based on natural variation, some researchers refer to these as nonequivalent comparison groups. They are nonequivalent because participants are not randomly assigned. Thus, the way in which researchers use existing natural variation to assign participants to treatment groups should be carefully considered. The goal is to use groups that are as equivalent as possible, and achievement of this goal relies primarily on the procedures chosen by the researcher.

Another example of the way in which quasi-experiments rely on natural variation is

demonstrated in a study investigating the influence of participating in a race relations program (Muthuswamy, Levine, & Gazel, 2006). The race relations program has been used at Michigan State University since 1996. It promotes integration among students by building a multiracial community of students from diverse backgrounds. Students who participate in the program engage in frank discussions on controversial issues and interact in exercises and experiences to foster friendships and to create and cultivate the experience of multiracial unity. The research team invited individuals who had been part of the program for at least two years prior to data collection, individuals who had joined the program two weeks before data collection, and individuals who had not participated in the program. Thus, the variation on this independent variable—degree of participation in the program—existed naturally.

In this study, the group of students who had the longest experience were considered the treatment group, while the students who had just joined were considered a baseline control group. Why? As the authors explain, the voluntary and

Is One Study Ever Enough?

Imagine the following: In doing an assignment for one of your communication courses, you find a journal article that addresses the very constructs in which you are interested. Even though you use several electronic databases to search for more articles like the one you have, you are not successful. So, with one article in hand, you set out to complete the assignment. As you read about the hypotheses and the quasi-experimental design used in the study, several questions arise:

- Is there anything about the way in which the research was designed that would detract from its findings, even though the study examines exactly the variables in which you are interested?

- To what degree did the researcher's procedures create control over the natural variation in the independent variables?

- Are the research procedures reported in enough detail and to your satisfaction?

- Could there be explanations for the findings other than what the researcher offers?

- Would the results from one study, even if it were an experiment, ever be enough?

topical nature of the program was likely to attract participants who were different from nonparticipants to begin with. Thus, it was likely that self-selection and not the program would account for any potential differences, posing a threat to internal validity. Because the researchers could not eliminate self-selection, this baseline control group of new recruits was included in addition to the control group of students who had chosen not to participate in the program. Students in all three groups completed a questionnaire measuring attitudes toward race relations. An example item was, "Diversity should be highly valued."

But the question remains, could the results of the study be based on preexisting differences? Or were the results based on students' participation in the program? To answer these questions, the researchers conducted closer examinations of the ways in which students were different or similar. After carefully guiding readers of the research article through these differences and similarities, the research team provides compelling arguments and data to demonstrate that effects of the race relations program were positive for both existing members and new members. But overall, students who had been part of the program longer had more positive attitudes toward race relations.

Field Experiments

As the name implies, **field experiments** are like experiments in terms of researcher control over the manipulation of independent variables and random assignment of participants. However, the research environment is realistic and natural. Participants are not asked to come to a laboratory environment that is used exclusively for experimentation. Rather, the research is conducted in environments with which participants already are familiar. This provides another advantage—field experiments are better suited for observing and evaluating complex and unfolding interaction events. But in field experiments, researchers also lack the degree of control they have in true experiments.

Clearly, as a researcher moves from the lab into a natural environment, some control is lost. Although researchers can control nearly all outside interferences (for example, people interrupting the research process, intruding noises) in the lab, they will be less likely to control outside interferences in the field because they are not in charge of the environment in which the research is taking place. Although some control is lost, realism is increased (Kerlinger, 1986). When realism is increased, findings have greater generalizability.

Field experiments are particularly effective for studying communication in context, especially the effect of media or political campaigns. For example, Shaw and Gimpel (2013) used a field experiment to examine the effectiveness of personal appearances of an incumbent governor in his campaigning for re-election. While popular wisdom suggests that candidate appearances have positive effects, the researchers designed a field experiment to test if candidate appearances would attract local news media attention, as well as increase volunteer signups to help with the campaign. Using the incumbent governor's campaign schedule, the research team searched local newspaper and television news coverage before and after the governor's public appearances. Thus, public campaign appearance was the independent variable; in this case, the research team used the city of the appearance as one category of the independent variable and a control city (the governor did not make an appearance that day) as a second category of the independent variable. The number of news stories was the dependent variable. Most local newspapers and television stations did not focus on the candidate for re-election the day prior to his visit. But after his visit, local news coverage was "pervasive after a visit" (p. 144). Thus, the research team concluded that campaign visits help to drive news coverage. A similar effect was found for volunteer sign-ups, a dependent variable in a separate hypothesis. As predicted, volunteer sign-ups rose from 2.6 before the campaign appearance to 6.8 after the appearance.

Obviously, the research questions addressed in this study could not have been studied in a laboratory environment. Using a field experiment was practical because the results help document the effect of this politician's campaign visits. By designing the project to compare news coverage in cities where the candidate made appearances with news coverage in cities where the candidate did not make appearances on the same day, the research team could assess the effectiveness of the candidate's visits. Thus, this campaign strategy was studied in its natural environment without researcher interference. Thus, the results from this research design had high generalizability because researcher intrusion was minimized to the greatest extent.

Strengths and Limitations of Quasi-Experimental Research Designs

The obvious strength of quasi-experimental designs is that the variation that communication scholars are often interested in exists naturally. Thus, these research designs can address the real world in a way that experimentation cannot; indeed it could be difficult, impossible, or unethical for a researcher to re-create these conditions. Quasi-experimental designs build on differences that naturally exist rather than rely on researcher-controlled differences through random assignment.

But the lack of random assignment brings up the question: Are the groups studied equivalent? Research designs that are carefully thought through and those which collect data on other variables that could potentially confound the results may help alleviate that concern. So, while a quasi-experimental design does not allow researchers to infer cause and effect, a well-designed and theoretically grounded quasi-experiment does enable researchers to demonstrate that rival interpretations are implausible.

DESCRIPTIVE DESIGNS

Descriptive designs, sometimes called **cross-sectional** or **non-experimental** designs, differ from experimental and quasi-experimental research designs in three fundamental ways. Although the study is still systematic, the researcher does not have direct control over the independent variables, nor are participants randomly assigned. Additionally, data are collected in such a way that temporal order cannot be determined. Despite these differences, the logic is basically the same—researchers want to demonstrate that differences or relationships exist between the independent and dependent variables.

These differences in descriptive designs decrease the degree to which causation can be ensured. Because a researcher has less control, variables other than those selected as independent variables may be responsible for changes in the dependent variable (Kerlinger, 1986). This characteristic makes it difficult for inferences to be made from the independent variables to the dependent variables (Pedhazur & Schmelkin, 1991). Because of this issue, some researchers substitute the terms *predictor variable* and *criterion variable* for *independent variable* and *dependent variable*, respectively. Using these two terms is more appropriate because they do not imply causality. Nevertheless, the tradition of naming variables as independent and dependent is very strong, and many researchers use these terms even when their research design is non-experimental. Although some researchers believe that experimental research is always superior to other research designs (Kerlinger, 1986), descriptive research can paint a picture of a communication phenomenon as it naturally occurs without relying on an intervention or a designed condition (Bickman, Rog, & Hedrick, 1998).

One type of descriptive communication research occurs when researchers want to demonstrate that categorical differences exist on some dependent variable. When a researcher limits interpretation of results from this type of study to a description of differences, descriptive forms can be successful in identifying variables that may later be used to build a theoretical explanation of the relationship between the independent variable and the dependent variable. However, researchers overstep the boundaries of descriptive research if they try to offer the differences they find as an explanation.

For example, finding the answer to the research question "What are research participants' attributions for the disclosure and nondisclosure of highly personal information?" (Derlega, Winstead, Mathews, & Braitman, 2008, p. 117) is a question for which a descriptive answer can be found. But knowing the reasons participants gave for disclosing or not disclosing does not explain how disclosure of personal information influences communication in relationships.

In this descriptive study, more than 200 college students described something personal about themselves that they considered to be sensitive.

Then they were asked why they disclosed or did not disclose this personal information to a mother, father, same-sex friend, or dating partner. Participants were not randomly assigned to conditions, nor did the researchers manipulate any variables. Rather, participants reported on their decisions to disclose or not disclose sensitive information. And, as in most descriptive research, the data were collected simultaneously through written self-report questionnaires. Data analysis resulted in identifying 11 reasons for disclosing to significant others and 12 reasons for not disclosing to significant others. The research report does not venture beyond description. However, the researchers do suggest that these findings are consistent with theories of privacy and social exchange. The research team also suggests that to be more comprehensive, these theories need to incorporate the type of relationships in explaining decision making about self-disclosure.

As another example, Rosaen and Dibble (2008) investigated the question, "Is there a relationship between social realism and parasocial interaction?" (p. 149). Children between the ages of 5 and 12 were asked to identify their favorite television characters. Over 70 characters were identified; Lizzie McGuire and SpongeBob SquarePants were most frequently mentioned. Children also provided responses to a questionnaire of parasocial interaction items. "I would invite SpongeBob SquarePants to my birthday party" is an example of how the researchers measured parasocial interaction, or the imaginary friendships that viewers form with media characters. To get a measure of social realism, three coders made a coding judgment for each character on appearance and behavior. In other words, did the character look like a real person? Did the character act like a real person? The researchers used a statistical test to answer their question; they found that, yes, there is a relationship between social realism and parasocial interaction. It was a positive and weak relationship, but it was significant. Thus, parasocial interaction is greater when social realism of the character is stronger.

"Although finding that two variables are correlated does not establish cause it does mean that a causal explanation is possible" (de Vaus, 2001,

p. 178). Thus, it would be inappropriate to claim that the social realism of characters caused children to have parasocial relationships with the characters or that having a parasocial relationship with a media character caused the character to seem more real. In the discussion section of the research article, Rosaen and Dibble (2008) explore the nature of their findings. The researchers admit that the strength of the relationship found was weak, and that the study did "not directly address what a child will select as his or her favorite character" (p. 151). This type of research design cannot explain why relationships or differences occur, but it can describe their occurrence.

Strengths and Limitations of Descriptive Research Designs

Simply, some of the research issues that exist in the study of communication do not lend themselves to experimental or quasi-experimental designs. So, clearly, descriptive research has merit. The most obvious advantage is that descriptive studies are most often conducted in more realistic environments with participants who are more like the individuals to whom the researcher wants to generalize. Also important, descriptive studies can be used in an exploratory manner to provide an orientation to a topic (Henry, 1998).

You have already seen that the differences between experimental and descriptive research—inability to manipulate the independent variable and lack of power to randomly assign participants—create two of the fundamental limitations of this type of research design. These two weaknesses lead to a third limitation, and that is the risk of improper interpretation of the research findings. With significant findings, researchers are eager to accept these as meaningful and real, despite the possibility that other explanations for the findings may exist. Thus, descriptive research designs can be more powerful when researchers offer several alternative hypotheses as explanations and test each one. When one hypothesis is supported and other alternatives are not, the findings of the significant hypothesis are strengthened (Kerlinger, 1986).

ONLINE EXPERIMENTS

Some of the problems inherent in conducting all types of experimental design can be overcome by conducting studies online instead of having participants come to a research lab or other controlled environment. Generally, an online, or Web-based, study can be developed for experimental, quasi-experimental, and descriptive designs, and include longitudinal and factorial aspects. Of course, online studies can also be designed as a field experiment—if online behavior is the natural environment being examined.

Some researchers use software provided by their universities (for example, Qualtrics™); other researchers use software available to the public (for example, SurveyMonkey™). These software programs can help you move your research design from a face-to-face environment to the Web. In some unique cases, programming skills are needed to design your own website and online experiment. But, generally, software programs like the ones mentioned above allow you to select or design the template (or look) for your study, and provide standard options for presenting questions and responses to participants (for example, Likert-type scales, categorical choices).

Online software can be valuable for research designs in which you want a participant to respond to a certain set of items based on how they answered a previous item. Known as *skip logic*, this technique allows you to determine, for example, that participants who watch television shows with violence read your survey items with "violent" as the adjective in the item. On the other hand, participants who watch situation comedies on television can read your survey items with "funny" as the adjective in the item. Skip logic is customized based on the research design and hypotheses, and it is controlled by rules you define as you set up in the program.

Online experiments offer several advantages (Iyengar, 2011), such as greater reach to more diverse populations. It is also efficient and effective to present text, audio, and video stimuli because these stimuli can be embedded easily in the online environment. A participant can read, listen to, or watch the stimuli and then move directly to the items to evaluate the stimuli. Web-based surveys and other technology can now self-administer experimental manipulations that previously took several people to administer in the lab. Moving experiments online is exciting, but it does not resolve all problems. Sampling remains problematic as online users are more representative of some demographic groups than others (Iyengar, 2011). If your experimental study is to be conducted online, be sure to think carefully through how to promote your study to reach the population and sample you desire.

RESEARCHER EFFECTS AND PROCEDURAL BIAS

Regardless of the degree of control offered by experiment and its alternative forms, researchers or other members of the research team can introduce bias and error into the research process through their interaction with research participants. Researchers can influence participants' behaviors during the research session, or they can create effects on the data itself (Brooks, 1970). All types of quantitative research designs—experimental, quasi-experimental, and descriptive forms—are susceptible because each requires a researcher or assistant to conduct or facilitate the process.

It is easy to see that researchers and research participants interact in a social environment. Who the researcher is (for example, age, sex, and race or ethnicity) and how the researcher communicates with participants or other members of the research team can create influences on participants' responses. Imagine the difference in your reaction as a research participant if you are met warmly and cordially by the researcher as contrasted to being met in a hostile and rejecting manner. How would you respond if you heard two research assistants arguing over research procedures before your experimental session began? Likewise, the degree of experience or expertise demonstrated by a researcher can influence research participants' responses to stimuli.

Researchers' expectations can also create unwanted effects on participants' responses (Abelson, 1995). Remember that researchers develop hypotheses before a study is conducted.

As a result, a researcher may unknowingly encourage participants to respond in the way that supports the predictions. Even subtle nonverbal cues may be perceived by participants and, as a result, influence their responses and measurements. Each of these biases can occur in quasi-experimental and field designs as well.

One way to overcome researcher expectancy is for individuals other than the researcher who designed the study to conduct the experiment without knowing anything about the hypotheses or the conditions to which participants are assigned (Abelson, 1995). When this occurs, the research report will indicate that the study facilitator or research assistant was *blind* to, or did not know, the hypotheses or conditions of the experiment.

Expectancy bias can also occur when researchers use participants with whom they are acquainted. This can occur when researchers conduct studies on student populations with whom they are familiar or in field settings where familiarity with potential participants eased their access into the field location. Even if the researcher does not know the students, it is very likely that students in the same department or university know of, or know something about, the researcher. These types of acquaintanceship between researcher and research participant can influence the way research participants react or respond. As a research participant, would you knowingly or unknowingly alter your behavior if the researcher were your advisor? If you were going to take a class from that professor next semester? If he or she were the department chair?

Students as research participants are also sensitive to demand characteristics, a situation that creates a bias based on participants' perceptions and interpretations of the research procedures. Students, particularly those with knowledge of research methods and communication theory, may try to second-guess what the researcher is looking for—the demand—and then try to provide answers to fulfill it.

Demand characteristics are also created when the research topic has some socially desirable element. For example, in conducting research on topics like sexual harassment, date rape, or deceptive practices, researchers need to develop procedures that encourage participants to answer honestly. Honesty is encouraged when research procedures do not create the perception for participants that they can be identified as victims or perpetrators of these socially undesirable acts.

To counter these effects, researchers write **research protocols** detailing each procedural step of the study. If the study is conducted face-to-face, protocols should be practiced with individuals similar to the research participants and evaluated for their effectiveness before data are collected. For online studies, a protocol should be developed before creating the online research environment. Then, individuals similar to the research participants should test the online study to be sure it presents stimuli and questions to participants as you expected. In either case, if pre-testing the research design leads you to changing something about the protocol, be sure to document those changes. An example of a research protocol is available at www.mhhe.com/keyton4 in the Student Learning Center. Standardizing how the researcher and his or her assistants interact with participants and how research procedures are administered ensures more control.

COMPARING RESEARCH DESIGNS

For the study of relationships among and differences between communication phenomena that can be quantified, experimental research designs are the most powerful. However, in many cases they simply are impractical or impossible. Thus, researchers turn to quasi-experimental and descriptive forms for their quantitative research.

Ideally, the authors of research reports would always explicitly describe the research design they used, explain why that design was selected, and then identify the design by name. Figure 7.6 can

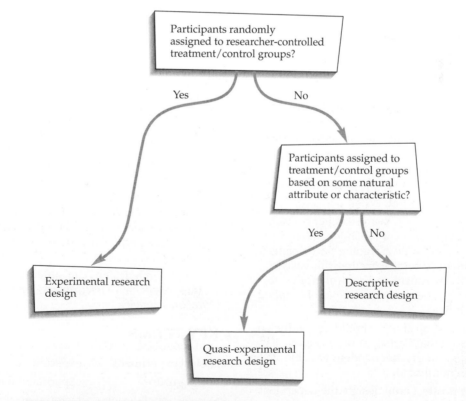

FIGURE 7.6 How Is the Study Designed?

help you decipher the methods section of a research report when these issues are not made explicit.

After you have identified the type of quantitative research design, the next step is to identify what was measured. You should be able to identify a specific operationalization of each variable included in the research hypotheses and research questions. This information should be included in the method section of the research report. Finally, you should examine how the research procedures were carried out, particularly with respect to the temporal order of measurement.

By independently checking these issues, you can critically assess the results the researcher presents and draw your own conclusions. You should be satisfied that the researcher used a design that was appropriate for the communication phenomena, setting, and participants, as well as effective in answering the hypotheses and research questions. With a good understanding of the research design and the implications of the choices made, you can make an independent assessment of the researcher's interpretations.

SUMMARY

1. There are three categories of quantitative research design: experimental forms, quasi-experimental forms, and descriptive forms.

2. Experimental research is used to establish cause–effect relationships between or among variables, and is most often conducted in a laboratory.

3. In an experiment, the researcher controls the manipulation of the independent variable by randomly assigning participants to treatment or control groups; this ensures that the treatment and control groups are equivalent before any treatment is applied or withheld.

4. Manipulation checks should be conducted to ensure that participants perceived variation in the independent variable as the researcher intended.

5. In the posttest only design, the dependent variable is measured only once—after participants are exposed to the stimulus.

6. In the pretest–posttest design, only individuals in the treatment group are exposed to the stimulus; the dependent variable is measured for all participants prior to and after the treatment group receives the stimulus.

7. In the factorial design, treatment groups are based on two or more independent variables, with random assignment occurring on one of the variables.

8. The time between the multiple measurements of the dependent variable in a longitudinal design is based on the communication phenomena under study and the theoretical foundation of the study.

9. In quasi-experiments, the researcher uses the natural variation that exists on the independent variable to assign participants to treatment and control conditions.

10. Field experiments are a form of quasi-experimental research design conducted in a naturalistic setting.

11. Descriptive designs are those studies that do not use random assignment of participants or researcher manipulation of the independent variable; as a result of lacking these controls, these research designs cannot demonstrate causation.

12. Communication researchers often use descriptive designs when communication phenomena do not lend themselves to experimental or quasi-experimental designs.

13. Online survey software can be used effectively, especially when a condition or manipulation is dependent on a participant viewing a particular text, audio, or video stimuli.

14. All research designs can suffer from bias from researcher effects or procedural inconsistencies.

KEY TERMS

classical experiment	experiment
control group	experimental research
cross-sectional design	factorial design
descriptive design	field experiment

interaction effect
longitudinal design
main effect
manipulation
manipulation check
non-experimental
  design

posttest only
pretest–posttest
quasi-experiment
random assignment
research protocols
treatment
treatment group

See the website www.mhhe.com/keyton4 that accompanies this text. For each chapter, the site contains a:

- chapter outline
- chapter checklist
- chapter summary
- short multiple-choice quiz
- PowerPoint presentation created by Dr. Keyton

For a list of internet resources, visit http://www.joannkeyton.com/CommunicationResearch-Methods.htm.

CHAPTER EIGHT

Surveys and Questionnaires

Chapter Checklist

After reading this chapter, you should be able to:

1. Design a survey or questionnaire to answer a research question or test a hypothesis.
2. Select the survey format (self-report, face-to-face, phone, or online) that will best serve the purpose of the survey.
3. Select existing or develop appropriate questionnaire items and response sets.
4. Use open and closed questions appropriately.
5. Design an uncluttered and easy to read survey.

6. Pretest the method of data collection.
7. Collect the data in an honest and ethical manner.
8. Analyze the data completely and appropriately.
9. Draw conclusions that do not overstate the limitations of your data or sample.
10. Present the data to others in an appropriate fashion.

Surveys and questionnaires are the most common quantitative method for collecting data about communication phenomena. You have probably responded to a questionnaire as part of a research project at school. Or maybe you were selected to participate in a political poll (or survey) conducted by a local or national news organization.

Surveys and questionnaires are excellent methodological tools for obtaining information about what people do (for example, how many times a week a person reads a newspaper), identifying what people believe influences their behavior (for example, how a television commercial affects views of a political candidate), and identifying respondents' attitudes or characteristics (for example, identifying a person's level of relational uncertainty or leadership style).

WHAT IS A SURVEY?

A **survey** is a system for collecting information. By asking questions or having participants respond to stimuli statements, researchers can collect data that can be used to describe, compare, or explain knowledge, attitudes, or behavior (Fink, 1995b). Also known as a questionnaire or a poll, a survey is probably the most commonly used (and perhaps misused) methodological tool for gathering information about almost any communication concept or topic. Generally, the purpose of asking questions in survey form is to produce comparable information across many people so that data from the sample can be generalized to the population from which respondents were selected.

Survey is the appropriate term when a questionnaire is the only method of data collection, such as in a phone, face-to-face, or online survey. A poll, like a survey, collects data only through a questionnaire, generally addresses issues of national or societal concern, and is conducted with a nationwide or statewide sample. In these instances, the questionnaire is the single or primary method of data collection, and is considered a type of descriptive research design. **Questionnaires,** however, can be used with other data collection methods in many research

designs and are frequently used in experimental, quasi-experimental, and descriptive research designs—in the lab and the field.

Whether a questionnaire, survey, or poll, there are four commonalities for this method of quantitative data collection. First, each is part of a fixed design; that is, the design of the questionnaire, survey, or poll does not change; it is standardized. All participants are asked the same questions and asked to respond on the same scales or categories. Second, all three forms of data collection help researchers collect data from a large number of people. Third, data are collected from a sample of individuals from an identified population. Finally, the data are **cross-sectional.** That is, data are treated as if all data were collected at the same time, even if takes a few days or weeks to collect the data.

Types of Surveys

Surveys come in many forms. Regardless of how a survey is administered, the goal is to design and conduct the survey in such a way that valid and reliable conclusions can be generalized to a larger population (Bracken, Jeffres, Neuendorf, & Atkin, 2009). Of course, each has advantages and disadvantages.

Self-Reports   The most common survey form is one that is self-administered in written form. In a **self-administered** survey, individuals read and select a response on their own. Often called **self-reports,** these can be done onsite, as in the research setting, mailed or e-mailed to individuals at work or home, or administered through online survey software. An advantage of self-reports for the participant is that the survey can be completed anonymously at the respondent's own pace.

This advantage also creates a disadvantage for researchers in that completing a survey may take longer than planned. In a laboratory setting, there is often a set amount of time between research sessions. A person who reads slowly may take longer than the 20 minutes you allowed for participants to complete this part of the research process and might hold up the group as a whole or the next set of participants. If the survey is delivered online, a person can be distracted by other activities and may not finish or submit it. Another disadvantage is that some respondents may have difficulty interpreting the instructions or the questions. Without someone to ask, the respondent is left to his or her own interpretation. One way to overcome this disadvantage is to be specific in the survey instructions.

Face-to-Face Interviews   As an alternative, some researchers use interviewers to facilitate the question-and-response process in a one-on-one, or face-to-face, interview. The advantages of one-on-one interviewing is that the data collector can create a personal and trusting relationship with the respondent, which makes it more likely that the participant will answer questions about sensitive topics. However, the presence of the interviewer may create a **social desirability response,** or the potential for the participant to respond with answers he or she believes the interviewer will perceive as favorable. Another way to minimize the effects of threatening questions in the face-to-face format is to lead into an open question with a qualifier phrase such as, "We know many people try using drugs when they are teenagers," and then continue with: "This next set of questions is about your experiences with drugs as a teenager. I'd appreciate your response to each question by using [this scale]." In the face-to-face format, it is also important to remind participants about the anonymity or confidentiality that is part of the research design.

Phone Surveys   Collecting survey data over the telephone is popular, particularly for polls about political issues and candidate preferences. Generally, participants for phone polls are selected through random-digit dialing (RDD). In this case, the phone number, not the person, is the sampling unit. Generally, researchers select a frame of telephone numbers, a large set of numbers in a particular area code that is coupled with a particular telephone exchange (e.g., 910-555-xxxx). This method overcomes problems caused by relying on outdated phone directories and the move from landlines to cell phones. If you want to use this form of data collection for your survey, be sure to have all callers, or interviewers, use a standardized introduction that identifies who they are, what the research is about, who is conducting the research, and the purpose for

collecting the information. Presenting yourself and the reason for your call is important given that many households have listed their phone number on the national do-not-call registry. Unsolicited phone calls for research purposes are excluded (Gwartney, 2007). However, that does not mean that a phone call from you will be welcomed. It is your job to distinguish your research purpose from a telemarketing call.

Callers should also verify that the right person, household, or telephone number has been reached, state any conditions of the interview (for example, confidentiality), and then ask for permission to proceed (Frey & Oishi, 1995). Using this type of introduction will distinguish your telephone survey from those phone callers who use a short survey as a way to introduce and market their products or services. However, phone survey responses are declining (Kemph & Remington, 2007). The proliferation of cell phones, screening technologies, and consumer opportunities to block unknown callers have become barriers to collecting telephone survey data.

Online Surveys   Because of their convenience for both researcher and participants, **online** or **web surveys** have become popular. They are also cost effective, do not have geographic restrictions, and can include color, graphics, and multimedia stimuli. Because digital media are used, survey responses are efficiently collected and managed in databases (often downloadable in an Excel file). Online survey programs, such as Qualtrics™, SurveyMonkey™, and QuestionPro™, have a distinct advantage in that designing a professional-looking survey is relatively easy. Further, these programs provide options for automatically directing respondents to a section or skip questions based on their responses to a previous question. Known as *skip logic*, this easy to use tool allows researchers to customize surveys based on participants' responses. For example, your survey is designed to capture responses from students at your university about their public speaking apprehension. One potential question you might ask is, "Have you had formal training in public speaking?" The response choice would be "yes" or "no." If the respondent answered "yes," you could automatically direct that person to a section to describe or evaluate his or her public speaking training. Likewise, for a respondent without public speaking training, the program could be set to automatically let this person skip these items.

Although online survey programs are effective, free versions often have limits on the number of items that can be asked or the number of respondents that can be accommodated. The most common method for delivering online surveys to participants is to send an e-mail with a link to the survey. This method works best if the researcher has legitimate access to potential participants' e-mail addresses. Or, the researcher can advertise a survey's unique URL on other websites or flyers. In this case, the respondent comes to the survey rather than the survey going to the respondent, which is typical in other survey research designs. If the sample was specifically recruited for an online survey research design, the researcher can give a password to this specific group of people.

Online surveys are an effective technique for collecting data if your sample is geographically dispersed. Another advantage is improved efficiency and effectiveness in data collection and management. Data will already be in a format that can easily be used for statistical analysis. Regardless of which online survey option you choose, questions about how well the sample represents the population of interest is always in question. Using online surveys creates physical distance between the researcher and respondents; thus, there is less control over who responds, when, and how. Although collecting data online may appear to be more efficient, researchers must still address various challenges.

One problem of online surveys is the potential of collecting low-quality data. For example, evidence shows that respondents who complete online surveys quickly are more likely to make cognitive shortcuts in answering questions or responding to items. Research comparing the responses of college freshmen in face-to-face and Web surveys demonstrated that Web surveys resulted in more respondents giving "don't know" answers and higher nonresponse rates. Moreover, respondents of Web surveys were more likely to use fewer of the available response alternatives (Heerwegh & Loosveldt, 2008), resulting in less variation. Research has demonstrated that

participant response to online surveys can be improved by (a) not relying solely on e-mail to make contact with potential respondents, (b) creating a complete and persuasive e-mail invitation, even if doing so increases the length of the invitation, (c) placing the link to the survey at the bottom, not inside, the invitation, (d), not overestimating the time it will take to complete the survey, and (e) using a subject line that potential participants would find familiar and authoritative (Kaplowitz, Lupi, Couper, & Thorp, 2012).

Most online survey software can capture completion time, or how long it takes a respondent to finish the survey. Malhotra (2008) recommends that researchers should report survey completion time and consider the use of completion time as a variable in the analysis. One way to deal with quick completion of online surveys is to include audio to guide respondents. This may result in higher-quality data. Another way to produce higher-quality data is to randomly order the presentation of items to respondents.

Because most people are becoming accustomed to reading information on computer screens, and mobile digital devices, such as iPads and smartphones, the design of an online survey should be considered. There are three general designs of online surveys (Norman, Friedman, Norman, & Stevenson, 2001; Sue & Ritter, 2012). The first is the welcome screen. Not only should it introduce the survey to potential participants, but it also should provide clear directions about how to proceed, as well as a brief description of the topic and who is conducting the research. The consent statement, required by a university's Institutional Review Board, would be on the next screen. After this introductory material, the next section displays the closed- or open-ended questions for participants to answer. Questions can be provided as one long form through which respondents scroll. Or, each group of similar items, such as a section or subscale, can be presented on a separate screen requiring the respondent to click "next" to advance through the survey. Many different formats for presenting items can be created with HTML or chosen from a menu in the survey software programs. These include common forms, such as Likert-type items or semantic differential scales. Often these types of items are presented as a matrix with items listed down the

---

*DESIGN
CHECK*

Are All Polls the Same?

You have probably noticed national news media use of public opinion polls. Often at the conclusion of news coverage on a controversial issue (for example, gun control, abortion, potential tax increase), a news program will provide a question with two or more response options. Viewers are provided instructions to text in their preference. For example, texting "yes" means you advocate stronger gun control; texting "no" means you do not. How do these types of instant polls differ from the more traditional random sampling public opinion polls? No research has investigated this question recently. However, the results of text polls are likely to differ substantially from those of random phone surveys. Why? First, selection bias is at work. It's not likely that you would take the time to text in your response unless you felt strongly about the issue. Second, public opinion polls conducted by researchers or public polling firms are more likely to be better designed and seek a population wider than just the viewers of a particular television station. If you see or hear the results of one of these polls, listen carefully for the description of how the poll was conducted.

---

left column and the response choices presented in a row across from each question. This design reduces the amount of scrolling a respondent needs to do. However, do not place too many items on one screen. Research findings suggest that 4 to 10 items per screen is optimum (Toepoel, Das, & Van Soest, 2009); moreover, including too many can increase the likelihood that participants will not respond to all of the questions (Sue & Ritter, 2012). Across all screens, how many questions should an online survey have? Lumsden (2007) suggests no more than 60 because participants tend to abandon longer surveys.

Other design choices for an online survey include the use of color, which can assist with navigation. When choosing colors, readability is the most important criterion. Generally, there should be a high contrast between the color of the text and the background. A dark color for the text with a light background color is easiest to read (Sue & Ritter, 2012). The font and its size should also be considered.

The type of design influences how respondents make sense of the questions. Toepoel, Das, and Van Soest (2008) explain that respondents "seem to use the proximity of the items as a cue to their meaning, perhaps at the expense of reading each item carefully" (p. 989). In designing

an online survey, the researcher has to make a choice: randomize items so that respondents read more carefully or group items together for better sensemaking. Which design choice you make, of course, depends on the wording and topic of the questions.

Comparing Survey Types　Will how you collect survey data affect its results? Yes, but there is no easy answer for which method of surveying will be effective. You must carefully consider the population you are interested in reaching and how best to obtain a meaningful sample. You must also consider the topic of the research questions or hypotheses, as well as the type of information you seek. Unfortunately, there are no clear answers. It is easy to assume that online and mobile technologies are preferred by potential respondents. But that is not always the case. In one study that compared how survey respondents evaluated different survey methods, participants preferred to use iPads over online and mail surveys, but iPad response rates were similar to response rates for face-to-face administration of surveys (Davis, Thompson, & Schweizer, 2012).

Obviously, each type of survey has advantages and disadvantages. See Table 8.1 for a summary

TABLE 8.1 Comparison of Types of Surveys

Type of Survey	Advantages	Disadvantages
Self-administered	• Can easily present visual information • Best for complex or long response sets • Respondent does not need to share information with interviewer	• Good reading and writing skills needed by respondents • Researcher cannot answer respondent questions • If using open-ended questions, limit to 1 or 2
Face-to-face survey	• Effective for encouraging participation, building rapport • Allows probing of responses • Can capture nonverbal cues • Probably best for longer surveys	• Costly in terms of personnel and time • Interviewers must be trained • Impractical for geographically dispersed sample • Interviewer bias or error
Phone survey	• Cost and time efficient • Random-digit dialing can be used for random sampling • Can be done at a geographical distance • Better response rate than mail	• Nonresponse or refusal rate can be high • Not suited for lengthy surveys • Inappropriate for sensitive or personal topics
Online survey	• Cost effective • Time efficient • Respondents can return data quickly • Easy to present visual information • Survey programs make it easy for respondents to skip items or branch to sections based on their responses to previous items	• Challenging to identify populations and samples • Concerns of computer security • Must have skills to create web page or will need to purchase survey software services • Must have accurate e-mail addresses
Mail survey	• Does not require many personnel • Easy to access geographically dispersed sample • Respondents have time to give thoughtful answers	• Nonresponse rate can be high • Cost of mailing • Need for accurate mailing addresses • Delay in getting surveys returned

(Fowler, 2009; Robson, 2011). These issues should be taken into consideration as part of your survey design. One caution is warranted here: Perhaps you are thinking that it would be a good idea to offset the limitations of one type of survey methodology with the advantages of another. Although it may seem logical to use, for example, self-report, telephone, and online methods to ask the same questions in a research project, people respond differently to different types of survey presentations (Weijters, Schillewaert, & Geuens,

2008). So rather than minimizing the limitations of one method by using another, you may introduce more error and bias.

DESIGNING A SURVEY

To be the most effective, surveys should have the following features (Fink, 1995b). First, the survey should be used as part of a sound research design. Second, the questions or items in the survey

TRY THIS!   ## Survey Design

Think of two communication issues on your campus. Perhaps problems exist with availability of parking on campus, or faculty and students are having discussions about the appropriateness and effectiveness of the current method by which students evaluate faculty. Isolate each problem, and write research questions to guide the design of a survey. Given the focus of your research questions, can you use existing questionnaires, or will you need to develop new ones? How would you select an appropriate sample for the survey? Would you use probability or nonprobability sampling? What survey technique would you use: self-report, face-to-face, phone, or online? What are the potential challenges in distributing the survey and collecting data to answer your research questions?

should be straightforward. Third, survey respondents, or the sample, should be chosen to be representative of a population by procedures that are appropriate, given the research question or hypothesis. Fourth, a survey should be both reliable and valid. Fifth, participants' responses to survey questions should be analyzed within the context of the questions asked. Sixth, survey results should be reported accurately and ethically. This includes not using the data out of context.

The research questions or hypotheses developed in the early stages of the research project's design will guide you in developing the survey. Generally, researchers use multiple items to help capture the complexity or depth of the concept associated with the objective. Of course, if you have multiple objectives for a survey or if a survey needs to capture data about several variables, the survey is likely to need multiple items for each objective or variable. To develop your survey objective, define your information needs.

For example, researchers want to know how to construct and target media campaigns for teenagers on the risks of smoking cigarettes. In this case, there are multiple objectives. One objective is to find out which media teenagers use. Another objective is to determine the degree to which informational messages (as contrasted to entertainment messages) in these media are heard and heeded. A third objective could be to find out what teenagers know (and don't know) about risks associated with smoking. Thus, the survey developed for this example would have

multiple items and sections. Survey items can be designed only after the research questions or hypotheses have been developed.

Evaluating Existing Questionnaires or Surveys

Fortunately for communication researchers, there are many established questionnaires that can be adopted. *Communication Research Measures II: A Sourcebook,* edited by R. B. Rubin, A. M. Rubin, E. E. Graham, E. M. Perse, and D. R. Seibold (2009), is a collection of scales that measure communication constructs in the cross-cultural and intercultural, family, group, health, interpersonal, instructional, organizational, and mass communication contexts. Besides providing the scale itself, the book describes scale background, validity, and reliability, and also provides primary citations. These scales are available to researchers and may be used for research without gaining additional permission from the authors of the scales. You can also find scales and questionnaires in some journal articles.

Although in many occasions these questionnaires can be used exactly as they were designed, some contexts may require minimal changes to be used effectively. What kinds of modification are appropriate? Minor wording changes may be necessary so that the survey is appropriate for the respondent population. But even this type of change is tricky. Most questionnaires are developed for adult audiences, and changing the items for teenagers and children, for example, may substantially alter the intent as well as the validity and reliability of the scale. Likewise, translating a questionnaire developed in English into another language may create similar difficulties.

Are there modifications that are inappropriate and should be avoided if possible? Some instruments are lengthy and it is tempting to use only some of the items. Copyright restrictions may prohibit this type of altering. If the instrument is not copyrighted, you should contact the scale's author and ask his or her advice on selecting only some of the survey items for your particular use. Be aware that making any changes or modifications to an existing questionnaire or scale will require that you pilot test, or pretest, the questionnaire after modifications have been made (more on this later in the chapter).

Even with these warnings, it is still recommended that you adopt or adapt questionnaires and scales from other studies whenever possible rather than create your own (Bourque & Fielder, 1995). These scales have undergone extensive testing, refinement, and competitive selection for publication. Using them also creates the opportunity to compare your results with results obtained by others. Moreover, building on the work of others is one way to maximize the clarity of your own research. Remember to document where you obtained the instrument and give credit to the authors of the questionnaire.

Writing Your Own Questionnaire

If you cannot find an appropriate survey instrument or questionnaire, you will have to develop your own. Start by conducting a literature review of the appropriate research literature to learn what might be included. For example, for her thesis, a student wanted to study the communication competence of members of top management teams (CEO, president, vice presidents, and others who report directly to the CEO or president of the organization). As she explored this literature, she found very few studies of top management teams, and none of these directly examined their communication competence. She had some choices. She could have used one of the existing communication competence questionnaires.

She reviewed those options and decided that they were too global or general for her research questions because she wanted her participants to respond to behaviors that constitute communication competence at this organizational level (for example, specific leadership and decision-making communication behaviors).

In reading reports of top management teams, she compiled a list of behaviors that would be described as positive or competent for executives in these positions. Working from that list, she developed a questionnaire that asked respondents to make a judgment about how often they used each particular behavior. And so, working from the literature, she developed a questionnaire about the communication competence of executives. Before using it as part of her thesis, though, she needed to pilot test the questionnaire with a handful of executives to make sure that each item was understood by respondents and that the items generated the types of responses she desired.

Designing Survey Items

A survey or questionnaire is only as good as the items it includes. What is a good survey question? A good question provides answers that are a reliable and valid measure of something we want to describe (Fowler, 2009). To obtain such results, survey items or questions should be straightforward. An item is straightforward, or concrete, when it is precise and unambiguous. Each item should be one complete thought written in sentence or question format. The sentence, or question, should be written in such a way that the respondent is given a choice in how to answer, and knows how to answer. In some cases, open questions are preferred over closed questions. Both forms are explained later in this chapter.

Regardless of which question form you select, how you word survey or questionnaire items is crucial to obtaining the information you desire. Even small changes in wording can create large differences in participant responses (Sudman & Bradburn, 1982). As a result, you should consider several issues as you write survey items (Fink, 1995a; Fowler, 2009; Robson, 2011). First, respondents must be able to understand the terminology used in questions. Because your interpretation of the data will rely on how easily and accurately respondents can answer the questions, you need to consider the literacy and language-proficiency levels of your respondents. Second, each survey item should have a purpose. If you believe respondents will have a difficult time identifying the purpose of the question, give them a reasonable explanation for asking for that information as a lead-in to the question.

The third and fourth issues are related: Third, all respondents should have access to the information needed to answer your question. You would not want respondents to answer a question if they lacked the knowledge or ability to do so. For example, respondents are unlikely to have the exact figure for the crime rate in their neighborhood. But they will be able to provide answers about their own status as a victim of crime or respond to questions about their perceptions of crime. The fourth issue is one of social desirability. Respondents must be willing to provide answers called for by the question and not feel pressured to give an answer that is socially desirable. For example, in sexual harassment research, the socially desirable answer to "Have you sexually harassed someone where you currently work?" is "no." It is unlikely that someone would volunteer that they have, in fact, sexually harassed another employee. As you can see, some types of questions, regardless of how they are asked, may not produce the type of results in which you are interested.

These next issues are practical ones: Fifth, avoid using abbreviations. Rather, use both the abbreviation and the full name or term, at least the first time the abbreviation is used. For example, in collecting data on sexual harassment, a question might include the abbreviation EEOC. Rather than assume that respondents know that EEOC stands for Equal Employment Opportunity Commission, use the full name followed by the abbreviation in parentheses—for example, "Have you read the Equal Employment Opportunity Commission's (EEOC's) guideline on sexual harassment?" Sixth, avoid using slang expressions or jargon. Such expressions change quickly and are used differently by subgroups. Seventh, short questions are better than long questions. Eighth, questions should be administered in a

consistent way. Generally, multiple items measuring the same construct use one set of instructions and the same response set.

Remember that respondents pay close attention and infer meaning from how the question or statement is worded; thus, taking these issues, as well as conversational norms, into account will help you write questions and statements that elicit the type of response you desire (Dillman, Smyth, & Christian, 2009; Schwarz et al., 1998). Pretesting survey items with individuals with the same characteristics as potential respondents can help assure you that your question is meaningful and understandable.

Closed Questions   There are two question formats. The first is the closed question. When respondents are asked a question (or given a statement) and then given a set of responses to select from, the question is **closed.** Questions that require a simple "yes" or "no" answer are closed questions. Likewise, questions that ask for a specific piece of information are closed. For example, "How old are you?" is also a closed question because simply answering "I'm 23" answers the question. No other explanation or description is required. Closed questions are the most frequently used type of question on surveys and questionnaires because their responses can be assigned a numerical value.

Closed questions are also ideal for capturing attitudes or perceptions. Generally, constructs (for example, interaction involvement, communication adaptability) require multiple items. On these types of scales, a standardized set of response items can be provided for the questions or items. For example, each item of the relational maintenance scale (Stafford et al., 2000) is paired with a 7-point Likert-type scale. Participants read each item (e.g., "I show love for my partner") and then select one response from the response set provided (for example, 1 = *strongly disagree* to 7 = *strongly agree*). Each response has a numerical value and a score can be created by totaling responses to all items in the scale. Those values and scores can be used in statistical tests.

Many communication constructs have been operationalized into scales. Before you begin to develop your own measures, check the research literature or the collection of scales in Rubin, Rubin, Graham, Perse, and Seibold (2009).

Whether you use an existing measure or create one of your own, a stimulus statement or stimulus question is required to help respondents contextualize their responses and understand what you are looking for. For instance, the stimulus statement for the Family Communication Standards Instrument (2003) reads:

> Different people have different beliefs about how family members should communicate with each other. Family members may live up to those standards sometimes but not other times. For this questionnaire, think about what you think counts as good family communication. Then, respond to each of the following items in terms of the extent to which it reflects good family communication. Remember, these are your beliefs about what things should be, it doesn't necessarily mean your own family always lived up to these expectations. (Graham, 2009, p. 152).

As you can see, the stimulus statement directs the respondent's attention to the type of questions he or she will be answering and gives general instructions for completing the questionnaire. If several constructs are measured in your survey, you need a separate stimulus statement for each section as well as general instructions as an introduction to the survey.

Response Sets for Closed Questions

There are many different types of response sets for closed questions. One type is *nominal,* or *categorical.* This means that responses in the set do not have a numerical equivalent. In a survey about communication choices at work, the researcher asks

Are you (check the appropriate box):

☐ a member of the clerical staff?
☐ a member of the maintenance team?
☐ a member of the management team?
☐ a member of the production team?

Respondents are being asked to name or categorize themselves. The answers have no natural numerical value. In other words, one answer has no more or no less value than another. Thus,

these types of questions can be used only to create frequency counts of each category.

As explained in Chapter 5, nominal or categorical responses are often used to obtain demographic information about respondents (for example, age, sex, marital status, employment status, socioeconomic status, education, income, occupation, religious preference or affiliation, race and ethnic background), and there are special considerations in developing these response sets. Options in a response set should be exhaustive, mutually exclusive, and equivalent. *Exhaustive* means that all possible choices are represented. *Mutually exclusive* means that the respondent will view only one of the choices in the response set as the correct or best answer. The response set is not mutually exclusive if a respondent finds two choices that can represent his or her answer. *Equivalent* means that the response choices are equal to one another.

In the previous example about communication choices at work, it may appear at first glance that all employees will be able to select a response that best identifies them. But, an engineer might not know where he or she fits. Is an engineer with supervisory responsibility a member of the management team or a member of the production team? Thus, the response set is not satisfactory because it is neither exhaustive nor mutually exclusive, although the response choices appear to be equivalent, because each is a choice about job function.

Many times, researchers add the response of "other" to catch the responses they have not considered or identified or to cover categories for which they believe there will be only a few respondents. Relying on this strategy too frequently will produce data that are not interpretable. To develop exhaustive, mutually exclusive, and equivalent response sets, think of the context and the population. Looking at response sets on other closed-question survey items will help you in developing your own. Be careful, however, about including too many demographic items. Some respondents will regard these as sensitive inquiries and may not answer these items. It is best to ask for only the demographic information that you need to answer your research questions or test your hypotheses. If you find that you need

Racial and Ethnic Group Identification

Many respondents are confused or frustrated when asked to identify their race or ethnicity on a survey or questionnaire. In some cases, the terminology used is unfamiliar to respondents. In other cases, individuals with mixed racial or ethnic backgrounds are uncomfortable when asked to "select the category that best describes you." As a result of these and other problems in how people use racial and ethnic identifiers, the Office of Management and Budget (OMB) in the United States created standards for maintaining, collecting, and presenting federal data on race and ethnicity. All other federal programs adopted these standards. The categories used by the OMB are often applied in research projects as well, especially those funded by U.S. government agencies. Working from the position that the categories represent a social–political construct for collecting data on race and ethnicity of broad population groups in the United States, the OMB recognizes that the recommended minimum categories are not anthropologically or scientifically based. The OMB recommends that, whenever possible, respondents should self-identify their ethnicity and race using the following two-part question:

Race (Select one or more)

- American Indian or Alaska Native
- Asian
- Black or African American
- Native Hawaiian or Other Pacific Islander
- White

to collect demographic data, consider collecting these data at the end of the survey.

Likert-Type Scales   The most common way to present closed questions and response options is the **Likert-type scale.** This multi-item scale asks respondents to respond to survey items with these (or similar) choices: strongly agree, agree, neutral, disagree, strongly disagree. Technically, a single item is a Likert item; multiple items comprising a measure of a construct is a Likert scale (Uebersax, 2006). To treat the data statistically, numerical values are assigned to each of the response choices. Because the numerical values are considered interval level data, or equal distance apart, the responses to a set of questions can be added together to create a total score for that variable.

Most survey response sets have a 5-point scale as response choices. Sometimes the response sets are expanded to a 7-point scale. For example,

a 7-point scale can have a response set, such as "always, very often, often, sometimes, seldom, very seldom, never." Typically, larger numerical values are associated with the response choice that represents the most positive rating. For the most commonly used Likert-type response scale, 5 is commonly anchored with "very often" or "completely agree."

However, you may want to leave off the numerical values and use only the word anchors, particularly if the scale measures sensitive items or negatively worded items (e.g., I fight with my family members). If the word anchors are in logical order from strongest to weakest, the respondent does not need a numerical equivalent. Indeed, some survey experts recommend leaving off the numerical labels unless there is specific and intentional purpose for including them (Dillman, Smyth, & Christian, 2009). Another way to handle items for which respondents may not have a high degree

Ethnicity (Select one)

- Hispanic or Latino
- Not Hispanic or Latino

When race data are collected separately, researchers should report the number of respondents in each racial category who are Hispanic or Latino. Researchers are also encouraged to report detailed distributions, including all possible combinations of multiple responses to the race question. Minimally, responses should be reported for participants who select more than one race.

Alternatively, a combined format can be used, especially when observers collect data on race and ethnicity. For this format, researchers should try to record ethnicity and race or multiple races, but it is acceptable to indicate only one category of the six. For the combined format, the minimum categories are

- American Indian or Alaska Native
- Asian
- Black or African American
- Hispanic or Latino
- Native Hawaiian or Other Pacific Islander
- White

If data are collected this way, researchers should provide the number of respondents who marked only one category as well as the number of respondents who marked multiple categories.

of motivation for providing honest answers is to change the order of the response set. In the example that follows, Form B is recommended over Form A (Barnette, 2000) because the question is positively and directly stated. If a measure has several items like Form B, these items should be grouped together so the respondent is not switching back and forth between response sets from question to question.

Form A

I do not like to talk with my parents.

Strongly   Disagree   Neutral   Agree   Strongly
Disagree   Agree

Form B

I like to talk with my parents.

Strongly   Agree   Neutral   Disagree   Strongly
Agree   Disagree

Likert-type response sets generally have an odd number of response options and offer a middle, or neutral, response like "agree and disagree" or "undecided." Although this sometimes accurately captures the respondent's belief or answer, many respondents will use this middle category when they do not have enough information about the question or have not formed an opinion. Table 8.2 can help you identify appropriate and meaningful response sets for different types of closed questions.

Notice how these response sets are balanced (Fink 1995a). In other words, the two end points represent the opposite of each other. Also notice that the intervals between the choices are about equal. Remember that using the neutral category may capture data different from what you intend or that respondents may use the neutral choice as an excuse for not answering the question. Thus, use a neutral category as a middle point only when it could be a valid response. Beware

TABLE 8.2 Response Set Alternatives for 5-Point Likert-Type Scales

Type of Survey Item	*Examples of Response Set Alternatives*				
Frequency	Very often	Fairly often	Occasionally	Rarely	Never
	Always	Usually	Sometimes	Rarely	Never
Feelings	Very positive	Generally positive	Mixed	Generally negative	Very negative
Evaluation	Excellent	Very good	Good	Fair	Poor
Satisfaction	Completely satisfied	Mostly satisfied	Unsure	Mostly dissatisfied	Completely dissatisfied
Agreement	Completely agree	Generally agree	Unsure	Generally disagree	Completely disagree
Accuracy or endorsement	Completely true	Somewhat true	Unsure	Somewhat untrue	Completely untrue
Intensity	None	Very mild	Mild	Moderate	Severe
Comparison	Much more than others	Somewhat more than others	About the same as others	Somewhat less than others	Much less than others

of using "no opinion" or "don't know" as a neutral choice. Having no opinion is different from having an opinion that is partially favorable *and* partially unfavorable. Do use "no opinion" or "don't know," however, when that response could be appropriate for your questionnaire or survey topic (Schwarz et al., 1998).

Finally, select the word anchors carefully. Although you may clearly discriminate among *usually, sometimes,* and *seldom,* others using the scale may view these three words as synonyms for one another. Use the exercise in the Try This! box ("How Different Are *Usually, Sometimes,* and *Seldom?*") to gauge the type of responses these words evoke.

Semantic Differential Scales   Another common response set for closed questions is a **semantic differential scale** (Osgood et al., 1957). For each question or item, a respondent is given a numerical scale anchored by word opposites, or bipolar adjectives. Look at the following

examples. Notice how the adjectives in the pairs are complete opposites of each other. The 7-point number continuum between the word anchors represents the degree to which the respondent agrees with one or the other anchor.

Unfriendly	1	2	3	4	5	6	7	*Friendly*
Not satisfied	1	2	3	4	5	6	7	*Satisfied*

In the first example, if respondents circle 7, they are indicating that the person they were asked about is friendly. If the respondents choose 3, they are indicating that the target person is more unfriendly than friendly. The midpoint of the scale, indicated by the number 4, is used if the respondent is unsure if the target person is friendly or unfriendly. In the second example, respondents would circle 7, 6, or 5 to indicate some level of satisfaction with their performance on a particular communication behavior.

Notice that only the ends of the continuum are anchored with words. This allows the respondent to select the meaning he or she has for the stimulus or target, which can be an object, a communication practice or process, him- or herself, or another person, or even an abstract concept. A continuum and its pair of opposing adjectives captures respondents' evaluations and is commonly used to measure attitudes or predispositions toward the stimulus or target.

Open Questions

The second type of question is open-ended. When respondents use their own words to respond to a question, it is an **open question.** This question form gives you data from a respondent's point of view rather than your own (Fink, 1995a). Responses to open questions are difficult to translate into numerical equivalents for use in statistical tests. For that reason, open questions are used sparingly, and often at the end of the survey after the closed-ended questions.

Open questions are particularly helpful when the topic you are studying is relatively new. For example, a researcher wants to know if, and to what degree, the respondent uses websites to obtain information in making voting selections about candidates. An open question could be a good way to find out how influential websites are after the researcher has asked closed questions about computer availability and Web usage. Look at Table 8.3 for examples.

Open questions will create multiple responses. As a result, responses from participants may not be comparable. For example, one respondent can provide the URLs of websites he frequently visits, whereas another respondent admits she has trouble distinguishing between web pages sponsored by a candidate's political party and unofficial web pages that describe the candidate and her views. As you can imagine, responses to open questions are often difficult to compare and interpret. If you must use open questions in a survey design, use them sparingly.

Open questions rely on how people respond. Thus, researchers need to consider what constitutes an adequate answer and build that request into the question. A good open question is one that is communicated in the same way to all respondents. Simply, if respondents differ in their perceptions of what constitutes an adequate answer, their answers will differ for reasons that have nothing to do with what you are trying to measure. For example, in a study on how students identify with their university, a researcher wanted to ask, "How would you describe North Carolina State University?" Possible answers could include "it's a public university," "it's where I'm getting my degree," "it has a great engineering school," "it's a school with tradition; both my mom and dad graduated from there," and so on. All of these and more are possible and reasonable. A better way to state the question would be to ask, "How would you, as a student, describe North Carolina State University to a

TABLE 8.3 Examples of Open and Closed Questions in a Phone or Face-To-Face Interview

Type of Question	Example
Closed	Do you have access to the Internet?
Closed	(If the respondent's answer is "yes") Do you use Google™ to search online?
Open	(If the respondent's answer is "yes") What do you look for online?
Closed	Do you ever look for information about political candidates or political parties?
Open	(If the respondent's answer is "yes") What types of information are helpful on those sites? Or, What appeals to you about sites with political information?

potential student?" because it better specifies the kind of answer the researcher was seeking.

In other open formats, participants are directed to recall episodes or past interactions they participated in. Researchers use a **recall cue** to draw participants' attention to the issue they are interested in or to restrict their attention to a particular type of interaction. For example, in a study of rituals in marriages, Bruess and Pearson (1997) used the following recall cue:

Below, please list and EXPLAIN in DETAIL all of the "routines" (or "rituals") that you and your spouse have developed either presently or have had in the past. Some of these routines might be very silly and trivial (such as regularly tugging on each other's ears to say "I love you") or they might involve elaborate planning (such as taking a "get away weekend" every fall).

We are interested in "routines" (or "rituals") that you and your spouse repeatedly do together, or for one another. For instance, other couples have reported that they regularly called each other during the day, go to particular restaurants or other favorite spots together, have a ritual of eating out on certain nights, take walks together at certain times, or regularly purchase special treats for one another [that have] special meanings.

Another couple reported regularly playing cribbage and drinking a cocktail together which served as a prelude to love making. Another couple regularly planned "adult dinners" after the children were in bed; they explained that no food was on the floor, they ate [slowly], were able to talk with another, and shared a glass of wine.

Please describe ANY routine (or "ritual") shared with your spouse no matter how small or large it is. After explaining each routine (or "ritual") completely, please respond to the questions which follow it. (p. 31)

This recall cue is very specific and should restrict the answers respondents give. When you need to include a recall cue, try it out before administering the survey. Recall cues are effective when they make reference to what happened, where it happened, and who was involved.

Recall cues that ask participants to begin with the most recent event are generally more effective unless the material has an inherent temporal or historical order—such as recalling where someone has lived since graduating from high school (Schwarz et al., 1998). Because recalling may take several seconds, give participants plenty of time to respond if you are using recall cues in face-to-face or telephone surveys.

If you are using open questions in an interactive format (by phone or face-to-face), capture everything the respondent says in exactly the way he or she says it. Do not try to code or abbreviate responses while the person is talking. Coding procedures are best done after all data have been collected. If you are using open questions in a written or online survey format, leave more space than you believe respondents will need to write their response. You do not want participants to base their response on the amount of space. Rather, you want them to be motivated to write as much and in as much detail as they would like.

Choosing Between Open and Closed Questions

To summarize survey design issues, use open questions if

1. Respondents' own words are important and you want to be able to quote what respondents say.
2. Respondents are willing and can answer the question in their own words.
3. The set of response choices is unknown.
4. You are willing to analyze the text of the responses.

Alternatively, use closed questions if

1. There is agreement on what the response set should be.
2. Statistical analysis and reporting of the data is desirable or necessary.

Regardless of your choice, remember these caveats. It is easier for respondents to endorse an opinion in a closed-response format. If you rely on an open-response format, the opinion may

How Different Are *Usually, Sometimes,* and *Seldom?*

In developing a questionnaire item, you must carefully consider how to word the statement or question. You should also be careful in choosing the response set for each item. In response to questions that ask about frequency of behaviors, some researchers use *always, usually, sometimes, seldom,* and *never.* Whereas most people would agree that *always* means 100% and *never* means 0%, what percentages would you infer from *usually, sometimes,* and *seldom?* Ask three people to identify the percentages they associate with *usually, sometimes,* and *seldom.* In each of these trials, change the order of word anchors. Compare the responses they provide with the responses others in your class receive. Are the percentages similar enough for you to have confidence in using this terminology to capture participants' responses? Were the percentages given in the same frequency order in which you would have ordered the words?

not be volunteered. On the other hand, if your response set is written in such a way as to omit a potential response, the opinion will not be reported at all (Schwarz & Hippler, 1991). As you can see, both response-set formats have clear and profound implications for data collection.

DESIGNING THE FLOW OF THE SURVEY

Whether you use an existing questionnaire or measure or create your own, the survey itself must be designed so that it is presented logically and clearly to research participants. These principles can help guide you.

First, the survey and each of its sections need a brief and clear set of instructions (Nardi, 2006). The first set of instructions should contextualize the survey. If you are collecting data about communicating at work, the instruction might read, "As you respond to the survey, please keep your current or most recent work experience in mind," or "As you respond to the survey, please focus on how you communicate at work." Although the consent form or agreement that participants read will also include this basic description of the survey, that information should be repeated in the general instructions of the survey.

In addition to general instructions, each section of the survey needs instructions. Do not

expect that participants will understand what you want them to do by looking at the survey. Instructions should be explicit: "Answer each question by circling your response" or "In this next section, respond to each question by selecting the degree to which you agree or disagree with the statement."

It is common to ask for demographic information in survey research. Your research questions or hypotheses may depend on this type of information. But be sensitive to including too many requests for demographic information. Although it may be interesting to know this information, ask for only the data you will need to answer your research questions or hypotheses. Generally, it is recommended that you ask for demographic information at the end of the survey (Nardi, 2006).

Of course, the survey should end with a "thank you" from the researcher. Researchers often put their contact information here as well. If the survey should be returned, give complete information, instructions, and a deadline for return.

How the Survey Looks

A list of questions you want respondents to answer and a survey are not the same thing (Dillman, Smyth, & Christian, 2009). Regardless of how you deliver the survey to respondents, the design of the survey must be clear and uncomplicated. Why? How the survey looks to respondents needs to motivate them to respond. If you are using face-to-face interviews, the survey also needs to be clear and uncluttered so you can easily read the questions to participants and record their answers. A well-designed survey also reduces nonresponses.

One way to think about designing the survey is as a conversation with potential respondents (Dillman, Smyth, & Christian, 2009). Questions and sections of questions should be in a logical order. It's also best to begin the survey with questions that are salient, or interesting and important, to your sample. Through the survey, its visual presentation should be attractive and consistent. A simple use of color or gray shading can help respondents navigate through the survey.

Although survey software can help achieve an effective design, be careful about adding too much visual interest for any type of online survey. Putting too many visual elements on a page or including too many horizontal lines will draw respondents' attention away from answering the questions. Survey software provides a variety of ways to present questions or items. While a matrix format (see Figure 8.1) may reduce the space needed, it is also the most difficult format for participants to respond to. As Dillman, Smyth, and Christian (2009) describe: "One survey we saw recently had 19 items on a single screen, and each item was to be rated on a scale of 1 (poor) to 10 (excellent). That's 190 radio buttons on one screen!" (p. 180).

PRETESTING THE SURVEY OR QUESTIONNAIRE

As you can see, a researcher can spend considerable time and energy either in looking for and adopting an existing questionnaire or in developing a new questionnaire. This energy should not be wasted. Thus, it is a good idea to pretest the instrument. **Pretesting,** sometimes called **pilot testing,** occurs when, before data collection actually begins, the researcher tries the survey or questionnaire with a small group of participants who are similar to those individuals who form the population. Note that this form of pretesting

is not the same as pretesting as part of experimental or quasi-experimental research designs. Data are not collected when a researcher is pretesting the survey or questionnaire.

There are four approaches to pretesting a survey: cognitive, conventional, behavior coding, and expert panels (Presser & Blair, 1994). The cognitive approach to pretesting helps uncover questions that can stimulate multiple interpretations. For example, your survey includes the question and response set "Do you own your own home?" followed by "yes" and "no." This seems a simple and straightforward question. Researchers would likely expect individuals participating in the survey to be able to answer the question. With **cognitive pretesting,** you would ask questions about the question "Do you own your own home?" When a participant answers "yes" to this question, does that mean personally owning the place where he or she lives, or does it mean owning the home with someone else? In answering "yes," does the person mean that he or she owns the home outright or that there is a mortgage on the home? In answering "yes," does the participant mean a single-family home or a condo, a high-rise apartment, or a duplex? If these differences are important to your survey, you would need to rephrase the question to be more specific. Thus, cognitive pretesting allows the researcher to test for semantic problems, or problems affecting how easily the questions are understood. As another example, if you were researching the social network of individuals and looking at their living arrangements as a predictor of the breadth of their network, making specific distinctions in living arrangements could make a difference in the interpretation of your results.

Cognitive pretesting is best done face-to-face with a person who is similar to those who will participate. Being face-to-face allows the researcher to watch the nonverbal expressions as individuals try to answer the questions. Probing questions and follow-up questions can be used to capture what the individuals think questions mean. The advantage here, obviously, is that the researcher can ask questions and try rephrasing questions until she is receiving exactly the type of data she wants.

Thinking of your preferences for working in groups and teams, please respond to the question and then move on to the next question.

1. **I like working in groups.**
    ○ Strongly agree   ● Agree   ● Undecided   ● Disagree   ● Strongly disagree

Exit this survey

Next

(a) Screen with one question

Exit this survey

Thinking of your preferences for working in groups and teams, please respond to each question.

1.   **I like working in groups.**
    ○ Strongly agree   ○ Agree   ○ Undecided   ○ Disagree   ○ Strongly disagree

2.   **I would prefer to work in an organization in which teams are used.**
    ○ Strongly agree   ○ Agree   ○ Undecided   ○ Disagree   ○ Strongly disagree

3.   **My ideal job is where I can be interdependent with others.**
    ○ Strongly agree   ○ Agree   ○ Undecided   ○ Disagree   ○ Strongly disagree

4.   **Group work is fun.**
    ○ Strongly agree   ○ Agree   ○ Undecided   ○ Disagree   ○ Strongly disagree

5.   **I would rather work alone.**
    ○ Strongly disagree   ○ Disagree   ○ Undecided   ○ Agree   ○ Strongly agree

6.   **Groups are terrible.**
    ○ Strongly disagree   ○ Disagree   ○ Undecided   ○ Agree   ○ Strongly agree

Prev   Next

(b) Screen with multiple questions with response sets

Thinking of your preferences for working in groups and teams, please respond to each question.

	Strongly Agree	Agree	Undecided	Disagree	Strongly Disagree
I like working in groups.	○	○	○	○	○
I would prefer to work in an organization in which teams are used.	○	○	○	○	○
My ideal job is where I can be interdependent with others.	○	○	○	○	○
Group work is fun.	○	○	○	○	○
I would rather work alone.	○	○	○	○	○
Groups are terrible	○	○	○	○	○

(c) Screen with matrix format

FIGURE 8.1 Three Designs for Online Surveys

TRY THIS!

Does This Questionnaire Need Modification?

Review the questionnaire below. How do its overall design and item design adhere to the principles described in this chapter? Are there changes or modifications you believe are necessary? Would you design the questionnaire differently for self-report use in written format from the design you would recommend for online format?

Communicative Adaptability Scale

Instructions: The following are statements about communication behaviors. Answer each item as it relates to your general style of communication (the type of communicator you are most often) in social situations. Please indicate the degree to which each statement applies to you by circling the appropriate number (according to the scale below) for each item.

5	4	3	2	1
Almost Always true of me	*Often true of me*	*Sometimes true of me*	*Rarely true of me*	*Never true of me*

1.	I feel nervous in social situations.	5	4	3	2	1
2.	People think I am witty.	5	4	3	2	1
3.	When speaking I have problems with grammar.	5	4	3	2	1
4.	I enjoy meeting new people.	5	4	3	2	1
5.	In most social situations I feel tense and constrained.	5	4	3	2	1
6.	When someone makes a negative comment about me, I respond with a witty comeback.	5	4	3	2	1
7.	When I embarrass myself, I often make a joke about it.	5	4	3	2	1
8.	I enjoy socializing with various groups of people.	5	4	3	2	1
9.	I try to make the other person feel important.	5	4	3	2	1
10.	At times I don't use appropriate verb tense.	5	4	3	2	1
11.	I often make jokes when in tense situations.	5	4	3	2	1
12.	While I'm talking I think about how the other person feels.	5	4	3	2	1
13.	When [I am] talking, my posture seems awkward and tense.	5	4	3	2	1
14.	I disclose at the same level that others disclose to me.	5	4	3	2	1

15.	I find it easy to get along with new people.	5	4	3	2	1
16.	I sometimes use words incorrectly.	5	4	3	2	1
17.	When I self-disclose I know what I am revealing.	5	4	3	2	1
18.	I try to be warm when communicating with another.	5	4	3	2	1
19.	I am relaxed when talking with others.	5	4	3	2	1
20.	When I am anxious, I often make jokes.	5	4	3	2	1
21.	I sometimes use one word when I mean to use another.	5	4	3	2	1
22.	I do not "mix" well at social functions.	5	4	3	2	1
23.	I am aware of how intimate the disclosures of others are.	5	4	3	2	1
24.	I am verbally and nonverbally supportive of other people.	5	4	3	2	1
25.	I sometimes use words incorrectly.	5	4	3	2	1
26.	I have difficulty pronouncing some words.	5	4	3	2	1
27.	I like to be active in different social groups.	5	4	3	2	1
28.	I am aware of how intimate my disclosures are.	5	4	3	2	1
29.	My voice sounds nervous when I talk with others.	5	4	3	2	1
30.	I try to make the other person feel good.	5	4	3	2	1

Circle the appropriate response for each of the following items:

31.	I am a college: freshman sophomore junior senior
32.	I currently attend college: full time part time
33.	I am: a Communication major not a Communication major undecided or have not declared my major
34	I am: female male

Thank you. Please return this survey to the session facilitator.
You may leave when you are finished.

SOURCE: Duran, R.L. (1983). "Communicative Adaptability: A Review of Conceptualization and Measurement," *Communication Quarterly, 40,* pp. 253–268. Used by permission of Eastern Communication Association.

AN ETHICAL
ISSUE

Would You Participate?

Survey research relies on the extent to which people are willing to respond to and answer the questions presented them. This self-selection bias on the part of participants creates a tension with researchers' desire to obtain responses from all members of a selected sample. Obviously, researchers cannot require, threaten, or force individuals to participate or respond. As a result, a tension exists between the scientific needs of a survey study and the rights of people to decline to participate partially or in total. Are there survey topics that would cause you to decline to participate? Is there anything the researcher or interviewer could say or do to make you change your mind? Think of at least three sensitive survey topics. How would you design the survey and its administration to increase the likelihood of participation?

A second type of pretesting is the **conventional pretest.** In this type of pretest, the researcher selects several individuals who are like persons in the population. The survey is completed just as it will be done in the study. This type of pretest allows the researcher to reflect on the survey process and make any changes to the administration of the survey before it is given or sent to members of the sample. Conventional pretesting captures the experience of the interviewers, or survey administrators, but it does not capture information from the perspective of those who participate in the survey.

This was the strategy used by Ellis (2000), who developed a questionnaire to assess students' perceptions of teachers' confirmation behaviors. She pretested the questionnaire on a group of 24 students before it was used with the larger sample in the study.

Behavior coding is the third type of pretesting and is used only when the survey is conducted in the face-to-face format. The idea in this type of pretesting is to have a third person monitor the interaction between the interviewer and respondent. The monitors are outside the survey process and, as a result, are more objective in identifying problems. The monitor observes the interaction as it happens. This means that he or she can look for only a few problems at a time. A monitor can look for problems from the perspectives of both the interviewer and the respondent. These include the interviewer changing how a question is read across many participants, interviewer probing for additional answers from some respondents and not others, respondent asking for clarification, and respondent giving uncodable or unexpected answers.

A fourth type of pretesting is the use of **expert panels.** In this type of pretesting, experts in research methodology or in the survey's content read through the questionnaire together and discuss potential problems they see with the survey. Because they are experts, this type of pretesting can point out semantic problems in how questions are worded and interviewer administration techniques, as well as potential problems with analyzing the data after the survey is complete. For example, Mueller and Lee (2002) used graduate communication students with work experience to compose an expert panel to examine a questionnaire on leader behavior and communication satisfaction. The panel was asked to identify any unclear wording, evaluate the ease of response, and indicate the time it took them to complete the survey. Based on feedback from the expert panel, the research clarified some terminology and how respondents would mark their answers on the survey. The survey was then used to collect data from full-time employees. Although it is time consuming and sometimes difficult to find experts who are willing to help you out, pretesting with expert panels is the most productive way to identify problems with survey and questionnaire administration.

At the completion of pretesting, make the final changes. Before copying the survey, proofread it one last time. At the end of the survey, be sure that a thank you is the last thing respondents see. If you collect the survey data in person, be sure to thank the respondent for his or her time and cooperation. If respondents must take an additional step to return the survey by mail or e-mail, be sure to give specific instructions and a reasonable deadline for doing so. Also consider using pre-addressed and stamped envelopes to increase the response rate for mailed surveys.

SAMPLING ISSUES FOR SURVEYS

In addition to the sampling issues presented in Chapter 6, using surveys requires the researcher to consider some unique issues.

Response Rate

A common error is to confuse sample size with response rate. They are not the same. **Response rate,** or return rate, is the number of people who respond after they have been contacted as part of the sample and asked to participate. An easy way to calculate response rate is to divide the number of people who responded by the number of respondents identified as part of the sample. For example, if you identified 300 potential individuals as the sample for your survey and 175 responded, your response rate would be 58.33% (175 divided by 300 equals 0.5833).

Although researchers wish for a high response rate, there is no standard, and response rates vary by survey technique, the interest your survey topic generates, and the type of respondent you are seeking. How will you know what an acceptable response rate is? A study analyzed 463 studies published in management and behavioral science academic journals for the years 2000 to 2005 (Heerwegh & Loosveldt, 2008). Across these studies, the average of the response rates of individuals was 52.7% ($SD = 20.4$) across all types of surveys. This suggests that a normal response rate could range from 32.3% to 73.1%. But remember that response rates vary. Hoonakker and Carayon (2009) found that mail surveys had the highest response rate (52.4%), followed by web surveys (50.5%), and e-mail surveys (32.8%).

One technique often used by communication researchers is to have students distribute questionnaires for them. Students are given instructions on the type of participant to seek. Kassing (2009a) used students to locate full-time working adults for his study. Of the 240 questionnaires distributed, 60% were returned. To find international students, Sheldon (2009) sent e-mails to 1,433 international students enrolled at a university. The e-mail contained a link to the online questionnaire. The response rate was 12%; 172 students completed the questionnaire. If you believe that the response rate will be low, you could choose to oversample. By increasing your sample size, you might also increase your response rate—but this is no guarantee.

Unfortunately, all surveys will suffer from **nonresponse,** or the failure to obtain data from individuals in the sample. One other problem exists: Some questionnaires or surveys are returned in an unusable form. In most of these cases, participants fail to fill out the survey in its entirety. Sometimes, participants write in remarks instead of using the response categories provided. When calculating the response rate, be sure to identify the number of usable surveys returned.

SURVEY RELIABILITY AND VALIDITY

The most common form of reliability for questionnaires and surveys is internal reliability, because multiple items are used to measure one construct. As you recall from Chapter 5, *reliability* means consistency. For example, the Communicative Adaptability Scale contains 30 items. Of the 30 items, five are associated with each of the six following subconstructs: social composure, social confirmation, social experience, appropriate disclosure, articulation, and wit.

Internal reliability is the degree to which each set of five items was consistent in measuring the subconstruct. Referred to as Cronbach's alpha, the measurement of internal reliability is expressed in value from 0 to 1.00, with 0 indicating that the five items had no internal consistency and 1.00 indicating that respondents answered each of the five questions for a particular construct in a similar way. Perfect internal reliability is rare. Generally, an internal reliability of .70 or greater is considered adequate and acceptable in communication research. This level of reliability means that in most cases, respondents gave the same response or a similar response to most items in that particular construct. Statistical programs can compute a scale's or subscale's internal reliability using Cronbach's alpha.

Also recall that *validity* means accuracy, or that the survey or questionnaire assesses what it purports to measure. Surveys should have high *content validity*. This means that the survey instrument or items measure thoroughly and appropriately what they are intended to measure. For example, a questionnaire investigating the construct of marital conflict should include items about arguments over household and childcare responsibilities, as well as items about the influence of third parties (e.g., in-laws) in creating tension between husband and wife. The most basic form of validity for survey questions is *face validity*. A good way to establish face validity is to ask yourself the question "Does this item (or items) ask all the needed questions in language that is appropriate?" For example, in measuring sexual harassment, a researcher would achieve face validity by including items that address actions frequently associated with sexual harassment, such as telling sexual jokes or inappropriate touching.

With respect to surveys, *construct validity* is established when a survey in fact does distinguish between people who do and do not have certain characteristics. Researchers use surveys to establish or identify levels or types of communication behavior. For example, a survey might ask about a respondent's media usage. The survey has construct validity to the extent that it distinguishes between people who are heavy and light media users.

ANALYZING AND REPORTING SURVEY DATA

After survey or questionnaire data are collected, the data must be interpreted. Researchers collect survey data from a sample of many individuals so the results can be generalized to the population from which the sample was selected. This is an important point! The researcher should not be interested in the responses of any individual, or even a set of individuals. Data are interpreted as a whole. In other words, the data of all participants are combined to create a picture of the population.

One of the weaknesses of using questionnaires or surveys as the only data collection method is that the data produced are largely descriptive and can only describe relationships between variables (see correlation as one test of variable relationships in Chapter 11). Because the data are collected at one point in time on all variables, it is difficult to demonstrate that one variable caused a change in another variable (Schwarz et al., 1998).

One way to overcome this weakness is to use a panel survey design. **Panels** are longitudinal research designs. Data are collected through survey techniques at more than one point in time. In this case, a sample of persons is repeatedly measured over time. If the same individuals participate in each survey, or wave, then the panel is fixed. If some of the same individuals participate, and in addition, new participants are added, the panel design is rotating (see Peng, Zhu, Tong, & Jiang, 2012). Still, problems exist. One is with participants who leave the panel survey because of some reason connected with the survey variables (for example, a married couple participates in the first wave but separates before the second wave of questioning). There is also some evidence that measuring a variable at time 1 causes changes in how the variable is measured at time 2 (Schwarz et al., 1998).

Although panel surveys allow the researcher to draw causal inferences and to assess change over time (Eveland & Morey, 2011), panel surveys are also subject to practical problems as well as measurement error. For example, Peter and Valkenburg (2009) used a panel survey designed to discover how exposure over time to sexually explicit Internet material influenced postadolescents' sexual satisfaction. Three waves of surveys with the same sample were conducted. The first was in May and June 2006; the second occurred later that year in November and December; the final wave occurred in May and June of 2007. From the first wave of 2,341 participants to the third wave, 1,052 or 54% responded to all three surveys. In this study and others, panel attrition not only reduces sample size, it reduces the representativeness of the sample because nonresponse is not random (Eveland & Morey, 2011).

Communication scholars can also overcome this weakness by testing data on models developed from theory. For example, the Peter and Valekenburg (2009) study was based on the research literature and a well-developed theory allowing them to advance and test hypotheses.

Generally, the data produced by closed questions, which is the most typical type of response for surveys, questionnaires, and polls, can be interpreted using conventional statistical tools. These data can be organized and described using the descriptive statistics explained in Chapter 9. These tools assist the researcher in developing basic reports and explanations of the data. More complex interpretations can be made by using the statistical tools that test for differences and relationships (Chapter 10 and Chapter 11, respectively). Responses to open questions first need to be categorized or content analyzed, as described in Chapter 12. After this is done, frequency counts are useful tools for organizing and reporting data.

Once analyzed, the results are written as a research report. Chapter 13 describes, in detail, how to write a quantitative research report. If survey data will be presented to respondents, charts, tables, and graphs are effective ways to present this data. By viewing the survey data in a graphic form, most people will be able to make sense of the information, even without having a background in research or statistics. If you entered the data on a spreadsheet or statistics program, graphic functions available there will produce a variety of visual displays.

Regardless of their use, the data and their results should never be reported out of context or without describing the respondents or context of the survey or questionnaire. If you used graphics, data reports should be appropriately labeled to allow others to make their own interpretation of the data at a glance. This does not mean that you should refrain from interpreting the data first. Rather, whoever reads or uses the report of the data should be able to come, independently, to the same conclusions that you have drawn. Forcing the data or results to fit your need or to satisfy a survey objective when it does not is unethical.

SUMMARY

1. Surveys and questionnaires are the most common quantitative method used in communication research.

2. Often self-administered, surveys can be distributed in written format through the mail, the Web, or e-mail, or interviewers can ask questions face-to-face or over the phone.

3. Research questions or hypotheses drive the survey or questionnaire design.

4. Existing and established questionnaires can be used in some instances; otherwise, the researcher has to develop the questionnaire.

5. Recall cues, or stimulus statements, are needed to direct or restrict participants' responses.

6. Open questions allow the respondent to use his or her own words in responding to a question or statement.

7. Closed questions are complete with standardized response sets; respondents choose from the responses provided by the researcher.

8. Many closed questions can be adequately responded to using a 5-point or 7-point Likert-type response scale, and must be exhaustive as well as mutually exclusive.

9. How the survey looks can affect if and how respondents will answer; it should be uncluttered and readable and respondents should be told explicitly how and where to mark their responses.

10. Before using the survey in a research project, it should be pilot tested, or pretested.

11. Response rate, or the number of people who respond after they have been contacted to participate, should not be confused with sample size.

12. An aspect of reliability central to questionnaires is internal reliability, or the degree to which multiple questions or items consistently measure the same construct.

13. After data is collected, the researcher must analyze and interpret the data as a whole, rather than focusing on the responses of any individual.

14. Survey data are collected at one point in time, which weakens their predictive ability unless theoretical models have been developed before the survey data are collected.

KEY TERMS

behavior coding

closed question

cognitive pretesting

conventional pretesting

cross-sectional

expert panel

Likert-type scale

nonresponse

online survey

open question

panel

pilot testing

pretesting

questionnaire

recall cue

response rate

self-administered survey

self-reports

semantic differential scale

social desirability response

survey

web survey

See the website www.mhhe.com/keyton4 that accompanies this text. For each chapter, the site contains a:

- chapter outline
- chapter checklist
- chapter summary
- short multiple-choice quiz
- PowerPoint presentation created by Dr. Keyton

For a list of internet resources, visit http://www.joannkeyton.com/CommunicationResearch-Methods.htm.

CHAPTER NINE

Descriptive Statistics, Significance Levels, and Hypothesis Testing

Chapter Checklist

After reading this chapter, you should be able to:

1. Explain the concept of the normal curve.
2. Assess data for its distribution and compare it to the normal curve.
3. Create a frequency distribution and polygon for each variable in a dataset.
4. Compute and interpret the mean, median, and mode for each variable in a dataset.
5. Compute the range and standard deviation for each variable in a dataset.
6. Explain the relationship between the mean and standard deviation for scores on a variable.
7. Use frequencies and percentages to provide a summary description of nominal data.

8. Accurately calculate descriptive statistics.
9. Accurately report descriptive statistics.
10. Choose an appropriate level of significance for each statistical test used in your research project.
11. Make a decision about a hypothesis based on the stated level of significance.
12. Explain the relationship among sampling techniques, significance levels, and hypothesis testing.
13. Identify when an alternative hypothesis is accepted and when a null hypothesis is retained.

Numbers are just one tool researchers can use to collect **data,** or information about communication phenomena. In their most basic function, numbers can capture the quality, intensity, value, or degree of the variables used in quantitative communication studies. Recall from Chapter 5 on measurement that numbers have no inherent value. Rather, a numerical value is meaningful and can be interpreted only within the context in which the number was collected. Also recall that each variable must be operationalized, meaning that the researcher must specify exactly what data were collected and how. These processes are valuable to scholarly research because they help researchers say precisely what is being studied and what is not.

In addition to descriptive statistics, this chapter also explains two concepts critical to quantitative communication research: statistical significance and hypothesis testing. These scientific traditions are so strong and so widely accepted among communication researchers who use quantitative research designs that they are often applied or adapted to other forms of quantitative communication research, such as surveys. To begin, let's examine how data are used to create descriptive statistics.

NUMBERS INTO STATISTICS

The numerical data, or **raw data,** collected from each participant is compiled into a **dataset** or collection of the raw data for the same variables for a sample of participants. A dataset is shown in Figure 9.1. In this dataset, except for the first column, the columns represent variables in the study, while the rows represent the responses of individuals. In this dataset, there are eight variables (*train* through *beh3*) and the responses of

Participant identification number

Variable names

id	train	tolerate	livesup	type1	type2	beh1	beh2	beh3
703	1	0	5	3	3	0	0	1
704	1	0	3	3	3	0	0	0
706	1	0	4	1	2	0	0	0
707	1	0	2	3	3	1	1	1
708	1	0	4	3	3	1	1	1
709	1	0	4	1	4	1	1	1
710	1	0	3	1	2	1	1	1
711	1	0	4	3	3	1	1	1
712	1	0	2	1	2	1	0	1
713	1	1	3	3	0	1	1	1
714	1	0	3	0	2	0	0	1
715	1	0	4	3	2	1	1	1
716	1	0	4	1	2	1	1	1
717	1	0	5	3	3	1	1	0
901	1	0	4	1	2	0	1	1

Raw data

Descriptive statistics for the variable *livesup*:
N (or number of cases) = 15
mean = 3.6 (sum of 54 divided by 15, the number of cases)
standard deviation = 0.91
range = 2 to 5, or 3

FIGURE 9.1 Example of a Dataset

15 participants. Using the numbers in the dataset, researchers compute another set of numbers, called **descriptive statistics,** which convey essential basic information about each variable and the dataset as a whole.

Look at the data in Figure 9.1. From the raw data, a researcher can compute four numbers to summarize and represent each variable in the dataset regardless. The *mean, standard deviation, range,* and *number of cases* are commonly used to provide a summary interpretation of each variable. Each of these is discussed in detail in this chapter.

Besides their descriptive, or summarizing, function, numbers are also used in more complex ways to provide information about the relationships between or among variables in the study and to help researchers draw conclusions about a population by examining the data of the sample. This use of numbers is known as **inferential statistics;** several types of inferential statistics, or statistical tests, are covered in Chapters 10 and 11.

Regardless of which statistical test may be called for by a hypothesis or research question, researchers must interpret and report basic information about the participants and each variable in a research study. Having a basic understanding of how researchers use numbers as a tool in collecting and interpreting data can help you make an independent assessment of a researcher's conclusion.

But before we can turn to those summary descriptive statistics, we need to introduce the properties of the normal curve. Descriptive statistics and their interpretation are inextricably linked to it.

NORMAL CURVE

It is not meaningful to analyze or interpret a score from one individual on one variable. Without other data to compare the score to, the researcher would be left with an isolated data point. Interpreting and reporting individual scores is neither practical nor meaningful.

More interesting and useful is the comparison of data collected from many individuals on one variable. For example, knowing how individuals in one sample scored on a leadership assessment provides the opportunity to examine one score

against other scores in the sample and the opportunity to examine the set of scores as a whole. As scientists over time and across disciplines have collected data from natural sources, they have discovered that frequency distributions of datasets tend to have a particular shape (Jaeger, 1990). This shape is the normal curve and represents one of the primary principles of statistics. While the normal curve is less likely to occur in the measurement of communication phenomenon (Hayes, 2005), the normal distribution is used as the basis of hypothesis testing and inferential statistics.

The **normal curve,** or bell curve, is a theoretical distribution of scores or other numerical values. Figure 9.2 illustrates the normal curve. The majority of cases are distributed around the peak in the middle, with progressively fewer cases as one moves away from the middle of the distribution. That is, in this theoretical distribution, more responses are average or near-average than extremely high or extremely low. The normal curve is recognizable because of its distinct bell shape and symmetry—one side of the curve is a mirror image of the other side.

The horizontal axis represents all possible values of a variable, whereas the vertical axis represents the relative frequency with which those values occur. In a normal curve—and remember that it is a theoretical model—the mean (the average score), median (the score in the middle of the distribution), and mode (the score that occurs most frequently) would have the same value and would divide the curve into two equal halves. Although it is highly unlikely that data for a variable would be represented as a true normal curve, scientists look for the normality of their data and the degree to which the distribution of their data deviates from the normal curve.

Skewed Distributions

When a distribution of scores is not normal, it is referred to as a **skewed distribution.** One side is not a mirror image of the other. Rather, the curve is asymmetrical; one side is different from the other. Thus, the mean, median, and mode will not be at the same point. Skewness, or the degree to which the distribution of data is bunched to one side or the other, is a direct reflection of the variability, or dispersion, of the scores.

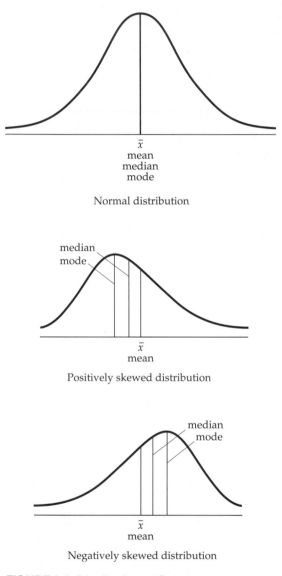

FIGURE 9.2 *Distribution of Scores*

A **positively skewed curve** represents a distribution in which there are very few scores on the right side of the distribution (see Figure 9.2). Thus, there are very few very high scores. The long tail pointing to the right indicates this. In a positively skewed curve, most of the scores are lumped together on the left side of the curve, below the mean. For example, students from a communication department with a strong focus on practicing communication skills would likely have a positively skewed distribution of communication apprehension scores. Why? The department's curriculum requires each course to include a communication skill or performance element. As students take communication classes, they become more comfortable communicating, and their communication apprehension decreases significantly. As a result, very few students in the department have very high communication apprehension scores.

Alternatively, a **negatively skewed curve** represents a distribution in which there are very few scores on the left side of the distribution (see Figure 9.2). Thus, there are very few very low scores. The long tail pointing to the left indicates this. In a negatively skewed curve, most of the scores are lumped together on the right side of the curve, above the mean. If we return to the example of communication students, this sample of students is also likely to have a negatively skewed distribution of communication competence scores. As students complete the skill or performance element in each class, they become more competent in their interactions. As a result, very few students in the department would have very low communication competence scores.

Notice the relative positions of the mean, median, and mode on the skewed distributions. The mean is always pulled to the skewed side (or side with the tail) of the distribution. Thus, the mean will always be the largest value of the three measures of central tendency in a positively skewed distribution and the smallest in a negatively skewed distribution. When distributions are skewed, the median is a better measure of central tendency than the mean.

Distributions of Data

Anytime you collect data, your first step should be to develop a frequency distribution for each variable in the dataset for which you have collected quantitative data.

Creating a frequency distribution is simple. List the scores in order, from highest to lowest, and then identify the number of times each score occurs (Figure 9.3). With these steps completed,

Data as they were collected	Data ordered from highest to lowest	Scores x	Frequency f
73	83	83	1
82	82	82	1
76	81	81	1
75	80	80	2
83	80	79	3
79	79	78	4
77	79	77	4
76	79	76	4
69	78	75	3
78	78	74	3
71	78	73	1
78	78	72	1
80	77	71	1
77	77	70	1
74	77	69	1
81	77		
74	76		
79	76		
80	76		
78	76		
78	75		
77	75		
77	75		
74	74		
76	74		
79	74		
75	73		
76	72		
70	71		
72	70		
75	69		

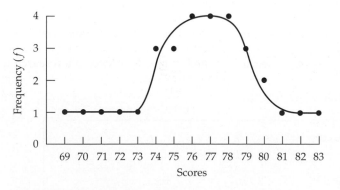

FIGURE 9.3 Developing a Frequency Distribution

you can create a polygon to get a good sense of the normality of the distribution. In this type of diagram, the range of possible scores for the variable is displayed on the horizontal axis. The frequencies with which those scores occur are listed on the vertical axis. With the axes defined, plot each data point according to its frequency of occurrence. Now draw a line to connect each of the points you plotted. How would you interpret the polygon in Figure 9.3 for this dataset? Is it normal? Or is it skewed positively or negatively?

DESCRIPTIVE STATISTICS

Descriptive statistics are those numbers that supply information about the sample or those that supply information about variables. They simply describe what is found. Having this information, researchers and consumers of research reports can make value judgments or inferences about what the data mean.

Researchers describe data for each quantitative variable in three ways: the number of cases or data points, central tendency, and dispersion or variability. Each of these descriptions provides information about the frequency of scores. The number of cases simply indicates the number of sources from which data were collected. Measures of central tendency describe how the majority of participants responded to a variable. Dispersion describes the spread of scores from the point of central tendency. Each of these concepts is described in the following sections. Figure 9.4 shows abbreviations commonly used in descriptive statistics.

Descriptive statistics provide a standardized method and procedure for summarizing and organizing all cases of one quantitative variable. In a research study, descriptive statistics are computed for each variable. When this step is complete, researchers use this information to assess differences and relationships between variables.

Recall from Chapter 5, on measurement, that data can be captured in four levels: nominal, ordinal, interval, and ratio. Data must be collected at interval or ratio levels for the mean and median to be computed. Of course, the number of cases and the mode can be computed for data at any level.

Number of Cases

Generally, the greater the **number of cases,** or data points, the more reliable the data. One way for consumers of research to make this determination is to look for this information in the methods or results section of the written research report. The number of cases for which data are reported is represented by the letter n or N (for example, $N = 231$). Although styles vary by journals, generally N refers to the total number in a sample, whereas n refers to a subsample, or a group of cases drawn from the sample.

Remember that the number of cases may not always be the number of people. Rather, cases may be the number of speaking turns, arguments, conflict episodes, or commercials—virtually any type of communication phenomenon that a researcher has identified in a research question or hypothesis.

Number of cases	n	N
Frequency	f	
Mean	M	$\overline{X}$
Median	Mdn	
Mode	Mo	
Standard deviation	sd	SD

FIGURE 9.4 Symbols Used to Represent Descriptive Statistics

TRY THIS!   ## Are the Data Normal or Skewed?

One of the best ways to learn about the normal curve, and potentially skewed distributions, is to collect data and diagram the data. Collect data from at least two of the following populations (admittedly, you will not be conducting a random sample) and plot the data as a frequency distribution. Try to get at least 50 cases in your sample.

- Shoe sizes of other students (do not mix men and women)
- Number of contacts in the address book of their mobile device
- Number of pets other students have
- Number of times other students have been issued a traffic violation ticket

After plotting your data on a frequency distribution, assess the normalcy of the curve. Does it look more like the normal curve or like a skewed distribution? If it is skewed, what could account for that type of distribution?

Measures of Central Tendency

Measures of **central tendency** are the primary summary form for data. One of the most common summaries is the average. One number, the average, can represent the sample of data on one variable. In other words, this one number acts as a summary of all the scores on one variable. Research reports do not report the data collected for every case on every variable. Instead, researchers report summary statistics for each variable. But there are several measures of central tendency in statistics. In research, we must specify which one we're using.

Mean   The arithmetic **mean,** or simply the mean, is the most common measure of central tendency. Commonly referred to as the **average,** the mean is computed by adding up all the scores on one variable and then dividing by the number of cases, or *N* for that variable. In this and other statistics, the mean should be calculated to include two decimal points. Because all the scores are added together, the mean depends upon each and every score available. If one score is changed, the mean will also change. The mean is the most sensitive to extremely high or extremely low values of the distribution, and it is the most commonly reported measure of central tendency.

Median   Another measure of central tendency is the **median.** The median is the middle of all the scores on one variable. To compute the median, the data (or scores) must be arranged in order from smallest to largest. If there is an uneven number of cases, the median is the score exactly in the middle of the distribution. If there is an even number of scores, the median is found by counting equally from the smallest and largest numbers to the midpoint where no number exists. Take the numbers above and below this midpoint, add them together, and divide by 2. This calculation is the median. It may or may not be the same as the mean for a set of scores. Because the median is always in the middle, scores in the dataset can change without the median being affected.

Look at Figure 9.5. Notice the line between 76 and 75 on the numbers in the ordered list. This is the midpoint of the dataset. Because a researcher cannot report the midpoint as "between 76 and 75," he or she adds the two numbers together (76 + 75 = 151). This total is divided by 2 (151/2 = 75.5) to find the median of the dataset, or 75.5.

Mode   A third measure of central tendency is the **mode.** The mode is the score that appears

Data in its raw order form	Data in order from highest to lowest
73	83
83	83
75	80
83	80
79	79
69	78
78	78
71	78
62	78
78	76
80	75
74	75
73	74
80	73
78	73
56	71
78	69
64	64
76	62
75	56

Descriptive statistics for the dataset:
mean = 74.25
standard deviation = 7.00
median = 75.5 (the two middle scores of 76 and 75 are averaged)
mode = 78
range = 27, from 56 to 83
$N = 20$

FIGURE 9.5 The Data from a Measure of Communication Competence

most often in a dataset. If datasets are large, it is common for the dataset to be bimodal or multimodal, which means that more than one score has the largest frequency of occurrence. In fact, most distributions of scores are bimodal or multimodal, making it impossible for a researcher to use the mode to represent the average in later statistical calculations.

Looking at the dataset in Figure 9.5, you can see that the value of 78 is the most frequent score. Thus, 78 is the mode for this dataset.

If a distribution of scores is normal, or completely symmetrical, the mean, median, and mode will be the same number. But data are seldom this perfect. It is far more likely that a distribution of scores will be somewhat asymmetrical. Thus, the mean, median, and mode will be different.

Most researchers report and use the mean in describing the data for a variable. It is an appropriate choice if the distribution is relatively normal. But if a set of scores is skewed, it may be better to report the median and use it in later calculations because it better reflects the middle of the distribution. Computing the variability in the scores can help you determine whether the mean or median is most appropriate. Mode scores are infrequently reported. When they are, the mean or median scores accompany them as well.

Measures of Dispersion

To fully describe a distribution of data, a measure of dispersion, or variability, is also needed. Two distributions can have the same mean but different spreads of scores. Whenever a measure of central tendency is used, a measure of dispersion should also be reported. The two most commonly reported are the range and the standard deviation; both provide information about the variability of the dataset.

Range   The simplest measure of dispersion is the **range,** or the value calculated by subtracting the lowest score from the highest score. Generally, the range is used to report the high and low scores on questionnaires. For example, for the data shown in Figure 9.5, the range of 27 is the result of subtracting 56, the lowest score, from 83, the highest score. The range is a crude measure of dispersion because changing any values between the highest and lowest score will have no effect on it.

The range can also be used to describe demographic characteristics of the research participants. In these instances, however, the lowest value is not subtracted from the highest value. Rather, the researcher simply reports the highest and lowest values. For example, Sidelinger, Frisby, and McMullen (2009) describe their participants in the following way:

> The female ($n = 145$) participants' mean age was 28.66 ($SD = 12.14$), range 18 to 66, and the mean age of the male ($n = 145$) participants was 30.43 ($SD = 12.40$), range 18 to 67. (p. 170)

Some scholars might report the range for females in age here simply as a range of 48 years (for example, $66 - 18 = 48$). However, reporting just the distance between the smallest and largest value does not tell us what part of the age continuum participants represent. It is more effective to report the smallest and largest value, as Sidelinger et al. demonstrate.

Standard Deviation   Even when the range is reported, it is impossible to determine how close or how far apart the scores are from one another. Thus, researchers use **standard deviation** as the standard calculation and representation of the variability of a dataset. The formula for computing a standard deviation is available at www.mhhe.com/keyton4 in the Student Learning Center. Of course, you can use any spreadsheet or statistical software program to calculate

the standard deviation. Both the mean and standard deviation are commonly reported; see the previous example—for each mean reported, the researchers also reported the standard deviation. In fact, the mean reported by itself is not interpretable. For instance, the larger the standard deviation, the greater the degree the scores differ from the mean. Alternatively, if the standard deviation is small, this indicates that the scores were very similar or close to one another. Or, if the standard deviation is zero, all the scores are the same.

Notice the vertical markers in the normal distribution in Figure 9.6. The middle marker is the point at which the mean exists. Now notice the two points on either side of the mean where the curve changes direction from convex to concave. These are the inflection points at which the +1 and −1 standard deviations are placed. The perpendicular lines to the right of the mean are positive standards of +1, +2, and +3. The perpendicular lines to the left of the mean are negative standards of −1, −2, and −3. The distances between the perpendicular lines are equal and, in turn, divide the horizontal axis into standard deviations.

Regardless of what your data are measuring or the range of scores in your dataset, the normal curve and this set of standards are always the same. This is a property of the theoretical normal curve. The more normal a distribution of scores, the more this property, or rule, applies. The less normal the distribution, the less accurate this rule. Using the normal curve as a base and the standard deviation for a set of scores, the distribution of scores for a variable can be compared to the normal curve. Thus, researchers use the theoretical normal curve to assess the distribution of the data they obtained. When a distribution is not normal, researchers should provide some explanation for this phenomenon.

The area of the curve between the +1 and −1 standards is identified in a variety of ways, including "within one standard deviation of the mean" and "one standard deviation above and below the mean." According to the theoretical normal curve, 68.26% of the cases in a dataset will fall within the +1 to −1 standards (see Figure 9.6).

To find the range of scores from a dataset that would fall within the +1 to −1 standard deviations, simply add the standard deviation to the

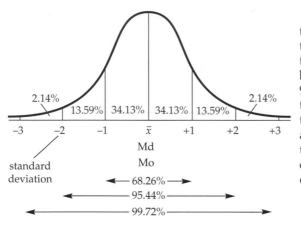

FIGURE 9.6 *Standard Deviations of the Normal Curve*

The further out a score on the distribution, the more extreme the score. The area between the +2 and −2 standard deviations would contain 95.44% of the scores in that dataset. The area between +3 and −3 standards would contain 99.72% of the scores in the dataset. Notice that the normal curve does not touch the horizontal axis. Rather, it extends infinitely to the right and the left. Remember that the normal curve is theoretical and must allow for the most extreme cases, even those that fall outside +3 or −3 standard deviations.

mean (or subtract it). When researchers refer to the typical participant or typical score, they are referring to the range of scores within this area. For example, if your score on some measure of communication apprehension fell within these standards, you would be considered as average, or someone for whom apprehension is not exceptional in either direction.

For the set of scores used in Figure 9.5 ($M = 74.25$; $SD = 7.00$), the following would represent the range of scores within the +1 to −1 standard deviations:

$M = 74.25$: Add the standard deviation of 7.00 to equal 81.25, or the score at the +1 standard deviation.

$M = 74.25$: Subtract the standard deviation of 7.00 to equal 67.25, or the score at the −1 standard deviation.

Thus, in this case, scores from 67 to 81 would be within the +1 to −1 standards and considered typical for this sample. To check, count the frequency of scores with values from 67 to 81. That count should be 15 out of 20, or 75% of total number of cases. When the curve is normal, about 68% of the cases should lie between these two values. The remaining cases are above and below these values.

APPLICATION OF DESCRIPTIVE STATISTICS

One reason the mean, median, and standard deviation are reported in the method section of a written research report is so the reader can assess the normalcy of the data. Descriptive findings also help the reader interpret the conclusions drawn from data (Levine, Weber, Park, & Hullett, 2008). The following excerpt from a research report characterizes one way researchers (Mendelson & Thorson, 2004) report this information:

> Participants in the study had a mean visualizer score of 23.67 ($SD = 8.35$) on a scale that varied from 10 to 70, with 10 being most visual. The *most visual* person in the samples scored a 10 and the *least visual* scored a 53. Cronbach's α for the 10 items on the visual scale was .71. (p. 482)

With this information, the mean and standard deviation can be interpreted to reveal the normalcy of the scores for the visualizer variable. In this case, it is easy to see that the variable had a positively skewed distribution, or very few very high scores.

Alternatively, when the distribution of scores appears normal, researchers indicate this by phrases such as "The distribution of scores approximated the normal curve" or "The distribution of scores appeared normal."

Frequencies and percentages are also commonly used to provide summaries of nominal data. Examples of each will demonstrate their utility.

AN ETHICAL ISSUE

Mistakes in Calculations

Whether you collect data by yourself or with the help of others, whether you calculate with a spreadsheet or statistical program, and whether you interpret data by yourself or with the help of an expert, as the researcher who reports the data, you are ultimately responsible for all aspects of data collection. Why? Because the researcher is the author of the research report. Thus, double-checking the procedures for data collection, the validity of the data as it is entered, and the results are all responsibilities of the researcher—no one else. Failing to take the time to double-check and failing to correct mistakes when they are found are ethical violations of scientific standards. People trust what they read to be accurate. In fact, they may use reported results to develop a communication training program to help others or to alter their own communication behaviors. A researcher's credibility—past, present, and future—rests on the extent to which consumers trust what they read. If you are collecting data for a project, you should double-check everything.

Frequencies

A commonly used descriptive statistic is **frequency**, or the number of times a particular value of a variable occurs. Communication researchers often use frequency data to report on the occurrence of communication events. This type of data is actually at the nominal level, because the researcher is making a decision for each occurrence—did this communication phenomenon occur or did it not?

For example, Roberts (2013) explored how television and Web-only ads were used in the 2004 and 2008 U.S. presidential elections. The researcher reported the findings of the analysis as frequencies, as shown in Table 9.1.

The table provides basic descriptive information about what the researcher discovered. Across the 817 advertisements that were included in the study, ads were first coded by media type (television or Web). Next ads were coded for the function they served (candidate acclaims himself as better than other candidate, candidate attacks opponent, or candidate defends against opponent's attack) and their theme (ad addresses

TABLE 9.1 Number and Percentage of All Spots by Presence of Function and Theme

	Acclaim*		Attack**		Defend		Policy***		Character	
	f	%	f	%	f	%	f	%	f	%
Television (n = 742)[a]	565	76.1	402	54.2	32	4.3	643	86.7	572	77.1
Web only (n = 75)[a]	33	44.0	54	72.0	4	5.3	52	69.3	64	85.3
Total (N = 817)	598	73.2	456	55.8	36	4.4	695	85.1	636	77.8

[a]n is total spots in a row.
*$\chi^2(1, N = 817) = 35.841, p < .001, \Phi$ Cramer's $V = -.210$.
**$\chi^2(1, N = 817) = 8.773, p = .003, \Phi$ Cramer's $V = -.210$.
***$\chi^2(1, N = 817) = 16.094, p < .001, \Phi$ Cramer's $V = -.140$.
SOURCE: "A Functional Analysis Comparison of Web-Only Advertisements and Traditional Television Advertisements from the 2004 and 2008 Presidential Campaigns," by Chris Roberts, *Journalism and Mass Communication* (Vol. 90, Issue 1), p. 16, copyright © 2013 by SAGE Publications. Reprinted by Permission of SAGE Publications.

policy issues, or ad addresses character or personal issues). Because political ads are often complex, coders could assign more than one function or theme to each advertisement. By looking at the frequencies in Table 9.1, you can determine that television ads were more frequent than Web-only ads. You can also tell that ads acclaiming, or promoting, the candidate were most frequent, and that ads in which the candidates defends himself are less frequent. With respect to theme, you can tell that the advertisements that addressed policy issues were only slightly more frequent than ads that addressed a candidate's character. Examining the frequencies the researcher reports indicate what functions and what themes presidential campaign ads are more likely to promote.

Percentages

Most commonly, we think of a **percentage** as being a number that represents some part of 100. But not all variable scores use 100 as the base or foundation. Thus, it is more accurate to describe a percentage as a comparison between the base, which can be any number, and a second number that is compared to the base. Look again at the previous example for the frequencies and percentages reported in Table 9.1. The number of ads on television is the basis for the percentages on the top row, the number of ads on the Web is the basis for the percentages on the middle, and the total number of advertisements coded is the basis for the percentages on the bottom row.

Percentages are also frequently used to describe attributes of participants or characteristics of their communication behavior. For a study that examined how parents mediate their tweens' (for example, ages 8 to 14) disclosure of information online (Wonsun, Jisu, & Faber, 2012), the following percentages are reported:

> The tween sample consisted of 201 boys (52.8%) and 177 girls (46.5%). Three did not indicate their gender. Nine out of ten tweens (89.8%) reported they had computers that they could use at home, and 98% of those computers were connected to the Internet. About 33% of computers were located in tweens' own rooms and 49% were in their parents' room or the living room. Fifty-seven percent of tweens had their own personal Web sites. (p. 641)

By putting data from the study's participants in percentage form, the researchers make it easy for the reader to get an idea of the degree to which tweens in the study had access to online technology and the degree to which their technology use was private. With that information, readers can make an assessment about the degree to which the sample is relevant and appropriate for the study.

CRUNCHING THE NUMBERS

In research, enough data are collected that computing statistics by hand is generally out of the question. But for small datasets, you will be able to

---

DESIGN CHECK

Describing Variables

When reading a research report, look for the descriptive statistics for each variable in the methods section or in a table. Here you should find

1. The number of cases for this variable

2. The mean or median

3. The standard deviation

4. The range of scores possible or the range of scores obtained

With this information you can make a determination of the normalcy of the data even if the researcher omits this description.

perform the needed calculations with a calculator, as long as it has a square root function. The square root function is indicated by the symbol $\sqrt{}$.

With medium or large datasets, you will need to use a spreadsheet program (such as Excel) or a statistics program (such as SAS or SPSS). A spreadsheet program works just fine for simple data analysis projects and is easy to use. Programs specifically designed for statistical use require a more specialized knowledge of statistics and programming.

One caution, however, about using any software program to help compute statistics is that although programs compute the statistical tests, the program relies on you to request the appropriate test and to make the appropriate interpretation of the outcome. Likewise, the program relies on you to indicate which data should be included in the test. If you specify the wrong test or indicate the wrong data to be used for that test, the software program will still do the calculation and provide a result—but it will be the wrong result or a noninterpretable result! If you are going to use any of these programs, you need basic instruction on how to set up the spreadsheet or statistical program, how to enter data, and how to appropriately run and interpret the statistical tests.

Despite the obvious advantages, the use of spreadsheet or statistical software can create a false sense of security. There are five issues that you should consider if you use these programs for data entry and statistical computation (Pedhazur & Schmelkin, 1991). First, computers can fail. Programs can stall. Never trust all your data to one file on one storage device. Second, results can only be as good as the data entered. Whereas a spreadsheet or statistical package may decrease the number of computational errors, data-entry errors can still occur. Errors such as entering the wrong value or omitting a value are common. Because your conclusions and interpretations rest on the validity of the data, it is wise to double-check all data entered.

Third, researchers—even experienced ones—tend to limit their thinking to statistical procedures they know they can do on the computer. Researchers always need to be mindful of this and periodically stretch their statistical knowledge

and expertise. Fourth, the power of computing makes it possible to create an abundance of analyses. Do not be tempted to "see what will happen" by running any and all statistics. Rather, the techniques and statistics chosen should be driven by your research questions and hypotheses. Finally, as the researcher, you are the person responsible for the results and their interpretations, even if someone else does your statistical programming.

For quantitative research, descriptive statistics simply describe the data. To provide answers to hypotheses and research questions, researchers then set significance levels.

SIGNIFICANCE LEVELS

A **significance level** is a criterion for accepting or rejecting hypotheses and is based on probability. *Probability* is a scientific term to identify how much error the researcher finds acceptable in a particular statistical test. But you are also familiar with the concept of probability in a less scientific sense. You have made many decisions in your life based on the degree of probability for some event occurring. Did you ever drive to the beach even though rain clouds were approaching? Have you ever gambled that you had enough gas to get you to your destination? Did you choose to ask either your mother or your father for money based on the likelihood of which one would give it to you? In these decisions and others similar to them, you were basing your actions on your informal rules of probability. In other words, you accepted a certain degree of risk, or error, in making these decisions. It probably would not rain, but what if it did? The last time your fuel gauge was close to empty you drove another 50 miles without a problem. And you knew it was better to ask your mom than ask your dad, as your mom usually said yes.

In scientific research, **probability** is an estimate of "what would happen if the study were actually repeated many times, telling the researcher how wrong the results can be" (Katzer et al., 1978, p. 60). In other words, probability is a calculation about the validity of the results. Researchers could choose to conduct the same survey or experiment many times, but calculating the probability, or significance, of a statistical test for a sample of data has become the accepted manner in which scientists deal with this issue. As a result, the level of probability provides an estimate of the degree to which data from a sample would reflect data from the population the sample was drawn from.

Perhaps you are thinking, "Why wouldn't the results of a study be valid?" In some cases, researchers are looking to make inferences from the sample, or people who participated in their particular study, to the population, or larger group from which the sample was pulled. Accepting the conclusions derived from the sample and assuming that those conclusions are also applicable to the population is known as **population inference.** More commonly in communication research, studies are designed to test the predictions of a theory (Hayes, 2005). In other words, are the data consistent with the predictions the researcher drew from the theory? If so, then the researcher can claim that the theory would likely work in similar situations. This is known as **process inference.** Social scientists base this inference on the probability level computed for each statistical test. The **probability level,** or significance level, which is established for each statistical test prior to computing the statistical test, is the level of error the researcher is willing to accept. You will find this symbolized in written research reports as the letter p or referred to as the **alpha level.** If the probability level of the statistical test is acceptable, or within the traditions of the discipline, then the findings are believed to be real, not random, and the inference can be presumed to be valid. If the probability level is unacceptable, no conclusion can be drawn (Boster, 2002).

Generally, the probability level of .05 is accepted as the standard in the communication discipline. This means that 5 out of 100 findings that appear to be valid will, in fact, be due to chance. When the probability level of a statistical test is .05 or less, the finding is real, and labeled as statistically significant. Setting the standard as a .05 probability level is arbitrary; generally, communication researchers have adopted this standard (.01 and .001 are other common standards). You should note, however, that the selection of a .05

probability level was not based on mathematical, statistical, or substantive theory (Henkel, 1976).

If the probability level of a statistical test is greater than .05 (for example, $p = .15$, $p = .21$), the finding is labeled nonsignificant. This means that the difference could easily be caused by chance or random error. What causes the probability level to be unacceptable, or higher than .05? Many things can contribute to high probability levels.

Items on a survey or questionnaire intended to measure a construct may be so poorly written that participants respond inconsistently to them. The researcher or assistants conducting an experiment can also create bias that generates unacceptable levels of probability. For example, male participants may be treated differently from female participants. Research assistants may unconsciously smile at participants they know and ignore those with whom they are unfamiliar. Or, the theory, which was the foundation of the study, is not accurate or the theory was not adequately or appropriately tested (Hayes, 2005). It is important to remember that setting the significance level at .05 is arbitrary. There can be good reasons to make the probability level more rigorous, setting it, for example, at .01. In their study of the effectiveness of message strategies for talking about AIDS and condom use, Reel and Thompson (1994) set the level at < .01. Why? The probability level needed to be more rigorous because the results of the study have direct implications for AIDS education efforts. Thus, the researchers had to create greater certainty about the results they achieved. Because a person's health could be at risk, they would not want to recommend strategies as being effective when that effectiveness in the study could have resulted from random chance or error.

Seldom is there a good reason to set the probability level at a more generous level of .10. If the researcher does set a higher probably level, he or she would be allowing more opportunity for research results to support a claim when, in reality, it is not supported.

It is tempting to believe that achieving statistical significance proves something. Recognize, however, that achieving statistical significance does not guarantee **social significance** of the result (Selltiz et al., 1959). Using a very large sample can create statistically significant differences that have little relevance in application. Also recognize that how a researcher interprets a statistical finding is as important as the level of significance the researcher chooses. The research process is more subjective than objective. Thus, statistical significance must always be interpreted with respect to social and practical significance—or how the results might actually be applied or used in everyday life (Kirk, 1996). Statistical significance must also be interpreted with respect to how the population was defined and to how the sample was selected.

HYPOTHESIS TESTING

Recall from Chapter 4 that hypotheses state the expected relationship or difference between two or more variables. Also recall that whereas scientific tradition privileges the alternative hypothesis in the writing of journal articles, it is technically the null hypothesis that is statistically tested. Hypothesis testing, relies on the two scientific techniques, significance testing and sampling (Chapter 6).

Testing the null hypothesis is, in essence, an act of decision making. Do you accept the alternative explanation, or do you retain the null hypothesis? Most researchers rely on the conventions of hypothesis testing because, combined with random sampling and significance testing, they can be effective in separating those hypotheses and their results that deserve additional attention from those that do not (Harlow, 1997). But, as with significance levels, these traditions are not absolute.

Researchers develop an alternative hypothesis, an assertion that states how they believe the variables are related or are different. However, in hypothesis testing, belief in the null hypothesis continues until there is sufficient evidence to make the assertion of the null hypothesis unreasonable. This decision is based on a comparison between the significance level established by the researcher prior to conducting the study, usually .05, and the significance level produced by the calculation of the statistical test. If the significance level computed for the statistical test is .05 or less, the alternative hypothesis is accepted. However, if the significance level computed for the statistical test is greater than .05, the null hypothesis is retained, as no conclusion can be drawn about the relationship or difference between the variables tested.

In the hypothesis testing process, two types of error can occur. Known as Type I and Type II errors, these represent decision errors in accepting or rejecting the null hypothesis. **Type I error** occurs when the null hypothesis is rejected even when it is true. The level of Type I error is set or controlled by the researcher when he or she chooses the significance level for the statistical test. Often called the alpha level, it is the same as the level of significance described earlier. Thus, if the significance level is set at .05, there is a 5% chance that the null hypothesis will be rejected even though it is true. This means that you run some risk in accepting the premise of the alternative, or research, hypothesis when in fact the premise would not hold. Another way of interpreting the .05 alpha level is to recognize that this significance level will retain a true null hypothesis 95% of the time. Recognize that anytime hypotheses are tested, some error of this type will occur.

Alternatively, **Type II error** occurs in the opposite case. Now the level of significance is not met. Thus, the researchers simultaneously fail to reject, or they accept, the null hypothesis and reject the alternative hypothesis. Type II error results when the alternative hypothesis is rejected even when it is true. One way the researcher can control the level of Type II error is to increase the sample size.

Table 9.2 can help you see the relationship between Type I and Type II errors. With each hypothesis tested, four outcomes are possible. Obviously, the goal of research is to make good decisions. However, the research process is not perfect, and error and bias can be introduced in many places—for example, errors can occur in selection of sample and in measurement. Hypothesis testing allows the researcher opportunities to control some of the error. Type I error can be controlled in setting a significance level that is appropriate. Type II error can be controlled by increasing the sample size.

TABLE 9.2 Relationship Between Type I and Type II Errors

	In Reality, the Null Hypothesis Is True	*In Reality, the Null Hypothesis Is False*
Researcher uses level of significance to reject the null hypothesis.	**Type I Error**—The null hypothesis is rejected even though it is true, OR researcher claims some difference or relationship exists when one does not.	**Decision 1**—The null hypothesis is rejected when it is false (or the alternative hypothesis is accepted), OR researcher claims some difference or relationship exists and that difference or relationship is found.
Researcher uses level of significance to retain the null hypothesis.	**Decision 2**—The null hypothesis is retained (or the researcher fails to reject the null hypothesis) when it is true, OR researcher does not claim a difference or relationship, and one is not identified.	**Type II Error**—The null hypothesis is retained even though it is false, OR researcher misses claiming a difference or relationship that is real.

You will find both types of decisions about hypotheses—Decision 1 and Decision 2 in Table 9.2—in the research literature. Looking at an example for each will help you apply these decision rules about hypotheses to a research setting. For example, the purpose of one study (Schrodt, 2009) was to test if family communication environments build family strength. In essence, the prediction was that families that created environments characterized by open expression of feelings for the purposes of problem solving and easing tensions would influence the commitment of family members to one another and the family as a unit.

To explore those interactions, 426 young adult children from first-marriage families in the midwest ($M = 19.54$, $SD = 1.31$, range 18 to 24) participated in a survey. The survey included measures of the family communication environment and family strength. For example, one item of the first scale was "My parents often ask my opinion when the family is talking about something;" an example item from the second was "We share similar beliefs and values as a family." Based on the literature, Schrodt (2009) hypothesized that "family expressiveness is positively associated with family strength" (p. 175). Results from this descriptive study supported the hypothesis. Schrodt reports "The results indicate that family expressiveness has a strong, positive association with family strength" (p. 181). These

decisions, like Decision 1 in Table 9.2, are presented in research reports in the following ways:

- The hypothesis is supported.
- The alternative hypothesis is accepted.
- Support was found for this hypothesis.
- The results were statistically significant.
- Results support this prediction.
- Results support this hypothesis.
- The hypothesis is confirmed.

In essence, the researcher is saying that the alternative hypothesis asserted some difference or relationship and that the research succeeded in finding that very difference or relationship. Many researchers do not use phrases like "reject the null hypothesis" because technically, the null hypothesis can never be rejected since there is always some possibility that it is true. This is where the level of significance comes into play. Remember that researchers set the alpha level, usually at .05 and never at .00. Thus, we can never be absolutely certain about the truth of the null hypothesis.

Now, lets' examine Decision 2 from Table 9.2. Recall that researchers are usually interested in the research, or alternative, hypothesis even though they are statistically testing the null hypothesis. It is unusual for researchers to want to confirm the null. So how do researchers describe Decision 2 when their results do not support the alternative hypothesis?

One research study (Richards & Nelson, 2012) explored if children of adult alcoholics were different with respect to their perceptions of health self-efficacy, or one's belief in their ability to achieve health-related goals, from children whose parents were not alcoholics. There have been only a few studies that examine the communication-related issues of being a child of alcoholic parents. But there is evidence that suggests that parental alcoholism has consequences for their children. Research has demonstrated that health self-efficacy is important to family-related health outcomes, as well as disease management. Thus, it makes sense that the researchers would hypothesize that a difference on health self-efficacy would exist for those who do and do not self-identify as children of adult alcoholics. Over 300 college students participated in the study. On average, participants were 20.76 years of age. Participants self-identified themselves as children of adult alcoholics using a 30-item scale with items, such as "Have you ever felt sick, cried, or had a knot in your stomach after worrying about a parent's drinking?" If participants responded yes to six or more of the 30 questions, they were categorized as adult children of alcoholics. Health self-efficacy was operationalized with five items (for example, "I am confident I can have a positive effect on my health."). However, this hypothesis was not supported. Health self-efficacy scores did not differ between those who had alcoholic parents and those who did not. These decisions, like Decision 2 in Table 9.2, are presented in research reports in the following ways:

- The [alternative] hypothesis was not supported.
- The results were not statistically significant.
- The null hypothesis is accepted.
- Results failed to support the [alternative] hypothesis
- No support emerged for the [alternative] hypothesis.
- The [alternative] hypothesis is rejected.

In essence, the researcher is saying that the alternative hypothesis asserted some difference or relationship and that findings from the study could not confirm the difference or relationship proposed. Thus, the null hypothesis is retained.

How do significance level and these principles of hypothesis testing apply to research questions? Recall that a research question is used because there is not enough prior evidence from which to develop a position or an assertion for a hypothesis. When a research question is used, the researcher uses the results to answer the question. Whereas hypotheses make assertions that must be responded to with a "yes, you are correct" or "no, you are not correct" type of decision, a research question poses a question that can be answered in a greater variety of ways. Thus, even though researchers set a significance level for statistical tests associated with research questions, there is no way to accept or reject a research question.

A FINAL WORD

One of the difficulties in learning about scientific traditions is to recognize that the principles addressed in this chapter are just that, traditions. There is not an absolute or objective set of research procedures that guarantee correct interpretation of results or that can be justified in every case (Abelson, 1997). In fact, the traditions used for setting significance levels and hypothesis testing have been widely disputed by scientists from many disciplines (Boster, 2002; Harlow, Mulaik, & Steiger, 1997; Hayes, 2009; Judd, McClelland, & Culhane, 1995; Levine, Weber, Hullett, Park, & Lindsey, 2008).

One way to integrate the use of scientific traditions but still honor the subjective interpretations of researchers is to view these traditions as interpretive tools rather than as absolute decision makers. These traditions invoke strong language—fail to reject the null hypothesis, accept the alternative hypothesis—that overemphasizes an either/or decision. A more contemporary view is that scientific traditions should aid the judgment of the researcher, not dictate it (Abelson, 1995).

SUMMARY

1. Numbers are one of many tools researchers use to collect data.

2. From the raw data collected, researchers compute the descriptive statistics that convey essential summary data of the dataset as a whole.

3. The normal curve is a theoretical distribution in which the majority of cases peak in the middle of the distribution, with progressively fewer cases as one moves away from the middle of the curve.

4. In normal distributions, one side mirrors the other; the curve is symmetrical.

5. In positively or negatively skewed distributions, the curve is asymmetrical.

6. Frequency distributions and polygons are the first step in analyzing a set of scores for one variable.

7. Descriptive statistics—number of cases, central tendency, and dispersion—are summary information about the dataset for one variable.

8. The number of cases is the number of data points.

9. Measures of central tendency—mean, median, or mode—reflect different types of average or typical data.

10. Measures of dispersion—range and standard deviation—provide a description of the variability of the data.

11. Researchers also use frequencies and percentages to describe their data.

12. Researchers are responsible for the results and their interpretations, even if an expert helps them in this aspect of the research process.

13. Significance levels are set for each statistical test used in a research project; generally, the probability level of .05 is accepted as the standard in communication research.

14. Hypothesis testing is based on probability sampling techniques and the stated level of significance.

15. By convention, researchers are interested in the alternative hypothesis but statistically test the null hypothesis.

16. Hypothesis testing is an act of decision making—accepting the alternative hypothesis or retaining the null hypothesis.

17. Type I and Type II errors occur when researchers accept or reject results as valid when the opposite is true.

KEY TERMS

alpha level	percentage
average	population inference
central tendency	positively skewed curve
data	
dataset	probability
descriptive statistics	probability level
frequency	process inference
inferential statistics	range
mean	raw data
median	significance level
mode	skewed distribution
negatively skewed curve	social significance
	standard deviation
normal curve	Type I error
number of cases	Type II error

See the website www.mhhe.com/keyton4 that accompanies this text. For each chapter, the site contains a:

- chapter outline
- chapter checklist
- chapter summary
- short multiple-choice quiz
- PowerPoint presentation created by Dr. Keyton

For a list of internet resources, visit http:// www.joannkeyton.com/CommunicationResearch-Methods.htm.

CHAPTER TEN

Testing for Differences

Chapter Checklist

After reading this chapter, you should be able to:

1. Explain the difference between descriptive and inferential statistics.

2. Use the four analytical steps to design and evaluate research designs and statistical findings.

3. Develop a hypothesis or research question and select the appropriate statistical test of difference (chi-square, *t*-test, ANOVA).

4. Differentiate among the assumptions and functions of chi-squares, *t*-tests, and ANOVAs.

5. Interpret research findings developed from results of chi-squares, *t*-tests, and ANOVAs.

Whether the research design is experimental, quasi-experimental, or descriptive, many researchers develop their studies to look for differences. Recall from earlier chapters that some hypotheses and research questions contain independent or predictor variables for which the data are nominal or categorical. When this is the case, communication researchers can hypothesize that differences in the independent or predictor variable will result in differences in the dependent variable. In these instances, researchers are looking for differences between or among the groups or categories of the independent variable in relationship to the dependent variable.

In a study of how people evaluate the statements organizations release after a public relations crisis, Lee and Chung (2012) hypothesized that apology statements with active responsibility are more likely to relieve public anger than apology statements with passive responsibility. Here the independent variable would be type of organizational apology statement: an apology statement in which the organization clearly takes responsibility for the problem, or an apology statement in which the organization expresses concern for the problem but does not directly take responsibility. Participants were randomly assigned to one of the conditions in which they read the news story about the organization's public relations crisis, and then read one of the versions of the organization's apology. The dependent variable was anger toward the organization, which was captured by their reporting the degree to which they were angry, mad, irritated, annoyed, and outraged with the organization. The hypothesis states that participants' anger toward the organization would differ based on which apology statement they read. In other words, does it matter which *group* participants were assigned to? Does the group, or condition, the participants were randomly assigned to create a difference in their report of anger toward the organization?

Another example is a study that investigated if and how participants perceived the credibility of mainstream and independent online news sources (Chung, Nam, & Stefanone, 2012). The study's hypothesis stated the presumption, "There are differences in credibility assessments among online news sources" (p. 174). A statistical test of difference would ask if participants' perceptions of credibility, the dependent variable, is different for mainstream and independent online news sources (type of online news source as the independent variable). In either of these cases, we could look at the scores in the dataset to see if the mean scores for the dependent variable were different based on the categories of the independent variables. But knowing that a simple difference exists in mean scores is not enough. Rather, researchers use inferential statistics to ask, Are those differences big enough to make a real difference—are they statistically significant? In other words, are the differences observed greater than the differences that might occur due to chance? Before we discuss three types of tests for differences—chi-square, *t*-test, and analysis of variance (ANOVA)—a brief explanation of inferential statistics is in order.

INFERENTIAL STATISTICS

In contrast to descriptive statistics described in Chapter 9, **inferential statistics** are used to draw conclusions about a population by examining the sample. On a more basic level, inferential statistics help researchers test hypotheses and answer research questions, and derive meaning from the results. With these steps complete, the results or findings from a sample on a statistical test can be used to make inferences about the population. A result found to be statistically significant by testing the sample is assumed to also hold for the population from which the sample was drawn. The ability to make such an inference is based on the principle of probability. Recall from Chapter 9 that researchers set the significance level for each statistical test they conduct. By using probability theory as a basis for their tests, researchers can assess how likely it is that the difference they find is real, not due to chance.

Three other assumptions accompany inferential statistics. The first is that the populations from which samples are drawn are normally distributed on the dependent variable. Let's say that the dependent variable is communication competence. If the population is normally distributed, and the sample is randomly selected, the communication competence scores for this sample would also be expected to be normally distributed. When a normal distribution is not known or cannot be assumed, a statistical test can provide only approximations of the differences.

The second assumption is that participants are randomly sampled from a larger population. In random sampling, each person has the same chance as every other person in the population to be selected to participate in the study.

The third assumption is that participants are randomly assigned to categories or groups of the independent variable. Recall that random assignment occurs when participants have an equal chance of being assigned to any one of the treatment or control groups. Researchers use random assignment to help ensure that groups are similar to one another. In other words, the random assignment procedure is used to reduce bias. When participants are randomly assigned to treatment or control groups, differences found between these groups are presumed to be due to the effects of the treatments of the independent variables. This assumption is often violated, particularly in communication research in which naturally occurring groups are used as the independent variable.

Many researchers use chi-squares, t-tests, and ANOVAs when their research designs do not meet the basic assumptions on which inferential statistics are based—the principles of probability, normal distribution, random sampling, and random assignment. Generally, meeting these assumptions would require that all communication scholarship be based on experimental designs, and that is not possible or practical when studying some communication phenomena. Some scholars (Lacy & Riffe, 1993; de Vaus, 2001) argue that using inferential statistics when the assumptions cannot be met is inexcusable. Other scholars—by virtue of the many published articles using inferential statistics in quasi-experimental and descriptive research designs without meeting these assumptions—take a more liberal view. Even when all the conditions mentioned are not met, if the researcher bases the research design on theory and appropriate data are collected, inferential statistics can provide information about a particular dataset (Tabachnick & Fidell,

2007). In such a case, however, researchers have to be careful not to overgeneralize their results. It is also important to remember that inferential statistics examine the patterns of scores across a sample of collected data. Examining data at this more holistic level allows a researcher to make inferences from the sample to the population or to test theoretical predictions. Thus, any significant differences found are not differences between individuals; they are differences between groups of individuals.

Alternative and Null Hypotheses

Inferential statistics test the likelihood that the alternative, or research, hypothesis is true and the null hypothesis is not. In testing differences, the alternative, or research, hypothesis would predict that differences would be found, whereas the null hypothesis would predict no differences. By setting the significance level (generally at .05), the researcher has a criterion for making this decision. If the .05 level is achieved (p is equal to or less than .05), then a researcher rejects the null hypothesis and accepts its alternative hypothesis. If the .05 significance level is not achieved, then the null hypothesis is retained. Recall from Chapter 9 that the null hypothesis (for example, that no difference exists) is retained until sufficient statistical support exists for accepting the research hypothesis.

Degrees of Freedom

Degrees of freedom are the way in which the scientific tradition accounts for variation due to error. Represented by the abbreviation *df*, it specifies how many values vary within a statistical test. In other words, scientists recognize that collecting data can never be error free. Each piece of data collected can vary, or carry error that we cannot account for. By including degrees of freedom in statistical computations, scientists help account for this error.

Another way of looking at degrees of freedom is as the latitude of variation within a statistical test (Kerlinger, 1986). For nominal or categorical variables, the general rule is that degrees of freedom will be the number of categories for the variable minus 1. So, if a variable has six categories representing choices the participant could make, the degrees of freedom associated with that variable are 5 (*df* = number of categories − 1). A participant had the opportunity to select five options other than the one chosen.

Although the concept of degrees of freedom can be difficult to comprehend (and such an explanation certainly is beyond this introduction to statistics), there are clear rules for how to calculate the degrees of freedom for each statistical test. These rules will be explained as each test is discussed.

Four Analytical Steps

With inferential statistical tests, there are four major steps to any statistical analysis the researcher undertakes (Simon, 1969). First, the statistical test is applied to determine whether differences or relationships exist. This chapter describes statistical tests of difference (used when data for the independent variable is categorical, or nominal). Chapter 11 describes statistical tests for relationships. In this step, the researcher selects the appropriate statistical test as indicated by the hypothesis or research question. The hypothesis and the statistical test must be parallel. If the hypothesis makes a presumption about differences, a statistical test designed to capture differences must be used. Moreover, which statistical test is used will depend on the type of data collected by the researcher (such as nominal or continuous level data).

The second analytical step characterizes the type of difference or relationship. Sometimes, the difference that appears in the data may not be the difference the researcher predicted. For example, Wong and Householder (2008) induced participants to be in a happy or sad mood by watching a short segment of a situation comedy (*Friends*) or crime drama (*Law & Order*). Next, participants were shown an anti-smoking ad that graphically shows a man dying on an operating table because of smoking. Specifically, the researchers hypothesized that "individuals in a positive mood will report less positive attitudes toward the ad than individuals in a negative mood" (p. 406). However, after running the statistical test, the exact opposite finding was found: Participants who were induced to be in a positive mood reported more positive attitudes toward the ad than negative mood participants. Thus, researchers must check to make sure that the differences they find are indeed the differences they predicted.

The third analytical step assesses the statistical importance of the difference or relationship. Recall from Chapter 9 that a probability level, or significance level, is established for each statistical test used. Knowing that a difference exists and whether it is the difference that is expected is not enough. A researcher must go one step further. Using the significance level, usually set at .05, a researcher can determine if the size of the differences he or she finds can be accepted as real, not random. Alternatively, if the probability level is not achieved, then any differences found are not statistically significant, and no conclusion can be drawn.

Finally, researchers want to move beyond the data tested into the future. Thus, the fourth analytical step evaluates the importance of the observed differences or relationships and then generalizes the findings. To make this evaluation, researchers must assess all the steps in the research process:

- How was the sample obtained?
- Were participants randomly selected?
- Were participants randomly assigned to treatment or control groups?
- To what extent does the sample represent the population in which the researchers are interested?
- Was the research design appropriate for the hypothesis and research question?
- Were the data collected in reliable and valid ways?

By asking and answering these questions, researchers can determine the extent to which they can generalize from the findings of the sample to the population.

Each of these four steps must be completed for each statistical test conducted. Recognize, however, that even with the most effectively designed research study, there is never a guarantee that results from the sample will reflect what happens in the population (Simon, 1969).

How do these analytical steps apply when experimental assumptions are violated? The four steps should be thought of as an ideal practice and should be followed for quasi-experimental and descriptive research designs as well. Obviously, in these cases, the fourth step is most jeopardized and is the one with which researchers must take the most caution.

CHI-SQUARE

Researchers choose **chi-square,** or χ^2, as the statistical test when they want to determine whether differences among categories are statistically significant. Thus, a chi-square is the appropriate test when data for one or more variables are nominal, or categorical. In principle, a chi-square examines the data to see if the categorical differences that occurred are the same as would occur by chance. Researchers compare the **observed frequency,** or the number of times the category actually appears, with the **expected frequency,** or the number of times the category was expected to appear. If the observed frequency exactly matches the expected frequency, then χ^2 is zero. The greater the difference between the observed and expected frequency distributions, the larger the value of χ^2. And, the larger the value of χ^2, the more likely that the difference will be statistically significant.

Researchers obtain observed frequencies from the collected data, but how are expected frequencies obtained? Generally, researchers work from a no-differences model specifying that frequencies for each category of a variable are equal. In this model, an expected frequency is calculated by dividing the number of observations by the number of categories, or cells, for that variable. This results in the same expected frequency value for each cell or category. As an alternative to the no-differences model, researchers can use the published research literature to establish expected frequencies that favor one category over another.

Recall from Chapter 5 that nominal variables do not have a numerical value. Rather, in a chi-square, the frequency for each category is used as the numerical value. As an example, for the nominal variable sex, the frequencies of females and males were 57 and 83, respectively. Each number represents the number of times, or the frequency with which, participants identified themselves as female or male. These values are used to calculate the chi-square. Both types of chi-squares—one-dimensional chi-square and the contingency analysis—rely on frequency data. Each is detailed in the sections that follow.

One-Dimensional Chi-Square

A **one-dimensional,** or **one-way chi-square,** is the statistical test for determining if differences in how the cases are distributed across the categories of one categorical, or nominal, variable are significant. In this case, the chi-square allows the researcher to test the question, "Are the differences found real or due to chance?"

In a study designed to examine how organizational dissent, or employee dissatisfaction, was portrayed on television, Garner, Kinsky, Duta, and Danker (2012) hypothesized that "Organizational dissent portrayed on television will be expressed to supervisors more often than to coworkers" (p. 613). This hypothesis simply stated that one audience for organizational dissent, or employee dissatisfaction, would be found more frequently than another. As is the tradition, the null hypothesis is unstated. If it were stated, it would be something like "Organizational dissent will be offered to supervisors and coworkers equally."

For this study, the researchers identified four potential receivers for organizational dissent: supervisors, coworkers, subordinates, and other dissent audiences. Across 99 dramas and 46 comedies, the research team identified 146 instances of organizational dissent; next they coded to whom the dissent was directed. But just coding and counting which character received the organizational dissent from the sender into the four categories would not reveal if there were statistically significant differences for which type of character was most likely to receive organizational dissent messages. These differences could have occurred by chance. The chi-square is used to demonstrate that the differences in frequencies are real by comparing the observed frequencies to expected frequencies.

TABLE 10.1 Frequency Chart for Organizational Dissent Messages

Supervisors	Coworkers	Subordinates	Other Dissent Targets
82.2%	12.3%	2.7%	2.7%
$n = 120$	$n = 18$	$n = 4$	$n = 4$

Because the null hypothesis states that all types of characters will receive equal amounts of organizational dissent, then the expected frequencies for the four types of receivers should be equal. For the null hypothesis to be retained, the 146 instances of organizational dissent coded for this hypothesis must be distributed equally among supervisors, coworkers, subordinates, and other dissent targets. Each target of organizational dissent should have been used about 36.5 times. But look at Table 10.1, which displays the frequencies and percentages of the data. You can see that television characters did not express their dissent equally across the four categories. The observed frequencies were not the same as the expected frequency of 36.5.

In this case, the chi-square was statistically significant, and the research hypothesis is accepted. Organizational dissent portrayed on television was expressed to supervisors more often than to coworkers. Of the 146 portrayals of organizational dissent, 82.2% were directed to supervisors, 12.3% were directed to coworkers, 2.7% were directed to subordinates, and 2.7% were direct to other dissent audiences. The significant chi-square demonstrates that the distribution of target for messages of organizational dissent on television did not occur by chance.

Now, take a look at how this chi-square was reported by the authors in the journal article. The hypothesis Garner and colleagues (2012) proposed was supported ($\chi^2 = 258.27$, $df = 3$, $p < .001$). The calculated chi-square value of 258.27 results from the statistical computation of the test. The formula and steps can be found at the website www.mhhe.com/keyton4 that accompanies this text. The degrees of freedom, or df, of 3 indicates that four coding categories were used. For one-way chi-squares, df is equal to the number of categories minus 1,

or in this case, $4 - 1 = 3$. You know that the chi-square was statistically significant by the reported significance level of $p < .001$. This means that the significance level of the computed chi-square was smaller than .001, which is less than the generally set standard of .05. Thus, the researchers could reject the null hypothesis (that organizational dissent messages will be communicated equally to the four types of receivers) and accept the research hypothesis (that organizational dissent will be expressed more often to supervisors than to coworkers).

You should note, however, that obtaining a significant χ^2 value is not enough to provide total support for the research hypothesis. A chi-square cannot tell researchers where the significant difference occurred—only that one exists. In this case, the significant difference could have potentially occurred between any of the four potential audiences for the dissent messages. With chi-square, researchers must visually inspect the frequencies and percentages to determine if the significant difference is, in fact, the difference they predicted.

Contingency Analysis

Obviously the chi-square just presented is fairly simple. The researcher was looking at the frequency distribution on only one nominal variable. The chi-square can also be used for examining the association between two nominal variables. In this case, participants are classified on two variables in relationship to each other. This statistic is also known as a **contingency analysis, two-way chi-square,** or **two-dimensional chi-square.** The two nominal variables are arranged in a table where rows represent one nominal variable and columns represent a second nominal variable. The display of frequency data in this type of table is called a **contingency table.** Such an arrangement

TABLE 10.2 Japanese and American Young Adults' Reported Conflict Strategies

	Young Adults' Conflict Strategy			
	Avoidance	Distribution	Integration	Total
Country				
Japan	13	73	61	147
	8.8%	49.7%	41.5%	100%
U.S.	90	47	64	201
	44.8%	23.4%	31.8%	100%
Total	103	120	125	348
	29.6%	34.5%	35.9%	100%

% within each country.

makes it easy to see how frequencies for one variable are contingent on, or relative to, frequencies for the other variable.

The simplest form of a two-dimensional chi-square would be composed of two nominal variables, each with two levels. This would be a 2 × 2 chi-square. But in reality, this chi-square design is not often used because most nominal variables have more than two categories. More frequently used are contingency analyses of two variables with multiple categories. The formula and steps can be found at the website www.mhhe.com/keyton4 that accompanies this text. The formula requires that besides having the frequency for each cell (where a row and column meet), the expected frequency for each cell must also be calculated. Although few articles report the expected frequencies, they are a necessary component to the computation.

Shearman, Dumlao, and Kagawa (2011) used this type of contingency analysis, or chi-square, to determine if and how conflict management strategies differ for American and Japanese young adults when dealing with parental conflict (see Table 10.2). In this case, the research queston was, "What strategies do the American and Japanese young adults report for dealing with a major conflict with their parents?" (p. 111). Culture was the first nominal variable, as participants were either Japanese or American. Conflict strategy type (avoidance, distribution, integration) was the second nominal variable. This 2 × 3 chi-square—two cultures and three types of conflict management strategy—was significant, $\chi^2(2) = 56.24, p < .001$. Thus, the researchers could conclude that frequency of use of the three types of conflict management strategies is contingent upon culture. The most frequent conflict management strategy for Japanese young adults was the distributive strategy, followed by the integrative and the avoidance strategies. American young adults reported a different frequency pattern. Avoidance was the most frequently used conflict management strategy, followed by the integrative and distributive strategies. As a consumer of research, you can tell the chi-square was significant by looking at the significance level, or p. When it is .05 or less, it is considered significant and the alternative hypothesis is accepted.

Degrees of freedom (df) for a contingency analysis depend on the number of rows and columns in the contingency table. Specifically, degrees of freedom equal the number of rows minus 1 times the number of columns minus 1 [(no. of rows − 1) × (no. of columns − 1)]. In the example in Table 10.2, conflict management strategy is represented by the columns (3 − 1 = 2) and culture is represented by the rows (2 − 1 = 1). Multiplying those two (2 × 1 = 2) together results in $df = 2$.

*DESIGN
CHECK*

Interpreting Chi-Squares

1. Identify the research hypothesis or research question. Develop the related null hypothesis or statement of no differences.

2. From information presented in the method section, verify that each variable in the chi-square hypothesis is at the nominal or categorical level. Identify the categories or groups for each variable.

3. In the results section, look for the specific test results. You must find the χ^2 and the significance level, or p.

4. If the p of the χ^2 is .05 or less, accept the differences in the chi-square test. The differences found are statistically significant. Determine if the differences found are the differences predicted by the hypothesis.

5. If the p of the χ^2 is greater than .05, retain the null hypothesis. Any differences reported are due to chance or are not different enough to be statistically significant.

6. In the discussion section, look for the researcher's interpretation of the chi-square. To what degree are the statistically significant results practical or relevant to the issue being studied? Independently come to your own conclusion. Do you agree or disagree with the researcher?

Limitations of Chi-Square

Besides being limited to variables of nominal data, the chi-square has other limitations. One limitation is that the chi-square is a test of frequencies. As a result, when the observed frequency is zero in any cell or when the expected frequency is less than 5 in any cell, the test may not be accurate. The second limitation addresses the number of variables the chi-square can test. Although the chi-square is not limited to testing only two variables, the results from chi-squares with more than three variables can be very difficult to interpret (Kerlinger, 1986). A more sophisticated statistical test, log-linear analysis, is available when three or more nominal level variables need to be simultaneously examined.

Finally, the primary design limitation is that the test cannot directly determine causal relationships. It would be inappropriate to say that categorization on one variable caused categorization on another variable. However, logical interpretation of the variables in a contingency table analysis can help a researcher make causal statements about the data. Even so, causation is not absolute because the variables are not independent and dependent in the truest sense.

As a result, it is easy for both researchers and consumers to overextend the results from chi-square analyses. Most commonly, overgeneralization of the findings would be found in the discussion and implication sections of a research report. Clearly, there are limitations to the extent to which researchers should use findings from chi-squares to draw conclusions about the population from which participants are drawn. However, this does not mean that findings from chi-square analyses have no utility.

THE *t*-TEST

The *t*-test, represented by the symbol t, is used to test hypotheses that expect to find differences between two groupings of the independent variable on a continuous-level dependent variable. First, participants or elements are categorized according to one of two levels of the independent variable. Second, the dependent variable is measured for all participants. Then, the dependent variable scores of one group are compared to the dependent variable scores from the other group.

In experimental research designs, the *t*-test is used to test the significance of difference between the means of two populations based upon the means and distributions of two samples. However, the *t*-test is also regularly used in quasi-experimental and descriptive research designs.

In a *t*-test, the independent variable must be a nominal variable composed of only two groups. Only one independent variable can be tested. For example, sex could be an independent variable because it is typically operationalized as two groups, females and males. The *t*-test is also restricted to one dependent variable. The dependent variable must be of continuous level data at the interval or ratio level.

Referring back to the four analytical steps introduced earlier in this chapter, the *t*-test asks, "Are the sample means different from each other?" If the answer is "yes," then, as suggested earlier, the researcher must continue with the other three analytical steps. A researcher must determine if the difference was in the direction it was expected. The statistical significance of the *t*-test must be determined. Finally, the difference must be interpreted for what it means or how it is to be applied.

Common Forms of *t*-Test

Several common forms of the *t*-test are used in communication research. The first investigates differences between the means of two independent samples. The formula and steps can be found at the website www.mhhe.com/keyton4 that accompanies this text. This type of *t*-test is commonly used because researchers want to compare the mean scores of the dependent variable for two different groups of people.

For the **independent sample *t*-test,** degrees of freedom are calculated according to the sample size for each of two categories of the independent variable. Thus, if the *t*-test is calculated for 100 cases, 50 of which are assigned to one category of the independent variable and 50 assigned to the other category of the independent variable, the equation for calculating degrees of freedom would be $df = (n_1) + (n_2) - 2$. In this case, the calculation is $df = (50 + 50 - 2) = 98$.

For example, in exploring how marital partners flirt, Frisby and Booth-Butterfield (2012) asked this research question: "How do men and women differ in their reports of flirting behaviors, flirting motivations, and relational maintenance behaviors?" (p. 470). Essentially, this type of research question requires a series of comparisons between married women and married men. Let's explore one type of relational maintenance behavior—assurance, or the behaviors men and women use to demonstrate their ongoing interest in their partner. Using independent samples *t*-tests, the researchers found that women reported using more assurances with their marital partner ($M = 43.71$) than men reported using with their marital partners ($M = 39.39$). This difference was significant, $t(156) = 3.69$, $p < .005$. Using assurances is the dependent variable. Because participants are in one category of the independent variable or the other, the samples are independent. A participant cannot be identified with both categories of the independent variable.

A second type of *t*-test is known as a **paired comparison** (also called a paired samples *t*-test) because it compares two paired or matched scores. In this case, scores on the dependent variable are not independent. One participant provides two scores that can be compared. For example, a study investigating infidelity over the Internet (Docan-Morgan & Docan, 2007) used a paired samples *t*-test to answer the research question, "Which types of Internet infidelity acts, if any, are considered more severe than others?" (p. 321). Participants provided responses to two types of Internet infidelity. The first type was superficial/informal acts, such as joking around, catching up, small talk, and other non-intimate acts. The second type was involving/goal-directed acts, such as disclosing love, making plans to meet, and other acts of sexual or emotional intimacy. The results of a paired samples *t*-test revealed that a statistically significant difference existed between the two types of acts. Superficial/informal acts ($M = 1.68$) were rated less severe than involving/goal-directed acts ($M = 3.74$), $t(199) = -32.46$, $p < .001$.

The formula and steps can be found at the website www.mhhe.com/keyton4 that accompanies this text. For the paired sample *t*-test, degrees

Interpreting *t*-Tests

1. Identify the research hypothesis or research question. Is the hypothesis or research question directional or nondirectional? Develop the related null hypothesis or statement of no differences.

2. From information presented in the method section, verify that the independent variable in the *t*-test hypothesis is at the nominal, or categorical, level. Identify the two categories or groups for this variable. Verify that the dependent variable is continuous-level data (interval or ratio).

3. In the results section, look for the specific test results. You must find the *t* and the significance level, or *p*. Also look for the mean scores of the dependent variable for each category or grouping of the independent variable.

4. If the *p* associated with the *t* is .05 or less, accept the differences in this *t*-test. The differences found are statistically significant. Determine if the differences found are the differences predicted by the hypothesis.

5. If the *p* of the *t* is greater than .05, retain the null hypothesis. Any differences reported are due to chance or are not different enough to be statistically significant.

6. In the discussion section, look for the researcher's interpretation of the *t*-test. To what degree are the statistically significant results practical or relevant to the issue being studied? Independently come to your own conclusion. Do you agree or disagree with the researcher?

of freedom are calculated for the total number of cases. Thus, if the *t*-test is calculated for 50 paired cases, the equation for calculating degrees of freedom would be $df = (n - 1)$, or $df = (50 - 1) = 49$.

To summarize, the *t*-test examines the data for significant differences. The mean and standard deviation of the dependent variable are calculated for both groups of the independent variable. The test compares the two sets of descriptive statistics to determine if differences between them are statistically different. Without a statistical test, you can compare the means and interpret one as higher or lower than another. But you will not know if the difference is real or simply due to chance.

With these principles in mind, the *t*-test can be further distinguished by the extent to which its hypothesis or research question specifies the difference the test is intended to find. Two-tailed *t*-tests are used when differences are not specified. One-tailed *t*-test is used when differences are specifically identified in the hypothesis or

research question. Both are described in the sections that follow.

Two-Tailed *t*-Test

When a researcher asks a research question or states a hypothesis for which a difference in either direction is acceptable, the *t*-test is called a **two-tailed test.** Using this form of hypothesis or research question to guide the examination of the data, it would not matter which group had the higher or lower score on the dependent variable. Researchers use the two-tailed *t*-test when they presume a difference exists but they cannot predict the direction of the difference.

For example, in a study investigating how viewers respond to the practice of placing branded products within films (for example, when a character drinks or eats a popular soda or snack), researchers asked, "How do attitudes towards the ethical aspects of product placements differ by demographic characteristics?" (Sung, de Gregorio, & Jung, 2009,

p. 262). Although the practice is widespread, little research has been done with nonstudent film patrons. When they considered sex (female or male) as the demographic characteristic, they were unable to predict whether women or men would perceive branded products in films as unethical. Thus, the two-tailed t-test was used. Using data collected from over 3,000 adults they found a statistically significant difference ($p = .01$). Male respondents ($M = 2.58$, $SD = 0.86$) believed more strongly than female respondents ($M = 2.47$, $SD = 0.81$) that product placement was an unethical practice. Although the difference is statistically significant, notice, however, that mean scores for men and women represent a neutral attitude toward being influenced by product placement in movies.

One-Tailed t-Test

Alternatively, a t-test is said to be **one-tailed,** or directional, if a specific difference is identified in the research question or hypothesis. For example, Chory and Cicchirillo (2008) hypothesized that men will report more frequent video game play than women. Stating the hypothesis in this way presumes that one group, men, will play more video games than the other group, females. This stated, or expected, difference requires a one-tailed t-test. Results of the t-test analysis revealed that there was a statistically significant difference, $t(155) = 5.53$, $p < .001$, between men and women and their frequency of video game playing: Males played, on average, 6.63 times per week ($SD = 9.64$), whereas females played, on average, 0.64 times per week ($SD = 2.18$). The t value is significant because the significance level, or p, is less than the standard of .05. Given the direction of the hypothesis, the t-test confirms that men play video games more frequently than women.

But for a moment assume that the t statistic was −5.53 instead of 5.53. A negative t value carries no implication for the significance of the difference between the groups, as the absolute value (5.53) is used to interpret the statistic. The t-test would still be significant, but the effect of the difference would be in the opposite direction. To be clear about which group has a higher score on the dependent variable, look for the mean scores on the dependent variable for both groups.

Limitations of the t-Test

The primary limitation of the t-test is that it is designed to examine the differences on one dependent variable according to two groupings, or categories, of the independent variable. Thus, researchers cannot use the t-test to examine more complex communication phenomena. See An Ethical Issue, "Are Two Categories Fully Representative?" for some of the issues related to this limitation.

ANALYSIS OF VARIANCE

Analysis of variance is generally referred to with the acronym **ANOVA.** This statistical test compares the influence of two or more groups (the independent variable) on the dependent variable and is represented by the symbol F. **Variance** is the dispersion of the distribution of scores on the dependent variable. The greater the variance, the more the scores deviate from the mean. Alternatively, the smaller the variance, the closer the scores are to the mean. ANOVA examines the degree to which categories of the independent variable can explain the variance of the dependent variable.

As with the t-test, the independent variable must be nominal data and the dependent variable must be continuous level data. But ANOVA extends the t-test in two ways. First, ANOVA can accommodate more than two categories of the independent variable. Second, the test can accommodate more than one independent variable. Thus, the difference between the t-test and ANOVA is the number of categories of the independent variable that can be tested and the number of independent variables that can be tested.

Researchers have long noticed that testing one independent variable and one dependent variable cannot capture the complexity of communication phenomena. They have also noticed that variables do not always act independently (Kerlinger, 1986). Being restricted to using t-tests would mean that researchers could test only one independent variable at a time and thus lose the ability to test for the complexity of most communication phenomena. In its simplest form, ANOVA can test one independent with more than two categorical levels (for example, school

AN ETHICAL ISSUE

Are Two Categories Fully Representative?

Using a *t*-test is a good statistical choice for simple comparisons. But can two categories really represent the characteristics or attributes of individuals? Suppose for a moment that handedness, or the dominance of your right or left hand, is a characteristic you want to study with respect to how people greet one another and shake hands (see Provins, 1997). The independent variable would be handedness; right or left would be its two categories. The dependent variable would be comfort in extending the right hand for a handshake. Is the *t*-test an appropriate statistical test if it limits the independent variable to two categorical levels? Besides right-handedness and left-handedness, what other hand-dominance attribute could be important? Did you consider someone who is truly ambidextrous? What about sex (female, male), marital status (married, single), or hierarchical status (subordinate, superior)? Can two categorical levels accurately represent these as independent variables? What ethical issues would the researcher need to address when using variables with only two categories like these that capture most, but not all, of the differentiation on a characteristic?

standing: freshman, sophomore, junior, senior). In its more complex form, ANOVA can test two or more independent variables simultaneously. These ANOVAs are known as one-way and two-way ANOVAs, respectively.

ANOVA Basics

Because ANOVA can deal with greater complexity in testing for differences, several other basic issues must be addressed. These issues—planned or unplanned comparisons, between-groups and within-groups variance, degrees of freedom, between-subjects and within-subject designs—are described in the sections that follow.

In either form, ANOVA allows the researcher to compare individuals' scores on the dependent variable according to the groups or categories they belong to for the independent variable. These comparisons can be planned or unplanned. **Planned comparisons** are those comparisons among groups that are indicated in the research hypothesis. These comparisons are specified before the data are gathered. Alternatively, unplanned comparisons, called **post hoc comparisons,** are conducted after the researcher finds that a significant ANOVA exists. Post hoc comparisons are not predicted by the research hypothesis. Thus, when used

they are considered exploratory. After finding a significant *F* value, the researcher realizes that some statistically significant difference or differences exist. Then the researcher must use post hoc comparisons to find what differences exist among which groups or categories of the independent variable.

Although ANOVAs are commonly referred to as looking for differences between groups of the independent variable, ANOVA actually tests differences between and among means. When differences are found, **between-groups variance** exists. The groups vary enough to distinguish themselves from one another. To be significant, the between-groups variance must be greater than **within-groups variance,** or the variation among individuals within any category or level. The difference between these two types of variance can be explained with Nathanson and Rasmussen's (2011) study of the amount and style of communication mothers have with their children while playing with them in different contexts. Their hypothesis states, "Mothers will communicate more frequently (beyond the communication required by reading) with their young children while reading books than while playing with toys and while watching TV" (p. 470). Thus, three mother-child entertainment contexts were the conditions of the nominal independent variable: watching television, reading a book, and playing with toys. The continuous level dependent variable is the mothers' communication with their children. Variation in the frequency of mothers' communication in the different play settings would be between-groups variance. This is the variance the researcher is interested in testing. Alternatively, variation in mothers' communication with their children in any one play setting (for example, watching television) would be within-groups variance.

For ANOVA, degrees of freedom are computed for each independent variable and for the number of participants. Between-groups degrees of freedom are based on the number of categories in an independent variable. The number of categories minus 1 equals the degrees of freedom and is calculated for each independent variable. Thus, sex as an independent variable would result in one degree of freedom (2 categories—female and male—minus 1). An independent variable with three categorical levels, like the study of mothers' communication just mentioned, would have two degrees of freedom, and so on.

Within-groups degrees of freedom are based on the number of participants and the between-groups degrees of freedom. There are several steps to calculate the within-groups degrees of freedom. For an ANOVA research design with one independent variable with 3 categorical levels and 200 participants, the within-groups degrees of freedom would be calculated as follows. First, subtract 1 from the number of participants (or, $n = 1$). Second, calculate the between-groups degrees of freedom. For this ANOVA with one independent variable with three categorical levels, this df would be 2 (df = number of categories − 1). Third, subtract the between-groups degrees of freedom from the number computed in step 1.

Number of participants $n = 200$
providing data for this F test

1. $n − 1$ $200 − 1 = 199$
2. Between-groups degrees $3 − 1 = 2$
   of freedom or number
   of categories − 1
3. Within-groups degrees $199 − 2 = 197$
   of freedom

Both degrees of freedom are reported with the F value. Between-groups degrees of freedom are reported first, followed by the within-groups degrees of freedom. Thus, the $F(2, 197)$ notation indicates that the independent variable has three categorical levels. The notation also indicates that data from 200 participants were included in this ANOVA.

The researcher must calculate the F statistic to determine if differences between groups exist and if those differences are statistically significant, or not due to chance. Although a researcher can simply compare the means for each group, which are likely to be different, the statistical test is precise and takes into account each group's mean and variation (standard deviation) on the dependent variable.

The F is really a measure of how well the categories of the independent variable explain the variation in scores of the dependent variable. If the categories explain no variation, F is zero. The better the categories of the independent variable explain variation in the dependent variable, the larger F becomes. When the F statistic is statistically significant, researchers can interpret the differences of the means between groups as real. In other words, the differences are not due to chance. If the F statistic is not significant, then the null hypothesis is retained, indicating no differences between or among means for the groups.

There are two alternatives to the null hypothesis. First, the research hypothesis could predict specific differences between groups, indicating which group would be higher or lower than another. This would be a directional hypothesis, and planned comparisons would be built into the statistical test. For example, Bisel and Messersmith (2012) investigated if and how training would influence participants' abilities to develop persuasive apologies. Participants were randomly assigned to receive the training (the treatment) or not (the control group). The training session included both lecture and written material that focused on the four components of organizational apology for the work setting. The hypothesis predicted: "Participants who receive organizational apology training craft more persuasive apologies in eliciting feelings of forgiveness than those who do not receive training" (p. 435). In this hypothesis, there are two conditions of the independent variable: participants who are trained and participants who are not trained. Thus, because of the training, those participants are predicted to design more persuasive apologies than those not trained.

Second, the research hypothesis could predict differences between groups but not specify which group will be more effective in developing apologies. This would be a nondirectional hypothesis. Post hoc comparisons would be required if the overall ANOVA is significant. Using the preceding study, the hypothesis could be restated in this nondirectional form: There will be differences in the persuasiveness of organizational apologies based on training condition. Stated in this form, there is no prediction as to which group will perform better. In this case, comparisons between the two groups would be computed post hoc only if the F statistic proved to be significant.

ANOVAs also differ with respect to another design feature—**between-subjects design** or within-subject design. Between-subjects design is one where each participant is measured at only one group or category, or under only one condition. The ANOVA design is called between-subjects because the researcher wants to examine differences across individuals in the study. The study described previously is a between-subjects design because participants were in one of two conditions and their effectiveness in developing organizational apologies was to be compared. Between-subjects comparisons occurred on the independent variable—receiving training or not receiving training. Thus, participants' scores on the dependent variable were independent of one another.

Alternatively, a **within-subject design** measures each participant more than once, usually at different levels or for different conditions. Researchers often use the term **repeated measures** to describe a within-subject design. A within-subject design can be used to compare the differences between participants' scores prior to training with their scores after training. Or, a within-subject design could be used to test participants' frequency of use of several media (for example, Facebook, YouTube, and Twitter). The key to a within-subject design is that each participant provides data on each category of the independent variable.

One-Way ANOVA

One-way ANOVA (or one-way analysis of variance) tests for significant differences in the dependent variable based on categorical differences on one independent variable. For this test, one independent variable is measured at a nominal, or categorical, level. There must be at least two categories for the independent variable, but there can be many more. Because only one independent variable is tested, a between-subjects design must be used.

The statistical test, F, examines the distributions by comparing the means and standard deviations of the dependent variable for each group, category, or level of the independent variable. If the difference between groups is larger than the difference within groups, the ANOVA is significant. In this case, the researcher would reject the null hypothesis and accept the research hypothesis.

In its original formulation, the ANOVA was designed to make comparisons of groups of roughly equal size. In communication research, in which many comparisons are among naturally occurring groups, meeting this assumption is often impossible and impractical. Computer programs used to compute ANOVA can overcome this problem by making programmatic adjustments. In most statistical software packages, there will be one statistical test for comparing groups of equal size (usually called ANOVA) and another statistical test for comparing groups of unequal size (usually called general linear model).

A study of information requests from website users (Cha, 2011) is a good example of how researchers use one-way ANOVA. Two one-way ANOVAs were computed for the research question "Is there a difference between Korea- and U.S.-based Web sites with respect to the amount and breadth of information requests?" (p. 616); both were significant. The result for the amount of requested information was $F(1,255) = 308.45$, $p < .001$. Korean websites requested significantly more information from users ($M = 25.46$, $SD = 7.38$) than U.S. websites requested from users ($M = 10.22$, $SD - 6.42$). Likewise, the result for the breadth of information requested was significant, $F(1,255) = -307.94$, $p < .001$. Korean

TABLE 10.3 Two-Way ANOVA for Organ Donation Study

Message Frame	Level of Ambivalence	
	High Ambivalence	Low Ambivalence
Loss	Participants with high level of ambivalence about organ donation read news story that patient will die if he does not receive organ donation and transplant.	Participants with low level of ambivalence about organ donation read news story that patient will die if he does not receive organ donation and transplant.
Gain	Participants with high level of ambivalence about organ donation read news story that patient will live if he receives organ donation and transplant.	Participants with low level of ambivalence about organ donation read news story that patient will live if he receives organ donation and transplant.

websites requested more types of information ($M = 15.27$, $SD = 4.25$) than U.S. websites did ($M = 6.69$, $SD = 3.50$) In this study, the independent variable had two categories, but ANOVA can be used with an independent variable composed of two, three, four, and even five categories.

Two-Way ANOVA

In a **two-way ANOVA,** there are two categorical independent variables and one continuous level dependent variable. In testing the effects or influence of two independent variables, ANOVA can determine the relative contributions of each independent variable, or a *main effect,* to the distribution of the dependent variable. Additionally, ANOVA can test for the *interaction effect,* or the combined influences that can occur from both independent variables simultaneously.

For example, Cohen (2010) designed a study to examine if and what types of messages encourage people to become organ donors by signing an organ donation card. The research team created a quasi-experimental design by exposing participants to two versions of a human interest news story on organ donation. To manipulate the first variable, the frame of the story, one version of the news story presented how someone who was critically ill would die if he did not receive an organ donation and transplant. In the other news story, the framing condition was presented as the person surviving if the organ donation

and transplant was completed in time. Thus, the first independent variable was the framing of the story as a loss or a gain; and participants were randomly assigned by the researcher into one of these two groups. The second independent variable was the degree of ambivalence participants felt about becoming an organ donor, which was measured by participants' responses to a questionnaire. One hypothesis in the study predicted that ambivalence level would moderate the relative effect of the loss frame over the gain frame.

A two-way ANOVA was used to test for the effects of two independent variables—message frame with two levels (loss or gain) and ambivalence level (high or low)—on the continuous-level dependent variable, willingness to donate (see Table 10.3). With a two-way ANOVA, the research team could test for the main effects of each independent variable and the predicted interaction effect. A main effect occurs when one independent variable influences scores on the dependent variable, and this effect is uninfluenced by the other independent variable. In other words, are participants' willingness to donate an organ due to the type of message they read, one main effect? Or are differences in willingness to donate an organ due to their level of ambivalence about becoming an organ donor, another main effect? Because two independent variables are used in a two-way ANOVA, researchers can also test for an interaction effect. An interaction effect occurs when the results of one main effect cannot be interpreted without acknowledging the results of the other main effect.

TRY THIS!

Should Differences Be Significant or Practical?

Communication researchers explore a variety of applied communication problems and issues. In some cases, differences on the dependent variable would need to be large to persuade policy makers to change their practices or procedures. In other cases, differences—even small ones—could positively benefit people. Take a look at each of the situations that follow. How much of a difference would be enough to persuade you that a policy needs to be developed and implemented or that a procedure needs to be changed? Does the difference need to be statistically significant? Even if testing a hypothesis produces statistical significance, policy makers must also consider practical significance. Assess both the advantages and disadvantages of basing policy or procedure changes on statistically significant differences.

Situation	*Communication Phenomena*	*Questions*
Police responding to domestic violence calls	Assertiveness and sex of police officers in talking with victim	How assertive should officers be in persuading victims to file complaints against their attackers? Would the impact of assertiveness differ if female officers talked with female victims and male officers talked with male victims?
Elementary school teacher controlling students in classroom	Loudness of teacher's voice and directness of eye contact in talking with students	How loudly should the teacher talk when the classroom is unruly? Should his or her eye contact be directed at all students or only at those who are disruptive?

The F statistic revealed a main effect for ambivalence, $F(1, 145) = 6.96$, $p < .05$, eta$^2 = .05$. This is interpreted as individuals who have low ambivalence about becoming an organ donor expressed more willingness to become an organ donor ($M = 3.48$) than those with high ambivalence ($M = 2.89$). That is, the scores for the dependent variable, willingness to become an organ donor, were higher for those in the low ambivalence group than those in the high ambivalence group. There was no main effect for message frame. In other words, participants' willingness to become an organ donor was not influenced by which news story they read. In responding to the hypothesis, the interaction between type of framing message and level of ambivalence did not exist. If a significant interaction had been present, then any significant main effects would be ignored. You probably noticed the report of eta$^2 = .05$ in this example. **Eta squared,** or η^2, is an assessment of the proportion of variance in the dependent variable, willingness to be an organ donor, associated with the categories of the independent variable, level of ambivalence about becoming an organ donor. When you see this symbol, it is an indication of the degree of that association, which in this case is small. Whereas the F test indicates that a statistically significant difference exists, η^2 allows the researcher to determine if this statistical difference is practically or socially meaningful. That, of course, depends

DESIGN CHECK

Interpreting *F*

1. Identify the research hypothesis or research question. Does the hypothesis or research question include planned comparisons among categories of the independent variable? Develop the related null hypothesis or statement of no differences.

2. From information presented in the method section, verify that each independent variable is at the nominal, or categorical, level. Identify the number and type of categories or groups for each variable. Verify that the dependent variable is continuous level data (interval or ratio).

3. In the results section, look for the specific test results. You must find the *F* and the significance level, or *p*. Also look for the mean scores of the dependent variable for each category or group on each independent variable.

4. If the *p* associated with the *F* is .05 or less, accept the alternative hypothesis. The differences found are statistically significant. Determine if the differences found are the differences predicted by the hypothesis. If planned comparisons were not directed by the hypothesis, what post hoc comparisons did the researcher test?

5. If the *p* of the *F* is greater than .05, retain the null hypothesis. Any differences reported are due to chance or are not different enough to be statistically significant.

6. In the discussion section, look for the researcher's interpretation of *F*. To what degree are the statistically significant results practical or relevant to the issue being studied? Independently come to your own conclusion. Do you agree or disagree with the researcher?

upon the hypothesis or research question asked and the setting of the research study.

Factorial ANOVA

ANOVA is not limited to a two-way design. Rather, it can also be used for more complicated *factorial* designs with three or even four independent variables. At a minimum, a factorial design would include at least two categorical independent variables, each with at least two levels. Often factorial designs have more than two independent variables. For example, a 2 × 2 × 2 would indicate three independent variables; each variable has two categories. As another example, a 3 × 2 × 2 factorial design, would also indicate three independent variables. The first variable would have three categories, and

the second and third variables would have two categories each. Regardless of the number of independent variables or the number of categories for a variable, there is still one dependent variable.

This complex ANOVA addresses another issue—that is, in complex designs with multiple independent variables of nominal data, researchers will often choose regression over ANOVA as their statistical test. Although traditionally reserved for examining the effects of a continuous level independent variable on a continuous level dependent variable, the regression test can accommodate nominal level independent variables. Some statisticians have argued that regression is preferred over ANOVA because the regression test is more comprehensive and can be applied equally to experimental and descriptive research designs (Hayes, 2005; Pedhazur & Schmelkin, 1991). Regression is described in more detail in Chapter 11.

Limitations of ANOVA

The obvious limitation of ANOVA is that it is restricted to testing independent variables made up of nominal, or categorical, data. The other limitation is really one of complexity. When researchers use three or four independent variables, differences found can be significant, but confusing and difficult to interpret.

ASKING FOR STATISTICAL HELP

The statistics presented in this chapter are appropriate for testing differences between groups or categories. Figure 10.1 can help you determine the appropriate test of difference by identifying the number and types of variables in the research questions or hypotheses. Having a basic understanding of chi-squares, t-tests, and ANOVAs can help you interpret the research literature, making the results more meaningful for you.

After you enter the raw data, you must select which data are to be used for the test and select the appropriate statistic. For t-tests and ANOVAs, the spreadsheet or statistical program will calculate the statistic, the significance level, or p, and the degrees of freedom and will also calculate the mean scores and standard deviations for each category of the independent variable.

However, the use of these and other statistics is subjective because there are many variations for each of the tests described. I strongly suggest that you ask someone with statistical expertise to look over your research plan and that you seek help at any confusing point in the research process (for example, when generating hypotheses, developing method and procedure of data collection, using statistical programming or spreadsheets, interpreting statistical tests). Although researchers tend to follow a generally accepted series of steps in the research process and in using statistics, even professors benefit from expert advice. Most universities have statistical experts or workshops available to both students and faculty to help them with their research activities.

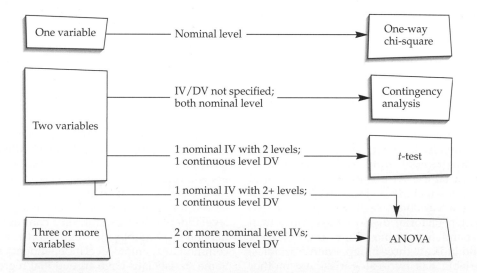

FIGURE 10.1 Identifying the Appropriate Statistical Test of Difference: IV = Independent Variable; DV = Dependent Variable

SUMMARY

1. Chi-square, *t*-test, and ANOVA are statistical tests of difference.

2. The function of inferential statistics is to draw conclusions about a population by examining the sample.

3. Inferential statistics rely on several assumptions: the use of probability in establishing significance levels, normal distribution of populations and samples, and random assignment of participants to groups.

4. Meeting these assumptions may not always be possible; thus, some scholars use these tests of differences outside the experimental design framework.

5. Four analytical steps assist the researcher through statistical interpretation of tests of differences: (1) conducting the statistical test to determine if differences exist; (2) characterizing the differences found as expected or not expected; (3) assessing differences for statistical significance; and (4) interpreting differences found with respect to the population from which the sample was drawn.

6. A one-way chi-square looks for statistically significant differences in categories within one nominal variable; contingency analysis looks for categorical differences between two or more nominal variables.

7. The *t*-test is used to test hypotheses that expect to find a difference between two groupings of the independent variable on a continuous level dependent variable.

8. A *t*-test can be two-tailed, in which any difference found is accepted, or one-tailed, in which the direction of the difference is specified by the research question or hypothesis.

9. Analysis of variance, or ANOVA, compares the influence of two or more groups of the independent variable on the dependent variable.

10. Design issues to consider in using ANOVA include planned or post hoc comparisons, and between-subjects and within-subject forms.

11. A one-way ANOVA tests for significant differences in the continuous level dependent variable based on categorical differences of one independent variable.

12. A two-way ANOVA tests for the effects of two categorical independent variables on a continuous level dependent variable.

13. Both main effects and interaction effects are possible in a two-way ANOVA.

14. Factorial ANOVA can accommodate three or four independent variables.

KEY TERMS

analysis of variance	one-tailed *t*-test
ANOVA	one-way ANOVA
between-groups variance	one-way chi-square
between-subjects design	paired comparison *t*-test
chi-square	planned comparisons
contingency analysis	post hoc comparisons
contingency table	repeated measures
degrees of freedom	*t*-test
eta squared	two-dimensional chi-square
expected frequency	two-tailed *t*-test
independent sample *t*-test	two-way ANOVA
inferential statistics	two-way chi-square
observed frequency	variance
one-dimensional chi-square	within-groups variance
	within-subject design

See the website www.mhhe.com/keyton4 that accompanies this text. For each chapter, the site contains a:

- chapter outline
- chapter checklist
- chapter summary
- short multiple-choice quiz
- PowerPoint presentation created by Dr. Keyton

For a list of internet resources, visit http://www.joannkeyton.com/CommunicationResearch-Methods.htm.

CHAPTER ELEVEN

Testing for Relationships

Chapter Checklist

After reading this chapter, you should be able to:

1. Explain the difference between tests of differences and tests of relationships.

2. Use the four analytical steps to design and interpret research designs and statistical findings.

3. Know which assumptions of inferential statistics your research project meets and which assumptions it does not meet.

4. Develop a hypothesis or research question and select the appropriate statistical test of relationship (correlation or regression).

5. Differentiate among the assumptions and functions of correlation and regression.

6. Interpret research findings developed from results of correlation and regression.

7. Identify structural equation modeling as tests of relationships.

Besides looking for statistically significant differences, researchers are also interested in looking for statistically significant relationships between and among variables. There are three statistical tests for examining relationships between and among continuous level variables—correlation, regression, and structural equation modeling. This chapter examines correlation and regression in detail and then introduces structural equation modeling.

Correlation, a statistical test that describes the type of relationship between two continuous variables, is the simplest of these tests. A test of correlation allows you to determine if scores on both variables increase or decrease, or if one score increases while the other score decreases. A correlation can also help you determine if there is no relationship between the two variables.

For example, Doss and Hubbard (2009) investigated the communicative role of tattoos. Based on the literature, they predicted a relationship between two constructs with the hypothesis, "For people with a single tattoo, there will be a positive linear association between reports of the communicative value of a tattoo and the visibility of a tattoo" (p. 65). The null hypothesis or statement of no relationship would be: There is no relationship between reports of the communicative value of a tattoo and the visibility of a tattoo. In other studies, researchers use a research question to explore a relationship without predicting how the variables will be related. Using the same study, the research question could be: Will there be a relationship between reports of communicative value of a tattoo and its visibility? Whether a hypothesis is posed or a question asked, the relationship to be examined is simple and straightforward; only two variables are included. The correlation statistic is used to test these types of relationships.

Of course, not all relationships are this simple. Some communication phenomena are more complex, and researchers need to develop hypotheses and research questions to examine more than just the relationship between two variables. It is not unusual for three or more independent variables to be hypothesized as influencing a dependent variable; in such a case, regression is the appropriate statistic. Although correlation is restricted to describing the nature of the relationship, the regression statistic allows researchers to examine causal or predictive relationships among continuous level variables.

As an example of the type of complexity regression can handle, Kinnally and Brinkerhoff (2013) designed a study to test the hypothesis, "Participants' intentions to donate to a public radio station are a positive function of their (a) beliefs about donating, (b) subjective norms, and (c) perceived behavioral control" (p. 5). Participants' scores on three independent variables—listeners' beliefs about donating, subjective norm regarding the degree to which a donor thinks that peers and family members hold positive or negative attitudes toward donating, and behavioral control to make a donation (that is, the resources and desire)—were used to predict participants' intentions to donate. Using multiple regression, the researchers could test to see which of the three independent variables had the most influence, relative to one another, on the dependent variable. Using regression, the unique influence of each variable could be identified.

In their simplest form, tests of relationship look for **linear** relationships. This means that a one-unit change in one variable is associated with a constant change in the other variable. Because this discussion is an introduction to statistics, the examples and methods described here are restricted to tests of relationships for two or more continuous level variables. Restricting the discussion this way will help you grasp the basic principles behind the statistical tests. Realize, however, that various forms of both correlation and regression can address categorical variables. Also, not all relationships are linear. Some are **curvilinear**, representing a ∪-shaped curve (both concave and convex forms). The regression statistic can be useful in testing for curvilinear relationships, but that discussion is beyond the scope of this chapter.

Why do researchers need to turn to statistics to look for these patterns or relationships? Without statistical tests, researchers would have to visually examine the raw data for patterns, which can be elusive and difficult, depending on the size of the dataset and the number of related variables. Even if a pattern were detected, knowing that a

---

DESIGN CHECK

Paying Attention to Details

A correlation or regression is only as meaningful as the theoretical model or basic assumptions about the relationships for which the researchers can argue. Thus, selection of the correlation or regression statistic should be based on a theory or on the findings of previous research studies. Spreadsheet and statistical programs can determine the relationship between and among sets of variables—even nonsensical relationships. As you read a research report, the authors should persuade you that they have selected the most appropriate set of variables to be studied. As a consumer, you should always be asking yourself if the variables for which a relationship is tested make sense.

---

relationship exists is not enough. Researchers use statistics to ask, "Is the relationship strong enough to be real—is it statistically significant?" In other words, is the relationship observed in the data stronger than the relationship that might occur due to chance? The three statistics this chapter addresses share a common logic.

BASIC ASSUMPTIONS

Before describing these tests, however, we need to return to the discussion of inferential statistics, alternative and null hypotheses, degrees of freedom, and the four analytical steps introduced in Chapter 10. As with the statistical tests for differences, the tests for relationships are used to draw conclusions about a population by examining the sample. In claiming that a finding from a sample holds true for its population, the researcher must meet four assumptions. Just as in difference tests, researchers set the significance level for each statistical test they conduct to assess how likely it is that the relationship found is real and not due to chance. Second, the data assumption must be met. Data are assumed to come from a normally distributed population. If not, a statistical test can provide only an approximation of the relationship.

The third assumption, very important to tests of relationships, is that the appropriate variables are selected to be tested. Thus, the theoretical model researchers use to specify which variables are to be included in a hypothesis and to specify which variable influences another is essential.

Finally, individuals participating in the research project should be selected through probability sampling. Recall from Chapter 10 that these principles are the ideal from which statistical tests were developed. If at all possible, these assumptions should be addressed and met in the research design phase of the research project. However, not all research meets these assumptions. As with the limitations and cautions for statistical tests of differences, violating these assumptions means that researchers need to be careful to not overextend research findings.

Remember that tests of relationships are not pertinent to the scores of any one participant in the research project. It would not be appropriate to investigate or report the relationship of variables for any one person. Rather, it is the pattern of scores across the sample that is of interest. When the basic assumptions listed earlier are met, examining the data at this holistic level allows a researcher to make inferences from the sample to the population or to test theoretical predictions. Thus, any significant relationship found is not significant for any specific participant, but representative of the population from which participants were selected or from participants providing data for similar situations.

Alternative and Null Hypotheses

Tests of relationships, like tests of differences, test the likelihood that the alternative hypothesis is true and the null hypothesis is not. The alternative, or research, hypothesis would predict that a relationship will be found, whereas the null hypothesis predicts that no relationship will be evident. The significance level is usually set at .05 to provide a criterion for making this decision. If the .05 level (or a lower one) is achieved, then a researcher rejects the null hypothesis and accepts the alternative hypothesis. If the .05 significance level is not achieved, the null hypothesis is retained.

Degrees of Freedom

As with statistical tests of differences, correlations and regressions require that degrees of freedom be calculated. Represented by the abbreviation *df*, degrees of freedom specify how many values vary within a statistical test. Again, there are clear rules for calculating the degrees of freedom for each statistical test. These rules are explained in the sections that follow.

Four Analytical Steps

The four analytical steps introduced in Chapter 10 can also be applied to statistical tests of relationships. First, the statistical test is applied to determine if a relationship exists between or among variables. Here, the researcher selects the appropriate statistical test—correlation or regression—as indicated by the hypothesis or research question. The hypothesis and the statistical test must be parallel.

The second analytical step characterizes the type of relationship found. Sometimes the relationship that appears in the data may not be the relationship predicted. Thus, researchers and consumers must check to make sure that the relationship found is indeed the relationship predicted.

The third analytical step assesses the statistical importance of the relationship. A researcher, generally using the significance level set at .05, determines if the strength and direction of the relationship found can be accepted as real, not random. If the probability level is not achieved, any relationship found is not significant and no conclusion can be drawn.

Finally, the researcher wants to move beyond the data tested into the future. Thus, this fourth analytical step evaluates the importance of the observed relationships in the sample and then generalizes the findings. Again, the researcher must make an assessment of all the steps in the research process:

- How was the sample obtained?
- Were participants selected through probability sampling?
- To what extent does the sample represent the population in which the researcher is interested?
- Was the research design appropriate for the hypothesis and research question?
- Were the data collected in reliable and valid ways?

Only by asking and answering these questions can a researcher determine the extent to which he or she can generalize from the findings of the sample to the population.

CORRELATION

Correlation, also known as the **Pearson product-moment correlation coefficient,** is represented by the symbol *r*. It is a statistical test that examines the linear relationship between two continuous level variables. Generally, a correlation can answer one of the following questions about the type of relationship between two variables:

- Do the scores on both variables increase?
- Do the scores on both variables decrease?
- Does one score increase at the same time the other score decreases?

The correlation coefficient indicates the degree to which two variables are related. To use a correlation as a statistical test, each participant must have provided measurements on two separate variables; that is, data on one variable must be paired with data on another variable. It is the pattern of the relationships between these two variables across all participants that correlation examines. If a correlation is statistically significant, then some type of relationship exists between the two variables. If a correlation is not significant, no conclusion can be drawn about the relationship between the two variables. The formula and steps for calculating the correlation coefficient can be found at the website www.mhhe.com/keyton4 that accompanies this text.

The degrees of freedom in a correlation are based on the number of variables in the test. A correlation tests for the relationship between two variables, X and Y. So, degrees of freedom for correlation are calculated as $df = n - 2$, with n referring to the pairs of data, not the individual data points. In a study with 100 participants providing scores on two continuous variables, the df would be 98 ($n - 2$, or $100 - 2 = 98$).

The one thing that a correlation cannot do is determine causation. Even when a correlation is significant, the statistical test does not provide any information about the cause-and-effect relationship between the two variables. The first variable could cause the second. Or vice versa; the second could cause the first. But, most important, a third variable could be the cause of both.

When two variables are statistically correlated, but not causally linked, a third variable creates the spurious relationship. A **spurious correlation**, or *spurious relationship,* is one in which a third variable—sometimes identified, at other times unknown—is influencing the variables tested. The correlation coefficient does not test for the existence of this third variable.

Interpreting the Coefficient

After the coefficient, or r value, is calculated, its interpretation requires two steps. The first addresses the direction of the relationship. The second deals with the strength of the relationship. Look at Figure 11.1 to see how these two interpretive steps work together.

Relationships can be positive or negative. In a positive relationship, values on one variable increase as values on the other variable increase. Alternatively, you could interpret a positive relationship as one in which values on one variable decrease as values on the other variable decrease as well. Either way, the principle behind a positive correlation is that the relationship is linear and both variables change in the same direction. A positive correlation coefficient is expressed as a positive number; some researchers include a plus sign to emphasize the positive nature of the relationship. Thus, both .79 and +.79 represent the same positive correlation.

In a negative relationship, the relationship is still linear, but now the variables change in directions opposite to each other. Thus, values on one variable increase, whereas values on the other variable decrease. A negative correlation coefficient is expressed as a negative number (for example, −.79).

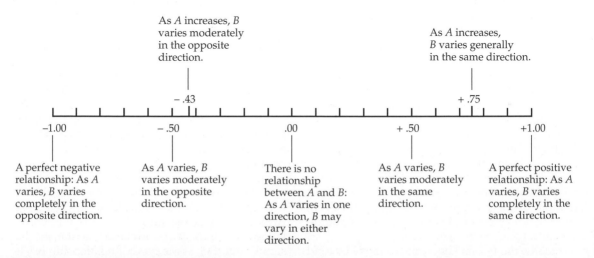

FIGURE 11.1 The Scale of Correlation

Therefore, the direction of the correlation coefficient represents how the two variables change with respect to one another. The positive or negative symbol of the r value is the indicator that the correlation is positive or negative.

The second interpretive step is an interpretation of the strength, magnitude, or size of the correlation. A simple principle aids the interpretation. The greater the absolute value of a correlation coefficient, or r, the stronger the relationship between the two variables. The numerical value of a correlation coefficient is restricted in range from -1.00 to $+1.00$. If you calculate a correlation and get a number less than -1.00 or greater than $+1.00$, an error exists in the calculation of r.

Interpreting the absolute value of the correlation in this step, the positive or negative nature of the r value is ignored. A perfect linear relationship would have an r value of $+1.00$ or -1.00. In this type of relationship, for every unit one variable increased, the other variable would also increase a unit. Or for every unit one variable increased, the other variable would decrease a unit. These are extreme cases and seldom found in communication research. The other extreme is a correlation coefficient of zero. In this case, no relationship exists between the two variables. In other words, no pattern can be discerned between the two distributions.

Practically, interpreting r values is subjective. Other than for the extreme values described, interpreting the magnitude of the correlation depends on what is being studied. However, researchers use some general rules to begin the process. Communication scholars, like other social scientists, generally follow these rules for interpreting the magnitude or strength of a correlation coefficient (Guilford, 1956; Hayes, 2005; Williams, 1968):

$< .30$	Weak correlation; slight relationship
$.30 - .70$	Moderate correlation; substantial relationship
$> .70$	Strong correlation; very dependable relationship

These rules apply whether the correlation is positive or negative. So, a correlation of $+.63$ is of the same strength as a correlation of $-.63$.

Recognize, however, that these are rules, and there are often exceptions to rules. For example, a statistically significant correlation coefficient may have little practical relevance. The only way to tell if a correlation coefficient is large or small is to know what is typical for similar measures of the same variables (Jaeger, 1990). Thus, the practical significance of the relationship must be determined not only by obtaining a statistically significant r but also by reading the scholarly literature.

Finally, in comparing one r value with another, it is inappropriate to compare their relative size. A correlation of .40 is not twice the relationship of a correlation of .20 (Williams, 1968). The r value is simply an index, not a measurement in and of itself.

Amount of Shared Variance Because of this interpretation problem, researchers use r^2 to represent the percentage of variance two variables have in common. Transforming r to r^2 allows comparisons between and among different correlated variables. Also known as the **coefficient of determination,** r^2 is found by simply squaring the r value. Researchers frequently do not report this calculation because it is easy for consumers of research to calculate it themselves. Take a look at Table 11.1. Notice how little variance is accounted for by low values of r. Alternatively, the amount of variance accounted for is closer to the r value when r is large.

When a correlation is presented as a statistical result, you should always mentally calculate r^2. Why? A correlation, or r, of .40 can be interpreted as a moderately positive result. But when you recognize that this r value accounts for only 16% of the variance, you must also acknowledge that the correlation did not account for 84% of the variance between the two variables. Simply stated, other variables, not the ones tested, were influencing the relationship. Thus, both researchers and consumers must be cautious in interpreting correlation coefficients and not confuse correlation with causation.

Notice that both positive and negative correlation coefficients result in the same level of r^2. A negative correlation of $-.63$ would account for 40% (.3969 rounded) of the variance, just as

TABLE 11.1 Determining Variance Accounted For

r Correlation Coefficient	r^2 Amount of Variance Accounted For
.2 or −.2	.04
.3 or −.3	.09
.4 or −.4	.16
.5 or −.5	.25
.6 or −.6	.36
.7 or −.7	.49
.8 or −.8	.64
.9 or −.9	.81

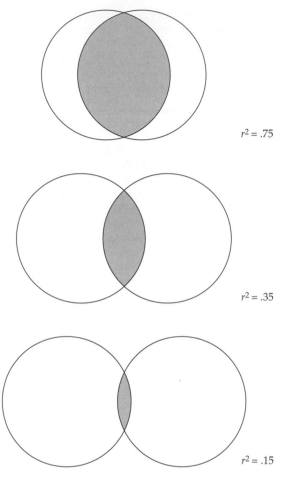

FIGURE 11.2 Venn Diagrams Representing Amount of Shared Variance in Correlations

the positive correlation of +.63 would. The Venn diagrams in Figure 11.2 demonstrate different sizes of correlations. The shaded and overlapping parts of the circles represent the variance accounted for, or the common variance between the two variables.

Plotting the Data   As a researcher, you should first plot out the data on a scattergram to verify that a linear relationship exists between the variables. A correlation is not a suitable test if the relationship is not linear. You can plot data for the two variables on a graph, or scattergram. An Excel spreadsheet program can do this for you: Highlight the data and, select the scatter function; data entered on a spreadsheet are automatically transformed into a scattergram. Statistical software can also provide this same function.

To check for linearity, draw a straight line through the middle of the data points. If a straight line *fits* the data, then there is some linearity to the relationship between the variables, and you can continue with calculating and interpreting the correlation coefficient. If a straight line cannot be drawn among the data points, the relationship is likely to be curvilinear and the correlation coefficient is an inappropriate test. Some statistical software packages can draw and fit the line for a relationship between two variables.

Examples of Correlation

A correlation provides descriptive information about the relationship between two variables. For example, Johnson (2013) predicts such a relationship with the hypothesis, "Perceived teacher clarity will be negatively related to reported in-class text messaging" (p. 58). Over 300 undergraduate students representing 48 different majors responding to a survey were asked to think of the instructor in the class where their participation was solicited. The survey included items related to four variables: teacher clarity (10 items), student communication satisfaction with the instructor (8 items), classroom climate (18 items), and in-class texting behavior (2 items).

Using the scores for the first and fourth of these variables, Johnson (2013) used correlation to test if the relationship predicted was true for this sample. In the results section of the journal article, Johnson reports the result as, "H1a, predicting a negative association between instructor clarity and texting, was supported ($r = -.35$)" (p. 60).

Looking at the table in the article, we can determine that r of $-.35$ was significant at p .001. Simply stated, the higher students' perceptions of their teachers' clarity of communication, the less frequently they texted while in class. Johnson suggests the implications of this relationship in the discussion section.

> Classroom texting potentially compromises students' engagement and the instructor-student relationship. Correlations linking texting and ... teacher clarity (H1a) ... suggest[s] that instructor behavior and classroom relationships influence student texting. (Johnson, 2013, p. 61)

This use of correlation is fairly simple and straightforward. The researchers hypothesized a correlation between two continuous-level constructs; found a significant negative relationship as hypothesized; reported their findings of the statistical test in the results section of the research report; and described the findings and their implications in the discussion section of the research report.

In another example of correlation analysis on the same topic of student-instructor communication, Shimotsu-Dariol, Mansson, and Myers (2012) hypothesized relationships about student and instructor communication. Two of the hypotheses in the study are

> H2: Students' self-reported academic competitiveness will be related positively to their out of classroom communication with their instructors.
>
> H3: Students' self-reported academic competitiveness will be related positively to their classroom participation. (p. 312)

Academic competitiveness is described by the authors as that behavior which occurs when

students strive to out perform themselves and other students. Sample items on the 18-item scale include: "Sometimes, I view a test as an opportunity to prove that I am intellectually superior to others," and "Academic competition inspires me to excel." Participants in the study self-reported their responses to these items on a 7-point Likert scale ranging from 1 (*strongly disagree*) to 7 (*strongly agree*).

The researchers reported their findings in the results section of the article. As predicted, students' self-reported academic competitiveness was positively related to their out of classroom communication with instructors ($r = .18, p < .01$) and their in-class communication ($r = .17, p < .05$). Note that both relationships are positive indicating that as one variable increased, so did the other. Also note the strength of the relationships. Although the relationships are positive, they are weak. The **correlation matrix** is displayed in Table 11.2. It contains the r statistic for each correlation used to test the three hypotheses in the study. The table also contains the mean, standard deviations, and internal reliability (α) for these variables.

When correlations are displayed in a table like this, it is called a correlation matrix because it is possible to see how every variable is correlated with every other variable. Notice how the variable names are numbered and in the same order across the top row of the table as well as down the far-left column of the table. With this type of table, you can select any two variables and determine the correlation between them.

For example, find the variable out-of-class communication in the far-left column in Table 11.2 and follow that row until you have reached the column identified as 1 to represent academic competitiveness. Here you should find the correlation between the two variables represented as $r = .18$. Do the same for in-class participation. Locate it in the far-left column and follow that row until you reach the column for out-of-class communication. Here you should find the correlation between the two variables represented as $r = .34$. Also notice that the significance level for all the correlations is presented as a note to the table.

You have probably also noted that the matrix is incomplete—that values are not presented in the top-right triangle of the table. A matrix

TABLE 11.2 Correlation Matrix for Student-Instructor Communication Study

Variable	M	SD	α	1	2	3	4	5	6	7	8
1. Academic competitiveness	68.81	13.28	.80	–							
2. Relational	14.51	5.03	.87	.19***	–						
3. Functional	22.39	4.92	.86	−.12	.14*	–					
4. Excuse making	14.41	5.58	.86	.21***	.32***	.18***	–				
5. Participatory	14.64	5.35	.87	.33***	.56***	.21***	.46***	–			
6. Sycophancy	14.01	5.20	.88	.35***	.60***	.10	.49***	.74***	–		
7. Out-of-class communication	24.48	5.73	.75	.18***	.50***	.20*	.23***	.44***	.36***	–	
8. In-class participation	14.70	4.22	.87	.17*	.45***	.24***	.24***	.51***	.41***	.34***	–

Note. *p < .05 **p < .01 ***p < .001.

repeats all the variables across the top and down the left column. A fully completed matrix would mean that correlations are reported twice. This is unnecessary because the correlation between two variables is the same regardless of their order. That is, the correlation between in-class participation and out-of-class communication is the same as the correlation between out-of-class communication and in-class participation. Finally, notice in the table that columns provide the mean, standard deviation, and Cronbach's alpha for each variable. With this additional information, you can fully interpret the variables and their relationships to one another.

Limitations of Correlation

Correlation is limited to finding a relationship for two variables, and the relationship between the variables is presumed to be linear, another limitation. These limitations severely restrict the development of hypotheses and research questions.

But the primary limitation is the degree to which inferences can be made from correlations. Even when all the assumptions described at the beginning of this chapter are met, correlation does not *necessarily* equal causation (Hayes, 2005; Vogt & Johnson, 2011). The strength and

direction of the correlation coefficient do not speak to the likelihood that one variable caused the other variable to increase or decrease in the way that it did. Rather, causality would be more directly inferred from the theoretical foundation for testing the two variables.

When two variables are known to be causally linked, the correlation coefficient can provide some evidence of that link. Still, it is important to remember that "statistics do not establish causation; *causation depends on the logic of relationships*" (Hoover & Donovan, 1995, p. 118). This logic is established by providing evidence from theory, previous research studies, and from practical knowledge of the sequence of events. As a researcher and consumer, you should be careful not to overextend findings about correlations as evidence of causation. Interpretation of the causal aspect of the relationship between two variables should be based on the foundation presented in the literature review, not just on the size of the correlation coefficient.

REGRESSION

Whereas correlations describe the relationship between two variables, predicting relationships

Interpreting Correlations

1. Identify the research hypothesis or research question. Develop the related null hypothesis or statement of no relationship.

2. From information presented in the method section, verify that each variable in the correlation hypothesis is measured continuously.

3. In the results section, look for the specific test results. You must find the r and the significance level, or p.

4. If the p of the r is .05 or less, accept the relationship in the test of correlation. The relationship found is statistically significant. Determine if the relationship found is the relationship predicted by the hypothesis.

5. If the p of the r is greater than .05, retain the null hypothesis. Any relationship reported is due to chance, or the variables are not related enough to be statistically significant.

6. In the discussion section, look for the researcher's interpretation of the correlation. To what degree are the statistically significant results practical or relevant to the issue being studied? Independently come to your own conclusion. Do you agree or disagree with the researcher?

among continuous variables is the task of regression. **Regression**—actually, a set of statistical techniques that predict some variables by knowing others—is a highly flexible statistical procedure that allows researchers to address many types of research questions and hypotheses and different types of data. The most common use of regression is to assess the influence of several continuous level predictor, or independent, variables on a single continuous criterion, or dependent, variable. But to understand the concept behind regression, we will begin with a model of simple linear regression with just two variables. One variable will serve as the independent variable; one will serve as the dependent variable. Both are measured at the continuous level.

It is worth mentioning here that even though regression is used to test for causation, it does not necessarily rely on an experimental research design. Regression is particularly well suited for testing the relationship between naturally occurring variables. In other words, the researcher does not manipulate anything. It is this characteristic of regression that is of particular advantage to communication researchers, because regression allows researchers to study variables that cannot be experimentally manipulated.

For example, to study the influence of social and emotional support on attributional confidence, or the ability to predict another's behavior, Avtgis (2003) asked men with brothers to respond to questionnaires to capture their perceptions on these variables and test these relationships. As you can imagine, it would be impractical and difficult to ethically manipulate one brother's perception of another brother in an experimental design. Thus, the research question "How do each of the social support styles and emotional support contribute to attributional confidence in the brother-brother relationship?" (p. 343) was answered using regression in a descriptive research design. Many concepts of interest to communication scholars would be difficult to manipulate experimentally. Thus, regression is an attractive alternative for testing naturally occurring phenomena.

As in correlation, "variance accounted for" is a phrase commonly associated with regression. In using this phrase, a researcher is describing the percentage of variance in the criterion variable accounted for by the predictor variable. In research reports, you are likely to find many ways of interpreting regression. Phrases that researchers use include

- the proportion of variance due to regression
- the proportion of variance predicted by the independent variable
- the proportion of variance accounted for by the independent variable
- the proportion of variance explained by the independent variable

The one chosen is based upon researcher preference, and that selection should be based upon the research context, the design of the research project, and the theoretical foundation for the regression model (Pedhazur & Schmelkin, 1991).

Linear Regression

Linear regression is a form of regression in which the values of a dependent, or criterion, variable are attributed to one independent, or predictor, variable. Without getting too technical, this statistical technique finds the **regression line,** a line drawn through the data points on a scattergram that best summarizes the relationship between the independent and dependent variables (or the predictor and criterion variables). Unless a perfect one-to-one relationship exists between the two variables, the line can only represent a best fit. The regression line of best fit is the one that minimizes the distances of the data points from the line (Cader, 1996). The better the fit of the regression line, the higher the correlation. In regression, this value is identified by the symbol R.

As in correlation, squaring R provides the proportion of variance explained or accounted for on the dependent variable by the independent variable. It is symbolized by R^2. Statistical software provides an adjusted R^2 that is often preferred by researchers, because the nonadjusted R^2 can be an inappropriately high estimate of the variance accounted for (Wright, 1997).

The value of R ranges from -1.00 through .00 to 1.00. Values close to zero indicate a very weak relationship between the predictor and criterion variables. As R values become larger and approach 1.00 (or -1.00), they indicate stronger relationships between the variables. Researchers consider R^2, the squared multiple correlation coefficient, to

be more meaningful. An R^2 value of .48 indicates that 48% of the variance of the dependent variable is accounted for, or determined, by the combination of the independent variables. As in correlation, R^2 is called the coefficient of determination.

In most cases, the independent (predictor) variables in a regression will not be based on the same unit of measurement. Even when all measures of the variables are based on a 5-point response set of a Likert-type scale (strongly agree to strongly disagree), variables are likely to be composed of different numbers of items, making direct comparisons among mean scores problematic. Statistical software transforms each of the measurements for each variable into standard deviations. In this form, the variables can be compared more easily. Despite their original measurement scales, variables with high variability will have large standard deviations. Conversely, variables with low variability will have much smaller standard deviations.

These standardized scores are referred to as **beta coefficients,** also known as **beta weights.** The greater the beta coefficient, or β, the greater the variability of that variable. Thus, β can be interpreted as the effect of the independent variable on the dependent variable. As with correlation coefficients, beta coefficients range from $+1.00$ to -1.00. A beta coefficient of $+1.00$ would indicate that a change of one standard deviation in the predictor variable is associated with a change of one standard deviation in the criterion variable and that the changes are both in the same direction. Of course, if the beta coefficient were -1.00, the changes would be in the opposite direction.

To summarize, you will need to look for several symbols or descriptions as you read research reports in which the hypotheses or research questions have been tested with regression. Identify the R, R^2, and β. Looking at the examples later in this chapter will help make this clearer.

Multiple Regression

Of course, most communication phenomena are more complicated than can be tested by the simple linear regression model with one independent and one dependent variable; thus, our need for multiple regression. **Multiple regression** allows a researcher to test for a significant relationship between the dependent variable and multiple independent variables separately and as a group. The test is symbolized by *R*, which is known as the **multiple correlational coefficient.** This is the type of regression most commonly seen in the communication literature. Like a correlation coefficient, it is an index of the magnitude of the relationship among the variables.

Theoretically, there is no limit to the number of independent, or predictor, variables tested. But, practically, communication researchers seldom test more than four in any one regression model. With the ability to test multiple independent, or predictor, variables, we need to consider another set of Venn diagrams (Figure 11.3). Diagram I demonstrates how the three predictor variables—*A, B,* and *C*—are correlated with each other and together influence the criterion variable as a group. Diagram II shows that predictor variable *A* is not correlated with predictor variables *B* and *C* and that *B* and *C* are correlated with each other. This diagram demonstrates how *A* influences the criterion variable separately from the *B* and *C* variable combination. Finally, Diagram III demonstrates the degree to which predictor variables *A* and *C* influence the criterion variable, whereas *B* has no influence on it. This diagram also shows how predictor variables can be unrelated to one another yet still influence the criterion variable.

By looking at the amount of overlap, or the degree to which the predictor variables influence the criterion variable, you can estimate the amount of variance accounted for, independently or in combination with one another. By diagramming regression relationships in this way, you should be able to get a feeling for the relative importance of each variable to the regression relationship.

Degrees of freedom, *df*, for regression are calculated by first identifying the number of independent variables in the full multiple regression equation. If there are three predictor variables, the first degree of freedom is 3. Then use the formula $n - k - 1$, where *n* equals the number of observations for the statistical test and *k* equals the number of independent variables in the test. So for 200 observations and a regression with three predictor variables, the second degree of freedom is 196 ($n - k - 1$, or $200 - 3 - 1$). In the results section, *df* is reported as 3,196 in parentheses after the *F* value.

Interpreting Multiple Regressions   Because multiple regressions allow a researcher to test both the separate and common influences of predictor variables on the criterion variable, interpreting multiple regressions can get a little tricky. First, the calculated *F* ratio indicates whether the squared multiple correlation coefficient, R^2, is significant. If the significance level, or *p*, for *F* is .05 or less, at least one of the relationships among the variables is significant.

Researchers rely on the beta weights, or β, to interpret the relative contributions of each independent, or predictor, variable. But this interpretation is not absolute, because independent variables are often correlated with one another. The ideal predictive situation is when the correlations between independent variables and dependent variable are high, and the correlations among the independent variables are low (Kerlinger, 1986). Thus, the greater the correlations among the independent variables, the more difficulty in establishing the unique contribution of each independent variable.

Interpretations of multiple regression are also more difficult as independent variables can both positively and negatively influence the dependent variable in the same model. Thus, whereas increases in one independent variable are related to increases in the dependent variable, decreases in another independent variable may be related to increases in the dependent variable. Given the objectives of this introduction to statistical methods, know that the researcher, guided by β, is ultimately responsible for interpreting the influence of individual independent variables.

Regression Examples

Fay and Kline (2011) were exploring how the informal communication between coworkers influences the organizational commitment and job satisfaction of workers who telecommute, or work from home rather than work at the office. They asked several research questions and hypotheses. Let's focus on their first research question (p. 150):

RQ₁: To what extent do informal communication practices and informal communication satisfaction predict coworker liking?

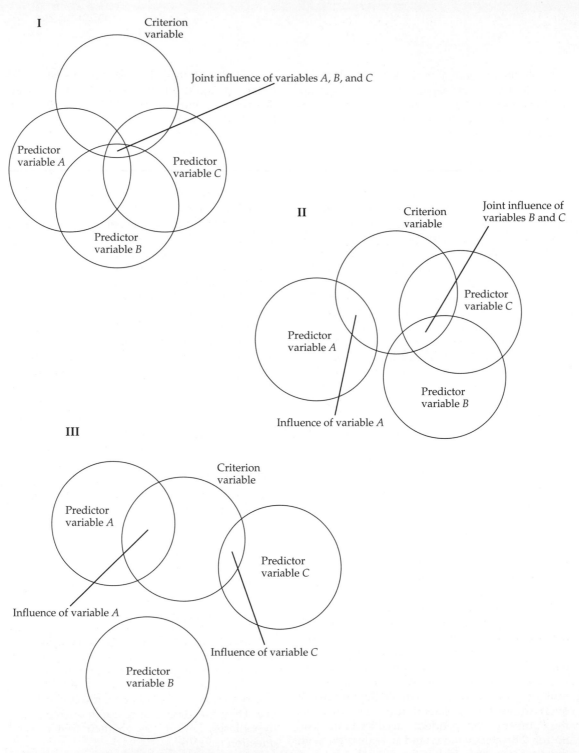

FIGURE 11.3 Venn Diagrams of Multiple Regression

To eliminate measurement error, the researchers chose multiple regression to simultaneously test the influence of the two independent variables (informal communication practices and informal communication satisfaction) on the dependent variable of coworker liking. An example of informal communication includes coworker to coworker communication practices, such as talking to learn more about each other as individuals, providing expertise, and complaining about other coworkers.

The researchers report their results in this way:

> This regression was statistically significant, F (4, 93) = 6.38, $p < .01$, $R = .46$, adjusted $R^2 = .18$, with informal communication satisfaction the only significant predictor, uniquely accounting for 14% of variance in coworker liking" (Fay & Kline, 2011, p. 155).

Notice how the researcher provides you with the test results. First, the F value is presented. The overall test of the influence of the two independent variables on the dependent variable was statistically significant and accounted for 18% of the variance. When the regression test is significant, that signals the researcher to look for which independent variables contributed to that finding. In this case, the researchers state that only one of the two independent variables, informal communication satisfaction, was a significant predictor. That is, the beta weight, or β, for informal communication satisfaction is statistically significant, but not the beta weight for informal communication practices. Thus, the result of the regression test could be interpreted this way: Coworker liking is influenced by informal communication satisfaction.

In another example of regression, Young, Kelsey, and Lancaster (2011) used multiple regression to answer their research question about students' perceptions of instructor e-mail. They asked "To what extent do students' perceptions of their instructor's e-mail communication (including frequency and level of immediacy) and their own reasons for contacting their instructor via e-mail predict students' perceived future rewards in developing a student-teacher relationship?" (p. 376). Data were collected from undergraduates about one of their instructors who used e-mail as out-of-class communication.

There were three independent variables. The first was frequency of instructor e-mail communication. The second was students' perception of instructor immediacy in e-mails (for example, "The teacher uses humor in the messages he/she sends to me," and "The teacher self-discloses personal information in his/her e-mails to me"). The third independent variable was student reasons (personal, procedural, and efficiency) for using e-mail with their teachers (for example, "get to know the teacher better," "ask for guidance on assignments," and "avoid speaking to the teacher by phone or in person"). The dependent variable was the value of student-teacher relational development (for example, "based on my e-mail interactions with this instructor, I believe that continuing our student-teacher relationship is likely to be positive"). The research team reports the results of the regression test of this research question this way:

> The group of instructor-based (perceived frequency of mass e-mails, perceived frequency of personalized e-mails, and perceived immediacy contained within the e-mails) and student-based (students' reasons for e-mailing the instructor, including: personal/social reasons, procedural reasons, and efficiency reasons) variables accounted for 30% of the variance with four variables emerging as significant predictors of the students' perceived rewards in developing a student-teacher relationship. . . . The findings revealed that when students believe their teacher e-mails the class frequently, when students view e-mails from their teachers as being immediate, when students e-mail teachers for procedural/clarification reasons, and when students do not e-mail teachers simply as a means of efficiency, then these factors increase students' positive predicted outcome value of fostering a student-teacher relationship. (p. 381)

A multiple regression was computed, F (6, 321) = 24.15, $p < .001$. The combination of the independent variables accounted for 30% of the variance in the model. The researchers report specifically how each independent variable influenced the dependent variable in a table. Four of the six independent variables were statistically significant in predicting the value of developing a student-teacher relationship. In order of the magnitude of the relationship, the R^2s for immediacy of instructor email $= .51$, frequency of instructor e-mail $= .14$, student efficiency reasons for emailing instructor $= -.13$, and student procedural reasons for e-mailing instructor $= .11$.

Regression tests the influence of multiple independent or predictor variables on one dependent or criterion variable. If the overall F statistic is significant, each predictor variable should be examined for the degree to which it influences the criterion variable. As with any statistical test, be sure to examine the degree of variance explained or accounted for by the predictor or independent variables. Although the overall F statistic is significant, that will not ensure that all the predictor variables significantly contribute to predicting the criterion variable. Statistical significance may be accounted for, but practical or social significance is also important in interpreting results.

Other Forms of Multiple Regression   Multiple regression is a flexible and sophisticated test,

and many other types of regression analyses are beyond the scope of this introductory chapter. Although the discussion here has focused on the use of continuous level variables, regression can also accommodate nominal variables. This introduction also focused on linear relationships. Yet, multiple regression can detect curvilinear relationships as well.

Hierarchical regression is commonly used in communication research. This regression form allows the researcher to enter independent variables in the order or sequence in which the variables are presumed to influence the dependent variable. Variables are grouped and called *sets* or *blocks*. A block can be a single variable, but more commonly a block consists of several related variables. Researchers rely on the theoretical connections among the variables to determine which blocks of variables are first, second, and so on. Perhaps you are wondering why a block of variables would be used. This next example can help to explain that.

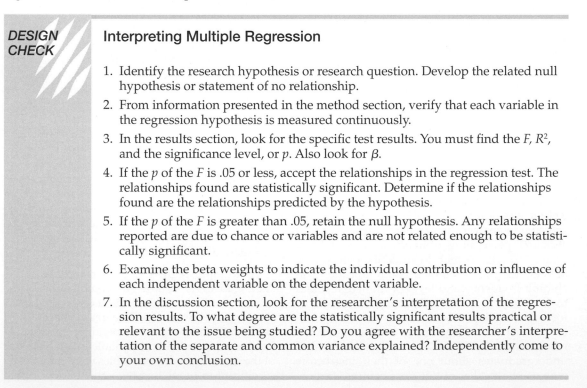

DESIGN CHECK

Interpreting Multiple Regression

1. Identify the research hypothesis or research question. Develop the related null hypothesis or statement of no relationship.

2. From information presented in the method section, verify that each variable in the regression hypothesis is measured continuously.

3. In the results section, look for the specific test results. You must find the F, R^2, and the significance level, or p. Also look for β.

4. If the p of the F is .05 or less, accept the relationships in the regression test. The relationships found are statistically significant. Determine if the relationships found are the relationships predicted by the hypothesis.

5. If the p of the F is greater than .05, retain the null hypothesis. Any relationships reported are due to chance or variables and are not related enough to be statistically significant.

6. Examine the beta weights to indicate the individual contribution or influence of each independent variable on the dependent variable.

7. In the discussion section, look for the researcher's interpretation of the regression results. To what degree are the statistically significant results practical or relevant to the issue being studied? Do you agree with the researcher's interpretation of the separate and common variance explained? Independently come to your own conclusion.

TRY THIS!

Identifying Independent Variables for Multiple Regression

The primary advantage of multiple regression for communication research is that it allows researchers to measure relationships among variables that cannot be manipulated by the researcher, as some forms of experimental designs would require. The first example identifies the dependent variable and independent variables, as well as reasoning for why the independent variables cannot be manipulated. For the remaining four dependent variables listed, identify the accompanying independent variables you believe communication researchers should investigate, explaining the reasoning for capturing the independent variables in their naturally occurring form without manipulation. To start, consider the following combination of variables:

Dependent Variable	Independent Variables	Reasoning
Marital satisfaction	Amount of time talking with partner about the relationship	It would be unethical for researchers to require participants to stop talking to their spouse.
	Quality of marital communication	Quality of conversation cannot be practically or logistically controlled by researcher.
Intercultural assimilation		
Political cynicism among new voters		
Belief in news first reported on the Internet		
Adopting practices promoted on television public service announcements		

Malachowski and Dillow (2011) used a hierarchical regression to examine the effect of three blocks of independent variables on relational satisfaction of cross-sex (or female-male) relationships. Of the three hypotheses in the study, let's focus on the final prediction: "Relational uncertainty, romantic intent, and attraction will be positive predictors of maintenance behaviors in cross-sex friendships" (p. 359). Using a survey, data were collected from 352 individuals who were involved in a cross-sex friendship with someone with whom they had never been romantically associated. Participants reported on a specific cross-sex relationship; these relationships ranged in length from one month to eight years.

Friendship length was entered in the first block; physical attraction and social attraction to the cross-sex partner were variables in the second block; and romantic intent was the third block followed by relational uncertainty in the fourth and final block. The variables in these blocks are the independent variables. Relational maintenance behavior was the dependent variable. It was operationalized by 34 items that described how the participant maintained the relationship with their cross-sex partner. Items for this variable addressed routine contact, emotional support and positivity, relational talk, instrumental support, social networking, antisocial behavior, humor and gossip, talk about romance in this relationship, flirtation, and avoiding of negativity or criticism. The researchers report the results of this statistical test in this way:

> The analysis indicated that only Step 4 (i.e., relational uncertainty) was significant. As indicated by a closer exploration of the results, however, only social attraction ($\beta = .13$), $t = 2.30$, $p < .05$; and relational uncertainty ($\beta = -.32$), $t = -5.01$, $p < .001$, emerged as significant predictors of relationship talk maintenance behaviors. (p. 362)

See Table 11.3. Notice the beta weights, or β, for the variables in each model (or block) of the regression. Also notice ΔR^2. Recall that R^2 is a measure of the proportion of variability of the dependent variable predicted by the independent variables. ΔR^2 is the incremental increase in R^2 values when additional blocks of predictors are added to the regression equation. Thus, the researchers conclude in the discussion section of the journal article that: "Social attraction increased, whereas relational uncertainty decreased, the use of relationship talk, routine contact and activity, and emotional support maintenance behaviors in cross-sex friendships" (Malachowski & Dillow, 2011, p. 365).

Stepwise regression is a similar form of regression in that independent variables are entered in some sequence or order. But in this case,

TABLE 11.3 Hierarchical Regression Table from Relational Satisfaction Study

Variable	F	ΔR^2	β	t
Step 1	.03	.00		
Friendship length			.01	.17
Step 2	2.48	.02		
Physical attraction			.02	.40
Social attraction			.13	2.30*
Step 3	2.15	.00		
Romantic intent			.07	1.08
Step 4	6.85**	.07		
Relational uncertainty			−.32	−5.01**

*p < .05. ** p < .001.

the order of variables is determined by the statistical program (in essence, the computer), not the researcher. Generally, the steps of entry are based on the degree of influence the independent variables have on the dependent variables.

Limitations of Regression

Because regression is based on correlations between and among variables, it is inappropriate, even when significant relationships are found, to unequivocally state that the relationship is evidence of cause-and-effect relationships. Although a certain asymmetry is established by the hypotheses and research questions tested, it is often more appropriate to indicate that significant relationships found are consistent with what the researcher hypothesized or expected to find. It would be overextending the results to suggest an absolute cause-and-effect relationship; however, regression is an excellent statistical tool for determining if one or more independent (predictor) variables explain the variation in the dependent (criterion) variable.

Scientists use regression to continue to confirm their beliefs about the causal links among variables. Cause-and-effect relationships are never proven with one study. Rather, consistent results over a period of time combined with practical reasoning provide the cumulative evidence and logic needed to establish causal links.

STRUCTURAL EQUATION MODELING

Recall that multiple regression allows communication researchers to expand the complexity of their analyses by determining how multiple independent variables affect a single dependent variable. When communication researchers want to test for significant associations among multiple independent *and* multiple dependent variables, they often employ **structural equation modeling (SEM).** This statistic allows researchers to test whether a theoretical model (or hypothesized associations among independent and dependent variables) is statistically different from their collected data. If the theoretical model is statistically different from the collected data, the researcher's

model needs to be revised. So where do models come from in the first place? Ideally, researchers who employ SEM specify their theoretical models based on theory and previous research.

In SEM, researchers calculate a variety of measures of fit to determine whether their theoretical model is similar to their collected data. The most basic test of fit is the chi-square statistic (see Chapter 10). However, when models are tested against large sample sizes with large correlations among variables, alternative fit indices are necessary. A fit index is a numerical representation of how similar a theoretical model is to the data collected by the researcher. A popular index of model fit is the **root mean square error of approximation (RMSEA)**. As a general rule, a RMSEA less than .05 indicates excellent model fit, whereas a RMSEA above .10 indicates poor model fit.

In SEM, when a variable is hypothesized to be caused by another variable, that variable is called an **endogenous variable** (similar to criterion variables in multiple regression). Alternatively, a variable that is not caused by another variable in the model is known as an **exogenous variable** (similar to predictor variables in multiple regression). There is no limit to the number of exogenous and endogenous variables a researcher can specify in a theoretical model; however, as the complexity of a theoretical model increases, the researcher's dataset must increase in size. Another unique aspect of SEM—different from any other statistical analysis presented in this book—is that SEM allows communication researchers to model multiple paths, such as in the theoretical model: $X \rightarrow Y \rightarrow Z$. In this theoretical model, both Y and Z are endogenous variables, whereas X is an exogenous variable.

Similar to linear and multiple regression, an analyst can determine the strength of associations among variables in SEM by computing a beta weight, or β. Additionally, an analyst can determine how much variance in the endogenous variable is explained by variance in the exogenous variable using a R^2 statistic.

SEM Example

In one example of communication research that employed SEM, Serewicz, Hosmer, Ballard, and Griffin (2008) wanted to determine how

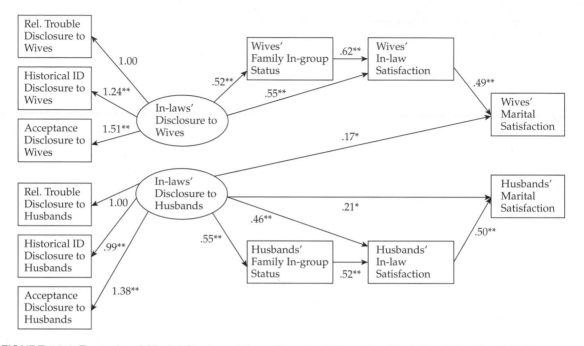

FIGURE 11.4 Example of Model Produced from Structural Equation Modeling (Significant Paths are Displayed).

disclosure from in-laws related to martial satisfaction. The investigators surveyed married couples. The researchers reviewed family and interpersonal communication research literature to discern what forms of in-law self-disclosure—according to theory—should enhance spousal satisfaction with their in-laws, and then, in turn, enhance their marital satisfaction. Then, Serewicz and her colleagues proposed their theoretical model, which included two exogenous (the disclosure variables) and six endogenous variables. See Figure 11.4. Based on their review of the literature, the authors hypothesized that the spouses' satisfaction with their in-laws mediates the association between in-laws' self-disclosure and spouses' marital satisfaction. In other words, the researchers argued that parents who self-disclosed appropriately to their child's spouse will raise the likelihood that their son- or daughter-in-law will be satisfied with them, which will enhance their son- or daughter-in-law's marital satisfaction (i.e., X → Y → Z). That portion of their theoretical model fit their data collection. Their model fit their data well, $\chi^2[35]$

$= 48.08, p > .05$, RMSEA $= .05$. Notice that $p > .05$. Recall that with SEM, the purpose is to test the goodness of model fit. When tests result in $p < .05$, that is an indication that the observed dataset is significantly different from the theoretical model. Also, notice that RMSEA $= .05$, which indicates that their theoretical model fit the data they collected.

Other Forms of SEM

There are other forms of SEM. In journal articles you will see confirmatory factor analysis (CFA), path analysis, latent composite SEM, and hybrid SEM. These variations are used for specific analyses, but they have the same basic characteristics of SEM as described previously.

CAUTIONS IN USING STATISTICS

The statistics presented in this chapter allow a researcher to test for relationships between and among variables. Figure 11.5 is attached can help

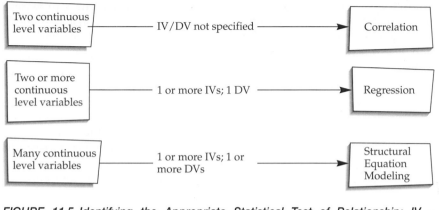

FIGURE 11.5 Identifying the Appropriate Statistical Test of Relationship: IV = Independent Variable; DV = Dependent Variable

you determine the appropriate test of relationship by identifying the number and types of variables in the research question or hypothesis. Having a basic understanding of correlations and regressions can help you understand findings presented in the research literature, and make the results more meaningful for you. With the help of spreadsheet and statistical programs, you can also collect and interpret data using these tests. However, just as with the statistical tests for differences, use of these statistical tests is subjective, and many variations exist for each of the tests described. Thus, the advice given at the end of Chapter 10 is repeated here.

If you assume the role of the researcher, I strongly suggest that you ask someone with statistical expertise to look over your research plan, and you should seek help at any point in the research process that includes the use of statistics (for example, in generating hypotheses, determining method and procedure of data collection, using statistical programming or spreadsheets, and interpreting statistical tests). A statistical expert can help you use these statistics in an appropriate and valid way. Seek expert advice anytime you have a question. Consult your instructor or your university's statistical expert when you need assistance with your research activities.

Beyond this general recommendation for seeking statistical help, three questions can help you assess the use of statistics (Katzer et al., 1978).

First, are the results worth interpreting statistically? You have probably heard the phrase "garbage in, garbage out." With respect to statistics, this means that despite the sophistication of any statistical test or procedure, if the data used are invalid (for example, collected in an ambiguous or suspect manner), then any result, even a significant one, is invalid. A sophisticated statistical test cannot overcome the problems of a bad dataset or provide meaning to unmeaningful data. Statistics are a tool, not a panacea.

If you can argue for the use of statistics, then ask the next questions: Are the results statistically significant? Was the appropriate statistical procedure selected and then used appropriately? If not, then the statistical significance of the test is called into question. Remember, too, that if the results were nonsignificant, there are multiple reasons for this outcome. A nonsignificant finding for one cause or relationship does not suggest that another causal factor or relationship is valid. Rather, a nonsignificant finding means that the cause or relationship tested could not be verified in this particular examination. If you believe the appropriate statistical test was effectively used, error could have been introduced into the process at many junctures (for example, in how the sample was selected, how the variables were operationalized, or how data were collected). And you must not dismiss the possibility that the assumption presumed by the researcher may have been wrong or not well founded.

The third question is more personal: Are the results meaningful to you? Statistical significance does not always equal social significance. Thus, you, the consumer of research, must decide if the results have meaning and utility within the context in which you will use the information.

SUMMARY

1. The degree to which the following assumptions are met determine the degree to which findings from the tests can be generalized from the sample to the population: (a) significance level of the test is based on probability theory, (b) data are assumed to come from a normally distributed population, (c) the appropriate variables are included in the test, and (d) individuals participating in the research project should be selected through probability sampling.

2. A correlation is a simple description of the degree to which two variables are related.

3. Causation cannot necessarily be established with correlation.

4. A correlation coefficient must be interpreted for its direction and its strength or magnitude.

5. In a correlation, researchers rely on r^2 to describe the amount of variance shared between the two variables.

6. Regression is an extension of correlation; however, multiple regression can test for the influence of multiple independent or predictor variables on the dependent or criterion variable.

7. Regression is particularly well suited for communication research because it tests the relationship among naturally occurring variables.

8. R^2 provides information about the amount of variance of the dependent variable explained by the independent variables separately or in common.

9. The beta weight, or β, provides information about the direction and strength of influence for each independent variable.

10. Structural equation modeling (SEM) allows a researcher to test whether a theoretical model (or hypothesized associations among multiple independent and dependent variables) is statistically different from their collected data; if the theoretical model is statistically different from the collected data, the researcher's model needs to be revised.

KEY TERMS

beta coefficients

beta weights

coefficient of determination

correlation

correlation matrix

curvilinear

endogenous variable

exogenous variable

hierarchical regression

linear

linear regression

multiple correlational coefficient

multiple regression

Pearson product-moment correlation coefficient

regression

regression line

root mean square error of approximation (RMSEA)

spurious correlation

stepwise regression

structural equation modeling (SEM)

See the website www.mhhe.com/keyton4 that accompanies this text. For each chapter, the site contains a:

- chapter outline
- chapter checklist
- chapter summary
- short multiple-choice quiz
- PowerPoint presentation created by Dr. Keyton

For a list of internet resources, visit http://www.joannkeyton.com/CommunicationResearchMethods.htm.

CHAPTER TWELVE

Quantitative Analysis of Text

Chapter Checklist

After reading this chapter, you should be able to:

1. Differentiate between manifest and latent content in content analysis.

2. Explain the basic processes for conducting a content analysis.

3. Identify appropriate uses of interaction analysis.

4. Explain the basic processes for conducting a research study using interaction analysis.

5. Assess the appropriateness and adequacy of a category scheme.

6. Identify suitable texts or messages to be coded and analyzed.

7. Reliably identify units of analysis.

8. Reliably apply the coding scheme.

9. Assess the validity of a coding scheme.

10. Assess the utility of the coding results with respect to the research questions and hypotheses.

Despite the variety of communication phenomena and contexts available for examination, most researchers would agree that the study of messages or message content is central to the communication discipline. As a result, what constitutes message content, or the text of messages, is broadly defined. Some communication scholars use the terms *content* and *text* only as a referent for spoken discourse, such as discourse that occurs in a policy team's interaction, a couple's conversation, or a speaker's public presentation. Other scholars use the terms *content* and *text* more broadly to include any form of discourse (written, spoken, or visual) that can be captured in some form with which the researcher can work.

The methods for coding and analyzing messages presented in this chapter—content analysis and interaction analysis—are two ways in which researchers can analyze content. These methods allow researchers the opportunity to analyze the content of messages, or what participants actually say in interaction. In contrast, communication research designed as experimental, quasi-experimental, or descriptive research projects often rely on participants' perceptions of their interaction. This distinction can be crucial to the practical significance of research, especially when senders' own words or the interactions among people are crucial to the investigation.

Content analysis is the most basic method of analyzing message content. In addition to providing researchers with a quantitative method for examining what people say, content analysis can also be used to examine emerging themes in participants' retrospective accounts of interaction situations, what participants believe they might say in hypothetical interaction settings, and mediated communication (for example, song lyrics, political advertisements). Like content analysis, interaction analysis is a quantitative method of coding communication into categories. However, interaction analysis is restricted to examining the ongoing communication between two or more individuals, and its focus is on identifying the features or functions of the stream of conversational elements.

CONTENT ANALYSIS

Content analysis integrates both data collection method and analytical technique as a research design to measure the occurrence of some identifiable element in a complete text or set of messages. Neuendorf (2002) defines content analysis as the "summarizing, quantitative analysis of messages that relies on the scientific method and is not limited as to the types of variables that may be measured or the context in which the messages are created or presented" (p. 10). Thus, content analysis can answer research questions such as: How often are older adults shown in television commercials? How much violence are children exposed to by watching television? What kinds of conflicts do employees have with one another at work? Each of these questions, and others like them, can be answered through content analysis. As a technique, content analysis helps researchers make inferences by identifying specific characteristics of messages in their context of use (Krippendorff, 2013).

Researchers agree that content analysis should be objective and systematic and meet the requirement of generality (Berleson, 1952; Holsti, 1969). This method can be used to provide a description of the characteristics of the content itself— the **manifest content.** Or content analysis can be used to study the **latent content**—interpretations about the content that imply something about the nature of the communicators or effects on communicators. An example will help clarify the difference.

In a study of gender and racial distortion in rap music videos (Conrad, Dixon, & Zhang, 2009), coders looked for the main and supporting characters, and if any of those characters were carrying any type of weapon (manifest content). The coders also made coding judgments about demographic characteristics of the characters, such as age, race, and sex (latent content). The presence or absence of main and supporting characters and the presence or absence of weapons is manifest content because this element is physically present in the data, countable, and easily verified (Gray & Densten, 1998). But making coding judgments about characters' age, race, and sex is more subjective, especially in the music video format in which costumes and special effects are frequently used. Thus, coders must infer these characteristics from what was said or how the character acted. Coders also made another coding decision about the use of common themes found in rap and hip-hop videos as suggested by the existing body of literature (for example, materialism, violence, love, expression of culture). These latent content decisions were made based on how characters behaved and what stories were portrayed in the videos. Thus, researchers used both the surface (manifest) content as well as interpretations of the content (latent) to respond to their research question and hypotheses.

Initially, it may seem easier to restrict content analysis to coding manifest content, but that would not always be interesting, or perhaps even meaningful, unless the content's latent value is also analyzed. If a researcher addresses the latent content, he or she is assuming that the behaviors, attitudes, meanings, and values found in the text reflect the behaviors, attitudes, and values of the people who create the material. Thus, content analysis is an indirect way to make inferences about people (Berger, 1998).

But for such inferences to have value, content analysis must be objective. That is, each step must be carried out according to specified rules and procedures. This differentiates content analysis from literary criticism or rhetorical criticism. Having objective codes and procedures for coding established before the coding is conducted helps decrease coders' subjective analysis. If a coding is objective, another coder should be able to use the same procedures with the same data and arrive at similar conclusions (Holsti, 1969).

Likewise, content analysis must be systematic in both identifying content and interpreting it (Kaid & Wadsworth, 1989). In other words, what is to be included or excluded for coding is decided systematically, making it more difficult for researchers to include only those elements that support the research question or hypothesis.

Finally, *generality* means that findings must have theoretical relevance (Holsti, 1969). Simply put, coding text for its content is of little value unless the results of the coding are related to other attributes of the text or characteristics of the message senders or receivers. So researchers would not code the content of something simply because the technique could be applied. Rather, content analysis is used because the results it produces can answer a

---

DESIGN CHECK

Content Analyzing Big Data

Content analysis is often used to examine media messages, as online data are proliferating. Online news stories, tweets, Facebook status updates, and reviews of products and services are just a few types of the "overwhelming volume of information produced by and about human activity" (Lewis, Zamith, & Hermida, 2013, p. 34), which is known as *Big Data*. Using scripts and software, researchers can easily collect and capture thousands of pieces of data. This should make a researcher's job easier in doing content analysis, right? Lewis, Zamith, and Hermida (2013) argue, however, that it is the combination of computational and manual methods that will result in the most reliable and valid research findings. These researchers argue that computers, software, and scripts can help freeze or trap online data that is structural in nature, but manual coding is required to capture the latent content that provides meaning to that data. That is, humans, not computers, are superior in "remaining sensitive to contextual nuance" (p. 41). As you read studies that employ content analysis, ask yourself these questions: Does the method of collecting of online data create barriers to how the data are interpreted? How do the authors of the study address manifest and latent characteristics of the content analyzed?

sufficiently interesting research question or hypothesis that can confirm, extend, or challenge theory.

Procedurally, the central idea behind content analysis is that regardless of the size of text or the number of messages, meaning can be classified into fewer categories (Weber, 1990). Thus, content analysis is one type of data reduction technique, used in much the same way researchers use numbers and statistics to represent participants' actions and perceptions about communication. The assumption here is that elements classified together have similar meanings.

An example of how content analysis serves as a data reduction technique will help clarify this. In a study of characteristics of prosocial behavior in animated Disney films popular with children, the research team (Padilla-Walker, Coyne, Fraser, & Stockdale, 2013) identified all 61 animated films produced by Walt Disney and Disney/Pixar films since 2011 (or 5,128 minutes of viewing time). Operationalizing prosocial behavior as "any voluntary act meant to benefit another, beyond mere sociability or cooperation" (p. 397), the research team identified 5,530 acts of prosocial behavior. These acts were then coded as being physical (51.16%) or verbal (48.86%). Next, based on the research literature, the prosocial acts were coded into one of six motivations: public, emotional, dire, anonymous, altruistic, and compliant. Thus, data found in over 5,000 minutes of film were reduced in two steps: first to two categories of behavior and then to six categories of motivation type, which could be meaningfully analyzed to answer the research questions.

Researchers use content analysis to produce frequency counts for each coded element so that comparisons can be made among them. However, restricting content analysis to a simple analysis of frequencies would dilute some interesting findings and perhaps place undue emphasis

---

DESIGN CHECK

What Content Can Be Analyzed?

What constitutes appropriate content to be analyzed? Literally, any message, or aspect of a message, that can be captured in some permanent form, such as in writing or in a digital format, can be content analyzed. The messages may exist naturally, such as in newspaper comic strips, or the messages may be created in response to a researcher's request. Content that can be analyzed includes the following (Holsti, Loomba, & North, 1968; Neuendorf, 2002):

- Sources, senders, or receivers of messages
- Functions or types of messages
- Message channels
- Implicit or explicit content of the message
- Message effects
- Nonverbal cues or behaviors
- Sounds
- Visual images (drawings, photos)
- Webpages
- Text messages or tweets
- Topics

Typically, a study focuses on one, perhaps two, of these elements. Regardless of what is analyzed, content analysis achieves its best results when the researcher has a well-developed research design with hypotheses or research questions.

on frequency of occurrence. Consider this: Just because an element occurs many times, does it necessarily have greater value than one essential element mentioned fewer times? In addition to using the frequency counts generated by the content coding, a researcher should also address the relevance of the frequencies to the theoretical propositions supporting the study.

The Content Analysis Process

After the researcher has identified the hypotheses or research questions that call for a content analysis research design, the steps of content analysis are the same as for any sound quantitative research design. That is, the researcher should identify a problem, review theory and research, and then finalize research questions or hypotheses. Then specific to content analysis, the process continues with (1) selecting the text or messages to be analyzed, (2) selecting categories and units by which to analyze the text or messages, (3) developing procedures for resolving differences of opinion in coding, (4) selecting a sample for analysis if all the messages cannot be analyzed, (5) coding the messages, (6) interpreting the coding, and (7) reporting the results relative to the research questions or hypotheses (Kaid & Wadsworth, 1989; Riffe, Lacy, & Fico, 1998; Thayer, Evans, McBride, Queen, & Spyridakis, 2007). During the content analysis process, a researcher will have to make both substantive decisions (for example, what to code and how to code it), but also technical decisions (for example, how the coders will mark selections of text and how coding will be interpreted; Hargittai & Karr, 2009).

Selecting What to Code   First, the researcher must identify the universe of messages to which the hypotheses or research questions apply. Second, the researcher must ask, "Do the messages I am interested in exist?" If no, then they must be created. After text or messages are available for coding, the next question to answer is, "Do I need to code all the messages in the population?" In some cases, the answer will be yes. In other cases, far too many data exist to practically code each message or piece of data. Thus, the text or messages must be narrowed to a reasonable and practical sample size. At the same time, a sample must be representative of the whole from which it was drawn.

The first narrowing technique is to cull the dataset for the element of interest. For example, if the research question directs you to code arguments, it is not necessary to code statements or messages that are not arguments. If this produces a reasonable number of messages to be coded (for example, 500 or fewer), then the researcher codes all the arguments. But, for sake of example, let us assume that even after eliminating all other elements, more than 5,000 arguments still exist. Now the researcher can turn to the probability or random sampling techniques (see Chapter 6), such as systematic or stratified sampling.

As an example of systematic sampling, Grimm and Andsager (2011) conducted a content analysis of California newspaper coverage of a proposed immigration-related law that sought to prevent undocumented immigrants from having access to public services. The proposed legislation prompted a number of protest marches across the United States; shortly after these protests, the bill died in committee. To create a sample of news stories for the analysis, the researchers had to select a set of newspapers, which they did based on circulation, geography, and racial diversity of area served by the newspaper; only one newspaper per county was included. Next, the researchers used systematic sampling to create a random sample of news stores from those newspapers. They describe their procedure this way:

> News stories were placed in chronological order within newspapers. Using a random number generator, we started on a random article and used three as the sampling interval in order to achieve a representative sample size across the newspapers included, so that every third article in the sample was coded. This strategy resulted in 280 articles. (p. 776)

Do you ever read the online reviews of products you are thinking about purchasing? One content analysis study examined what characteristics of those reviews are useful to purchasers. Given the prevalence of online shopping, the number of online reviews is considerable. The researchers, Willemsen, Neijens, Bronner, and de Ridder (2011), employed stratified sampling to identify both a reasonable number of reviews of cameras, DVD players, running shoes, and sunscreen. First, the research team identified all online reviews of these products on Amazon.com for a four-year period that had been marked as "useful" by another person. This resulted in 42,700 reviews. The next step was to identify a representative sample. The research team stratified the reviews by product type and randomly selected 400 reviews equally distributed across the two types of products (cameras and DVD players that can be evaluated prior to purchase because of their concrete and functional attributes; running shoes and sunscreen that cannot be evaluated until after purchase because their benefits are intangible until they are experienced). The stratified sampling process significantly reduced the population to a manageable and codeable sample that was representative across each of the four products for which reviews were collected.

As you can see, some populations, especially media and online content, can be difficult to first, identify, and then, second, reduce to a manageable and representative sample. Why? Because identifying the population of interest is difficult to define, and, typically, the population is constantly changing. These are instances in which nonprobability sampling is the most logical for content analysis research designs. Here, the researcher must design the selection of the sample in such a way as to systematically decrease the number of units to be considered for coding. By taking a number of systematic steps, the researcher has reduced the population of relevant texts. The following is a good example of such a sampling procedure.

Hurley and Tewksbury (2012) studied cancer news on the Internet. As you know, content on the Internet is constantly changing, and is personalized to the searcher based on which search engine is used and how that person has used the search engine in the past. To create a sample, the researchers took these steps using the search word "cancer":

1. Used the four most frequented news websites based on reported data.

2. Searched for four contiguous months (March through June)

3. Stratifying by day of the week, seven days were randomly selected from each month

4. For each sampled date, a research team member conducted four searches on each news website in 6-hour intervals

5. The first three pages from each search were included in the sample. This yields 30 stories for each search.

6. Finally, 10 articles were randomly selected from set of 30 stories.

Their procedure created a sample of 1,120 cancer news articles representing each website for each time period. Designing the search in this way ensured that the 24-hour news cycle was covered. Finally, by restricting the search to the first 30 news stories ensured that the sample included the stories most likely read.

Other types of content used as data in content analysis also present some unique challenges with respect to sampling. For example, a unit to be analyzed may be of considerable length, like the interaction between a sales associate and customer—especially one in which the sales associate is helping the customer make a decision between options. In these types of long exchanges of interaction, there is generally a beginning, middle, and end. Certain types of statements may appear at the beginning of exchanges (for example, questions to find out what the customer wants) and not at the end, and vice versa (for example, attempts to persuade the customer toward a choice). Group discussions are another special case. Information is shared among group members in the beginning; evidence is likely to be presented in the middle; and arguments for selecting a solution are more frequently given toward the end of the discussion. Thus, for any dataset in which there is a cycle to the data (e.g., Sunday newspapers have different sections than do newspapers published other days of the week; in a public relations or political campaign, issues or language may change), random sampling may weight the dataset in an unfavorable manner. Stratified random sampling may be the best choice—so that the selected data to code are proportional to the entire dataset (Riffe, Lacy, & Fico, 1998).

Developing Content Categories Content categories are the useful distinctions a researcher makes and are often based on previously reported research. At the same time, the categories must represent the phenomenon the research question or hypothesis calls on to be examined (Kaid & Wadsworth, 1989). Some categorical schemes might call for the researcher to content analyze *what* was said. Other schemes might call for the researcher to content analyze *how* the messages were said (or visualized). As with responses to questions in survey research, content categories must be exhaustive, equivalent, and mutually exclusive. Thus, the categories must cover all possible occurrences and be of the same type. Moreover, a unit cannot be coded into multiple categories. There are, however, rare exceptions to the mutual exclusion criterion.

It is not uncommon to see coding schemes with one category identified as "other." This category typically represents those elements that could not be coded according to one of the specific categories. In essence, then, the *other* category reflects a failure of the classification scheme (Kumar, 1996). Using the *other* category too often usually means that the category system is not as developed as it should be (Krippendorff, 2013). As a general rule, if more than 5% of the coded elements fall into the *other* category, the category system needs to be revised, or coding procedures need to be reexamined.

For example, in coding memorable messages regarding aging for their valence or tone, Holladay (2002) initially conceptualized the coding categories for this variable as positive, negative, or neutral. However, in coding the data, a fourth category was added to code messages that contained both positive and negative elements. Because the coding unit was an entire message, it was possible, of course, for some messages to be of such a length or complexity that both positive and negative tone could be detected by the coders.

Alternatively, content categories can also emerge from the data in what is known as the grounded theory approach of constant comparison (Glaser & Strauss, 1967; Strauss & Corbin, 1998). The relevant categories are derived directly from the data. Such was the case in Rains, Tumlin, and Knapp's (2009) study of electronic bumper stickers, or the sayings or quotations that e-mail users sometimes add at the end of their messages. After collecting over 300 electronic bumper stickers, all three authors first read through all of the sayings, and one author constructed categories of message content. These categories were discussed with the other two authors and refined, resulting in the five categories of wisdom, humor, advice, religious, and sociopolitical commentary. An *other* category also emerged, including a wide range of electronic bumper stickers with organizational slogans, quotes in other languages, or names of fraternities or sororities.

Units of Analysis The **unit of analysis** is the discrete thing that is coded and counted. It is an observable and measurable unit that provides a standard way of dissecting the text into elements to be analyzed. Without a standard or uniform unit, the analysis will be flawed because comparisons will be either impossible or meaningless.

In some cases, the unit of analysis is obvious. Often, these are physical units, such as a website. For example, Cai and colleagues (2003) examined children's websites to see how many collected personal information from children, included privacy statements, and required parental permission for children to participate or give personal information. The website was the unit of analysis regardless of the number of links or subpages it had. Coders aggregated their codings across a website's various pages to create one coding sheet per site. Even so, the rules for identifying the unit should be explicit.

In other cases, the unit of analysis is dependent on the context of the interaction. For example, for a study of impression management strategies used in spoken and written corporate discourse, Allen and Caillouet (1994) used the statement as the unit of analysis. They defined a statement as "a sentence or set of sentences which expressed a complete thought interpretable as a strategic act (i.e., influencing or describing the corporate actor's public image)" (p. 50). With this definition, some statements were as short as one sentence, whereas over half of the statements were longer.

Some typical units of analysis in communication research include the following:

- Words or phrases. For example, Cressman, Callister, Robinson, and Near (2009) analyzed the content of popular teen movies for the seven dirty words that the FCC has deemed unspeakable for broadcast.

- Complete thoughts or sentences. As an example of the most common unit of analysis, one research team (Pratt, Wiseman, Cody, & Wendt, 1999) examined how questions were used to develop relationships between senior citizens and children over e-mail. Normally, a question is easily identified by the question mark at the end of a sentence. However, in e-mail format, where speed is valued and grammatical accuracy is not, question marks do not always appear. Thus, the research team had to more closely assess the e-mails for instances when requests for information and implicit pressure to respond were made.

- Themes, or a single assertion about some subject. For example, Hefner and Wilson (2013) coded the themes in romantic comedy movies that were evidence of the four parts of the romantic ideal (i.e., love conquers all, idealization of partner, soul mate/one and only, or love at first sight).

- Paragraphs or short whole texts. As an example, Keyton and Smith (2009) coded employees written responses to an open-ended question at the end of a survey.

- Full articles. Meeks (2013) coded newspaper articles about male and female political candidates.

- Characters or speakers. For example, Ricke (2012) content analyzed the characters who sent and received derogatory messages on the TV show *Family Guy*.

- Photographs. As an example, Baiocchi-Wagner (2012) coded photographs from brochures about long-term care facilities. Photos of residents of these facilities were identified and coded for age, sex, affect (for example, did they appear to be enjoying themselves?), and pose (the resident only, or the resident with others).

- Advertisements. Roberts (2013) examined Web-only video ads and television ads used in campaigns of presidential candidates.

- Television programs, films, or scenes. To study the differences in films that had both R-rated versions and NC-17 rated versions, Vandenbosch, Vervloessem, and Eggermont (2013) analyzed scenes from music videos and programs broadcast on music entertainment television channels.

With the current emphasis on written or visual texts that can be captured digitally and the ease with which interaction can be audio- or videotaped, one additional step may be needed before the unitizing and categorizing steps already discussed. When continuous streams of interaction are to be coded and the unit of analysis is theoretically driven (for example, violent scenes in film, topics of conversation, conflict episodes) rather than natural (for example, words, sentences, questions), coders must first identify whether the interaction called for by the unit of analysis exists (Krippendorff, 2013). Regardless of what unit is selected, it remains consistent throughout the research process. For example, if the unit chosen is a complete sentence, then only complete sentences are unitized and coded. A researcher could not analyze words or phrases that are part of the complete sentence. Thus, once a unit is decided upon, it remains constant through coding and analysis processes, as well as in the presentation of findings (Kripendorff, 2013).

Besides making decisions about what to code, researchers conducting content analyses must also establish how they will quantify the coded content. Codes could be simply counted for frequency—the most common way to analyze this type of data. But others are possible. For example, seconds and minutes or inches and pages could quantify media messages. Recognize the assumptions accompanying both units of enumeration (Holsti, 1969). With these, the researcher is assuming that frequency, length of interaction, and message size are valid indicators of concern, focus, intensity, value, importance, and so on. Finally, after units of analysis have been identified, coders can also rate the unit. For example, in a study of police-civilian interactions (Dixon, Schell, Giles, & Drogos, 2008), coders were asked to rate the officer's respect and politeness on a Likert-type item anchored by 0 for *not at all respectful/polite* and 10 for *very respectful/polite.*

Training Coders   Because content coding should be systematic and objective, all coders, including the researchers who develop the coding system, must be trained. Research has demonstrated that training can increase agreement among coders. But to achieve increased agreement, training must be more than a simple discussion of the coding categories (Kaid & Wadsworth, 1989).

The coding system should be committed to paper so that all coders are trained from the same category scheme and they can return to it at any time. Many researchers prepare a codebook to identify coding content, coding units, and rules for coding. As part of their training, coders generally practice on text or messages similar to those that must be coded. After a sufficient degree of reliability is established among coders, they work individually. See the codebook (Figure 12.1) for Ricke's (2012) content analysis of *Family Guy*, an adult animated sitcom. Notice how each category, and the codes within categories are exhaustive, mutually exclusive, and equivalent. With this type of precision in the codebook, it is more likely that coders will achieve reliability in their coding.

Coding Reliability   Several reliability issues exist with respect to content analysis. In content analysis, reliability is identified as **interrater reliability, interrater agreement,** or **intercoder reliability** and it must be calculated for two different sets of coding decisions. Interrater reliability must be calculated for two types of content coding decisions (Cappella, 1987). The first is **unitizing reliability,** or the degree to which two or more observers agree that communication action has taken place and can identify the action in the stream of interaction (Krippendorff, 2013). In other words, do the coders agree on what is to be coded? Units can be small, such as phrases, sentences, or complete thoughts, or units can be large, such as a lengthy turn at talk or a news story. Essentially, unitizing requires raters to identify the beginning and ending of what they will code. If

the unit to be coded is a sentence, then agreement should not be too much of a problem. Natural units, like complete sentences, have standardized identifiers for marking their beginning and ending. But if the text is naturally occurring conversation, and speakers do not speak in complete sentences, then identifying the unit to be coded is far more difficult. Coding units, like themes or stories, are more abstract, and it will generally take more time to train coders to identify the unit. After the units to be coded have been identified, each coder decides independently into which category the unit will be placed. The more frequently coders choose the same category, the greater their degree of coding or **categorizing reliability.** This is the second type of interrater reliability that must be established.

Several formulas exist for determining the degree of intercoder or interrater reliability in coding content. **Scott's *pi*** is commonly used in communication research when two coders are used because it accounts for the number of categories in the coding scheme as well as for the probable frequency for each category. The formula and steps for calculating intercoder reliability can be found at the website www.mhhe.com/keyton4 that accompanies this text.

Calculating intercoder reliability is fairly straightforward; identifying an acceptable level of intercoder reliability is far more subjective. Generally, researchers must make this judgment based on the research question or hypothesis and the context of the coding. As the number of categories increases or as the coding process becomes more complex, lower levels of reliability can be acceptable. In general, intercoder reliability of .90 is nearly always acceptable, and .80 is acceptable in most situations. Intercoder reliability of .70 is appropriate in some exploratory studies and the lower end limit for acceptable coding decisions (Lombard, Snyder-Duch, & Bracken, 2002). The degree of intercoder reliability and the procedures used to obtain it should be reported in the research study.

For example, in a study of a series of weekly business meetings, Beck and Keyton (2009) wanted to examine how messages function in the meetings. The meetings were audio and video recorded. Working from the transcripts, two coders independently

Example of Content Analysis Codebook

A. Season (Write In)
B. Episode (Write In)
C. Scene
   1. A scene is marked:
      i. Every time a new character enters the frame
      ii. Every time a character leaves the frame
      iii. Every time the setting changes
D. Aggressor [who was the aggressor of the violence]
   1. Male (=1)
   2. Female (=2)
   3. Animal (=3)
   4. Multiple (=4)
   5. Cannot Determine/Unknown [We cannot see] (=5)
   6. Spontaneous (=6)
E. Recipient [who was the recipient of the violence]
   1. Male (=1)
   2. Female (=2)
   3. Animal (=3)
   4. Multiple (=4)
   5. Cannot Determine/Unknown [We cannot see] (=5)
   6. No Recipient/ Phantom Recipient (=6)
   7. Spontaneous (=7)
F. Aggressor Race [Physical Violence]
   1. White (=1)
   2. Black (=2)
   3. Asian (=3)
   4. Hispanic (=4)
   5. Multiple (=5)
   6. Cannot Determine (=6)
G. Recipient Race [Physical Violence]
   1. White (=1)
   2. Black (=2)
   3. Asian (=3)
   4. Hispanic (=4)
   5. Multiple (=5)
   6. Cannot Determine (=6)
H. Aggressor Age [Physical Violence]
   1. Young (=1)
   2. Middle Aged (=2)
   3. Older (=3)
   4. Multiple Aggressors (=4)
   5. Cannot Determine (=5)
I. Recipient Age [Physical Violence]
   1. Young (=1)
   2. Middle Aged (=2)
   3. Older (=3)
   4. Multiple Recipients (=4)
   5. Cannot Determine (=5)

J. Aggressor Sexual Orientation [Physical Violence]
   1. Straight (=1)
   2. Gay (=2)
   3. Cannot Determine (=3)
K. Recipient Sexual Orientation [Physical Violence]
   1. Straight (=1)
   2. Gay (=2)
   3. No Receiver (=4)
   4. Cannot Determine (=3)
L. Aggressor Disabled? [Physical Violence]
   1. Yes (=1)
   2. No (=2)
   3. Cannot Determine (=3)
M. Recipient Disabled? [Physical Violence]
   1. Yes (=1)
   2. No (=2)
   3. Cannot Determine (=3)
N. Reciprocal [was the violence reciprocated by the recipient?]
   1. Yes (=1)
   2. No (=2)
O. Type of Violence
   1. Punch (=1)
   2. Kick (=2)
   3. Slap (=3)
   4. Poke (=4)
   5. Pushing (=5)
   6. Forcibly Holding (=6)
   7. Grabbing (=7)
   8. Shaking (=8)
   9. Throwing (=9)
   10. Cannot Determine (=11)
   11. Various types of violence (=12)
   12. Other (=10)
P. Aggressor [Language]
   1. Male (=1)
   2. Female (=2)
   3. Animal (=3)
   4. Multiple (=4)
   5. Cannot Determine/Unknown [We cannot see] (=5)
   6. Spontaneous (=6)
Q. Recipient [Language]
   1. Male (=1)
   2. Female (=2)
   3. Animal (=3)
   4. Multiple (=4)
   5. Cannot Determine/Unknown [We cannot see] (=5)
   6. No Recipient/ Phantom Recipient (=6)
   7. Spontaneous (=7)
R. Aggressor Race [Language]
   1. White (=1)
   2. Black (=2)

   3. Asian (=3)
   4. Hispanic (=4)
   5. Multiple (=5)
   6. Cannot Determine (=6)
S. Recipient Race [Language]
   1. White (=1)
   2. Black (=2)
   3. Asian (=3)
   4. Hispanic (=4)
   5. Multiple (=5)
   6. Cannot Determine (=6)
T. Aggressor Age [Language]
   1. Young (=1)
   2. Middle Aged (=2)
   3. Older (=3)
   4. Multiple Aggressors (=4)
   5. Cannot Determine (=5)
U. Recipient Age [Language]
   1. Young (=1)
   2. Middle Aged (=2)
   3. Older (=3)
   4. Multiple Recipients (=4)
   5. Cannot Determine (=5)
V. Aggressor Sexual Orientation [Language]
   1. Straight (=1)
   2. Gay (=2)
   3. Cannot Determine (=3)
W. Recipient Sexual Orientation [Language]
   1. Straight (=1)
   2. Gay (=2)
   3. No Receiver (=4)
   4. Cannot Determine (=3)
X. Aggressor Disabled? [Language]
   1. Yes (=1)
   2. No (=2)
   3. Cannot Determine (=3)
Y. Recipient Disabled? [Language]
   1. Yes (=1)
   2. No (=2)
   3. Cannot Determine (=3)
Z. Reciprocal [was the violence reciprocated by the recipient?]
   1. Yes (=1)
   2. No (=2)
AA. Language Type
   1. Hate Speech (=1)
   2. Sexist Speech (=2)
   3. Homophobic Speech (=3)
   4. Racist Speech (=4)
   5. Religious Intolerant (=5)
   6. Disability Intolerant (=6)
   7. Overtly Sexual (=7)
   8. Multiple Types of Aggressive Language (=8)
   9. Other (=9)

SOURCE: LaChrystal Ricke.

FIGURE 12.1 Codebook for Family Guy Content Analysis

TRY THIS!

Identifying Themes of Freshman Socialization

Try this as a class exercise in collecting and coding content data. Ask 10 freshmen at your university or college to finish the statement "Being a freshman at [college/university] is like _____" on an index card. Combine the responses you collect with those of another member of your class. Individually, each of you should read each index card. Now, working in pairs, examine the cards and identify the evident themes. When you find cards that are similar, start a stack. Continue this until every card is in a stack. If a card is truly distinct from the others, it is okay for that one card to be by itself. Now look at the stacks you created. Do the stacks need refining? The next step is to begin creating labels for the stacks. After this step, examine each card in each stack to verify that the card is representative of the stack label. Adjust stacks and labels as necessary. To what extent did you and your coding partner agree on identifying the themes? How did you resolve any disagreements? Were there disagreements that could not be resolved? Did you find themes similar to those identified by Jorgensen-Earp and Staton (1993), which are presented below?

Themes of Newness	Themes of Status	Themes of Engagement	Themes of Satisfaction
New environment	Back to square one	Cut adrift	Rude awakening
New experience	Low prestige	Stranger in a strange land	Prison
New chapter	Accomplishment	Lost	Unpleasant experience
New beginning	Moving up	Isolated	Survival
Clean slate		Small	Ordeal
Metamorphosis	*Themes of Control*	Freedom	Self-discovery
Adult	Overwhelmed	Breaking away	Enlightenment
Rebirth	Pressure	Journey	Challenge
Freshness	Confusion	Explorer	Contented
	Competition	Belonging	Supportive
	Struggle		Learning
	Command		
	Self-discipline		
	Poised on the brink		
	Receptive		

How Did the Researcher Perform the Content Analysis?

1. How did the researcher define the coding unit?
2. How did the researcher define the categories for coding the units? Are the categories exhaustive, mutually exclusive, and equivalent?
3. Was the coding system tested before being used to answer the research question or hypothesis?
4. What steps were taken to train coders? Was coder training adequate?
5. How reliable were coders?
6. How was the coding conducted?
7. How well did the coding scheme relate to the issues posed by the research question or hypothesis?
8. Do you agree with the researcher's interpretation of the coding results?

---

identified complete thought units. Then, the coders compared their decisions. Their agreement would be the basis of the unitizing reliability calculation, or .92. In communication research, this level of coder reliability is generally acceptable.

In the next step, the two coders independently identified which of 12 message functions best characterized each thought unit. After comparing their ratings, the research team calculated **Cohen's kappa,** a measure of interrater reliability for categorical data. Just like Cronbach's alpha, this reliability measure ranges from perfect agreement (1.0) to agreement that is no better than would be expected by chance (0.0). For the coding of message function, or categorizing reliability, Cohen's kappa was .90. Because an acceptable level of coding reliability was established, the rest of the transcripts could be coded.

Another example of intercoder reliability is demonstrated in Malone and Hayes (2012) examination of employees' perceptions of backstabbing in the workplace. The researchers asked participants to fill out a survey, after which participants responded to three open-ended questions. For example, participants were asked to describe in writing "an incident in detail that occurred at work when they felt they were 'backstabbed'" (p. 203). These open-ended responses were coded by two coders, which resulted in 8 types of backstabbing incidents,

13 types of motives for backstabbing, and 20 types of responses to backstabbing at work. After each coder independently coded the responses, Scott's *pi* (Holsti, 1969) was used as an index of coding reliability. This technique is often used for intercoder reliability because it accounts for the number of categories in the coding scheme as well as the frequency with which each code is used. The intercoder agreement, or reliability was .95.

Validity   In content analysis, *validity* refers to the appropriateness and adequacy of the coding scheme for the text or messages being coded. Researchers increase the validity of their coding schemes by examining previous research on the same and similar issues and by basing their coding schemes on theory (Potter & Levine-Donnerstein, 1999). At a minimum, any categorical coding scheme must have face validity. Recall, however, that face validity is generally weak in establishing the accuracy or truthfulness of what is being measured. Researchers using content analysis produce the most valid results when content coding schemes are examined for construct validity by comparing the results of coding with another external measure (Weber, 1990). Return to Chapter 5 to review issues of construct validity.

Krippendorff (2013) also recommends that researchers using content analysis should be concerned about **semantic validity.** That is, to what degree do the analytical categories of the content coded have meaning for individuals in a particular context? Content coding of messages and symbols depends upon both denotative and connotative meaning. Considering semantic validity reminds researchers to code content and interpret those codings within the context from which the texts were selected.

Interpreting the Coding Results

After the coding is complete, the researcher must interpret what was coded. Just like any other research method, content analysis must be relative to the initial research question or hypothesis and interpreted back to the context from which the data were selected. Researchers can analyze content coded data in several ways. The simplest, and most common, method of analysis is to look for the frequency of categorical occurrences. Remember, however, that the underlying assumption here is that frequency can be interpreted as a measure of importance or value. A closely related, but more sophisticated interpretive approach is to look for differences in the application of categories. Researchers using these interpretive frames often use chi-squares to determine if significant differences exist in the frequencies of the categories (see Chapter 10).

Trends, patterns, and structures of communication phenomena can also be revealed through content analysis (Krippendorff, 2013). These types of analysis seek to identify which elements precede or succeed other elements. An example of each is described in the paragraphs that follow.

For example, when researchers look for trends, they examine how the data move or change over time. For example, Rowling, Jones, and Sheets (2011) examined U.S. political and news discourse surrounding the Abu Ghraib prison scandal. To look at how the presentation of this event changed over time and in response to previous stories about the event, the researchers conducted three content analyses. First they coded speeches, interviews, press conferences, and press releases by members of the White House and U.S. military. In the second content analysis, the research team coded statements by Democratic and Republican members of the

U.S. Senate and House of Representatives. Last, the research team coded news coverage of Abu Ghraib on CBS News and in the *Washington Post*. Thus, the unit of analysis was the source of the messages, and the sources were coded for types of sources and the types of claims they made about the events. Types of sources were: (a) U.S. government and military officials, (b) U.S. academics, members of think tanks, members of nongovernmental organizations, and former government and military officials, (c) those accused, (d) U.S. news media and U.S. citizens, and (e) foreign sources, such as detainees, governmental officials, experts, media, and citizens from other countries. The claims sources made were coded if it was congruent with the administration's message, challenged the administration's messages, or was mixed/neutral. Looking at how these different sources described and explained, or commented on, the Abu Ghraib event, the research team could demonstrate that news from the White House and formal sources made attempts to contain the event by constructing their messages as frames of national identity protection. They could also demonstrate that Democratic congressional members did challenge the national identity frame. However, the national identity frame was repeated, or echoed, by the press. In the conclusion of their journal article, the research team argues that their study "illuminates the complex process through which the press aligns its coverage with government communications, suggesting that both the source and content of political frames deeply matters in determining which frames manifest in the press" (p. 1058). This content analysis reveals how an important news event is first presented, the way in which it was challenged, and how news sources relied on framing by the administration in its presentation of the event.

Computers and Content Analysis

As with most processes, computers and content analysis software programs are invaluable tools. Some researchers who conduct content analysis studies use simple spreadsheets to keep track of the content and the coding. Even the search or find function in a word document program can

AN ETHICAL ISSUE

Taking Content Out of Context

Content analysis is a useful method for finding themes in a great number of messages. Because the sample is generally several hundred or more, a researcher typically presents the category scheme, a few examples for each category, and the frequencies and percentages of themes for each category. Thus, a consumer must trust that the researcher is not interpreting the findings out of the context in which participants provided them. For example, a researcher asks participants to write a brief description about what they would consider to be unethical communication practices. From these descriptions, the researcher identifies a handful of themes to include, for example, dishonesty in representing one's self, telling a small lie to protect someone else, telling a small lie to be polite, and so on. It would be unethical for the researcher to interpret these results as unethical communication practices *committed* by participants. They are only the communication practices participants *consider* to be unethical. Because participants wrote about these themes does not mean they are guilty of the practices. Researchers using content analysis want to make inferences from their findings, but they must retain the contextuality participants used in providing the descriptions.

be helpful. For example, if your unit of analysis is a discrete unit (for example, a word or phrase), and you have a large quantity of messages or text to examine, the search or find function in a word processing program will speed up the identification process. Some researchers use more sophisticated software programs as an aid in their coding and analytical tasks. But even these programs do not allow the researcher to turn over the entire coding and interpretation process to the computer. Although computers can speed up the mechanical process, limitations exist to what they can do.

Furthermore, computers will not decrease the need for developing the coding scheme. In fact, using a computer will force you to identify coding units more explicitly because all judgments must be built by you into the software program. As a result, coding reliability will increase as long as the researcher has done the necessary foundational work. After the categories and assumptions are prescribed, the computer is capable of using them over and over without variation. This could certainly be an advantage over human coders. Recognize, however, that if the categories and assumptions built into the program are in error, the results obtained will contain those same errors.

Strengths of Content Analysis Research

Clearly, a strength of content analysis is that the data are close to the communicator. In some cases, communicators naturally generate text or messages prior to the researcher's involvement. Written texts are also available widely in libraries (for example, magazines, newspapers, books) and over the Internet (for example, chat room discussions, web pages, archived materials). Audio- and videotapes can be made of broadcast materials with home equipment (for research purposes only), or researchers can ask people to participate in a study to create or develop texts or messages to be coded. In either case, the communicators themselves generate text or messages to be coded. As a result of this closeness, it is easy for the researcher to argue that the messages produced are valid and representative and that inferences drawn from the categorical analysis of these texts and messages are plausible.

This method is also unobtrusive. After texts or messages are captured, researchers can analyze the messages without participants' awareness. Some publicly available texts are available without the knowledge or approval of the message creator. Thus, a researcher can study the texts of a person whom they would likely never meet or be granted the opportunity to interview. Finally, the method is applicable to texts or messages of any structure. This advantage increases the scope of research as content analysis can be used on nearly any type of message in any form.

Limitations of Content Analysis Research

Despite these strengths, content analysis also has its limitations. First, if text or messages cannot be captured, the content cannot be coded. Second, coding schemes can contain too few or too many categories, decreasing the likelihood that nuances of the text or messages will surface.

INTERACTION ANALYSIS

Like content analysis, **interaction analysis** is systematic in the way it codes communication into categories. However, interaction analysis codes the content of *ongoing* communication between two or more individuals. Thus, the focus of interaction analysis is to identify the verbal or nonverbal features or functions of the stream of conversational elements. Besides being systematic, interaction analysis is also sequential (Bakeman & Gottman, 1997). Using a standard set of rules for coding the interaction, researchers can conduct more complex analyses, including analyzing the intent and function of messages, determining the effects of messages, and examining messages for their relationship to one another over time (Tucker, Weaver, & Berryman-Fink, 1981). Why? Because messages are captured in the order in which they occurred.

The most effective coding schemes are those based on theories. Much time and energy is involved in developing coding schemes, and they are usually refined and revised over time as researchers—those who originated the coding scheme and others—work with the coding scheme, apply it to different types of interaction, and ask different research questions. Thus, most scholars would agree that interaction coding schemes are always in some stage of development.

You can use several interaction analysis coding schemes in research projects, especially for the study of interpersonal and group communication. For example, Siminoff and Step (2011) analyzed the dyadic interactions of clinicians and patients in health settings. The Siminoff Communication Content and Affect Program (SCCAP) has demonstrated reliability and validity for coding both the relational and persuasive aspects of conversation in health settings. Interaction analysis is also a good choice for studying the complexity of interaction that occurs between and among group members. Bales's (1950) Interaction Process Analysis (IPA) has long been used to study the task and relational elements of group interaction. The coding scheme identifies interaction as task or relational based on the function the interaction serves in the group members' conversations (see Keyton, 1997). Another coding scheme for group and team communication focuses on conflict. Poole and Dobosh (2010) used the Group Working Relationships Coding System, or GWRCS (Poole,1983a; Poole & Roth, 1989), to code conflict process in the interactions of a jury making a decision about an accused's guilt or innocence, and a decision about the sentence. As you can imagine, conflict is likely to occur when jurors are making such important and consequential decisions. The GWRCS allows researchers to identify patterns of conflict interaction and to track how the jury managed its conflict processes. A third coding scheme is the Conversational Argument Coding Scheme (Canary & Seibold, 2010; Meyers & Brashers, 2010; Seibold, Lemus, & Kang, 2010), developed to code the structure of arguments in group decision making. This scheme is used in an example later in this chapter (see Table 12.1).

Gathering and Preparing the Interaction for Coding

Interaction coding requires that researchers listen to the conversation and determine how the conversation is structured and how meaning is created relative to what happens before and after each unit of interaction. This type of coding complexity is easier to handle when researchers create a written transcription of the interaction from

TABLE 12.1 Example of Interaction Analysis Coding

Unit #	Speaker	Complete Thought	Coding of Complete Thought
329	Larry	Is not getting a degree from there, is getting the degree from (a less prestigious university) better than going four years and not getting a degree from Harvard?	Proposition
330	Tom	(Better than) Let's say a 90% chance of getting a degree from the (less prestigious university).	Assertion
331	Larry	Is better than a 10% chance?	Proposition
332	Tom	A 10% chance from Harvard.	Assertion
333a	Larry	You say yes.	Assertion
333b	Larry	I say no way.	Objection
334	Kathy	I say no way.	Objection
335	Tom	I say it's better to go to Harvard.	Proposition
336a	Terry	You guys really think if he goes to school and he flunks out he can't go for a degree anywhere?	Proposition
336b	Terry	He can.	Assertion
336c	Terry	He can still go to the other place and still get his degree there.	Elaboration
337a	Tom	Oh good point.	Agreement
337b	Tom	I mean, why not go for it?	Proposition

SOURCE: "Argument in Initial Group Decision-Making Discussions: Refinement of a Coding Scheme and a Descriptive Quantitative Analysis," by R. A. Meyers, D. R. Seibold, and D. Brashers, 1991, *Western Journal of Speech Communication, 55,* pp. 47–68. Used by permission of the Western States Communication Association.

audio- or videotapes before they begin the process of unitizing and then coding the interaction. As with content analysis procedures described earlier, the data to be coded must first be unitized. This means that independently two or more judges identify the units of analysis to be coded. Unitizing reliability is computed to determine the degree of consistency in how the judges are unitizing the conversation. Disagreements about their choices must be resolved before coding the interaction by categories can begin. Obviously, judges or coders must be trained as to what constitutes the unit of analysis before they begin this phase of the analysis. Often, judges are trained on conversations that are similar to but not part of the dataset for the research project.

One of the most frequently used units of analysis in interaction analysis is the complete thought. This means that any statement that functions as a complete thought or change of thought is considered one unit. This is an intermediate position between coding words or phrases at a more microlevel and coding complete speaking turns or utterances at a more macrolevel. Look at the example in Table 12.1, drawn from Meyers et al. (1991), to understand how complete thoughts are captured and coded.

Coding the Interaction

As with unitizing, coders must be trained in the specific coding scheme for the research project. For the project from which Table 12.1 was selected, Meyers and colleagues (1991) reported that two pairs of two coders were trained over a period of 5 weeks for more than 40 hours of training and practice coding sessions. The four coders worked until their coding decisions achieved 80% agreement. From then on, each pair of coders independently coded half of the transcripts. Although coders worked primarily from the typed transcripts, they could refer to groups' videotaped interaction at any time. Even with this training, independent coding of the transcript resulted in differences between coders. To reduce these differences, teams of coders discussed and clarified each of these instances. Again, the coding reliability between coders was computed. Disagreements between coders were discussed until coders could agree on a coding selection. Although specifics may differ slightly from research project to research project, the procedures described here are fairly common.

Analyzing and Interpreting the Coding

After the interaction is coded, it is time to analyze the codings. Again, the researcher returns to the research question or hypothesis that provides a foundation for the study. In the example from Meyers et al. (1991), the researchers asked, "What is the distribution of argument acts across all group discussions?" (p. 52). Thus, researchers were examining group conversations to discover the ways in which argument is used in group decision making.

In a common type of analysis, researchers conduct frequency analyses for each of the coding categories. At that point, a researcher has summarized the raw data and can now analyze these results against the theoretical position posited in the literature review. But researchers also examine the coded transcripts for evidence of patterns that simple frequency analyses cannot illuminate. Meyers and colleagues (1991) examined the coded transcripts to determine how argumentative elements were placed or sequenced relative to one another.

More sophisticated analyses can also be conducted on coded interaction units. For example, Keyton and Beck (2009) used Bales's (1950) Interaction Process Analysis (IPA) to code each complete thought of the conversations from five meetings of a breast cancer support group. Next, the researchers identified each instance in which a relationally coded thought unit was preceded and followed by a task-oriented thought unit. Agreement, one type of relationally oriented thought unit, was identified most frequently, or 136 times across the five meetings. A closer examination of the instances in which agreement was positioned between task-oriented thought units revealed that agreement was used in three ways in these support group meetings. Acts of agreement by support group members (a) confirmed information from another speaker, (b) signaled the direction of the conversation, and (c) signaled identification of other members. In a different analysis of the same support group conversations, Beck and Keyton (2014) used IPA to identify in detail how the support group's leader facilitated conversation among group members to provide the social support group members were seeking. The turn-by-turn analysis demonstrated that social support is not given like advice, rather it is interactive.

Strengths of Interaction Analysis

An obvious strength of interaction analysis is that elements preceding and subsequent to the element being coded are considered in placing conversational elements into categories. Thus, most interaction coding schemes place considerable emphasis on the relative position of any category to the context and the entirety of the conversation. Although interaction coding schemes can be developed for virtually any communication phenomenon, communication scholars have continued to use and develop several coding schemes that are fundamental to our understanding of communication. This type of scholarship development encourages theoretical insight, a quality missed by developing novel coding schemes for specific research projects.

Limitations of Interaction Analysis

Of course, interaction analysis is limited to the degree the coding scheme is valid and representative of the communication phenomenon being explored. Therefore, the development of the coding scheme is critical to the success of its results.

Unitizing conversation into elements that can be coded is generally a greater problem in interaction analysis than in content analysis because interaction analysis relies solely on ongoing streams of conversation, which are not always neat and tidy. Thus, researchers must train coders to select and identify units consistently. The other limitation is that coding in interaction analysis generally takes longer because it is a more laborious process.

DESIGN CONSIDERATIONS

Whether your research design calls for content analysis or interaction analysis, several criteria are important for designing an effective study (Waitzkin, 1993). First, there should be a balance between method and meaning. Although procedures for validity and reliability should be used, these and the procedures used for data coding and analysis should not overwhelm or distort the meaning of the text. Second, if not all text or content can be coded, texts should be selected through some type of sampling procedure to ensure the representativeness of the analysis. Third, selected texts should be available to others so that researchers can question or build upon what was found. Fourth, if it is necessary to transcribe audio or video data into written text, standardized rules for transcribing text from spoken or visual form to written form should be developed and applied, and the reliability of the transcription process should be assessed. Fifth, procedures for interpreting the text should be decided in advance and in consideration of the content and structure of the text, as well as in consideration of the research question or hypothesis. Most important, the interpretation procedures should be designed in accordance with the theory or perspective providing the foundation for the analysis.

If you use one of the quantitative methods for analyzing content, you need to consider three general limitations (Street, 1993; Waitzkin, 1993). First, quantifying codes of a text cannot capture the complexity of discourse. Regardless of how discrete a coding scheme appears, some information about the conversation is lost when it is coded quantitatively. Second, quantitative coding cannot capture the contextuality of conversation. In fact, much of the context from which the text is taken or captured cannot be retained. Third, coding interaction into categories cannot represent the quality of messages (for example, meaningfulness, appropriateness) as interpreted by those in the conversation.

SUMMARY

1. Content analysis and interaction analysis are two quantitative methods for analyzing communication texts.

2. Content analysis is the most basic methodology for analyzing message content; it integrates the data collection method and analytical technique in a research design to reveal the occurrence of some identifiable element in a text or set of messages.

3. Category schemes allow researchers to code the manifest and latent meanings to text.

4. Content analyses are often reported and analyzed using frequency counts and chi-square.

5. Coding schemes can be developed from existing theory or other published research findings, or coding schemes can emerge from the data.

6. Virtually any communication phenomena can be content analyzed; codable elements include words or phrases, complete thoughts or sentences, themes, paragraphs or short whole texts, characters or speakers, communicative acts or behaviors, advertisements, and entire television programs.

7. At least two trained coders code the selected content; interrater reliability must be calculated for both unitizing and coding decisions.

8. Validity issues for content coding rest primarily with the appropriateness and adequacy of the coding scheme.

9. Content analysis can be used to identify frequencies of occurrence, differences, trends, patterns, and standards.

10. Computer software is available to assist the researcher in the coding process.

11. Interaction analysis, especially suitable for interpersonal and group communication, codes the ongoing conversation between two or more individuals into categories.

12. Interaction analysis focuses on the features or functions of the stream of conversational elements.

13. Coding of interaction elements is based on the element itself, and what happens before and after it.

KEY TERMS

categorizing reliability

Cohen's kappa

content analysis

interaction analysis

intercoder reliability

interrater agreement

interrater reliability

latent content

manifest content

Scott's *pi*

semantic validity

unitizing reliability

unit of analysis

See the website www.mhhe.com/keyton4 that accompanies this text. For each chapter, the site contains a:

- chapter outline
- chapter checklist
- chapter summary
- short multiple-choice quiz
- PowerPoint presentation created by Dr. Keyton

For a list of internet resources, visit http://www.joannkeyton.com/CommunicationResearch-Methods.htm.

CHAPTER THIRTEEN

Reading and Writing the Quantitative Research Report

Chapter Checklist

After reading this chapter, you should be able to:

1. Review and revise your literature review to ensure that the literature review aligns with the designed and tested study.

2. Review and revise, if necessary, the problem statement.

3. Review and revise, if necessary, the research questions and hypotheses presented in your study.

4. Write a method section describing the participants, research procedures, and variables.

5. Write a results section that presents the findings in a straightforward manner.

6. Write a discussion section that provides interpretations and implications of the research findings.

7. Identify the limitations of your study and interpret the limitations with respect to your findings.

8. Recommend future research ideas and methods.

9. Finish the research report with an appropriate title, title page, abstract, and list of references.

10. Use APA style for direct and indirect citations and for developing the reference list.

11. Use the revision process to enhance the quality of the written research report.

12. Submit your paper for review to a communication association convention.

No study is complete until the researcher writes the research report to communicate the findings to others. Just as researchers draw from previously presented and published research, they are also responsible for preparing a research report for use by others. Thus, the typical audience for a research report is other researchers and scholars, including students like you.

Following one of the traditions of science, disciplines that study human behavior (such as communication, management, psychology, sociology) and the physical world (such as biology and chemistry) rely upon the same basic format for presenting research results. This chapter focuses on the four basic sections of a quantitative research paper written to be published in communication journals: literature review, method, results, and discussion. See Figure 13.1.

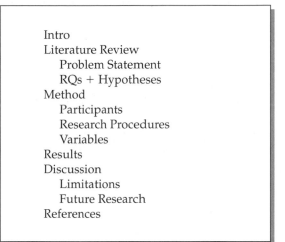

Intro
Literature Review
    Problem Statement
    RQs + Hypotheses
Method
    Participants
    Research Procedures
    Variables
Results
Discussion
    Limitations
    Future Research
References

FIGURE 13.1 The Primary Sections of a Quantitative Research Report.

REVIEWING THE LITERATURE REVIEW

Now that your data have been collected and analyzed, it is time to go back to the *literature review* you developed at the beginning of the research process (see Chapter 2). As you worked through the design of the research project, you may have encountered additional journal articles and book chapters that should be included in the literature review section of the research report.

Taking the time to read the literature review, and revise if necessary, ensures that the literature review section of your research report is parallel with the study you designed and completed. If you answer "yes," to these questions, you are ready to move onto the other sections of the research report.

- Does the title of the literature report reflect what happened or was found in the study?

- Are all of the terms defined and documented the first time they are used in the literature review?

- Does the problem statement still reflect the social or practical significance of your study?

- Have you added any additional journal articles or book chapters that strengthen your arguments?

Reviewing the Research Questions and Hypotheses

As you finalize the literature review, it is also a good time to reflect on the best placement for the research questions and hypotheses. There are two general forms for presenting research questions and hypotheses. The first is to display the questions and hypotheses as they emerge from the literature review. In this form of presentation, these elements are interspersed throughout the literature review, and the literature review has a repetitive broad-to-narrow structure as each hypothesis or research question flows from the narrative before the next broad-to-narrow section begins. The alternative is to present the research questions and hypotheses together as a summary to the literature review.

As a reminder, each hypothesis or research question should be separately stated as a simple sentence or simple question. And each hypothesis or research question should be identified as such, usually with the notations H_1, H_2, or RQ_1, RQ_2, and so on. Besides helping to identify specific questions and hypotheses, this notation form creates a shortcut in the results section because the researcher can simply refer to H_1, or the first hypothesis, without restating it again. Null hypotheses are not provided.

THE METHOD SECTION

The **method section** describes how the research study was executed. By describing the research procedures, the researcher allows readers to make a determination about the appropriateness and adequacy of the method for meeting the purpose of the study. At a minimum, the method section should include descriptions of the research participants and the research procedures, as well as descriptive information for each of the variables included in the study.

Describing Participants

Most published research reports describe the setting and the participants of the research project in an anonymous fashion. Given the topic or focus of some studies, some scholars now recognize that the political, historical, legal, economic, social, and cultural environment of the population, organization, or geographic area studied are important to the research process and the interpretation of data (Ryan, 1998). Although you should not report the identity of participants or organizations without their consent, you should provide a description that details the age range, composition of sex, and the nationality, racial, or ethnic characteristics of those who participated in the study. If there are other demographic characteristics important to the study and results, those should also be reported. This remains, however, an individual or journal-specific editorial preference.

As a general rule, researchers report demographic information about participants in this section of the research report even when the categories of information (sex, ethnicity, age) represent independent variables in the research study. Keyton et al. (2013) provide an example of the way in which demographic information can be reported:

> Snowball sampling and an online survey were used to reach participants who were currently employed full-time or part-time. One hundred and twenty-six respondents (female = 68.9%,

$N = 87$; male = 31.1%, $N = 39$; M age = 35.74, $SD = 11.80$) completed the survey checking off the verbal workplace communication behaviors they heard or observed in the previous day of work. More than 90% of participants had college degrees, most (81.9%) worked full time; more than half (61.9%) did not supervise other employees. Respondents were nearly equally distributed among being in their current position 1 year or less (30.1%), 1 to 2 years (25.7%), 3 to 5 years (25.7%), or 6 years or more (18.6%). Respondents reported being in their current profession 1 year or less (11.5%), 1 to 2 years (20.4%), 3 to 5 years (20.4%), and 6 or more years (47.8%). (p.158)

This type of description paints a picture of the participants and their work situations, which helps readers evaluate the study's outcomes as relevant to a particular group or type of individual.

In an article on how people respond to conversations about managing their weight, different characteristics about the participants are reported to help readers understand the personal situations in which the conversations occurred. The sample was described in this way (Thompson, Romo, & Dailey, 2013, p. 37):

> The sample was fairly evenly divided between men ($n = 78$, 49.4%) and women ($n = 80$, 50.6%), with their ages ranging from 24 to 69 years ($M = 39.80$, $SD = 9.98$). Participants were largely White/Caucasian (74.7%); other ethnicities included Asian or Pacific Islander (14.6%), Black or African-American (3.8%), Hispanic or Latino/a (1.9%), and multiple or other ethnicities (5.1%). Most (77.8%) were in married or long-term relationships, 15 were engaged, 16 were dating, and four described their current relational status as "other." Couples' relationship length ranged from 1.17 to 45 years ($M = 11.10$, $SD = 8.89$). Individuals reported that their household income (combined with their partner) ranged from less than $20,000 ($n = 1$) to more than $100,000 ($n = 40$); the median income was between $80,000 and $100,000. Participants' body mass indexes or BMIs (weight in pounds $\times$ 703/[height in inches]^2) ranged from 17.71 to 71.32 ($M = 26.69$, $SD = 6.81$), and the 65 partners' BMIs were substantially correlated ($r = .51, p < .001$).

Do You Have the Basic Information?

As a researcher writing a research report or a consumer reading a research report, you should check for the adequacy of the following components (Katzer et al., 1978):

1. Does the introduction contain a statement of the problem and some justification for its importance?
2. Does the summary and evaluation of literature in the literature review put the current study into historical and scientific perspective?
3. Is an adequate description of the research method and procedures given?
4. Does the information in the results section answer the research questions and hypotheses?
5. In the discussion section, are the specific findings generalized to the larger issues?

This subsection should also include any information about the sampling techniques used to select participants. Researchers also report the size of the sample here. Finally, this subsection should also present any special conditions regarding informed consent, confidentiality, or anonymity.

Describing the Research Procedure

In the second part of the method section, the researcher should describe in sufficient detail what was done in the research study. The research design should be fully described. In other words, after reading this subsection, you should know what the researcher did to collect the data. The research design should be detailed and transparent, as should all of the research procedures.

What kinds of detail are necessary? Stimuli used to create experimental conditions need to be completely explained. If confederates were used, the role of the confederate should be explained in detail. The researcher should also note whether interactions were audio- or videotaped. If other equipment or technologies were used to collect data, this should be described as well.

The scientific ideal requires that researchers describe their research procedures with enough detail that other researchers could easily replicate the research design. In practice, however, a method section with that much detail would be too cumbersome. Most scholars take a more moderate approach by describing the basic procedures for each aspect of the research design. This should give readers enough information on which to evaluate the adequacy and appropriateness of the research procedures. If you decide to replicate a study, you will probably need to contact the researcher directly. Contact information for authors is usually provided on the first or last page of the journal article.

Describing the Variables

The third element of the method section is devoted to describing the variables used in the study. An operationalization, or specific way in which the variable is observed or measured, must be provided for each variable. A variable's operationalization specifies the steps or procedures for creating and measuring the variable.

When data are collected through an existing questionnaire, the researcher should provide a brief description of the questionnaire, including the number of items, an example of an item, the type of response scale, and a citation where readers can locate the scale. Information about the questionnaire's reliability and validity should also be included.

If a questionnaire is developed specifically for a study, the researchers should describe the steps taken to construct the scale, indicate if and how the scale was pilot tested, and provide information about the steps the researcher took to address issues of reliability and validity. In this case, most researchers will include the entire instrument as an appendix to the research report.

If data were collected through content or interaction analysis, the researcher should provide a description of how the category scheme was developed and pilot tested, as well as information about how coders were trained and how intercoder reliability was established. Also important in this description would be how disagreements between coders were resolved.

Each category of a nominal variable should be described by the percentage of respondents. Continuous-level variables should each be described by the mean, standard deviation, range of scores, and, if appropriate, internal reliability. If several continuous variables are used in the study, researchers should consider adding a correlation matrix to describe the relationships among them and for presenting this descriptive information. Refer back to Table 11.2 for a typical correlation matrix. Generally, researchers add a row or column to the matrix so that the mean, standard deviation, and internal reliability of each variable can be included.

Finally, each variable should also be identified as an independent (predictor) or dependent (criterion) variable. Readers should not have to guess how the researcher situated or sequenced the variables in the study.

THE RESULTS SECTION

Traditionally, results are presented in the order of the research questions and hypotheses. In the **results section,** results are presented as information without interpretation. Thus, accuracy of reporting is critical. All numbers used as results should be double-checked. And complete consistency should exist between the numerical report and textual description of the numbers.

At a minimum, several pieces of information need to be presented for each hypothesis or question:

- The statistical test used
- The results of the test

- The significance level of the test
- A written description connecting the result of the statistical test as support for or rejection of the research hypothesis, or connecting the result of the statistical test to the answer of the research question

The scientific tradition also requires researchers to report all results, even if they do not support the researcher's expectations. If a hypothesis or research question is provided, the results from the associated test must be reported. It would be unethical not to do so.

Notice how McManus and Nussbaum (2013) follow these guidelines.

> Children's perceptions of parents' ambiguity were the focus of H_2 and RQ_2. Results supported H_2: Children perceived parents to use ambiguity in negatively valenced discussions, $t(38) = 17.73, p < .01$, and positively valenced topics, $t(38) = 20.96, p < .01$. However, a paired samples t-test showed no differences in the amount of ambiguity children perceived in negatively versus positively valenced discussions, RQ_2: $t(38) = 1.74, p > .05, r = .74, p < .01$. (p. 207)

Using Tables and Graphs

Tables are used to graphically display numerical data. Tables should be well identified in the title, and all rows and columns should be labeled; all abbreviations should be explained. A good table is one that supplements rather than repeats information in the text of the report. Authors should point out each table and indicate its importance. But it is unnecessary to discuss every item of a table in the text. Tables are commonly used to present descriptive statistics, such as frequencies and percentages, a matrix of correlations among variables, and results of ANOVA and regression results.

Figures are used sparingly in research reports, but they are useful when important or complex findings could be otherwise overlooked. Figures can display graphs (for example, bar or column charts) or other illustrations of data. A photograph or drawing can also be used in a figure. Like a table, all of the information needed to interpret the figure should be contained in the figure, its title, and notes. Tables and figures should be interpretable by the reader without referring to the article.

THE DISCUSSION SECTION

In the **discussion section** of the written research report, researchers provide an interpretation of the results based on the research questions and hypotheses posed in the literature review. In this section the researcher tries to answer the question "What do these results mean?" As a researcher, you need to provide a full, fair, and detailed account of the implications of the data. As a consumer, you need to make an assessment of the results independently of what is written.

The discussion section is the place for the author to interpret the results. Although interpretations are linked to information presented in the results section, the discussion section should not be a simple restatement of significant and non-significant findings. Rather, the discussion section is an interpretation that indicates what the results mean and why the results are important or meaningful. Conclusions presented in this section should be linked to the theories or previous studies presented in the literature review. Furthermore, the author should describe how the conclusions of this study confirm, extend, or challenge theory. The discussion section also includes brief subsections on the limitations of the research design and suggestions for future research.

As you read or write a discussion section, three questions can guide you (Katzer et al., 1978). We will look at each question first from the reader's point of view and then from the researcher's point of view. First, as a reader, do you know how the author arrived at the interpretation or summary? It should be clear to you what observations, measurements, or data were used to draw the stated conclusions. If you are not sure how the researcher came to the conclusions, you need to refer back to the method section of the document. As the researcher writing the discussion section, you should be sure to expand on any procedural or descriptive details that will help readers agree with your conclusions.

Second, as a reader, does the conclusion given make sense? Are there alternative interpretations of the data that the author ignores or dismisses? Seldom is there a correct or single interpretation of the data. Rather, the author has formed his or her conclusions based on the framework established in the literature review and in response to the research questions or hypotheses. As a consumer, can you follow the path (literature review to hypotheses to data collection to results) that leads the author to this particular conclusion? Are the results linked to the theory presented in the literature review? Is the interpretation of results consistent with other research findings presented in the literature review? If not, does the author provide a sufficient explanation for why these results might be different?

An author can use this same logic as the discussion section is developed. Remember that as the researcher and author of the research report, you are inherently more familiar with why and how the data were collected. These elements influence the conclusions you present. You must remember that anyone reading your report will not be as familiar with the research setting. Develop and describe your interpretations and conclusions with enough detail to make them credible.

Third, can you think of anything that could have been left out? Rereading the method section again can help you identify potential gaps between data collected and data interpreted. Check to see if each hypothesis or research question was answered. If any were eliminated, what reason was given for doing so? Was any part of the data reported and published elsewhere? As a researcher and writer of a research report, remember that a conscientious researcher will account for everything that was assumed from the beginning. Give honest and fair explanations if data were not meaningful, if variables did not predict as hypothesized, or if questions were dropped from your study.

Developing Interpretations from Results

It is not always straightforward or easy to explain what the results mean. But you must. You cannot assume that the brief conclusion and description of statistical tests in the results section

AN ETHICAL
ISSUE

Dealing with Unexpected Results

Imagine yourself as a researcher who has just spent several months designing and conducting a study. Looking at your statistical findings, you see several alarming results. One hypothesized difference is not significant, and one hypothesized relationship runs in the direction opposite to your expectation. Now what? Before you panic, consider the following:

- Are you certain that the data were entered accurately and in the required format?

- Is the statistical programming correct and appropriate?

If the data and programming are not suspect, you have several alternatives:

- Consider alternative explanations for the findings. Reread everything you can find about your topic and methodology.

- Reexamine the methods and procedures of the previous studies to determine the extent to which differences in methodologies could create different results.

- Talk to others with expertise in your research topic and research methodology. They may provide useful insight.

- Determine the consequences of these unexpected results to the overall worth and conclusion of your study.

After taking these steps, you will have to decide whether to continue with your plan to write the research report. If you decide to continue, taking these steps should help you write about the unexpected results with more confidence. Although researchers are not fond of unexpected results, the scientific process allows for them. Never hide a result, even if it is not the result you expected. You and other scholars will benefit from your straightforward and realistic description and assessment of them.

eliminate the need for you to describe in writing the results found.

Most research projects seek to answer a set of research questions or hypotheses, and the answers to these are not always consistent. Not only must a researcher interpret findings for each question or hypothesis, but he or she must also be able to reconcile the findings as a whole—across the research questions and hypotheses.

One way to do so is to return to the study's main objective (Bouma & Atkinson, 1995). What did the study seek to find? Starting with the answer to this question can help a researcher frame the discussion section. If the results are the answers the researcher expected, writing the discussion section will be more straightforward. But

if the results do not answer the main objective directly or if findings contradict one another, the researcher must address these inconsistencies or unexpected findings.

As part of interpreting the results, the researcher should address to whom the research findings apply (Bouma & Atkinson, 1995). In the strictest sense, research findings are limited to the participants who were part of the research project. However, most researchers want to extend the application of their findings to larger issues and individuals beyond the sample of participants. Findings can be stated firmly with respect to the sample, but when researchers make broader generalizations, they should be tentative.

TRY THIS!   ## How to Read a Research Report

In reading research reports, you should act like a critic. This means that you should bring a healthy level of skepticism as well as an open mind to reading research reports. The following recommendations will help you become a better consumer of research (Katzer et al., 1978; Tucker et al., 1981):

1. Read the entire article.
2. Do not evaluate the research as good or bad because of one aspect of the research that you liked or disliked.
3. Do not be easily impressed, positively or negatively.
4. Recognize that something can be learned from every study. Even if you discount a study's results, you should be able to learn something about how to conduct, or not conduct, research from reading the research report.
5. Acknowledge that all research has limitations.
6. Seek to identify the assumptions that are unwritten but at the foundation of the research report. Ask if these assumptions are acceptable to you.

Manner of Presentation

There are several forms for providing interpretation of research results in the discussion section. One way is to simply interpret the results for each research question and hypothesis in order. Another is to discuss the most important result first and then continue the discussion with the interpretations of results that are secondary. A third way is to respond to the study's primary objective and then provide detail about each research question and hypothesis.

However the discussion section is organized, this section usually starts with a one-paragraph summary of the overall results. An example of this type of summary is provided by Cingel and Krcmar (2013):

> In the present sample, very young children are using computers an average of 15 minutes a day. However, parents indicate that children are using significantly more television and DVDs, averaging approximately an hour each of use per day. Furthermore, babies are first exposed around 6–12 months and use it as part of their daily routine between 18 and 24 months, well before they are recommended to do so by the American Academy of American Academy of Pediatrics. (p. 389)

This one paragraph generally summarizes the results before the researcher addresses each finding more specifically.

One other feature of a discussion section is consistent regardless of how it is organized—the researcher should link the findings back to the literature described in the literature review. Doing this completes the research cycle by demonstrating how new results are consistent or inconsistent with previous findings. Generally, researchers should avoid presenting new citations in the discussion section.

Presenting the Limitations

It is also customary for the researcher to acknowledge any methodological limitations that may affect the results or interpretation of the results. Sometimes researchers present a limitations subsection; in other cases, limitations are presented near the end of the discussion section.

All research designs and all methodologies have limitations. Although the point in this section is not to address each and every potential limitation, researchers should draw readers' attention to those that are most likely to influence the research results and implications drawn from the findings. Often, limitations of a research study are linked to the demographic characteristics of participants included in the sample, the size of the sample, or some aspect of the research design. By acknowledging the limitations, authors engage in self-reflexive criticism, which is part of the scientific tradition.

Recommending Future Research

Recommendations about future research may be presented as a separate subsection or as a conclusion to the discussion section. In the future research subsection, authors give advice about what they believe should be studied next or how they believe the next study should be designed. These recommendations should be specific, rather than a vague statement to the effect that "Future research is needed."

Both the limitations and future research material in a research report are important information. If you are reviewing articles to help you design a research project, pay careful attention to the information here. The limitations section can help you avoid problems or weaknesses of previous research. Information in the future research section can provide insight and direction for your project.

FINISHING THE QUANTITATIVE RESEARCH REPORT

After the major sections of the research report are written, the researcher must complete several more elements that help introduce the manuscript and make it appealing for readers.

Title

Researchers generally have a tentative, working title even before they start writing the research report. But now, with the report essentially finished, that title must be checked to see if it is still representative of what was written. The guidelines that follow can help you create an effective title:

1. The title should identify the theory or variables.

2. Indicate in the title what was studied, not the results or conclusions of the study.

3. If the population is important, identify it in the title (for example, adolescent Internet users).

With your title written according to these guidelines, examine it more closely. Is the title as concise and succinct as possible? Generally, a title should not be longer than 12 words. Is it consistent with the research questions or hypotheses in your study? The title provides readers with a framework for engaging what you have written, and should be written as a simple summary of the main idea of the study. And, many times, readers make a decision to read or not read a research report by examining the title. Make sure yours reflects the study you completed.

Title Page

Obviously, the title goes on the title page. Other information that goes here includes the author's name, contact information, and the date the report was written or submitted. The title page is also the place to acknowledge and thank anyone who helped during the research process. Almost all researchers get help from others in data collection. The rule is, if someone helped on your project and is not one of the report's authors, this person should be thanked in an acknowledgment sentence at the bottom of the title page.

Abstract

An abstract is not always required. If it is, it can be written only after the research manuscript is complete. Generally, an abstract is very short, 75 to 250 words, and has three objectives (Bouma & Atkinson, 1995). First, the abstract states the aim or overall objective of the research. Second, the abstract gives a brief explanation of the research method. Finally, the abstract briefly summarizes the results of the study. Researchers should write the abstract carefully because it is potentially the first—and perhaps the only—element a consumer will read. The abstract should help a reader find the potential value of the study for his or her research project.

In their 155-word abstract, Vanden Abeele and de Cock (2013) describe the topic of the study, briefly describe the participants, and briefly explain the results of the study.

> This article presents the results of a study in Flanders (Belgium) ($N = 264$) on the relationship between adolescents' peer group status, their gender and their involvement in different types of mobile phone cyberbullying. By means of a (within-classroom) free nominations procedure, likeability and perceived popularity scores were calculated for each respondent. Based on these scores, four groups were identified: popular controversial, popular liked, average, and rejected adolescents. Even after controlling for age, gender, the frequency of voice calling and the frequency of text messaging, popular controversial adolescents were significantly more likely to make or send threatening/insulting voice calls or text messages. They also gossiped significantly more frequently by means of voice calls or text messages. No relationship was found between peer group status and making hurtful pictures or videos. A significant interaction effect with gender was found for mobile phone gossiping: Popular controversial girls were more involved in gossiping than popular controversial boys. (p. 107)

References

The **reference list** is an alphabetical listing by author's last name of all materials cited in the research report. It must be complete and without error because it is the mechanism by which readers trace backward from your document to other research reports. It should not include materials you examined or consulted but did not use to write your research report. A reference list must follow an academic style. The information you need is provided in the next section of this chapter.

USING APA STYLE

The scientific tradition requires that researchers use one of many standardized styles for citing the work of others and for providing a list of material used in writing the research report. Typically, in the communication discipline, the preferred style is that of the style book of the American Psychological Association (APA). Its formal title is *Publication Manual of the American Psychological Association* (6th ed., 2010). APA style is used in this book.

Citing Others' Work

Citing the work of others is essential. It would be unethical not to give other researchers credit for their ideas or conclusions. Recall from Chapters 2 and 3 that you need to be familiar with two types of citations.

The first is the direct citation. Here, you are using word for word what others have written. The phrases or sentences of others that you want to use must be indicated with opening and closing quotation marks or by block indent. The author or authors, the year of publication, and the page number(s) are also required. With this information, a reader of your report can turn to the reference list and find the original source of the material.

The second type is the indirect citation. Here, you are paraphrasing the words, phrases, and sentences of other researchers. In this case, quotation marks and page numbers are not required. Refer back to Chapter 2 for a complete description of how to use both direct and indirect citations. Also check with the writing center at your university for additional resources.

Creating the Reference List

When you are ready to create the reference list for your research article, you can turn to several resources to guide you through the process. Obviously, you should check your library or writing center for a copy of the APA style manual. Your writing center will likely have handouts and online resources for creating reference lists and placing citations in the text of your manuscript.

The guidelines for citing Web-based sources suggest the following format:

> The Annenberg Public Policy Center of the University of Pennsylvania. (n.d.). Retrieved from http://www.annenbergpublicpolicycenter.org

TRY THIS!

Submit Your Research Paper to a Communication Convention

You may write a research paper for your research methods class or some other class. Given your hard work, why not submit your paper to be reviewed and considered for presentation at a conference or convention of one of the communication associations? Although the dates do vary, the following table lists several of the communication associations, a general time frame for their submission deadlines and convention dates, and websites you can check for their submission requirements. Some associations have sections or units especially for students. For example, see the Undergraduate Honors Conference at the SSCA website, the Graduate Student Caucus at the CSCA website, and the Student Section at the NCA website. Another outlet for your research is your state communication association.

Convention	General Time Frame for Submission Deadlines & Convention Dates	Association Website
Association for Education in Journalism and Mass Communication	Submissions are due early April for the next August's convention.	http://www.aejmc.org
Broadcast Education Association	Submissions are due early December for the next April's convention.	http://www.beaweb.org
Central States Communication Association	Submissions are due mid-September to early October for the next April's convention.	http://www.csca-net.org
Eastern Communication Association	Submissions are due mid-October for the next April's convention.	http://www.ecasite.org
International Communication Association	Submissions are due in November for the next May/June convention.	http://www.icahdq.org
National Communication Association	Submissions are due in March for the next November's convention.	http://www.natcom.org
Southern States-Communication Association	Submissions are due mid-September for the next April's convention.	http://www.ssca.net
Western States Communication Association	Submissions are due early September for the next February/March convention.	http://www.westcomm.org

If you submit your paper, it will be reviewed by several evaluators and judged for its quality. If the quality of your paper is acceptable and competitive with other submissions, your paper will be programmed on a panel with other presentations. At the convention, each participant on a panel has 10 to 15 minutes to present the major ideas of his or her paper. After all paper presentations are complete, a respondent will provide constructive feedback about the papers. Good luck!

The notation n.d. indicates that the website was not dated. On some websites the word "updated" followed by a date is provided. This date should be inserted in parentheses after the name of the website.

ISSUES IN WRITING

The writer's presentation of his or her efforts is crucial to how the written report is received. Unfortunately, writers call negative attention to their writing when they fail to recognize some common writing problems. Several of these common to writing research reports are described here (Ryan, 1998).

The first common problem is carelessness. Although you have heard this advice before, it is repeated here as well—proofread your document. Use the spell checker on your word—processing program and then read your manuscript to double-check for problems the computer will not find. Manuscripts should be error-free—no typographical errors, spelling mistakes, or grammatical problems. Errors like these cause readers to doubt the credibility of your findings. After all, if you are not careful with the written manuscript and make noticeable mistakes, readers will wonder to what extent you were careful with data collection and interpretation.

Beyond being error-free, your research report should not include rambling, ambiguous, or wordy phrases. Simple, basic sentences are better than complex ones. Carelessness can also extend to the style in which citations and references are included. When you can follow a style, the implication is that you can follow procedures in other aspects of the research process as well.

The second common problem is making unspecified assumptions. Remember that the written research report is the only conversation you will have with readers. Thus, your major assumptions should be specified. Do not expect the reader to piece together your assumptions based on your literature review, hypotheses, and methodology. The best way to help a reader understand your point of view is to describe it and its supporting framework.

A third type of common problem with written research reports is the authors' failure to place their study within the context of published research. You should describe the literature on which your study is based. If special circumstances prevailed at the time of data collection, you should contextualize your research with respect to these events. For example, if you are collecting data on employee perceptions of corporate scandals and a high-profile case is featured prominently in the news immediately preceding or during your data collection, you should include this information in the method section and consider its influence in the interpretation of the findings.

The fourth writing problem is lack of clarity of the research questions and hypotheses. If you can answer "yes" to each of the following, you have succeeded in avoiding this common problem:

- Do your research questions or hypotheses provide a clear focus and direction for the research?
- Do your hypotheses predict relationships or differences between or among variables?
- Do your research questions and hypotheses suggest how the relationships or differences will be tested?

These questions can be used as criteria to test the clarity of research questions and hypotheses regardless of a study's methodological approach or research design.

The fifth common problem is the use of vague and undefined terms. Dictionary definitions are generally not suitable for scholarly writing. All concepts, constructs, and variables should have clear definitions that flow from prior research or from the theoretical perspective guiding the study. These definitions should be provided in the literature review, with the operationalizations described in the method section.

The Revision Process

Finally, be prepared to revise and rewrite your manuscript. It is unlikely that you will be able to create the most effective presentation of information in the first draft. Effective writing is both precise and clear; it is achieved through rewriting. As you review the manuscript, also check for spelling, punctuation, and grammar errors.

You should make certain that every citation in the text of your paper is listed in the reference section. Likewise, every item in the reference list should be found somewhere in the paper. Finally, every item in the reference list should have complete information.

Most important to the revision process is to look for the clarity and strength of your arguments. Ask others, even if they are not experts on your topic or method, to read your research report. Responding to the questions they have is likely to make your report clearer and more succinct. Every claim should be based on evidence, and you should not make claims that overstate the findings.

SUMMARY

1. A study is not complete until the researcher writes a research report to communicate his or her findings with others.

2. Following the scientific tradition of many disciplines, there are four major parts to the written quantitative research report: literature review, method section, results section, and discussion.

3. The literature review is comprised of the literature the researcher sought and studied to design the research project. It provides a brief historical background of the variables, issues, and topics studied and goes beyond simple description of previous work to analyze and integrate this work into a coherent whole.

4. Literature reviews usually begin with a problem statement, can be organized in several ways, are written in third person, and present research questions and hypotheses.

5. The method section describes how the research study was executed and includes descriptions of the participants, the research procedures, and the research variables.

6. The results section presents the findings as information without interpretation.

7. In the discussion section, the researcher provides the interpretation and implications of the results to answer the question, "What do these results mean?"

8. Researchers include subsections on the limitations of their research design and methodology as well as recommendations for future research in the discussion section.

9. To complete a research report, the researcher must develop a title, finalize the title page, construct an abstract, and create the reference list.

10. Most quantitative research reports are written in APA style.

11. Researchers need to be very careful in their written work because their level of carelessness translates to readers' perceptions of lack of credibility.

12. Researchers should be prepared to spend time in the revision process.

KEY TERMS

discussion section	reference list
method section	results section

See the website www.mhhe.com/keyton4 that accompanies this text. For each chapter, the site contains a:

- chapter outline
- chapter checklist
- chapter summary
- short multiple-choice quiz
- PowerPoint presentation created by Dr. Keyton

For a list of internet resources, visit http://www.joannkeyton.com/CommunicationResearch-Methods.htm.

CHAPTER FOURTEEN

Introduction to Qualitative Research

Chapter Checklist

After reading this chapter, you should be able to:

1. Describe qualitative research and its assumptions.
2. Identify examples of qualitative research.
3. Explain inductive analysis.
4. Explain the qualitative research model.
5. Describe issues of credibility that must be addressed in qualitative research.
6. Explain the role of a research question in qualitative research.
7. Assess the effectiveness of research questions in qualitative research.
8. Describe different ways meaning is derived from data in qualitative research.
9. Distinguish among the different levels of data in qualitative research.
10. Explain the advantages and disadvantages of qualitative research.

Communication researchers recognize that human interaction is complex and intricate, especially communication processes that unfold over time. Qualitative research methods are especially effective in capturing this type of complexity. Why? Because qualitative methods are sensitive to the social construction of meaning (Lindlof, 1991) and to the experiences of individuals and their communication partners. This means that qualitative research illuminates the meanings and actions of participants. In qualitative methods, researchers emphasize the communication environment, or the social environment, of interactants, allowing researchers to explore everyday social phenomena in a way other methods do not.

WHAT IS QUALITATIVE RESEARCH?

Qualitative research preserves the form and content of human interaction. Often in the form of text, audio, or video, these data are analyzed for their characteristics as they occur in natural settings. Lindlof and Taylor (2011) describe qualitative research as that which focuses on "the performances and practices of human communication" (p. 4). Communication performances are creative and collaborative in-the-moment interaction events, whereas communication practices are more routine and standardized. Lindlof and Taylor argue that communication performances and practices constitute the texture of everyday life. To be true to communication viewed in this way, qualitative research methods emphasize empirical, inductive, and interpretive approaches applied to interaction within a specific context.

Qualitative researchers are interested in the whole of the communication phenomenon or process, regardless of how complex or messy it gets. Qualitative methodologies described in this book include participant observation, interviews, focus groups, narrative analysis, and ethnography. Other forms of qualitative research are used to study communication phenomena, but those listed are some of the most common.

Sometimes qualitative methods are referred to as naturalistic research, ethnography, field research, or participant observation, although the term *qualitative research* is preferred by communication scholars and is the broadest and most inclusive term (Lindlof & Taylor, 2002). Regardless of how it is labeled, qualitative research uses discourse (Anderson, 1996) or symbolic interaction (Lindlof & Taylor, 2011) as its data. In qualitative research, the **discourse,** or naturally occurring talk or gestures, is captured in a variety of forms and remains as it occurs. Qualitative research aims for **subjectivity** rather than objectivity. This means that researchers use interpretive research processes to make the subject of the interpretation meaningful (Anderson, 1996). This definition differs from the definition of the term *subjective* as meaning "individual" or "idiosyncratic." Rather, the qualitative researcher uses both data collection and analytic techniques from which research claims can be tested. In the strictest sense, the qualitative research tradition rejects the objectivity and absolute truth that is associated with quantitative methods and accepts that multiple interpretations are possible. In practice, however, both subjectivity and objectivity are matters of degree. For qualitative researchers, subjectivity is primary.

Subjectivity is favored over objectivity in qualitative research because researchers using qualitative methods have a strong concern for the context in which the interaction occurs. The qualitative researcher takes a more subjective frame in the research process because he or she must rely on research participants for their understanding of the interaction context. More precisely, qualitative researchers favor subjectivity because they are interested in exploring **intersubjectivity,** or the social accomplishment of how people co-construct and co-experience the interaction of social life and their rules for doing so (Gubrium & Holstein, 2000). Intersubjectivity refers to shared understanding, and the act of speaking is the action that accomplishes that act (Lindlof & Taylor, 2011).

Although differing in techniques for collecting data, qualitative methods share certain characteristics (Chesebro & Borisoff, 2007, Denzin & Lincoln, 2000; Lindlof & Taylor, 2002). First, qualitative methodologies have a theoretical interest in how people understand and interpret communication processes. Second, each of the methodologies is concerned with the study of communication as socially situated human action and artifacts. This means that qualitative research is conducted in the field as opposed to simulated or lab environments. It also means that qualitative researchers use interpretive lenses to capture and explore how social experience is created in a specific time and space, and how communicators develop and derive meanings from those experiences. Third, each method uses human investigators as the primary research instrument. This means that the researcher can capture rich descriptions of the interaction field and capture interactants' points of view more intimately. Finally, all qualitative methodologies rely on textual, usually written, forms for coding data and presenting results to participants and other audiences. As a result of these characteristics, qualitative research reports rely heavily on the use of expressive language and, as the author allows, participants' voices.

Qualitative research is grounded in the premise of **mutual simultaneous shaping** (Lincoln & Guba, 1985)—meaning that in the natural world, it is difficult to distinguish cause from effect. From this perspective, "everything influences everything else, in the here and now. Many elements are implicated in any given action, and each element interacts with all the others in ways that change them all while simultaneously resulting in something that we, as outside observers, label as outcomes or effects" (p. 151). With so much going on at once, identifying specific causality is difficult, if not impossible. As a result, qualitative researchers focus on processes rather than outcomes.

Many qualitative researchers argue that interaction has no directionality (Lincoln & Guba, 1985) and maintain an emphasis on processes and meanings (Denzin & Lincoln, 1994). Likewise, they see no need to identify outcomes of actions. Qualitative researchers argue that events are mutually shaped by other events and that dissecting events into parts for study, as is done in quantitative research, is inappropriate. Thus, the strength of qualitative research is that it captures the complexity of the interaction event because it does not artificially limit observation to one or a few aspects or components.

As a result, researchers using qualitative methods search for plausible explanations based on what is observed. At the same time, qualitative researchers acknowledge that the particular web or pattern of interactions observed may never occur again in that same way. So explanations are unique in that they represent how the interaction was enacted and influenced in this particular case.

Examples of Qualitative Research

Qualitative research is particularly useful for studying personal or sensitive topics. For example, Romo (2011) interviewed parents who had a child or children over the age of 5. The researcher used interviews to understand how parents disclose financial information to their children. To find participants, the researcher recruited individuals through a posting on an online neighborhood listserv and through an announcement on a popular mothers' blog. Snowball sampling was also used. Twenty-three parents were interviewed; each was interviewed individually for about 35 minutes. The age of the participating parents ranged 32 to 54 ($M = 39.5$); most were female (74%) and White/Caucasian (87%).

The interview schedule contained 12 open-ended questions. The first few questions focused on demographics and then on the participants' working situation. The next set of questions focused on the family financial situation. Then questions focused on participants' financial conversations with their children (for example, "What are your thoughts on sharing your financial information with your kids?" p. 281) and on questions on their experience in talking about family financial issues with their parents (for example, "How did your parents communicate to you about financial information growing up? What kind of economic background did you grow up in?" p. 281). All interviews were audio-recorded with the consent of participants. The researcher also made field notes immediately after the interviews.

In analyzing the data for one research question, "What motivates parents to conceal financial information from their children (i.e., what rules do parents use to determine not to disclose)?"

(p. 267), Romo found that parents presented two different reasons for not sharing family financial information with their children. Parents' responses revealed two privacy concerns: (a) personal financial issues should not be a child's concern, and (b) children should not be made to worry about financial issues. After analyzing the data for all three research questions, Romo concluded:

> The findings of this study indicate that parents choose to socialize their children about personal financial issues through the information they decide to disclose. In this way, parents must negotiate managing privacy with the financial knowledge and wellbeing of their children. (p. 278)

Using focus groups, another qualitative method, Zerba (2011) collected data to answer this research question: "What would the 'ideal print newspaper' be like for 18- to 24-year-old and 25- to 29-year-old nonreaders of daily print newspapers?" (p. 600). Focus groups were conducted in Chicago, Dallas, and San Antonio separately for the two age groups (18- to 24-year-olds, 25- to 29-year-olds). Focus group conversations were audio recorded, and a research assistant took notes. In describing the ideal newspaper, focus group participants commented that an ideal paper, in part, would be brief and to the point, focused on local news with diverse perspectives, look like a glossy magazine or book, have a table of contents, and use more pictures and colors.

To analyze the participants' verbal contributions to the focus group discussion, Zerba (2011) developed an initial set of categories and subcategories based on the research questions and the research literature. The researcher reported that she read and re-read the transcripts to further develop categories and subcategories. Some categories and subcategories were added or removed before the final coding scheme was established. The researcher also reports that each category and subcategory was illustrated with an example from the transcripts. This analytical process was conducted separately for each age group, and then responses for the two age groups were compared.

As a third example of qualitative research, Porter (2012) used three qualitative data collection techniques to study the role of technology used in the response to Hurricane Katrina: indepth interviews with technology volunteers, participant observation of technology volunteers in their post-response meetings, and messages from an e-mail listserv that was created during the Katrina response to coordinate the volunteers at the shelter. By examining and cross-referencing these three data sources, Porter sought to answer two research questions: "RQ1: How does situational boundary-making occur in emergent disaster response efforts?" and "RQ2: How do situational boundary-making practices shape the design and use of technology?" (p. 12). Data were coded and arranged in a timeline to identify significant events during the response to the hurricane and to identify the elements, actors, and technologies important to those events. Analyses of the data revealed that the situational demands placed on volunteers rendered them as responsive or reactive. "Reactive volunteers responded to the situation with inaction or delay, while responsive volunteers responded

Qualitative Research Preserves the Natural Interaction of Participants.
Keith Brofsky/Getty Images

TRY THIS!

Identifying Contexts for Qualitative Research

Qualitative methods are very useful in answering questions about communication contexts that are difficult to replicate in the lab or other controlled environments. Often the biggest advantage of qualitative methods is that the researcher can go into interaction contexts or capture interaction from contexts that would otherwise not be accessible. In the following table, after the examples given, identify five other communication contexts and the respective research question you believe deserves the attention of communication researchers.

Interaction Context	*Research Questions*
Family reunion	How do distant relatives reestablish connections and relationships with one another during family reunion activities?
Employee dining room	In what ways do employees use informal lunch-time conversations to release work stress?
Police-citizen interaction	How is communication characterized when police interact with community members from cultures different from their own?

to extraordinary situational demands through the design of responsive technologies" (p. 24). Unfortunately, the technology failed, which compounded situational demands. Moreover, as volunteers focused on fixing the technology, they became more dependent on it. Findings such as these not only explore the relationship between technology and the process of organizing, but also can be useful to technology volunteers in future crisis situations.

Each of these qualitative studies asks different research questions, focuses on different communication contexts, and uses different qualitative methods. But the common thread to the three—and qualitative research in general—is the way in which researchers conceptualize what counts as data. In all three examples, researchers captured or observed the interaction they were interested in studying. In all cases the researchers were immersed in the interaction context, either by being there or by obtaining detailed records of the interaction. The communication environments were real, the participants were natural actors in these settings, and, most important, the communication consequences to the participants were real. These three elements represent the ideal against which qualitative research is measured.

Inductive Analysis

Qualitative methods rest on inductive reasoning, moving from the specific to the general. **Inductive analysis** is the reasoning used by qualitative researchers to discover and develop theories as they emerge from the data.

This process of analysis has several steps (Janesick, 2000; Lindlof & Taylor, 2002). First, the researcher becomes intimately familiar with the field of interaction and observes firsthand the interaction of participants in an effort to grasp its implicit meaning. After being immersed in the setting or in the data, the researcher needs to allow time to think and become aware of the nuance of the communication and its meaning in the setting. Being immersed allows the researcher to create better descriptions of what is occurring. Thus, by taking time to complete more observations, or reading and rereading through the

data, the researcher becomes intimately familiar with the setting, the interactants, their communication, and potential interpretations. But the process of inductive analysis does not stop with description.

As the researcher becomes more familiar with the setting or data, a process of analysis and interpretation begins as the researcher tests alternative and tentative explanations. More formally, there are several methods for analyzing qualitative data. All include comparing and contrasting data for themes and patterns. Several of these will be explained in detail in Chapter 16. As the data are being analyzed, the researcher begins to synthesize and bring together pieces into a whole. This allows the researcher to make tentative and plausible statements of the phenomenon being studied. Inductive analysis continues as the qualitative researcher begins to write the research document. For most qualitative researchers, the process of writing is where knowledge claims are solidified. Thus, the researcher moves from specifics of the data (i.e., transcripts, observations) to identification of patterns and themes to general conclusions.

A Model for Qualitative Research

Qualitative research requires forethought and planning, just as quantitative research does, although the process is slightly different and is often revisited. The model of qualitative research design presented in Figure 14.1 demonstrates how the stages of the qualitative research process are interdependent, emergent, cyclical, and, at times, unpredictable (Lindlof & Taylor, 2002, 2011; Maxwell, 1996).

Conducting qualitative research is not linear, as it cannot be planned out in its entirety before entering the field. Because the researcher enters an existing interaction context, the researcher cannot control it the way a quantitative researcher can control what happens in a laboratory experiment. However, that does not mean that the researcher enters the field unprepared.

The circle in Figure 14.1 identifies the activities the researcher should undertake in preparing for a qualitative research project. Most qualitative researchers are motivated to conduct

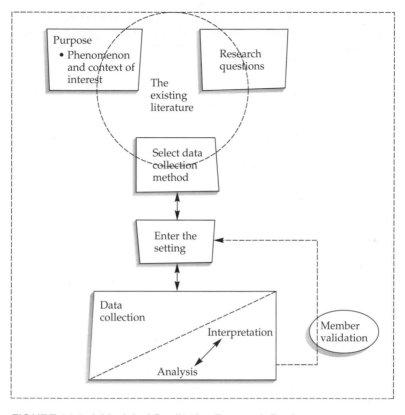

FIGURE 14.1 A Model of Qualitative Research Design

an investigation because they have experienced a communication situation that the research literature has not adequately explored. As the researcher begins to establish the phenomenon and context of interest, he or she should turn to the existing research literature. Searching the literature for studies about the phenomenon and studies about the context will help prepare the researcher to make the most of his or her time in the field.

The researcher must be able to identify the tentative goals of the study. Not only does the researcher have to address the academic research audience, but he or she should also address the concerns of communicators. The first question—What communication practices or processes will be illuminated?—helps provide the academic focus. The second question—For whom will the

results be beneficial?—helps provide the practical focus. Because researchers using qualitative methods are entering or assessing natural communication and, in some cases, entering the lives of research participants, they must be able to answer the question "What is the most effective argument for pursuing this particular research project?"

Next, the researcher must develop tentative research questions. This component should not be overlooked simply because the research is qualitative. Research questions can be developed to help uncover greater understanding of or to determine what is not known about the communication phenomenon. If a study requires multiple questions, these need to be articulated in such a way that the relationships among them are clear.

Likewise, the researcher turns to the existing literature to address previous findings and conceptual frameworks that are related to the phenomenon of interest. In some cases, theory may exist that can provide a temporary or plausible explanation about the communication process. In qualitative research, existing theory can inform the research process. Qualitative researchers vary to the degree that they use theory in this development phase of a research project. When theory does exist, researchers should "carefully suspend its use" (Lindlof & Taylor, 2011, p. 35) when entering the data collection and data analysis stages of the research project.

Why would researchers consider a theory and then suspend it? One of the hallmarks of qualitative methods is its focus on developing interpretations from what researchers observe participants saying or doing. Since all theory is partial, it would be unlikely that a theory could describe or explain the depth and intricacy of the whole of a particular communication phenomenon or process in its natural setting. Indeed, in observing participants, the researcher may discover additional aspects of the phenomenon or process that is different from what the theory offers as description and explanation of events. After these initial steps, the researcher designs the research project by selecting a data collection method or set of methods. This part of the process is at the bottom of the circle in Figure 14.1 to suggest that the method does not lead the inquiry. Rather, the method should be selected because it is the most appropriate for investigating the communication phenomenon or process of interest and for its ability to answer the research question. Here, some practical issues exist. What qualitative research skills do you, as a researcher, possess? What skills can be learned or enhanced? Finally, the researcher must be able to give an answer to the question "What qualitative techniques and approaches are appropriate for answering the research questions and can be effectively used in *this specific communication environment?*" Both parts of this question must be satisfied. Besides identifying the methods for collecting the data, the researcher should plan the method of data analysis. This decision must be made before data are collected.

Now the researcher is ready to enter the setting—after securing the permission and consent of participants, if this is required. Although data collection is now the primary activity, the researcher needs to remain flexible. Once in the setting, the researcher may recognize that the planned research design and selected method are not the most effective or appropriate. Thus, adjustments may be made. The two-way arrows between method and setting and between setting and data collection emphasize the need for flexibility.

In the setting, the researcher begins data collection; that is the primary activity. However, analyzing and interpreting data can begin as soon as data are collected, or shortly thereafter. As mentioned earlier in this chapter, data collection is closely followed by data analysis and interpretation. In some cases—for example, in interview and focus group research—all the data may be collected before data analysis begins. In other cases, particularly when the researcher is making observations in the field, data analysis will begin while the researcher is still collecting data. In either case, making tentative and plausible statements of the phenomenon being studied gives the researcher the opportunity to expand or restrict questions that are being asked or observations that are being made. The long dashed line separating data collection from analysis and interpretation indicates this relationship. The two processes can be separate activities, or they may become integrated activities. This type of continuous comparison is common in qualitative research methods and may suggest that the researcher make adjustments to what is being asked or observed.

There is a process to qualitative research with a beginning, middle, and end. But the process is more cyclical than linear. Thus, the researcher is likely to revisit some steps in the process and reconsider some decisions "until the researcher 'gets it right'" (Lindlof & Taylor, 2002, p. 67). Indeed, Tracy, Scott, and Richard (2008) argue that qualitative research is not only inductive, but also iterative. They describe entering the field to collect and analyze data with a rough idea of their direction, but they also found that they needed to return to the research literature—repeating this process several times before the research design and topic became more focused. From this perspective, the model for qualitative research design is more fluid. As researchers learn more from their work in the field, they adjust their topic and methods. While overall the process is inductive, the steps that researchers take to collect and analyze data are iterative.

Issues of Credibility in Qualitative Research

Qualitative researchers focus on the issue of credibility to assess the quality of their interpretations. **Credibility,** or the extent to which interpretations can be validated as true, correct, and dependable (Lindlof & Taylor, 2002) is enhanced when the perspective of participants is authentically represented in the research process and research report (Fossey, Harvey, McDermott, & Davidson, 2002) Qualitative data and the interpretations drawn are also evaluated for their *fit*— that is, how well do the findings fit the data and social context from which they were collected.

Credibility is essential to qualitative research findings because the process of qualitative research could result in multiple interpretations (Lindlof & Taylor, 2002). A caution here: Seeking credibility should not be confused for seeking a single truth. Indeed, different interpretations of communication processes are likely to exist in any group of research participants. The subjective nature of qualitative research seeks credibility for the multiple situated and constructed realities of the persons from whom data are collected. Thus, researchers design their projects and then analyze and interpret their data to create "plausible, insightful and/or useful" interpretations (Lindlof & Taylor, 2002, p. 240). Triangulation and member validation are two ways qualitative researchers enhance the credibility of their findings.

Researchers use **triangulation,** or the use of several kinds of methods or data, to bring credibility to their findings. If the analyses of two or more methods of data collection or two or more investigators point toward the same conclusion "then validation is enhanced" (Lindlof & Taylor, 2011, p. 274). Communication scholars can

triangulate their findings in several ways (Denzin, 1978; Janesick, 1994). The first method of triangulation common to qualitative research is **data triangulation.** By using a variety of data sources and data types in one study, researchers are more confident about their findings and conclusions. Humphreys (2012) describes how data triangulation was achieved in his case study analysis of mobile social networks (i.e., Dodgeball, BEDD, sms.ac, Socialight, and Twitter). First, the author was in the field for each case ranging from 6 months to 2 years. Second, he and other researchers conducted in-depth-interviews with 70 users and employees of the mobile social networks. Third, Humphreys conducted textual analyses of user profiles, corporate press releases, websites, and popular press for each of the cases. Finally, he and others conducted a content analysis of tweets.

A second method of triangulation common to qualitative research is **investigator triangulation.** When several researchers or evaluators participate in the research, researchers have greater confidence in their findings because no result is dependent on one person's observations or interpretations. Qualitative methods frequently use multiple observers or coders to reduce the subjective bias that can be introduced when only one researcher acts as the observer and data collector. For example, Smith, Coffelt, Rives, and Sollitto (2012) conducted an interview study to answer the research question "How do natural disaster crisis victims frame their experience during the remembering phase of sensemaking?" (p. 55). The authors report that all of them interviewed participants and participated in the analysis through discussion before, during, and after data collection to apply diverse perspectives to the process" (p. 56). The authors report this step in the method section as an explanation of how they addressed the credibility and transferability of the results.

Finally, **interdisciplinary triangulation** is possible when researchers from a variety of disciplines work together on a research project. Interdisciplinary triangulation is becoming more popular as communication researchers enter into highly specialized interaction environments. For example, two communication scholars teamed with a physician to examine how physician–patient interaction was influenced by the presence of a third person, an intern or resident (Pomerantz, Fehr, & Ende, 1997). The research team represented both communication and medical expertise, creating greater ecological validity for their analysis. By working together as a team, researchers can question one another's biases and perspectives to find the most effective way to study and then analyze the phenomenon of interest.

Thus, triangulation through the use of multiple sources of data or multiple investigators from the same or different disciplines is used to dispel doubts about the reality of a finding and enhance the credibility of the qualitative research process (Lindlof & Taylor, 2002). Let's turn now to member validation.

Member validation, or **member check,** is the process of taking the research findings back to individuals from whom data were collected or were observed. Research participants can comment on, even edit, the preliminary research report. What the researcher hopes for is that the participants will recognize the findings as true or accurate (Lindlof & Taylor, 2011). Participants' contributions are often the source of valuable insight for the researcher, which enhances the credibility of data interpretation for participants (Ellingson, 2009). For example, Goins (2011) conducted member checks with participants she observed in a study about Black female friendship groups. The member check occurred after the researcher analyzed the data by identifying themes and acknowledging tensions.

In this case, the researcher checked her findings directly with the research participants she observed. However, some member checks can be conducted with individuals who are knowledgeable about the context in which the study was conducted but did not participate in the project (Janesick, 2000). For example, if you were unable to validate your findings with the teacher and teacher's aide from an observation study in a second-grade classroom, you could review your findings with other second-grade teachers. Having individuals who are intimately familiar with the generalized context (i.e., a second-grade classroom) review your findings may generate questions to uncover assumptions that the

teacher who participated in the project might overlook.

Building one or more of these methods of triangulation or member checks into a qualitative research design is essential. Their use coupled with the iterative process researchers use to become more familiar with the communication context results in systematic, rigorous research that is informed by the literature.

CONCEPTUALIZING RESEARCH QUESTIONS FOR QUALITATIVE RESEARCH

The model of qualitative research provides an overview of what researchers encounter and must consider in designing and conducting qualitative research. Because research questions are central to the qualitative approach, let's return our attention there.

A researcher's interest in conducting a qualitative study often starts from a personal experience with a particular type of communication. Or, a researcher might start asking questions about topics that are personally and socially relevant. Or, a researcher can use a theory or set of theories as a basis for developing research questions. Because of these differences, research questions for qualitative research are broadly stated and generally nondirectional. For example, Stephens, Cho, and Ballard (2012) asked this question in their qualitative study of organizational communication (p. 27):

RQ1: What types of temporal values do Millennials express for multiple-task completion?

Also typical are Kosenko's (2011) research questions for an interview study (p. 479):

RQ_1: How do transgender individuals describe the process of safer sex communication?

The use of research questions accomplishes two objectives simultaneously. First, the research question provides the researcher with a focus. At the same time, the generalized nature of the research question allows the researcher considerable latitude in following interesting paths that

What If Research Questions Are Not Presented?

Whereas quantitative research follows fairly strict traditions, authors of qualitative research have more flexibility in how they approach what they study and how they report their findings. In writing qualitative research reports, many authors will explicitly state the research question that provides the focus for the study. However, you will read some that do not. When this is the case, you must look for the implied research questions. Generally, you can find these in two places: in the opening paragraphs of the article or at the end of the literature review, just before the section in which the researcher explains the method and analytical process for the study. If you are still having trouble identifying the research question, read the conclusion or implications section at the end of the research report. With that information you should be able to work backward to develop the question that framed the researcher's study. If you are still having trouble identifying the research question, ask yourself, "What is the central communication phenomenon or process being explored?"

appear as the researcher collects the data. Thus, many qualitative studies are structured around just a few questions, an overall research question, or one central question with a couple of subquestions.

Most qualitative research questions focus on some specific interaction context. As a result, the research questions are specific to a type of communication and specific communicators. Good examples of this type of qualitative research question are found in a study of the boys who were part of a refugee settlement, commonly referred to as the Lost Boys of Sudan (McKinnon, 2008, p. 399):

RQ$_1$: How are the "Lost Boys of Sudan" discursively situated as refugee subjects?

RQ$_2$: What does this positioning mean for the ways they experience and/or negotiate resettlement in the United States?

RQ$_3$: How does this positioning work in relation to the ways that the men negotiate identity and belonging in resettlement?

Assessing Research Questions

Typically, qualitative research questions start with *how* or *what*. By using these openings, researchers can pose questions to discover, explain

or seek to understand, explore a process, or describe the experiences of participants (Creswell, 2014). All these objectives are particularly well suited to qualitative research. Notice that each of the research questions given in the examples begins with *what* or *how*. Asking research questions this way suggests a research design that is open to the possibilities that the data provide (Creswell, 2014). Because of the open and subjective nature of qualitative research, expect your research question to change as you plan for and as you conduct the study. It is quite common for research questions to evolve as you become more familiar (or maybe less familiar) with the research settings, the participants, and the communication process being explored.

Although not always the case, research questions developed for qualitative studies usually use nondirectional wording. Words such as *affect, influence, impact, determine, cause,* and *relate* all have a directional orientation (Creswell, 2014). If possible, research questions should reference the research site (Creswell, 1994). Qualitative research is conducted on specific interaction with specific interactants in a specific context. Thus, results from such a study are less generalizable to other interactions, other interactants, or other contexts. By identifying contextual elements in your research question, you remind the reader and yourself of this issue. Finally, can the research question be answered with the qualitative method you expect to use?

What kinds of questions are best answered with qualitative research methods? Qualitative methods can be effectively used when researchers ask questions about (1) a specific type of interaction, (2) how meaning is developed and shared by a specific set of interactants in a specific interaction context, (3) naturally occurring issues that would be difficult or unethical to replicate in experimental conditions, (4) unanticipated phenomena and influences, (5) communication processes that occur over time, and (6) a particular communication context and the influences of the context on the interactants (Creswell, 2014; Erickson, 1986; Maxwell, 1996).

In asking these types of questions, qualitative research brings the "invisibility of everyday life" (Erickson, 1986, p. 121) to the surface. Sometimes interaction events that are familiar escape our assessment and analysis. Qualitative methods can bring an enhanced level of detail to familiar interaction events. Such detail allows researchers to examine message construction and the ways in which messages create meanings for individuals in intimate ways.

Thus, a researcher must plan for intensive study of the interaction, be especially complete in recording observations and taking notes, and be willing to spend considerable time in reflection to develop an appropriate analysis. Although qualitative methods focus the researcher's attention on common interaction events, the researcher must carefully scrutinize these events for their significance as well as consider the various points of view of the interactants or participants (Erickson, 1986).

WHAT COUNTS AS DATA IN QUALITATIVE RESEARCH?

What counts as data, or evidence, in qualitative research is a difficult matter because anything that the researcher could observe or capture could count as data. Often the initial question

that guides the development of the qualitative research project will broadly identify the phenomena the researcher wants to examine. But in qualitative research, the researcher seldom fully understands the communication phenomenon or process being studied before entering the research field. How, then, can the researcher construct meaning or develop interpretations of what he or she heard and saw? Two issues—the construction of meaning and the level of data representation—can help researchers determine what counts as data in qualitative research studies.

Interpreting Meaning

Researchers interpret meaning in qualitative research in three ways (Potter, 1996). The first is **researcher construction.** From his or her personal, subjective position or perspective on the experience, the researcher develops an interpretation. Thus, evidence is fully the construction of the researcher. This would be the position a researcher would have to take if he or she were unable to communicate directly with the research participants. In some studies, the researcher takes on the role of the strict observer and does not interact with participants in their interaction environment. Thus, in analyzing the data, researchers are forced to rely upon their interpretation of what happened and why. As a result, the researchers write the qualitative research report using their perceptions and insights.

The second method of interpretation is **subjective valuing.** This interpretation of meaning relies on a mix of both objective and subjective elements. Subjective valuing acknowledges that there are tangible artifacts, or objective sources of meaning. However, the researcher must make some interpretation of these objective elements. As a result, the researcher's subjectivity is introduced into the interpretation of meaning. With this type of meaning construction, the researcher mixes his or her interpretations with interpretations received directly from participants.

The third interpretation of meaning, **contingent accuracy,** relies on tangible artifacts, which are believed to be accurate representations of the phenomenon. This is the most objective of the three positions. However, some subjectivity is introduced when the researcher selects some elements over others to use as evidence. Well-trained researchers are capable of making the best selections; little interpretation is required. Thus, if direct quotes from research participants are available and the researcher selects the ones that require the least additional interpretation, then contingent accuracy has been achieved.

Level of Evidence

Evidence, or data, in qualitative research can range, for example, from the one-word quotation of an employee to the lengthy storylike description of an organization's culture. Microlevel evidence can be identified and stand on its own. Macrolevel evidence is broad-scale and many similar data belong to the same classification. Midlevel data, obviously, are somewhere between the two extremes. Examine Table 14.1 for examples of evidence at the three levels (Potter, 1996).

Whereas quantitative methods rely on comparisons among data at the same level of analysis, qualitative methods are not as restrictive. Some qualitative studies will focus on the same level of evidence, or unit of analysis, throughout the study. In other qualitative studies, researchers will integrate levels of evidence in order to answer the research question.

MAKING THE CASE FOR QUALITATIVE RESEARCH

Qualitative research is widely known and accepted in the study of communication. Some qualitative research is reported in such detail and depth that the study is published as a book (for example, see Goodall, 2006 or Miller-Day, 2004) or as book chapters. Regardless of where it is found in the scholarly literature, qualitative research provides an intimate view of human communication.

Advantages of Qualitative Research

What advantages does qualitative research enjoy? First, the researcher documents what is going on in a way that individuals participating in the interaction event may not be able to see. Some communication features or functions are often taken for granted by those who use them. A researcher can uncover such phenomena by carefully planned observation. Second, qualitative research can provide information about communication processes that cannot be replicated in the lab or for which surveys are not suitable. For example, a researcher using qualitative methods can enter participants' communication environments (for example, workplaces) and discover how communication functions for them. Third, qualitative data can provide a detailed picture of many aspects of communication phenomenon. Because a researcher using

TABLE 14.1 Evidence at Three Levels

Microlevel Evidence	Midlevel Evidence	Macrolevel Evidence
Direct quotations from one person	Interaction patterns	Organizational norms
Answers to specific questions in an interview	Conversational structures	Cultural values
Diaries, memos, letters	Leadership behaviors	Rituals
A book	Genres of television shows	Cultural values demonstrated through a variety of sources
A television show	A body of work	All television shows

qualitative methods has direct access to participants, probing questions and observation can reveal detail that neither the participant nor the researcher initially considered part of the communication environment or process.

Limitations of Qualitative Research

As with any research method, qualitative research has limitations. The communication environment must be accessible to researchers. Thus, some communication environments (for example, parents talking with their children about sex) may be off-limits to researchers. Another limitation occurs because people being observed can consciously, or sometimes unconsciously, change their behavior as a result of being observed. Thus, what the qualitative researcher sees and hears may not occur when the researcher is not there. A third limitation is that all observations are filtered through the interpretive lens of the researcher. Finally, qualitative research is often time consuming. Thus, the researcher may attempt to limit observations to times and situations that are comfortable and convenient or may limit observing to when something is expected "to happen." As a result, the representativeness of the observations may be in question.

Lindlof and Taylor (2011) offer four challenges of qualitative data that some would see as limitations. First, qualitative research designs produce a great deal of data that must be read, re-read, and re-read again to make sense of it. Second, qualitative data analysis often results in multiple decision points that inevitably result in a set of plausible interpretations that might not otherwise develop. Third, qualitative designs are circular. As Lindlof and Taylor describe, "sometimes the researcher isn't able to identify the real research problem until the data analysis is well underway" (p. 242). The fourth challenge is that a qualitative research report must be judged as meaningful and credible by the participants, as well as be judged by the academic audience the report is written for. While some may see these four challenges as limitations, they really are just peculiarities that arise from learning anything new.

Threats to Credibility in Qualitative Research

A primary threat to the credibility of a qualitative research study is inaccuracy or incompleteness of the data (Maxwell, 1996). Audio- and videotaping largely resolve this problem. But what if it would be difficult or impossible to make such recordings? Then your field notes must be as complete and accurate as possible. Techniques for taking notes and other methods of qualitative data collection are described in detail in Chapter 16.

A second threat to your study is a problem of interpretation. Using yourself as the data collection instrument in qualitative methodologies requires that you carefully consider whose interpretation is being imposed upon the data. Is the interpretation your understanding? Or does the interpretation represent the perspective of the people you studied? You can counter this threat by carefully listening for the participants' interpretation of the interaction. Viewing the interaction from the perspective of those you study can overcome this threat to validity. In some cases you will be able to verify your interpretation with the interactants, and it is always a good practice to do so if the situation allows.

Depending on yourself as both data collector and interpreter requires attention to the way in which you treat similar and different cases. Are two similar instances of communication behavior—from observations of different people or from the same person at different times—interpreted differently or similarly? If different interpretations are created, on what basis can you justify the differences?

A third threat in qualitative research is the threat to theoretical validity (Maxwell, 1996) that can occur if you do not pay attention to data that fail to fit the explanation or interpretation you are developing. These data cannot simply be dismissed. Rather, they must be considered and analyzed.

Finally, qualitative researchers must always be sensitive to selection bias and reactivity bias (Maxwell, 1996). Selection bias occurs when data stand out to the researcher. To counter

AN ETHICAL ISSUE

Is Anything Off-Limits?

Communication researchers are especially interested in sexual harassment because communication is the medium for the inappropriate act as well as a medium for resisting it. Moreover, organizations communicate to their employees about sexual harassment through their sexual harassment training programs, policies, and procedures. Communication researchers have captured the narratives of those who have been harassed. But researchers have not been able to document firsthand occurrences of sexual harassment. Why? Even when researchers spend considerable periods of time within an organization, some types of interaction are performed out of the researcher's view. This is the case with sexual harassment. Researchers can identify symptoms of a sexually harassing culture and other evidence that harassment has occurred (for example, negative attitudes toward women, victims' self-reports). But, generally, researchers will not see the harassment. How does this affect the researcher's attempt to study sexual harassment? Will this create any ethical dilemmas? How much verification does a researcher need or should a researcher seek when an employee describes a sexually harassing incident? Can you think of other interaction situations similar to this?

this bias, the researcher must always be asking, "Why do these data stand out or seem unique to me?" Perhaps the data are really unique and should be captured for analysis. Or is it possible that the observed phenomena mirror an extreme example in the researcher's own life, and he is reacting to it because it has personal relevance for him?

Reactivity bias is the influence of the researcher on the interaction setting or the interaction among participants. In most qualitative studies, participants will know that you are the researcher and that you are there to observe them or to ask them questions. It is unlikely that anything you do or say will eliminate this bias completely. However, you should try to minimize this bias by monitoring your interactions and activities.

How can these biases be overcome? Using methods of triangulation, discussed earlier in this chapter, will certainly help. Researchers should get feedback from those who were observed, if at all possible. If multiple researchers conduct observations, they should regularly check with one another about their interpretations. In some cases, training observers might be necessary.

ONE LAST THOUGHT

Communication scholars have varying positions on the philosophical foundations of and theoretical contributions to qualitative research. Likewise, they have different views about the role and the goal of the researcher (Lindlof & Taylor, 2011). Regardless, communication scholars generally view qualitative research as the process of collecting and analyzing data for which the researcher is responsible for developing precise reports that reveal how communicators construct patterns, meanings, and interpretations in their day-to-day interactions with others.

SUMMARY

1. Qualitative research methods are sensitive to the social construction of meaning, and they explore social phenomena through an emphasis on empirical, inductive, and interpretive approaches.

2. Qualitative methods aim for subjectivity and intersubjectivity.

3. Qualitative methods are characterized by the following: a theoretical interest in how humans interpret and derive meaning from communication practices, concern with socially situated interaction, reliance on the researcher as the data collection instrument, and reliance on textual data.

4. Qualitative research recognizes that everything in the communication environment influences everything else and generally does not seek to ascertain causality.

5. Qualitative research uses inductive reasoning, which requires the researcher to become intimately familiar with the field of interaction.

6. The qualitative research process is comprised of processes that are interdependent and cyclical.

7. Triangulation and member checks help establish credibility in qualitative research findings.

8. Research questions guide qualitative research projects.

9. The concept of data is broadly defined in qualitative research.

10. Researchers assess data for the way in which meaning is constructed and the level of the evidence.

11. Advantages of qualitative research include being able to study communication features or functions taken for granted, collect information about those who cannot or will not participate in more traditional quantitative research designs, and enter the communication environments of those who are deviant or hostile.

12. Limitations of qualitative research include difficulty in accessing or gaining entry to the desired communication environment, participants changing their normal behavior due to the presence of the researcher, and having the researcher being the sole interpretive lens of the interaction.

KEY TERMS

contingent accuracy

credibility

data triangulation

discourse

inductive analysis

interdisciplinary triangulation

intersubjectivity

investigator triangulation

member check

member validation

mutual simultaneous shaping

researcher construction

subjective valuing

subjectivity

triangulation

See the website www.mhhe.com/keyton4 that accompanies this text. For each chapter, the site contains a:

- chapter outline
- chapter checklist
- chapter summary
- short multiple-choice quiz
- PowerPoint presentation created by Dr. Keyton

For a list of internet resources, visit http://www.joannkeyton.com/CommunicationResearch-Methods.htm.

CHAPTER FIFTEEN

Designing Qualitative Research

Chapter Checklist

After reading this chapter, you should be able to:

1. Identify the role of the researcher in qualitative research designs and explain the potential effects of different researcher roles on the research process.

2. Select and argue for an appropriate researcher role for a specific research project.

3. Develop a purpose statement and research question for a qualitative research project.

4. Create a research design for a qualitative study.

5. Develop a technique for gaining entry to a research site.

6. Use sampling strategies to identify potential participants or other sampling units.

7. Select effective and appropriate data observation strategies.

8. Document data as evidence in complete and detailed notes.

9. Consider and, if appropriate, moderate your impact as researcher on participants and the research process.

This chapter explores the process of designing and conducting qualitative research. The term *qualitative research* represents a variety of methodologies for data collection and data analysis (Denzin & Lincoln, 2005). Recall that qualitative research is distinguished by the role the researcher assumes in collecting data. In qualitative methodologies, the researcher assumes the role of an observer or interviewer, collecting data from participants in as descriptive and detailed a manner as possible. Thus, the researcher assumes an active, fluid, and subjective role. As a result, participation and observation are integrated (Lincoln & Guba, 1985).

As with any type of data collection, qualitative data collection should be well planned using credible methods, carried out effectively, and subject to the scrutiny of others (Phillips, 1992). The caveat is that the researcher using qualitative methods of data collection is entering a setting over which he or she has little control; thus, the researcher must be sensitive to the site or setting in which data are collected. The researcher must be able to be fluid and adapt plans, and perhaps even ways, of collecting data once on the site.

The way qualitative research is conducted is often less apparent in a research article because some design decisions are made in the field and this flexibility is not easily captured in the traditional journal article form (Tracy, Scott, & Richard, 2008). Still, the process of conducting qualitative research does have standards by which it is evaluated. You will need to plan and make decisions for four main components (Maxwell, 2005). First, what settings and individuals do you want to observe or interview? What other data are available for your use? Second, you need to establish relationships with those you want to study. Third, how will you gather data? And, fourth, what will you do with the data to make sense of it? This chapter explains the preparations a researcher should make and describes the standards that have been accepted by researchers across disciplines. Chapter 16 describes some basic methods for collecting qualitative data. Chapter 17 focuses on how researchers make sense of and analyze qualitative data.

RESEARCHER SKILLS FOR QUALITATIVE METHODOLOGIES

What skills do researchers working with these qualitative methods need? First, to work effectively with qualitative methods, a researcher needs both theoretical knowledge and social sensitivity (Strauss & Corbin, 1998). This means that the researcher must balance what is being observed with what he or she knows or can draw upon from the scholarly literature. The researcher must know and understand the literature and the research process and, at the same time, be immersed in the interaction environment. This characteristic allows the researcher to maintain the distance necessary to complete the data analysis.

Second, a researcher must be able to recognize his or her subjective role in the research experience (Strauss & Corbin, 1998). Some qualitative methods create greater distance between the researcher and participants. Even so, in collecting qualitative data, the researcher is always part of the interaction environment. For example, in focus groups, researchers need to be able to avoid asking questions that lead participants toward a particular answer. Without the ability to recognize and avoid this type of bias, it would be impossible for the researcher to gather credible data. On the other hand, some qualitative methods, like ethnography, create very little distinction between the researcher and the researched. In this case, the researcher's bias and point of view are central to interpretation of the observations, but they still must be recognized and acknowledged.

Finally, a researcher needs to be able to think abstractly (Strauss & Corbin, 1998). This ability allows the researcher to make connections among the collected data, even though no relationships are obvious at first glance. Drawing upon his or her ability to view the world in conceptual terms, the researcher can uncover meanings and relationships that were hidden or obscured.

THE RESEARCHER'S ROLE IN QUALITATIVE METHODOLOGIES

Qualitative methodologies are used by communication researchers to study the performance, process, and practice of communication. By choosing to use qualitative methods to answer research questions, the researcher is *in* the communication context being studied or is interacting directly with research participants. In qualitative practices, the role of the researcher is integrated within the context of the individuals who are being observed. Gold (1958) explains:

> Every field work role is at once a social interaction device for securing information for scientific purposes and a set of behaviors in which an observer's self is involved. . . . He [sic] continually introspects, raising endless questions about the informant and the developing field relationship, with a view to playing the field work role as successfully as possible. (p. 218)

Researchers are in the research context for extended periods of time—days, weeks, months, even years—giving them the opportunity to sequentially examine in depth the experiences and insights of participants. As a result, researchers observe the communication firsthand rather than through secondhand verbal or written reports of participants. This type of researcher involvement is labeled **participant observation.** Its various forms are described in the sections that follow. However, it is best not to view the four roles as discrete. Rather, the roles exist on a continuum from mostly participant to mostly observational. The role of researcher interacting with and collecting data from participant can be quite fluid.

Forms of Participant Observation

As a researcher, you may take a passive role, only observing what is going on. This would be the case if you observed your city council in action. For example, you would take a seat in the audience, would not identify yourself as a researcher, and would not talk to those around you. Your activity would consist of taking notes about the meeting, detailing who said what and how. Alternatively, your role could become active. You could join in the debate before the council by raising your hand and asking a question. Now you would be participating in the interaction. There are four types of roles researchers assume with respect to observing and participating (Adler & Adler, 1987; Gold, 1958; Lindlof & Taylor, 2011).

Complete Participant   In the **complete participant** role, you are fully functioning as a member of the scene, but you do not reveal to others that you are simultaneously observing and assessing their actions. In other words, you disguise your role as researcher through your role as participant. Permission to observe is legitimated through your role as participant. In this way, you are using yourself as a participant to understand the interaction behavior. And in your role as a complete participant, you are affecting what happens in the interaction.

In this role, the researcher observes from a perspective of full membership. Full membership is achieved when researchers choose to study a group with which they have prior membership (for example, their family) or by seeking and obtaining membership in a group (for example, joining the Chamber of Commerce in their position as business owner). Of course, in an ethnography, the researcher may be the central character as the ethnography details the interactions of his or her specific experience, such as Frentz's (2009) tale of his hip replacement.

What risks are involved if you take on this research role? First, others in the interaction setting will see you as a full participant and create expectations for you in that role. As a result, you may find it very difficult and perhaps even intrusive to take notes during the interaction. You must maintain your role as a complete participant. Second, you are likely to receive or hear information that is not intended for outsiders. The private information you receive is given to you based on the nature of your personal relationship with others. You must react to this information as an insider, not as an outsider. Doing otherwise can reveal your identity as a researcher and will encourage others to negatively assess you and the research role when it is uncovered. Third, you can only observe the actions and interactions available to someone in your role, as you "can only go where those members typically go and only do what they do, when and how they do it" (Lindlof & Taylor, 2011, p. 145). It is impossible to temporarily step outside your role as a participant to ask questions. Fourth, because you are involved in the interaction, it may be more difficult for you to detach yourself to analyze it. It may also be difficult to identify the effects of your participation on the group's interaction. Would the group have taken a certain step if you had not been there? These risks raise ethical questions about the role of complete participant. As a result, few communication researchers approach qualitative data collection from the complete participant role.

Participant as Observer   In the **participant as observer** role, the researcher is both participant and observer. While openly acknowledging the research purpose, the researcher also takes an active role in the interaction. In this way, the researcher is viewing the interaction as someone inside the system, even though others know and accept that research is being conducted. As an active member, the researcher participates in the core activities of the group and in some ways is the same as any other individual being observed. At the same time, the researcher retains his or her research focus and refrains from committing totally to the group.

As an example of participant observation, Wieland (2011) spent 6 months, or about 700 hours, in a multinational research and development firm. By shadowing employees for a half day at a time, going to meetings and coffee breaks, and observing them in their offices, she was able to immerse herself into the culture. Wieland did not have a formal role in the organization, but she did immerse herself as a typical employee by going to orientation, attending the organization's company parties, and meeting with employees after work. In this participant-observation role, Wieland collected observational data in 700 pages of **fieldnotes** and interviewed 59 employees. Her participant-observer role also allowed her to collect thousands of pages of organizational documents. Wieland describes her role as a "moderate participant" (p. 168). The advantage of this researcher role is that the researcher need not pretend about his or her presence. Not having to pretend to take on a role in the setting, the researcher is free to ask naïve questions. For example, Wieland describes that she often asked participants to "tell me what just happened" (p. 181). Another advantage is that being relieved of secrecy allows open and honest relationships to be negotiated, which presumably encourages more meaningful interactions—and more credible data (Lindlof & Taylor, 2011). The biggest risk

of the participant-as-observer role stems from the extra demands it places on the researcher, who is creating social relationships with people whom he or she is also observing.

Observer as Participant   The primary focus in the **observer as participant** role shifts to the role of observer. In other words, the researcher has negotiated entrance into an interaction setting to observe with the intention of allowing the interaction to proceed as it naturally would.

In this role, the researcher participates but does not take on a central role in the group being observed; the researcher still interacts with participants casually and occasionally, often indirectly. For example, the researcher might fulfill a secondary role within a group—perhaps helping a baseball team keep score or keeping their playing equipment organized, for example. However, the researcher would not offer or agree to a request to play in one of the team's key positions or participate in the team's decision making. Engagement with participants in the interaction scene is possible, but the interaction is not driven or motivated by the researcher being an actor within the interaction scene.

For example, McKinnon (2008) created interpersonal engagements at the Arizona Lost Boys Center, which assists Sudanese refugees. She engaged in interviews with individuals whom she interacted with most at the center and who understood well the intent of the research project. Acknowledging her status as an outsider, McKinnon reports: "I realized that my role was to listen carefully and well, to rigorously examine the meanings I attached to interactions because of my positionality, to tentatively make connections and to share such ideas with the men" (p. 401). She also conducted informal focus groups, being careful to fit the interviews into the flow and structure of the center. McKinnon observed social gatherings such as monthly dances, workshops, sporting events, and cultural activities. Finally, she was invited to observe the leadership council meetings, which provided greater insight in the needs and issues of the center's community.

In such a role, you would not interrupt the roles and interactions of those observed because your participation would be limited to observing

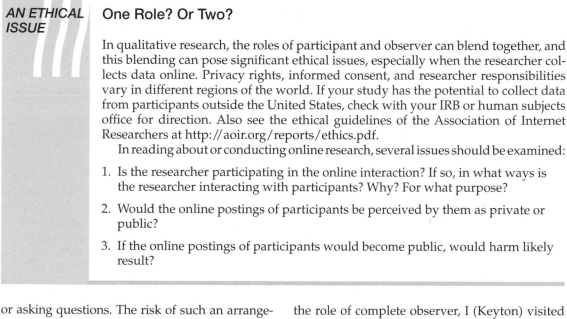

One Role? Or Two?

In qualitative research, the roles of participant and observer can blend together, and this blending can pose significant ethical issues, especially when the researcher collects data online. Privacy rights, informed consent, and researcher responsibilities vary in different regions of the world. If your study has the potential to collect data from participants outside the United States, check with your IRB or human subjects office for direction. Also see the ethical guidelines of the Association of Internet Researchers at http://aoir.org/reports/ethics.pdf.

In reading about or conducting online research, several issues should be examined:

1. Is the researcher participating in the online interaction? If so, in what ways is the researcher interacting with participants? Why? For what purpose?

2. Would the online postings of participants be perceived by them as private or public?

3. If the online postings of participants would become public, would harm likely result?

or asking questions. The risk of such an arrangement is that your minimal participation may make it more difficult to complete full observations or valid assessments of the interaction making it more likely for the research to favor his or her interpretation of events. While this researcher role is easy to negotiate and carry out, it can blind you to the complexity of the interaction.

Complete Observer   In the **complete observer** role, the researcher enacts only the observer role. As a result, the researcher is hidden completely from the interactants in the scene. Thus, data are limited to what one can see or hear. In this role, the researcher does not engage interactants in any fashion. Interviews are not conducted; questions are not posed; people are not asked to explain their comments. Interactants in the setting may not even know the researcher is there as he or she blends into, but does not interact with, the scene and its participants. Of course, the greatest risk is that the researcher's interpretations of what is observed are totally reliant on what is personally observed. The complete observer does not verify or check interpretations with others because doing so would expose this covert role.

For example, Smith and Keyton (2001) reported and interpreted data collected when, in

the role of complete observer, I (Keyton) visited the production of one episode of the television series *Designing Women*. With approval of the show's producer, I observed all rehearsals of the show, the filming of the show before a studio audience, and some postproduction activities. Although the producer was aware of my research role and knew that I was there to observe and take notes, we did not meet or have any communication during my visit to the set. Nor did I have any conversations with cast and crew members. Rather, I sat alone in the stands, as did extras, staff and crew members who were idle, and visitors to the set. No one asked who I was and I was able to remain anonymous. From this vantage point, I had visual and auditory access to cast and crew interactions during the rehearsals and filming. Thus, the job-related interactions and some informal interactions among the cast, directing staff, and crew could be observed and recorded in my fieldnotes.

The risks of the complete observer role are that it does not allow the researcher to develop social relationships and interactions with participants, thereby missing their interpretations of events. While I could easily hear all conversation in the stands and on the set, I could not see or hear what was being said backstage. I did have some

---

TRY THIS!   ## Assuming Researcher Roles

Over the next few days, identify interaction settings in which you can assume each of the four roles just described: complete participant, participant as observer, observer as participant, and complete observer. Stay within the interaction setting long enough to experience the differences in the four roles. After you have had these experiences, answer the following questions: (1) Which role was most comfortable for you? Least uncomfortable? Why? (2) In which role do you believe you could most effectively collect data? Why? (3) To what extent do you believe research participants were aware of your roles?

---

participants' interpretation of unfolding events during rehearsal as they talked to one another, but I did not have first-hand knowledge of how these events were unfolding among actresses and the directing staff backstage. My observer role was enhanced, however, as the producer gave me access to the scripts and all script rewrites as they occurred.

Committed Membership   Another way of conceptualizing the researcher role in qualitative research is based on the degree of researcher's commitment to being a member of that scene (Adler & Adler, 1987). The three researcher roles are: complete member, active member, and peripheral member. **Peripheral members** are insiders, but they do not take on activities central to the participants being observed. **Active members** participate in the interactions and activities like members of the scene do, but they refrain from making full commitment to the goals and values of participants. **Complete members** conduct research in settings and and collect data from participants in situations in which they already have membership, or for which membership can be legitimately obtained.

Researcher as Interviewer   Of course, some qualitative research designs require that the researcher interview participants in one-on-one interviews or in focus groups. For the first type, interviews may be the only method used, or one of many methods used. Thus, the familiarity of the interviewer to participants can vary widely from a one-time relationship established for the sole purpose of collecting data to an established

relationship based on a significant amount of time interacting in the setting with participants. For focus groups, the researcher may be the interviewer, or not. In either case, the focus group interviewer does not know the participants.

Moving Between Researcher Roles   In some qualitative studies, it is necessary (and even desirable) to move among the different researcher roles. For example, David Novak (Novak & Harter, 2008) attended various StreetWise settings and events during the first four months of the research project. This allowed him the opportunity to build rapport with the director and board members, understand the history of the organization, and identify other opportunities for collecting field data. StreetWise is a name of a newspaper and an organization that provides symbolic and material support for people without homes or those at risk. During the next four months, he became completely immersed in the day-to-day activities of participants. During the last four months of fieldwork, he returned periodically to StreetWise to engage in informal member checking about emergent themes and lingering questions and maintained contact with the organization through e-mail. Throughout the project, Novak spent 367 hours in the research setting. Sometimes he was observing vendors sell newspapers. Sometimes he was observing interactions in the office or at staff meetings. Sometimes, he participated in StreetWise by writing an article for the newspaper. As you can see, Novak moved among the different types of researcher roles, each affording him a different perspective from which to gain information and insight.

Regardless of which research role you assume, remember that you are conducting research. The role exists because of your research objective. These researcher role distinctions are from the researcher's point of view. In designing a qualitative study, it is helpful to consider how participants in your study will perceive your role.

IDENTIFYING THE RESEARCH FOCUS

How does a researcher plan for a qualitative study? After the researcher identifies a general research problem or topic, the next step is to articulate a compelling and researchable question that is salient to one or more audiences. Recall the inductive research model presented in Chapter 2. These two steps are the paths through which the researcher enters the research process.

Practically, then, the researcher is the first audience for the research study. If the question is not personally interesting or compelling, you may lack the stamina or motivation to stay in the setting long enough to collect an adequate amount of data, analyze and interpret the data, finish the project, or conduct the study in an effective and ethical manner.

As the researcher enters the field to investigate, however, the question may change as evidence of the problem is observed (or not observed). Even though the question is likely to change, the researcher must still have a question with which to begin. With that question in mind, researchers expecting to use qualitative methods can then use the qualitative model of research design, discussed in Chapter 14, developed specifically for projects using qualitative methods.

Because qualitative research is contextually bound to specific interaction and specific interactants, each research project will result in a unique design solution (Lindlof & Taylor, 2002). Often, researchers cannot determine which method or methods will be best until they spend some time in the interaction context. If researchers are not familiar with the interaction setting, they need time to become acquainted with the parameters of the interaction. What might initially seem confusing might be a regular part of ongoing interaction to the interactants. Alternatively, if the interaction setting is very familiar to the researcher, time is needed within the interaction context to develop a critical, or researcher, view of the interaction. In either case, researchers might choose methods to be used even before the observation and participation begins, but they must ask if these methods are best after they are in the interaction setting. Thus, methodological solutions must be both unique and flexible.

At this point in designing the qualitative study, it is helpful to develop a purpose statement as a road map for your project (Creswell, 2014). You may even use this map later when you write your research report. But its purpose now is to make sure you are ready to collect data. By filling in the blanks in the following sentences, you can articulate what you are investigating and how:

> The purpose of this _____ (type of qualitative method) study will be to _____ (describe? understand? discover?) the _____ (communication phenomenon you are interested in studying) for _____ (the unit of analysis: a person? a group of people? a process?) at _____ (a particular research site). At this stage in the research project, the _____ (communication phenomenon you are interested in studying) is generally defined as _____ (provide a general definition of the central concept).

Consider this completed purpose statement:

> The purpose of these face-to-face interviews and focus groups will be to discover the way in which employees of Organization ABC express acceptance or rejection of the organization's family leave policy. At this stage in the research project, the expression of acceptance or rejection of the policy is generally defined as the acceptance or rejection expressed in the stories or accounts employees give about the policy, expected changes that employees relate about their future use of family leave, and employees' abilities to repeat or paraphrase the policy.

Obviously, in a project of this scope, it is likely that many researchers will be conducting interviews and focus groups. Thus, it is important that all members of the research team have the same road map by which to conduct their research activities. After the first round of interviews and focus groups, research team members will want to meet to consider their ability to fulfill this purpose statement. A rephrasing of the statement may occur. Rephrasing, or revisiting, the initial research problem or question is a natural part of qualitative research because collecting data continually informs or reinforms the researcher about the subject of the research. This reflexive nature of qualitative research is, in part, what distinguishes qualitative from other approaches.

Another aspect of the planning process is to consider one's flexibility as a researcher (Lindlof & Taylor, 2002). The researcher will not have control over what happens in the field. This means that the researcher must be able to fit in with events, people, and interaction with which he or she is unfamiliar. The researcher does not evaluate others by his or her personal rules or standards of conduct. In qualitative research, these come from individuals in the interaction situation, not from the researcher. As a result, the researcher needs to develop a sense of knowing what constitutes important information or actions that should be documented: Events may erupt or develop in a monotonous drone. The researcher must be able to decipher which events and interactions are important and when development (or lack of development) of the interaction creates new questions.

Consulting the Literature

While identifying the research focus, the researcher should simultaneously become involved with the research literature as it relates to the content area and the qualitative method about to be undertaken. By searching the research literature, the researcher can become familiar with terminology or practices used in a particular interaction setting or context, and can identify theories that can support observations or be refuted with observations. Lindlof and Taylor (2011) argue that theory should be used as "resources for developing insights" (p. 78). Reading and becoming familiar with theory can sensitize you to concepts or foreshadow concepts that may be relevant in the interaction context you are studying. At later stages in a qualitative project, going back to theory

can help you test ideas and work out puzzles or tensions you have noticed in the data.

Most qualitative research takes an inductive stance toward theory. Still, Maxwell (2005) describes two ways to think of and use existing theory about your topic or context of interest. First, theory can be a *coat closet*. This means that a theory provides a framework from which to start collecting data and analyzing it. As questions and data are hung together in the closet, it may be possible to see relationships that would have otherwise remained disconnected. Second, theory can be used as a *spotlight*. This means that an existing theory can be used to illuminate or draw your attention to particular communication events or phenomena. Using theory in these ways provides both background for your research design as well as opportunities to develop new theoretical stances, or challenge or extend theory.

Concept Map

If you are unsure about how to begin, you can use theory and empirical findings to create a **concept map,** or diagram of the research project. This is particularly helpful because the map is a conceptual tool that will help you think through a qualitative project (Maxwell, 2005). Because it is visual, the map can help you see what concepts can be grouped together, and how relationships form among groups of concepts. It can also help you uncover holes or contradictions. The map can help you work through your implicit theory or clarify or extend an existing theory. The map can also be used as a tentative understanding of the communication phenomenon, as well as a tentative direction of the research design. Thus, you will generate many maps throughout a project as you take on the reflexive position required by qualitative methods. A concept map can be sketchy or as detailed as you like and prefer. It can be written on paper, the computer, or an erasable surface. The point is not to create a concept map and then be bound to it. Rather, the point of a concept map is to let it be an aid to your creativity and thinking about the research project as you prepare for the project, as you are engaged in the project, and as you reflect on it after collecting data. Figure 15.1 is a series of concept maps developed for a research

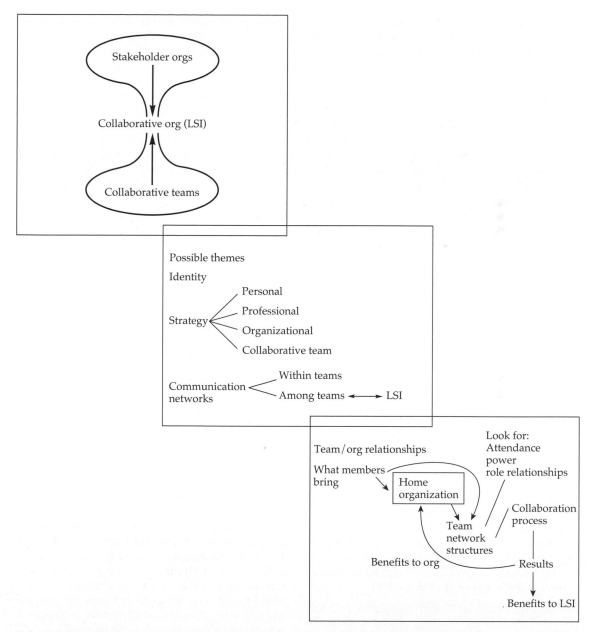

FIGURE 15.1 *Three Concept Maps Developed for a Qualitative Research Project. Maps 1 and 2 Were Developed from the Literature Before Entering the Field; Map 3 Was Developed During Participant Observation.*

project that became the basis for theory development presented in Keyton, Ford, and Smith (2008). Concept maps are particularly helpful when working in a research team. The maps can become the basis of team conversations, planning, and reporting to one another.

Finally, a concept map can help you discover what is *in* your study and what is outside the scope of the study. All research projects have boundaries. What remains in a study should have some degree of coherence and sequence (Stake, 2005); a concept map should help you identify these. With these identifications made, the next step is developing the research questions or research objectives.

Research Questions and Objectives

Recall that qualitative research tends to emphasize description and explanation rather than prediction (Fitch, 1994). Research questions, or a series of research questions, specify the expectations of what the researcher will describe and explain (Lindlof & Taylor, 2002). Different forms of research questions for qualitative studies can be found in Chapter 14.

Alternatively, the research purpose or objective can be stated in a declarative sentence. For example, in her ethnographic study of her father's letters from World War II, Miller (2008) states her purpose

> In this paper, I consider one of the most central aspects of how my father "became a man" during his World War II experiences. Specifically, I examine the transition from "boyhood" to "manhood" through a consideration of how the letters address his relationship with his mother and his father, especially with regard to his father's death in June of 1945. (p. 150)

As another example, Turner and Reinsch (2007) stated the following research objective to examine how employees manage multiple communication tasks:

> To better understand multicommunicating and decisions leading up to it, the first author interviewed 20 individuals at a large, high-tech organization at which we had observed frequent examples of multicommunicating. (p. 42)

Whether a research question or statement of the research purpose is used, the researcher should include enough contextual information to help the reader understand the context of the study. Remember that being reflexive and flexible are key characteristics of the researcher's role in qualitative research. The first research questions and research objectives should be considered tentative, or provisional, until the researcher has experience in the field as an observer or participant. The initial questions and objectives may stay the same; they may change. The goal is to develop questions or objectives that are not too broad (for example, "What's going on here?") or so focused that important communication aspects are overlooked or ignored (Maxwell, 2005).

SAMPLING IN QUALITATIVE DESIGNS

Although researchers are in the field and want to capture the complexity of communication events, the reality is that one researcher, or even a team of researchers, cannot capture the totality of the experience. Thus, qualitative designs require a sampling strategy to guide researcher choices about what to observe or whom to interview. While people (or research participants) are the most likely sampling unit, researchers can also sample physical and online sites and settings. The latter is particularly useful if the research question or purpose is to examine how people use an environment, or how people vary their communication based on a context. Activities can also be sampled (Lindlof & Taylor, 2011). Think of returning a purchase to a store. Waiting in line is an activity in which nonverbal or informal communication could be studied. Another activity is the conversation between the shopper and the sales associate as the return is finalized. Several sampling strategies can be used.

Snowball sampling is often employed in qualitative studies because this technique helps the researcher find potential participants who share some characteristic that is required for the person to participate in the research. **Snowball sampling** is accomplished by getting referrals from individuals who already are participating in the research. Because it is common for people to know and interact with people like themselves, research participants are a good source of additional participants. Favero and Heath (2012) collected qualitative data through focus groups to explore women's perspectives on work/life balance. To assess if different generations of females view work/life issues differently, the research team held a focus group for Gen X and Gen Y women, and another focus group for Boomers. To initiate invitations to the focus group, the research team recruited participants through convenience sampling. This type of sampling was appropriate as the researchers needed to populate the focus groups with women of appropriate ages. To add variability to the sample, these participants were encouraged to bring a guest who also met the study criteria. Thus, snowball sampling added women to the focus group study, but these women were not known to the researchers.

Purposive sampling is often used in qualitative research designs when the researcher is seeking people or other sampling units. A researcher selects a person or site to be included in the study because the person or site is thought to be typical of the communication being investigated. That is, researchers "make informed judgments about what to observe or whom to interview" (Lindlof & Taylor, 2011, p. 110). Usually working from inclusion criteria, researchers purposively seek some people or sites over others. For example, Oliveria (2013) designed a qualitative study to explore how crisis communication experts dealt with cultural issues that surround organizational crisis. The study was conducted in Charlotte, the biggest city in North Carolina, which is home to a variety of national and multinational companies. A purposive sample was appropriate as Oliveria needed to identify currently employed crisis communication professionals with experience in managing crisis situations. Thus, the inclusion criteria were: (a) currently employed as a crisis communication professional, (b) has had experience managing an organizational crisis, and (c) lives within Charlotte or the surrounding business area.

Maximum variation sampling is based on two criteria. First, the researcher seeks participants for the study who vary with respect to the focus of the study. Second, the researcher continues to seek additional participants until the data received are redundant with, or the same as, previously collected data. In other words, the data are saturated with the same information. This is the sampling Lucas (2012) employed to explore the job socialization messages exchanged by parents and their children. Lucas sought participants for her sample by e-mailing individuals who were members of an online alumni network representing all high schools in the community, posting flyers on bulletin boards (for example, in grocery stores and banks), and placing stories about the study in the local media. This method of seeking participants resulted in 25 adults who grew up with fathers who worked in the mining industry. As Lucas explains,

> They [the 25 adults] were evenly split among several key characteristics: sex (13 male; 12 female); age (average age was 37; range 32 – 41); and geographic location (13 moved away; 12 lived in their hometown). Their educational attainment ranged from high school diplomas through graduate degrees. They worked in a variety of industries, including financial, medical, engineering, nonprofit, education, military, corrections, and construction/skilled trades. (pp. 102–103)

Thus, the 25 participants who were children of fathers who worked in the mining industry were considerably varied providing "demographic richness" (Lindlof & Taylor, 2011, p. 113) to the data.

Sample Size

With these types of sampling procedures, what constitutes an acceptable sample size for a qualitative study? Lindlof and Taylor (2011) explain that sample size usually cannot be predetermined. Rather, the researcher usually begins with a few instances (people, sites, activities, etc.) that fit the interest of the study. From there, sampling proceeds in serial fashion—that is, one adds new instances "depending on who and what has come before, so that ongoing sampling supports the emerging theorizing (Tuckett, 2004, p. 49)" (p. 117).

Depending on the research question, one fully developed case may be enough (see Keyton, Ford, & Smith, 2008), or a great number of interviews may need to be done. Most researchers sample until a "critical threshold of interpretation has been reached" (Lindlof & Taylor, 2002, p. 129), or when new information is not being added or existing information is unchallenged.

Other considerations for identifying sample size include the scope of the project and the complexity of the communication being explored, as well as the practicalities of time, money, and assistance in analyzing the data. But Tracy (2014) gives this warning: "Not enough interviews will result in shallow and stale contributions. Too many will result in a paralyzing amount of data, which discourage transcription and penetrating interpretations" (p. 138).

Special Considerations for Sampling in Qualitative Research

To make sense of what you see or hear you must employ some type of strategy for making comparable observations or notes. Thus, the question is, "Of all the interactions available to you, what do you sample?" In the field, the choices can be overwhelming, and over a period of time you may want to sample different units or things. Initially you will want to determine the sample in terms of settings, persons, activities, events, and time (Lindlof & Taylor, 2002).

The setting in which the interaction occurs is more narrowly defined than the context. For example, in my study of resident physicians (Keyton, 1995), the context was a medical teaching hospital, whereas the setting was resident interaction with attending physicians and nurses in the intensive and critical care units. Limiting observations to this setting provided one of many focuses available in this context. Residents' interactions over lunch or coffee breaks were excluded, as were residents' conversations with patients and their families. Identifying the setting is important because it defines the physical, social, and cultural parameters of what is being observed.

The persons who were investigated in this study were the resident physicians. Although I also observed attending physicians and nurses, my primary focus was on the resident physicians and their relationships with people in these two other groups. Thus, who is being observed must be salient and related to your research question. By identifying the setting and persons, as a researcher I could also identify the activity in which I was interested. My primary focus was on their decision-making interactions. Although other communication functions were intertwined with decision-making activities, I was interested in them only to the extent that they informed or provided information about decision making.

Specific events, of course, are related to the settings, persons, and activities previously described. Yet, generally, there are three types of events (Schatzman & Strauss, 1973). The first type includes routine events. These happen regularly or are a regular feature of the interaction. The people involved expect this activity to occur in this setting with these interaction partners. A second type of event is a special event, or an event that does not occur regularly, but when it does is not surprising. For example, celebrating a physician's birthday in the setting of the intensive or critical care unit is a special event. It does not occur every day. Although it may seem odd to an outsider, this setting was the only place the medical staff could gather to celebrate. The third type of event is an untoward event, or an event that results from an emergency. It is unexpected by the people in the setting.

Caution should be exercised in determining what is a routine, special, or untoward event. For example, in my first few days observing in the intensive and critical care units, I did not see physicians yelling and screaming at nurses. Thus, the first time I observed such an event, I believed it to be an untoward event. But over time, I came to realize that screaming and yelling regularly occurred, and being civil to one another (what I observed in my first few days of observation) was really the anomaly (and was probably caused by my presence).

Time is the last sampling unit. A good example of this would be in observing the call-receiving behavior of phone reservationists. Because the downtime between calls is controlled by a computer, what reservationists do or say during this time period can be a valuable indicator of

---

Why Was the Researcher There?

Sometimes researchers and field settings coincide, and the researcher is able to take advantage of the opportunity to collect data. At other times, the researcher actively searches for a specific type of setting in which to collect data to answer a research question. Sometimes someone inside the interaction setting wants the interaction diagnosed or wants help in managing the interaction environment and so invites the researcher to collect data. As you read qualitative research reports, it should be clear how the researcher came to this particular research setting. The motivation for being in a particular setting can influence what the researcher sees and how he or she analyzes and reports the data. Information about how the researcher gained access to the interaction studied is usually presented in the method section of the written research report. Knowing how the researcher gained access and the motivation for conducting the study will help you assess the researcher's claims.

---

employee mood and commitment. Alternatively, time can be helpful for analyzing rhythm and pace of interactions. For example, what does your instructor do in the 10 minutes immediately preceding the class for which you are reading this book? How do his or her activities in that time period compare or contrast to how other instructors spend their 10 minutes before class?

By altering when you observe, you are more likely to observe different aspects of routine behavior. Morning rituals are different from evening rituals. This same strategy also applies to other cycles of times. For example, observing college students at the end of the semester would certainly leave a researcher with one impression, whereas observing them at the beginning of a semester would likely create a completely different impression.

One way to overcome the patterns that time cycles impose is to make observations at irregular time points. For example, if courses at your university started on the hour and finished at 50 minutes past the hour, you might select every 7 minutes as your time point for making observations about the interaction activities in the main lobby of your student center. Finally, you can randomly select the days and times of your observations.

Which sampling unit should be used? Most researchers use several in the same study or use several to define a specific interaction event in which they are interested. When sampling units are consistent, data are more easily compared. Also, by having identified the sampling units of your observations, you are more likely to identify anomalies when they occur.

GAINING ACCESS

Gaining access to, or getting into, the research setting is not always easy. For example, you want to study family interaction at dinnertime. To assess some of the difficulties of gaining access to such interaction, think about your family's dining experiences. What does your family talk about at dinnertime? Is the conversation always friendly? Are dinner topics suitable for a nonfamily audience? How would the presence of an outsider (not at the dinner table, but in close proximity to view and hear the conversation) affect family members' conversation?

Now reflect on how you would approach others with a request to study their family dinnertime interactions. How would you ask friends if you could observe their family dinnertime conversations? How would you approach strangers and make this same request?

In qualitative research, what seems easy and doable often requires finesse to accomplish. Before you approach anyone to ask for access to collect data, you should consider the following questions: What would you tell the people you approach that you wanted to study? What if they asked why you wanted to study them? Finally, you should consider alternative ways of gaining access to the setting you are interested in studying. A research project can start out with a great topic or question but be impossible to complete because access to the interaction event is not practical or is difficult—even denied.

In practice, gaining access includes making the initial contact, negotiating access, establishing entry and operational parameters, becoming known to the participants, and observing the interaction. Returning to the family dinnertime-conversation project, you could begin to negotiate access and establish entry by getting yourself invited to dinner at the homes of friends and relatives. With these invitations, you could *case the scene,* or become familiar with interactions in this setting. By casing the scene (Lindlof & Taylor, 2002), you can develop a better awareness of the interaction you want to study and can refine the research question. More important, observing these interactions may provide you with clues to the best way to ask others to let you observe their dinnertime conversations.

Of course, if your research question takes you to a public setting, gaining access and casing the scene is all that much easier. In the role of visitor, you can hang out and do what visitors do in this public space. You can engage others in conversation, ask questions, and get directions or advice. Of course, it is still difficult to observe all interactions, even in public spaces. Some people will feel as if you are invading their personal space if you try to get too close to their private conversations in public spaces. As an example, how would you observe the interaction at a bus stop to collect data about the function of nonverbal behavior in such settings? What difficulties would you expect to encounter observing in this public space?

As discussed earlier, gaining access to some settings may require that you assume a research role of participant or member. If you take on one of the covert roles, your acceptance by others as a participant or member is dependent on your ability and willingness to play the part (Foster, 1996). Thus, your physical appearance, impression

management skills, and communication competence may need some adjustment to give you the credibility needed to gain access to some settings.

In some settings, particularly organizational ones, you may need to gain the permission of a **gatekeeper,** or a person who has authority or credibility with the group or organization. Alternatively, someone already in the group or organization can act as your **sponsor.** A sponsor can vouch for you to others who will be observed as well as validate and legitimize your presence. Even with such an advocate, the process of gaining access to an organization can be a lengthy one. For example, Pitts, Fowler, Kaplan, Nussbaum, and Becker (2009) relied upon agricultural extension agents to make initial contact with farm families about the research project because the research team needed families who were experiencing or had recently experienced a farm succession. The agent forwarded the names and contact information of those farm families who were willing to discuss their experiences to members of the research team. Of 40 families, 9 agreed to participate in the study.

Part of gaining access is also figuring out if this setting and your observations here will provide you with the data you need. You should ask yourself, (a) Is this setting suitable? (b) Can I observe what I want to observe? (c) Will my observations be feasible? and (d) Can I observe in such a way that my tactics will not be suspect to others? (Schatzman & Strauss, 1973). In fact, during the process of gaining access, the researcher is actively negotiating a role regardless of which level of participant observation he or she plans to use.

Becoming Familiar with People and Places

Because the researcher is always the guest, he or she must take all responsibility for becoming familiar with the setting and the interactants. You can use several techniques to do this. One way to familiarize yourself with the setting is to draw a map. By sketching out the physical nature of the interaction context, you orient yourself to the place in which the interaction occurs. Taking a tour through the interaction setting is another way to observe, ask questions, and learn information about the communication environment. Shadowing a potential participant by following him or her through a typical day is also a good way to become familiar with people and places. A tour or shadowing is a good idea even if the interaction setting is familiar to you. By asking one of the individuals you want to observe or interview to take you on a tour or to allow you to shadow lets you see the interaction context from the participant's unique perspective.

Another way is to seek or ask for relevant background information. In organizations, this might include copies of annual reports or newsletters, public relations or other marketing materials, or reprints of feature stories about the organization or its key members. If you are observing a formally organized group, you could ask for copies of minutes or reports the group has produced. For families or individuals, you might look at scrapbooks or pictures.

Developing Trust

Due to the nature of the researcher's role in qualitative research, trust must be attended to from the first contact with research participants (Lincoln & Guba, 1985). In this situation, trust has some critical characteristics. First, trust is person specific. This means that the researcher will have to develop trust with each person individually. Second, trust is established developmentally and slowly over time. Moreover, trust is fragile and must always be nurtured. Third, trust—even when it has been steadily growing—can be destroyed with one improper action.

Trust between participants and researcher is paramount, and researchers can establish trust in a variety of ways. For her study of a witches' coven, Lesch (1994) describes how she attended regular open meetings of the coven to give participants a chance to know her before she attended with a tape recorder to take notes. Witmer (1997) studied the interaction of an Alcoholics Anonymous group, but only after seeking and gaining permission from the group's founder and informal leaders. Even though the meetings she observed were open to anyone, she felt that getting permission was needed as a matter of both ethics and courtesy.

Developing Rapport In addition to developing trust with others and facilitating participants' trust with the research process, you must also develop rapport with those whom you will be observing and interacting.

Often asking simple questions is a good way to start. Most people are eager to answer questions because it gives them the opportunity to demonstrate their expertise or skill. This technique has several benefits. Asking questions yields basic information you will need to avoid making assumptions. Additionally, it provides a cover for your research role, because it minimizes your role as an observer and heightens your role as a participant. Individuals may feel threatened if some stranger (you in the role of researcher) suddenly shows up without explanation to observe them. People are usually more open to your observations if they have some one-on-one contact with you.

When it is not possible to talk with everyone, maintaining a pleasant conversational posture with the person you are speaking with is important. The tone of the conversation carries over into your nonverbal behavior, which can be interpreted by anyone who is looking on.

If your research role allows it, learn the names and titles of people with whom you will be interacting. In some cases you can ask for a list of names and titles ahead of time. Asking for someone by name is an immediate conversation starter, even if that person is not available.

Another way in which researchers can build rapport with participants is to help with tasks and activities that participants are doing as a normal part of the interaction setting. These types of **commitment acts** (Feldman, Bell, & Berger, 2003) require an investment of time and energy on the part of the researcher but can yield considerable information in learning about the routine and mundane tasks of the setting. For example, Edwards and Kreshel (2008) used several qualitative methods to collect data from participants about their participation in a three-day breast cancer walk. Edwards participated in the walk as a crew member, which stimulated rapport with participants when she facilitated focus groups and interviews. Tasks do not need to be dramatic; mundane or routine tasks can also demonstrate a researcher's trustworthiness and willingness to listen.

Locating Key Informants In some qualitative research settings, there will be one or a few people without whom your project could not be completed. These are your **key informants.** You can identify key informants by asking about the interaction environment beforehand. In an organizational setting you might ask, "Who has worked here the longest? To whom do others turn when they need help? Who always knows the latest rumors?"

Another way to identify a key informant is through your observations. As you watch the interaction, does one person seem more central to the interaction than others? If you are observing a formal setting, who seems to be at the center of the informal conversations? In informal settings, who talks the most or the longest? To whom do others direct their questions? Who tells the jokes? Although you certainly cannot rely solely on one, or even two, key informants, their position in the interaction setting is likely to be essential to your research project.

Key informants are valuable for a variety of reasons. As Rudd (2000) explained, his informants at the symphony were from three groups: musicians, board members, and administrators. "These individuals explained 'native' terms to me, gave me guidance regarding how to pursue additional information and sources, and assisted me in confirming or disconfirming initial interpretations" (p. 121).

Stumbling Onto Something Interesting

Sometimes, of course, and despite the research plan, the researcher will stumble onto something unexpected or unusual. When this happens, the researcher must make a decision to continue with the original project and look for ways the new situation influences what is being observed or to be flexible enough to change course and pursue the new activity, particularly when it replaces or overshadows routine interaction.

For example, something unexpected happened while I was observing the preproduction and production activities of the television show *Designing Women* (Keyton, 1994; Smith & Keyton, 2001). I had asked to observe the rehearsals, taping, and postproduction of the last episode of the 1989–1990 season. My research purpose was to observe the group interaction necessary to produce a television show. The day I arrived on the show's set to begin observations, rehearsals and all other preproduction activities were halted as one of the show's actresses made public what had been a private show-business feud.

This event overtly influenced all the activities leading up to and including the production of the show. How the various production teams worked together no longer seemed very interesting. Rather, my attention shifted to how the producer/writer spoke to the actress via the script because the interaction on the set among cast and crew had shifted to that issue. Events of two days of rehearsals and the night of filming were captured using extensive fieldnotes. I was also able to capture each revision of the script and later compared how the characters' interaction was scripted and filmed with the final aired version. After I returned home, I found additional information about the relationships among the ensemble's actresses and the producer/writer in media reports and additional factual information about the show in organizational reports. Had I not been able to redesign the study spontaneously, I would have lost the opportunity to capture this crisis that eventually prompted the demise of the production company that produced the series.

Given that qualitative research focuses on the specifics of the here and now, is it possible to plan for a qualitative research project? Broadly, yes (Lincoln & Guba, 1985). Researchers start with a focus but are open to the possibility that the focus might change as they observe the interaction. Second, researchers can plan to use certain qualitative methods, depending upon the initial focus. Here, too, they must recognize that the research method or procedure might change if the focus changes or if the research technique is inadequate or inappropriate once in the interaction setting. Third, theory tends to emerge from the inquiry or observation. Questions can be posed before observation begins, but researchers must be flexible and develop theory from what is observed regardless of their initial assumptions. This is an important point, because the data cannot be specified at the beginning of the project. Thus, the form of analysis is inductive rather than deductive.

You can see, then, that a researcher cannot lay out or specify all the details of a qualitative inquiry in advance. Rather, some design issues must be decided as the interaction unfolds. This aspect of qualitative research illuminates its reflexive nature; that is, qualitative research is designed and adapted to the environment in which the research is conducted.

DESIGNING A QUALITATIVE RESEARCH PROJECT

It should be clear that designing a qualitative research is possible, but must remain tentative. Stake (2005) describes qualitative research as seeking the common and the uncommon aspects of the communication phenomenon of interest. To accomplish both, a qualitative research design should consider the following: First, what communication phenomenon (issue, practice, process) do you want to capture and study? Second, what is the historical, economic, political, and cultural background of the phenomenon? In other words, what other elements about the communication phenomenon should you become informed of to understand and represent it? Third, how will you determine that what you are studying is the phenomenon of interest? This is a definitional question. For example, perhaps you want to study conflict in friendships. What is a conflict? A friendship? Is it conflict because you identify it as such? Or, is it conflict because participants label it that way? A highlighting feature of qualitative research is that it can be designed to explore both "What is conflict?" as well as "What is occurring in the conflict?" or "What is it that is going on that makes this interaction conflictual?" Fourth, where is the physical setting of the communication phenomenon? Is it accessible to you as a researcher? This is a central question in the design process. If you can enter the interaction setting and interact with participants, your researcher role and the methods you can choose from will be different than if you can only observe the interaction from a more distant place. Fifth, how will you enter the interaction environment? Do you need a sponsor or key informants? Do you need to work through a gatekeeper to access the population of interest?

Finally, I add two related issues to be considered in the design of a qualitative research project. Do you have the time to commit to the participants and the research environment? Qualitative data are not collected quickly. Qualitative research projects also produce a large amount of data. Do you have the time and resources to manage, review, integrate, analyze, and interpret the data? Consider the following researchers' reports of the time they spent in the field and amount of data they collected:

- Barge, Lee, Madux, Nabring, and Townsend (2008) gathered over 500 pages of documents about a dialogue-centered change program and another 80 pages of evaluations from participants. The team also conducted eight interviews, which ranged from 25 to 75 minutes and produced 87 single-spaced typed transcripts.

- Braithwaite, Toller, Daas, Durham, and Jones (2008) conducted eight focus groups over three months. Tapes from the focus groups were transcribed resulting in 493 pages of interview transcripts.

- Canary (2008) interviewed the parents and children in four families. Interviews varied in length. Approximately two hours were spent in each family's home; a total of 122 pages of interview transcripts and notes were collected.

- Smith, Coffelt, Rives, and Sollitto (2012) conducted 29 interviews with 29 victims of an ice storm. Interviews averaged 27 minutes with the longest interview lasting 52 minutes. The transcribed interviews resulted in 186 single-spaced typed pages.

- Prentice (2008) examined how the newcomer in-law became part of the family. She conducted interviews with 42 participants. Transcribed interviews resulted in 534 single-spaced pages.

- Unson, Trella, Chowdhury, and Davis (2008) interviewed 38 women in their homes; each interview lasted between one and a half and two hours.

As you can see, qualitative research projects require researchers who are committed to being in the field at the convenience of participants. Researchers must also be committed to following through in the analysis and interpretation of the data they gather. A qualitative project you design and conduct may not be as involved as these examples and, as a result, not take as much time nor produce as much data. But a researcher should stay in the field until he or she has discovered what participants would consider *normal.* If a researcher leaves the field too early, he or she may compromise the data by using what the researcher considers normal instead.

What Constitutes Data in Qualitative Research?

The concept of data is broadly cast in qualitative research. Generally, qualitative data are continuous rather than discrete (Fitch, 1994); thus, data often represent a stream or unfolding of events or interactions. Obviously, the notes you take that reflect your observations are data. Recordings of interviews in written, audio, or video form are also data. Written documents—including letters, reports, magazine articles, e-mails, journals, and minutes—are data. Visual documents that you collect or draw are data. Photos and artifacts can also be collected or captured as data. Thus, if you can collect, record, or capture it in some way, it can be used as data.

Qualitative data exist on a continuum from public to private. Some data represent private or personal phenomena (such as a family scrapbook), available to you only because participants willingly provide you access to them. Other data represent more public phenomena, such as an interaction that occurs in an open and public space or a document from an organization's website. Some communication scholars (Fitch, 1994; Tompkins, 1994) argue that at least some of the qualitative data used by researchers should be drawn from public or publicly accessible sources or records. The obvious advantage is that others can verify such data, which adds to the credibility of the research and its findings.

Your Impact as a Researcher

The usefulness of your data will depend to some degree on your ability to acknowledge that who you are will affect what you observe and how you observe it. For example, how does your sex, age, or ethnicity affect your observations? In my observations of a corrections facility (Keyton & Rhodes, 1999), I was made very aware of my sex even though female prisoners were incarcerated and many female officers were present. The severity and controlled structure of the environment confronted me, making me feel uncomfortable dressed in a business suit. I felt more comfortable dressed in a blazer, shirt, and slacks because, in this outfit, I was dressed more like the officers. The point here is that on that first day I was uncomfortable, and those feelings affected my observations.

One way to address these issues is to keep a separate personal journal of your research experience (Lindlof & Taylor, 2011). A private journal or diary of your experiences can be a place to capture emotions, acknowledged prejudices, doubts about the research process, and reflections on your role as a researcher. Although it is impossible for researchers to completely remove themselves from the notes they are taking, having a place to vent can be used as a tool for learning about yourself in the researcher role and improving your researcher performance.

There is another impact you have as a researcher: The amount of similarity between your physical and cultural attributes and those of the people you are observing will also affect your comfort level. It may also positively affect your ability to gain access. Being similar can even enhance the quality of the data you collect because you possess some degree of insider knowledge or have some familiarity with the interaction event. But drawbacks also exist. Being similar to the people you are observing may make you blind to differences that exist between you and them. Similarities may make it less likely that you evaluate them or their interactions negatively. Because you look alike, or place yourself in the same or similar categories, you believe you have a common grounding with others. Making harsh evaluations of them is likely to be perceived as

DESIGN CHECK

Are the Data Credible?

After reading a qualitative research report, use the following questions to assess the credibility of the data. Later, if you conduct a qualitative research project, you can use this same set of questions to help you describe the observation process more fully.

1. What observer role did the researcher assume? Was he or she also a participant?
2. Did the researcher enter the interaction environment in such a way as to develop trust and intimacy with research participants?
3. Does the researcher provide information about how rapport or credibility was established with participants?
4. Does the researcher identify key informants?
5. What interaction setting did the researcher observe?
6. What was the time frame of the observations?
7. Does the researcher explain how notes were collected, managed, and interpreted?
8. Did the researcher use any form of triangulation?
9. Does the researcher address his or her biases or the impact of his or her role on the data collected?

How do your responses to these questions influence your confidence in the findings reported in the research report? If there was one question you could ask the author(s) about the qualitative method, what would that be?

an evaluation of yourself. Thus, researchers must be aware of the possible consequences of their identities on the ethics and politics of conducting research (Lindlof & Taylor, 2002).

Researchers often report their similarities and differences as part of the methodological description in research reports. In that way, readers can also make their own analysis of the degree to which the identity of the observer affected the collection of data and the interpretation of the results. For example, Goins (2011) reports on an observational study of two friendship groups to examine Black female friendship. In a note at the end of the manuscript Goins acknowledges, "Both the author and research assistant are Black females. The author purposely chose a Black female assistant so the women in the friendship group would continue to feel safe (during the research project) in their spaces of Black women" (p. 545).

Authors of qualitative research often reveal themselves in the method section of the research report. For example, Goltz (2009) acknowledges himself in the following way:

I, as researcher and participant, am a 31-year-old, gay, White, Jewish male. My interest in this research is deeply informed by my own personal experience; I make no claims of distance from the study. I have witnessed more than half of my gay friends test positive for HIV, although each of them understood safe sex practices years before infection. I spent a good part of my late teens and 20s on drugs, unconcerned with the dangers. As a teen, I was suicidal, and I was hospitalized on three separate occasions. I've lived most of my life with a reckless ambivalence toward life and anticipated being dead many years ago. My past has led me to this research project. (pp. 566–567)

For both articles, author similarities with the research participants was influential in the research design. It is unlikely that Goltz would have succeeded in drawing gay, lesbian, and bisexual participants together to talk about themes of queerness, feminism, and fantasy without his declaring the ways in which he was similar to them. Likewise, it is unlikely that a White male would have succeeded in being allowed to observe the informal interactions of a Black female friendship group.

In other settings, using research teams composed of male and female investigators of different ages, races, or cultural groups can help researchers gain broader perspectives on research issues. Because researchers bring their backgrounds, personal experiences, and demographic characteristics to the collection and interpretation of data, having a diversified research team can help researchers overcome inherent biases.

FINALIZING THE RESEARCH DESIGN

You must make many decisions before you enter the interaction field. The following list of questions can help you determine if you are ready to conduct a qualitative study (Janesick, 1994):

1. What questions guide your study?
2. Have you identified a site and participants?
3. Have you negotiated access and entry to the site and participants?
4. Have you considered potential ethical issues associated with your study?
5. Do you need informed consent?
6. What is the time frame for your study?
7. Have you selected one or more qualitative techniques for collecting data?
8. Have you addressed credibility issues?
9. Have you considered how theory informs your study? Are you working from an established theory? Or are you attempting to contribute to theory development?
10. Have you identified and acknowledged the biases you bring to the research process?

If you cannot answer one or more of these questions, you are not adequately prepared to enter the field. Collecting data without adequate preparation can waste your (and participants') time. More important, without adequate preparation you may unknowingly engage in activities that are unethical or that can physically or psychologically harm participants.

SUMMARY

1. The role of the researcher is a primary consideration in qualitative research because the researcher is the primary data collection instrument.
2. Researchers can use various roles (complete participant, participant as observer, observer as participant, or complete observer) to immerse themselves in the interaction setting to collect firsthand data.
3. Developing the purpose for the research project will create a road map for a qualitative study.
4. The focus of a qualitative research study is a broadly stated research question or statement of the researcher's expectations.
5. Researchers plan and design their qualitative study recognizing that flexibility in the field will likely be required.
6. To find their samples for qualitative research, researchers use snowball, purposive, or maximum variation sampling.
7. Gaining access, or getting in, to the research setting includes making the initial contact, negotiating access, establishing entry and operational parameters, and becoming known to the participants.
8. Qualitative data is collected through observation and note taking.
9. The researcher must become immersed in the interaction setting, utilize a variety of observation strategies, and take complete and detailed notes.
10. What counts as data in qualitative research is broadly defined.
11. Who the researcher is—his or her qualities and attributes—will affect what and how he or she observes.

KEY TERMS

active members

commitment acts

complete members

complete observer

complete participant

concept map

fieldnotes

gatekeeper

key informant

maximum variation
sampling

observer as participant

participant as observer

participant observation

peripheral members

purposive sampling

snowball sampling

sponsor

See the website www.mhhe.com/keyton4 that accompanies this text. For each chapter, the site contains a:

- chapter outline
- chapter checklist
- chapter summary
- short multiple-choice quiz
- PowerPoint presentation created by Dr. Keyton

For a list of internet resources, visit http://www.joannkeyton.com/Communication ResearchMethods.htm.

CHAPTER SIXTEEN

Qualitative Methods of Data Collection

Chapter Checklist

After reading this chapter, you should be able to:

1. Select effective and appropriate data observation strategies.

2. Document data as evidence in complete and detailed notes.

3. Distinguish among the various forms of qualitative research methods.

4. Select the most appropriate qualitative research method for your research purpose or research question.

5. Identify the basic steps or process the researcher uses to collect qualitative data.

6. Evaluate the method used for its ability to produce credible data.

7. Conceptualize and plan for a field interview.

8. Use open questions in conducting a field interview.

9. Conceptualize and plan for a focus group.

10. Find and select appropriate focus group participants.

11. Develop a focus group outline.

12. Conduct a focus group.

13. Identify several ways to collect narratives.

14. Describe the benefits of ethnographic research.

15. Explain the researcher's role in ethnography.

There are a variety of methods for collecting qualitative data. The qualitative methods described in this chapter—interviews, focus groups, narratives, and ethnography—are common ways of collecting qualitative data about communication phenomenon. Although they differ with respect to how the relationship between researcher and participant is constructed and formalized, each requires design and planning before the researcher enters the interaction environment.

As you might expect, many communication researchers can and do use several techniques in one study. Being familiar with a number of these broadens your skills as a researcher. This chapter provides guidance in planning and conducting field interviews and focus groups and in collecting stories for narrative analysis. Next, the chapter describes ethnography and how the researcher collects data while immersed in the field. Each of these techniques produce textual data in the form of participants' transcribed or researchers' descriptive accounts. Before moving to specific techniques, however, observation and note taking are discussed; they are two fundamental skills used in all qualitative research. These deserve our attention first.

COLLECTING QUALITATIVE DATA

What makes for successful data collection and observation? It should be coming clear that simply observing what is going on, as you would do in your normal day-to-day activities, is not the same as observing in the role of a researcher. The researcher must employ systematic observation (Lindlof & Taylor, 2002; Weick, 1985), which means that the researcher observes and is aware of the interdependence among the people observed, the social situation, and the context in which the interaction occurs. Moreover, the researcher is engaged in the interaction for prolonged periods of time, is conscious and observant of his or her observing ability and activities, and is analyzing the interaction within the complexity of the situation. Thus, when done by a researcher, observing is purposeful, not accidental.

Observation Strategies

Regardless of which qualitative method you use, you will be making observations of interaction. Some methods are more dependent upon observation than others. Even in conducting field interviews, you should practice observation before, during, and after each interview. Doing so engages you with the interaction setting. You can use several methods for making successful observations. A few are explained here. Your instructor is likely to have other observation techniques to share with you. If you propose and conduct a qualitative study, you, too, are likely to develop a strategy that works well. Remember, however, that each qualitative problem requires a unique solution. Do not become too reliant on one or two methods.

The Seamless Container   One way to structure your observations is to conceptualize the setting and context before you as a seamless container. Think of the interaction setting as being round or oval. Starting to your left, describe what you see and what you hear. When you feel as if you cannot add any other detail to this observation, slowly scan your eyes farther to the left, stopping at the next detail that catches your attention (for example, a male student walks into the room with earbuds hanging around his neck, a noise sounds from a vending machine outside in the hall, a brightly colored poster on the wall draws your attention). Again, make as many detailed observations as you can. When finished, once again slowly scan your eyes farther to the left and up to the top of the circle until something else catches your attention. Repeat this process until you have scanned the entire container from your near left, up to the top of the circle, down to the right, and back down to your near right. Now you must include yourself in the observation. How is your presence part of the setting?

A container is a good metaphor for making observations because it can help you describe how things enter or leave the setting. How do people enter the setting—quickly, slowly, or hesitantly? Where do sound and noises come from—inside or outside the space? Are interactions spread throughout or concentrated in one part of the

TRY THIS! **Your Classroom as a Seamless Container**

Sitting in your classroom, start to describe the room according to the seamless container metaphor. Be sure to follow the pattern from your near left, up through the left and to the top of the circle, and to the right and down to your near right. Do not forget to include yourself. Compare your description with that of your colleagues. In what ways do your descriptions differ? Do descriptions differ based on where your seat is located in the room? Do your descriptions differ based on your comfort level in the class? If you were training others to make this type of description, what advice would you give them?

space? Using the container metaphor can help you isolate the setting and interaction but also can make you cognizant of what is outside the setting and how what is outside becomes part of or affects what is going on inside the setting.

Ask Questions to Aid Observation When researchers use observation in a qualitative study, they are often entering unfamiliar territory. In such a situation, it is natural to ask questions. It is also natural (and often satisfying) to try to answer those questions too quickly. Your first answer may not be the best or the correct answer. One way to overcome this natural tendency to respond too quickly is to restrict yourself to asking questions about the people, the setting, and the context.

Researchers using qualitative methods must become good observers, but observations should be "evidence of something" (Lindlof & Taylor, 2011, p. 139). This means that your observations should be tied to the communication phenomenon or processes of your research question or purpose. Imagine that you are in a meeting room observing a community group that decides which nonprofits to support with financial contributions. Let's also assume that your observations are intended to help you answer the research question, "How does following Robert's Rules of Order help or hinder the group from making decisions?" So as you observe, you must ask yourself, "Is what I'm observing now an example of decision making? Is what is occurring helping or hindering the group?" Or, "Is the interaction

I'm watching an example of something else?" If so, "Is this interaction influencing their decision making?"

Observations and your questions about them occur rapidly because most communication processes occur quickly. Once complete, they are gone. As Lindlof and Taylor (2011) argue, "Observers never get a chance to notice any particular event twice" (p. 139). As you practice making observations, your skill will improve.

As another example, assume you are in a doctor's waiting room. You are seated in the area where patients wait to be called back to the examining rooms. To your right is a glass panel that divides the waiting area from the office area. Behind the glass you see a woman who appears to be in her mid-30s. She is a tall brunette and wears a white coat over street clothes. You can see her interact with others in the office, but it is difficult to hear entire conversations. Occasionally, she slides back the glass partition and calls someone to the window to talk with her. After these very short conversations, the person either leaves the doctor's office or returns to wait some more. What questions would you ask about these people, the setting, and the context?

After you jot down your questions, look at them for underlying assumptions you hold. Who is the tall brunette? What is her role in this interaction? What type of interaction is she having with those who appear to be patients? What kind of patients are they? If they are not patients, who are they? What are they doing in this setting? What is the context of the setting? If you have provided answers to these questions or if you restricted your questioning to a particular line of questioning, you may be assuming too much. When you ask questions, your attention is on finding answers. Just be sure that you allow the answers to emerge from the interaction setting and context. Do not assume answers to questions prematurely. If you do so, you are limiting your ability to observe the interaction from a perspective other than your own.

Taking Notes

How does a researcher capture what is seen or heard? Researchers using qualitative methods take **fieldnotes,** or notes that are created on the spot while the interaction occurs. Fieldnotes create a continuous, or sequential, record of what was observed. Be sure to read through and reflect on your notes immediately after you leave the interaction setting. At this point you will want to add detail or jot down questions to consider. Also remember to number and date each page of notes. If your observations are made while moving from one interaction scene to another, be sure to identify the place and people you are observing.

The importance of fieldnotes regardless of which qualitative method you are using cannot be overstated. Fieldnotes are a detailed and "permanent record that verifies field events did in fact occur as the researcher has otherwise stated" (Lindlof & Taylor, 2011, p. 157). Your fieldnotes are the only record of what occurred. You may have audio- or videotape as documentation as well, but fieldnotes do more than document what occurred. They are the beginning of your interpretation of the events.

If you can do so without disrupting the communication process being observed, you should take fieldnotes as the communication activity is occurring and developing before you. If you cannot do this, then it is important to write your fieldnotes as soon as possible after the observation.

It is better to take more notes than fewer. Because the interaction is unfolding before you, you never know what detail will become important later on. What may seem trivial initially may become an important link to understanding interaction occurring hours, even days or weeks, in the future. How many notes does qualitative research typically generate? There is really no easy answer to this question. A better criterion for answering this question is to consider whether you took full advantage of capturing what you heard or observed in the interaction setting.

When taking fieldnotes, move whenever possible from generalized descriptions of observations to capturing *participants'* words, phrases, or comments. To represent the participants' meaning, it is essential to capture the words they use and to note the context or situation in which the words were spoken (Emerson, Fretz, & Shaw, 1995). For example, in observing a workshop on facilitation skills, I took the following notes:

> Carl did an excellent debrief. He described— To get people's attention: "If you can hear my voice, clap one time; if you can hear my voice, clap two times; if you can hear my voice, clap three times."
>
> Carl modeled excellent facilitation skills and process
>
> - Modeled way to get attention (see above)
> - Defined nonprofit
> - Described importance of board participation
> - Then used discussion questions about these issues to create interaction with large audience
> - Related own experiences
> - Described legal obligations of board members

I successfully captured Carl's technique for getting people's attention at meetings. Notice how I set it off with quotations? I failed, however, by describing Carl's debriefing and facilitation skills as "excellent." Who thought they were excellent? Me! I have no idea how the people in the workshop evaluated his skills. Certainly, they did clap when they heard Carl's voice (eventually), and then quieted down to participate in the group activity. However, they might have done so out of a politeness norm, not because they believed Carl's facilitation skills were effective. Thus, in these fieldnotes I made two errors. First, I collapsed description with analysis. Description and analysis should be distinct. Second, I failed to take any notes that could be used as evidence of how the group evaluated or responded to Carl.

Lindlof and Taylor (2002) recommend that fieldnotes contain enough description so you can write answers to the following questions after you leave the interaction setting:

Who are these people?

What are their roles and their relationships with each other?

What is this activity they are performing?

How, when, and where is it performed?

What artifacts are usually involved?

Who uses these artifacts and how is their use determined? (p. 162)

Notice how the questions begin: Who? What? How? When? Where? Just keeping these simple questions in mind will help you take effective fieldnotes. As Lindlof and Taylor remind us, nothing is so trivial or obvious that it should not be noticed and documented. In writing your fieldnotes, you rely heavily on descriptive writing. Tracy (2013) suggests that fieldnotes *show rather than tell*. To show, or demonstrate, your fieldnotes must be detailed "so that readers may come to a conclusion about its meanings on their own" (p. 118). This is the opposite of *telling* in which your notes provide the conclusion. For example, compare these two descriptions: (a) The meeting room was small and cramped. All of the surfaces were white or gray. Team members sat around a rectangular table; there were few conversations as team members came into the room and took a seat. Joe, the team leader, sat at one end of the table. He began the meeting by reading the agenda; no other team members were paying attention; (b) The meeting began appropriately with Joe reviewing the meeting agenda. Notice how the last statement *squeezes* the detail of the first descriptive statement into an evaluative statement that the researcher has no way of knowing is true.

Describing versus Analyzing in Fieldnotes

Describing and analyzing are two different activities. Describing means that you are identifying *what* is going on with *whom*. What are you doing right now? Can you describe your actions and the actions of those around you? After the description is complete, you can begin to analyze *why* or *how* the interaction occurred. Why are you doing what you are doing? How are you doing it? Techniques for analyzing qualitative data are described in Chapter 17.

One good way to distinguish between description and analysis is to draw a vertical line down the middle of a piece of paper. On the left, describe the activities as they occur. You should regularly note the time so that you can create a timeline of action as well. Do not write anything in the right column of your paper until the action is over and the description is complete. When it is complete, go back to the top of your description column. Directly opposite in the right column, analyze what happened by asking "Why?" and "How?" When you are finished with the analysis step, go back to the top and ask if alternative explanations could exist. See Figure 16.1 for an example. This process of describing–analyzing–providing alternative explanations is particularly effective when the interaction or activity is ongoing, making it difficult to stop for periodic assessments and analyses. Practice this technique by watching a situation comedy on television. Remember to describe first, then analyze, and then look for alternative explanations.

Digital Note Taking

Is it ever possible to take your notes with audio or video recording? Yes, but it depends on the situation and your role as researcher. It is unethical to audio- or video-record others without their permission. In some cases (for example, a city council meeting), audio, video, or written records of the interaction are likely to exist as part of the public record. If you do take audio- or video-recording notes, be aware of the following issues. First, some people are uncomfortable talking with recording devices on. They may be afraid of telling you the complete story, or they may be afraid of how they will sound when you play the recording back. Second, if you do make audio or video recordings, offer participants the right to turn off the recording device at any point in your conversation. Always honor their

Information/Facts/Quotes	Questions/Analyses
8:50 I arrived 10 minutes early and signed in on the sign-in sheet. Staff members sign in as well when they arrive. Overall, area is quiet. Employees speak to each other when they walk in, but not much. Receptionist does not know where meeting will be held; has to ask someone else.	Wonder why staff signs in and out? This is a regularly scheduled staff meeting; why wouldn't the receptionist know where it is to be held?
9:10 Meeting is supposed to start at 9; meeting leader still not arrived. I ask the receptionist what might be happening and she said, "Shirley is sometimes late and the meeting does not start until 9:30."	I am feeling frustrated. Staff members do not appear to be upset that the meeting has not started. They appear quite calm and nonchalant. No one mentions or gives any other indication that the meeting is late.
9:25 Several employees walk into Richard's office as if it is time for the meeting. I go in as well. Chris indicates to me that he is going to run the meeting in Shirley's absence.	This appears to be planned. No one acts as if the meeting is late. Does Chris always lead the meeting when Shirley is absent?
9:30 Staff members sit around the conference table in Richard's office; Richard takes a seat at the head of the table. There is not room for everyone to sit around the table; some staff members sit in a second row behind the people at the table.	Are meetings always held in Richard's office? Although Richard's office is neat and clean, the room has a temporary feeling. The room is not conducive for the entire group to meet and discuss issues.
9:35 Chris excuses himself and leaves the meeting. He gives no explanation. While he's gone, Candace asks Julianna to start.	Wonder why Candace took over Chris's role as leader?
9:37 Julianna starts to give her report when Chris comes back in the room.	Difficult to tell if Julianna waited on purpose for Chris to come back in to the meeting, or if this was just coincidence.
9:38 Julianna's report is interrupted by other staff members as they request answers to questions. During her report, Verna came in and sat in the second row of chairs.	Julianna spoke loudly with strength, but others do not appear to be overly interested in her report. Julianna makes eye contact with all other staff members sitting around the table.
9:48 After Julianna finishes, Chris asks Richard to give his report next.	Is there some pattern to the reports? Where is Shirley?

FIGURE 16.1 Capturing Description and Analysis

request and do not resume recording until you have cleared it with them.

Third, you are ethically responsible for maintaining recordings you make and playing them only for those on the research team who must hear or see the recording to complete their data collection or interpretation. There is a distinct difference between making recordings as a researcher and making recordings for distribution to the public. Fourth, do not forget that even the most sophisticated recordings cannot capture the full spectrum of accompanying nonverbal behavior. Likewise, the best video recordings leave out interaction that occurs outside its lens direction and focus. Finally, remember that technical problems can accompany use of these devices (for example, low battery power, lack of available outlets, equipment failure, and so on).

What about taking notes on your laptop computer? This is not recommended unless you can take notes in a place where using a laptop would be considered a routine feature of the interaction space and where you would not disturb others by tapping on the keyboard. Technical breakdowns and human error here, too, can destroy hours of detailed observation notes.

Transcribing Fieldnotes   Most researchers who take handwritten notes in the field usually transcribe them into written form to make these data easier to analyze and compare with other data. Some researchers transcribe their written notes word-for-word as they were written in the field. Other researches use the transcription process as an opportunity to add additional reflection and questions. I have done it both ways and found that the second manner of transcription works best for me. I do, however, use italics or boldface to indicate what I have added since being in the field.

Your fieldnotes should have also captured some word-for-word conversation of the individuals you were observing. Unless you have audio or video to back up a change in what they said, do not tidy up what was said. And do not turn spoken language into conventional or traditional written form. People speak differently from how they write. One

of the unique contributions of communication scholars is that we capture and analyze data as people produce it, not as it is edited. If you arbitrarily change what someone said, it can influence the shape and form of your fieldnotes, which could ultimately influence the analysis of the data (Tilley, 2003).

If you are creating notes from an audio or video recording, you should listen to the tape and verify the transcription. This may take two or three passes through the data. Also remember that putting notes into writing eliminates many nonverbal cues. After your notes are transcribed, you should listen to the recordings again and insert any nonverbal cues that could influence how something was said and would provide a different meaning than its textual representation.

What If You Cannot Take Notes?   Some interaction settings would make it difficult to take notes. At a wedding, for example, your note-taking behavior would seem strange and inappropriate to others, as well as focus unwanted attention on you. In situations like this, you must retreat to a suitable setting (for example, a break room, a private office, your car) for note taking. Take frequent breaks during observations so that you do not overload your memory. Then, when you leave the interaction setting completely, take additional time to review your notes and add to or clarify them.

FIELD INTERVIEWING

Interviews are a practical qualitative method for discovering how people think and feel about their communication practices. But an interview is more than a simple linear process of asking questions and getting answers, and "a much harder task than it may seem at first" (Fontana & Frey, 2005, p. 697). **Field interviewing** as a qualitative research method is a semidirected form of discourse or conversation with the goal of uncovering the participant's point of view. Thus, field interviewing goes beyond simply asking questions to obtain factual information that is common in other types of interview situations.

Field interviewing requires that the interviewer develops intimacy with the interviewee by using interpersonal interaction to create a social atmosphere similar to that one would find in talking with friends (Johnson & Rowlands, 2012).

Field interviews can be challenging because they are minimally structured and conducted in an unstructured environment (Mason, 1993). The interviewer and questions asked act as a catalyst for interviewees so they can communicate information and opinions, and clarify their responses (Wang & Yan, 2012). The interviewer has a general idea of what topics to cover but, at the same time, he or she must draw on terminology, issues, and themes introduced into the conversation by the respondent. Thus, to get the data needed to answer his or her research question, the researcher must have both theoretical and contextual knowledge as well as possess and be comfortable with a variety of communication skills.

Sometimes referred to as the *long interview* (McCracken, 1988) or the *depth interview* (Berger, 1998), face-to-face interviewing is a powerful method for seeking deep information and understanding about the way people order and assess their world and their interactions in it (Fontana & Frey, 2005). In conducting an interview, the researcher is trying to meet at least one of the following objectives (Lindlof & Taylor, 2002, 2011):

1. Inquire about occurrences in the past.

2. Learn about events and interactions that cannot be directly observed.

3. Develop a relationship with the participant to infer communication properties and processes.

4. Gain an understanding of a communication event or process from the participant's perspective.

5. Uncover the distinctive language and communication style used by the participant in his or her natural communication environment.

6. Verify or validate data obtained from other sources.

To these ends, interviews can be formal or informal. Researchers often use both types because the different types of information produced by each complement the other. But in either type, effective interviews occur when interviewers see themselves in the role of students learning from interviewees (Johnson & Rowlands, 2012).

As an example of field interviewing, Petronio and Sargent (2011) recruited registered nurses as potential participants through snowball sampling in a large urban medical center. The interview study was designed to explore how nurses address issues of privacy management. During their duties caring for convalescents, patients may disclose private information. Interviews were conducted in the hospital "where the participants confirmed they felt comfortable revealing their stories," and at a time doing the interview "would not disturb patient care" (p. 257). Eleven nurses (9 female, 2 male; representing the proportion of males to females employed at the hospital) were interviewed with a semi-structured interview guide that focused on "eliciting retrospective narratives about disclosure predicaments in which nurses felt uneasy, puzzled, awkward, distressed, uncomfortable, or perplexed about the information revealed by patients and families" (p. 25). Interviews lasted from 30 to 90 minutes and they were transcribed, resulting in 145 pages.

To reach participants with a wide range of occupations, Hastings and Payne, (2013) used snowball and purposive sampling. To be included in the study, participants had to meet the inclusion criterion of having significant experience in using e-mail at the workplace. Fourteen females and seven males met the criterion and participated in interviews. To be able to uncover rules for e-mail use at work that are common across organizational boundaries, participants represented a variety of professions and organizations. The study was designed to answer two research questions: (1) "What are employees' perceptions of communication rules for expressing dissent through email?", and (2) "What role(s) do interviewees suggest email plays in organizational dissent? (p. 315). The researchers describe the interviews as moderately scheduled, as they were used to probe participants' reports about favorite and least favorite e-mails, as well as how dissent was accomplished through e-mail. One author served as the interviewer. Before answering the researcher's questions about the use of e-mail with respect to organizational dissent, participants read a definition of dissent from the research literature. Participants "were then asked to offer examples and stories that involved using e-mail for dissent at the workplace" (p. 316). The interviews took between 20 to 45 minutes, and were tape recorded and transcribed. The number of transcript pages devoted to participants' reports of using e-mail for organizational dissent totaled 73 single-spaced pages.

Most qualitative studies using the interview method are conducted so that the interviewer and participants are face-to-face. However, Bute and Jensen (2011) chose to use telephone interviews to speak with low-income women. These women had income levels at 200% of the poverty level or below, and participated in statewide university-wide extension programs. Staff members, who also participated in the programs, asked women if they were interested in participating in a study about sexual health and education. Why did the research team use telephone rather than face-to-face interviews? The research team wanted to accommodate the complicated circumstances many participants faced. Some women lived in temporary housing or with a relative; some women had limited transportation or childcare. But all of the women had telephone access. While being more convenient for participants, the researchers do admit that:

> Although this meant that a number of the interviews were conducted while women were also watching their children or otherwise multitasking, the majority of women in this sample would not have been able to participate in this study without the flexibility that a telephone interview afforded them. (p. 217)

Online Interviewing

Although most researchers prefer to conduct interviews in face-to-face settings, there is a trend for collecting interview data through mediated channels, such as e-mail, chat rooms, and VOIP (voice over Internet protocols) and other text, audio, and video online formats (James & Busher, 2012). Three advantages are obvious: One advantage is the low cost of communicating with participants, or setting up a project-dedicated website with a list of open-ended questions on a web form to which participants reply and click to send. Another advantage is that electronic interviewing is a way to collect data from participants who are geographically dispersed or unable to meet with researchers. The third advantage is that conducting interviews online conceals some aspects of the interviewee, perhaps making it more likely that people who are reticent or cautious might participate or be more willing to discuss sensitive topics.

Technology allows interviews to be conducted synchronously and asynchronously. The former more closely aligns with face-to-face interviewing. Still there can be transmission delays and errors. In asynchronous online interviewing, interviewers can motivate their respondents to reply by creating a friendly atmosphere and by being prompt in replying. Finally, and regardless if the interview is synchronous or asynchronous, be careful of contacting people to participate in research through the e-mail address connected to their work or professional life, as many of these systems archive all e-mail sent and received. Unless you are given permission by potential participants, it is better to use their personal e-mail addresses for research to avoid the risks of threatening their privacy and anonymity.

A number of disadvantages also exist. Electronic forms of interviewing make it particularly difficult to develop rapport and relationships with participants. Moreover, participant commitment may be difficult to develop or sustain. Markham (1998) describes another disadvantage: Online interviewing can result in fictional social realities. Without the face-to-face interaction and the corresponding nonverbal cues, the opportunity is missed to check out participant sincerity or confusion. Markham's experience with online interviewing suggests that this form can take longer than face-to-face interviews and result in cryptic responses and less depth.

Of course, online interviewing may be the only way to reach some populations. Researchers who conduct interviews online must recognize that the online space changes the context of interviewing, as well as altering how knowledge

DESIGN CHECK

Where Did the Interviews Occur?

When you read research reports in which interviewing is the primary data collection method, identify where the interviews occurred. Picture yourself in your professional or career role and being asked to participate in a research study about a work topic. Where would be the most likely place for that interview to occur? Would that location give you and the interviewer the privacy you needed? If not, what other locations would be appropriate? If the only office with a closed door is your boss's office, would you feel comfortable being interviewed there? What other locations would hinder truthful responses to the interviewer's questions? As a consumer of research literature, you can make your own assessments of data credibility by putting yourself in the participant's role.

is constructed through an interview (James & Busher, 2012). Just as a researcher would practice face-to-face interviewing, he or she would also practice conducting an interview using technology.

The Interview Process

Research investigations that rely on interviewing are composed of seven steps (Kvale, 1996; Seidman, 2013). First, the researcher must conceptualize the study and design the research questions. Second, the researcher must design the interviews so that the research questions can be addressed. Next, the researcher conducts the interviews. In the fourth step, the interviews, if they were recorded, need to be transcribed. Fifth, the researcher analyzes the data produced by the interviews. Verification is the sixth step; and seventh, the description and analyses of the interviews are reported. Thus, interviewing, as a research methodology, is systematic and planned.

Conceptualizing the Interview Study As with most qualitative methods, standards exist for conducting research interviews. However, many points in the interview investigation require thoughtful selection of alternatives by the researcher. Your objective as a researcher should be to make choices from the methodological options available based on knowledge of the topic (Kvale, 1996). When selecting interviewing as a method, a researcher must

ask him- or herself if the structure of an interview can be adapted to the communication phenomenon or process of interest (Seidman, 2013). These choices should be made while not losing sight of the whole—the entirety of the interview as a research process. Because interviewing as a research technique is so flexible, the researcher should be able to prepare in advance and argue for the choices made.

In this first stage, the why and what of the research study must be clarified before methodological choices can be made. As with any other research project, the qualitative project begins by examining the published literature.

With this foundation, you should be ready to clarify the purpose of your study. For example, is your study exploratory, seeking to describe or understand a communication phenomenon for which little background research exists? If so, then your interviews will likely be more open and less structured, allowing you to seek new information and create new ways of looking at the topic. Alternatively, if your study builds on a substantial foundation of knowledge, your interviews are likely to be more structured. This structure allows you to compare interview responses from different participants to make comparisons to previously published results. In either case, you cannot design an interview without specifying the research questions that guide your study.

Designing the Interview With the purpose clarified and research questions developed, you are ready to make specific methodological choices. At a minimum, you will need to decide how to find and select your interview participants and then determine how many participants you will need. Often, the focus and context of a qualitative study is so narrowly or specifically defined that not just any participant will do. Generally, researchers are looking for participants with knowledge of a specialized communication environment or for those representing a certain demographic group. Recall the examples of snowball sampling earlier in this chapter. This sampling procedure is frequently used to identify participants for interview studies, as are purposive sampling and maximum variation sampling. Seidman (2013) offers additional advice about selecting participants for research studies designed for the interview method. He encourages researchers to avoid individuals who are too enthusiastic and persuasive about why they should be interviewed. Likewise he recommends that researchers should encourage those initially reluctant to participate. He argues that those potential participants who appear too eager may have a particular bias and want to be sure that you get their side of things. People who are initially reluctant may be a key person from whom the interviewer would learn a great deal.

For some research projects, the number of respondents might be limited by the number of people you can identify who have knowledge about your topic, interact in a particular role you are studying, or represent the characteristics related to your research question or objective. As with other qualitative research projects, two key criteria can guide your decision to stopping or continuing with data collection. Sufficiency, or the range of participants (or sites), included in your data is the first criteria. Saturation (or redundancy) of data collected is the second criterion. When finding enough respondents is not a problem, researchers sometimes stop interviewing when the interviews are producing essentially the same data or when they are able to answer their research questions. If the data you collect are redundant, you have two choices: You may decide that your interviewing is complete, or you may want to revise your interview schedule, taking into consideration what you have learned from participants thus far. In either case,

the researcher must be able to describe how he or she reached the decision not to seek other interviews. If information collected is redundant, you should be able to write a short description of that redundancy. Simply indicating that "I'm not getting new information" is not enough.

Conducting the Interview

In an interview, the researcher needs to quickly establish a context for the questioning. Often it helps to frame the interview for the participant. The researcher should start with small talk appropriate for the setting, briefly explain the purpose of the interview, ask about recording the interview, and ask if the participant has any questions before beginning (Johnson & Rowlands, 2012; Kvale, 1996).

It is also important to select locations and times that are comfortable and accessible for respondents. Making participants comfortable might require other steps as well. For example, the interview teams in Braithwaite and Eckstein's (2003) study of individuals with disabilities consisted of one interviewer and an informant with a disability. In Butler and Modaff's (2008) study of in-home day care providers, interviews were conducted either in person or by telephone. Some of the interviews were conducted in participants' homes; some interviews were conducted during the evening when the day care providers did not have children other than their own present. When interviews were conducted during the day, participants requested that the interviews be conducted while the children napped or were having quiet time. Because interviews are neither neutral nor anonymous (for the researcher at least), creating comfortable settings allows the interview to develop as a conversation. This encourages the researcher–participant dyad to move beyond polite conversation between two strangers.

Of course, interviews do not have to be located in a fixed place. Brown and Durrheim (2009) describe mobile interviewing in which the researcher and participant drive together or walk alongside each other. As the researcher and participant move through space and time, the conversation inevitably becomes situated, or contingent, on what they see, hear, and feel as they walk or drive. Generally, interview experts recommend that the researcher "avoid getting involved in a 'real' conversation in which he or she answers questions asked by the respondent or provides personal opinions on the matters discussed" (Fontana & Frey, 2005, p. 713). However, with mobile interviewing, that would be difficult to avoid. Indeed, an authentic conversation between the interviewer and interview may be the type of data necessary to answer the research question.

Interviews generally last between 30 minutes and 1 hour, although some can be considerably longer. For example, in Butler and Modaff's (2008) study, they reported their interviews as lasting from 30 minutes to 3½ hours. Unless there is an important reason for not doing so, researchers often find that interviewing is best done in pairs. In the team approach, one team member serves as the interviewer, while the other team member is responsible for recording or note taking. After the interview is complete and the research team has left the interview site, the team of researchers can discuss and compare their observations and interpretations.

Asking Questions Conducting an interview is more complex than simply asking questions. Rather, the interviewer must carefully construct questions to obtain the needed information or to prompt discussion of the topic of interest. This means that the researcher has thoroughly reviewed the literature for help in defining, narrowing, or extending the area of questioning. It will be difficult to construct a meaningful list of questions, or an **interview guide,** without this preparation. The interview guide may not be followed in exactly the same way in each interview, but it does remind the researcher of which topics to cover.

The interview guide is an important aspect of the research design for field interviewing. The schedule indicates what topics will be talked about and when. It also dictates when and how shifts from one topic to another will occur (Wang & Yan, 2012). Some schedules of questions will be more precise or have little flexibility; some schedules will be more flexible allowing, for example, the interviewee to signal shifts in topic. Good interviewers listen carefully to the interviewee's response, as the information contained in their answer gives guidance to the interviewer about asking a follow-up question on the same topic or moving on to the next topic.

The interview guide for Green-Hamann, Eichhorn, and Sherblom's (2011) investigation of individuals who belong to social support groups on Second Life (for example, One Cancer Caregivers, Alcoholics Anonymous) on why people belong to these types of virtual support groups (p. 473). Notice how it guides participants through a series of linked stages (Rubin & Rubin, 2005).

1. I know you attend the Second Life support group:

    1.a Do you also go to face-to-face meetings outside Second Life?

    1.b How does your participation in the Second Life support group differ from your face-to-face support group participation?

2. Have you participated in any online discussion boards in addition to the support group in Second Life?

    If yes: How does participation in Second Life support group differ from a typical online discussion board?

3. What motivated you to participate in the Second Life support group?

4. On a scale from 1–7, where 7 is very satisfied, how satisfied are you with your experience in this support group in Second Life?

5. What influences your satisfaction?

6. In what ways do you believe the Second Life support group is helpful to you?

7. What do you like least about participating in this support group in Second Life?

8. What is your relationship with the group members in the Second Life support group?

9. Have you developed any personal friendships with group members? In what capacity?

10. What surprised you the most as a participant in the Second Life support group?

Notice how the interview schedule starts with simple and broad questions to get the process started. Interviewee's responses to these questions provide the interviewer with background information that will help the interviewer interpret other responses. In the next phase of the interview, the questions become more specific, but always open-ended. Looking at the interview schedule, notice how each question asks for descriptive or evaluative information from the respondent, and how questions build on one another. Designing interviews in this way, helps to build rapport with respondents and assists respondents in self-disclosing.

Regardless of the interview topic, you may want to ask some biographical questions to help you understand the contextual nature of the interaction you are studying. These demographic questions should be pertinent to the research question for the interview study. Some researchers ask participants about their age, sex, race/ethnicity, occupation, highest level of education, and state of residence. This is appropriate if responses to these questions will inform the data analysis. But some participants find general demographic questions, like these, as unrelated to the topic of the interview and invasive.

As you construct the interview guide, different questions serve different purposes. The main questions should be developed in such a way to obtain the information you know you need (Rubin & Rubin, 2005). That is, the main questions ask information directly related to the study's research question or objective. Probing or follow-up questions are meant to explore something the participant said in further detail (Rubin & Rubin, 2005). Probing questions might take the form of urging a participant to continue ("What do you mean by that?"), elaborate ("Can you tell me more about that?"), clarify ("You said 'they' want to be sure they're first. Who is 'they'?"), or steer the participants back to the topic ("Can you go back to talking about your team?").

Main and probing questions should be developed in such a way as to allow the respondent to tell his or her own story (McCracken, 1988). Your questions should encourage respondents to provide their point of view without biasing their response. Open questions are better than closed questions for initiating dialogue and obtaining fuller descriptions and answers. An open question

does not suggest or imply any particular answer. Alternatively, a closed question suggests a certain type of answer based on how the question is constructed. Take a look at some examples:

Open Questions	*Closed Questions*
How would you describe your conflict management style?	Do you always succeed in getting your point across during a conflict?
Why do you believe you are a competent communicator?	Are you a competent communicator?
Why do you watch police dramas on television?	Do you watch police dramas on television because of the suspense in the plot?

Open questions specify the topic or issue you want the respondent to cover. Yet they do not overly restrict how the respondent addresses the issue. Alternatively, notice how closed questions suggest one or two alternative answers to the respondent. In each case, the question implies that a "yes" or "no" response is appropriate.

Open questions can help a researcher probe for more detail. Here are ways in which open questions invite respondents to talk about their experiences (Janesick, 2004):

Type of Open Question	*Examples*
Descriptive question	How would you describe your relationship with your father after you went away to college? Tell me how your relationship with your father changed after you went away to college.
Follow-up question	You mentioned that "winning your way" is important to you. How would you describe "winning your way"?
Experience/example question	You indicated that you believe you were a competent communicator. What examples of your communication style exemplify this?

Type of Open Question	Examples
Clarification question	You used the term "democratic leader." How would you define that term?
	You used the term "democratic leader." How would you describe someone who has those characteristics?
	You used the term "democratic leader." What do you mean by that?
Structural/paradigmatic question	You indicated that you had difficulty talking with your sister. What would you describe as the cause of this problem?
Comparison/contrast question	You described several different decisions made by your council. How would you describe the differences in the decisions?

Regardless of which type of question you are using, be careful not to introduce new language or terminology into the interview. Rather, be sensitive to the terminology used by the respondent. If you are unsure of what is meant, ask probing questions to gain clarity and definition.

Interviewing Technique   Using interviews to collect data, the researcher obviously asks questions. This puts the interviewer in the role of listener. Being a good listener will encourage participants to talk. In listening to participants, pay attention by looking at the participant and displaying pleasant and inviting nonverbal cues.

As Seidman (2013) explains, "the hardest work for many interviewers is to keep quiet and to listen actively" (p. 81). Additionally, the interviewer must listen on three levels. First, the interviewer must listen to what the participant is saying by concentrating on the substance of the response. Second, the interviewer must listen to discern when the participant is talking about him- or herself, or representing him- or herself by talking about others in a general way. If it is

unclear who the referent of the participant's response is, ask in a gentle way. A good technique here is, "Can you give me an example of that?" Third, the interviewer must listen to the process of interaction with the interviewee. How is the conversation going? Are the questions being answered? Are my follow-up questions appropriate? Effective? What am I learning now? What else should I learn? How much time is left? Do I need to move this participant onto the next issue? Is the participant tired of talking to me? What can I do to help the participant to express him- or herself?

Interviewer technique also includes asking questions when you do not understand. If the interviewee uses language with which you are unfamiliar, do not let this moment pass. Instead ask, "I heard you use the word *pirouette*. What do you mean by that?" You should also use a question to follow up on language that is vague. If an interviewee describes something as effective, you can ask "In what way is that effective? Can you give me an example?" Interviewer technique also includes asking questions to hear more of what a participant has to offer. Perhaps the participant believes that more detail is boring; but that detail could be important to your interpretation of the data. Anytime you do not understand or want to hear more, ask the participant. Generally, more detail is better than less for your research project. Details are important when interviewing about communication phenomenon and processes.

Sometimes a participant can seemingly talk forever, and in doing so comments on something you believe deserves to be followed up. What do you do? Jot down a key word or two in your notes while the person talks. Do not interrupt the interviewee. Rather, use these keywords to bring up the issue later. You can get back to topic with, "Earlier you talked about the difficulty in communicating with people who are older than you. Would you talk about that in more detail?" If you use this technique, be sure to use the same words or phrases that the participant used earlier. Do not introduce new terminology into the conversation.

There are two ways in which an interviewer can unknowingly influence what the interviewee says. First, be careful of sharing your experiences.

Occasionally sharing a short, similar experience may help encourage the interviewee to talk more. But too much sharing of your personal experiences can distract the participant and perhaps cause the interviewee to become impatient with you. Another way in which interviewers unknowingly influence the interviewee occurs when the interviewer reinforces what the participant is saying with "yes," "okay," or a strong positive nod of the head. It may seem polite to do so, but these verbal and nonverbal cues can influence how the participant responds. Finally, tolerate silence during the interview. If the questions are personal or difficult to answer, the participant may need a few moments to develop a thoughtful response.

As you can see, effective interviewer technique requires that the interviewer practice a delicate balance (Seidman, 2011). An effective interview should flow "from an interviewer's concentrated listening, engaged interest in what is being said, and purpose in moving forward" (p. 95). An interview is not like a conversation between friends (Packer, 2011). It is different in several ways. The interviewer is in a professional role and has a specific goal. It is scheduled and not spontaneous. The interview focus is often on something in the past for which the participant is asked for details and elaboration. So while a conversation is often more symmetrical, a research interview is asymmetrical. Thus, it can take some practice to do it well.

Concluding the Interview   At the conclusion of the interview, the researcher needs to debrief the participant (Kvale, 1996). A good way to conclude the interview and start the debriefing segment is to summarize the main points gleaned from the interaction. And because the participant has been polite in responding to the researcher's questions, the researcher should ask if the participant has any questions. If yes, the researcher answers. If not, the researcher thanks the participant, the interview is concluded, and the recording device is turned off.

Researchers also use the debriefing segment to explain the purpose of the study, what is known about the problem or topic and the questions asked or the objectives guiding the study, why the study is important, and what they hope to find. If information was withheld from participants before the interview, now is the time to share it. This is also an appropriate time to remind participants about the confidentiality and anonymity associated with the data.

After the interviewee leaves, it is both necessary and helpful to spend a few minutes reflecting on what the interviewee said. Capturing your immediate reactions to the interview, the participant, or the setting in fieldnotes can be helpful later in the analytical steps of the research project.

Transcribing the Interview   In most situations, recording the interview is recommended. Recording interviews allows the researcher to concentrate on the interview interaction instead of taking notes. Professional typists or transcriptionists can prepare transcripts. However, many researchers prepare their own transcripts because it provides an opportunity to become familiar with the data. Regardless of how it is produced, the written record should be a verbatim account of what was said by both the interviewer and the respondent.

The goal of transcription is to create a verbatim record of the interaction. Whether you do your own transcribing or have someone do it for you, the first rule is: Do not *tidy up* the transcripts (Poland, 1995). Transcripts are data and should not be edited. One of the unique contributions of communication scholars is that we capture and analyze data as people produce it, not as it is edited. Reflecting critically on qualitative data she collected, Tilley (2003) explores how the interpretive frame of the transcriber she hired influenced the shape and form of the transcription. In turn, the transcription ultimately influences the analysis of the data. Before you or someone else transcribes data, reviewing Tilley's experience can help you make better decisions about transcribing recordings of communication. Bird (2005) also explores her researcher role in transcribing interview data; she recommends learning how to transcribe before working on data.

After an audio or video recording is transcribed, you should listen to the tape and verify the transcription. This may take two or three passes through the data. However, even an accurate transcription will miss important nonverbal cues from an audio or video recording. Whenever possible, take the extra steps to ensure that written transcripts include the following conversational elements: pauses, laughing, coughing, interruptions, overlapping speech, garbled speech, emphasis, held sounds, and paraphrasing or quoting others.

One thing to remember in transcribing interviews is that the process of transcribing strips away all nonverbal cues, such as facial expressions and tone of voice, as well as any contextual cues present in the space in which the interview occurred. Moreover, physical descriptions of the participants are not captured in the transcription (Ellingson, 2012). One way to overcome this loss of data is to make notes about the physical space, as well as physical characteristics of participants, including their locations relative to one another. Making a seating map can also help. Ellingson (2012) reminds us that "moving from oral to written speech involves not accurate dictation but translation . . . writing down oral speech renders it a different entity altogether" (p. 530). The best practice, if possible, is to listen to the audio of the interview as you read through the transcript. You can make notes on the transcript about tone of voice and other emotional expressions, as well as anything unusual that occurs. This will help your interpretation and analysis of the written transcript.

Strengths and Limitations of Interview Research

One obvious advantage of interview research is that the research participant is in front of you for an extended period of time. During your conversations, you can probe more deeply, follow up on a response, or pursue a topic that you did not expect to address. A second advantage is that interviews often provide the only opportunity to collect data on communication that cannot be directly observed.

Because of the strengths noted, interviews often produce an enormous amount of material

to be reviewed and analyzed. For example, Giannini's (2011) interviews resulted in 13 hours and 27 minutes of recorded data. The transcriptions of these interviews resulted in 206 double-spaced pages of text-based data. As another example, Smith (2013) interviewed 32 employees; interviews ranged from 30 minutes to 2 hours for a total of 31 hours of interview time. Moving to text, the interviews were transcribed verbatim resulting in 579 single-space pages. You can see the importance for having a method for managing and analyzing the data after it is collected.

As with any conversation, the interviewing method can replicate many problems found in other dyadic interactions. It is easy to stray off course, particularly if the respondent is talking. If your respondent strays, you must carefully and politely refocus the conversation (Mason, 1993). However, be careful of cutting off your respondents too quickly. They might be telling you about other events as background to help you understand the point they are trying to make.

Alternatively, a respondent consents to be interviewed but is hesitant to talk. Two techniques can help. First, be able to ask each question in multiple ways. Although you may prefer one wording of the question, it may not make sense to the respondent. Second, if the respondent has difficulty responding to direct questions, use broadly based questions (for example, "Tell me about your day yesterday") to get the respondent talking, and then use follow-up questions to guide the respondent toward the areas of your research study.

FOCUS GROUPS

Another qualitative method that depends on developing conversations with others is the focus group. A **focus group** is a facilitator-led group discussion used for collecting data from a group of participants about a particular topic in a limited amount of time. But it is also more than that. Focus groups allow researchers to study deliberation, dialogue, and democratic practice—issues central to the study of communication. Moreover, focus groups are intended to stimulate

Research or Selling?

Many consumers are familiar with focus groups because they are a popular technique for companies to learn how to better market their products and services. Even political candidates use focus groups to test how campaign messages and slogans will be received. Because of the widespread popularity of focus groups as a marketing or public relations tool, individuals selected to participate may be hesitant to agree even if the focus group is for a research project because they question the ethics (and motivation) of the person who invites them to participate.

To counter this hesitancy, researchers must develop carefully planned invitations to participate. Think of yourself as an individual receiving a phone call or e-mail and being asked to participate in a focus group for a research project. What information would you want to know before you agree to participate? What clues would you use to distinguish between an invitation to participate in a marketing focus group and an invitation to participate in a research focus group? Are there any persuasive strategies that could convince you to participate in a focus group research project? What could the researcher offer as an incentive to encourage your participation?

conversation among participants, conversations much like the ones people have in team or family discussions and negotiations. Focus groups are different from interviews because they give researchers the opportunity to explore what is happening in the participants' conversation as well as what participants say about the topic or issue (Kamberelis & Dimitriadis, 2005). Of special interest to communication scholars, a focus group as a research method provides the researcher the opportunity to hear first-hand what language and terms people use for speaking about communication phenomena and processes.

Although many variations exist, a focus group is typically a facilitator-led group discussion of 5 to 10 people (Krueger & Casey, 2000). The group meets for 60 to 90 minutes to give participants the opportunity to respond to the facilitator's questions. The facilitator (who may or may not be the researcher) coordinates the focus group interaction by using a discussion guideline. Like the interview guide described earlier, the **focus group schedule**, or discussion guideline, is a series of questions to help the facilitator prompt participant interaction. It provides a semistructured interaction experience but is flexible enough to allow the facilitator to take advantage of unexpected twists and turns in the group's conversation.

Respondents are encouraged to interact with one another, not just respond to the facilitator's questions. In fact, one of the advantages of using the focus group methodology is the opportunity it provides to listen to participants talk about the topic among themselves without direction or input from the facilitator. A focus group is not a decision-making group because there should be no pressure for the participants to reach any type of consensus.

As an example, Quick, Fiese, Anderson, Koester, and Marlin (2011) conducted six focus groups to explore the health benefits of shared family mealtimes. Twenty-four parents who had at least one child under the age of 5 years were the participants. Participants represented a range of socio-economic characteristics. To encourage sharing and discussing, participants were scheduled to participate in groups with similar others. One focus group was conducted in Spanish, assisted by a translator. Participants in the focus groups were asked the same nine questions (see Table 16.1). The focus group method made it possible both to hear participants' descriptions of their family mealtimes and their perceived benefits and barriers to doing so. To assist prevention of AIDS in Kenya, Muturi and Mwangi (2011) conducted a focus group study; 56 people participated in

TABLE 16.1 Focus Group Question Schedule for Shared Family Mealtime Study

1. What are the challenges that your family experiences when trying to eat meals together as a family?

2. Can you describe a typical mealtime in your house? (Think about the following: who eats together; where do family members eat—table, counter, living room, etc.; does everyone eat the same thing or do people choose own food; do people do other things while eating, like talking, watching TV, reading, texting, other?)

3. If you were to paint a picture of the ideal mealtime, what would it look like?

4. Do you remember having meals together as a family when you were growing up as a child? Can you describe a typical mealtime?

5. What do you think might be benefits of eating meals together as a family?

6. What are some reasons for not eating meals together as a family? What would make it easier for your family to eat meals together as a family?

7. If you could make shared family mealtimes better, how would you do it?

8. What strategies does your family use to make sure you eat meals together as a family? Which strategies are most effective? Which strategies are ineffective? (Have you ever tried to make sure you eat meals together as a family? If so, how did you do that? What worked for you and what didn't work for you?)

9. If you were to create a message to parents encouraging them to eat meals together as a family, what would it say? How would you say it (print, radio, television)? Who would say it (spokesperson)? How would it look? What would attract a parent's attention?

six focus-group discussions that lasted about 2 hours each. Participants lived in a rural region of Kenya that had a high incidence of AIDS infection. Both men and women, ages 55 to 75, participated in same-sex groups. The goal of the focus group design was to seek the perspectives of older adults on HIV/AIDS prevention and their recommendations on appropriate strategies for their communities. Focus groups were used to mirror the community-based culture of this nation. After collecting and analyzing the data, one recommendation of the researchers was to increase interpersonal communication about AIDS prevention through existing community and cultural structures, such as churches, schools, families, clans, and age groups.

The unique advantage of using focus groups to collect data is that it allows participants to offer their viewpoints relative to the viewpoints of others. For example, Dougherty (2001) investigated the different ways men and women used sexually laden interaction in a stressful hospital setting. Specifically, the researcher was interested in discovering how male and female employees differed in their labeling of interaction as sexual harassment. Look at the excerpt that follows. Dougherty used this segment of interaction from the focus group to demonstrate how men perceived sexual behavior as functional rather than as sexual harassment.

Jack (the moderator): Let me ask you this. What is your definition of sexual harassment?

Male B: I think it's more of a, something personal to person. You know?

Male C: Yeah.

Male B: You do something to that person. Um, I tell a dirty joke out loud, I don't think that's sexual harassment. I don't think a funny joke posted on a board is sexual harassment. If I do something either physical or directly toward, directed toward you. If I make a comment about you, or I tell a joke maybe strictly toward you, or I physically touch you in a [sexual] way, yeah, that is. But I think something. I think like [Male C] said, that stress reliever. That's how our department runs. I mean boy.

Jack: Talk about that stress reliever.

Male B: Oh, telling dirty jokes.

Male C: Yeah.

Male A: Something to lighten up the mood.
(p. 381)

Notice how participants in the group develop an explanation for how sexually laden interaction is not sexual harassment in their work setting. In a focus group, participants have the opportunity to refer to other participants' comments, and confirm or challenge what someone else says. Most important, participants are stimulated by the ideas of others, often resulting in a chaining or cascading of information, as the preceding example demonstrates.

Thus, this focus group interaction and others like it succeed in exploiting the group effect (Carey, 1994). Whereas a single participant may be reluctant to talk about sensitive topics in an one-on-one interview, the group dynamics of many participants in a focus group make it more likely that participants will open up and explain their disagreement when ideas they disagree with are presented by others in the group (Liamputtong, 2011). In other words, the group setting provides an opportunity for participants to create insights about a topic that otherwise would not be easily discovered or easily accessible.

Planning Focus Group Research

It may seem relatively easy to invite a group of people to meet together and discuss a topic. Yet, to conduct focus group research, a more systematic process is required. The researcher must identify selection criteria for the type of participant desired and then figure out how to locate individuals meeting those criteria

for three to five focus groups. The researcher must develop a discussion guide and then train or practice for this specialized form of group interaction.

The Focus Group Schedule   Although some focus group facilitators prefer to strictly follow a **focus group schedule** or topic guide, other facilitators use the outline for themselves to identify which topics have or have not been covered. Depending on the context and participants, some focus group discussions can evolve very quickly into dynamic discussions. Thus, the facilitator may need only to start the discussion with a series of opening questions and then let the discussion among participants develop from there. During the group's discussion, however, the facilitator should be checking to determine if all of the desired topics have been covered. If not, introducing questions may be necessary.

As with any research design, a search of the published research literature will provide you with ideas for developing questions or topics for your outline. In particular, look for research suggestions at the end of the discussion section after the results have been interpreted. Some research reports identify a special section of the report for future research considerations. These can be valuable sources for focus group questions and topics.

Generally, the discussion outline is planned as a funnel to take advantage of the types of responses both structured and less-structured discussions provide (Morgan, 1997). With this strategy, opening questions are broad to encourage free discussion among participants. A good opening question to start discussion follows the form of "One of the things we are especially interested in is _____ . What can each of you tell us about that?" All participants should be able to respond to this question because they were invited to participate based on their expertise, knowledge, or experience with the issue. A good starter has two other criteria. It should motivate participants to listen to what others have to say, and it should create opportunities for participants to express a wide range of views (Morgan, 2012). Although it is critical that each participant have the opportunity to talk, this type of broad opening question also allows you to identify what other topics or issues participants associate with the issue of the focus group.

As participants become comfortable hearing themselves talk and at ease when discussing the issues, the moderator can move to a more structured phase of the discussion and ask specific questions. This strategy allows the researcher to capture participants' more spontaneous ideas and comments early in the discussion as well as participants' responses to more specific questions. Table 16.1 displays the focus group schedule of the Quick, et al. (2011) study of the health benefits of shared family mealtimes.

Selecting Participants Like research designs that use interviews to collect data, focus group participants are usually solicited through snowball, network, or purposive sampling.

In addition to finding appropriate participants, researchers must also be concerned with how participants are grouped together. Generally, it is best to select individuals who possess similar characteristics and meet your selection criteria but who are also strangers. Ideally, the selection goal is to create a group of participants with homogeneous backgrounds but dissimilar attitudes and perspectives. The homogeneity among participants ensures some degree of shared experience and encourages free-flowing conversation (Liamputtong, 2009; Morgan, 1997). Alternatively, when the focus group topic is sensitive or controversial, it is best to invite respondents who are familiar with one another and who hold similar attitudes. Although this level of familiarity may be beneficial in such cases, the moderator must be aware that participants familiar with one another may avoid talking frankly about the most intimate, personal, or controversial topics (Morgan, 1997).

Whether you use participants who are strangers or who are familiar with one another, potential participants should be screened before the focus group meets. Using a few well-selected questions during an e-mail or a phone call provides assurance that participants meet your inclusion criteria.

After the researcher has found appropriate participants, they must be motivated to actually attend the focus group discussion. You are more likely to secure their agreement if you provide participants with a few details. They should be informed of the location, time, date, duration, and general topic of the focus group. Because many marketing firms conduct focus groups, be sure to indicate that your focus group is part of a research project and not associated with the marketing or selling of any product. A follow-up e-mail or phone call a day or two before the focus group event will help maintain participants' interest and motivate their attendance.

Most focus groups range in size from 5 to 10 participants. With fewer than 5 participants, the facilitator may have difficulty sustaining a conversation. With more than 10 participants, it may be difficult for the facilitator to control the discussion or for every participant to have the opportunity to talk. As a practical matter, the researcher should over-recruit by 20% for each group, because it is likely that some participants will not follow through on their commitment to participate (Morgan, 1997).

Most researchers follow the general rule of scheduling three to five focus groups for a research study (Morgan, 1997). Research and experience have demonstrated that conducting more groups does not usually result in additional meaningful insights. But conducting fewer than three groups increases the likelihood that the researcher will miss an important aspect of discussion. However, the greater the diversity within each focus group, the more likely it is that a greater number of focus groups will be needed (Liamputtong, 2011). Practically, researchers should plan to conduct three to five focus groups, with the possibility of holding more if the last scheduled focus group is still producing new and helpful data.

Conducting Focus Group Research

The group discussion to which you have invited participants is not a freewheeling conversation, nor is it rigidly controlled or structured. The researcher makes decisions about how much structure the discussion will require and how conversation among participants will be encouraged. More structured focus group discussions use a standardized set of questions for every group. Less structured discussions may be stimulated by just a few questions and rely more heavily on group dynamics that develop among participants. You may choose one strategy over another or combine the two.

Most focus group discussions require 90 minutes. In that length of time, the moderator can facilitate introductions of the participants, serve refreshments, conduct the discussion according to the outline, and summarize what he or she heard to receive feedback from the participants. In recruiting participants, it is wise to identify their expected time commitment as 2 hours. This provides the moderator with a cushion of time and some flexibility. A good moderator will never run over the time commitment expected by participants.

In addition to the moderator, each focus group needs a note taker and an assistant. The moderator role is demanding. Having a note taker releases the moderator from this task. The note taker sits outside the circle of participants to take notes as unobtrusively as possible. Although introduced to participants at the beginning of the focus group, there is no further interaction with the note taker. Focus groups are also likely to run more smoothly with the help of an assistant. The person in this role can take on a variety of tasks. The assistant can help escort participants to the focus group room, assist with refreshments, and manage latecomers. He or she can also help with note taking if recording equipment fails.

Guiding and Maintaining the Conversation Choosing an appropriate and effective moderator, or facilitator, for a particular focus group situation is critical. The researcher does not need to be the moderator and should not be if he or she knows some of the participants and not others. Ideally, the focus group moderator is someone with whom participants can identify. It is also important to select a moderator the participants will perceive as credible. In most cases, this means that the moderator should share important characteristics with participants. For example, to study sexual harassment, Dougherty (2001) used a male facilitator to conduct a focus group with men while she conducted a focus group with women. Both facilitators conducted

the focus group when participants of both sexes were included.

At the very beginning of the focus group, the moderator should introduce him or herself, and the topic and goal of the group discussion. Next the moderator should address issues of confidentiality and anonymity, and emphasize that what other participants say in the focus group should not leave the room. Permission to record the conversation should be requested at this stage, as well as participants' right to turn off the recorder if requested. Finally, the moderator should explain that there are no right or wrong answers, and that participants are likely to disagree with one another as the discussion develops. At this point, the focus group discussion is ready to begin. The moderator should ask participants to introduce themselves by asking each person to say their first name and to answer a question about the research topic. Do not discount this portion of the focus group, as it is the first time participants will hear each other speak.

Thus, it is important for the moderator to have the communication skills to gently guide a group during its discussion (Herndon, 1993). The moderator must communicate in a style that encourages participants to talk and must also be able to identify when probing questions are required to gain clarity and depth. The moderator is not an interviewer. Thus, he or she needs skill to avoid the spoke-and-wheel pattern of communication, in which participants talk only to the moderator. The moderator sometimes must remain silent to encourage participants to respond to one another.

What are the characteristics of an effective focus group moderator (Liamputtong, 2011)? Obviously, the moderator must ensure that all participants are included in the discussion. He or she must also be able to identify disagreement or conflict and help to temper it. To facilitate the conversation among focus group participants, the moderator should be sensitive to the needs of participants so that those who want to speak can. The moderator should also be open-minded and non-judgmental. Because focus groups are intended to raise a variety of ideas and issues, it is important that the moderator not leak positive or negative nonverbal cues as people present their ideas and opinions. Essentially, an effective moderator is respectful of people and ideas and demonstrates these qualities by being a good listener, and having good leadership skills, good observation skills, and patience and flexibility.

One interactive technique designed to encourage interaction among participants is for the moderator to ask one participant about his or her reaction to something said by another participant. This style of moderating which asks focus group participants to share and compare (Morgan, 2012) is especially helpful when participants have, a wide range of responses. The moderator might ask someone who has not shared recently in the conversation, "We've heard about different responses to [the topic], Sam—In what ways are your experiences similar or different?"

Data from Focus Group Discussions

The data collected in this method are recorded or transcribed group interactions. In addition to the recording and transcribing of the focus group conversation, the moderator should also make his or her own fieldnotes immediately after each session. The moderator should identify what issues or topics were talked about most, what issues or topics appeared to be most salient for participants, what issues or topics participants appeared to avoid, even after direct questioning, and any contradictory information participants provided. These elements should be reviewed later in conjunction with analysis of the transcribed group interaction.

The same techniques used and standards applied to transcribing individual interviews are also used to transcribe focus group interviews. But most researchers who have transcribed focus group interaction describe it as more difficult, as the interaction is not back and forth between the interviewer and interviewee. Because the focus group method hinges on group dynamics, it is important to note in the transcript where nontextual conversational characteristics occur. See Table 16.2 for a list of these. Interruptions and overlapping speech are especially important in focus group transcribing as these can indicate that a participant did not have the opportunity to complete a thought.

TABLE 16.2 Transcribing Non-textual Communication Characteristics of Focus Groups

Pauses	Specify short pauses of 1 to 3 seconds during talking by a series of dots (. . .); for longer pauses use (pause)
Laughing, coughing	Use (coughs) or (laughs)
Interruptions	Use a hyphen (-) at the point someone's talk is broken off
Overlapping speech	For the initial speaker, use a hyphen (-) at the point his or her talking is truncated by another speaker; for the second speaker place (overlapping) before his or her speech
Garbled speech	Use (inaudible) when you cannot understand what the speaker is saying
Emphasis	Strongly emphasized words can be emphasized with capital letters or underlining; WHAT or <u>what</u>
Held sounds	Repeat the sound which is held by repeating the letter held; "that is no-o-o-o-o-t true"
Paraphrasing or imitating others	If a participants talks in a different voice to indicate he or she is talking as another person, use (mimicking voice) and place what is said in this voice in quotes

Adapted from Pranee Liamputtong, *Focus Group Methodology: Principles and Practice*

TRY THIS!

Motivating Attendance at Focus Groups

Below are focus group topics for both proprietary and academic research. For each of the focus group topics that follow, what ideas do you have for finding focus group participants?

Focus Group Topic	*What Type of Participants Would You Seek?*	*How/Where Would You Seek Them?*
Investigation commissioned by the humane shelter in your community for developing persuasive messages to spay and neuter dogs and cats.		
Proprietary research for the local committee of the Republican Party who want to develop a campaign to increase voter turnout at local elections.		
Scholarly investigation to discover why parents allow their children to watch programming of which they disapprove.		
Scholarly investigation for developing more effective methods of doctor–patient interaction.		

Compare your ideas for finding focus group participants with those of others in your class. What would motivate individuals to participate in these focus groups?

As with individual interviews, focus groups can produce a large amount of data—data that are useless unless they are analyzed and summarized in some fashion. As with interviews, the analytical process should stem from the research literature and the research questions that prompted the study.

Focus Group Strengths and Limitations

Probably the greatest strength of focus group research is that it directly stimulates interaction among participants on the topic in which the researcher is interested. Although a facilitator directs the interaction, the group discussion format provides views and opinions in the participants' own words. Moreover, the discussion format allows consensus or conflict among participants to emerge, and these interactions could not occur if participants were interviewed separately (Morgan & Krueger, 1993). Thus, a focus group can produce concentrated amounts of information on a specific topic. The discussion format also allows the moderator to follow conversation paths that were not expected.

Focus groups are a good research method to select for the following situations (Janesick, 2004). If you are new to an area or topic of research or new to studying communication of a particular target group, a focus group can help you orient yourself to the area. Information from participants can help you identify issues that need to be addressed and identify areas that you need to learn more about before conducting additional research. Focus groups can also help you become familiar with the language and behavior of people with whom you have little familiarity.

Focus group methodology is extremely flexible. In some cases, researchers enter with a broad research question with the intent to discover the themes that emerge naturally from the interaction. From the emergent themes, research questions and hypotheses can be generated for future studies. For example, Ballard and Seibold (2004) conducted a focus group with employees in the organization in which they planned to conduct a subsequent research project. Their goal was to learn more about the nature of the work performed, the challenges and rewards employees encountered in conducting their work, and their experiences surrounding the specific topic of the subsequent research project. Using a focus group first, the research team was able to gain a better understanding of the environment in which employees worked and interacted.

Another strength of focus groups is their ability to generate information about the same topic from different types of people. For example, if you are interested in how children make media choices, you could conduct focus groups with a variety of people who can give you that information. Conducting focus groups separately with parents from two-parent households, parents from one-parent households, children, and baby-sitters would provide different perspectives on the same topic. Thus, focus groups are an excellent choice for gathering comparative data about complex behaviors.

The advantages of the focus group method occur through participants' interaction. Likewise, so do the disadvantages. Depending on the mix of focus group participants, a talkative or opinionated member of the group can dominate the discussion, inhibiting others' contributions. Another risk is that participants in the group will come to a quick consensus because some participants are hesitant to express opinions that are the opposite of the opinions held by other participants (Morgan, 1997). Both of these limitations artificially restrict individual input and generalizability of the data.

Because a focus group is stimulated by the moderator's questions, the interaction that results is not completely natural. Thus, there is always some concern that the moderator has overly influenced participants and their reactions (Morgan, 1997). Some researchers avoid this bias by asking someone else to assume the moderator role. When this is the case, the researcher maintains the research focus by generating the focus group outline for the moderator to use and by observing (if possible) all focus group interactions. There is a certain amount of skill needed to conduct a focus group. Researchers need to honestly assess this skill set before making a decision about who will moderate the groups.

Another risk of focus groups is that it is easy for researchers to overgeneralize focus group findings. After having listened to participants' interaction and having facilitated several focus groups, researchers find that the issues participants talk about seem real and valid. Researchers must balance their findings, however, with respect to how focus group participants were found, selected, and even encouraged to participate. How widely was the net cast for participants? Thus, researchers must carefully assess the degree to which their focus group results can be applicable to others from the same or similar populations.

COLLECTING NARRATIVES

Many communication scholars look to the **narratives**, or stories, people tell as a way of knowing, understanding, and explaining their lives. Stories are a natural part of interaction in many contexts because people create and tell stories to organize and interpret their experiences. As a result, narratives can be a reliable guide to the storyteller's beliefs, attitudes, values, and actions. **Narratives** are characterized by a focus on events; that is, the story is about something specific. That specificity, of course, is directed by the research question. Second, narratives reveal the speaker's point of view, which often is value laden. Third, narratives are told, more or less, in a chronological order. Fourth, narratives end with or reveal an explanation of meaning for the speaker (Gergen, 2009; Wells, 2011). Some narratives may be *big* in nature. In other words, the participant has distance from the event and has had an opportunity to reflect on what happened and his or her role in the event. Other narratives may be *small*. That is, these stories are centered on aspects of everyday life and very recent events (Chase, 2013).

Harter (2009) argues that narratives endow experience with meaning as the stories told become temporally organized with characters distinguished and links between disparate events identified. Most important, narratives communicate the narrator's, or teller's, point of view (Chase, 2005). As a result, narratives tell about events, as well as express emotions and interpretations. By telling or communicating the narrative, the narrator is explaining, entertaining, informing, defending, complaining, confirming, or challenging what happened and why.

By their very nature, stories are subjective because participants relate their conceptualization and understanding of events. Collecting and analyzing stories, or narratives, can provide a method for uncovering how seemingly isolated events are actually part of a larger interaction environment, identifying the explanations and justifications people give for their past actions, and determining how participants make sense of particular communication events.

Sources for Stories

Stories can be invited or captured in several ways (Brown & Kreps, 1993; Query & Kreps, 1993). First, stories can be collected from one-on-one interviews. For example, Fine (2009) asked women in senior leadership positions three open-ended prompts to solicit their stories without directing their responses. The questions in the individual interviews were: "(1) What events in your life led you to taking leadership positions? (2) Describe a situation in which you think you exercised leadership well. (3) Describe a situation in which you think you did not exercise leadership well" (pp. 187–188). Each transcript was analyzed for its narratives themes; then themes were compared across interviews.

Narratives can also be captured through online survey software. Kranstuber and Kellas (2011) asked this research question, "RQ1: What are the themes in adoption entrance narratives from the perspective of adopted individuals?" (p. 182). After responding to an online survey, the researchers elicited narratives from participants. This is the way the researcher translated their research question for participants:

> An adoption entrance narrative is an adoptive family's version of the birth story. Adoption entrance narratives teach adoptive children what adoption means, why they were placed for adoption, and why they were adopted into their family. (p. 186)

This prompt was followed by unlimited space in which participants could write. Participants were then given unlimited space to provide their response. The stories participants provided ranged from 19 to 835 words.

Second, stories can be collected through the critical incident technique (Flanagan, 1954). **Critical incidents** are those events in an individual's life that stand out as being memorable, positively or negatively. For example, participants are asked to focus on a specific relationship (such as their relationship with their first-grade teacher) or reflect on a specific event (such as their last birthday) or behavior (such as their last disagreement with their supervisor). By focusing the respondent's attention in this way, the story told is the individual's first-hand account of events, not a story he or she has heard from others. The researcher then uses probing open-ended questions to elicit detailed accounts, or stories, about a specific interaction context.

For example, Bryant and Sias (2011) asked participants "to provide an account of an incident in which they were deceived by a co-worker and

The Difference Between the Research Question and Asking Questions

The outcome of your preparation (reviewing the existing literature, getting familiar with the context) for a qualitative study is often a set of research questions. These are the questions that guide choosing a method and then later guide analysis and presentation of the research findings. But the research questions are not the questions asked of participants. Why? The question developed to guide data collection and analysis are phrased more formally and often include words or phrases that would not be understood by participants. Rubin and Rubin (2005) recommended rewording research questions (or objectives) into the vocabulary and concepts participants will recognize. The questions asked of participants should be answerable in terms of their experiences and knowledge. To ensure that an effective translation has occurred from research questions to interview questions, you should try out the interview questions on people like those you want to include in your study. Watch for their reaction to the question. Encourage them to give you feedback.

include any information they felt was relevant" (p. 120). Follow-up questions were also employed.

Less directly, stories can exist naturally in the course of everyday conversation. Coopman and Meidlinger (2000) examined how stories told in a Roman Catholic parish confirmed or challenged the organization's power structure. The first author unobtrusively collected stories, as she was an active member of the parish in which the research was conducted; she also had been employed by the parish. In the participant observer research role, she ate lunch with parish staff members over a period of 6 months. Immediately, or as soon as possible after lunch, Meidlinger created fieldnotes to capture the stories, responses to the stories, and general topics discussed.

Narratives can also be found in many print and online forms. For example, Jodlowski, Sharf, Nguyen, Haidet, and Woodard (2007) secured narratives from an online message board for individuals coping with opiate addiction. The research team describes their collection of narratives as posts and responses: Some were as short as a few sentences, whereas others were a page or longer. All posts generated at least a few responses, but some posts received more attention than others. After reading the posts, the research team identified those narratives that were representative of many of the other posts and responses.

As you can see, narratives can be invited or found, but differences exist in the presentation and preservation of the narrator's voice. When narratives are collected in person, the researcher can attend to who is telling the story and take those characteristics and experiences into consideration during analysis. When narratives are collected in ways removed from the narrator, the story, not the storyteller, becomes the focus.

Strengths and Limitations of Narrative Research

One of the advantages of collecting narratives is the richness and depth of the data collected. Moreover, stories can be collected about communication events that would be difficult or impossible to observe. There are, of course, risks when researchers ask participants to remember some types of stories. In collecting stories that are potentially troubling or negative, participants may re-create past trauma in their retelling (Clair, Chapman, & Kunkel, 1996). Wittenburg-Lyles (2006) avoided problems asking for narratives about the experience of death and dying;

she collected narratives from hospice volunteers rather than family members.

Whereas collecting stories can create a rich qualitative database, some narratives can be very long, and not all story elements are equally important. Part of your job as the researcher in analyzing the narratives is to draw the readers' attention to the most compelling parts of the story.

ETHNOGRAPHY

Ethnography is the study and representation of people and their interaction. Usually, it is the holistic description of interactants in their cultural or subcultural group, but the method of data collection is not restricted to any particular qualitative method (Lindlof & Taylor, 2002, 2011). In conducting ethnographic studies, researchers immerse themselves in the interaction field for long periods of time—often, but not necessarily, becoming one of the interactants. This immersion allows the researcher to observe and understand how communication is generated and responded to in a particular context. Thus, ethnography relies on some form of participant observation. But from an ethnographic viewpoint, almost anything can count as data. So, ethnographers must notice everything—informal and formal talk, posted written messages, written reports and letters, as well as the design, layout, and use of the interaction space. But most important, ethnographers take voluminous notes.

Here are the details of Gunn's (2008) participation and observation experiences of the closing of a hospital and its impact on its workers:

> I conducted fifty-five in-depth ethnographic interviews, produced observation fieldnotes, and collected more than 200 newspaper articles covering the closing of Dorothea Dix Mental Health Hospital (Dix) in Raleigh, North Carolina. During the time of the interviews, Dix was scheduled to close sometime in 2007 or 2008; many suspect that it will take longer. (p. 690)

With this description Gunn situates herself in a context and explains how data were collected. But ethnographers move more deeply (and often emotionally) into the context, which serves to draw readers in. Gunn continues:

> Regardless of the timeline, 1,200 employees will be displaced. A total of 400 of these employees have a high school degree or less and make no more than $22,000 a year. They are the focus of this project. The intent of this essay is not to critique the complex historical, social, and political experience of job loss. The intent of this essay is to offer the reader a glimpse into, and a moment to feel, the emotions of those individuals who live on the margins and who are living job loss. (p. 690)

You will also see the label **ethnography of communication** to describe some ethnographic accounts. Ethnography of communication is a theoretically driven method of ethnography in which researchers focus on language or speech communities to produce highly detailed analyses of how symbolic practices are expressed in a particular social structure (Lindlof & Taylor, 2002). Three key assumptions provide a foundation for studies from the ethnography of communication tradition (Phillipsen, 1992). First, "speaking is structured" (p. 9) and rules guide the structure. An ethnographer seeks to identify the code, or rules, of communication that a speech community uses. Second, "speaking is distinctive" (p. 10). Each speech community differs in its code of community. Thus, communication can only be understood by studying it in its cultural setting. Third, "speaking is social" (p. 13). As members of a speech community communicate with one another they are constructing their social lives and social identities.

Scholars who do the fieldwork to produce such data are called ethnographers. As an ethnographer, the scholar shares the environment of those he or she is studying. The ethnographer experiences firsthand the environment, problems, background, language, rituals, and social relations of a specified group of people. In becoming intimate with the communication, the ethnographer should then be equipped to develop a rich, complex, yet truthful account of the social world being studied (Van Maanen, 1988).

Communication scholars use ethnography to investigate a wide variety of interaction contexts that are impossible to simulate. For example, Ballard and Ballard (2011), as researchers and parents, tell a series of stories about international adoption, especially how it influences their family identity. There are three interesting aspects of this research. First, it is both scholarly writing and personal writing. Second, it foretells the future by exploring the past and present. Third, it suggests a unique way for exploring family communication. The researches begin their article by telling a story about telling a story. The impetus is their daughter asking, "Daddy, tell us again how you were adopted" (p. 69).

Autoethnography is autobiographical; the researcher is also a participant. Autoethnography "zooms backward and forward, inward and outward, distinctions between the personal and cultural become blurred, sometimes beyond distinct recognition" (Ellis & Bochner, 2000, p. 739). This type of research is embodied in its writing and is highly personal and emotional. Because the writing is personal, autoethnography may not have the same structure as other research articles.

In her autoethnography, Defenbaugh (2008) tells her personal story that describes and explains how her sensemaking emerged through numerous doctor–patient encounters as she suffers with and learns about her chronic disease. As a patient, she writes about the anxiety of not knowing what ails her, and then the anxiety of knowing how the doctor labels her illness. The essay reveals how her voice as a patient and person is concealed or ignored by others. Thus, in her autoethnography Defenbaugh demonstrates herself as powerless against the medical establishment. Further, she acknowledges the importance of emotions, how body and voice are inseparable, and how stories help create, interpret, and change our social worlds (Jones, 2005).

Practically, ethnography is the label applied to research with the following features (Atkinson & Hammersley, 1994):

1. There is a strong interest in exploring a particular social phenomenon. Researchers are unlikely to have well-developed research questions from which to begin the study because the phenomenon has been unexplored or underexplored.

2. Because the field is underexplored, the researcher must work with data that are unstructured or data that do not fit neatly into categories.

3. Research is focused on a small number of cases—even one case in detail can be sufficient.

4. Analysis of the data produces deep, thick descriptions and explanation of meanings and functions of communication behavior.

Entering the Scene

Generally, researchers conducting ethnography do not go through a formal process to gain entry to the research setting. Rather, ethnographers become part of the interaction environment, even if they only observe the interaction. If researchers are already natural actors in that environment, others may not know that they are also researchers. If researchers are entering a new interaction context, they must join the interaction in a presumably normal way and gain the confidence of those they are observing. Thus, the researchers become integrated within the interaction and the surroundings so that others interact with and toward the researchers as if they are normally a part of that interaction environment.

In some cases where physical characteristics or formal rules of membership would exclude a researcher from joining the interaction without notice, the researchers declare their research status, negotiate permission to do research, and then assimilate themselves into the interaction setting. Thus, with respect to the participation–observation roles of qualitative research described in Chapter 15, ethnographers assume a role more influenced by participation than observation. As a result, researchers are often unable to take fieldnotes while participating. They must find time and space away from the environment and interactants to write down or audiotape their observations.

Of course, authors of autoethnography do not enter a scene or research setting. They use their own communication experiences as the basis of their study.

DESIGN CHECK

Reading Ethnography

1. Does the author give details about how he or she entered the scene?
2. Does the author describe the type and length of involvement and interaction with participants?
3. How does the author describe the method of data collection?
4. Is the description of the researcher's experience detailed enough for you to feel as if *you are there*?
5. Are the details of the methodology sufficient to warrant the claims made by the researcher?
6. Are there plausible explanations for the communication described other than the ones presented by the ethnographer?

As technology use increases, however, the scene for ethnographers may shift from face-to-face communication to online communication or a blend of the two. Garcia, Standlee, Bechkoff, and Cui (2009) provide recommendations for doing ethnography virtually. While traditional methods are used in online ethnography, researchers must also learn "how to translate observational, interviewing, ethical, and rapport-building skills to a largely text-based and visual virtual research environment" (p. 78).

Strengths and Limitations of Ethnographic Research

An obvious benefit to ethnography is the rich, deep description that it offers. Reading ethnography is often like being inside the communication environment, rather than being an outsider. Because the researcher is immersed in the cultural and social context where the communication occurs, he or she is able to develop an intimacy with both the communication context and its interactants in a way not possible through other methods.

The most obvious limitation of ethnographic research is the time researchers must commit to the project. Conducting ethnography requires learning and then understanding the language, concepts, categories, practices, rules, beliefs, and values of those being studied (Van Maanen,

1988). Only after researchers are saturated in the data can they write the research report that does descriptive and analytical justice to the communication environment observed. Thus, ethnographers must commit the time and energy necessary to become more than just familiar with their research surroundings—they must become intimate with the communication environment. As a result of such intense involvement, researchers can overidentify with the participants and lose distance and analytical objectivity.

SUMMARY

1. Observation and taking notes are two skills required for collecting qualitative data.

2. Describing what is occurring is different from analyzing what occurred.

3. Different qualitative research methods create different relationships between researcher and participants.

4. Interactions with participants and observations of their interactions with others are captured as textual data.

5. Field interviewing is a practical qualitative method for discovering how people think and feel about communication practices.

6. Researchers use an interview guide composed mostly of open questions to encourage the respondent to tell his or her own story.

7. Most interviews are recorded, transcribed, and verified back to the recording.

8. Guided by a facilitator, a focus group is composed of 5 to 10 people who respond to the facilitator's question in a group discussion format.

9. Focus groups are a practical method for addressing applied communication problems and capturing the ideas of difficult-to-reach populations.

10. Focus groups take advantage of the chaining or cascading of conversation among participants.

11. Narratives, or stories, can be collected in interviews, as critical incidents, from questionnaires, from the course of everyday conversation, and in many forms of printed communication.

12. Ethnography is a qualitative research method in which the researcher immerses him- or herself in the communication environment for a long time, often becoming one of the interactants.

13. Autoethnography is autobiographical, reveals the author's emotions, and is often written in first person.

14. Ethnography of communication is a theoretically driven method in which researchers focus on language or speech communities to produce highly detailed analyses of how symbolic practices are expressed in a particular social structure.

15. The advantage of ethnography is that it allows researchers to collect communication in its natural state.

KEY TERMS

autoethnography

critical incidents

ethnography

ethnography of communication

field interviewing

fieldnotes

focus group

focus group schedule

interview guide

narratives

See the website www.mhhe.com/keyton4 that accompanies this text. For each chapter, the site contains a:

- chapter outline
- chapter checklist
- chapter summary
- short multiple-choice quiz
- PowerPoint presentation created by Dr. Keyton

For a list of internet resources, visit http://www.joannkeyton.com/Communication ResearchMethods.htm.

CHAPTER SEVENTEEN

Analyzing Qualitative Data

Chapter Checklist

After reading this chapter, you should be able to:

1. Distinguish between emic and etic readings of data.
2. Distinguish between the analysis and interpretation of qualitative data.
3. Write an analytical memo.
4. Search textual data for relevant codes to be analyzed.
5. Create a coding scheme for qualitative data.
6. Use grounded theory and constant-comparative method to analyze qualitative data.
7. Recognize when qualitative data analysis is theoretically saturated.
8. Decide whether a computer program will be helpful in the data analysis process.
9. Create an interpretation for categories or themes of qualitative data.
10. Enhance the credibility of a qualitative research design.
11. Conduct a member check or member validation.
12. Use triangulation to strengthen data analysis and interpretation.

Qualitative data analysis is the process of moving from raw data to evidence-based interpretation (Rubin & Rubin, 2005). The data analysis process brings "order, structure, and interpretation to the mass of collected data. It is a messy, ambiguous, time-consuming, creative, and fascinating process. It does not proceed in a linear fashion; it is not neat" (Marshall & Rossman, 1999, p. 150). Simply said, qualitative data are complex because participants do not talk or behave in standardized or comparable units. Thus, even a well-thought-out qualitative research design will need strategies to order and structure data. How does a researcher know when the analyses are complete? Usually, analyses are considered done when the researcher can construct "informed, vivid, and nuanced reports that reflect" what participants said; these reports must also answer the research questions or objectives (Rubin & Rubin, 2005, p. 201). Various techniques exist for analyzing qualitative data. Several of the more common methods are described in this chapter.

One caution should be noted: There is not a one-to-one relationship between how the data are collected and how the data are analyzed. All focus group data are not analyzed one way. All observational data are not analyzed the same way. It is easier, I believe, to think of qualitative research methods as producing some type of textual data that needs some type of qualitative data analytical technique.

AN OVERVIEW

Qualitative data analysis is described by Ellingson (2013) as "the process of separating aggregated texts (oral, written, or visual) into smaller segments of meaning for close consideration, reflection, and interpretation" (p. 414). These smaller segments, or data, are then examined repeatedly by the researcher who extracts themes or patterns from them. She also reminds us that these two processes of separating data and identifying themes or patterns overlap. With some qualitative data collection methods, the overlap is less (for example, interviews and focus groups); with other qualitative methods (for example, fieldnotes from observing and participating), the overlap is greater. When the researcher is involved or invested in the process of producing data, it is difficult for the researcher to separate these two processes.

Analyzing qualitative data generally takes some form of identifying themes (Bouma & Atkinson, 1995). The analytical process often begins just after the first data collection session. Remember that one advantage of qualitative research is its reflexive nature. Thus, the researcher can move back and forth between stages of data collection and data analysis. This allows the researcher to facilitate the emerging design of the qualitative study as well as tease out the structure of future observations (Lincoln & Guba, 1985). Remember, too, that qualitative research is inductive, which means that the researcher is working from the specific to the general. The collection of data and generation of tentative conclusions makes the inductive process cyclical and evolutionary.

Most researchers start by reading through every note or other piece of data they have acquired to get a sense of the overall data and to start a list of the broad themes that exist. Ideally, you should read the entire database several times to immerse yourself in the details. You are likely to discover something new each time you read through your notes. It's important to have a sense of the whole before you begin to break down the data into more manageable parts. After broad themes are identified, read your notes again. In this step look for significant quotes for each theme, relationships among themes, and for other salient issues that do not fit easily within the themes identified earlier.

Another technique for analyzing qualitative data is to start by rereading the literature that initially prompted or guided your study. This body of literature should suggest themes or broad categories that should be evident in your data. Then examine the data to see if the categories suggested by the literature can be confirmed or challenged.

A good standard to apply in analyzing qualitative data is to spend as much time analyzing data as collecting data in the field (Janesick, 1998). Time spent in examining the data will allow you to move beyond simply describing what happened to an analytical or theoretical level. Where should the analysis start? One place to begin is with points of conflict, tension, or contradiction. These are often fruitful points of departure for analysis or for developing theoretical premises.

Regardless of the analytical method chosen, the researcher works back and forth in an iterative fashion between "emic, or emergent, readings of the data and an etic use of existing models, explanations, and theories" (Tracy, 2013, p. 184). A researcher takes the **emic** view when he or she reads and interprets the data from the participants' point of view in the context in which the data are collected. Other phrases to describe an emic view are insider, inductive, and bottom up. In an emic view, the researcher works from the perspective and words of the participants. A researcher takes the **etic** view (or outsider, deductive, top-down) when interpreting data in comparison to theories or perspectives. In other words, participants' behavior or talk is analyzed more conceptually and more generally and without specific regard to the context.

Admittedly, it is difficult to know exactly how researchers analyze and interpret qualitative data. Both of these are cognitive activities. One of the advantages of having team members to conduct research with you is that these cognitive activities can occur through your interactions. It is very helpful to ask, "Why do you think that?" or "Why does this data fit that and earlier in a similar case, you said it didn't." Whether you work alone or with teammates, it is important to document the analytical and interpretive steps taken. Sagar and Jowett (2012, p. 154) described their process this way:

> Trustworthiness and credibility of the research was obtained through several steps designed to ensure rigor in data analyses. First, we maintained an audit trail, which is a record of the analytical decisions and processes that allowed us to verify rigor and to minimize interpretive bias. Second, taking a collaborative approach (e.g., ongoing peer debriefing) in the analytical process helped to reduce interpretive bias and continually to examine the credibility of the researchers. Third, maintaining a reflexive journal forced us to reflect on our biases and values (Malacrida, 2007) including our beliefs on what constitutes effective or ineffective coach communicative acts of interaction. We recorded these biases and reflections in a journal during the analysis phase, which helped to challenge them and, thereby, minimize bias in the course of the study.

Whatever analytical and interpretative strategies you select, documenting each step is essential. Do not rely on your memory or the memory of others.

Choosing an Analytic Method

As suggested, the initial process of analyzing qualitative data begins when the data are being collected. But a more holistic analytical process begins when the researcher can examine the whole of the dataset. Because so much data can be produced using qualitative data collection methods, the choice of analytical method for a qualitative research design must be made carefully (Lindlof & Taylor, 2002). First, the quantity of data that the researcher will sort through is more difficult to reduce to a coherent or meaningful representation. Second, multiple plausible interpretations can exist. Third, the research question that initiated the study may have changed during data collection as the researcher became more involved in the communication setting and more knowledgeable about the communication problem or issue being investigated. Fourth, the researcher's interpretation of the data must remain true to participants' localized meanings; that is, the interpretation must make sense to the participants who provided the data.

Regardless of which analytical technique you use, Lindlof and Taylor (2002) suggest that researchers think of the process as two distinct steps: analysis and interpretation. **Analysis** is the process of labeling and breaking down raw data to find patterns, themes, concepts, and propositions that exist in the dataset. **Interpretation** is making sense of or giving meaning to those patterns, themes, concepts, and propositions.

THE PROCESS OF ANALYSIS AND INTERPRETATION

One of the first steps in analyzing qualitative data is to capture your reactions to and impressions of the people, setting, and interactions. Researchers use analytical memos to separate out their analysis from data collection. The second step is the process of categorizing the data into meaningful units.

Analytical Memos

Although the researcher enters the communication setting with a design in mind, recall that qualitative design is more flexible due to its reflexive nature. Thus, what the researcher encounters in the field may not be what he or she had in mind before entering the setting. Even when a researcher's expectations and experience in the setting are similar, it is a good practice to begin the analytical process as data are collected. Thus, researchers use **analytical memos** to capture their first impressions and reflections about the setting, people, and interactions.

Analytical memos are both part of the process and an outcome of the analysis (Tracy, 2013).

Written as memos to yourself, analytical memos are informal. They capture first impressions, tentative conclusions, and descriptions of communication events with which you are not familiar. It is important to point out that analytical memos are not part of the data. Rather, they are accompaniments to the data and your first attempt at analyzing what is going on in a particular interaction scene. Look at the two segments of an analytical memo in Figure 17.1

Fieldnotes

Donna took over, listing all of the towns they've worked in, claiming "resident status." She was very complimentary of the state and its people, saying "you are cutting edge." She explained her role as to set the stage and provide simple instructions and rules. She encouraged people to talk with one another and keep their hands busy with the toys on the tables. She continued to affirm participants, saying they were the "future of [the state]." She gave more background of why the foundation sponsors such leadership training and parallels to programs in other states. Said that the foundation came to her and Barbara to answer the questions:

- What is it that groups need to be like?
- What do leaders need to be like/do?

Additional comments from Barbara:
- Communities (2 or more people) that work/are effective have visions, strategic actions, they are leader-full
- Leaders don't have to all wear different hats
- The goal of the foundation is to transform community leadership programs in the state
- During these 2 days: workshops that model ways to create leaders who create leaders who create leaders . . .
- You'll leave with processes/practices/materials from participatory workshops
- Our Philosophy: Serve one another, we do this as we work together

Corresponding Segments of an Analytical Memo

1. In the introduction, Barbara and Donna were touted as having extensive experience in leadership training, but no single organization was listed other than the foundation sponsoring the training. This left me wondering about their credentials.

2. Donna said that the foundation served to transform leadership programs in the state. From my understanding then, every leadership program is "transformed" in the exact same way, through their training program. Is this wise to have every community working in the same way, or would the state benefit from communities working from a variety of perspectives? Who is to say that their [the trainers'] perspective is the "right" one? Is there ever any evaluation of or follow-up on these techniques?

FIGURE 17.1 Fieldnotes and Corresponding Analytical Memo

and compare them to the fieldnotes. These are taken from a project in which the researcher was a complete observer; she was visible to the group she was observing and they were aware they were being observed. The notes are taken from the first day of observation—the first of eight full days of training.

While observing and taking fieldnotes, the researcher was struck by two statements that she believed deserved further attention. But the pace of the interaction did not allow her to stop and make these analytical comments and develop these questions in the field. Nor was it appropriate for her to make this type of analytical note during short breaks in the training, as the room in which the training was being held was not large enough for her to find a more private space to work. Written immediately after the training session, the analytical memo provided her the opportunity to capture reactions and ask questions that could be explored when collecting other observational data from this same group and through other methods. Whereas fieldnotes are written in the field, analytical memos are more commonly written after the researcher leaves the research setting field.

However you develop analytical memos, it is important to remember that they are not part of the data. They are initial reactions to and impressions of the data. Thus, analytical memos can suggest potential avenues of additional data collection, or become the first version of a categorizing or analytical scheme, and tentative conclusions, as well as biases that you should be aware of in data collection and data analysis. See Figure 17.2 for an analytical memo written by Suter and Daas (2007) in their study of self-identified members of lesbian couples. The researchers were investigating how lesbian couples uphold or challenge norms of heterogeneity as they negotiate, through the nonverbal symbols in their relationship with a partner.

Heather and Amber talked about choosing rings as a private visual sign of their commitment. However, they struggled with a label for the ring. The couple resisted traditional (heteronormative) terms such as a promise or engagement ring while drawing on the traditional (heteronormative) meanings attached to the symbol as a way to gain recognition for their relationship.

Like Mindy and Christy, Heather and Amber were concerned how others, particularly those who are not supportive of their relationship, would react to their revelation of commitment. Heather commented:

> But like even my mom recognized it [the ring], which she's not always the most observant and, while I think she supports us in our relationship, but she's definitely not necessarily happy about it, but she tries really hard. And so when I was home for Christmas she like commented on it, and it was positive I mean in her kind of way, it wasn't like oh I'm so happy for you, but she kind of acknowledged it which I thought, in some ways kind of served its purpose. I mean for me I was really nervous about wearing the ring home and having my family kind of comment on it, and so that went kind of really well. (17: 304–312)

Heather clearly articulates her concerns about how her family would react to her and Amber's relationship while also expressing how the ring "served its purpose" in securing acknowledgement of the relationship from her mother. Heather's use of the ring as a symbol of commitment illustrates how Heather is drawing on the traditional (heteronormative) symbol of a ring to gain public recognition for her and Amber's relationship, which is contested even among some members of her family. (p. 182)

SOURCE: Suter, E. A., & Daas, K. L. (2007) Negotiating heteronormativity dialectically: Lesbian couples' display of symbols in culture. *Western Journal of Communication, 71*, 177–195. Used by permission of the Western States Communication Association.

FIGURE 17.2 Analytical Memo

The use of analytical memos should be reported in the research report. For example, Becker, Ellevold, and Stamp (2008) describe their use of analytical memos in their interview study of romantically involved heterosexual couples in this way: "Specifically, each researcher prepared analytical memos to capture insights and reflections. They shared and discussed these memos with each other and compared them to the data" (p. 92).

Diagramming the Data

At this point, some researchers reduce their data by transforming it into graphical form (Creswell, 1998). By placing data in tables, diagrams, or graphs, researchers make relationships among data become more evident. In this form, data can be displayed by case, subject, theme, or interaction event. Clearly at this point, the researcher will confirm that he or she has more data than can possibly be used. Yet, it is essential that no data be discarded. Rather, continue to use data sorting and reduction strategies to begin isolating the data that will answer your research questions or hypotheses.

Coding and Categorizing Data

For qualitative research designs, the data will consist of pages and pages of notes, or written text or transcripts. The text can be your notes from observing participants in the field. The text might be transcriptions of audiotapes from interviews and focus groups. Or the text could be participants' written narratives.

In almost every case, a researcher will have the need to categorize and code data. Doing so helps the researcher reduce the data into a manageable size from which an interpretation can be made. Some researchers start this process as soon as data are collected; other researchers wait until all the data are collected. The larger the potential dataset, the more practical it will be to begin categorizing the data at intermediate points during data collection.

As you observe participants in their interaction settings and listen to participants in interviews and focus groups, you will naturally start to link statements and behaviors and distinguish those from other statements and behaviors. Figure 17.3 depicts how categories are identified in the data and then linked to research questions.

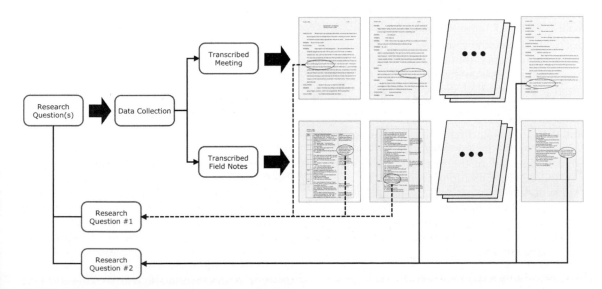

FIGURE 17.3 Linking Data to Research Questions

This is the beginning of the categorizing process. A **category** is a label for a set of excerpts, examples, or themes that are similar. Categories may be drawn from the literature used to build a foundation for the qualitative research design. For example, Martin (2004) used existing categories of humor to begin her categorization of how humor was used in an organizational setting. She describes the process of using existing categories in this way:

> It is important to note that humor categories fundamental to extant theories served only as initial categories. For example, the idea of humor as play and lightness does emerge from the data as an important nuance not usually distinct among humor typology. Holding extant humor labels lightly, as guiding constructs rather than final categories, served to fulfill the communicative approach to organizational studies suggested by Pacanowsky and O'Donnell-Trujillo (1982). (p. 155)

Notice that Martin used the existing categories, but used them as a reference point and not as an absolute. Even when categories are determined beforehand, researchers are wise to let unique or novel categories emerge. As a result, a category scheme may be revised or reformulated.

On the other hand, categories may emerge from the data. Following the inductive model used in most qualitative research, researchers inductively derive the categories as representative of the phenomenon they are investigating. At the first attempt, these are likely to be "fuzzy categories due to a certain degree of ambiguity in their definition" (Lindlof & Taylor, 2002, p. 215). They are not distinct, nor are they conceptually clear. But they are a starting point for the analysis. Most likely, the initial categories will be somewhat different than the final categories used to develop an interpretation of the data.

If you are having trouble identifying categories, try the following steps. First, return to your research question. Your research question is likely to help you explore one of these paths (Lofland & Lofland, 1995):

- If something exists, what are its types?
- How often does a communication phenomenon occur?

- How big, strong, or intense is a communication phenomenon?
- Is there a process, a cycle, or phases to the interaction?
- How does one event influence another?
- In what ways do consequences follow an event or interaction?
- How do people use interaction in a specific way? To accomplish a specific goal?

Regardless of how you analyze your data, your analysis must be responsive to the constructs identified in the research question.

Rubin and Rubin (2005) argue that researchers should be able to recognize and label each concept by answering the following five questions:

1. How will I label this construct? What am I calling it?
2. How will I define it? You should be able to write out a definitional statement.
3. How will I recognize it in the data? What likely implicit and explicit ways will participants express this construct?
4. What does this construct not include?
5. What are a few examples of this construct in these data?

Simply, it is difficult to code data effectively if the researcher does not have working definitions. For example, the first of several research questions often seeks to establish that a type of interaction exists. To answer this type of question, search data for evidence of the existence and the types of interaction in which you are interested. Ellingson's (2003) research question "What are the communication processes among team members in the clinic backstage?" (p. 96) is this type of question. Thus, she looked for "similarities and differences in content and structure of interactions among team members as they communicated in the clinic backstage" (p. 98). Her analyses resulted in seven categories of backstage communication processes, each with two or more subtypes. Thus, she confirmed that the type of interaction she was seeking did take place and was able to make distinctions among the various types.

Another strategy is to have a set of questions to reflect on as you read through the data. Lofland and Lofland (1995, p. 186) suggest asking the following:

1. What is this? What does it represent?
2. What is this an example of?
3. What do I see going on here? What are people doing? What is happening? What kind of events are at issue here?

As categories emerge, you should begin labeling with a code, one word or a short phrase. For example, two of Ellingson's (2003) codes are "training students" and "handling interruptions." These codes represent the categories, which are more fully described by the examples within them. Writing notes in the margins and drawing arrows or using highlighters will assist in this process.

As categories are identified, researchers should test the category system being discovered by looking for the opposite or negative cases and searching for other plausible explanations. "Alternative explanations *always* exist" (Marshall & Rossman, 1999, p. 157). Thus, the researcher must explain why a particular set of categories is the most plausible of all.

If the dataset consists of notes from separate meetings or as transcripts from multiple interviews, a researcher will need to decide how best to analyze the data. Depending on the research question guiding the investigation, a researcher might decide to treat the data as a whole. When the data are collected from a homogeneous sample, this can be an effective strategy. But, more frequently, a researcher will want to retain the uniqueness of each interaction event or each individual. Thus, most researchers analyze notes for each meeting or each interview in its entirety and then compare and contrast findings across the dataset. In this way, researchers can isolate any unique circumstances (e.g., comparison of categories in first meeting to second and subsequent meetings) or characteristics (e.g., sex, race, ethnicity, hierarchical status) to create a more sophisticated and integrated analysis.

Categorizing and coding data, however, is the most elementary of qualitative analytical techniques.

Most communication scholars use one of the two following perspectives for analyzing qualitative data: grounded theory and thematic analysis.

GROUNDED THEORY

Many researchers use grounded theory, introduced by Glaser and Strauss (1967) and modified by Charmaz (2000; see also Charmaz & Belgrave, 2012), as an iterative approach for coding their data. The **grounded theory** approach is based on three specific features:

1. Emergent theory is "grounded in" the relationships between data and the categories in which they are coded;
2. Categories develop through an ongoing process of comparing units of data with each other (a process known as the **constant-comparative method**); and
3. Codes, categories, and category definitions continue to change dynamically while the researcher is still in the field, with new data altering the scope and terms of the analytic framework. (Lindlof & Taylor, 2011, p. 250)

Categories are mutable, or can be changed, because the researcher is constantly identifying new categories and comparing them to the existing categories as the researcher continues to analyze the data or collects new data. Thus, grounded theory can be used to analyze textual data regardless of its type of data collection method.

One caution must be given here. Grounded theory is not a method for identifying categories. Rather, grounded theory requires that researchers examine the relationships between the data and its category, and the relationships among categories. It is a theorizing activity (Charmaz, 2005).

The first step using this approach is to become very familiar with the data. Often researchers do not try to code on their first pass through the data. The second step is to code the data. A typical approach is to use a highlighting pen to identify parts of the transcript or fieldnotes that are relevant to the research questions. The third pass is then made to identify the initial categories that emerge from the data. The fourth and subsequent passes

AN ETHICAL ISSUE

Considering Relational Ethics with Participants During Data Analysis

Researchers apply to their university's Institutional Review Board to obtain approval to conduct research. Generally speaking, the ethical issues in an IRB application address how participants will be identified and selected, what role the researcher will use to interact with participants, how the researcher will address participants' anonymity, and how researchers will uphold the confidentiality of their data. But what are ethical responsibilities of researchers to their participants in qualitative communication studies while the data are being analyzed? Clearly issues of anonymity and confidentiality are still present. Are there other ethical issues that researchers should be aware? Here are some to consider:

- Is the analysis truthful to the data? Or is the data being stretched in some way?
- If a participant read the research report, would he or she accept my analysis of his or her data?
- Is it possible that participants have different interpretations of the data than what is presented?
- Was something left out of the analysis because it did not fit?

What other ethical issues do you believe are important and should be considered in the analysis and interpretation of data collected from others?

---

through the data are used to compare and contrast the categories that emerge. Harter (2004) explains her emergent categorizing process using grounded theory in this way:

> I read all transcripts and documents in their entirety to develop a sense of these data as a whole. I re-read the transcripts while playing the original tapes to ensure accuracy of transcriptions and to note special emphases or cues that might affect interpretation but did not appear on the transcripts. After gaining a holistic sense of the discourse, I started the actual analysis. A constant comparative method allowed themes representing recurring patterns of behavior and meaning to emerge from subjects' own words. The process began with manually coding the data on the actual transcripts. By engaging in a constant comparative analysis of data I continually compared specific incidents in the data, refined concepts, and identified their properties. (p. 98)

The process is iterative, meaning that the process is repeated until the researcher believes all

relevant categories have been identified. Lammers and Garcia (2009) describe how they worked together as a research team using grounded theory:

> In our initial analysis of the field data, the three researchers read all of the field notes, transcripts, and documents and individually sorted the texts into thematic groups using the grounded theory method of constant comparison in a search for themes and affinities in the data. . . . Specifically each researcher separately read the corpus of research materials, sorted the texts into themes on notecards, and reported the themes in several group meetings. . . . Researchers then shared their themes and reviewed each other's notes. After long discussions of the themes each had identified (and without reference to the literature on professions at this time), researchers created a list of themes and agreed on coding the categories. (p. 365)

Their description demonstrates the multiple steps taken to identify and justify themes that the researchers believed to be characteristics of how managers, veterinarians, knowledge management staff, toxicologists, and veterinary assistants communicated their *profession* to others at work.

The steps of grounded theory and the constant-comparative method are coding data, developing inductive categories, revising categories, and writing memos to explore preliminary and tentative ideas. Throughout the process, the researcher is continually comparing parts of the data to other parts and the research literature.

In the coding process, researchers use two types of categories. The first is **open coding,** or unrestricted coding, and is the first pass through the data. Open coding is unrestricted because the researcher is not looking for data that fit a set number or type of categories. Nor is the researcher interested in how categories fit together. Rather, the researcher is *open* to all possibilities of categories. In later passes, the researcher uses **axial coding,** or the process of linking categories in a meaningful way. In the process of axial coding, categories are collapsed or relabeled into fewer categories. Hamel (2009) describes her use of open and axial coding in this way:

> The data from the in-depth interviews and focus group were analyzed by first using an open-coding process to identify and differentiate between discrete concepts that were then labeled and sorted. Similar concepts were then grouped under conceptual categories. This process was followed by axial coding where relationships within and among the categories were identified to verify their discreteness. (pp. 244–245)

Another example of open and axial coding is described by Gallagher and Sias (2009) in their study of employees' impressions and uncertainty about newcomers to their organizations. They also asked a research question about how employees seek information to reduce uncertainty about newcomers.

> Data analysis was carried out in several steps. First, the primary researcher examined all interview transcripts using an open-coding process to identify general themes relevant to the types of uncertainty experienced by veteran employees and the information-seeking tactics used to reduce that uncertainty. The primary researcher and a second coder then worked together on one randomly selected transcript by making general lists and labels next to each paragraph. General themes (e.g., uncertainty about how the newcomer might transform the work environment) identified during this process were used by the coders to separately code two more randomly selected transcripts. The coders then reconvened to compare their coding decisions and, using axial coding, together developed a code book for coding the remaining transcripts. The code book was tested (by separately coding randomly selected transcripts) and revised several times until categories and subcategories were identified within each general theme (e.g., comments regarding how the newcomer might affect the veteran employee's job and task assignments were grouped together under the subcategory "Job Changes" under the broad category "Transformation Uncertainty"). (p. 28)

When all the data relevant to the research question can be coded into a category, researchers label the data as being **theoretically saturated** (Glaser & Strauss, 1967). New categories are not emerging, and the existing category structure appears stable. After the categories are stable, the researcher explores the relationships among the categories. How are the categories similar? Different?

But simply having saturation of categories is not enough. Charmaz (2005) suggests that grounded theory research should be based on four criteria. The first is the credibility of the data collection. For example, has the researcher achieved and demonstrated familiarity with the setting or topic? Do the range, number, and depth of observations merit the researcher's claims? Are there strong logical links between the data gathered and presented and the researcher's arguments? The second criterion is originality of the analysis and its significance. Do the categories offer new insights? What is the social and theoretical significance of the work? How do the findings challenge, extend, or refine ideas or concepts? The third criterion for evaluating grounded theory research is resonance. Do the categories identified reflect the full domain of the communication studied? Does the analysis make sense to those who were interviewed or observed? The fourth criterion is the usefulness of findings in everyday life and for future research. Can the researcher's interpretations be used by people in their everyday communication practices? Can the analysis stimulate future research on other issues?

THEMATIC ANALYSIS

Thematic analysis, sometimes identified as thematic interpretation (Owen, 1984), is based on participants' conceptions of actual communication episodes. A **theme** is a conceptualization of an interaction, a relationship, or an event. Themes are identified in textual data based on three criteria: recurrence, repetition, and forcefulness. Recurrence is present when at least two parts of a report have the same thread of meaning. Recurrence is not simply repetition of the same words or phrase; different wording may result in the same meaning. Thus, this criterion focuses on salient meaning.

The second criterion, repetition, is the explicit repetition of key words, phrases, or sentences. The third criterion, forcefulness, is present when the data reveal

> vocal inflection, volume, or dramatic pause which serve to stress and subordinate some utterances from other[s] . . . it also refers to the underlining of words and phrases, the increased size of print or use of colored marks circling or otherwise focusing on passages in the written reports. (Owen, 1984, pp. 275–276)

The three criteria—recurrence, repetition, and forcefulness—are found in participants' vocal or written records. Thus, when used they identify what the salient issues are and demonstrate the degree of salience for participants.

Suter, Reyes, and Ballard (2011) explain their use of thematic analysis. The authors posed this research question for a focus group study: "What is the primary metaphor underlying transracial, international adoptive parents' talk about how they make sense of laypersons' remarks about their families?" (p. 44). The research team collected data from 12 focus groups; each focus group was audiotaped and transcribed verbatim. Using Owens' three criteria, the research team searched each transcript to identify metaphors to answer their research question. Next, the team met to discuss the themes and the analytical memos they created for each focus group. Their discussion allowed them

to reach consensus on how data from each focus group were coded. The researchers describe how they continued with the analytical process:

> Only after consensus did we move on to analyze the next focus group. This process was followed for all 12 focus groups. After this, we independently reanalyzed each of the 12 analytic tables, memos, and transcripts to abstract the larger, more overarching metaphor that brought our analysis into a coherent whole. (p. 45)

CODING AND ANALYZING WITH SOFTWARE

Software known as computer-assisted qualitative data analysis programs is available to aid researchers in the task of analyzing qualitative data. Researchers wanting to use such a program should examine several because programs vary widely in what data management and data analysis steps they provide. (Data management includes data entry, searching and retrieving data, and coding data; data analysis includes analyzing data codes, linking data, and analyzing links.) Clearly, researchers should assess a program and its capabilities based on the type goodness of data collected for the research project. Before deciding to use a computer program, other scholars' evaluation of their use and experiences with computer-assisted qualitative data analysis will be helpful. As software is regularly updated, I encourage you to do an online search for qualitative software reviews to find information about the most recent releases of software packages.

Communication scholars who use computer-aided qualitative data analysis software should report its use in a research article with a brief description. For example, Smith, Coffelt, Rives, and Sollitto (2012) report: "Transcripts were imported into NVivo qualitative data management software, which aids the researcher in sorting qualitative data sets. Once added to the program, transcripts were coded based on emergent themes" (p. 55). Another research team reports on their use of NVivo,

> First, each researcher independently coded several transcripts using NVivo version 8.0 to develop an initial list of codes describing process and content of decision-making meetings. These

separate lists were then discussed to develop a common list of codes and higher-order categories to reflect themes emergent in the data. Coding continued until a complete list of codes and categories was developed, which we agreed faithfully represented the data and could be used to address the research questions. (Canary & Cantu, 2012, p. 277)

Jian (2008) reports how she used a software program to assist in the analysis of data from a information-technology provider in more detail:

I started my analysis with three root categories: "identity," "Alpha [a state of the art information and computer technology] use," and "control." I coded data line-by-line into these categories. . . . data points that were interesting but did not fit into these categories, I created what N4 calls "free codes" to hold these data points for potential later use. The second round of coding was to examine the data within each root category and split them into sub-categories. In fact, while conducting the first round of coding, some subcategories began to emerge and were created along the way. (p. 65)

Using this type of software is particularly helpful if you have a large volume of data, or if the research project explored multiple sites or collected data from multiple interviewees. Despite the advantages such programs can offer, seasoned researchers acknowledge that the hard work of analyzing qualitative data remains because the work is intellectual, not mechanical (Dohan & Sanchez-Jankowski, 1998). The researcher still must create the categories, determine the parameters of categories, and link categories together. Computer-aided qualitative data analysis software can offer help and efficiency in coding, sorting, querying, and retrieving data. But these programs can be costly; check to see if your college or university offers a student version that is free or less costly.

THE PROCESS OF INTERPRETATION

No matter how much time is spent coding and categorizing, these steps do not "guarantee a sensitive reading of a life, a social ritual, or a cultural scene" (Lindlof & Taylor, 2002, p. 232). Thus, interpretation is critical in analyzing qualitative data. And interpretation is never neutral. Both the researcher and the data collection and analytical methods come from particular standpoints. Qualitative research does not occur in a vacuum—for those being observed or interviewed, as well as the interviewer. Both bring past experiences, interests, and values to the research experience.

Thus, **interpretation** is making sense of or giving meaning to patterns, themes, concepts, and propositions. It is the act of translating categories into a meaningful whole by switching from a micro frame, which consists of the coding and categorizing, to a macro frame, which analyzes the data as a whole.

When coding has been completed and categories or themes are stable, researchers again turn to memos as an "intermediate step between coding and the first draft of the completed analysis" (Charmaz, 2000, p. 517). Researchers use the memo writing step to "elaborate processes, assumptions, and actions that are presumed" in the coding and categorizing process (p. 517). **Memo writing** encourages researchers to detail the properties of each category and to suggest how each category or theme fits with others. Quotes from participants or phrases from field notes are used in memo writing first to test the specificity of the analysis, and then later as exemplars of the category. These memos are used as the basis for organizing the research report, and often they become drafts of the results section of the research report.

Evaluating Interpretation

How does the researcher evaluate his or her results after the coding, categorizing, and interpretations are completed? What cues can a consumer use in reading a research report to assess the soundness of a qualitative study and its claims? Participant quotes, credibility, member validation, and triangulation are the primary tools researchers use to enhance the quality of their findings.

Participant Quotes The initial test of the researcher's ability to analyze and interpret qualitative data is the degree to which participant

How Are Participant Quotes Used?

Researchers use participant quotes to document emergent themes from qualitative data. The following criteria can guide you in deciding which quotes to use. First, the quoted material should fully describe the point the researcher is claiming to make. There should be a one-to-one comparison between the researcher's claim and participants' quotes. Second, participants' quotes should illuminate the claim with detail and specifics. Third, quotes selected should not be open to an alternative plausible interpretation. Fourth, at least one quote should be given word-for-word in the research report.

quotes illuminate the analysis and interpretation. In other words, quotes from participants must be provided in the research report as evidence that the analysis and interpretation are plausible. By reading the examples provided, it should be obvious to the reader of the report that the categories described are based on the qualitative data collected. Thus, researchers often use quotes from several participants or segments of fieldnotes from different parts of a meeting to document the existence of a category and to distinguish this category from others.

But how does a researcher select which quotes to use? Ellingson (2013) provides some direction. Returning to the research question or research purpose is the first step, as the participant quotes selected should illustrate and illuminate the substance of the question or purpose. Quotes or examples that bring strong images to mind are usually longer; they are one type of quote to use as evidence. Shorter quotes are also useful for identifying and describing themes. But, be sure to select those that provide an illustration easily to readers unfamiliar with the deep background of the research design. Most important, make every data example count. Quotes should be selected because they illuminate and illustrate the communication phenomenon or communication processes studied.

How many examples are needed? Generally, researchers need to give enough examples to demonstrate the breadth and depth of a category or theme. Many times, three examples are enough to convey the researchers' analysis and interpretation of a category. Overall, researchers should work for balance between the presentation of the categories and themes with the presentation of data as examples (Lofland & Lofland, 1995).

Credibility   The criterion used to assess the effectiveness and accuracy of a qualitative research design and findings drawn from its data is *credibility* (see Chapter 14). How does a researcher enhance credibility? First, the researcher must plan for and carry out the inquiry in such a way that the findings are believable to others. How can this be achieved? With prolonged and persistent engagement with the interactants and the interaction setting, you have the opportunity to develop a real sense of the interaction culture as well as test for any misinformation introduced through distortion or bias. And, as a result of prolonged interaction, the researcher has additional opportunities to build trust.

Second, credibility is enhanced when the findings are agreeable to those who were research participants. Recall that *member validation* is the process of asking those observed to respond to your observation summaries. Besides giving you the opportunity to correct errors, participants can also challenge your interpretations and provide insight from their point of view. By providing participants with the details or interpretation of the interaction, you might also stimulate their recall of additional information or insight. This is what Pierce and Dougherty (2002) did to enhance the credibility of their findings. By taking their findings back to the pilots who provided the data, they were able to assess how well they had captured the pilots' experiences. Besides these opportunities to correct or gain information, your willingness to share what you found with participants strengthens the researcher–participant bond. These activities inherently enhance your credibility as a researcher and the credibility of your findings.

Triangulation Researchers often rely on **triangulation** to increase the credibility of their research. Refer to the initial discussion of triangulation in Chapter 14. The most common form is *data triangulation,* in which a variety of qualitative methods are used to produce different types of data. The validity of a finding is enhanced if the researcher comes to similar or complementary conclusions using two or more methods. For example, one way to triangulate findings is through the process of gathering data from different sources. Finding redundancy, or the repetition and overlapping of interpretations, is another form of data triangulation. A third form of data triangulation is to challenge the explanations you and other members of the research team create. When there is a research team, members should work to clarify meaning by exploring different ways in the data are seen (Stake, 2005).

Investigator triangulation is another form of triangulation. Two researchers observing the same interaction are likely to capture a more complete view of what happened in the interaction than would one observer, due to differing vantage points or differing perspectives. Their interpretations may blend into one as they talk about what happened, or their interpretations may remain separate and distinct accounts of what transpired. Researchers have even studied the extent to which multiple coders agree on the thematic analysis of focus group interaction. Armstrong, Gosling, Weinman, and Martaeu (1997) found that even though researchers have their own views, which are part of the subjective nature of qualitative research, the themes that the coders found were similar. Divergence among the coders occurred as they packaged or bound the themes together in different frameworks. Two or more researchers are likely to provide alternative frameworks from which the data can be interpreted.

Another way to triangulate findings is to observe at different times. Capturing data across time and at different intervals or times of day provides a greater variety of data from which to draw conclusions and, as a result, creates greater reliability.

Triangulation is especially important in overcoming threats to external validity. One of the most frequent criticisms of qualitative research is that the qualitative method creates an overreliance on one case or a series of cases (Denzin, 1970). By observing multiple parties over a period of time, researchers can overcome biases believed to exist either because the individuals studied have unique properties or characteristics or because there is instability in the population under observation. Thus, researchers must demonstrate that the individuals or cases studied are representative of the class of units to which generalizations are made. To avoid a threat to external validity, researchers should become familiar with the social and personal characteristics of individuals observed and be sensitive to any biasing features they possess.

Although the practice of triangulation can be planned for, it is actually carried out as the research is being conducted (Hickson & Jennings, 1993). Thus, triangulation practices can also be added to a research project after it is underway. This points to the greater flexibility of qualitative methods over quantitative methods. As you can see, the role of the researcher (or research team members) can be enhanced or expanded to meet the demands of the interaction situation as it occurs.

A FINAL WORD

Across the qualitative analytical methods described here, some commonalities exist. Qualitative analytical methods are progressive, meaning that data are continually compared and contrasted to create a sophisticated interpretation (Fossey, Harvey, McDermott, & Davidson, 2002). All qualitative data analysis starts with reading the transcripts and reviewing all data collected. Depending on the complexity of the data, a researcher may read the data several times. If data were recorded, listening to or viewing the recordings should also be done. During reading, listening, and viewing, researchers generally take notes to help them conceptually organize the material. Because a central characteristic of qualitative research is its ability to capture the complexity of communication, keep transcriptions and other documents in their original form. Literally, breaking a transcript or document into categories will interfere with how the researcher makes sense of the data.

At this point, the researcher makes a decision about how to proceed. Will analytical memos be written? Will diagrams of ideas be drawn? Will transcripts be coded? Will the researcher choose grounded theory or thematic analysis, or some other inductive analysis technique? Next, a researcher needs to connect the analyses in a framework and compare the emerging framework to existing theory as a challenge or extension or develop and pose a new theory.

Throughout the analytical process, revisiting the data will help the researcher confirm, question, and reject tentative findings. Revisiting the data is always a good choice.

SUMMARY

1. Because qualitative research is inductive, data collection and analysis can be cyclical and evolutionary.

2. Analysis of qualitative data, or identifying patterns and themes, is distinct from interpreting, or making sense of the patterns and themes.

3. Generally, a researcher spends as much time analyzing qualitative data as collecting data.

4. Researchers write analytical memos to capture their first impressions and reflections of the data.

5. Diagramming the data, or putting the data into some graphical form, can help a researcher find relationships among the data.

6. Coding and categorizing qualitative data reduces it to a manageable size.

7. Categories may be drawn from the literature or emerge from the data.

8. Grounded theory, or the constant-comparative method, is an iterative process that guides a researcher through identifying categories and identifying relationships among categories.

9. Data are saturated theoretically when all data can be coded into a category.

10. Thematic analysis of data is based on the criteria of recurrence, repetition, and forcefulness.

11. After data are analyzed, or categorized, a researcher must develop an interpretation of the patterns, themes, and concepts.

12. Researchers use participant quotes, credibility, member validation, and triangulation to affirm the quality of their findings.

KEY TERMS

analysis	grounded theory
analytical memo	interpretation
axial coding	memo writing
category	open coding
constant-comparative method	thematic analysis
	theme
credibility	theoretical saturation
emic	triangulation
etic	

See the website www.mhhe.com/keyton4 that accompanies this text. For each chapter, the site contains a:

- chapter outline
- chapter checklist
- chapter summary
- short multiple-choice quiz
- PowerPoint presentation created by Dr. Keyton

For a list of internet resources, visit http://www.joannkeyton.com/Communication ResearchMethods.htm..

CHAPTER EIGHTEEN

Reading and Writing the Qualitative Research Report

Chapter Checklist

After reading this chapter, you should be able to:

1. Select the writing style for your qualitative report.
2. Decide whose voice will be the primary storyteller.
3. Identify the core ideas you want to present.
4. Write a description about how the data were collected.
5. Make decisions about revealing the identity of participants.
6. Include both description and analysis in the written report.
7. Select the most appropriate quotes from participants to support your analysis.
8. Write a discussion section that reviews what was attempted, what has been learned, and identifies new questions.
9. Refine your written report through several revisions.
10. Write a title that accurately introduces your study in an interesting way.
11. Write an abstract for the written report.
12. Develop a complete and accurate list of references used in the report in the preferred style.

As with other research designs, a qualitative study is not complete until the researcher writes the research report to communicate findings to others. Although similarities exist between qualitative and quantitative research reports, there are significant differences. The primary differences are based on the process of the back-and-forth reflective steps in collecting and analyzing qualitative data. Some differences are based on the greater flexibility some journals allow for the presentation of qualitative research (for example, see *Qualitative Inquiry*). Regardless of the form a report of qualitative research takes, the researcher usually uses some of the memos or other analytical writing he or she used in interpreting the data.

In any report of qualitative research, legitimacy is at stake. The writer's job is to convince readers that the description is authentic and significant. In some sense, the writer of a qualitative research report becomes a guide helping the reader move through unfamiliar interaction (Lindlof & Taylor, 2002). If the interaction being reported belongs to the familiar and everyday, the writer's objective is to help the reader see it in a new way or to expose some aspect that is often overlooked. Whether the interaction is new or familiar, researchers using qualitative methods can increase our understanding about how humans construct and share meanings (Potter, 1996). Therefore, the researcher-now-writer must pay special attention to what is written and how it is written.

Generally, writing qualitative research reports can be difficult. Why? First, there are fewer conventions or traditions for writing the qualitative research report. So the researcher has more decisions to make about what to present as data and how to present data to support conclusions. Second, qualitative research by its very nature is more difficult to report, because data or evidence cannot be reduced into discrete units the way it is in quantitative reports. For example, researchers using qualitative methods do not rely on descriptive statistics to summarize and represent a group of data. Thus, a central evaluation criterion to use at each stage of the qualitative writing process is to ask yourself how your description and analysis is increasing the reader's understanding of how humans construct messages and share meaning.

REPRESENTING QUALITATIVE RESEARCH

Qualitative research reports vary considerably in their structure and writing style. For example, see Gunn's (2008) article, which is written as a poem that is followed by a section explaining why and how data from interviews were used. This chapter focuses on the more traditional manner of presenting qualitative research. Admittedly, scholars using qualitative methods (Tracy, Scott, & Richard, 2008) have struggled with, and sometimes challenged, this traditional and dominant format of scholarly presentation associated with quantitative research. Ellingson (2009) argues that she felt "stuck" as she chose between qualitative writing styles that "privileged story over theory and evocative details over patterns on the other" (p. xi). Taking a more eclectic approach, Ellingson introduces **crystallization,** which

> combines multiple forms of analysis and multiple genres of representation into a coherent text or series of related texts, building a rich and openly partial account of a phenomenon that problematizes its own construction, highlights researchers' vulnerabilities and positionality, makes claims about socially constructed meanings, and reveals the indeterminacy of knowledge claims even as it makes them. (p. 4)

More simply said, crystallization is the combination of forms of analysis, and presentation and representation of qualitative data in written research reports.

Despite this move to greater flexibility in reporting qualitative research, most studies are still presented in a form more like the traditional reporting of social science. With that in mind, a research report should include an introduction, a summary of the literature that provided a foundation for the study, a description of data collection and analytic techniques, and a report of the interpretation and analyses. In addition to these sections, many qualitative reports include sections on implications of the findings and research questions that remain to be explored or research questions that develop as a result of the study. Each of these is explored in turn.

Beginning the Research Report

Most qualitative studies begin with an introductory premise that serves as a frame for the descriptions and analyses that follow. One way to begin is to explain why a particular setting is important or interesting. For example, examine how Schultz, Hoffman, Fredman, and Bainbridge (2012, pp. 44–45) use the introduction to create relevance for their study of work-life balance by grounding their research in prior studies:

> Over the past decade, scholars have surveyed the literature and posed problematics concerning the relationship between work and life (Cowan & Hoffman, 2007; Golden, Kirby, & Jorgenson, 2006; Kirby, Golden, Medved, Jorgensen, & Buzzanell, 2003). They have also explored how balance is defined and negotiated by individuals and organizations (Hoffman & Cowan, 2008; Kirby & Krone, 2002; Medved, 2004).

This is the traditional approach to an introduction. In this case, you would use the opening paragraphs to demonstrate your familiarity with similar studies or to position your study in opposition to what has been previously studied.

Or, the manuscript can begin more dramatically with an excerpt from fieldnotes or a quote from a participant. For example, Dennis and Wood (2012) set the scene and create interest for the reader with this opening paragraph:

> Twenty-two-year-old Rhea fondly recalls that, starting at age eight or nine, she and her mom had open, frank conversations about sex. Rhea says being able to talk so comfortably about sex with her mother was a "bonding experience between a mother and her daughter, and I think that something that's missed a lot, especially in the Black culture." (p. 204)

By starting with this compelling excerpt from their interviews, Dennis and Wood foreshadow the emotional interaction of talking about sex.

Many introductory techniques will work. The one that works best will depend upon the subject matter and the audience. Regardless of how you begin, your goal is to draw the reader into your experiences of being in and with the participants in the communication environment you studied. One piece of writing advice that many researchers share is that to begin writing you must know the story you want to tell. This is why the introduction is so important: It frames the rest of the manuscript. In fact, it is likely that you will write the introductory paragraphs several times, perhaps even revising them after the rest of the manuscript is complete.

The Literature Review

After the introduction, qualitative research reports generally transition into the literature review. Ethnographies are one type of qualitative research report that most often break with this tradition. If you wrote a research proposal, then you should return to that document and revise it now that the data are collected and analyzed. Why not just use the literature review from the proposal? While it is a good reference point and starting place, your experience in the field collecting data has given your research question life. Look back at Dennis and Wood's (2012) opening paragraph. Could that paragraph have been written before the researchers collected and analyzed data? No. Does that paragraph help you understand the topic of the research article? Yes. Not all qualitative research needs this type of alternative beginning, but you should not dismiss the possibility.

Regardless of how the literature review begins, Tracy (2013) recommends that literature reviews for qualitative research reports should include a rationale (an argument for the study); a review of the literature, concepts, and theories; and the research problem or research question. Ellingson (2009) suggests that literature reviews for qualitative research reports be short. Why? Reporting qualitative data generally takes a great deal of space. The focus should be on your new findings.

Although qualitative research is generally inductive, presenting theory in the literature review can be beneficial. Reviewing theory can create a focus, as doing so will alert you to language or terminology that can be used in the data analysis or interpretation; and it can reveal your position in extending or challenging theory

(Anfara & Mertz, 2006). It is precisely because of the inductive and subjective qualities of qualitative research that the literature review is different. Lindlof and Taylor (2011) recommend using a mix of conceptual discussions and empirical studies to situate the context of the study as well as situate the study in the existing literature.

WRITING ABOUT THE METHOD

The second section of a qualitative research report is the method section. Sometimes it is called *research procedures*, or *design of the study*.

Someone reading a qualitative research study should know, at a minimum, (1) when the fieldwork was conducted, (2) the extent or length of your involvement in the interaction environment, (3) information about the participants and the communication context and scene, (4) the steps and methods for analyzing the data, and (5) to what extent the data were triangulated, or cross-checked (Kvale, 1996; Wolcott, 2001). Information about research methods and procedures should always be included in the written research report. As Ellingson (2009) describes, "be absolutely clear about what you did (and did not) do in producing your manuscript" (p. 119).

For example, Dougherty, Baiocchi-Wagner, and McGuire (2011) start their method section with one paragraph describing their theoretical framework for the inductive design of their data analysis.

In the following two paragraphs, the research team describes the participants by providing information about the number of nurses who participated in the study, and where they lived, as well as other demographic information. Next, the research team describes nurses' experience with sexual harassment or inappropriate sexual conduct from patients. The next paragraph describes the procedures the research team used, including IRB approval. They detail how the interview guide was developed and how and where the interviews were conducted.

Finally, Dougherty et al. describe their analytical method in a subsection labeled *data analysis*. What follows is slightly more than half of their

description of what was presented in the journal article:

> Consistent with the interpretive paradigm, an emergent thematic analysis was conducted. It is essential that findings emerge inductively from the data instead of deductively being imposed by the theory (Putnam, 1983). The following process was utilized. We began the analysis with a very general sense of theory. Specifically, during the interviews and transcription processes we came to believe that stereotypes were an important part of the coping mechanism for sexual harassment. During the analysis we were sensitized to intergroup theories, but maintained a careful openness to findings that could build and/or contradict these theories. The second author used the following coding processes: After transcription, the data were read and large chunks of text suggesting categories were identified. Then, transcripts were read again. In this process the emerging categories were solidified, and expanded. Some categories were dropped and others were combined. Categories were developed using a highlighter, underlining, and margin notes. Throughout this process, memoing on a separate pad of paper helped shape the interpretive process. Specifically, it was noted that many of the emergent categories involved stereotyping. This finding confirmed the earlier impression formed during the interview and transcription processes. Upon deeper examination, it became clear that two forms of stereotypes were being utilized: identifying stereotypes used by others, and stereotyping others. During this process, a few of the original categories were integrated, resulting in a final set of emerging categories and subthemes.

Notice the full description of what the data are and how the data were collected. This description is transparent, as the researchers walk readers through what they did and why.

Most of the time, information about the context of the communication you are reporting on is presented in the method section. Do not minimize this aspect of your report. Brann (2007) sets the context for her study by describing who she approached and how she gained access to a department of a hospital. She describes who she observed and how often. She describes the number of employees and their job responsibilities. She goes into detail about the demographic characteristics of the employees. In one paragraph the reader knows where the data were collected and who data were collected from.

In the next paragraph, Brann (2007) provides details about what data were collected and how, her researcher role in the data collection, and the number of hours of observations and how many fieldnotes and memos were created during the data collection process. She also explains that two participants could not be formally interviewed due to scheduling conflicts, but that she did have informal conversations with them. In the third paragraph, Brann describes in detail how the data were analyzed. With the information presented in three paragraphs (or 467 words), the reader can make an assessment of the credibility of her interpretations and claims about the data. Giving this detailed information is important because it helps readers evaluate the methodological rigor of your study (Ellingson, 2009).

Revealing the Identity of Participants

In writing about participants, the researcher must keep his or her agreement about confidentiality and anonymity with participants. If participants' privacy is to be maintained, you must develop fictitious names to refer to participants. There are several ways to do this. One method is to develop a set of substitute names that maintain the sex and ethnicity of participants. For example, Janice would be an appropriate substitute for Joann. But Joan or Joanne would be too similar to use. Changing Joann to Juanita or Juana would not be appropriate because it invokes a change in ethnicity. Another method is to refer to participants as Physician 1, Physician 2, and so on. Your readers will probably appreciate the first approach because it personalizes the description and makes the report more readable.

In some cases, you must go beyond simply changing the name. If a description of a participant is so unique as to allow the person to be identified, you should also change some of the participant's nonessential characteristics. In no case should

you camouflage an identity so that it is misleading. You would not want readers to accept the actions of a female as those of a male. Nor would you want readers to believe a participant was a child when he or she was an adult. Researchers report that these name and identity changes have been made either by stating so in the method or data analysis section or by adding an endnote to the report. For example, Maeda and Hecht (2012) report, "All names of the women presented here are pseudonyms and some personal information is modified to protect their confidentiality" (p. 53).

Recall the earlier recommendation that you are encouraged to make the detailed notes about data collection and data analysis steps. If you have made notes, the method section can be drafted early on in the process and later blended into the research report.

PRESENTING THE DATA

In qualitative research, data are textual. Whether the researcher recorded the interaction or observed the interaction firsthand, the observations end up in a written or textual form. In some cases, authors include visual elements as well (for example, drawings by participants; see Braithwate, Toller, Daas, Durham, & Jones, 2008). Because of the volume of data qualitative methods can produce, authors need to judiciously edit the data to a manageable amount (Wolcott, 1990). This is often a difficult process: The researcher has painstakingly collected the data and is reluctant to not include all the written data in the final research report. Besides reducing the amount of data to be presented, the researcher must also select data that provide a meaningful frame for interpretation. In other words, decisions must be made about what to tell and how to tell it (Van Maanen, 1988). Thus, Wolcott (1990) suggests that in planning to write the qualitative research report, you determine "the basic story you are going to tell, who is to do the telling, and what representational style you will follow for joining observer and observed" (p. 18). To help your readers understand your points, you will need to take extra care in presenting your analytical process in a clear way to your readers.

Authorial Voice

In qualitative research reports, the writer must make a decision about **authorial voice**—or who will tell the story. This question is critical in qualitative research (Wolcott, 2001). Because qualitative research is conducted with participants in the field, many scholars allow participants to tell the story in their voice. Interweaving the participants' voices with that of the writer (in the role of narrator) can be a successful approach.

Voice is different from writing style. Lindlof and Taylor (2011) comment that voice emerges out of the practical choices researchers make: (a) choices about relationships they want to construct with participants, (b) choices about the relationships they have developed with participants; and (c) how language is used to describe persons, events, and objects. Because these are individual choices for each qualitative research design, a researcher could choose an intimate voice or a highly analytical one.

For example, students in Communication Studies 298 at California State University, Sacramento, describe their experiences in an entertainment center that included a brew pub, a sports bar, a dance bar, a piano bar, a country-western bar, a comedy club, a game arcade, and two restaurants. The manuscript, team-written, flows effortlessly between their impressions and their interaction with the center's employees and customers. An excerpt demonstrates:

The dance bar is quiet now, the sweaty bodies gone. Steely energy lingers, pressing in on me from all sides. The man is here, leaning against the bar. He is wearing a name tag on his shirt that reads "Manager, Dance."

"It's the edge in the room," he whispers, moving closer. "You can feel it. Have you ever been outside just before a thunderstorm, and it's in the air?"

He snaps his fingers and the music, a primal heartbeat begins. It pulses around and through my body. It pierces my ears and throat. "These short, sharp pulses spread across the spectrum of sound our ears pick up," the man explains proudly, "overloading our hearing, inducing trance." He offers a beguiling smile. "Why don't you dance?" (Communication Studies 298, 1997, p. 261)

This approach interweaves multiple voices, acknowledging the roles of researchers and participants.

Descriptive accounts are generally written in the first person, although third-person language can be used. Be cautious, however. The impersonality of the third-person approach can make it appear that you are representing an objective truth (Wolcott, 2001)—an idea opposed in qualitative research.

Another common technique is to alternate between third person for the analysis and first person for the presentation of the data. Reporting on

---

AN ETHICAL ISSUE

Creating Something from Nothing

In writing qualitative research reports, researchers cannot be tempted to create quoted material from notes that are not in the direct words of participants. For example, your fieldnotes indicate, "Jerry was upset and seemed angry at Lisa's interpretation of their disagreement." That is how you, the researcher, described the interaction you observed. These are your words, not the words of Jerry, the participant. It would be unethical to turn those fieldnotes into the following description and quote in the written research report: "Jerry seemed upset at Lisa. 'I can't believe that's how you interpreted our disagreement.'" The rule here: Use only what you have captured as the direct words of participants as quoted material. Besides the prohibition against creating something from nothing, what other ethical concerns should researchers be aware of when they use quotes from research participants?

DESIGN CHECK

Who Did What? How? When?

When you read a qualitative research report, consider asking these analytical questions: Who did the observations? How did their background, training, expectations, or attitudes affect their collection and interpretation of the data? Was the context and manner in which the observations were made suitable and acceptable to you? Did the researcher use other data collection methods to account for or control for observer distortion? Are the interpretations acceptable to you? Are other interpretations of the data possible?

how and why students watch reality televisions shows, (Lundy, Ruth, & Park, 2008) demonstrates this technique:

> Escapism emerged from the data citing RT [reality television] as an escape from reality for participants. Participants felt that RT offered the viewer a "glimpse" into another world, for which a moment could take the viewer away from their own reality. One participant suggested,
>
>> I think because it is an escape from the reality of like the war and a lot of economic problems and like political problems. I mean you have the option of watching reality television, which although it can be extreme, it is amusing, as opposed to watching the news about Martha Stewart, Michael Jackson, Kobe Bryant or even the war. Basically something that is depressing as opposed to something, while ridiculous, is entertaining and an escape from some of the negative reality that people deal with day in and day out. (pp. 213–214)

To make their arguments, Lundy, Ruth, and Park (2008) alternate between analysis, written in the third person, and participants' presentation of data. This structure allows the voice of participants to be heard. Additionally, it integrates the data or evidence with the researchers' assessment of the data in a larger framework. "Skillfully weaving of the author's and participants' voices highlights the similarities and differences of their experiences and perspectives." Ellingson continues, "longer quotes do not always highlight participants' experiences better than shorter ones; selection of telling phrases

and revealing comments requires an artisan's touch" (p. 153).

Decisions about authorial voice are not trivial, as they relay information about the closeness of the researchers to the participants' experiences (Lindlof & Taylor, 2011). You may need to try writing a short section of the research report in different ways to find the authorial voice that makes the most sense for the research method used, the research context studied, and the participants represented.

FINDINGS AND INTERPRETATION

Rather than report results, researchers using qualitative methods often report *findings*. The volume of data in qualitative research makes it impossible for the researcher to present all the research data. Generally, the findings are integrated with interpretation of the findings. This is likely to be the largest section of a qualitative research report.

In this section, authors need to consider three issues: finding the appropriate balance between description and analysis, the organizing scheme for presenting the material, and decisions about how to use participants' quoted material. Each is addressed in the sections that follow.

Balancing Description and Analysis

If you have trouble starting the qualitative research report, describe the interaction by answering the question, "What happened?" Because analysis is based on description, the descriptive account of who, what, when, and where may be the most important contribution made in the

TRY THIS!   **Describe, Then Analyze**

Find a place where you can take notes freely and observe the interaction of two to four people. You might want to takes notes on the nonverbal behavior of the mother and her two children sitting across the aisle from you on the bus. You could take a seat in the entryway of the library and watch students interact with members of the library staff as they ask for information or check out books. For at least 15 minutes, take notes describing the interaction environment, the interactants, and the interaction. When you are through, review your notes to distinguish between notes that describe and notes that analyze. Descriptive notes answer "What?" "Who?" "When?" and "Where?" Analytical notes answer "Why?" and "How?" Try writing first a description of what you observed and then an analysis of those interactions. What could you do differently in how you took notes to improve both the description and the analysis?

research report. To begin descriptively, the writer takes on the role of the storyteller. In this role, the writer invites readers to see what he or she has observed or heard. A natural place to start is to begin with the details of the settings and events. These should be revealed in a fairly straightforward and journalistic manner.

What is enough detail? Being familiar with the research setting may cause you to omit important details readers unfamiliar with the setting will need to make sense of the description. Ask people unfamiliar with your research setting to read the description. If they need to ask questions after reading it, pay close attention to the types of questions they ask. These will guide you in adding detail that makes sense to readers.

Another way to gauge the adequacy of your descriptive passages is to shift between writing description and analytic passages. If the analysis or interpretation does not make sense without additional descriptive detail, then you know more description is needed. On the other hand, descriptive detail not referenced by the analysis is extraneous and can be edited—or else it needs to be explained.

It can be difficult to separate descriptive from analytical writing, especially when writing a qualitative manuscript. One way to make this distinction is to change the authorial voice mentioned earlier in this chapter. For example, Taylor (1996) first presents three episodes from a 3-month study of the Bradbury Science Museum located at Los

Alamos National Laboratory, a nuclear weapons facility. Each episode is his description of different voices and the accompanying political interests found in three different interaction environments in and around the museum. To signal that the descriptive part of the manuscript is finished, Taylor identifies the subsequent section as "Reflection." Here, he reemphasizes his role as a coparticipant in the production of the episodes. Then he moves the reader into his analyses of the episodes as well as an analysis of his methods by identifying specific themes revealed in his study.

Strategies for Writing the Findings and Analyses

Researchers collect a great deal of qualitative data. Finding the thread of the story you want to present is an important first step. Next, as you tell the story of your research, it can be helpful to find an organizing scheme so your readers can see the same patterns and themes that you saw so clearly.

A common way to structure this section is to use the study's research questions as a structure for presenting the data. But since there is flexibility in how qualitative research, and its findings, are presented, one of the following alternative methods of presentation may be a more compelling presentation.

Tracy (2013) describes four writing strategies, or styles, that are frequently used in communication journal articles; each can effectively present qualitative research findings. The first is a **thematic** or **topical focus.** Generally, the researcher uses the themes found in the data as a guiding structure for writing this section. Oliviera (2013) uses this writing strategy in her presentation of an interview study that explored the role of cultural influences in organizational crises. Using a grounded theory approach, the researcher identified four core categories. Each core category was presented in the order that they were discovered in the analysis of the interviews. In this writing style, the four categories (diversity and its various elements; cultural diversity and crisis strategies; proper planning, channels, and tactics; and addressing diversity) were used as subheadings. In the discussion and implication section of the report, the author draws connections among the four categories to deepen the analysis and interpretation.

A second writing style is one that is **chronological.** This is a particularly effective writing style if the research reports about the development of a process. By highlighting the timeline and timeframe of events, readers may find it easier to follow along. Toyosaki (2011) uses a chronological writing style in his ethnographic study based on his experiences and those of participants as he executed an earlier research project about Japanese international students' culturally specific understandings of American culture and communication styles. In the ethnography, Toyosaki treats his life stages, and those of participants in his earlier study, in chronological order from being born and early cultural socialization through high school, and preparing for study in the United States. This writing style is effective as it allows the reader to follow the author's life and experiences and understand more completely the challenges he and his research participants faced as they interacted with new cultures and encountered cultural hierarchy.

The third writing style is the **puzzle explication** strategy. Puzzles or tensions about communication are often the focus of qualitative research. This writing style helps to encourage the curiosity of the reader. Typically the puzzle is presented first, then the researcher leads the reader to an explanation of what seemed puzzling before. If this approach is used, the section can be organized in two ways. The first presents the puzzles, or critical points, regardless of the order of events. This approach can be effective if you are observing a series of similar events or if your data were collected from interviews or focus groups.

A second way to organize patterns is to present a series of problems in order of importance (from major to minor, from minor to major). In this case, the research report is organized in three-part sets that identify a problem, describe the interaction attributed to the problem, and then analyze the interaction with respect to the problem. This type of organization works better if your observations come from many similar events or from many similar people rather than from one long stream of interaction of a confined set of participants, as might be the case in an ethnographic study.

To help you find a pattern that is compelling and revealing, write a few words about each major event or each major issue revealed in the data on a note card. This is a practical way to sort and organize your findings. Try arranging the note cards differently—first in sequential order, and then in order of importance. As you read the layout of note cards, one of these organizing patterns should make more sense than the others, and that is the organizing scheme you should use to start writing your research report.

The fourth writing style is labeled **separated text.** In this case, the analysis and theoretical background are separated from the story or narrative, which is generally more descriptive. This is the style Johansson (2011) chose for presenting his qualitative study of men's construction of being a parent and father. The researcher presents four case studies, each following the same structure. First, a short descriptive case study is written to introduce the participants. Description of the participants and their relationship to fatherhood and quotes from the participants are interwoven in short blocks. The quotes of participants are used as evidence of the description written by the author. Then the author provides two or three paragraphs of interpretation of the short descriptive case. This writing style helps to make each case identifiable and unique. At the same time, the similar structure makes it easy to draw comparison across the four cases.

Letting Participants Speak

When you write a qualitative research report, you need to insert both long and short quotes from participants. The most traditional and neutral form would be a phrase such as: One participant said. . . . Using the word "said" is common. But it does not capture the nonverbal characteristics of participants' talk. Consider one of the verbs below in presenting quotations from participants.

- Commented
- Reported
- Argued
- Captured
- Stated the key challenge
- Stated the fundamental assumption
- Shared
- Observed

- Indicated
- Divulged
- Addressed
- Stated
- Suggested
- Noted
- Stressed

Regardless of the organizational pattern, there should be a rhythm to the presentation. That is, this section should be characterized by symmetry (Ellingson, 2009). Using the same form to present each theme or subsection of findings and interpretation will help the reader follow your claims and arguments.

When you've completed a draft of the findings and interpretation section, the following criteria, adapted from Lindlof and Taylor (2002), can be used to evaluate your writing:

- Is your manuscript written well? Does it engage the reader emotionally and intellectually? Does it evoke shared experiences or frames of reference?

- Does your manuscript effectively address multiple audiences?

- Are data in your manuscript credible and interesting?

- Did you reflect on your role in producing the interpretation of the data?

- Is your manuscript ethically produced and politically accountable?

- Did you balance the tension between coming to conclusions or resolutions and remaining open to other alternatives?

- Does your writing invite readers to actively participate in the interpretation?

- Does your writing alternate between the personal and the social, or the individual and the larger group?

- Does your manuscript contribute to our understanding of social life?

- Is your writing generalizable? Does the detail of a person, scene, or setting belong to a broader group or class?

Qualitative scholars generally agree on these criteria. However, the primary objectives of reporting qualitative data are to find your own voice and remain true to your data.

Using Participants' Quoted Material

Researchers strengthen their reporting and analysis of qualitative data by using the directly quoted interaction of participants. Several guidelines can help you in selecting and reporting this type of material (Kvale, 1996). First, provide a frame of reference or the interaction context for quoted material. Readers should not have questions about who said what, when, or where. Second, interpret all material quoted from participants. The researcher should clearly state what a quotation illuminates, illustrates, proves, or disproves. Quotes from participants, or descriptions from fieldnotes or analytical notes, are seldom presented without interpretation from the researcher.

Third, find an appropriate balance between use of quoted material and your descriptions and interpretations. One standard for evaluating this balance is that quoted material should not be more than half of the findings and interpretation.

Fourth, short quotations are better than long ones. If longer passages are necessary, consider breaking them up by interspersing them with your description and analysis. The fifth criterion is to use only the best quotations. In making choices about which of two similar quotations is better, ask which one is most extensive, illuminating, or well formulated. Finally, if participants' quoted material is edited in any way (for example, shortened), include a note about this fact. If symbols are used to note omissions, those should be included in a note as well.

DRAWING AND SUPPORTING CONCLUSIONS

A conclusion section generally ends the report of qualitative research. Some researchers portray the end of their research report as being decision oriented (Wolcott, 2001). In other words, what decisions can be made given the descriptions and analyses that have been presented? By its very nature, qualitative research is limited in its ability to draw generalizations. Writers should avoid the urge to draw conclusions larger than their findings. Hammersley (2008) recommends that the final conclusion of the report be inclusive of the claims, or findings, presented, but not be a simple restatement of those claims. In other words, it is the author's responsibility to integrate claims, or findings, into an integrated whole.

By all means, a qualitative research report should finish with closing paragraphs that review what has been attempted, what has been learned, and what new questions have been raised. A reader should be able to grasp an overall understanding of the data. This doesn't mean that contradictions do not exist. They often will. But the reader should understand what contradictions exist and why (Ellingson, 2009). Researchers often include summaries, recommendations, or implications—even a statement of personal reflections (Wolcott, 2001).

Alternatively, a more traditional closure can be developed. Summarizing and integrating the results of the research according to the research questions can be followed by limitations and suggestions for future research. However, it is important to end with a statement that reflects the specific research setting investigated in the study.

Revisiting Your Analysis

A qualitative research report will likely require many revisions. Why? Your analytical skills are constrained by your writing ability as you explore the assertions and research questions that guided your study.

After your report is written, use the following seven criteria to judge the adequacy of what you have written (Ellingson, 2009; McCracken, 1988). Revisiting your written analysis will help you sharpen your conclusions and extend the usefulness of your research. Reading your essay out loud will help improve the flow of writing, especially as you move back and forth between your claims in the third person and the first person account of participants.

The first step in revisiting your description and analysis of the data is to consider its accuracy and exactness, especially in the presentation of participants' data. It must be so complete that ambiguity does not exist. Second, your writing must be economical so that it forces the reader to make the minimum number of assumptions. Third, the analysis you expose through your writing must be consistent, or reliable. Moreover, the analysis must also be detailed enough to allow the reader to develop his or her conclusions.

The fourth criterion, being externally consistent, is tricky. Your descriptions and analyses should be consistent, or ring true, with what others have reported or with what is commonly known about a communication event. This does not mean that you ignore new or novel information or explanations. Rather, such novelty must be explained in relationship to more commonly held knowledge and assumptions. If you ignore what your reader would hold as true or expected, you risk the reader's not believing your description and analysis. Thus, you need to anticipate how others might develop alternative explanations or interpretations of your findings. If you

---

TRY THIS!   ## Submit Your Paper to a Communication Journal

You may conduct a qualitative research project for a research methods class, some other class, or as an independent study or thesis. Talk with your instructor and ask for his or her advice about further developing your research report for potential presentation at a conference or for publication.

Southern States Communication Association has an Ethnography Interest Group. The association holds its annual conference in April, with papers due in the prior September. As part of the conference, the association holds an Undergraduate Honors Conference; papers are due in December prior to the conference.

Western States Communication Association holds an Undergraduate Scholars' Research Conference during its annual conferences held in February. Papers are due in December prior to the conference.

National Communication Associations has a Student Section and an Ethnography Division. The association holds its annual conference in November, with papers due in the previous February.

The communication journals listed below exclusively feature qualitative research.

- *Kaleidoscope: A Graduate Journal of Qualitative Communication Research*
- *Qualitative Communication Research*
- *Qualitative Research Reports In Communication*

---

believe this will happen, you should address it by stating your explanations very clearly.

Fifth, you should scrutinize your writing for its unification and organization. Rather than presenting one conclusion after another, are your ideas organized in a framework that is, or becomes, apparent to the reader? Have you addressed relationships among the conclusions? Providing a clear and cohesive structure encourages your readers to accept your analyses.

The sixth criterion examines the power of your explanation. Does your written report explain as much of the data as possible? Your explanation should be complete and comprehensive. Alternatively, it should not compromise any of the data you presented. Finally, your description and analysis should be both heuristic and fertile. Your explanations and conclusions should suggest new opportunities and insights. At the same time, they should give readers a new way to explain this interaction phenomenon.

Evaluating your written description and analysis using these criteria is one way to judge the credibility and utility of your work. Asking someone whose opinion you trust to read your written work

is also advisable. The more subjective nature of qualitative research demands that you pay careful attention to both the level of detail in your descriptions and the quality of explanations.

FINISHING THE QUALITATIVE RESEARCH REPORT

Generally, as the written research report begins to look like a complete report, authors pay attention to three other details: the title, the abstract, and the references.

Title

Titles are important to the final written research report because they are the readers' introduction to what you have to say about a particular communication phenomenon. Thus, the title should reflect the content of your essay and not misguide readers into developing false expectations.

Some researchers draft a working title (Creswell, 1994) early in the writing process to help them develop the direction of the manuscript. Doing so helps you position the central ideas at an early stage of writing. It is unrealistic to think, however, that the working title will not change. It almost always does as your description and analysis become clearer throughout the writing and revising process.

Some title-writing advice follows (Creswell, 1994; Wilkinson, 1991):

1. Be brief.
2. Avoid wasting words.
3. Eliminate unnecessary words (for example, "A Qualitative Study of . . .").
4. Avoid long titles (more than 12 words).
5. Decrease rather than increase the number of articles and prepositions.
6. Include the focus of the study.

With that advice in mind, remember that titles remain a very individual choice. Because the title is the first thing your reader sees, it sets up expectations and provides an entry into your writing.

If you are submitting your written report to a conference or to be reviewed for publication, the title plays another important role. Your work will be indexed and referenced primarily by its title. So if you want someone to find your work on men's anger groups, then the phrase "men's anger groups" should be in the title. Alternatively, you could use the phrase "counseling groups." But if your title uses only the keywords "empathy" and "understanding," it is likely that others will miss your work on men's anger groups. Although they are short and often the last element to be determined, the importance of titles should not be downplayed.

Abstract   An abstract for a qualitative report has three objectives (Bouma & Atkinson, 1995). First, the abstract states the aim or overall objective of the research. Second, the abstract gives a brief explanation of the research method. Finally, the abstract briefly summarizes the findings of the study. But the elements are not necessarily in any specific order. Abstracts vary considerably in length; but generally they range from 75 to 250 words.

Two different examples illustrate how these elements can be presented in qualitative research abstracts.

In this critical qualitative examination of the "Lost Boys of Sudan" refugee resettlement, I explicate the ways that the "Lost Boys" negotiate discursive positioning by the U.S. state and nation in forging a sense of identity and belonging in resettlement. Specifically, I examine the ways that the men are recognized as subjects through the "Lost Boys" label and interpellated into U.S. belonging through racist discourses. Finally, I work to show how the particulars of exile and resettlement for the "Lost Boys" factor into the ways identity is communicated and belonging is negotiated for this particular community. (McKinnon, 2008, p. 397)

This project uses a narrative view of identity to interrogate how individuals construct notions of ability and disability within their families. Participants include children with disabilities from diverse ethnic backgrounds, their parents, siblings, and extended family members. Interactions within four families are explored as well as interactions family members have with people outside their families. Interview and observational data demonstrate ways that participants construct identities that highlight intersections of ability/disability and individuality/relationships. Results indicate that families primarily construct identities of "normal" through their interactions and routines as they negotiate contradictions inherent in their everyday lives. Theoretic implications of narrative dimensions of constructions and contradictions are offered. Finally, practical applications for professionals and families of children with disabilities are suggested with future directions for research and practice. (Canary, 2008, p. 437)

Notice that the author starts by stating the method and gives some information about the communication context of the study. Both abstracts provide the primary findings of the study.

Using the APA Style Manual

Generally, scholars who conduct communication research from the social science perspective use the *Publication Manual of the American Psychological Association* (6th edition, 2010). This is the reference and citation style preferred by most communication journals that publish quantitative and qualitative research; it was used in preparing the references and citations for this text.

Not only does the manual provide guidance in how to prepare your in-text citations and end-of-manuscript references, but it also provides invaluable advice for writing research reports. Its many sections on punctuation, spelling, abbreviations, capitalization, headings, and so on are also extremely useful to writers of qualitative research reports.

For class projects, you should always check with your instructor to determine which style manual he or she prefers. Learning a style requires discipline. At the same time, learning to use a standardized writing style helps you communicate your research ideas more clearly.

Probably the part of the style manual you will find most helpful is the information for using in-text citations and information for creating the reference list at the end of your written report. Your library and writing center will have a copy of the APA style manual.

SUMMARY

1. Researchers have flexibility, and therefore can make decisions about writing a qualitative research report.

2. One way to check on your writing process is to ask how the description or analysis is increasing the reader's understanding.

3. At a minimum, qualitative research reports should include an introduction; a summary of the literature; a description of data collection and analysis; and a report of the findings, interpretation, and analysis.

4. Qualitative research projects create too much rather than not enough data.

5. The researcher must decide whether he or she or the participants will have the responsibilities of authorial voice.

6. A good way to begin a qualitative research report is to explain why the setting was important or interesting.

7. In writing about data collection, the reader should know when the fieldwork was conducted, how long and in what way the researcher was involved with participants, descriptive information about the participants and their communication environment, steps taken in data collection and analysis, and if data collection was triangulated.

8. If the researcher has agreed to maintain the anonymity of participants, a system for referencing participants will need to be created.

9. Description and analysis must be balanced in a qualitative research report.

10. An effectively written qualitative research report has an organizing framework to guide the reader through description and analysis.

11. Participants' quotes are the data of qualitative research project; some directly quoted conversation of participants must be presented in the research report.

KEY TERMS

authorial voice	separated text
chronological	thematic
crystallization	topical
puzzle explication	

See the website www.mhhe.com/keyton4 that accompanies this text. For each chapter, the site contains a:

- chapter outline
- chapter checklist
- chapter summary
- short multiple-choice quiz
- PowerPoint presentation created by Dr. Keyton

For a list of internet resources, visit http://www.joannkeyton.com/Communication ResearchMethods.htm.

GLOSSARY

active member   In qualitative research, a type of committed membership in which the researcher becomes a member of the group being observed, but does not commit to the goals or values of the group.

alpha level   The significance or probability level set by the researcher for each statistical test prior to conducting the study; in communication research, most often set at .05; represented by the symbol *p*.

analysis   In qualitative research, the process of identifying and labeling raw data (text) to find patterns, themes, concepts, and propositions.

analysis of variance   Statistical test compares the influence of two or more groups of one or more nominal independent variables on a continuous level dependent variable; represented by the symbol *F*; also referred to as *ANOVA*.

analytical memo   Used in qualitative research to capture first impressions and reflections about the setting, people, and interactions; informal writing to distinguish the analysis from the data.

anonymity   Protection of names and other pieces of information that can identify participants; researchers do not ask participants to reveal information that would aid the researcher in identifying participants' individual data.

ANOVA   Statistical test that compares the influence of two or more groups of one or more nominal independent variables on a continuous level dependent variable; represented by the symbol *F*; also referred to as *analysis of variance.*

antecedent variable   Variable manipulated by the researcher; presumably, this manipulation, or variation, is the cause of change in other variables; also referred to as *independent variable, experimental variable, treatment variable,* and *causal variable.*

attrition   Threat to the internal validity of research when participants can no longer be observed or used for data collection because they have dropped out of the research project; also known as *mortality.*

authorial voice   The person(s), researcher or the participants, who tell the story in a qualitative research report.

autoethnography   A type of ethnography in which the researcher is also a participant; the research report is highly personal and emotional.

average   See *mean.*

axial coding   Used in coding qualitative data after open coding, this coding pass links categories together in a meaningful way.

behavior coding   Type of questionnaire pretesting for face-to-face surveys; a third person monitors the interaction between the interviewer and respondent to look for problems in the questionnaire or its administration.

beneficence   Protection of the well-being of participants; the researcher must meet the obligation to maximize possible benefits while minimizing possible harms.

beta coefficients   Unit of standardized scores in regression; indicates the difference in a dependent variable associated with an independent variable; also known as *beta weights.*

beta weights   Unit of standardized scores in regression; indicates the difference in a dependent variable associated with an independent variable; also known as *beta coefficients.*

between-groups variance   Variation of scores between categories or groupings of independent variable sufficient to distinguish themselves from one another.

between-subjects design   Design feature of ANOVA in which each participant is measured at only one level, group, or category, or under only one condition; designed to examine differences across individuals in the study.

biased   Favoring one attribute or characteristic more than another.

categorical data   Form of discrete data; describes the presence or absence of some characteristic or attribute; also known as *nominal data.*

categorizing reliability   Degree to which multiple coders make similar distinctions among the data to be coded in assigning data to categories; used in content analysis.

category   In qualitative research, a label for a set of excerpts, examples, or themes that are similar; may be drawn from the literature or emerge from the data.

causal variable Variable manipulated by the researcher; presumably, this manipulation, or variation, is the cause of change in other variables; also referred to as *antecedent variable, experimental variable, treatment variable,* and *independent variable.*

census Situation where every element of a population is included in a research project.

central tendency Term applied to any of several measures that summarize a distribution of scores; mean, median, and mode are common measures of central tendency; this one number acts as a summary of all the scores on one variable.

chi-square Represented by the symbol χ^2; statistical test used to determine if differences among nominal, or categorical, level data are statistically significant; examines the observed frequencies in comparison to the expected frequencies to determine if the categorical differences that occurred are the same as would occur by chance.

chronological Writing style that highlights the timeline and timeframe of events.

classical experiment Research design in which participants are randomly selected and the researcher controls the treatment or the manipulation of the independent variable by randomly assigning participants to treatment or control groups.

closed question Question form in which respondents are asked a question (or given a statement) and then given a set of responses to select from.

cluster sampling Form of random, or probability, sampling used when researchers do not have access to a complete list of population members; a two-stage or multistage process; in the first stage, groups, or clusters, of the population are selected; then simple random sampling is used in each cluster to select the research sample.

coefficient of determination The percentage of variance two variables have in common; represented by the symbol r^2; found by simply squaring the r value.

cognitive pretesting Type of questionnaire pretesting in which researcher asks questions about the stimulus question to eliminate alternative meanings.

Cohen's kappa Measure of interrater reliability for categorical data; ranges from perfect agreement (1.00) to agreement that is no better than would be expected by chance (0).

commitment acts In qualitative research, helping participants with routine tasks and activities to acquaint one's self with the research setting and to gain information.

complete member In qualitative research, a type of committed membership in which the researcher makes observations in settings in which he or she is already are a member, or can become a member

complete observer Form of participant observation; the researcher enacts only the observer role; the researcher is hidden completely from the interactants.

complete participant Form of participant observation; researcher is a fully functioning member of the scene; the research role is disguised through the role as participant.

concept Abstract idea or way of thinking about something that helps us distinguish it from other elements; can be an object, event, relationship, or process.

concept map A diagram of the research project used as a conceptual tool to assist in thinking through a qualitative project; used to find relationships among concepts and to uncover holes or contradictions.

conceptual scheme A set of concepts connected to form an integrated whole that specifies and clarifies the relationships among them; individually, each concept describes a unique process; as a group, the concepts still retain common characteristics.

concurrent validity Method for establishing criterion-related validity of a new measurement; demonstrates that the new measuring instrument and the established measuring instrument— both measuring the same or similar things— are related.

confederate Someone who pretends to also be participating in the research project but is really helping the researcher; a deceptive practice because research participants do not know that an individual is playing the confederate role; used when the researcher needs to create a certain type of interaction context or to provide a certain type of interaction to which an unknowing research participant responds.

confidence interval The range of responses generalized from the sample to the population based on the confidence level of a statistical test.

confidence level Degree of accuracy in predicting the result for a population from the result found by testing the sample.

confidentiality Protection of research participant; any information the participant provides is controlled in such a way that others do not have access to it.

constant-comparative method   An approach for coding qualitative data; the coding and categorizing process continues to change as the researcher analyzes the data and as additional data are collected.

construct   Theoretical definition of a concept; not directly observable.

construct validity   Extent to which measuring device measures the core concept that was intended to be measured and not something else; researchers use a different, but theoretically related, measure of the same or a similar phenomenon to establish construct validity.

content analysis   Quantitative research method that integrates both data collection method and analytical technique to measure the occurrence of some identifiable element in a complete text or set of messages.

content validity   Degree to which the measurement items are representative of all the potential items available for measuring the construct of interest.

contingency analysis   Form of chi-square in which frequency distributions are created simultaneously on two nominal variables; cases are classified on two variables in relationship to each other; also referred to as *two-way chi-square* or *two-dimensional chi-square*.

contingency table   Table in which two nominal variables are arranged; rows represent one nominal variable, and columns represent a second nominal variable; used to display data for contingency analyses.

contingent accuracy   Way to interpret meaning in qualitative research; relies on tangible artifacts, which are believed to be accurate representations of the phenomenon; most objective of the three interpretive positions.

continuous level data   Data for which values can differ in degree, amount, or frequency and for which these differences can be ordered on a continuum; also referred to as *quantitative data*.

control group   Group in which assigned participants receive no treatment or stimuli or receive the standard form of the treatment.

convenience sampling   Sampling technique not based on random selection or probability; the researcher simply selects those who are convenient as respondents; no guarantee that all eligible units have an equal chance of being included in the sample; also referred to as *opportunity sampling*.

conventional pretesting   Type of questionnaire pretest in which a researcher selects several individuals who are like persons in the population; the survey is completed just as it will be done in the study.

correlation   Statistical test that examines the linear relationship between two continuous level variables; represented by the symbol r; also known as *Pearson product-moment correlation coefficient*.

correlation matrix   Display of variables in a table; makes it possible to see how every variable is correlated with every other variable.

correlational design   See *descriptive design*.

credibility   The criterion used in qualitative research to assess the effectiveness and accuracy of the research design and findings drawn from its data.

criterion-related validity   Determination of whether one measurement can be linked to some other external measurement; achieved through two procedures—predictive validity and concurrent validity.

criterion variable   Variable that is influenced or changed by the predictor variable.

critical incidents   Positive or negative events remembered by participants.

Cronbach's alpha   Measure of internal reliability for a series of items across all respondents; also referred to as *internal reliability* or *internal consistency*; also known as *coefficient alpha*.

cross-sectional design   See *descriptive design*.

crystallization   In writing qualitative research, combines forms of analysis and representation of qualitative data.

curvilinear   Type of relationship between two variables represented by a U-shaped curve (either concave or convex).

data   Quantitative or qualitative information about any communication phenomenon.

dataset   Entirety of the data from each participant or about each element compiled by variables or by cases; also referred to as a *database*.

data triangulation   Method of triangulation in which a variety of data sources are used in one study.

debriefing   Interaction between researcher and participants immediately following the research activity; researcher explains the purpose of the study and what he or she hopes to find; any information that was withheld from participants before the research activity is shared at this time.

deception   Situation where researcher purposely misleads participants; should be used only if there is no other way to collect the data and the deception does not harm participants.

deductive   Reasoning process in which researcher begins with a theory and then gathers evidence, or data, to assess whether the theory is correct;

generally used with quantitative research methods.

degrees of freedom   Number of values that vary within a statistical test; represented by the symbol *df*; accounts for variation due to error.

dependent variable   Variable that is influenced or changed by the independent variable.

descriptive design   Type of research design in which a researcher lacks direct control over variation in the independent variables and temporal order of variables; participants are not randomly assigned to conditions; also called *correlational, cross-sectional,* or *non-experimental design.*

descriptive statistics   Numbers that summarize essential and basic information about the dataset as a whole.

directional hypothesis   A precise statement indicating the nature and direction of the relationship or difference between the variables.

discourse   Set of naturally occurring messages that serve as data in qualitative methodologies.

discussion section   Section of the written research report in which the authors provide an interpretation of the results.

ecological validity   Form of external validity; the degree to which participants are like those the researcher is really interested in and the degree to which the research setting is natural.

emic   View that interprets data from the participant's point of view in the context in which the data are collected.

empirical   Refers to observations or experiences; empirical methodologies in communication are based on or are derived from experiences with observable phenomena.

endogenous variable   In structural equation modeling, a variable is hypothesized to be caused by another variable.

equivalent   Characteristic of nominal or categorical response set; responses must be equal to one another or of the same type.

eta squared   The amount of variance in the dependent variable that can be accounted for by the independent variable; also represented by the symbol η^2.

ethnography   Detailed study and representation of people and their interaction; the holistic description of interactants in their cultural or subcultural group.

ethnography of communication   A theoretically driven method of ethnography; researchers focus on language or speech communities; the research report is detailed analyses of how

symbolic practices are expressed in a particular social structure.

etic   View in which the participant's talk or behavior is analyzed more conceptually without specific regard to context.

exclusion criterion   A standard or guideline that, if met, excludes participants from being selected as part of a nonprobability sample.

exhaustive   Characteristic of nominal, or categorical, response set; responses must represent the entirety of the variety of characteristics of the people or element being measured.

exogenous variable   In structural equation modeling, a variable that is not caused by another variable in the model.

expected frequency   The number of times a category was expected to appear in a test of chi-square.

experiment   Research design used to determine causation; the recording of observations made by defined procedures and in defined conditions; researcher must have control over manipulation of the independent variables and random assignment of participants to conditions.

experimental research   Type of research most often conducted in the laboratory or other simulated environments controlled by researchers.

experimental variable   Variable manipulated by the researcher; presumably, this manipulation, or variation, is the cause of change in other variables; also referred to as *antecedent variable, independent variable, treatment variable,* and *causal variable.*

expert panels   Form of questionnaire pretesting in which experts in research methodology or in the survey's content read through the questionnaire together and discuss potential problems with the survey.

external validity   Degree to which the findings of a research project can be extended to participants and settings beyond those studied.

face validity   Extent to which the items reference the construct intended to be measured; exists if the measurement looks and feels as if it will capture the intended construct.

factorial design   Type of ANOVA design based on two or more categorical independent variables, each with at least two levels; allows the researcher to test for the effects of each independent variable and the interaction effect on the continuous level dependent variable.

field experiment   Form of a quasi-experimental design; like an experiment in that researcher controls the manipulation of independent variables and random assignment of participants; the research environment is realistic and natural, so researcher lacks the degree of control found in classical experiments.

field interviewing   Qualitative research method; a semidirected form of discourse or conversation with the goal of uncovering the participant's point of view.

fieldnotes   Notes about observations made in the field, in the interaction setting, or while interaction occurs.

focus group   Qualitative research method; facilitator-led group discussion used for collecting data from a group of participants about a particular topic in a limited amount of time.

focus group schedule   A question or topic guide used to facilitate a focus group, usually structured as a funnel from broad to more specific questions or topics.

frequency   Number of times a particular value or category of a variable occurs.

gatekeeper   Person who has authority to allow the researcher into an environment to collect data.

generalizability   Extent to which conclusions developed from data collected from a sample can be extended to the population; the extension of the findings to similar situations or to similar others.

grounded theory   An approach to analyzing qualitative data in which theory emerges from the data and the relationships among the emergent categories of data.

heuristic   Characteristic of research; results of one study lead to more questions.

hierarchical regression   Form of regression in which the researcher determines the order or sequence in which the independent variables are presumed to influence the dependent variable.

human subjects review committee   University committee that uses a formal process for considering the soundness and reasonableness of research proposals; also known as *institutional review board (IRB)*.

hypothesis   Tentative, educated guess or proposition about the relationship between two or more variables; often, hypotheses take the form of statements like "If x occurs, then y will follow," or "As x increases, so will y."

inclusion criterion   A standard or guideline participants must meet to be included in a nonprobability sample.

independent sample *t*-test   Statistic used to compare means of two sets of scores, each set collected from a different set of people or collected about a different set of stimuli.

independent variable   Variable manipulated by the researcher; presumably, this manipulation, or variation, is the cause of change in the dependent variable; also referred to as *antecedent variable, experimental variable, treatment variable,* and *causal variable.*

inductive   Reasoning process in which data are gathered and examined, hypotheses are formulated, and eventually theories are developed in response to what the data reveal; generally used with qualitative research methods.

inductive analysis   Reasoning process in which researchers work from what emerges from the data to formulate hypotheses and eventually develop theories; generally used with qualitative research methods.

inferential statistics   Statistical tests that provide information about the relationships between or among variables in the study; used to draw conclusions about a population by examining the sample.

informed consent   Agreement participant gives to researcher to participate in the research project after having been given some basic information about the research process.

institutional review board (IRB)   University committee charged with the formal process of considering the soundness and reasonableness of research proposals; also known as *human subjects review committee.*

interaction analysis   Quantitative research method; codes the content of ongoing communication between two or more individuals; identifies the verbal or nonverbal features or functions of the stream of conversational elements.

intercoder reliability   *See* interrater reliability.

interrater agreement   *See* interrater reliability.

interrater reliability   Degree to which two or more coders assign communication behaviors to the same categories, or the degree to which two or more raters similarly evaluate a communicate act on a scale or index; also referred to as *interrater agreement* or *intercoder reliability.*

interaction effect   Combined and simultaneous influence of two or more independent variables on the dependent variable.

interdisciplinary triangulation   Form of triangulation in which researchers from a variety of disciplines work together on a research project.

internal reliability   Degree to which multiple items invoke the same response from a participant; expressed in value from 0 (no internal consistency) to 1.00 (complete internal consistency).

internal validity   Extent to which one can draw valid conclusions about the effects of one variable on another; depends upon how the research is designed and the data collected; addresses the relationship between the concept being measured and the process for measuring it.

interpretation   In qualitative research, making sense of or giving meaning to the identified patterns, themes, concepts, and propositions.

intersubjectivity   How people jointly construct their social lives through interactions with others and their rules for doing so.

interval   The distance between any two adjacent, or contiguous, data points.

interval data   Data measured based on specific numerical scores or values in which the distance between any two adjacent, or contiguous, data points is equal; scale without a meaningful zero.

interview guide   List of questions or topics used in interview research.

investigator triangulation   Method of triangulation in which several researchers or evaluators are used.

justice   Issue of fairness in conducting research; addresses who should receive the benefits of research and who should bear its burdens.

key informant   Individual from whom data must be collected for a research project to be complete.

latent content   Type of content coded in content analysis; inferences or interpretations about the content that imply something about the nature of the senders or producers of the content or effects on senders.

Likert-type scale   Type of interval scale measurement widely used in communication research; participants are given a statement and then asked to respond, indicating the degree to which they agree or disagree with the statement; a typical response set is "strongly disagree, disagree, undecided, agree, strongly agree."

linear   Type of relationship between variables in which a one-unit change in one variable is associated with a constant change in the other variable in the same or opposite direction; when plotted, forms a straight line.

linear regression   Form of regression in which the values of a dependent or criterion variable are attributed to one independent, or predictor, variable.

literature review   Section of the written research report that provides the framework of the research investigation; summarizes the literature the researcher sought and studied to design and develop the research study.

longitudinal design   Type of research design that allows for multiple measurements of the dependent variable over time.

main effect   Simple influence of independent variable on the dependent variable; the influence of one independent variable is examined without considering the influence of other independent variables.

manifest content   Type of content coded in content analysis; a description of the characteristics of the content itself.

manipulation   One of the ways in which the researcher varies the type of stimuli or the amount or level of stimuli presented to research participants; also referred to as *treatment.*

manipulation check   Verification that participants did, in fact, regard the independent variable in the various ways that the researcher intended; conducted prior to statistical analyses of the hypotheses.

maturation   Threat to the internal validity of research as participants change, or mature, over the course of the observations.

maximum variation sampling   Sampling technique used in qualitative research; based on informational redundancy; a researcher continues to seek additional participants until the data received are redundant with, or the same as, previously collected data.

mean   Most common measure of central tendency; commonly referred to as the *average;* computed by adding up all the scores on one variable and then dividing by the number of cases, or *n,* for that variable.

measurement   Use of numbers to represent a communication phenomenon; more broadly, a process that includes everything the researcher does to arrive at the numerical estimates, including the measuring device or instrument, how the device or instrument is used, the skill of the person using the device or instrument, and the attribute or characteristic being measured.

median   Measure of central tendency indicating the middle of all the scores on one variable; the point or score that divides a distribution of scores in half.

member check   See *member validation.*

member validation   The process of asking individuals from whom data were collected to verify the interpretation of the data.

memo writing   In qualitative research, a writing process that serves as an intermediate step between coding and the first draft of the analysis; used as the basis for organizing the research report.

method section   Section of the written research report that describes how the research study was executed.

mode   Measure of central tendency indicating the score that appears most often in a dataset.

mortality   Threat to the internal validity of research when participants can no longer be observed or used for data collection because they have dropped out of the research project; also known as *attrition.*

multiple correlational coefficient   Represented by the symbol *R;* an index of the magnitude of the relationship among the variables in a multiple regression.

multiple regression   Statistic to test for the significant relationships between the dependent variable and multiple independent variables separately and as a group.

mutual simultaneous shaping   In qualitative research, the belief that everything influences everything else in the here and now; with so many influences, it is difficult, if not impossible, to specify causality.

mutually exclusive   Characteristic of choices in a response set; categories should present only one option for which a person is able to identify him- or herself.

narratives   Stories people tell as a way of knowing, understanding, and explaining their lives.

negatively skewed curve   Distribution in which there are very few scores on the left side of the curve; there are very few very low scores; most of the scores are lumped together on the right side of the curve, above the mean.

network sampling   Form of nonprobability sampling in which researcher actively solicits individuals who fit a specific profile and asks them to participate in the research study.

nominal data   Discrete data that describe the presence or absence of some characteristic or attribute; data that name a characteristic without any regard to the value of the characteristic; also referred to as *categorical data.*

nondirectional hypothesis   Statement that a difference or relationship between variables will occur; does not specify the direction of the difference or the nature of the relationship.

non-experimental design   See *descriptive design.*

nonprobability sampling   Sampling technique that does not rely on any form of random selection.

nonresponse   Failure to obtain data from individuals in the sample.

normal curve   Theoretical distribution of scores, or other numerical values, in which the majority of cases are distributed around the peak in the middle with progressively fewer cases as one moves away from the middle of the distribution; has a distinct bell shape and symmetry—one side of the curve is a mirror image of the other side; the mean, median, and mode for the distribution are at the same point; also referred to as the *bell curve.*

null hypothesis   Implicit complementary statement to the research hypothesis that states that no relationship, except one due to chance, exists between the variables.

number of cases   A count of the data about which, or people from which, data were collected.

observed frequency   Used in chi-square; the number of times the category actually appears; is compared to the expected frequency.

observer as participant   Form of participant observation; researcher in both participant and observer roles, but the primary focus shifts to the role of observer, although the researcher has negotiated entrance into an interaction setting with the intention to allow the interaction to proceed as it naturally would.

one-dimensional chi-square   Statistical test to determine if differences in how the cases are distributed across the categories of one categorical, or nominal, variable are significant; also referred to as *one-way chi-square.*

one-tailed *t*-test   Statistic used to test for a specific difference on a continuous level dependent variable relative to one of two categories of a nominal level variable.

one-way ANOVA   One-way analysis of variance; statistical test to identify significant differences in the dependent variable based on categorical differences on one independent variable.

one-way chi-square   Statistical test to determine if differences in how cases are distributed across the categories of one categorical, or nominal, variable are significant; also referred to as *one-dimensional chi-square.*

online survey   Surveys conducted over the Internet.

open coding   The first and unrestrictive pass in coding qualitative data.

open question   Question for which respondents use their own words to formulate a response.

operationalization   Statement that denotes how the variable is observed and measured in a specific way; most variables can be operationalized in multiple ways.

ordinal data   Data measured based on the rank order of concepts or variables; differences among ranks need not be equal.

outcome variable Variable that is influenced or changed by the independent, or predictor, variable.

paired comparison *t*-test Statistic used to compare two paired or matched scores.

panel Longitudinal design for a survey in which data are collected from the same participants at more than one point in time.

participant as observer Form of participant observation; the researcher is both participant and observer; researcher openly acknowledges the research purpose, but also takes an active role in the interaction.

participant observation Data collection method used with qualitative methods; allows researchers to observe communication firsthand.

Pearson product-moment correlation coefficient Statistical test that examines the linear relationship between two continuous level variables; represented by the symbol *r*; also known as *correlation.*

percentage Comparison between the base number and a second number; represented by the symbol %.

peripheral members In qualitative research, a type of committed membership in which the researcher becomes a member of the group being observed, but does not take on central activities.

pilot testing Researcher's trial of a survey or questionnaire with a small group of participants who are similar to those individuals who constitute the population before data collection actually begins; also referred to as *pretesting.*

planned comparisons Hypothesized statistical comparisons used with ANOVA to compare individuals' scores on the dependent variable according to the groups or categories of the independent variable.

population All units or the universe—people or things—possessing the attributes or characteristics in which the researcher is interested.

population inference Accepting the conclusions derived from the sample with the assumption that those conclusions are also applicable to the population.

population validity Degree to which the sample represents the population of interest.

positively skewed curve Distribution in which there are very few scores on the right side of the distribution or very few very high scores; most of the scores are lumped together on the left side of the curve, below the mean.

post hoc comparisons Unplanned statistical comparisons used with ANOVA to compare individuals' scores on the dependent variable according to the groups or categories of the independent variable; conducted after the researcher finds a significant ANOVA.

posttest only Type of research design in which participants are assigned to treatment or control groups; the simple comparison between groups allows a researcher to conclude that any significant differences found are due to the fact that the treatment group received some stimulus that participants in the control group did not.

predictive validity Method for establishing criterion-related validity; exists when measurement predicts performance or behavior.

predictor variable Variable that causes change in the dependent, or criterion, variable; used in non-experimental research designs because the researcher cannot directly control manipulation of the independent variable.

pretesting Trial of a survey or questionnaire with a small group of participants who are similar to those individuals who constitute the population before data collection actually begins; also referred to as *pilot testing.*

pretest–posttest Type of research design in which the dependent variable is measured before the treatment group is exposed to the stimuli; after the stimulus is given, the dependent variable is measured again in exactly the same way with the same participants.

probability Degree to which a particular event or relationship will occur.

probability level Level of error the researcher is willing to accept; established for each statistical test; symbolized as *p* or referred to as the *alpha level*; also referred to as *significance level.*

probability sampling Most rigorous way for identifying whom to include as part of a sample; the probability, or chance, of any element being included in the sample is known and equal for everyone or every element in the sample: also referred to as *random sampling.*

process inference Accepting the conclusions derived from testing a theory with the assumption that those conclusions are also applicable in similar situations.

proprietary research Research that is commissioned by an individual or organization for its private use.

purposive sampling Form of nonprobability sampling; depends on the judgment of the researcher who hand-picks the cases to be included in the sample; used when researcher wants to select cases that are typical of the population of interest and when sensitive topics are of research interest or when very specialized populations are sought.

puzzle explication   Writing style where researcher presents the puzzle first, then leads the reader to an explanation of what seemed puzzling before.

qualitative methods   Research in which the researcher is the primary observer, or data collector.

quantitative data   Data that represent the values (degree, amount, or frequency) that can be ordered on a continuum; also known as *continuous level data*.

quantitative methods   Research that relies on numerical measurement.

quasi-experiment   Research design in which variation in the independent variable is natural, or not manipulated by the researcher; participants are not assigned randomly to treatment and control groups; also referred to as *natural experiment*.

questionnaire   A method of data collection, such as in a mail, phone, face-to-face, or online questionnaire; can be used by itself or with other data collection methods in many research designs.

questions of cause and effect   Questions that ask and answer if one or more variables is the cause of one or more outcome variables.

questions of definition   Questions that ask for definitions for or that help to describe the phenomena in which we are interested.

questions of policy   Questions that ask for evaluation of procedures or programs.

questions of relationships   Questions that examine if, how, and the degree to which phenomena are related.

questions of value   Questions that ask for individuals' subjective evaluations on issues and phenomena, usually about the aesthetic or normative features of communication.

quota sampling   Form of nonprobability sampling in which a researcher uses a target, or quota, as a goal for seeking people or elements that fit the characteristics of the subgroup; when the quota for each subgroup is met, data collection is complete.

random   Characteristic of a sample in which probability for selection is equal; decreases bias.

random assignment   Procedure in which each participant or element has an equal chance of being assigned to any one of the treatment or control groups of the independent variable.

range   Simplest measure of dispersion; the value calculated by subtracting the lowest score from the highest score.

ratio data   Measurement for which intervals between data points are equal; a true zero exists; if the score is zero, there is a complete absence of the variable.

raw data   Data in the form in which they are collected from each participant or about each element; compiled with data from all participants into a dataset.

recall cue   Statement preceding a survey or questionnaire designed to direct participants to recall episodes or past interactions in which they participated.

reference list   Section of the written research report that provides an alphabetical listing by authors' last names of all materials cited or referenced in the research report.

regression   Set of statistical techniques that predict some variables by knowing others; the most common use of regression is to assess the influence of several continuous level predictor, or independent, variables on a single continuous criterion, or dependent, variable.

regression line   Line drawn through the data points on a scattergram that best summarizes the relationship between the independent and dependent variables (or the predictor and criterion variables).

reliability   Achieved when researchers are consistent in their use of data collection procedures and when participants react similarly to them; other researchers using the same measure in another project with comparable participants would produce similar results; measurement is stable, trustworthy, or dependable; a reliable measure is one that is consistent or gives very similar results each time it is used.

reliability coefficient   Number between 0 and 1 to express the degree of consistency in measurement; 1.00 represents complete consistency or reliability; a score of 0 indicates that consistency or reliability was no better than would be due to chance.

repeated measures   Form of ANOVA design in which each participant is measured more than once, usually at different levels or for different conditions; also referred to as *within-subject design*.

replication   Design of current study to follow the procedures of other studies that have investigated the same topic, often using the same methods or procedures.

research   The discovery of answers to questions through the application of scientific and systematic procedures.

researcher construction   Way in which researcher interprets meaning in qualitative research; interpretation from researcher's personal, subjective position or perspective on the experience; evidence is fully the construction of the researcher.

research protocol   Written detailed procedures for conducting the research study and collecting data.

research question   Question that asks what the tentative relationship among variables might be or asks about the state or nature of some communication phenomenon.

respect for persons   Two separate principles: treating individuals as capable of making decisions and protecting those who are not capable of making their own decisions.

response rate   Number of people who respond after they have been contacted as part of the sample and asked to participate; divide the number of people who responded by the number of respondents identified as part of the sample; also referred to as *return rate.*

results section   Section of the written research report that provides the results of the study without interpretation.

root mean square error of approximate   A fit index, also known as RMSEA, used in structural equation model to indicate how similar a theoretical model is to the data collected by the researcher; a RMSEA less than .05 indicates excellent model fit, whereas a RMSEA above .10 indicates poor model fit.

sample   A subset, or portion, of a population; data are collected from a sample to make generalizations back to a population.

sample size   Number of people or elements from whom or on which data are collected.

sampling error   Degree to which a sample differs from population characteristics on some measurement; as sample size increases and becomes a larger proportion of the population, sampling error is reduced; also referred to as the *margin of error.*

sampling frame   Set of people or elements that are available to be selected as part of the sample; the list of the available population from which participants are selected.

Scott's *pi*   A measure of interrater reliability for coding categorical data; ranges from perfect agreement (1.0) to agreement that is no better than would be expected by chance (0); accounts for the number of categories in the coding scheme and the frequency with which each category is used.

self-administered survey   Data collection method in which a participant reads and selects a response without the researcher's aid; also called *self-report.*

self-report   Type of survey, questionnaire, or poll in which respondents read the question and select a response by themselves without researcher interference.

semantic differential scale   Form of interval measurement; using a stimulus statement, participants are asked to locate the meaning they ascribe to the stimulus on a response scale anchored by two opposites, usually bipolar adjectives.

semantic validity   The degree to which the analytical categories of a content analysis design have meaning for individuals in a particular context.

separated text   Writing style in which the analysis and theoretical background of the story are separated from the story or narrative.

significance level   Level of error the researcher is willing to accept; established for each statistical test; symbolized as *p* or referred to as the *alpha level*; also referred to as *probability level.*

simple random sampling   Sampling technique in which every person or unit—selected one at a time and independently—has an equal chance of being selected to participate in the study.

skewed distribution   Shape of a distribution of scores that is not normal; the curve is asymmetrical; the mean, median, and mode are not at the same point.

snowball sampling   Nonprobability sampling technique in which participants help the researcher identify other similar participants; used when the research topic is controversial or a specific population of participants is difficult to find.

social desirability response   Response for which there is the potential for participants to respond with answers they believe the interviewer will perceive as favorable.

social science research   Research conducted through the use of scientific and systematic methods; based on the assumption that research can uncover patterns in the lives of people.

social significance   The practical relevance of a statistically significant finding, or how the results might actually be applied.

sponsor   Someone to vouch for person in the role of researcher; also validates and legitimizes researcher's presence.

spurious correlation   Relationship between two variables in which a third variable—sometimes identified, at other times unknown—is influencing the variables tested. Also called *spurious relationship.*

standard deviation   Representation of the variability or spread of the dataset; the amount the scores in a distribution deviate from the mean.

stepwise regression   Form of regression in which independent variables are entered in sequence or order as determined by the statistical program based on the degree of influence the independent variables have on the dependent variables.

stratified random sampling   Form of random or probability sampling in which the population is divided according to subgroups of interest, or homogeneous groups; then elements are randomly selected from each homogeneous subgroup of the population with respect to its proportion to the whole.

structural equation modeling   Also identified by the acronym SEM; a statistic that allows researchers to test whether a theoretical model (or hypothesized associations among exogenous and endogenous variables) is statistically different from the collected data.

subjective valuing   Way in which researcher interprets meaning in qualitative research; interpretation relies on a mix of both objective and subjective elements; the researcher mixes his or her interpretations with interpretations received directly from participants.

subjectivity   Approach to research in which researcher uses interpretive research processes to make the subject of the interpretation meaningful.

survey   System for collecting information to describe, compare, or explain knowledge, attitudes, and behavior; also known as questionnaire or poll.

systematic sampling   Form of random or probability sampling in which every nth element is chosen after starting at a random point.

test–retest reliability   The expression of the relationship, or correlation between scores at two administrations of the same test, or measurement, to the same participants; 1.00 would indicate that the same participants evaluated the stimulus the second time exactly as they did the first time; a score of 0 would indicate that the two measurements were no better related than they would be by chance.

thematic analysis   A method of qualitative analysis based on participants' conceptions of actual communication episodes; a theme is identified based on recurrence, repetition, and forcefulness.

thematic focus   A strategy for writing qualitative research reports; researchers uses themes from the data as a guiding structure; also referred to as *topical focus*.

theme   A conceptualization of an interaction, relationship, or event drawn by the researcher from close reading and analysis of textual data.

theoretical saturation   The point at which all data can be coded into a category; new categories are not emerging, and the existing category structure appears stable.

theory   Related set of ideas that explains how or why something happens; presents a systematic view of the phenomenon; and specifies the relationships among the concepts with the objective of describing, explaining, or predicting the phenomenon.

topical focus   A strategy for writing qualitative research reports; researchers uses themes from the data as a guiding structure; also referred to as *thematic focus*.

treatment   One of the ways in which the researcher varies the type of stimuli, or the amount or level of stimuli, presented to research participants; also referred to as *manipulation*.

treatment group   The group of participants who receive a stimulus, or one manipulation of the independent variable.

treatment variable   Variable manipulated by the researcher; presumably, this manipulation, or variation, is the cause of change in the dependent variable; also referred to as *antecedent variable, experimental variable, independent variable,* and *causal variable.*

triangulation   Use of several kinds of methods or data to further validate research outcomes and results.

t-**test**   Statistic used to find differences between two groupings of the independent variable on a continuous level dependent variable.

two-dimensional chi-square   Form of chi-square in which frequency distributions are created on two nominal variables; cases are classified on two variables in relationship to each other; also referred to as *contingency analysis* or *two-way chi-square.*

two-tailed *t*-test   Statistic used to test for differences on a continuous level dependent variable relative to one of two categories of a nominal level variable; no specific difference identified in hypothesis or research question.

two-way ANOVA   Statistical test to examine the influence of two categorical independent variables on one continuous level dependent variable; can determine the main effect of contributions of each independent variable and the interaction effect.

two-way chi-square   Form of chi-square in which frequency distributions are created on two nominal variables; cases are classified on two variables in relationship to each other; also referred to as *contingency analysis* or *two-dimensional chi-square*.

Type I error   Error in hypothesis testing that occurs when the null hypothesis is rejected even when it is true; set or controlled by the researcher when choosing the significance level for the statistical test.

Type II error   Error in hypothesis testing that occurs when the alternative hypothesis is rejected even when it is true.

unitizing reliability   Degree to which two or more observers agree that communication action has taken place and can identify the interaction in the stream of interaction; used in content analysis.

unit of analysis   Discrete element coded and counted in content analysis; an observable and measurable unit that provides a standard way of dissecting the text or content into elements to be analyzed.

validity   Achieved when the measurement does what it is intended to do; related to truthfulness or accuracy in measurement.

variable   Element that is specifically identified in the research hypotheses or questions; must be able to be expressed as more than one value or in various categories.

variance   Dispersion of the distribution of scores.

volunteer sampling   Type of nonprobability sampling; research participants offer to participate.

web survey   Surveys conducted over the Internet; also referred to as *online survey*.

within-groups variance   Variation among scores within any category or level of an independent variable.

within-subject design   Form of ANOVA design in which each participant is measured more than once, usually at different levels or for different conditions; also referred to as *repeated measures design*.

REFERENCES

Abelson, R. P. (1995). *Statistics as principled argument.* Hillsdale, NJ: Erlbaum.

Abelson, R. P. (1997). The significance test ban of 1999. In L. L. Harlow, S. A. Mulaik, & J. H. Steiger (Eds.), *What if there were no significance tests?* (pp. 117–141). Mahwah, NJ: Erlbaum.

Adler, P. A., & Adler, P. (1987). *Membership roles in field research.* Newbury Park, CA: Sage.

Agarwal, V. (2013). Investigating the convergent validity of organizational trust. *Journal of Communication Management, 17,* 24–39. doi:10.1108/13632541311300133

Alexander, A. (2008). Relationship resources for coping with unfulfilled standards in dating relationships: Commitment, satisfaction, and closeness. *Journal of Social and Personal Relationships, 25,* 725–747. doi:10.1177/0265407508093783

Alhabash, S., & Wise, K. (2012). PeaceMaker: Changing students' attitudes toward Palestinians and Israelis through video game play. *International Journal of Communication, 6,* 356–380.

Ali, M., & Levine, T. (2008). The language of truthful and deceptive denials and confessions. *Communication Reports, 21,* 82–91. doi:10.1080/08934210802381862

Allen, M. W., & Caillouet, R. H. (1994). Legitimation endeavors: Impression management strategies used by an organization in crisis. *Communication Monographs, 61,* 44–62.

American Psychological Association. (2010). *The publication manual of the American Psychological Association* (6th ed.). Washington, DC: Author.

Ancu, M. (2012). Older adults on Facebook: A survey examination of motives and use of social networking by people 50 and older. *Florida Communication Journal, 40,* 1–12.

Andersen, P. A. (1989). Philosophy of science. In P. Emmert & L. L. Barker (Eds.), *Measurement of communication behavior* (pp. 3–17). New York, NY: Longman.

Anderson, J. A. (1996). Thinking qualitatively: Hermeneutics in science. In M. B. Salwen & D. W. Stacks (Eds.), *An integrated approach to communication theory and research* (pp. 45–59). Mahwah, NJ: Erlbaum.

Anfara, V. A., Jr., & Mertz, N. T. (Eds.). (2006). *Theoretical frameworks in qualitative research.* Thousand Oaks, CA: Sage.

Armstrong, D., Gosling, A., Weinman, J., & Martaeu, T. (1997). The place of inter-rater reliability in qualitative research: An empirical study. *Sociology, 31,* 597–606. doi:10.1177/0038038597031003015

Atkinson, P., & Hammersley, M. (1994). Ethnography and participant observation. In N. K. Denzin & Y. S. Lincoln (Eds.), *Handbook of qualitative research* (pp. 248–261). Thousand Oaks, CA: Sage.

Aubrey, J. S., Rhea, D. M., Olson, L. N., & Fine, M. (2013). Conflict and control: Examining the association between exposure to television portraying interpersonal conflict and the use of controlling behaviors in romantic relationships. *Communication Studies, 64,* 106–124. doi:10.1080/10510974.2012.731465

Austin, E. W., Miller, A. C., Silva, J., Guerra, P., Geisler, N., Gamboa, L. . . . Kuechle, B. (2002). The effects of increased cognitive involvement on college students' interpretations of magazine advertisements for alcohol. *Communication Research, 29,* 155–179. doi:10.1177/0093650202029002003

Avtgis, T. A. (2003). Male sibling social and emotional support as a function of attributional confidence. *Communication Research Reports, 20,* 341–347. doi:10.1080/08824090309388833

Baiocchi-Wagner, E. A. (2012). Framing the aging experience in care facility brochures: A mixed-method analysis. *Southern Communication Journal, 77,* 349–368. doi:10.1080/1041794X.2012.679991

Bakeman, R., & Gottman, J. M. (1997). *Observing interaction: An introduction to sequential analysis* (2nd ed.). Cambridge, UK: Cambridge University Press.

Bales, R. F. (1950). *Interaction process analysis: A method for the study of small groups.* Cambridge, MA: Addison-Wesley.

Ballard, D. I., & Seibold, D. R. (2004). Organizational members' communication and temporal experience: Scale development and validation. *Communication Research, 31,* 135–172. doi:10.1177/0093650203261504

Ballard, R. L., & Ballard, S. J. (2011). From narrative inheritance to narrative momentum: Past, present, and future stories in an international adoptive family. *Journal of Family Communication, 11,* 69–84. doi:10.1080/15267431.2011.554618

Barge, J. K., Lee, M., Maddux, K., Nabring, R., & Townsend, B. (2008). Managing dualities in planned change initiatives. *Journal of Applied Communication Research, 36,* 364–390. doi:10.1080/00909880802129996

Barker, D. A., & Barker, L. L. (1989). Survey research. In P. Emmert & L. L. Barker (Eds.), *Measurement of communication behavior* (pp. 168–196). New York, NY: Longman.

Barnette, J. J. (2000). Effects of stem and Likert response option reversals on survey internal consistency: If you feel the need, there is a better alternative to using those negatively worded stems. *Educational and Psychological Measurement, 60,* 361–370. doi:10.1177/00131640021970592

Beatty, M. J., & Friedland, M. H. (1990). Public speaking state anxiety as a function of selected situational and predispositional variables. *Communication Education, 39,* 142–147. doi:10.1080/03634529009378796

Beaulieu, A., & Estalella, A. (2012). Rethinking research ethics for mediated settings. *Information, Communication & Society, 15,* 23-42. doi:10.1080/1369118X.2010.535838

Beck, S. J., & Keyton, J. (2009). Perceiving strategic meeting interaction. *Small Group Research, 40,* 223–246. doi:10.1177/1046496408330084

Beck, S. J., & Keyton, J. (2014). Facilitating social support: Member-leader communication in a breast cancer support group. *Cancer Nursing.*

Becker, J. A. H., Ellevold, B., & Stamp, G. H. (2008). The creation of defensiveness in social interaction II: A model of defensive communication among romantic couples. *Communication Monographs, 75,* 86–110. doi:10.1080/03637750701885415

Berger, A. A. (1998). *Media research techniques* (2nd ed.). Thousand Oaks, CA: Sage.

Berger, A. A. (2011). *Media and communication research methods: An introduction to qualitative and quantitative approaches* (2nd ed.). Thousand Oaks, CA: Sage.

Berleson, B. (1952). *Content analysis in communication research.* New York, NY: Free Press.

Bickman, L., Rog, D. J., & Hedrick, T. E. (1998). Applied research design: A practical approach. In L. Bickman & D. J. Rog (Eds.), *Handbook of applied social research methods* (pp. 5–37). Thousand Oaks, CA: Sage.

Bird, C. M. (2005). How I stopped dreading and learned to love transcription. *Qualitative Inquiry, 11,* 226–248. doi:10.1177/1077800404273413

Bisel, R. S., & Messersmith, A. S. (2012). Organizational and supervisory apology effectiveness: Apology giving in work settings. *Business Communication Quarterly, 75,* 425–448. doi:10.1177/1080569912461171

Bodie, G. D. (2013). Issues in the measurement of listening. *Communication Research Reports, 30,* 76–84. doi:10.1080/08824096.2012.733981

Boruch, R. F. (1998). Randomized controlled experiments for evaluation and planning. In L. Bickman & D. J. Rog (Eds.), *Handbook of applied social research methods* (pp. 161–191). Thousand Oaks, CA: Sage.

Boster, F. J. (2002). On making progress in communication science. *Human Communication Research, 28,* 473–490.

Bostrom, R. N. (2003). Theories, data, and communication research. *Communication Monographs, 70,* 275–294. doi:10.1080/0363775032000179106

Bouma, G. D., & Atkinson, G. B. J. (1995). *A handbook of social science research* (2nd ed.). New York, NY: Oxford University Press.

Bourque, L. B., & Fielder, E. P. (1995). *How to conduct self-administered and mail surveys.* Thousand Oaks, CA: Sage.

Bracken, C. C., Jeffres, L. W., Neuendorf, K. A., & Atkin, D. (2009). Parameter estimation validity and relationship robustness: A comparison of telephone and internet survey techniques. *Telematics and Informatics, 26,* 144–155. doi:10.1016/j.tele.2008.03.001

Braithwaite, D. O., & Eckstein, N. J. (2003). How people with disabilities communicatively manage assistance: Helping as instrumental social support. *Journal of Applied Communication Research, 31,* 1–26.

Braithwaite, D. O., Toller, P. W., Daas, K. L., Durham, W. T., & Jones, A. C. (2008). Centered but not caught in the middle: Stepchildren's perceptions of dialectical contradictions in the communication of co-parents. *Journal of Applied Communication Research, 36,* 33–55. doi:10.1080/00909880701799337

Brandtzaeg, P. B. (2012). Social networking sites: Their uses and social implications: A longitudinal study. *Journal of Computer-Mediated Communication, 17,* 467–488. doi:10.1111/j.1083-6101.2012.01580.x

Brann, M. (2007). Health care providers' confidentiality practices and perceptions: Expanding a typology of confidentiality breaches in health care communication *Qualitative Research Reports in Communication, 8,* 45–52. doi:10.1080/17459430701617903

Brooks, W. D. (1970). Perspectives on communication research. In P. Emmert & W. D. Brooks (Eds.), *Methods of research in communication* (pp. 3–8). New York, NY: Houghton Mifflin.

Brown, L., & Durrheim, K. (2009). Different kinds of knowing: Generating qualitative data through mobile interviewing. *Qualitative Inquiry, 15,* 911–930. doi:10.1177/1077800409333440

Brown, M. H., & Kreps, G. L. (1993). Narrative analysis and organizational development. In S. L. Herndon & G. L. Kreps (Eds.), *Qualitative research: Applications in organizational communication* (pp. 47–62). Cresskill, NJ: Hampton Press.

Bruess, C. J. S., & Pearson, J. C. (1997). Interpersonal rituals in marriage and adult friendship. *Communication Monographs, 64,* 25–46.

Bryant, E. M., & Sias, P. M. (2011). Sensemaking and relational consequences of peer co-worker deception. *Communication Monographs, 78,* 115–137. doi:10.1080/03637751.2010.542473

Burgoon, J. K. (1976). The unwillingness-to-communicate scale: Development and validation. *Communication Monographs, 43,* 60–69. doi:10.1080/03637757609375916

Burgoon, J. K., Blair, J. P., & Strom, R. E. (2008). Cognitive biases and nonverbal cue availability in detecting deception. *Human Communication Research, 34,* 572–599. doi:10.1111/j.1468-2958.2008.00333.x

Bute, J. J., & Jensen, R. E. (2011). Narrative sensemaking and time lapse: Interviews with low-income women about sex education. *Communication Monographs, 78,* 212–232. doi:10.1080/03637751.2011.564639

Butler, J. A., & Modaff, D. P. (2008). When work is home: Agency, structure, and contradictions. *Management Communication Quarterly, 22,* 232–257. doi:10.1177/0893318908323151

Byrne, S. (2009). Media literacy interventions: What makes them boom or boomerang? *Communication Education, 58,* 1–14. doi:10.1080/03634520802226444

Cader, S. (1996). Statistical techniques. In R. Sapsford & V. Jupp (Eds.), *Data collection and analysis* (pp. 225–261). Thousand Oaks, CA: Sage.

Cai, X., Gantz, W., Schwartz, N., & Wang, X. (2003). Children's website adherence to the FTC's online privacy protection rule. *Journal of Applied Communication Research, 31,* 346–362. doi:10.1080/1369681032000132591

Campbell, D., & Stanley, J. (1963). *Experimental and quasi-experimental designs for research.* Chicago, IL: Rand McNally.

Campbell, S. (2008). Perceptions of mobile phone use in public: The roles of individualism, collectivism, and focus of the setting. *Communication Reports, 21,* 70–81. doi:10.1080/08934210802301506

Canary, D. J., & Seibold, D. R. (2010). Origins and development of the conversational argument coding scheme. *Communication Methods & Measures, 4,* 7–26. doi:10.1080/19312451003680459

Canary, H. E. (2008). Negotiating disability in families: Constructions and contradictions. *Journal of Applied Communication Research, 36,* 437–458. doi:10.1080/00909880802101771

Canary, H. E., & Cantu, E. (2012). Making decisions about children's disabilities: Mediation and structuration in cross-system meetings. *Western Journal of Communication, 76,* 270–297. doi:10.1080/10570314.2011.651252

Cappella, J. N. (1977). Research methodology in communication: Review and commentary. In B. D. Ruben (Ed.), *Communication yearbook 1* (pp. 37–53). New Brunswick, NJ: Transaction Books.

Cappella, J. N. (1987). Interpersonal communication: Definitions and fundamental questions. In C. R. Berger & S. H. Chaffee (Eds.), *Handbook of communication science* (pp. 184–238). Newbury Park, CA: Sage.

Carbaugh, D., & Buzzanell, P. M. (2010). Reflections on distinctive qualities in communication research (pp. 106–116). In D. Carbaugh & P. M. Buzzanell (Eds.), *Distinctive qualities in communication research.* New York, NY: Routledge.

Carey, M. A. (1994). The group effect in focus groups: Planning, implementing and interpreting focus group research. In J. Morse (Ed.), *Critical issues in qualitative research methods* (pp. 225–241). Thousand Oaks, CA: Sage.

Carmines, E. G., & Zeller, R. A. (1979). *Reliability and validity assessment.* Beverly Hills, CA: Sage.

Carusi, A., & De Grandis, G. (2012). The ethical work that regulations will not do. *Information, Communication & Society, 15,* 124–141. doi:10.1080/1369118X.2011.634015

Cha, J. (2011). Information privacy: A comprehensive analysis of information request and privacy policies of most-visited web sites. *Asian Journal of Communication, 21,* 613–631. doi:10.1080/01292986.2011.615942

Charmaz, K. (2000). Grounded theory: Objectivist and constructivist methods. In N. K. Denzin & Y. S. Lincoln (Eds.), *Handbook of qualitative research* (2nd ed., pp. 509–535). Thousand Oaks, CA: Sage.

Charmaz, K. (2005). Grounded theory in the 21st century. In N. K. Denzin & Y. S. Lincoln (Eds.), *The Sage handbook of qualitative research* (3rd ed., pp. 507–535). Thousand Oaks, CA: Sage.

Charmaz, K., & Belgrave, L. L. (2012). Qualitative interviewing and grounded theory analysis. In J. F. Gubrium, J. A. Holstein, A. B. Marvasti, & K. D. McKinney (Eds.), *The SAGE handbook of interview research: The complexity of the craft* (2nd ed., pp. 347–365). Los Angeles, CA: Sage.

Chase, S. E. (2005). Narrative inquiry: Multiple lenses, approaches, voices. In N. K. Denzin & Y. S. Lincoln (Eds.), *The Sage handbook of qualitative research* (3rd ed., pp. 651–679). Thousand Oaks, CA: Sage.

Chase, S. E. (2013). Narrative inquiry: Still a field in the making. In N. K. Denzin & Y. S. Lincoln (Eds.), *Collecting and interpreting qualitative materials* (pp. 55–83). Los Angeles, CA: Sage.

Cheney, G. (2008). Encountering the ethics of engaged scholarship. *Journal of Applied Communication Research, 36,* 281–288. doi:10.1080/00909880802172293

Chesebro, J. W., & Borisoff, D. J. (2007). What makes qualitative research qualitative? *Qualitative Research Reports in Communication, 8,* 3–14. doi:10.1080/17459430701617846

Cho, H., & Choi, J. (2011). Television, gender norms, and tanning attitudes and intentions of young men and women. *Communication Studies, 62,* 508–530. doi:10.1080/10510974.2011.577500

Chory, R. M., & Cicchirillo, V. (2008). The relationship between video game play and trait verbal aggressiveness: An application of the general aggression model. *Communication Research Reports, 24,* 113–119. doi:10.1080/08824090701304766

Chung, C. J., Nam, Y., & Stefanone, M. A. (2012). Exploring online news credibility: The relative influence of traditional and technological factors. *Journal of Computer-Mediated Communication, 17,* 171–186. doi:10.1111/j.1083-6101.2011.01565.x

Cingel, D. P., & Krcmar, M. (2013). Predicting media use in very young children: The role of demographics and parent attitudes. *Communication Studies, 64,* 374–394. doi:10.1080/10510974.2013.770408

Clair, R. P., Chapman, P. A., & Kunkel, A. W. (1996). Narrative approaches to raising consciousness about sexual harassment: From research to pedagogy and back again. *Journal of Applied Communication Research, 24,* 241–259. doi:10.1080/00909889609365455

Clark, R. A. (1990). Teaching research methods. In J. A. Daly, G. W. Friedrich, & A. L. Vangelisti (Eds.), *Teaching communication: Theory, research, and methods* (pp. 181–191). Hillsdale, NJ: Erlbaum.

Cohen, E. L. (2010). The role of message frame, perceived risk, and ambivalence in individuals' decisions to become organ donors. *Health Communication, 25,* 758–769. doi:10.1080/10410236.2010.521923

Communication Studies 298, California State University, Sacramento. (1997). Fragments of self at the postmodern bar. *Journal of Contemporary Ethnography, 26,* 251–292.

Conrad, K., Dixon, T. L., & Zhang, Y. (2009). Controversial rap themes, gender portrayals and skin tone distortion: A content analysis of rap music videos. *Journal of Broadcasting & Electronic Media, 53,* 134–156. doi:10.1080/08838150802643795

Coopman, S. J., & Meidlinger, K. B. (2000). Power, hierarchy, and change: The stories of a Catholic parish staff. *Management Communication Quarterly, 13,* 567–625. doi:10.1177/0893318900134002

Craig, R. T. (1993). Why are there so many communication theories? *Journal of Communication, 43,* 26–33. doi:10.1111/j.1460-2466.1993.tb01273.x

Craig, R. T. (1999). Communication theory as a field. *Communication Theory, 6,* 119–161. doi:10.1111/j.1468-2885.1999.tb00355.x

Cressman, D. L., Callister, M., Robinson, T., & Near, C. (2009). Swearing in the cinema. *Journal of Children & Media, 3,* 117–135. doi:10.1080/17482790902772257

Creswell, J. W. (1998). *Qualitative inquiry and research design: Choosing among five traditions.* Thousand Oaks, CA: Sage.

Creswell, J. W. (2014). *Research design: Qualitative, quantitative, and mixed methods approaches* (4th ed). Los Angeles, CA: Sage.

Cronbach, L. J. (1951). Coefficient alpha and the internal structure of tests. *Psychometrika, 16,* 297–334. doi:10.1007/BF02310555

Cushman, D. P. (1998). Visions of order in human communication theory. In J. S. Trent (Ed.), *Communication: Views from the helm for the 21st century* (pp. 8–12). Boston, MA: Allyn Bacon.

Dainton, M. (2003). Equity and uncertainty in relational maintenance. *Western Journal of Communication, 67,* 164–186. doi:10.1080/10570310309374765

Davis, S. K., Thompson, J. L., & Schweizer, S. E. (2012). Innovations in on-site survey administration: Using an iPad interface at national wildlife refuges and national parks. *Human Dimensions of Wildlife, 17,* 282–294.

Deetz, S. A. (1992). *Democracy in an age of corporate colonization: Developments in communication and the politics of everyday life.* Albany, NY: SUNY Press.

Defenbaugh, N. L. (2008). "Under erasure": The absent ill body in doctor-patient dialogue. *Qualitative Inquiry, 14,* 1402–1424. doi:10.1177/1077800408322579

Dennis, A. C., & Wood, J. T. (2012). "We're not going to have this conversation, but you get it": Black mother-daughter communication about sexual relations. *Women's Studies in Communication, 35,* 204–223. doi:10.1080/07491409.2012.724525

Dennis, M. R., Kunkel, A., & Keyton, J. (2008). Problematic integration theory, appraisal theory, and the Bosom Buddies Breast Cancer Support Group. *Journal of Applied Communication Research, 36,* 415–436. doi:10.1080/00909880802094315

Denzin, N. K. (1970). *The research act: A theoretical introduction to sociological methods.* Chicago, IL: Aldine.

Denzin, N. K. (1978). *The research act. A theoretical introduction to sociological methods* (2nd ed.). New York, NY: McGraw-Hill.

Denzin, N. K., & Lincoln, Y. S. (1994). Introduction: Entering the field of qualitative research. In N. K. Denzin & Y. S. Lincoln (Eds.), *Handbook of qualitative research* (pp. 1–17). Thousand Oaks, CA: Sage.

Denzin, N. K., & Lincoln, Y. S. (2000). Introduction: The discipline and practice of qualitative research. In N. K. Denzin & Y. S. Lincoln (Eds.), *Handbook of qualitative research* (2nd ed., pp. 1–28). Thousand Oaks, CA: Sage.

Denzin, N. K., & Lincoln, Y. S. (2005). Introduction: The discipline and practice of qualitative research. In N. K. Denzin & Y. S. Lincoln (Eds.), *The Sage handbook of qualitative research* (3rd ed., pp. 1–32). Thousand Oaks, CA: Sage.

Derlega, V. J., Winstead, B. A., Mathews, A., & Braitman, S. L. (2008). Why does someone reveal highly personal information? Attributions for and against self-disclosure in close relationships. *Communication Research Reports, 25,* 115–130. doi:10.1080/08824090802021756

D'Haenens, L., & Ogan, C. (2013). Internet-using children and digital inequality: A comparison between majority and minority Europeans. *Communications: The European Journal of Communication Research, 38,* 41–60. doi:10.1515/commun-2013-0003

de Vaus, D. A. (2001). *Research design in social research.* Thousand Oaks, CA: Sage.

Dillman, D. A., Smyth, J. D, & Christian, L. M. (2009). *Internet, mail, and mixed-mode surveys: The tailored design method* (3rd ed.). Hoboken, NJ: John Wiley.

Dixon, T. L., & Linz, D. G. (1997). Obscenity law and sexually explicit rap music: Understanding the effects of sex, attitudes, and beliefs. *Journal of Applied Communication Research, 25,* 217–241. doi:10.1080/00909889709365477

Dixon, T. L., Schell, T. L., Giles, H., & Drogos, K. L. (2008). The influence of race in police–civilian interactions: A content analysis of videotaped interactions taken during Cincinnati police traffic stops. *Journal of Communication, 58,* 530–549. doi:10.1111/j.1460-2466.2008.00398.x

Docan-Morgan, T., & Docan, C. A. (2007). Internet infidelity: Double standards and the differing views of women and men. *Communication Quarterly, 55,* 317–342. doi:10.1080/01463370701492519

Dohan, D., & Sanchez-Jankowski, M. (1998). Using computers to analyze ethnographic field data: Theoretical and practical considerations. *Annual Review of Sociology, 24,* 477–498. doi:10.1146/annurev.soc.24.1.477

Doss, K., & Hubbard, A. S. E. (2009). The communicative value of tattoos: The role of public self-consciousness on tattoo visibility. *Communication Research Reports, 26,* 62–74. doi:10.1080/08824090802637072

Dougherty, D. S. (2001). Sexual harassment as [dys]functional process: A feminist standpoint analysis. *Journal of Applied Communication Research, 29,* 372–402. doi:10.1080/00909880128116

Dougherty, D. S., & Baicchi-Wagner, E. A., & McGuire, T. (2011). Managing sexual harassment through enacted stereotypes: An intergroup perspective. *Western Journal of Communication, 75,* 259–281. doi:10.1080/10570314.2011.571654

Downs, E., Boyson, A. R., Alley, H., & Bloom, N. R. (2011). iPedagogy: Using multimedia learning theory to identify best practices for MP3 player use in higher education. *Journal of Applied Communication Research, 39,* 184–200. doi:10.1080/00909882.2011.556137

Duran, R. L. (1983). Communicative adaptability: A measure of social communicative competence. *Communication Quarterly, 31,* 320–326. doi:10.1080/01463378309369521

Durham, W. T. (2008). The rules-based process of revealing/concealing the family planning decisions of voluntarily child-free couples: A communication privacy management perspective. *Communication Studies, 59,* 132–147. doi:10.1080/10510970802062451

Dwyer, K. K., Bingham, S. G., Carlson, R. E., Prisbell, M., Cruz, A. M., & Fus, D. A. (2004). Communication and connectedness in the classroom: Development of the connected classroom climate inventory. *Communication Research Reports, 21,* 264–272. doi:10.1080/08824090409359988

Edwards, H. H., & Kreshel, P. J. (2008). An audience interpretation of corporate communication in a cause-related corporate outreach event: The Avon breast cancer 3-day walk. *Journalism & Communication Monographs, 10,* 175–244. doi: 10.1177/152263790801000203

Eisner, E. (1991). *The enlightened eye.* New York, NY: Macmillan.

Elgemsem, D. (1996). Privacy, respect for persons, and risk. In C. Ess (Ed.), *Philosphical perspectives on computer-mediated communication* (pp. 45–66). Albany: State Univeristy of New York Press.

Ellingson, L. L. (2003). Interdisciplinary health care teamwork in the clinic backstage. *Journal of Applied Communication Research, 31,* 93–117. doi:10.1080/0090988032000064579

Ellingson, L. L. (2009). *Engaging crystallization in qualitative research.* Thousand Oaks, CA: Sage.

Ellingson, L. L. (2012). Interview as embodied communication. In J. F. Gubrium, J. A. Holstein, A. B. Marvasti, & K. D. McKinney (Eds.), *The SAGE handbook of interview research: The complexity of the craft* (2nd ed., pp. 525–539). Los Angeles, CA: Sage.

Ellingson, L. L. (2013). Analysis and representation across the continuum. In N. K. Denzin & Y, S. Lincoln (Eds.), *Collecting and interpreting qualitative materials* (4th ed., pp. 413–445). Los Angeles, CA: Sage.

Ellis, C., & Bochner, A. P. (2000). Autoethnography, personal narrative, reflexivity: Researcher as subject. In N. K. Denzin & Y. S. Lincoln (Eds.), *Handbook of qualitative research* (2nd ed., pp. 733–768). Thousand Oaks, CA: Sage.

Ellis, K. (2000). Perceived teacher confirmation: The development and validation of an instrument and two studies of the relationship to cognitive and affective learning. *Human Communication Research, 26,* 264–291. doi:10.1093/hcr/26.2.264

Elm, M. S. (2009). How do various notions of privacy influence decisions of qualitative Internet research? In A. N. Markham & N. K. Baym (Eds.), *Internet inquiry: Conversations about method* (pp. 69–87). Los Angeles, CA. Sage.

Emerson, R. B., Fretz, R. I., & Shaw, L. L. (1995). *Writing ethnographic field notes.* Chicago, IL: University of Chicago Press.

Emmert, P. (1989). Philosophy of measurement. In P. Emmert & L. L. Barker (Eds.), *Measurement of communication behavior* (pp. 87–116). New York, NY: Longman.

Erbert, L. A., Perez, F. G., & Gareis, E. (2003). Turning points and dialectical interpretations of immigrant experiences in the United States. *Western Journal of Communication, 67,* 113–137. doi:10.1080/10570310309374763

Erickson, F. (1986). Qualitative methods in research on teaching. In M. C. Wittrock (Ed.), *Handbook of research on teaching* (3rd ed., pp. 119–161). New York, NY: Macmillan.

Eveland, Jr., W. P., & Morey, A. C. (2011). Challenges and opportunities of panel designs. In E. P. Bucy & R. L. Holbert (Eds.), *The sourcebook for political communication research: Methods, measures, and analytical techniques* (pp. 19–33). New York, NY: Routledge.

Eyal, K., & Kunkel, D. (2008). The effects of sex in television drama shows on emerging adults' sexual attitudes and moral judgments. *Journal of Broadcasting & Electronic Media, 52,* 161–181. doi:10.1080/08838150801991757

Fairhurst, G. T. (1993). The leader-member exchange patterns of women leaders in industry: A discourse analysis. *Communication Monographs, 60,* 321–351. doi:10.1080/03637759309376316

Favero, L. W., & Heath, R. G. (2012). Generational perspectives in the workplace: Interpreting the discourses that constitute women's struggle to balance work and life. *Journal of Business Communication, 49,* 332–356. doi:10.1177/0021943612456037

Fay, M. J., & Kline, S. L. (2011). Coworker relationships and informal communication in high-intensity telecommuting. *Journal of Applied Communication Research, 39,* 144–163. doi: 10.1080/00909882.2011.556136

Faylor, N. R., Beebe, S. A., Houser, M. L., & Mottet, T. P. (2008). Perceived differences in instructional communication behaviors between effective and ineffective corporate trainers. *Human Communication, 11,* 149–160.

Feldman, M. S., Bell, J., & Berger, M. T. (2003). *Gaining access: A practical and theoretical guide for qualitative researchers.* Walnut Creek, CA: AltaMira.

Fine, M. G. (2009). Women leaders' discursive constructions of leadership. *Women's Studies in Communication, 32,* 180–202.

Fink, A. (1995a). *How to ask survey questions* (Vol. 2). Thousand Oaks, CA: Sage.

Fink, A. (1995b). *The survey handbook* (Vol. 1). Thousand Oaks, CA: Sage.

Fisher, C. B., & Fryberg, D. (1994). Participant partners: College students weigh the costs and benefits of deceptive research. *American Psychologist, 49,* 417–427. doi:10.1037/0003-066X.49.5.417

Fitch, K. L. (1994). Criteria for evidence in qualitative research. *Western Journal of Communication, 58,* 32–38. doi:10.1080/10570319409374481

Fitch, K. L. (2005). Difficult interactions between IRBs and investigators: Applications and solutions. *Journal of Applied Communication Research, 33,* 269–276. doi:10.1080/00909880500149486

Flanagan, J. C. (1954). The critical incident technique. *Psychological Bulletin, 51,* 327–357. doi:10.1037/h0061470

Floyd, K., Boren, J. P., Hannawa, A. F., Hessee, C., McEwan, B., & Beksler, A. E. (2009). Kissing in marital and cohabiting relationships: Effects on blood lipids, stress, and relationship satisfaction. *Western Journal of Communication, 73,* 113–133. doi:10.1080/10570310902856071

Fontana, A., & Frey, J. H. (2000). The interview: From structured questions to negotiated text. In N. K. Denzin & Y. S. Lincoln (Eds.), *Handbook of qualitative research* (2nd ed., pp. 645–672). Thousand Oaks, CA: Sage.

Fontana, A., & Frey, J. H. (2005). The interviews: From neutral stance to political involvement. In N. K. Denzin & Y. S. Lincoln (Eds.), *The Sage handbook of qualitative research* (3rd ed., pp. 695–727). Thousand Oaks, CA: Sage.

Fossey, E., Harvey, C., McDermott, F., & Davidson, L. (2002). Understanding and evaluating qualitative research. *Australian and New Zealand Journal of Psychiatry, 36*, 717–732.

Foster, P. (1996). Observational research. In R. Sapsford & V. Jupp (Eds.), *Data collection and analysis* (pp. 57–93). Thousand Oaks, CA: Sage.

Fowler, F. J., Jr. (1993). *Survey research methods* (2nd ed.). Newbury Park, CA: Sage.

Fowler, F. J., Jr. (2009). *Survey research methods* (4th ed.).Thousand Oaks, CA: Sage.

Frentz, T. S. (2009). Split selves and situated knowledge: The trickster goes titanium. *Qualitative Inquiry, 15*, 820–842. doi:10.1177/1077800408329236

Frey, J. H., & Oishi, S. M. (1995). *How to conduct interviews by telephone and in person.* Thousand Oaks, CA: Sage.

Frisby, B. N., & Booth-Butterfield, M. (2012). The "how" and "why" of flirtatious communication between marital partners. *Communication Quarterly, 60*, 465–480. doi:10.1080/01463373.2012.704568

Gallagher, E. B., & Sias, P. M. (2009). The new employee as a source of uncertainty: Veteran employee information seeking about new hires. *Western Journal of Communication, 73*, 23–46. doi:10.1080/10570310802636326

Galvan, J. L. (1999). *Writing literature review: A guide for students of the social and behavioral sciences.* Los Angeles, CA: Pyrczak.

Garcia, A. C., Standlee, A. I., Bechkoff, J., & Cui, Y. (2009). Ethnographic approaches to the internet and computer-mediated communication. *Journal of Contemporary Ethnography, 38*, 5–84. doi:10.1177/0891241607310839

Garner, A. C. (1999). Negotiating our positions in culture: Popular adolescent fiction and the self-constructions of women. *Women's Studies in Communication, 22*, 85–111. Retrieved from http://www.cios.org/www/wommain.htm

Garner, J. T. (2009). When things go wrong at work: An exploration of organizational dissent messages. *Communication Studies, 60*, 197–218. doi:10.1080/10510970902834916

Garner, J. T., Kinsky, E., S., Duta, A. C., & Danker, J. (2012). Deviating from the script: A content analysis of organizational dissent as portrayed on primetime television. *Communication Quarterly, 60*, 608–623. doi:10.1080/01463373.2012.725001

Gergen, K. (2009). *An invitation to social construction* (2nd ed.). Los Angeles, CA: Sage.

Giannini, G. A. (2011). Finding support in a field of devastation: Bereaved parents' narratives of communication and recovery. *Western Journal of Communication, 75*, 541–564. doi:10.1080/10570314.2011.608406

Glaser, B. G. (1978). *Theoretical sensitivity.* Mill Valley, CA: Sociology Press.

Glaser, B. G., & Strauss, A. L. (1967). *The discovery of grounded theory: Strategies for qualitative research.* New York, NY: Aldine.

Goins, M. N. (2011). Playing with dialectics: Black female friendship groups as a homeplace. *Communication Studies, 62*, 531–546. doi:10.1080/10510974.2011.584934

Gold, R. L. (1958). Roles in sociological field observations. *Social Forces, 36*, 217–223.

Goltz, D. (2009). Investigating queer future meanings: Destructive perceptions of "The harder path." *Qualitative Inquiry, 15*, 561–586. doi:10.1177/1077800408329238

Goodall, Jr., H. L. (2006). *A need to know: The clandestine history of a CIA family.* Walnut Creek, CA: Left Coast Press.

Graham, E. (2009). Family communication standards instrument. In R. B. Rubin, A. M. Rubin, E. E. Graham, E. M. Perse, & D. R. Seibold (Eds.), *Communication research measures II* (pp. 149–153). New York, NY: Routledge.

Gray, J. H., & Densten, I. L. (1998). Integrating quantitative and qualitative analysis using latent and manifest variables. *Quality & Quantity, 32*, 419–431.

Green-Hamann, S., Eichhorn, K. C., & Sherblom, J. C. (2011). An exploration of why people participate in Second Life social support groups. *Journal of Computer-Mediated Communication, 16*, 465–491. doi:10.1111/j.1083-6101.2011.01543.x

Grimm, J., & Andsager, J. L. (2011). Framing immigration: Geo-ethnic context in California newspapers. *Journalism & Mass Communication Quarterly, 88*, 771–788.

Gubrium, J. F., & Holstein, J. A. (2000). Introduction: The discipline and practice of qualitative research. In N. K. Denzin & Y. S. Lincoln (Eds.), *Handbook of qualitative research* (2nd ed., pp. 487–508). Thousand Oaks, CA: Sage.

Guilford, J. P. (1956). *Fundamental statistics in psychology and education.* New York, NY: McGraw-Hill.

Gunn, A. M. (2008). "People's lives are hanging here": Low wage workers share their experience of job loss. *Journal of Contemporary Ethnography, 37*, 679–693. doi:10.1177/0891241608316666

Guthrie, J., & Kunkel, A. (2013). Tell me sweet (and not-so-sweet) little lies: Deception in romantic relationships. *Communication Studies, 64*, 141–157. doi:10.1080/10510974.2012.755637

Gwartney, P. A. (2007). *The telephone interviewer's handbook: How to conduct a standardized conversation.* San Francisco, CA: Jossey-Bass.

Hackman, J. R. (1992). Commentary: Time and transitions. In P. J. Frost & R. E. Stablein (Eds.), *Doing exemplary research* (pp. 73–76). Newbury Park, CA: Sage.

Hall, J. A., Carter, S., Cody, M. J., & Albright, J. M. (2010). Individual differences in the communication of romantic interest: Development of the flirting styles inventory. *Communication Quarterly, 58,* 365–393. doi:10.1080/01463373.2010.524874

Hamel, S. A. (2009). Exit, voice, and sensemaking following psychological contract violations. *Journal of Business Communication, 46,* 234–261. doi:10.1177/0021943608328079

Hammersley, M. (2008). *Questioning qualitative inquiry: Critical essays.* Los Angeles, CA: Sage.

Hammersley, M., & Traianou, A. (2012). *Ethics in qualitative research.* Los Angeles, CA: Sage.

Hargittai, E., & Karr, C. (2009). Wat R U Doin? Studying the thumb generation using text messaging. In E. Hargittai (Ed.), *Research confidential: Solutions to problems most social scientists pretend they never have* (pp. 192–216). Ann Arbor: University of Michigan Press.

Harlow, L. L. (1997). Significance testing introduction and overview. In L. L. Harlow, S. A. Mulaik, & J. H. Steiger (Eds.), *What if there were no significance tests?* (pp. 1–17). Mahwah, NJ: Erlbaum.

Harlow, L. L., Mulaik, S. A., & Steiger, J. H. (Eds.). (1997). *What if there were no significance tests?* Mahwah, NJ: Erlbaum.

Harrington, N. G., Lane, D. R., Donohew, L., Zimmerman, R. S., Norling, G. R., Jeong-Hyun, A. . . . Bevins, C. C. (2003). Persuasive strategies for effective anti-drug messages. *Communication Monographs, 70,* 16–38. doi:10.1080/036775032000104568

Harter, L. M. (2004). Masculinity(s), the agrarian frontier myth, and cooperative ways of organizing: Contradictions and tensions in the experience and enactment of democracy. *Journal of Applied Communication Research, 32,* 89–118. 10.1080/0090988042000210016

Harter, L. M. (2009). Narratives as dialogic, contested, and aesthetic performances. *Journal of Applied Communication Research, 37,* 140–150. doi:10.1080/00909880902792255

Harter, L. M., Berquist, B., Titsworth, S., Novak, D., & Brokaw, T. (2005). The structuring of invisibility among the hidden homeless: The politics of space, stigma, and identity construction. *Journal of Applied Communication Research, 33,* 305–327. doi:10.1080/00909880500278079

Hastings, S. O., & Payne, J. J. (2013). Expressions of dissent in email: Qualitative insights into uses and meanings of organizational dissent. *Journal of Business Communication, 50,* 309–331. doi:10.1177/0021943613487071

Hawes, L. C. (1975). *Pragmatics of analoguing: Theory and model construction in communication.* Reading, MA: Addison-Wesley.

Hayes, A. F. (2005). *Statistical methods for communication science.* Mahwah, NJ: Erlbaum.

Heerwegh, D., & Loosveldt, G. (2008). Face-to-face versus web surveying in a high-Internet-coverage population. *Public Opinion Quarterly, 72,* 836–846. doi:10.1093/poq/nfn045

Hefner, V., & Wilson, B. J. (2013): From love at first sight to soul mate: The influence of romantic ideals in popular films on young people's beliefs about relationships. *Communication Monographs, 80,* 150–175. doi:10.1080/03637751.2013.776697

Henkel, R. E. (1976). *Tests of significance.* Beverly Hills, CA: Sage.

Henry, G. T. (1990). *Practical sampling.* Newbury Park, CA: Sage.

Henry, G. T. (1998). Practical sampling. In L. Bickman & D. J. Rog (Eds.), *Handbook of applied social research methods* (pp. 101–126). Thousand Oaks, CA: Sage.

Herndon, S. L. (1993). Using focus group interviews for preliminary investigation. In S. L. Herndon & G. L. Kreps (Eds.), *Qualitative research: Applications in organizational communication* (pp. 39–45). Cresskill, NJ: Hampton Press.

Hickson, M., III, & Jennings, R. W. (1993). Compatible theory and applied research: Systems theory and triangulation. In S. L. Herndon & G. L. Kreps (Eds.), *Qualitative research: Applications in organizational communication* (pp. 139–157). Cresskill, NJ: Hampton Press.

Holladay, S. J. (2002). "Have fun while you can," "you're only as old as you feel," and "don't ever get old!": An examination of memorable messages about aging. *Journal of Communication, 52,* 681–697. doi:10.1111/j.1460-2466.2002.tb02568.x

Holsti, O. R. (1969). *Content analysis for the social sciences and humanities.* Reading, MA: Addison-Wesley.

Holsti, O. R., Loomba, J. K., & North, R. C. (1968). Content analysis. In G. Lindzey & E. Aronson (Eds.), *The handbook of social psychology* (Vol. 2, pp. 596–692). Reading, MA: Addison-Wesley.

Hoonakker, P., & Carayon, P. (2009). Questionnaire survey nonresponse: A comparison of postal mail and Internet surveys. *International Journal of Human-Computer Interaction, 25,* 348–373. doi:10.1080/10447310902864951

Hoover, K., & Donovan, T. (1995). *The elements of social scientific thinking* (6th ed.). New York, NY: St. Martin's Press.

Hopf, T., Ayres, J., Ayres, F., & Baker, B. (1995). Does self-help material work? Testing a manual designed to help trainers construct public speaking apprehension reduction workshops. *Communication Research Reports, 12,* 34–38.

Horan, S. M., & Chory, R. M. (2013). Relational implications of gay and lesbian workplace romances: Understanding trust, deception, and credibility. *Journal of Business Communication, 50,* 170–189. doi:10.1177/0021943612474993

Hullett, C. R. (2002). Charting the process underlying the chance of value-expressive attitudes: The importance of value-relevance in predicting the matching effect. *Communication Monographs, 69,* 158–178. doi:10.1080/714041711

Humphreys, L. (2012). Connecting, coordinating, cataloguing: Communicative practices on mobile social networks. *Journal of Broadcasting & Electronic Media, 56,* 494–510. doi:10.1080/08838151.2012.732144

Hurley, R. J., & Tewksbury, D. (2012). News aggregation and content differences in online cancer news. *Journal of Broadcasting & Electronic Media, 56,* 132–149. doi:10.1080/08838151.2011.648681

Israel, M., & Hay, I. (2006). *Research ethics for social scientists.* Thousand Oaks, CA: Sage.

Ivory, J., & Kalyanaraman, S. (2009). Video games make people violent—well, maybe not that game: Effects of content and person abstraction on perceptions of violent video games' effects and support of censorship. *Communication Reports, 22,* 1–12. doi:10.1080/08934210902798536

Iyengar, S. (2011). Experimental designs for political communication research: Using new technology and online participant pools to overcome the problem of generalization. In E. P. Bucy & R. L. Holbert (Eds.), *The sourcebook for political communication research: Methods, measures, and analytical techniques* (pp. 129–148). New York, NY: Routledge.

Jackob, N., Roessing, T., & Petersen, T. (2011). The effects of verbal and nonverbal elements in persuasive communication: Findings from two multi-method experiments. *Communications: The European Journal of Communication Research, 36,* 245–271. doi:10.1515/COMM.2011.012

Jaeger, R. M. (1990). *Statistics: A spectator sport* (2nd ed.). Newbury Park, CA: Sage.

James, N., & Busher, H. (2012). Internet interviewing. In J. F. Gubrium, J. A. Holstein, A. B. Marvasti, & K. D. McKinney (Eds.), *The SAGE handbook of interview research: The complexity of the craft* (2nd ed., pp. 177–191). Los Angeles, CA: Sage.

Janesick, V. J. (1994). The dance of qualitative research designs: Metaphor, methodolatry, and meaning. In N. K. Denzin & Y. S. Lincoln (Eds.), *Handbook of qualitative research* (pp. 209–219). Thousand Oaks, CA: Sage.

Janesick, V. J. (1998). *"Stretching" exercises for qualitative researchers.* Thousand Oaks, CA: Sage.

Janesick, V. J. (2000). The choreography of qualitative research design. In N. K. Denzin & Y. S. Lincoln (Eds.), *Handbook of qualitative research* (2nd ed., pp. 379–399). Thousand Oaks, CA: Sage.

Janesick, V. J. (2004). *"Stretching" exercises for qualitative researchers* (2nd ed.). Thousand Oaks, CA: Sage.

Jeffres, L. W., Neuendorf, K., & Atkin, D. J. (2012). Acquiring knowledge from the media in the Internet age. *Communication Quarterly, 60,* 59–79. doi:10.1080/01463373.2012.641835

Jian, G. (2008). Identity and technology: Organizational control of knowledge-intensive work. *Qualitative Research Reports in Communication, 9,* 62–71. doi:10.1080/17459430802400365

Jian, G., Pettey, G., Rudd, J., & Lawson, D. (2007). Masculinity/femininity and compliance-gaining in business negotiations: A cross-cultural comparison. *Journal of the Northwest Communication Association, 36,* 93–110. doi:10.1080/17459430802400365

Jodlowski, D., Sharf, B. F., Nguyen, L. C., Haidet, P., & Woodard, L. D. (2007). 'Screwed for life': Examining identification and division in addiction narratives. *Communication & Medicine, 4,* 15–26. doi:10.1515/CAM.2007.003

Johansson, T. (2011). Fatherhood in transition: Paternity leave and changing masculinities. *Journal of Family Communication, 11,* 165–18. doi:10.1080/15267431.2011.561137

Johnson, A. J., Becker, J. A., Wigley, S., Haigh, M. M., & Craig, E. A. (2007). Reported argumentativeness and verbal aggressiveness levels: The influence of type of argument. *Communication Studies, 58,* 189–205. doi:10.1080/10510970701341154

Johnson, D. I. (2009). Connected classroom climate: A validity study. *Communication Research Reports, 26,* 146–157. doi:10.1080/08824090902861622

Johnson, D. I. (2013). Student in-class texting behavior: Associations with instructor clarity and classroom relationships. *Communication Research Reports, 30,* 57–62. doi:10.108008824096.2012.723645

Johnson, J. M., & Rowlands, T. (2012). The interpersonal dynamics of in-depth interview. In J. F. Gubrium, J. A. Holstein, A. B. Marvasti, & K. D. McKinney (Eds.), *The SAGE handbook of interview research: The complexity of the craft* (2nd ed., pp. 99–113). Los Angeles, CA: Sage.

Johnson, T. J., Kaye, B. K., Bichard, S. L., & Wong, W. J. (2008). Every blog has its day: Politically-interested Internet users' perceptions of blog credibility. *Journal of Computer-Mediated Communication, 13,* 100–122. doi:10.1111/j.1083-6101.2007.00388.x

Jones, S. H. (2005). Autoethnography: Making the personal political. In N. K. Denzin & Y. S. Lincoln (Eds.), *The Sage handbook of qualitative research* (3rd ed., pp. 763–791).Thousand Oaks, CA: Sage.

Jorgensen-Earp, C. R., & Staton, A. Q. (1993). Student metaphors for the college freshman experience. *Communication Education, 42,* 123–141. doi:10.1080/03634529309378920

Judd, C. M., & McClelland, G. H. (1998). Measurement. In D. T. Gilbert, S. T. Fiske, & G. Lindzey (Eds.), *The handbook of social psychology* (Vol. I, 4th ed., pp. 180–232). Boston, MA: McGraw-Hill.

Judd, C. M., McClelland, G. H., & Culhane, S. E. (1995). Data analysis: Continuing issues in the everyday analysis of psychological data. In J. T. Spence, J. M. Darley, & D. J. Foss (Eds.), *Annual review of psychology* (Vol. 46, pp. 433–465). Palo Alto, CA: Annual Reviews.

Kaid, L. L., & Wadsworth, A. J. (1989). Content analysis. In P. Emmert & L. L. Barker (Eds.), *Measurement of communication behavior* (pp. 197–217). New York, NY: Longman.

Kaiser, K. (2012). Protecting confidentiality. In J. F. Gubrium, J. A. Holstein, A. B. Marvasti, & K. D. McKinney (Eds.), *The SAGE handbook of interview research: The complexity of the craft* (2nd ed., pp. 457–464). Los Angeles, CA: Sage.

Kamberelis, G,. & Dimitriadis, G. (2005). Focus groups: Strategic articulations of pedagogy, politics, and inquiry. In N. K. Denzin & Y. S. Lincoln (Eds.), *The Sage handbook of qualitative research* (3rd ed., pp. 887–907). Thousand Oaks, CA: Sage.

Kaplan, A. (1964). *The conduct of inquiry.* San Francisco, CA: Chandler.

Kaplowitz, M. D., Lupi, F., Couper, M. P., & Thorp, L. (2012). The effect of invitation design on web survey response rates. *Social Science Computer Review, 30,* 339–349. doi:10.1177/0894439311419084

Kassing, J. W. (2009a). Breaking the chain of command. *Journal of Business Communication, 46,* 311–334. doi:10.1177/0021943609333521

Kassing, J. W. (2009b). "In case you didn't hear me the first time": An examination of repetitious upward dissent. *Management Communication Quarterly, 22,* 416–436. doi:10.1177/0893318908327008

Katzer, J., Cook, K. H., & Crouch, W. W. (1978). *Evaluating information: A guide for users of social science research.* Reading, MA: Addison-Wesley.

Keaten, J. A., & Kelly, L. (2008). Emotional intelligence as a mediator of family communication patterns and reticence. *Communication Reports, 21,* 104–116. doi:10.1080/08934210802393008

Kemph, A. M., & Remington, P. L. (2007). New challenges for telephone survey research in the twenty-first century. *Annual Review of Public Health, 28,* 113–126. doi:10.1146/annurev.publhealth.28 .021406.144059

Kennedy-Lightsey, C. D., Martin, M. M., Thompson, M., Himes, K. L., & Clingerman, B. Z. (2012). Communication privacy management theory: Exploring coordination and ownership between friends. *Communication Quarterly, 60,* 665–680. doi:10.1080/01463373.2012.725004

Kerlinger, F. N. (1986). *Foundations of behavioral research* (3rd ed.). New York, NY: Holt, Rinehart and Winston.

Keyton, J. (1994). Designing a look at women. *The Mid-Atlantic. Almanack, 3,* 126–141.

Keyton, J. (1995). Using SYMLOG as a self-analytical group facilitation technique. In L. R. Frey (Ed.), *Innovations in group facilitation: Applications in natural settings* (pp. 148–174). Cresskill, NJ: Hampton Press.

Keyton, J. (1997). Coding communication in decision-making groups: Assessing effective and ineffective process. In L. R. Frey & J. K. Barge (Eds.), *Managing group life: Communication in decision-making groups* (pp. 236–269). Boston, MA: Houghton Mifflin.

Keyton, J. (2011). *Communication and organizational culture: A key to understanding work experiences* (2nd ed.). Thousand Oaks, CA: Sage.

Keyton, J., & Beck, S. J. (2009). The influential role of relational messages in group interaction. *Group Dynamics, 13,* 14–30. doi:10.1037/a0013495

Keyton, J., Bisel, R. S., & Ozley, R. O. (2009). Recasting the link between applied and theory research: Using applied findings to advance communication theory development. *Communication Theory, 19,* 146–160. doi:10.1111/j.1468-2885.2009.01339.x

Keyton, J., Caputo, J., Ford, E., Fu, R., Leibowitz, S., Liu, T., . . . Ghosh, P. (2013). Investigating verbal workplace communication behaviors. *Journal of Business Communication, 50,* 152–169. doi:10.1177/0021943612474990

Keyton, J., Ford, D. J., & Smith F. L. (2008). A meso-level communicative model of interorganizational collaboration. *Communication Theory, 18,* 376–406. doi:10.1111/j.1468-2885.2008.00327.x

Keyton, J., & Rhodes, S. C. (1997). Sexual harassment: A matter of individual ethics, legal definitions, or organizational policy? *Journal of Business Ethics, 16,* 129–146. doi:10.1023/A:1017905100869

Keyton, J., & Smith, F. L. (2009). Distrust in leaders: Dimensions, patterns, and emotional intensity. *Journal of Leadership and Organizational Studies, 16,* 6–18. doi:10.1177/1548051809334196

Kibler, R. J. (1970). Basic communication research considerations. In P. Emmert & W. D. Brooks (Eds.), *Methods of research in communication* (pp. 9–49). New York, NY: Houghton Mifflin.

Kim, H., K., & Niederdeppe, J. (2013). Exploring optimistic bias and the integrative model of behavioral prediction in the context of a campus influenza outbreak. *Journal of Health Communication, 18,* 206–232. doi:10.1080/10810730.2012.688247

Kim, J. Y., & Kiousis, S. (2012). The role of affect in agenda building for public relations: Implications for public relations outcomes. *Journalism & Mass Communication Quarterly, 89,* 657–676. doi:10.1177/1077699012455387

Kinnally, W., & Brinkerhoff, B. (2013). Improving the drive: A case study for modeling public radio member donations using the theory of planned behavior. *Journal of Radio & Audio Media, 20,* 2–16. doi:10.1080/19376529.2013.777733

Kirk, R. E. (1996). Practical significance: A concept whose time has come. *Educational and Psychological Measurement, 56,* 746–759. doi:10.1177/0013164496056005002

Kosenko, K. A. (2011). The safer sex communication of transgender adults: Processes and problems. *Journal of Communication, 61,* 476–495. doi:10.1111/j.1460-2466.2011.01556.x

Kramer, M. W. (1995). A longitudinal study of superior-subordinate communication during job transfers. *Human Communication Research, 22,* 39–64. doi:10.1111/j.1468-2958.1995.tb00361.x

Kramer, M. W., Meisenbach, R. J., & Hansen, G. J. (2013). Communication, uncertainty, and volunteer membership. *Journal of Applied Communication Research, 41,* 18–39. doi:10.1080/00909882.2012.750002

Kranstuber, H., & Kellas, J. K. (2011). 'Instead of growing under her heart, I grew in it': The relationship between adoption entrance narratives and adoptees' self-concept. *Communication Quarterly, 59,* 179–199. doi:10.1080/01463373.2011.563440

Krejcie, R. V., & Morgan, D. W. (1970). Determining sample size for research activities. *Educational and Psychological Measurement, 30,* 607–610.

Krippendorff, K. (2013). *Content analysis: An introduction to its methodology* (3rd ed.). Thousand Oaks, CA: Sage.

Krueger, R. A., & Casey, M. A. (2000). *Focus groups: A practical guide for applied research* (3rd ed.). Thousand Oaks, CA: Sage.

Kuhn, T., & Poole, M. S. (2000). Do conflict management styles affect group decision making? Evidence from a longitudinal field study. *Human Communication Research, 26,* 558–590. doi:10.1111/j.1468-2958.2000.tb00769.x

Kumar, R. (1996). *Research methodology: A step-by-step guide for beginners.* Thousand Oaks, CA: Sage.

Kvale, S. (1996). *InterViews: An introduction to qualitative research interviewing.* Thousand Oaks, CA: Sage.

Lacy, S. R., & Riffe, D. (1993). Sins of omission and commission in mass communication quantitative research. *Journalism Quarterly, 70,* 126–132.

Lammers, J. C., & Garcia, M. A. (2009). Exploring the concept of "profession" for organizational communication research: Institutional influences in a veterinary organization. *Management Communication Quarterly, 22,* 357–384. doi:10.1177/0893318908327007

Lange, J. I. (1990). Refusal to compromise: The case of Earth First! *Western Journal of Speech Communication, 54,* 473–494. doi:10.1080/10570319009374356

Lee, E. (2004). Effects of visual representation on social influence in computer-mediated communication: Experimental tests of the social identity model of deindividuation effects. *Human Communication Research, 30,* 234–259. doi:10.1093/hcr/30.2.234

Lee, E., & Oh, S. Y. (2012). To personalize or depersonalize? When and how politicians' personalized tweets affect the public's reactions. *Journal of Communication, 62,* 932–949. doi:10.1111/j.1460-2466.2012.01681.x

Lee, J. K. (2008). Effects of news deviance and personal involvement of audience story selection: A web-tracking analysis. *Journalism & Mass Communication Quarterly, 85,* 41–60.

Lee, M. J., & Chen, Y-C. (2013). Underage drinkers' responses to negative-restrictive versus proactive-nonrestrictive slogans in humorous anti-alcohol abuse messages: Are humorous responsible drinking campaign messages effective? *Journal of Health Communication, 18,* 354–368. doi:10.1080/10810730.2012.727949

Lee, S., & Chung, S. (2012). Corporate apology and crisis communication: The effect of responsibility admittance and sympathetic expression on public's anger relief. *Public Relations Review, 38,* 932–934. doi:10.1016/j.pubrev.2012.08.006

Leeman, M. A. (2011). Balancing the benefits and burdens of storytelling among vulnerable people. *Health Communication, 26,* 107–109. doi:10.1080/10410236.2011.527628

Leonardi, P. M., & Jackson, M. H. (2009). Technological grounding: Enrolling technology as a discursive resource to justify cultural change in organizations. *Science, Technology, & Human Values, 34,* 393–418. doi:10.1177/0162243908328771

Lesch, C. L. (1994). Observing theory in practice: Sustaining consciousness in a coven. In L. R. Frey (Ed.), *Group communication in context: Studies of natural groups* (pp. 57–84.). Hillsdale, NJ: Erlbaum.

Levine, T. R., Weber, R., Hullett, C., Park, H. S., & Lindsey, L. L. M. (2008). A critical assessment of null hypothesis significance testing in quantitative communication research. *Human Communication Research, 34,* 171–187. doi:10.1111/j.1468-2958.2008.00317.x

Levine, T. R., Weber, R., Park, H. S., & Hullett, C. R. (2008). A communication researchers' guide to null hypothesis significance testing and alternatives. *Human Communication Research, 34,* 188–209. doi:10.1111/j.1468-2958.2008.00318.x

Lewis, S. C., Zamith, R., & Hermida, A. (2013). Content analysis in an era of big data: A hybrid approach to computational and manual methods. *Journal of Broadcasting & Electronic Media, 57,* 34–52. doi:10.1080/08838151.2012.761702

Liamputtong, P. (2011). *Focus group methodology: Principles and practice.* London, United Kingdom: Sage.

Lim, T. S., & Bowers, J. (1991). Facework: Solidarity, approbation, and tact. *Human Communication Research, 17,* 415–450. doi:10.1111/j.1468-2958.1991. tb00239.x

Lincoln, Y. S., & Guba, E. G. (1985). *Naturalistic inquiry.* Beverly Hills, CA: Sage.

Lindlof, T. R. (1991). The qualitative study of media audiences. *Journal of Broadcasting & Electronic Media, 35,* 23–42. doi:10.1080/08838159109364100

Lindlof, T. R. (1995). *Qualitative communication research methods.* Thousand Oaks, CA: Sage.

Lindlof, T. R., & Taylor, B. C. (2002). *Qualitative communication research methods* (2nd ed.). Thousand Oaks, CA: Sage.

Lindlof, T. R., & Taylor, B. C. (2011). *Qualitative communication research methods* (3rd ed.). Los Angeles, CA: Sage.

Littlejohn, S. W. (1991). Deception in communication research. *Communication Reports, 4,* 51–54. doi:10.1080/08934219109367521

Liu, F. (2007). Determinants of cable system product diversification: An investigation of the U.S. cable systems. *The International Journal on Media Management, 9,* 9–18. doi:10.1080/14241270701193391

Lofland, J., & Lofland, L. H. (1995). *Analyzing social settings: A guide to qualitative observation and analysis* (3rd ed.). Belmont, CA: Wadsworth.

Lombard, M., Snyder-Duch, J., & Bracken, C. C. (2002). Content analysis in mass communication: Assessment and reporting of intercoder reliability. *Human Communication Research, 28,* 587–604. doi:10.1111/j.1468-2958.2002.tb00826.x

Longo, D. R., Ge, B., Radina, M. E., Greiner, A., Williams, C. D., Longo, G. S. . . . Salas-Lopez, D. (2009). Understanding breast-cancer patients' perceptions: Health information-seeking behavior and passive information receipt. *Journal of Communication in Healthcare, 2,* 184–206.

Loseke, D. R. (2013). *Methodological thinking: Basic principles of social research design.* Los Angeles, CA: Sage.

Lowry, D. T. (1979). Population validity of communication research: Sampling the samples. *Journalism Quarterly, 55,* 62–68, 76.

Lucas, K. (2011). Socializing messages in blue-collar families: Communicative pathways to social mobility and reproduction. *Western Journal of Communication, 75,* 95–121. doi:10.1080/10570314.2010. 536964

Lumsden, J. (2007). Online-questionnaire design guidelines. In R. A. Reynolds, R. Woods, & J. D. Baker (Eds.), *Handbook of research on electronic surveys and measurements* (pp. 44–64). Hershey, PA: Idea Group Reference.

Lundy, L. K., Ruth, A. M., & Park, T. D. (2008). Simply irresistible: Reality TV consumption patterns. *Communication Quarterly, 56,* 208–225. doi:10.1080/01463370802026828

Lustig, M. W. (1986). Theorizing about human communication. *Communication Quarterly, 34,* 451–459.

Lykken, D. E. (1968). Statistical significance in psychological research. *Psychological Bulletin, 70,* 151–159. doi:10.1037/h0026141

Mabry, L. (2009). Governmental regulation in social science. In D. M. Mertens & P. E. Ginsberg (Eds), *The handbook of social research ethics* (pp. 107–120). Los Angeles, CA: Sage.

Maeda, E., & Hecht, M. L. (2012). Identity search: Interpersonal relationships and relational identities of always-single Japanese women over time. *Western Journal of Communication, 76,* 44–64, doi:10.1080/10570314.2012.637539

Maki, S. M., Booth-Butterfield, M., & McMullen, A. (2012). Does our humor affect us? An examination of a dyad's humor orientation. *Communication Quarterly, 60,* 649–664. doi:10.1080/01463373.2012. 725006

Malachowski, C. C., & Dillow, M. R. (2011) An examination of relational uncertainty, romantic intent, and attraction on communicative and relational outcomes in cross-sex friendships. *Communication Research Reports, 28,* 356–368.; doi:10.1080/08824096. 2011.616245

Malhotra, N. (2008). Completion time and response order effects in web surveys. *Public Opinion Quarterly, 72,* 914–934. doi:10.1093/poq/nfn050

Malone, P., & Hayes, J. (2012). Backstabbing in organizations: Employees' perceptions of incidents, motives, and communicative responses. *Communication Studies, 63,* 194–219. doi:10.1080/10510974. 2011.635552

Mansson, D. H. (2013). College students' mental health and their received affection from their grandparents. *Communication Research Reports, 30*, 157–168. doi:10.1080/08824096.2012.763028

Manusov, V., Trees, A. R., Reddick, L. A., Rowe, A. M. C., & Easley, J. M. (1998). Explanations and impressions: Investigating attributions and their effects on judgments for friends and strangers. *Communication Studies, 49*, 209–223. doi10.1080/10510979809368532

Markham, A. N. (1998). *Life online: Researching real experience in virtual space.* Walnut Creek, CA: AltaMira.

Markham, A. N. (2004). The Internet as research context. In C. Seale, G. Gobo, J. F. Gubrium, & D. Silverman (Eds.), *Qualitative research practice* (pp. 358–374). London, United Kingdom: Sage.

Marshall, C., & Rossman, G. B. (1999). *Designing qualitative research* (3rd ed.). Thousand Oaks, CA: Sage.

Martin, D. M. (2004). Humor in middle management: Women negotiating the paradoxes of organizational life? *Journal of Applied Communication Research, 32*, 147–170. doi:10.1080/0090988042000210034

Martinson, B. C., Anderson, M. S., & de Vries, R. (2005). Scientists behaving badly. *Nature, 435*, 737–738. doi:10.1038/435737a

Mason, S. A. (1993). Communication processes in the field research interview setting. In S. L. Herndon & G. L. Kreps (Eds.), *Qualitative research: Applications in organizational communication* (pp. 29–38). Cresskill, NJ: Hampton Press.

Maxwell, J. A. (1996). *Qualitative research design: An interactive approach.* Thousand Oaks, CA: Sage.

Maxwell, J. A. (2005). *Qualitative research design* (2nd ed.). Thousand Oaks, CA: Sage.

Mazer, J. P., & Ledbetter, A. M. (2012). Online communication attitudes as predictors of problematic Internet use and well-being outcomes. *Southern Communication Journal, 77*, 403–419. doi:10.1080/1041794X.2012.686558

McCracken, G. (1988). *The long interview.* Newbury Park, CA: Sage.

McCroskey, J. C. (1970). Measures of communication-bound anxiety. *Speech Monographs, 37*, 269–277. doi:10.1080/03637757009375677

McCroskey, J. C., Beatty, M. J., Kearney, P., & Plax, T. G. (1985). The content validity of the PRCA-24 as a measure of communication apprehension across communication contexts. *Communication Quarterly, 33*, 165–173. doi:10.1080/01463378509369595

McCroskey, J. C. & Richmond, V. (1990). Willingness to communicate: Differing cultural perspectives. *Southern Communication Journal, 56*, 72–77. doi:10.1080/10417949009372817

McCroskey, J. C., Richmond, V. P., Johnson, A. D., & Smith, H. T. (2004). Organizational orientations theory and measurement: Development of measures and preliminary investigations. *Communication Quarterly, 52*, 1–14.

McGee, D. S., & Cegala, D. J. (1998). Patient communication skills training for improved communication competence in the primary care medical consultation. *Journal of Applied Communication Research, 26*, 412–430.

McKinnon, S. L. (2008). Unsettling resettlement: Problematizing "lost boys of Sudan" resettlement and identity. *Western Journal of Communication, 72*, 397–414. doi:10.1080/10570310802446056

McManus, T. G., & Nussbaum, J. F. (2013). Topic valence and ambiguity in parent-emerging adult child postdivorce discussions. *Communication Studies, 64*, 195–217. doi:10.1080/10510974.2011.646085

Meeks, L. (2013). He wrote, she wrote: Journalist gender, political office, and campaign news. *Journalism & Mass Communication Quarterly, 90*, 58–74. doi:10.1177/1077699012468695

Meltzer, C. E., Naab, T., & Daschmann, G . (2012). All student samples differ: On participant selection in communication science. *Communication Methods & Measures, 6*, 251–262. doi: 10.1080/19312458. 2012.732625

Mendelson, A. L., & Thorson, E. (2004). How verbalizers and visualizers process the newspaper environment. *Journal of Communication, 54*, 474–491. doi:10.1111/j.1460-2466.2004.tb02640.x

Meyer, P. (1973). *Precision journalism.* Bloomington, IN: University Press.

Meyers, R. A., & Brashers, D. (2010). Extending the conversational argument coding scheme: Argument categories, units, and coding procedures. *Communication Methods & Measures, 4*, 27–45. doi:10.1080/19312451003680467

Meyers, R. A., Seibold, D. R., & Brashers, D. (1991). Argument in initial group decision-making discussions: Refinement of a coding scheme and a descriptive quantitative analysis. *Western Journal of Speech Communication, 55*, 47–68.

Miller, G. R. (1970). Research setting: Laboratory studies. In P. Emmert & W. D. Brooks (Eds.), *Methods of research in communication* (pp. 77–104). New York, NY: Houghton Mifflin.

Miller, G. R., & Nicholson, H. E. (1976). *Communication inquiry: A perspective on a process.* Reading, MA: Addison-Wesley.

Miller, K. I. (2008). My father and his father: An analysis of World War II correspondence. *Journal of Family Communication, 8*, 148–165. doi:10.1080/15267430701857349

Miller, T. (2012). Reconfiguring research relationships: Regulation, new technologies and doing ethical research. In T. Miller, M. Birch, M. Mauthner, & J. Jessop (Eds.), *Ethics in qualitative research* (2nd ed., pp. 29–42). Los Angeles, CA: Sage.

Miller-Day, M. A. (2004). *Communication among grandmothers, mothers, and adult daughters: A qualitative study of maternal relationships.* Mahwah: NJ: Erlbaum.

Morgan, D. L. (1997). *Focus groups as qualitative research* (2nd ed.). Thousand Oaks, CA: Sage.

Morgan, D. L. (2012). Focus groups and social interaction. In J. F. Gubrium, J. A. Holstein, A. B. Marvasti, & K. D. McKinney (Eds.), *The SAGE handbook of interview research: The complexity of the craft* (2nd ed., pp. 161–176). Los Angeles, CA: Sage.

Morgan, D. L., & Krueger, R. A. (1993). When to use focus groups and why. In D. L. Morgan (Ed.), *Successful focus groups: Advancing the state of the art* (pp. 3–19). Newbury Park, CA: Sage.

Moriarty, C. M., & Harrison, K. (2008). Television exposure and disordered eating among children: A longitudinal panel study. *Journal of Communication, 58,* 361–381. doi:10.1111/j.1460-2466.2008.00389.x

Mueller, B. H., & Lee, J. (2002). Leader-member exchange and organizational communication satisfaction in multiple contexts. *The Journal of Business Communication, 39,* 220–244. doi:10.1177/002194360203900204

Muthuswamy, N., Levine, T. R., & Gazel, J. (2006). Interaction-based diversity initiative outcomes: An evaluation of an initiative aimed at bridging the racial divide on a college campus. *Communication Education, 55,* 105–121. doi:10.1080/03634520500489690

Muturi, N., & Mwangi, S. (2011). Older adults' perspectives on HIV/AIDS prevention strategies for rural Kenya. *Health Communication, 26,* 712–723. doi:10.1080/10410236.2011.563354

Nan, X., & Zhao, X. (2012).When does self-affirmation reduce negative responses to antismoking messages? *Communication Studies, 63,* 482–497. doi:10.1080/10510974.2011.633151

Nardi, P. M. (2006). *Doing survey research: A guide to quantitative methods* (2nd ed.). Boston, MA: Pearson.

Nathanson, A. I., & Rasmussen, E. E. (2011). TV viewing compared to book reading and toy playing reduces responsive maternal communication with toddlers and preschoolers. *Human Communication Research, 37,* 465–487. doi:10.1111/j.1468-2958.2011.01413.x

National Commission for the Protection of Human Subjects of Biomedical and Behavioral Research. (1979). *The Belmont report: Ethical principles and guidelines for the protection of human subjects of research.* Retrieved from http://www.hhs.gov/ohrp/humansubjects/guidance/belmont.html

Neuendorf, K. A. (2002). *The content analysis guidebook.* Thousand Oaks, CA: Sage.

Nir, L. (2012). Public space: How shared news landscapes close gaps in political engagement. *Journal of Broadcasting & Electronic Media, 56,* 578–596. doi:10.1080/08838151.2012.732145

Norman, K. L., Friedman, Z., Norman, K., & Stevenson, R. (2001). Navigational issues in the design of on-line self-administered questionnaires. *Behavior & Information Technology, 20,* 37–45. doi:10.1080/01449290010021764

Northey, M., Tepperman, L., & Albanese, P. (2012). *Making sense in the social sciences: A student's guide to research and writing* (5th ed.). Don Mills, Ontario, Canada: Oxford University Press.

Novak, D. R., & Harter, L. M. (2008). "Flipping the scripts" of poverty and panhandling: Organizing democracy by creating connections. *Journal of Applied Communication Research, 36,* 391–414. doi:10.1080/00909880802104890

Ntseane, P. G. (2009). The ethics of the researcher-subject relationship: Experiences from the field. In D. M. Mertens & P. E. Ginsberg (Eds), *The handbook of social research ethics* (pp. 295–307). Los Angeles, CA: Sage.

Oliveira, M. (2013). Multicultural environments and their challenges to crisis communication. *Journal of Business Communication, 50,* 253–277. doi:10.1177/0021943613487070

Oliver, M. B., & Raney, A. A. (2011). Entertainment as pleasurable and meaningful: Identifying hedonic and eudaimonic motivations for entertainment. *Journal of Communication, 61,* 984–1004. doi:10.1111/j.1460-2466.2011.01585.

O'Keefe, D. J. (2004). The unity of argument across methodological divides. Paper presented at the conference of the International Communication Association, New Orleans, LA.

Osgood, C. E., Suci, C. J., & Tannenbaum, P. H. (1957). *The measurement of meaning.* Urbana: University of Illinois Press.

Owen, W. F. (1984). Interpretive themes in relational communication. *Quarterly Journal of Speech, 70,* 274–287. doi:10.1080/00335638409383697

Packer, M. (2011). *The science of qualitative research.* New York, NY: Cambridge University Press.

Padilla-Walker, L. M., Coyne, S. M., Fraser, A. M., & Stockdale, L. A. (2013). Is Disney the nicest place on Earth? A content analysis of prosocial behavior in animated Disney films. *Journal of Communication, 63,* 393–412. doi:10.1111/jcom.12022

Paek, H. J., Lambe, J. L., & McLeod, D. M. (2008). Antecedents to support for content restrictions. *Journalism & Mass Communication Quarterly, 85,* 273–290.

Paek, H. J., Oh, H. J., & Hove, T. (2012). How media campaigns influence children's physical activity: Expanding the normative mechanisms of the theory of planned behavior. *Journal of Health Communication, 17,* 869–885. doi:10.1080/10810730.2011.65

Pazos, P., Chung, J. M., & Micari, M. (2013). Instant messaging as a task-support tool in information technology organizations. *Journal of Business Communication, 50,* 68–86. doi:10.1177/0021943612465181

Pearson, J. C., Child, J. T., DeGreeff, B. L., Semlak, J. L., & Burnett, A. (2011). The influence of biological sex, self-esteem, and communication apprehension on unwillingness to communicate. *Atlantic Journal of Communication, 19,* 216–227. doi:10.1080/15456870.2011.584509

Pedhazur, E. J., & Schmelkin, L. P. (1991). *Measurement, design, and analysis: An integrated approach.* Hillsdale, NJ: Erlbaum.

Peng, T-Q., Zhu, J. J. H., Tong, J-J., & Jiang, S-J. (2012). Predicting internet non-users' adoption intention and adoption behavior. *Information, Communication, & Society, 15,* 1236–1257. doi:10.1080/1369118X.2011.614628

Peter, J., & Valkenburg, P. M. (2009). Adolescents' exposure to sexually explicit Internet material and sexual satisfaction: A longitudinal study. *Human Communication Research, 35,* 171–194. doi:10.1111/j.1468-2958.2009.01343.x

Petronio, S., Reeder, H. M., Hecht, M. L., & Ros-Mendoza, T. M. (1996). Disclosure of sexual abuse by children and adolescents. *Journal of Applied Communication Research, 24,* 181–189. doi:10.1080/00909889609365450

Petronio, S., & Sargent, J. (2011). Disclosure predicaments arising during the course of patient care: Nurses' privacy management. *Health Communication, 26,* 155–266. doi:10.1080/10410236.2010.549812

Phillips, D. C. (1992). *The social scientist's bestiary: A guide to fabled threats to, and defenses of, naturalistic social science.* Oxford, United Kingdom: Pergamon Press.

Phillipsen, G. (1992). *Speaking culturally: Explorations in social communication.* Albany: State University of New York Press.

Pierce, T., & Dougherty, D. S. (2002). The construction, enactment, and maintenance of power-as-domination through an acquisition: The case of TWA and Ozark Airlines. *Management Communication Quarterly, 16,* 129–164. doi:10.1177/089331802237232

Pitts, M. J., Fowler, C., Kaplan, M. S., Nussbaum, J., & Becker, J. C. (2009). Dialectical tensions underpinning family farm succession planning. *Journal of Applied Communication Research, 37,* 59–79. doi:10.1080/00909880802592631

Ploeger, N. A., Kelley, K. M., & Bisel, R. S. (2011). Hierchical mum effect: A new investigation of organizational ethics. *Southern Communication Journal, 76,* 465–481. doi:10.1080/11111041794x201.500343

Poland, B. D. (1995). Transcription quality as an aspect of rigor in qualitative research. *Qualitative Inquiry, 1,* 290–310.

Pomerantz, A., Fehr, B. J., & Ende, J. (1997). When supervising physicians see patients: Strategies used in difficult situations. *Human Communication Research, 23,* 589–615.

Poole, M. S. (l983a). Decision development in small groups II: A study of multiple sequences in decision-making. *Communication Monographs, 50,* 206–232.

Poole, M. S., & Dobosh, M. (2010). Exploring conflict management processes in jury deliberations through interaction analysis. *Small Group Research, 41,* 408–426. doi:10.1177/1046496410366310

Poole, M. S., & McPhee, R. D. (1985). Methodology in interpersonal communication research. In M. L. Knapp & G. R. Miller (Eds.), *Handbook of interpersonal communication* (pp. 100–170). Beverly Hills, CA: Sage.

Poole, M. S., & Roth, J. (l989). Decision development in small groups IV: A typology of decision paths. *Human Communication Research, 15,* 323–356

Porter, A. J. (2013). Emergent organization and responsive technologies in crisis: Creating connections or enabling divides? *Management Communication Quarterly, 27,* 6–33. doi:10.1177/0893318912459042

Potter, W. J. (1996). *An analysis of thinking and research about qualitative methods.* Mahwah, NJ: Erlbaum.

Potter, W. J., & Levine-Donnerstein, D. (1999). Rethinking validity and reliability in content analysis. *Journal of Applied Communication Research, 27,* 258–284. doi:10.1080/00909889909365539

Pratt, L., Wiseman, R. L., Cody, M. J., & Wendt, P. F. (1999). Interrogative strategies and information exchange in computer-mediated communication. *Communication Quarterly, 47,* 46–66. doi:10.1080/01463379909370123

Prentice, C. M. (2008). The assimilation of in-laws: The impact of newcomers on the communication routines of families. *Journal of Applied Communication Research, 36,* 74–97. doi:10.1080/00909880701799311

Presser, S., & Blair, J. (1994). Survey pretesting: Do different methods produce different results? In P. V. Marsden (Ed.), *Sociological methodology* (Vol. 24, pp. 73–104). Washington, DC: American Sociological Association.

Provins, K. A. (1997). Handedness and speech: A critical reappraisal of the role of genetic and environmental factors in the cerebral lateralization of function. *Psychological Review, 104,* 554–571. doi:10.1037/0033-295X.104.3.554

Punch, M. (1994). Politics and ethics in qualitative research. In N. K. Denzin & Y. S. Lincoln (Eds.), *Handbook of qualitative research* (pp. 83–97). Thousand Oaks, CA: Sage.

Pyrczak, F., & Bruce, R. R. (2007). *Writing empirical research reports: A basic guide for students of the social and behavioral sciences* (3rd ed.). Los Angeles, CA: Pyrczak.

Quan-Haase, A., & Collins, J. L. (2008). "I'm there, but I might not want to talk to you." *Information, Communication & Society, 11,* 526–543. doi:10.1080/13691180801999043

Query, J. L., Jr., & Kreps, G. L. (1993). Using the critical incident method to evaluate and enhance organizational effectiveness. In S. L. Herndon & G. L. Kreps (Eds.), *Qualitative research: Applications in organizational communication* (pp. 63–77). Cresskill, NJ: Hampton Press.

Quick, B. L., Fiese, B. H., Anderson, B., Koester, B. D., & Marlin, D. W. (2011). A normative evaluation of shared family mealtime for parents of toddlers and young children. *Health Communication, 26,* 656–666. doi:10.1080/10410236.2011.561920

Rains, S. A., & Keating, D. M. (2011). The social dimension of blogging about health: Health blogging, social support, and well-being. *Communication Monographs, 78,* 511–534. doi:10.1080/03637751.2011.618142

Rains, S. A., Tumlin, G. R., & Knapp, M. L. (2009). Electronic bumper stickers: The content and interpersonal functions of messages attached to e-mail signatures. *Discourse Studies, 11,* 105–120. doi:10.1177/1461445608098500

Real, K. (2008). Information seeking and workplace safety: A field application of the risk perception attitude framework. *Journal of Applied Communication Research, 36,* 339–359. doi:10.1080/00909880802101763

Reel, B. W., & Thompson, T. L. (1994). A test of the effectiveness of strategies for talking about AIDS and condom use. *Journal of Applied Communication Research, 22,* 127–140. doi:10.1080/00909889409365393

Resnik, D. B. (2007, February 23). What is ethics in research & why is it important. Retrieved from http://www.niehs.nih.gov/research/resources/bioethics/whatis.cfm

Richards, S, T., & Nelson, C. L. (2012). Problematic parental drinking and health: Investigating differences in adult children of alcoholics status, health locus of control, and health self-efficacy. *Journal of Communication in Healthcare, 5,* 84–90. doi:10.1179/1753807612Y.0000000006

Ricke, L. D. (2012). Funny or harmful?: Derogatory speech on Fox's Family Guy. *Communication Studies, 63,* 119–135. doi:10.1080/10510974.2011.638412

Riffe, D., Lacy, S., & Fico, F. G. (1998). *Analyzing media messages: Using quantitative content analysis in research.* Mahwah, NJ: Erlbaum.

Roberto, A. J., Carlyle, K. E., Zimmerman, R. S., Abner, E. L., Cupp, P. K., & Hansen, G. L. (2008). The short-term effects of a computer-based pregnancy, STD, and HIV prevention program. *Communication Quarterly, 56,* 29–48. doi:10.1080/01463370701839255

Roberto, A. J., Meyer, G., Boster, F. J., & Roberto, H. L. (2003). Adolescents' decisions about verbal and physical aggression: An application of the theory of reasoned action. *Human Communication Research, 29,* 135–147. doi:10.1111/j.1468-2958.2003.tb00834.x

Roberts, C. (2013). A functional analysis comparison of Web-only advertisements and traditional television advertisements from the 2004 and 2008 presidential campaigns. *Journalism & Mass Communication Quarterly, 90,* 23–38, doi:10.1177/1077699012468741

Robson, C. (2011). *Real world research: A resource for users of social research methods in applied settings* (3rd ed.). Chicester, United Kingdom: Wiley.

Rogan, R. G., & Hammer, M. R. (1994). Crisis negotiations: A preliminary investigation of face work in naturalistic conflict discourse. *Journal of Applied Communication Research, 22,* 216–231. doi:10.1080/00909889409365399

Rold, M., F., Honeycutt, J. M., Grey, S. H., & Fox, A, J. (2011). Emotional management in the aftermath of hurricane Katrina: Coping with tragedy through biblical stories of destruction. *Journal of Communication & Religion, 34,* 128–143.

Romo, L. K. (2011). Money talks: Revealing and concealing financial information in families. *Journal of Family Communication, 11,* 264–281. doi:10.1080/15267431.2010.544634

Rosaen, S. F., & Dibble, J. L. (2008). Investigating the relationships among child's age, parasocial interactions, and the social realism of favorite television characters. *Communication Research Reports, 25,* 145–154. doi:10.1080/08824090802021806

Rowling, C. M., Jones, T. M., & Sheets, P. (2011). Some dared call it torture: Cultural resonance, Abu Ghraib, and a selectively echoing press. *Journal of Communication, 61,* 1043–1061. doi:10.1111/j.1460-2466.2011.01600.x

Rubin, A. M., & Perse, E. M. (1994). Measures of mass communication. In R. B. Rubin, P. Palmgreen, & H. E. Sypher (Eds.), *Communication research measures: A sourcebook* (pp. 37–56). New York, NY: Guilford Press.

Rubin, H. J., & Rubin, I. S. (2005). *Qualitative interviewing: The art of hearing data* (2nd ed.). Thousand Oaks, CA: Sage.

Rubin, H. J., & Rubin. I. S. (2012). *Qualitative interviewing: The art of hearing data* (3rd ed.). Los Angeles, CA: Sage.

Rubin, R. B., Rubin, A. M., Graham, E. E., Perse, E. M., & Seibold, D. R. (2009). *Communication research measures II: A sourcebook.* New York, NY: Routledge.

Rudd, G. (2000). The symphony: Organizational discourse and the symbolic tensions between artistic and business ideologies. *Journal of Applied Communication Research, 28,* 117–143. doi:10.1080/00909880009365559

Russ, T. L. (2012). The relationship between communication apprehension and learning preferences in an organizational setting. *Journal of Business Communication, 49,* 312–321. doi:10.1177/0021943612456035

Ryan, M. (1998). Pitfalls to avoid in conducting and describing scholarly research. *Journalism & Mass Communication Educator, 52*(4), 72–79.

Sagar, S. S., & Jowett, S. (2012). Communicative acts in coach–athlete interactions: When losing competitions and when making mistakes in training. *Western Journal of Communication, 7,* 148–174. doi:10.1080/10570314.2011.651256

Salkind, N. J. (2011). *Statistics for people who (think they) hate statistics* (4th ed.). Los Angeles, CA: Sage.

Sapsford, R., & Abbott, P. (1996). Ethics, politics, and research. In R. Sapsford & V. Jupp (Eds.), *Data collection and analysis* (pp. 317–342). Thousand Oaks, CA: Sage.

Sapsford, R., & Jupp, V. (1996). Validating evidence. In R. Sapsford & V. Jupp (Eds.), *Data collection and analysis* (pp. 1–24). Thousand Oaks, CA: Sage.

Schatzman, L., & Strauss, A. L. (1973). *Field research: Strategies for a natural sociology.* Englewood Cliffs, NJ: Prentice-Hall.

Schrodt, P. (2009). Family strength and satisfaction as functions of family communication environments. *Communication Quarterly, 57,* 171–186. doi:10.1080/01463370902881650

Schultz, N. J., Hoffman, M. R., Fredman, A. J., & Bainbridge, A. L. (2012). The work and life of young professionals: Rationale and strategy for balance. *Qualitative Research Reports in Communication, 13,* 44–52. doi:10.1080/17459435.2012.719208

Schwarz, N., Groves, R. M., & Schuman, H. (1998). Survey methods. In D. T. Gilbert, S. T. Fiske, & G. Lindzey (Eds.), *The handbook of social psychology* (4th ed., Vol. 1, pp. 143–179). New York, NY: McGraw-Hill.

Schwarz, N., & Hippler, H. (1991). Response alternatives: The impact of their choice and presentation order. In P. P. Biemer, R. M. Groves, L. E. Lyberg, N. A. Mathiowetz, & S. Sudman (Eds.), *Measurement errors in surveys* (pp. 41–56). New York, NY: Wiley.

Scott, C. R. (2005). Anonymity in applied communication research: Tensions between IRBs, researchers, and human subjects. *Journal of Applied Communication Research, 33,* 242–257. doi:10.1080/00909880500149445

Sears, D. O. (1986). College sophomores in the laboratory: Influences of a narrow data base on social psychology's view of human nature. *Journal of Personality and Social Psychology, 51,* 515–530. doi:10.1037/0022-3514.51.3.515

Seibold, D. R., Lemus, D. R., & Kang, P. (2010). Extending the conversational argument coding scheme in studies of argument quality in group deliberations. *Communication Methods & Measures, 4,* 46–64. doi:10.1080/19312451003680525

Seidman, I. (2013). *Interviewing as qualitative research* (4th ed.). New York, NY: Teachers College Press.

Selltiz, C., Jahoda, M., Deutsch, M., & Cook, S. W. (1959). *Research methods in social relations* (Rev. ed., one vol.). New York, NY: Holt, Rinehart and Winston.

Serewicz, M .C. M., Hosmer, R., Ballard, R. L., & Griffin, R. A. (2008). Disclosure from in-laws and the quality of in-law and marital relationships. *Communication Quarterly, 56,* 427–444. doi:10.1080/01463370802453642

Shapiro, M. A. (2002). Generalizability in communication research. *Human Communication Research, 28,* 491–500. doi:10.1111/j.1468-2958.2002.tb00819.x

Shaw, D. R., & Gimpel, J. G. (2012). What if we randomize the governor's schedule? Evidence on campaign appearance effects from a Texas field experiment. *Political Communication, 29,* 137–159. doi:10.1080/10584609.2012.671231

Shearman, S. M., Dumlao, R., & Kagawa, N. (2011). Cultural variations in accounts by American and Japanese young adults: Recalling a major conflict with parents. *Journal of Family Communication, 11,* 105–125. doi:10.1080/15267431.2011.554499

Sheldon, P. (2009). Being ill in a foreign country: International students' trust in American physicians. *Journal of Intercultural Communication, 19.* Retrieved from http://www.immi.se/intercultural

Shimotsu-Dariol, S., Mansson, D. H., Myers, S. A. (2012). Students' academic competitiveness and their involvement in the learning process. *Communication Research Reports, 29,* 310–319. doi:10.1080/08824096.2012.723643

Sidelinger, R. J., Frisby, B. N., & McMullen, A. L. (2009). The decision to forgive: Sex, gender, and the likelihood to forgive partner transgressions. *Communication Studies, 60,* 164–179. doi:10.1080/10510970902834890

Sieber, J. E. (1992). *Planning ethically responsible research: A guide for students and internal review boards.* Newbury Park, CA: Sage.

Sieber, J. E. (1994). Will the new code help researchers to be more ethical? *Professional Psychology: Research and Practice, 25,* 369–375. doi:1037/0735-7028.25.4.369

Sieber, J. E. (1998). Planning ethically responsible research. In L. Bickman & D. J. Rog (Eds.), *Handbook of applied social research methods* (pp. 127–156). Thousand Oaks, CA: Sage.

Siminoff, L. A., & Step, M. M. (2011). A comprehensive observational coding scheme for analyzing instrumental, affective, and relational communication in health care contexts. *Journal of Health Communication, 16,* 178–187. doi:10.1080/10810730.2010.535109

Simon, J. L. (1969). *Basic research methods in social science.* New York, NY: Random House.

Sirkin, R. M. (1995). *Statistics for the social sciences.* Thousand Oaks, CA: Sage.

Smith, F. L., & Keyton, J. (2001). Organizational storytelling: Metaphors for relational power and identity struggles. *Management Communication Quarterly, 15,* 149–182. doi:10.1177/0893318901152001

Smith, F. L. M., Coffelt, T. A., Rives, A. P., & Sollitto, M. (2012). The voice of victims: Positive response to a natural disaster crisis. *Qualitative Research Reports in Communication, 13,* 53–62. doi:10.1080/17459435.2012.719209

Smith, J. M. (2013). Philanthropic identity at work: Employer influences on the charitable giving attitudes and behaviors of employees. *Journal of Business Communication, 50,* 128–151. doi:10.1177/0021943612474989

Spack, J. A., Board, B. E., Crighton, L. M., Kostka, P. M., & Ivory, J. D. (2012). It's easy being green: The effects of argument and imagery on consumer responses to green product packaging. *Environmental Communication: A Journal of Nature and Culture, 6,* 441–458. doi:10.1080/17524032.2012.706231

Spitzberg, B. H. (2006). Preliminary development of a model and measure of computer-mediated communication (CMC) competence. *Journal of Computer-Mediated Communication, 11*(2), article 12. Retrieved from http://jcmc.indiana.edu/vol11/issue2/spitzberg.html

Sriramesh, K., Moghan, S., & Wei, D. L. K. (2007). The situational theory of publics in a different cultural setting: Consumer publics in Singapore. *Journal of Public Relations Research, 19,* 307–332. doi:10.1080/10627260701402424

Stacks, D. W., & Salwen, M. B. (2009). Integrating theory and research: Starting with questions. In D. W. Stacks & M. B. Salwen (Eds.), *An integrated approach to communication theory and research* (2nd ed., pp. 3–12). New York, NY: Routledge.

Stafford, L., Dainton, M., & Haas, S. (2000). Measuring routine and strategic relational maintenance: Scale revision, sex versus gender roles, and the prediction of relational characteristics. *Communication Monographs, 67,* 306–323. doi:10.1080/03637750009376512

Stake, R. E. (2005). Qualitative case studies. In N. K. Denzin & Y. S. Lincoln (Eds.), *The Sage handbook of qualitative research* (3rd ed., pp. 443–466). Thousand Oaks, CA: Sage.

Standards for reporting on empirical social science research in AERA publications. (2006). *Educational Researcher, 35*(6), 33–40. doi:10.3102/0013189X035006033

Stanovich, K. E. (1986). *How to think straight about psychology.* Glenview, IL: Scott Foresman.

Stephens, K. K., Cho, J. K., & Ballard, D. I. (2012). Simultaneity, sequentiality, and speed: Organizational messages about multiple-task completion. *Human Communication Research, 38,* 23–47. doi:10.1111/j.1468-2958.2011.01420.x

Stephens, K. K., & Dailey, S. L. (2012). Situated organizational identification in newcomers: Impacts of preentry organizational exposure. *Management Communication Quarterly, 26,* 404–422. doi:10.1177/0893318912440179

Strauss, A. L. (1987). *Qualitative analysis for social scientists.* New York, NY: Cambridge University Press.

Strauss, A. L. & Corbin, J. (1998). *Basics of qualitative research: Techniques and procedures for developing grounded theory.* Thousand Oaks, CA: Sage.

Street, R. L., Jr. (1993). Analyzing messages and their outcomes: Questionable assumptions, possible solutions. *Southern Communication Journal, 58,* 85–90. doi:10.1080/10417949309372891

Sue, V. M., & Ritter, L. A . (2012). *Conducting online surveys.* Los Angeles, CA: Sage.

Sung, Y., de Gregorio, F., & Jung, J.-H. (2009). Nonstudent consumer attitudes towards product placement. *International Journal of Advertising, 28,* 257–285. doi:10.2501/S0265048709200564

Suter, E. A., & Daas, K. L. (2007) Negotiating heteronormativity dialectically: Lesbian couples' display of symbols in culture. *Western Journal of Communication, 71,* 177–195. doi:10.1080/10570310701518443

Suter, E. A., Reyes, K. L., & Ballard, R. L. (2011). Adoptive parents' framing of laypersons' conceptions of family. *Qualitative Research Reports in Communication, 12,* 43–50. doi:10.1080/17459435.2011.601524

Swazey, J. P., Anderson, M. S., & Lewis, K. S. (1993). Ethical problems in academic research. *American Scientist, 81,* 542–553. Retrieved from http://www.americanscientist.org/issues/feature/ethical-problems-in-academic-research/1

Sypher, H. E. (1980). Illusory correlation in communication research. *Human Communication Research, 7,* 83–87.doi:10.1111/j.1468-2958.1980.tb00553.x

Tabachnick, B. G., & Fidell, L. S. (2007). *Using multivariatestatistics* (5th ed.). Boston, MA: Pearson.

Taylor, B. C. (1996). Make bomb, save world: Reflections on dialogic nuclear ethnography. *Journal of Contemporary Ethnography, 25,* 120–143. doi:10.1177/089124196025001007

Taylor, B. C. (1997). Home zero: Images of home and field in nuclear-cultural studies. *Western Journal of Communication, 61,* 209–234. doi:10.1080/10570319709374572

Thayer, A., Evans, M., McBride, A., Queen, M., & Spyridakis, J. (2007). Content analysis as a best practice in technical communication research. *Journal of Technical Writing and Communication, 37,* 267–279. doi:10.2190/TW.37.3.c

Thompson, B. (2006). *Foundations of behavioral statistics: An insight-based approach.* New York, NY: Guilford Press.

Thompson, C. M., Romo, L. K., & Dailey, R. M. (2013). The effectiveness of weight management influence messages in romantic relationships. *Communication Research Reports, 30,* 34–45. doi:10.1080/08824096.2012.746222

Tilley, S. A. (2003). "Challenging" research practices: Turning a critical lens on the work of transcription. *Qualitative Inquiry, 9,* 750–773. doi:10.1177/1077800403255296

Toepoel, V., Das, M., & Van Soest, A. (2008). Effects of design in web surveys: Comparing trained and fresh respondents. *Public Opinion Quarterly, 72,* 985–1007. doi:10.1093/poq/nfn060

Toepoel, V., Das, M., & Van Soest, A. (2009). Design of web questionnaires: The effects of the number of items per screen. *Field Methods, 21,* 200–213. doi:10.1177/1525822X08330261

Tompkins, P. K. (1994). Principles of rigor for assessing evidence in "qualitative" communication research. *Western Journal of Communication, 58,* 44–50. doi:10.1080/10570319409374483

Toyosaki, S. (2011). Critical complete-member ethnography: Theorizing dialectics of consensus and conflict in intracultural communication.

Journal of International & Intercultural Communication, 4, 62–80. doi:10.1080/17513057.2010.533786

Tracy, S. J. (2002). When questioning turns to face threat: An interactional sensitivity in 911 call-taking. *Western Journal of Communication, 66,* 129–157. doi:10.1080/10570310209374730

Tracy, S. J. (2013). *Qualitative research methods: Collecting evidence, crafting analysis, communicating impact.* Malden, MA: Wiley-Blackwell.

Tracy, S. J., Scott, C., & Richard, E. (2008, November). *What if the research questions really didn't come first?: The paradoxes and challenges of methodological conventions and interpretive qualitative research.* Paper presented at the conference of the National Communication Association, San Diego.

Tucker, R. K., Weaver, R. L., & Berryman-Fink, C. (1981). *Research in speech communication.* Englewood Cliffs, NJ: Prentice-Hall.

Turner, J. W., & Reinsch, Jr., N. L. (2007). The business communicator as presence allocator: Multicommunicating, equivocality, and status at work. *Journal of Business Communication, 44,* 36–58 doi:10.1177/0021943606295779.

Uebersax, J. S. (2006). Likert scales: Dispelling the confusion. Retrieved from http://www.john-uebersax.com/stat/likert.htm

Unson, C. G., Trella, P. M., Chowdhury, S., & Davis, E. M. (2008). Strategies for living long and healthy lives: Perspectives of older African/Caribbean-American women. *Journal of Applied Communication Research, 36,* 459–478. doi:10.1080/00909880802175627

Utz, S., Schultz, F., & Glocka, S. (2013). Crisis communication online: How medium, crisis type and emotions affected public reactions in the Fukushima Daiichi nuclear disaster. *Public Relations Reviews, 39,* 40–46. doi:10.1016/j.pubrev.2012.09.010

Vanden Abeele, M., & de Cock, R. (2013). Cyberbullying by mobile phone among adolescents: The role of gender and peer group status. *Communications: The European Journal of Communication Research, 38,* 107–118. doi:10.1515/commun-2013-0006

Vandenbosch, L, Vervolessem D., & Eggermont, S. (2013). "I might get your heart racing in my skin-tight jeans": Sexualization on music entertainment television. *Communication Studies, 64,* 178–194. doi:10.1080/10510974.2012.755640

Vanderpool, H. Y. (1996). Introduction to part I. In H. Y. Vanderpool (Ed.), *The ethics of research involving human subjects: Facing the 21st century* (pp. 33–44). Frederick, MD: University Publishing Group.

van Swol, L. M. (2003). The effects of nonverbal mirroring on perceived persuasiveness, agreement with an imitator, and reciprocity in a group discussion. *Communication Research, 30,* 461–480. doi:10.1177/0093650203253318

van Swol, L. (2009). Discussion and perception of information in groups and judge-advisor systems. *Communication Monographs, 76,* 99–120. doi:10.1080/03637750802378781

Van Maanen, J. (1988). *Tales of the field: On writing ethnography.* Chicago, IL: University of Chicago Press.

Vogt, W. P., & Johnson, R. B. (2011). *Dictionary of statistics & methodology: A nontechnical guide for the social sciences* (4th ed.). Los Angeles, CA: Sage.

Waitzkin, H. (1993). Interpretive analysis of spoken discourse: Dealing with the limitations of quantitative and qualitative methods. *Southern Communication Journal, 58,* 128–146. doi:10.1080/10417949309372895

Wang, J., & Yan, Y. (2012). In J. F. Gubrium, J. A. Holstein, A. B. Marvasti, & K. D. McKinney (Eds.), *The SAGE handbook of interview research: The complexity of the craft* (2nd ed., pp. 242–176). Los Angeles, CA: Sage.

Weber, K., & Martin, M. M. (2012). Designing and evaluating the campus organ donor project. *Communication Quarterly, 60,* 504–519. doi:10.1080/01463373.2012.704575

Weber, R. P. (1990). *Basic content analysis* (2nd ed.). Newbury Park, CA: Sage.

Webster, J. G., & Lin, S. (2002). The Internet audience: Web use as mass behavior. *Journal of Broadcasting & Electronic Media, 46,* 1–12. doi:10.1207/s15506878jobem4601_1

Weick, K. (1985). Systematic observation methods. In G. Lindzey & E. Aronson (Eds.), *Handbook of social psychology: Theory and method* (3rd ed., pp. 567–634). New York, NY: Random House.

Weijters, B., & Schillewaert, N., & Geuens, M. (2008). Assessing response styles across modes of data collection. *Journal of the Academy of Marketing Sciences, 3,* 409–422. doi:10.1007/s11747-007-0077-6

Wells, K. (2011). *Narrative inquiry.* New York, NY: Oxford University Press.

Westerman, C. Y. K., & Westerman, D. K. (2013). What's fair? Public and private delivery of project feedback. *Journal of Business Communication, 50,* 190–207. doi:10.1177/0021943612474991

Wieland, S. M. B. (2011). Struggling to manage work as a part of everyday life: Complicating control, rethinking resistance, and contextualizing work/life studies. *Communication Monographs, 78,* 162–184. doi:10.1080/03637751.2011.564642

Wilkinson, A. M. (1991). *The scientist's handbook for writing papers and dissertations.* Englewood Cliffs, NJ: Prentice-Hall.

Willemsen, L. M., Neijens, P. C., Bronner, F., & de Ridder, J. A. (2011). 'Highly recommended!' The content characteristics and perceived usefulness of online consumer reviews. *Journal of Computer-Mediated Communication, 17,* 19–38, doi:10.1111/j.1083-6101.2011.01551.x

Williams, F. (1968). *Reasoning with statistics: Simplified examples in communication research.* New York, NY: Holt, Rinehart and Winston.

Wintre, M. G., North, C., & Sugar, L. A. (2001). Psychologists' response to criticisms about research based on undergraduate participants: A developmental perspective. *Canadian Psychology/Psychologie Canadienne, 42,* 216–225. doi:10.1037/h0086893

Witmer, D. F. (1997). Communication and recovery: Structuration as an ontological approach to organizational culture. *Communication Monographs, 64,* 324–349.

Wittenberg-Lyles, E. M. (2006). Narratives of hospice volunteers: Perspectives on death and dying. *Qualitative Research Reports in Communication, 7,* 51–56. doi:10.1080/17459430600964935

Wolcott, H. F. (1990). *Writing up qualitative research.* Newbury Park, CA: Sage.

Wolcott, H. F. (2001). *Writing up qualitative research* (2nd ed.). Thousand Oaks, CA: Sage.

Wong, N. C. H., & Householder, B. (2008). Mood and ad processing: Examining the impact of program-induced moods on subsequent processing of an antismoking public service advertisement. *Communication Studies, 59,* 402–414. doi:10.1080/10510970802473658

Wonsun, S., Jisu, H., & Faber, R. J. (2012). Tweens' online privacy risks and the role of parental mediation. *Journal of Broadcasting & Electronic Media, 56,* 632–649. doi:10.1080/08838151.2012.732135

Wright, D. B. (1997). *Understanding statistics: An introduction for the social sciences.* Thousand Oaks, CA: Sage.

Wright, K. B. (2012). Emotional support and perceived stress among college students using Facebook.com: An exploration of the relationship between source perceptions and emotional support. *Communication Research Reports, 29,* 175–184. doi:10.1080/08824096.2012.695957

Young, S., Kelsey, D., & Lancaster, A. (2011). Predicted outcome value of e-mail communication: Factors that foster professional relational development between students and teachers. *Communication Education, 60,* 371–388. doi:10.1080/03634523.2011.563388

Zerba, M. (2011). Young adults' reasons behind avoidances of daily print newspapers and their ideas for change. *Journalism & Mass Communication Quarterly, 88,* 597–614.

NAME INDEX

Abbott, P., 53
Abelson, R. P., 142, 187
Abner, E. L., 16
Adler, P., 279, 282
Adler, P. A., 279, 282
Agarwal, V., 96
Albanese, P., 33
Albright, J. M., 95
Alexander, A., 15
Alhabash, S., 126
Ali, M., 52
Allen, M. W., 235
Alley, H., 75
Ancu, M., 116
Andersen, P. A., 11
Anderson, B., 314, 317
Anderson, J. A., 63, 262
Anderson, M. S., 39
Andsager, J. L., 233
Anfara, V. A., Jr., 346
Armstrong, D., 341
Atkin, D., 72, 147
Atkinson, G. B. J., 13, 254, 256, 329, 355
Atkinson, P., 325
Aubrey, J. S., 6
Austin, E. W., 113
Avtgis, T. A., 217
Ayres, F., 44
Ayres, J., 44

Bainbridge, A. L., 345
Baiocchi-Wagner, E. A., 236, 346
Bakeman, R., 243
Baker, B., 44
Bales, R. F., 243, 245
Ballard, D. I., 270, 321
Ballard, R. L., 225, 325, 338
Ballard, S. J., 325
Barge, J. K., 293
Barker, D. A., 112, 113, 118
Barker, L. L., 112, 113, 118
Barnette, J. J., 157
Beatty, M. J., 85, 94

Beaulieu, A., 56
Bechkoff, J., 326
Beck, S. J., 237, 245
Becker, J. A. H., 101, 333
Becker, J. C., 290
Beebe, S. A., 108
Beksler, A. E., 53
Bell, J., 291
Belgrave, L. L., 335
Berger, A. A., 36, 231, 305
Berger, M. T., 291
Berleson, B., 230
Berquist, B., 15
Berryman-Fink, C., 243, 255
Bevins, C. C., 76, 133
Bichard, S. L., 117
Bickman, L., 140
Bird, C. M., 312
Bisel, R. S., 21, 73, 201
Blair, J., 162
Blair, J. P., 124, 127
Bloom, N. R., 75
Board, B. E., 132
Bochner, A. P., 325
Bodie, G. D., 76
Booth-Butterfield, M., 71, 197
Boren, J. P., 53
Borisoff, D. J., 262
Boruch, R. F., 127
Boster, F. J., 6, 110, 184, 187
Bostrom, R. N., 3, 11
Bouma, G. D., 13, 254, 256, 329, 355
Bourque, L. B., 153
Bowers, J. W., 96
Boyson, A. R., 75
Bracken, C. C., 147, 237
Bradburn, N. M., 153
Braithwaite, D. O., 293, 308, 347
Braitman, S. L., 140
Brandtzaeg, P. B., 136
Brann, M., 346, 347
Brashers, D., 243, 244, 245
Brinkerhoff, B., 209

Brokaw, T., 15
Bronner, F., 233
Brooks, W. D., 19, 142
Brown, L., 308
Brown, M. H., 322
Bruce, R. R., 70
Bruess, C. J., 160
Bryant, E. M., 322
Burgoon, J. K., 86, 124, 127
Burnett, A., 85, 86
Busher, H., 306, 307
Bute, J. J., 306
Butler, J. A., 308, 309
Buzzanell, P. M., 8
Byrne, S., 134

Cader, S., 218
Cai, X., 235
Caillouet, R. H., 235
Callister, M., 63, 236
Campbell, D., 129
Campbell, S., 71
Canary, D. J., 243, 293
Canary, H. E., 339, 355
Cantu, E., 339
Cappella, J. N., 13, 237
Caputo, J., 14, 86, 250
Carayon, P., 167
Carbaugh, D., 8
Carey, M. A., 316
Carlyle, K. E., 16
Carmines, E. G., 93
Carter, S., 95
Carusi, A., 40
Casey, M. A., 314
Cegala, D. J., 57
Cha, J., 202
Chapman, P. A., 323
Charmaz, K., 335, 337, 339
Chase, S. E., 322
Chen, Y-C., 129
Cheney, G., 40
Chesebro, J. W., 262
Child, J. T., 85, 86

Cho, H., 109
Cho, J. K., 270
Choi, J., 109
Chory, R. M., 98, 199
Chowdhury, S., 293
Christian, L. M., 154, 156, 161,162
Chung, C. J., 190
Chung, J. M., 70
Chung, S., 190
Cicchirillo, V., 199
Cingel, D. P., 255
Clair, R. P., 323
Clark, R. A., 13
Clingerman, B. Z., 90
Cody, M. J., 95, 236
Coffelt, T. A., 269, 293, 338
Cohen, E. L., 203
Communication Studies 298, 348
Conrad, K., 230
Cook, K. H., 11, 33, 67, 84, 93, 104,
        108, 115, 183, 227, 251,
        253, 255
Cook, S. W., 80, 81, 93, 102, 117,
        126, 184
Coopman, S. J., 323
Corbin, J., 235, 278
Couper, M. P., 149
Coyne, S. M., 232
Craig, E. A., 101
Craig, R. T., 2, 7
Cressman, D. L., 63, 236
Creswell, J. W., 34, 271, 272, 283,
        333, 354, 355
Crighton, L. M., 132
Cronbach, L. J., 98
Crouch, W. W., 11, 33, 67, 84, 93,
        104, 108, 115, 183, 227, 251,
        253, 255
Cui, Y., 326
Culhane, S. E., 187
Cupp, P. K., 16
Cushman, D. P., 7

Daas, K. L., 293, 332, 347
Dailey, R. M., 250
Dailey, S. L., 77
Dainton, M., 74, 154
Danker, J., 193, 194
Das, E., 150
Daschmann, G., 115
Davidson, L., 269, 341
Davis, E. M., 293
Davis, S. K., 150

de Cock, R., 257
de Gregorio, F., 198
de Ridder, J. A., 233
de Vaus, D. A., 68, 96, 126, 129,
        134, 140, 191
de Vries, R., 39
Deetz, S. A., 7
Defenbaugh, N. L., 325
De Grandi, G., 40
DeGreeff, B. L., 85, 86
Dennis, A. C., 345
Dennis, M. R., 89
Densten, I. L., 230
Denzin, N. K., 262, 263, 269,
        278, 341
Derlega, V. J., 140
Deutsch, M., 80, 81, 93, 102, 117,
        126, 184
d'Haenens, L., 31
Dibble, J. L., 140, 141
Dillman, D. A., 154, 156, 161, 162
Dillow, M. R., 224
Dimitriadis, G., 314
Dixon, T. L., 49, 58, 230, 237
Dobosh, M., 243
Docan, C. A., 197
Docan-Morgan, T., 197
Dohan, D., 339
Donohew, L., 76, 133
Donovan, T., 21, 70, 80, 93, 99, 216
Doss, K., 209
Dougherty, D. S., 315, 318,
        340, 346
Downs, E., 75
Drogos, K. L., 237
Dumlao, R., 195
Duran, R. L., 165
Durham, W. T., 293, 347
Durrheim, K., 308
Duta, A. C., 193, 194

Easley, J. M., 53
Eckstein, N. J., 308
Edwards, H. H., 291
Eggermont, S., 236
Eichhorn, K. C., 309
Eisner, E., 46
Elgesem, D., 51
Ellevold, B., 333
Ellingson, L. L., 270, 313, 329, 334,
        335, 340, 344, 345, 346, 347,
        352, 353
Ellis, C., 325

Ellis, K., 166
Elm, M. S., 51
Emerson, R. B., 301
Emmert, P., 84, 96
Ende, J., 270
Erbert, L. A., 74
Erickson, F., 272
Estalella, A., 56
Evans, M., 233
Eveland, Jr., W. P., 169
Eyal, K., 130

Faber, R. J., 182
Fairhurst, G. T., 95
Favero, L. W., 287
Fay, M. J., 219, 221
Faylor, N. R., 108
Fehr, B. J., 270
Feldman, M. S., 291
Fico, F. G., 233, 234
Fidell, L. S., 191
Fielder, E. P., 153
Fiese, B. H., 314, 317
Fine, M., 6, 322
Fink, A., 113, 118, 147, 151, 153,
        157, 159
Fisher, C. B., 51, 52
Fitch, K. L., 45, 286, 294
Flanagan, J. C., 322
Floyd, K., 53
Fontana, A., 304, 305, 309
Ford, D., 286, 288
Ford, E., 14, 86, 250
Fossey, E., 269, 341
Foster, P., 290
Fowler, C., 290
Fowler, F. J., Jr., 118, 151, 153
Fox, A. J., 89
Fraser, A. M., 232
Fredman, A. J., 345
Frentz, T. S., 279
Fretz, R. I., 301
Frey, J. H., 148, 304, 305, 309
Friedman, Z., 149
Frisby, B. N., 179, 197
Fryberg, D., 51, 52
Fu, R., 14, 86, 250

Gallagher, E. B., 337
Galvan, J. L., 34
Gamboa, L., 113
Gantz, W., 235
Garcia, A. C., 326

Garcia, M. A., 336
Gareis, E., 74
Garner, A. C., 59
Garner, J. T., 193, 194
Gazel, J., 137
Ge, B., 87
Geisler, N., 113
Gergen, K., 322
Geuens, M., 151
Ghosh, P., 14, 86, 250
Giannini, G. A., 313
Giles, H., 237
Gimpel, J. G., 139
Glaser, B. G., 235, 335, 337
Glocka, S., 64
Goins, M. N., 270, 295
Gold, R. L., 279
Goltz, D., 295
Goodall, Jr., H. L., 273
Gosling, A., 341
Gottman, J. M., 243
Graham, E. E., 152, 155
Gray, J. H., 230
Green-Hamann, S., 309
Greiner, A., 87
Grey, S. H., 89
Griffin, R. A., 225
Grimm, J., 233
Groves, R. M., 154, 158, 160, 168
Guba, E. G., 263, 278, 291, 292, 329
Gubrium, J. F., 262
Guerra, P., 113
Guilford, J. P., 213
Gunn, A. M., 324, 344
Guthrie, J., 5
Gwartney, P. A., 148

Haas, S., 154
Hackman, J. R., 13
Haidet, P., 323
Haigh, M. M., 101
Hall, J. A., 95
Hamel, L. M., 337
Hammer, M. R., 96
Hammersley, M., 50, 325, 353
Hannawa, A. F., 53
Hansen, G. J., 15
Hansen, G. L., 16
Hargittai, E., 233
Harlow, L. L., 185, 187
Harrington, N., 76, 133
Harrison, K., 92
Harter, L. M., 15, 282, 322, 336

Harvey, C., 269, 341
Hastings, S. O., 305
Hawes, L. C., 65
Hay, I., 39
Hayes, A. F., 173, 184, 187, 206,
    213, 216
Hayes, J., 240
Heath, R. G., 287
Hecht, M. L., 117, 347
Hedrick, T. E., 140
Heerwegh, D., 149, 167
Hefner, V., 236
Henkel, R. E., 184
Henry, G. T., 110, 141
Hermida, A., 231
Herndon, S. L., 318
Hessee, C., 53
Hickson, M., III, 341
Himes, K. L., 90
Hippler, H., 161
Hoffman, M. R., 345
Holladay, L., 235
Holstein, J. A., 262
Holsti, O. R., 230, 231, 232,
    236, 240
Honeycutt, J. M., 89
Hoonakker, P., 167
Hoover, K., 21, 70, 80, 93, 99, 216
Hopf, T., 44
Horan, S. M., 98
Hosmer, R., 225
Householder, B., 192
Houser, M. L., 108
Hove, T., 14
Hubbard, A. S. E., 209
Hullett, C. R., 180, 187
Humphreys, L., 269
Hurley, R. J., 234

Israel, M., 39
Ivory, J., 64, 132
Iyengar, S., 141, 142

Jackob, N. 127
Jackson, M. H., 5
Jaeger, R. M., 108, 173, 213
Jahoda, M., 80, 81, 93, 102, 117,
    126, 184
James, N., 306, 307
Janesick, V. J., 13, 266, 269, 270,
    296, 310, 321, 329
Jeffres, L. W., 72, 147
Jennings, R. W., 341

Jensen, R. E., 306
Jeong-Hyun, A. , 76, 133
Jian, G., 115, 339
Jiang, S-J., 168
Jisu, H., 182
Jodlowski, D., 323
Johansson, T., 351
Johnson, A., 102
Johnson, A. D., 80
Johnson, A. J., 101
Johnson, D. I., 214, 215
Johnson, J. M., 305, 308
Johnson, R. B., 84, 216
Johnson, T. J., 117
Jones, A. C., 293, 347
Jones, S. H., 325
Jones, T. M., 241
Jorgensen-Earp, C. R., 239
Jowett, S., 330
Judd, C. M., 84, 187
Jung, J. H., 198
Jupp, V., 127, 135

Kagawa, N., 195
Kaid, L. L., 231, 233, 235, 237
Kaiser, K., 46
Kalyanaraman, S., 64
Kamberelis, G., 314
Kang, P., 243
Kaplan, A., 84
Kaplan, M. S., 290
Kaplowitz, M. D., 149
Karr, C., 233
Kassing, J. W., 15, 167
Katzer, J., 11, 33, 67, 84, 93, 104,
    108, 115, 183, 227, 251,
    253, 255
Kaye, B. K., 117
Kearney, P., 85, 94
Keaten, J. A., 77
Keating, D. M., 116
Kellas, J. K., 322
Kelley, K. M., 73
Kelly, L., 77
Kelsey, D., 221
Kemph, A. M., 148
Kennedy-Lightsey, C. D., 90
Kerlinger, F. N., 7, 9, 11, 103, 104,
    112, 118, 124, 125, 134, 139,
    140, 141, 191, 196, 199, 219
Keyton, J., 5, 9 14, 21, 86, 89, 236,
    237243, 245, 250, 281, 286,
    288, 292, 294

Kibler, R. J., 68, 71, 72, 74, 75
Kim, H. K., 63, 113
Kim, J. Y., 77
Kinnally, W., 209
Kinsky, E. S., 193, 194
Kiousis, S., 77
Kirk, R. E., 185
Kline, S. L., 219, 221
Knapp, M. L., 235
Koester, B. D., 314, 317
Kosenko, K. A., 270
Kostka, P. M., 132
Kramer, M. W., 15
Kranstuber, H., 322
Krcmar, M., 255
Krejcie, R. V., 111
Kreps, G. L., 322
Kreshel, P. J., 291
Krippendorff, K., 230, 235, 236, 237, 240, 241
Krueger, R. A., 314, 320
Kuechle, B., 113
Kuhn, T., 102
Kumar, R., 235
Kunkel, A., 5, 89, 323
Kunkel, D., 130
Kvale, S., 40, 41, 307, 308, 312, 346, 352

Lacy, S. R., 191, 233, 234
Lambe, J. L., 89
Lammers, J. C., 336
Lancaster, A., 221
Lane, D. R. , 76, 133
Lange, J. I., 59
Lawson, D., 115
Ledbetter, A. M., 74
Lee, E., 15
Lee, J., 166
Lee, M., 293
Lee, M. J., 129
Lee, S., 190
Leeman, M. A., 40
Leibowitz, S., 14, 86, 250
Lemus, D. R., 243
Leonardi, P. M., 5
Lesch, C. L., 291
Levine, T. R., 52, 137, 180, 187
Levine-Donnerstein, D., 240
Lewis, K. S., 39
Lewis, S. C., 231
Liamputtong, P., 316, 317, 318, 319
Lim, T. S., 96
Lin, S., 117

Lincoln, Y. S., 262, 263, 278, 291, 292, 329
Lindlof, T. R., 50, 262, 266, 268, 269, 270, 274, 275, 279, 280, 283, 284, 286, 287, 288, 290, 294, 295, 299, 300, 301, 302, 305, 324, 330, 334, 335, 339, 344, 346, 348, 349, 352
Lindsey, L. L. M., 187
Linz, D. G., 49, 58
Littlejohn, S. W., 51
Liu, F., 113
Liu, T., 14, 86, 250
Lofland, J., 334, 335, 340
Lofland, L. H., 334, 335, 340
Lombard, M., 237
Longo, D. R., 87
Longo, G. S., 87
Loomba, J. K., 232
Loosveldt, G., 149, 167
Loseke, D. R., 76
Lowry, D. T., 118
Lucas, K., 287
Lumsden, J., 150
Lundy, L. K., 349
Lupi, F., 149
Lustig, M. W., 19, 20, 21
Lyken, D. E., 110

Mabry, L., 39, 40
Maddux, K., 293
Maeda, E., 347
Maki, S. M., 71
Malachowski, C. C., 224
Malhotra, N., 149
Malone, P., 240
Mansson, D. H., 68, 215
Manusov, V., 53
Markham, A. N., 51, 306
Marlin, D. W., 314, 317
Marshall, C., 329, 335
Marteau, T., 341
Martin, D. M., 334
Martin, M. M., 15, 90
Martinson, B. C., 39
Mason, S. A., 305, 313
Mathews, A., 140
Maxwell, J. A., 266, 272, 274, 278, 284, 286
Mazer, J. P, 74
McBride, A., 233
McClelland, G. H., 84, 187
McCracken, G., 305, 310, 353
McCroskey, J. C., 80, 85, 94, 102

McDermott, F., 269, 341
McEwan, B., 53
McGee, D. S., 57
McGuire, T., 346
McKinnon, S. L., 271, 280, 355
McLeod, D. M., 89
McManus, T. G., 252
McMullen, A. L., 71, 179
McPhee, R. D., 100
Meeks, L., 236
Meidlinger, K. B., 323
Meisenbach, R. J., 15
Meltzer, C. E., 115
Mendelson, A. L., 180
Mertz, N. T., 346
Messersmith, A. S., 201
Meyer, G., 6
Meyer, P., 111
Meyers, R. A., 243, 244, 245
Micari, M., 70
Miller, A. C., 113
Miller, G. R., 7, 13, 21, 72, 76, 78, 124, 135
Miller, K. I., 286
Miller, T., 51
Miller-Day, M., 273
Modaff, D. P., 308, 309
Moghan, S., 114
Morey, A. C., 169
Morgan, D. L., 316, 317, 319, 320, 321
Morgan, D. W., 111
Moriarty, C. M., 92
Mottet, T. P., 108
Mueller, B. H., 166
Mulaik, S. A., 187
Muthuswamy, N., 137
Muturi, N., 314
Mwangi, S., 314
Myers, S. A., 215

Naab, T., 115
Nabring, R., 293
Nam, Y., 190
Nan, X., 6
Nardi, P. M., 161
Nathanson, A. I., 200
National Commission for the Protection of Human Subjects of Biomedical and Behavioral Research, 41, 43, 44
Near, C., 63, 236
Neijens, P. C., 233

Nelson, C. L., 187
Neuendorf, K. A., 72, 147, 230, 232
Nguyen, L. C., 323
Nicholson, H. E., 7, 13, 21, 72, 76, 78
Niederdeppe, J., 63, 113
Nir, L., 77
Norling, G. R. , 76, 133
Norman, K., 149
Norman, K. L., 149
North, C., 115
North, R. C., 232
Northey, M., 33
Novak, D. R., 15, 282
Ntseane, P. G., 39, 40
Nussbaum, J., 252, 290

Ogan, C., 31
Oh, H. J., 14
Oh, S. Y., 15
Oishi, S. M., 148
O'Keefe, D. J., 4
Oliveira, M., 287, 351
Oliver, M. B., 98
Olson, L. N., 6
Osgood, C. E., 90, 158
Owen, W. F., 338
Ozley, R. O., 21

Packer, M., 312
Padilla-Walker, L. M., 232
Paek, H. J., 14, 89
Park, H. S., 180, 187
Park, T. D., 349
Payne, J. J., 305
Pazos, P., 70
Pearson, J. C., 85, 86, 160
Pedhazur, E. J., 123, 135, 136, 140, 183, 206, 218
Peng, T-Q., 168
Perez, F. G., 74
Perse, E. M., 101, 152, 155
Peter, J., 169
Petersen, T., 127
Petronio, S., 117, 305
Pettey, G., 115
Phillips, D.C., 278
Phillipsen, G., 324
Pierce, T., 340
Pitts, M. J., 290
Plax, T. G., 85, 94
Ploeger, N. A., 73
Poland, B. D., 312
Pomerantz, A., 270

Poole, M. S., 100, 102, 243
Porter, A. J., 264
Potter, W. J., 240, 272, 273, 344
Pratt, L., 236
Prentice, C. M., 293
Presser, S., 162
Provins, K. A., 200
Punch, M., 50
Pyrczak, F., 70

Queen, M., 233
Query, J. L., Jr., 322
Quick, B. L., 314, 317

Radina, M. E., 87
Rains, S. A., 116, 235
Raney, A. A., 98
Rasmussen, E. E., 200
Real, K., 112
Reddick, L. A., 53
Reeder, H. M., 117
Reel, B. W., 184
Reinsch, N. L., Jr., 286
Remington, P. L., 148
Resnik, D. B., 40
Reyes, K. L., 338
Rhea, D. M., 6
Rhodes, S. C., 9, 294
Richard, E., 268, 278, 344
Richards, S. T., 187
Richmond, V. P., 80, 102
Ricke, L. D., 236, 237
Riffe, D., 191, 233, 234
Ritter, L. A., 149, 150
Rives, A. P., 269, 293, 338
Roberto, A. J., 6, 16
Roberto, H. L., 6
Roberts, C., 181, 236
Robinson, T., 63, 236
Robson, C., 151, 153
Roessing, T., 127
Rog, D. J., 140
Rogan, R. G., 96
Rold, M. F., 89
Romo, L. K., 250, 263, 264
Ros-Mendoza, T. M., 117
Rosaen, S. F., 140, 141
Rossman, G. B., 329, 335
Roth, J., 243
Rowe, A. M. C., 53
Rowlands, T., 305, 308
Rowling, C. M., 241
Rubin, A. M., 101, 152, 155
Rubin, H. J., 309, 310, 323, 329, 334

Rubin, I. S., 309, 310, 323, 329, 334
Rubin, R. B., 152, 155
Rudd, G., 292
Rudd, J., 115
Russ, T. L., 85
Ruth, A. M., 349
Ryan, M., 34, 118, 250, 259

Sagar, S. S., 330
Salas-Lopez, D., 87
Salkind, N. J., 70
Salwen, M. B., 14
Sanchez-Jankowski, M., 339
Sapsford, R., 53, 127, 135
Sargent, J., 305
Schatzman, L., 288, 290
Schell, T. L., 237
Schillewaert, N., 151
Schmelkin, L. P., 123, 135, 136, 140, 183, 206, 218
Schrodt, P., 186
Schultz, F., 64
Schultz, N. J., 345
Schuman, H., 154, 158, 160, 168
Schwarz, N., 154, 158, 160, 161, 168
Schwartz, N., 235
Schweizer, S. E., 150
Scott, C., 268, 278, 344
Scott, C. R., 54, 55
Sears, D. O., 115
Seibold, D. R., 152, 155, 243, 244, 245, 321
Seidman, I., 307, 308, 311, 312
Selltiz, C., 80, 81, 93, 102, 117, 126, 184
Semlak, J. L., 85, 86
Serewicz, M .C. M., 225
Shapiro, M. A., 22, 110, 115
Sharf, B. F., 323
Shaw, D. R., 139
Shaw, L. L., 301
Shearman, S. M., 195
Sheets, P., 241
Sheldon, P., 167
Sherbloom, J. C., 309
Shimotsu-Dariol, S., 215
Sias, P. M., 322, 337
Sidelinger, R. J., 179
Sieber, J. E., 40, 41, 45, 50, 57, 58
Silva, J., 113
Siminoff, L. A., 243
Simon, J. L., 93, 192
Sirkin, R. M., 84

Smith, F. L., 236, 281, 286, 288, 292
Smith, F. L. M., 269, 293, 338
Smith, H. T., 80, 102
Smith, J. M., 313
Smyth, J. D., 154, 156, 161, 162
Snyder-Duch, J., 237
Sollitto, M., 269, 293, 338
Spack, J. A., 132
Spitzberg, B. H., 88
Spyridakis, J., 233
Sriramesh, K., 114
Stacks, D. W., 14
Stafford, L., 154
Stake, R. E., 286, 293, 341
Stamp, G. H., 333
Standards for Reporting on
        Empirical Social Science
        Research in AERA
        Publications, 40
Standlee, A. I., 326
Stanley, J., 129
Stanovich, K. E., 115
Staton, A. Q., 239
Stefanone, M. A., 190
Steiger, J. H., 187
Step, M. M., 243
Stephens, K. K., 77, 270
Stevenson, R., 149
Stockdale, L. A., 232
Strauss, A. L., 235, 278, 288, 290,
        335, 337
Street, R. L., Jr., 246
Strom, R. E., 124, 127
Suci, C. J., 90, 158
Sudman, S., 153
Sue, V. M., 149, 150
Sugar, L. A., 115
Sung, Y., 198
Suter, E. A., 332, 338
Swazey, J. P., 39
Sypher, H. E., 100

Tabachnick, B. G., 191
Tannenbaum, P. H., 90, 158
Taylor, B. C., 50, 262, 266, 268,
        269, 270, 274, 275, 279, 280,
        283, 284, 286, 287, 288, 290,

294, 295, 299, 300, 301, 302,
        305, 324, 330, 334, 335, 339,
        344, 346, 348, 349, 350, 352
Tepperman, L., 33
Tewksbury, D., 234
Thayer, A., 233
Thompson, B., 75
Thompson, C. M., 250
Thompson, J. L., 150
Thompson, M., 90
Thompson, T. L., 184
Thorp, L., 149
Thorson, E., 180
Tilley, S. A., 304, 312
Titsworth, S., 15
Toepoel, V., 150
Toller, P. W., 293, 347
Tompkins, P. K., 294
Tong, J-J., 168
Townsend, B., 293
Toyosaki, S., 351
Tracy, S. J., 268, 278, 288, 302, 330,
        331, 344, 345, 350
Traianou, A., 50
Trees, A. R., 53
Trella, P. M., 293
Tucker, R. K., 243, 255
Tumlin, G. R., 235
Turner, J. W., 286

Uebersax, J. S., 156
Unson, C. G., 293
Utz, S., 64

Valkenburg, P. M., 169
Van Maanen, J., 324, 326, 347
Van Soest, A., 150
van Swol, L., 34, 129
Vanden Abeele, M., 257
Vandenbosch, L., 236
Vanderpool, H. Y., 44
Vervloessem, D., 236
Vogt, W. P., 84, 216

Wadsworth, A. J., 231, 233,
        235, 237
Waitzkin, H., 246

Wang, J., 305, 309
Wang, X., 235
Weaver, R. L., 243, 255
Weber, K., 15, 187
Weber, R., 180
Weber, R. P., 232, 240
Webster, J. G., 117
Wei, D. L. K., 114
Weick, K., 299
Weijters, B., 151
Weinman, J., 341
Wells, K., 322
Wendt, P. F., 236
Westerman, C. Y. K., 128
Westerman, D. K., 128
Wieland, S. M. B., 280
Wigley, S., 101
Wilkinson, A. M., 355
Willemsen, L. M., 233
Williams, C. D., 87
Williams, F., 213
Wilson, B. J., 236
Winstead, B. A., 140
Wintre, M. G., 115
Wise, K., 126
Wiseman, R. L., 236
Witmer, D. F., 291
Wittenberg-Lyles, E. M., 323
Wolcott, H. F., 346, 347, 348, 353
Wong, N. C. H., 192
Wong, W. J., 117
Wonsun, S., 182
Wood, J. T., 345
Woodard, L. D., 323
Wright, D. B., 218
Wright, K. B., 15

Yan, Y., 305, 309
Young, S., 221

Zamith, R., 231
Zeller, R. A., 93
Zerba, M., 264
Zhang, Y., 230
Zhao, X., 6
Zhu, J. J. H., 168
Zimmerman, R. S., 16, 76, 133

SUBJECT INDEX

abstract, 256–257, 355
access, for qualitative research, 289–293
alpha level, 184
American Psychological Association (APA)
citation style, 31, 257, 355–356
analysis of variance. *See* ANOVA
analytic memos, 331–333
anonymity, 54–55, 59–60, 347
ANOVA, 199–206
basics, 200–202
between-groups variance, 200–202
between-subjects design, 202
eta squared, 204–205
factorial, 205–206
interpretation, 205
limitations, 206
one-way, 202–203
planned comparisons, 200
post hoc comparisons, 200
repeated measures, 202
two-way, 203–205
within-groups variance, 200–202
within-subject design, 202
antecedent variables. *See* independent variables
attrition, 100–101
audiotaping, of research participants, 57
authorial voice, 348–349
autoethnography, 325
average. *See* mean
axial coding, 337

behavior coding, 166
bell curve. *See* normal curve
Belmont Report, 41
beneficence, 41–42
beta coefficients (beta weights), 218–219

between-groups variance, 200–202
between-subjects design, 202

categorical data, 86–88
categorical response set, 155
categorizing reliability, 97, 237
category, definition, 334
causal variables. *See* independent variables
census, 107
central tendency, measures, 177–178
chi-square, 193–196
contingency analysis, 194–196
contingency table, 194–195
expected frequency, 193
in content analysis, 241
interpretation, 196
limitations, 196
observed frequency, 193
one-dimensional (one-way), 193–194
two-dimensional (two-way), 194–196
chronological writing style, 351
citation of sources, 31, 32, 58–59, 257–259, 355–356
classical experiment, 125–129
closed questions, 154–159
choosing, *versus* open questions, 160–161
Likert-type scales, 90, 156–158
response sets, 155–156
semantic differential scale, 90–92, 158–159
cluster sampling, 113–114
Code of Professional Ethics for the Communication Scholar/ Teacher (NCA), 42–43
coefficient of determination, 213–214
cognitive pretesting, 162
Cohen's kappa, 240
commitment acts, 291

committed membership, 282
Communication & Mass Media Complete, 28
communication research
definition, 2
questions, 13–16
scientific approach, 9–11
social science perspective, 2–3, 7–13
complete members, 282
complete observer, 281–282
complete participant, 279–280
computer-assisted qualitative data analysis programs, 338–339
concept, 67–69
concept map, 284–286
conceptual scheme, 68
concurrent validity, 95
confederate, 52–53
confidence interval, 111
confidence level, 111
confidentiality, 55–56, 59–60, 347
consent, informed. *See* informed consent
constant-comparison method, 335–337
construct, 68, 69
construct validity, 95–96, 168
content analysis, 230–243
Big Data, 232
categorizing reliability, 237
codebook, 237, 238
coding reliability, 237–240
Cohen's kappa, 240
computers and, 241–242
definition, 230
design considerations, 246
developing content categories, 235
examples, 230–231
interpreting coding results, 241
interrater reliability, 237
latent, 230–231
limitations, 243

content analysis (*continued*)
    manifest, 230–231
    process, 233–241
    Scott's *pi*, 237
    selecting what to code,
        233–234
    semantic validity, 240
    strengths, 242–243
    training coders, 237
    unitizing reliability, 237
    units of analysis, 235–236
    validity, 240–241
content validity, 94, 168
contingency analysis, 194–196
contingency table, 194–195
contingent accuracy, 272–273
continuous level data, 88–93, 294
control group, 123, 127–128
convenience sampling, 115
conventional pretest, 166
correlation, 209–210, 211–217
    coefficient of determination,
        213–214
    correlation coefficient, 211–213
    correlation matrix, 215–216
    examples, 214–216
    interpretation, 212–214, 217
    limitations, 216–217
    plotting data, 214
    scale, 212
    shared variance, 213–214
    spurious, 212
credibility
    definition, 269
    in qualitative research,
        269–270, 295, 340–341
    threats, 274–275
criterion-related validity, 94–95
criterion variables. *See* dependent
    variables
critical incidents, 322–323
Cronbach's alpha, 98
cross-sectional data, 147
cross-sectional designs. *See*
    descriptive designs
crystallization, 344
curvilinear relationships, 209

data. *See* qualitative data;
    quantitative data
data interpretation, issues,
    103–104
dataset, 172–173
data triangulation, 269, 341

debriefing, 57–58, 312
deductive reasoning, 19, 65
deductive research model,
    21–22, 23
degrees of freedom, 191–192, 211.
    See also specific statistical
    tests
demand characteristics, 142–143
dependent variables, 74–75
    relationship with independent
        variables, 75
descriptive designs, 123, 139–141
    comparison with other
        designs, 143–144
    limitations, 141
    researcher effects and bias,
        142–143
    strengths, 141
descriptive statistics
    applications, 180–182
    calculation, 182–183
    definition, 173, 176
    inferential statistics *versus,* 190
    measures of central tendency,
        177–178
    measures of dispersion, 178–180
    number of cases, 176
    symbols, 176
determination, coefficient,
    213–214
df. See degrees of freedom
directional hypotheses, 70
discourse, 262
discrete data, 86–88
discussion section, of
    quantitative research
    report, 253–256
dispersion, measures, 178–180
documentation of sources, 31, 32,
    58–59, 257–259, 355–356

ecological validity, 102
emic view, 330
empirical methods, 3
endogenous variable, 226
equivalent categories, 88, 155
error
    calculation, 181
    researcher effects and,
        142–143
    sampling, 110–112
    scientific, 12
    Type I, 185–186
    Type II, 185–186

eta squared, 204–205
ethics. *See* research ethics
ethnography, 262, 324–326
    autobiographical, 325
    definition, 324
    entering scene, 325–326
    reading, 326
    research report, 345
    strengths and limitations, 326
ethnography of communication,
    324
etic view, 330
evidence, 11
evidence levels, 273
exclusion criterion, 116
exhaustive categories, 88, 155
exogenous variable, 226
expectancy bias, 142
expected frequency, 193
experiment, 10, 124. *See also*
    experimental research
experimental group, 123
experimental research, 123,
    124–139
    cause and effect, 126
    classical, 125–129
    comparison with other
        designs, 143–144
    control group, 123, 127–128
    design types, 129–139
    factorial design, 132–133
    field experiment, 138–139
    limitations, 134–135
    longitudinal designs,
        133–134, 136
    manipulation check, 128–129
    online, 141–142
    posttest only design, 129–130
    pretest–posttest design,
        130–132
    quasi-experiment, 135–138
    random assignment, 126–127
    researcher effects and bias,
        142–143
    strengths, 134
    treatment groups, 127–128
experimental variables. *See*
    independent variables
expert panels, 166
explanation of behavior, 6
external validity, 101–102

F. See ANOVA
f. See frequency

face-to-face interviews, 148, 151, 159
face validity, 94, 168
factorial ANOVA, 205–206
factorial design, 132–133
field experiments, 138–139
field interviews, 304–313
 conceptualizing study, 307
 concluding, 312
 conducting, 308–313
 designing, 307–308
 interviewing technique, 311–312
 long or in-depth, 305
 online, 306–307
 process for, 307–308
 questions, 309–311
 strengths and limitations, 313
 transcribing, 312–313
fieldnotes, 280, 301–304
 analytic memos and, 331–333
 describing *versus* analyzing, 302
 digital, 302–304
 showing *versus* telling, 302
 specificity, 301
 transcribing, 304
field research. *See* qualitative research
focus group(s), 313–321
 data from discussions, 319–320
 definition, 313
 effective moderator, characteristics, 318–319
 guiding and maintaining conversation, 318–319
 limitations, 320–321
 motivating attendance, 320
 schedule (discussion guide), 314, 315, 316–317
 selecting participants, 317
 size, 317
 strengths, 320–321
 transcribing non-textual communication characteristics, 319
frequency, 176, 181–182, 193
frequency distribution of data, 174–176, 177

gatekeeper, 290
generalizability
 content analysis, 230, 231
 definition, 109

inductive reasoning, 19
 sampling, 109–110, 118–120
 scientific research, 12
 surveys, 147
 theory development, 19–20
goals of research, 5–6
graphs, in research reports, 252–253
grounded theory, 335–338

harm, physical and psychological, 53–54
heuristic, 12
hierarchical regression, 224
human subjects, 39. *See also* research participants
human subjects review committee, 44. *See also* Institutional Review Boards
hypotheses, 9–11
 assessment, 70
 directional, 70
 nondirectional, 70
 null, 71
 for quantitative research, 68–71
 research traditions, 71
 variable identification, 75, 76, 77
hypothesis testing, 70, 185–187
 experimental research, 125–126
 inferential statistics, 191
 statistical tests 191–192, 210–211
 Type I error, 185–186
 Type II error, 185–186

inclusion criteria, 116
independent sample *t*-test, 197
independent variables, 73–74
 definition, 73
 descriptive designs, 139–140
 identifying, from hypotheses, 75, 76, 77
 manipulation, 123
 relationship with dependent variables, 75
inductive analysis, 266
inductive reasoning, 19, 266
inductive research model, 21–22, 23, 24
inference
 population, 184
 process, 184

inferential statistics, 173, 190–193
 analytic steps, 192–193
 assumptions, 190–191
 degrees of freedom, 191–192
 hypothesis testing, 191
informed consent, 45–50
 definition, 45–46
 determining need for, 47
 example, 48
 information provided, 46
 qualitative research, 50
 quantitative research, 49
Institutional Review Boards (IRBs), 41, 43, 44–45
interaction analysis, 243–246
 analyzing and interpreting coding, 245
 coding interaction, 245
 definition, 243
 design considerations, 246
 example, 244
 gathering and preparing interaction, 243–244
 limitations, 245–246
 strengths, 245
interaction effect, 132–133, 203
Interaction Process Analysis (IPA), 243, 245
intercoder reliability, 237–240
interdisciplinary triangulation, 269–270
internal reliability, 97–98, 167–168
internal validity, 93
Internet
 online experiments, 141–142
 online interviews, 306–307
 online narratives, 322
 online research, 29
 online surveys, 148–150, 151
 research ethics, 51, 56
interrater agreement, 237
interrater reliability, 237
intersubjectivity, 262
interval data, 90–92, 176
interview(s)
 conceptualizing study, 307
 conducting, 308–313
 designing, 307–308
 face-to-face, in surveys, 148, 151, 159
 field, 299, 304–313
 interviewing technique, 311–312

interview(s) (*continued*)
  limitations, 313
  online, 306–307
  process, 307–308
  questions, 309–311
  setting for, 307, 308–309
  strengths, 313
  transcribing, 312–313
interviewer, researcher as, 282
in-text citation, 5, 31, 32,
      255, 356
investigator triangulation,
      269, 341
IRBs. *See* Institutional Review
      Boards

journals
  finding articles, 27–28
  submission of research
      paper, 354
  theory in articles, 21
justice, 41, 43

key informants, 292

laboratory experiments,
      124–125
latent composite SEM, 226
latent content, 230–231
library resources, 27–31
Likert-type scales, 90, 156–158
linear regression, 218–219
linear relationships, 209
literature review, 33–36
  body, 34–35
  conclusion, 33, 36
  introduction, 33–34
  organization, 35
  problem statement, 33–34
  qualitative research report,
      345–346
  quantitative research report,
      249–250
longitudinal designs, 133–134,
      136, 168–169

M. See mean
mail survey, 151
main effect, 132–133, 203
manifest content, 230–231
manipulation
  in classical experiments, 125
  in quantitative research, 123
manipulation check, 128–129

maturation, participant, 101
maximum variation sampling, 287
Mdn. See median
mean, 176, 177, 178
measurement, 10, 12, 83–105
  continuous level, 88–93
  definition, 84
  discrete level, 86–88
  principles, 84–86
  reliability, 93, 96–99
  validity, 93–96, 99–103
median, 176, 177
member check, 270, 340
member validation, 270, 340
memo writing, 339
method section
  qualitative research report,
      346–347
  quantitative research report,
      250–252
Mo. See mode
mode, 176, 177–178
mortality, participant, 100–101
multiple correlational coefficient,
      219
multiple regression, 219–224
  hierarchical, 224
  identifying independent vari-
      ables for, 223
  interpretation, 219–221, 222
  stepwise, 224
  Venn diagrams, 219, 220
mutually exclusive categories,
      88, 155
mutual simultaneous
      shaping, 263

n. See number of cases
narratives, 321–324
  critical incidents, 322–323
  definition, 321
  online, 322
  sources for stories,
      322–323
  strengths and limitations,
      323–324
National Communication
      Association (NCA), code
      of ethics, 42–43
natural experiments. *See*
      quasi-experiments
naturalistic research. *See* qualita-
      tive research
negatively skewed curve, 174

network (snowball) sampling,
      116–117, 286–287
nominal data, 86–88, 176
nominal response set, 155
nondirectional hypotheses, 70
non-experimental designs. *See*
      descriptive designs
nonprobability sampling, 114–118
  convenience, 115
  inclusion and exclusion
      criteria, 116
  justifying, 116
  purposive, 117, 287, 305
  quota, 117–118
  snowball (network), 116–117,
      286–287, 305
  volunteer, 115–116
nonresponse, 167
normal curve, 173–176, 177
null hypothesis
  definition, 71
  testing, 185–187, 191, 210–211
number of cases, 173, 176

objectivity, 12
observation
  asking questions to aid,
      300–301
  fieldnotes, 301–304
  in qualitative research, 299–301
  in science, 10, 12
  setting as seamless container,
      299–300
  in theory development, 19, 20
observed frequency, 193
observer as participant, 280–281
Office for Human Research
      Protections (OHRP), 39, 47
one-dimensional (one-way)
      chi-square, 193–194
one-tailed *t*-test, 199
one-way ANOVA, 202–203
online experiments, 141–142
online interviews, 306–307
online narratives, 322
online resources, 29
online surveys, 148–150, 151
open coding, 337
open questions, 159–161, 310–311
operationalization, 68, 69, 76–78,
      79, 84
ordinal data, 89–90, 176
outcome variables. *See* dependent
      variables

p. See significance level
paired comparison *t*-test, 197–198
panels (panel surveys), 168–169
participant observation, 262,
        279–283
    active members, 282
    complete members, 282
    complete observer, 281–282
    complete participant, 279–280
    interviewer, 282
    observer as participant,
        280–281
    participant as observer, 280
    peripheral members, 282
participant quotes, 339–340, 348,
        352–353
path analysis, 226
Pearson product-moment cor-
        relation coefficient. *See*
        correlation
percentages, 182
peripheral members, 282
personal interest, in research,
        13–14
phone surveys, 148
physical harm, 53–54
pilot testing, of survey, 162–167
plagiarism, 31, 32, 58–59
planned comparisons, 200
poll, 147, 150. *See also* surveys
population, 107–109
    creating sample, 107, 119
    definition, 107
    identifying, 108–109
    size and sampling error, 111
population inference, 184
population validity, 118–120
positively skewed curve, 174
post hoc comparisons, 200
posttest only design, 129–130
prediction of behavior, 6
predictive validity, 95
predictor variable, 74
pretesting, of survey, 162–167
pretest–posttest design, 130–132
probability, 183
probability (significance) level,
        183–185
probability sampling, 110–114
    cluster, 113–114
    confidence interval, 111
    confidence level, 111
    random selection, 110
    simple random, 112

    stratified random, 113
    systematic, 112–113
process inference, 184
proprietary research, 3
protocols, research, 143
psychological harm, 53–54
public opinion polls, 150
purpose statement, for qualitative
        research, 283–284
purposive sampling, 117, 287, 305

qualitative data, 272–273, 294
    analysis of. *See* qualitative data
        analysis
    collection, 299–327. *See also*
        specific methods
    continuous, 294
    emic reading, 330
    etic reading, 330
    from focus groups, 319–320
    grounded theory, 335–338
    interpretation of. *See* qualita-
        tive data interpretation
    level of evidence, 273
    member validation or check,
        270, 340
    observation, 299–301
    presentation, in research
        report, 347–349
    public-to-private
        continuum, 294
    seamless container, 299–300
    taking notes, 301–304
    theoretically saturated, 337
    triangulation, 269–270, 341
qualitative data analysis, 328–342
    analytic memos, 331–333
    axial coding, 337
    choosing method, 330
    coding and categorizing,
        333–335
    constant comparative
        method, 335
    diagramming data, 333
    emic view, 330
    etic view, 330
    Grounded Theory, 335–338
    open coding, 337
    overview, 329–330
    process, 330–335
    relational ethics with partici-
        pants during, 336
    research report, 346–347
    software, 338–339

    thematic analysis, 338
    theoretically saturated, 337
qualitative data interpretation,
        330, 339–341
    credibility, 340–341
    evaluation, 339–341
    participant quotes, 339–340
    research report, 349–353
    triangulation, 341
qualitative research, 3, 7–8,
        261–276
    advantages, 273–274
    commitment acts, 291
    committed membership, 282
    concept map, 284–285
    contingent accuracy, 272–273
    credibility, 269–270, 274–275,
        295, 340–341
    data, 272–273
    definition, 262
    designing, 279, 293–296
    developing rapport, 291
    developing trust, 291–292
    discourse, 262
    ethnography, 262, 324–326
    examples, 263–264, 266
    familiarity with people and
        places, 290–291
    field interviewing, 299,
        304–313
    fieldnotes, 280, 301–304,
        331–333
    focus groups, 299, 313–321
    gaining access, 289–293
    gatekeeper, 290
    inductive analysis, 266
    informed consent and, 50
    interpreting meaning, 272–273
    intersubjectivity, 262
    key informants, 292
    level of evidence, 273
    limitations, 274
    literature/theory, 284
    member validation, 270
    model, 266–269
    mutual simultaneous
        shaping, 263
    narratives, 321–324
    observation strategies, 299–301
    participant observation, 262,
        279–283
    purpose statement, 283–284
    researcher as interviewer, 282
    researcher construction, 272

qualitative research (*continued*)
  researcher flexibility, 284
  researcher impact, 294–296
  researcher skills, 278
  researcher's role, 275, 278–283
  research focus, identifying,
      283–286
  research objectives, 286
  research questions,
      270–272, 286
  sampling, 286–289
  sponsor, 290
  stumbling into something
      interesting, 292–293
  subjective valuing, 272
  subjectivity, 262
  time, 288–289
qualitative research report,
      343–356
  abstract for, 355
  analytical questions about, 349
  authorial voice, 348–349
  balancing description and
      analysis, 349–350
  chronological writing
      style, 351
  criteria to evaluate writing, 352
  crystallization, 344
  difficulty, 344
  drawing and supporting
      conclusions, 353–354
  ethics of quoting, 348
  findings and interpretation,
      349–353
  introduction, 344, 345
  literature review 345–346
  method section, 346–347
  presentation of data, 347–349
  primary sections, 344
  puzzle explication writing
      style, 351
  quotations, 348, 352
  reference list, 355
  revealing identity of
      participants, 347
  revisiting analysis, 353–354
  separated text writing
      style, 351
  strategies for writing findings
      and analyses, 350–352
  submission to journal, 354
  thematic or topical focus
      writing style, 351
  title, 354–355

quantitative analysis of text,
      229–247
  content analysis, 230–243
  interaction analysis, 243–246
quantitative data, 88–93
quantitative research, 3, 7–8,
      62–82
  advantages, 78
  comparison of designs,
      143–144
  conceptual model, 65–67
  deductive reasoning, 65
  definition, 63
  dependent variable, 74–75
  descriptive, 123, 139–141
  descriptive statistics, 172–182
  error, 12
  examples, 63–65
  experimental, 123, 124–139
  field experiment, 138–139
  foundation for, creating,
      67–68, 69
  hypotheses, 68–71
  hypothesis testing, 185–187
  independent variable, 73–74
  informed consent and, 49
  limitations, 78
  longitudinal design, 133–134
  manipulation of independent
      variables, 123
  measurement, 83–105. *See also*
      measurement
  online design, 141–142
  quasi-experimental, 123,
      135–139
  random assignment, 123,
      126–127
  reliability and validity, 79–81
  researcher effects and bias,
      142–143
  research questions, 71–72
  statistical tests of difference,
      189–207
  statistical tests of relationships,
      208–228
  surveys, 146–170
  variable operationalization, 68,
      69, 76–78, 79
  variable types, 72–75
quantitative research report,
      248–260
  abstract, 256–257
  APA style, 257–259
  describing participants, 250

  describing research
      procedure, 251
  describing variables, 251–252
  discussion section, 253–256
  future research, 256
  how to read, 255
  hypotheses, 149–150
  literature review, 249–250
  method section, 250–252
  presenting limitations, 255–256
  primary sections, 249
  reference list, 257
  research questions, 149
  results section, 252–253
  revising, 259–260
  tables and graphs, 252–253
  title, 256
  title page, 256
  writing issues, 259
quasi-experiments, 123, 135–139
  comparison with other
      designs, 143–144
  field experiments, 138–139
  goal, 136
  limitations, 136, 139
  longitudinal designs, 136
  researcher effects and bias,
      142–143
  strengths, 139
question(s)
  closed, 154–161
  interview, 309–311
  open, 159–161, 310–311
  research. *See* research
      question(s)
  survey, 151–152, 153–159
questions of cause and effect, 14
questions of definition, 14
questions of policy, 16
questions of relationships, 14
questions of value, 15
questionnaires, 147. *See also*
      surveys
quota sampling, 117–118
quotes, participant, 339–340, 348,
      352–353

random assignment, 123, 126–127
random sampling, 110–113
  simple, 112
  stratified, 113
  systematic, 112–113
random selection, 110
range, 179

rapport, in qualitative research, 291
ratio data, 92–93, 176
raw data, 172–173
recall cue, 160
reference list, 257–259, 355
regression, 216–225
    beta coefficient, 218
    beta weight, 218
    definition, 217
    examples, 219–222
    hierarchical, 222, 224
    limitations, 225
    linear, 218
    multiple, 218–223
    stepwise, 224–225
regression line, 218
relationships, statistical tests, 208–228
    analytical steps, 211
    basic assumptions, 210–211
    correlation, 209–210, 211–217
    degrees of freedom, 211
    regression, 209–210, 216–225
    structural equation modeling, 209, 225–226
reliability
    categorizing, 237
    Cohen's kappa, 240
    in content analysis, 237, 240
    Cronbach's alpha, 98
    definition, 79–80, 96
    improving, 99
    intercoder, 237–240
    internal, 97–98, 167–168
    interrater, 237
    in measurement, 93, 96–103
    in quantitative research, 79–81
    in survey research, 167–168
    test-retest, 98–99
    threats, 80–81, 100–103
    types, 97–99
    unitizing, 97, 237
    validity and, 99–100
reliability coefficient, 96
repeated measures, 202
replication, 11, 110
research
    definition, 2–3
    generalizability, 12
    goals, 5–6
    heuristic, 12–13
    objectivity, 12

as process, 23–24. *See also* research process
    proprietary, 3
    scholarly, 4–7
    scientific tradition, 187
    social science, 2–3, 7–13
    student relationship to, 3–4
    summary, 32–33
    and theory, 7, 19–22
researcher
    ethical responsibilities, 39, 40–41
    impact in qualitative research, 294–296
    role in qualitative research, 275, 278–283
    student as, 2, 3–4
researcher construction, 272
researcher effects, 142–143
research ethics, 38–61
    accuracy in reporting, 58
    anonymity, 54–55, 59–60
    Belmont Report and, 41
    beneficence, 41–42
    conducting research, 50–58
    confederate use, 52–53
    confidentiality, 55–56, 59–60
    debriefing, 57–58
    deception, 51–52
    documentation of sources, 31, 58–59
    informed consent, 45–50
    IRBs, 41, 43, 44–45
    justice, 41, 44
    participant identities, 54–55, 59
    physical and psychological harm, 53–54
    plagiarism, 58–59
    planning research, 40–50
    professional association guidelines, 42–43
    qualitative research, 50
    quantitative research, 49
    questions for researcher to ask, 41
    reporting research, 58–59
    respect for persons, 41, 42–43
    videotaping and audiotaping of participants, 57
    U.S. federal standards, 39, 44, 45, 47
research participants, 39. *See also* specific research types and methods

research process
    deductive model, 23
    idea formulation, 24–25
    inductive model, 23, 24
    literature review, 33–36
    model, 22–24
    problem identification, 24–27
    scientific approach, 9–11
    theory, 19–22
research protocols, 143
research question(s), 9–11, 13–16
    adjusting, 30–31
    asking questions *versus*, 323
    assessing, 271–272
    of cause and effect, 14
    of definition, 14
    evaluation, 15, 26–27
    of policy, 16
    preliminary, framing, 25–26
    in qualitative research, 270–272, 286
    in qualitative research report, 350
    in quantitative research, 71–72
    of relationships, 14
    reviewing, 249–250
    significance, 13–14
    of value, 15–16
research report
    qualitative research, 343–356
    quantitative research, 248–260
respect for persons, 41, 42–43
response rate, 167
result(s)
    developing interpretations from, 253–254
    limitations, 255–256
    manner of presentation, 255
    unexpected, dealing with, 254
results section, of quantitative research report, 252–253
root mean square error of approximation (RMSEA), 225

sample
    creating, from population, 107, 119
    definition, 107
    generalizability from, 109–110, 118–120
    representativeness, 101–102, 109–110, 118
sample size, 111–112, 118, 287–288

sampling
    cluster, 113–114
    confidence interval, 111
    confidence level, 111
    in content analysis, 233–234
    convenience, 115
    exclusion criteria, 116
    generalizability, 109–110,
        118–120
    inclusion criteria, 116
    maximum variation, 287
    nonprobability, 114–118
    online, 141–142
    population validity, 118
    probability, 110–114
    purposive, 117, 287, 305
    qualitative research, 286–289
    quota, 117–118
    simple random, 112
    snowball (network), 116–117,
        286–287, 305
    stratified random, 113
    for surveys, 167
    systematic, 112–113
    volunteer, 115–116
sampling error, 110–112
sampling frame, 107
scholarly books, 28–29
scholarly journals
    finding articles, 27–28
    theory in articles, 21
scholarly research, 4–7
science, characteristics, 11–13
scientific approach, 9–11
scientific tradition, 187
Scott's *pi*, 237
SD. See standard deviation
seamless container, 299–300
self-correction, in science, 11
self-reports, 147–148, 151
SEM. *See* structural equation
        modeling
semantic differential scales, 90–92,
        158–159
semantic validity, 240–241
significance level, 182–185
simple random sampling, 112
skepticism, in science, 12
skewed distribution, 173–174
skip logic, 141, 148–149
snowball sampling, 116–117,
        286–287, 305
social desirability response, 148
social importance, of research, 13

social science research, 7–13
    definition, 2–3
social sciences, definition, 8
social significance, 184–185
sponsor, 290
spurious correlation, 212
standard deviation, 176, 179–180
statistical software, 182
statistical tests of difference,
        189–207
    ANOVA, 199–206
    chi-square, 193–196
    significant *versus* practical
        difference, 204
    t-test, 196–199
statistical tests of relationships,
        208–228
    analytical steps, 211
    basic assumptions, 210–211
    correlation, 209–210, 211–217
    degrees of freedom, 211
    regression, 209–210, 217–225
    structural equation modeling,
        209, 225–226
statistics
    calculation, 182–183
    cautions in using, 226–228
    descriptive, 172–182
    inferential, 173, 190–193
    seeking help with, 206,
        226–227
stepwise regression, 224
stories. *See* narratives
stratified random sampling, 113
structural equation modeling
        (SEM), 225–226
    definition, 225
    endogenous variables, 225
    example, 226
    exogenous variables, 225
    hybrid, 226
    latent composite, 226
    root mean square error of ap-
        proximation (RMSEA), 225
subjective valuing, 272
subjectivity, 262
surveys, 146–170
    analyzing and reporting data,
        168–169
    behavior coding, 166
    closed questions on, 154–159
    comparing question types,
        150–151
    cross-sectional data from, 147

definition, 147
designing, 151–161
existing, evaluation and use,
        152–153
face-to-face, 148, 151, 159
flow, 161–162
items (questions), 153–159
Likert-type scales, 156–158
look or appearance,
        161–162, 163
mail, 151
nonresponse, 167
online, 148–150, 151
open questions, 159–160
panel design, 168–169
phone, 148, 151
pretesting, 162–167
recall cue, 160
reliability and validity, 147,
        167–168
response rate, 167
response sets, 156–158
sampling issues, 167
self-administered, 147–148, 151
self-reports, 147–148, 151
semantic differential scales,
        158–159
social desirability
        response, 148
types, 147–151
web, 148–151
writing your own, 153
systematic sampling, 112–113

tables, in research reports,
        252–253
taxonomies, 22
telephone surveys, 148
testing
    hypothesis. *See* hypothesis
        testing
    in scientific research, 11
    in theory development, 20–21
test-retest reliability, 98–99
text
    content analysis, 230–243
    interaction analysis, 243–246
    quantitative analysis,
        229–247
thematic analysis, 338
thematic focus, 351
theme, definition, 338
theoretically saturated data, 337
theoretic significance, 13

theory
definition, 7, 19
development, 19–21
in journal articles, finding, 21
in qualitative research, 284, 345–346
research and, 7, 19–22
utility, 21–22
title, of research report, 256, 354–355
title page, 256
treatment (manipulation), in classical experiment, 125
treatment group, 123, 127–128
treatment variables. *See* independent variables
triangulation, 269–270, 341
t-test, 196–199
definition, 196
forms, 197–198
independent sample, 197
interpretation, 198
limitations, 199
one-tailed, 199
paired comparison (paired samples), 197–198
two-tailed, 198–199
two-dimensional (two-way) chi-square, 194–196

two-tailed *t*-test, 198–199
two-way ANOVA, 203–205
Type I errors, 185–186
Type II errors, 185–186

unitizing reliability, 97, 237
units of analysis, 235–237

validity
concurrent, 95
construct, 95–96, 168
content, 94, 168
in content analysis, 240–241
criterion-related, 94
definition, 80, 93
ecological, 102
external, 101–102
face, 94, 168
internal, 93
in measurement, 93–96, 99–103
population, 118–120
predictive, 95
in quantitative research, 80–81
reliability and, 99–100
semantic, 240–241
in survey research, 147, 167–168
threats to, 80–81, 100–103
types, 94

variables, 68, 69, 72–75
antecedent, 73
causal, 73
definition, 72
dependent, 74–75
description, in research report, 251–252
descriptive statistics on, 182
endogenous, 226
exogenous, 226
experimental, 73
identifying, from hypotheses, 75, 76, 77
independent, 73–74
operationalization, 76–78, 79
predictor, 74
relationship between independent and dependent, 75
treatment, 73
videotaping, of research participants, 57
voice, authorial, 348–349
volunteer sampling, 115–116

Web-based experiments, 141–142
Web surveys, 148–150
within-groups variance, 200–202
within-subject design, 202